Andrew Bain, Ethan Gelber

D0558176

Cycling
AUSTRALIA

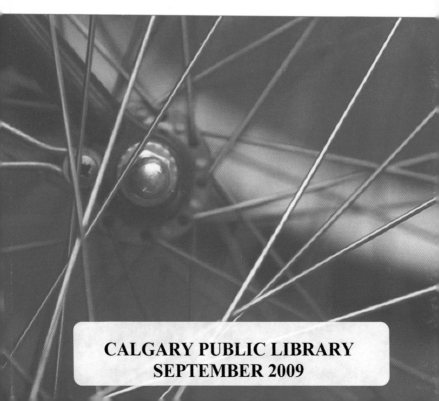

NEW SOUTH WALES

1 HILL END

Hill End is an historic town that once housed 30,000 gold-hungry prospectors. As you roll through its near-deserted, almost nostalgic main street, you'll pass a single store and the lone pub that remains from a heyday of more than 50 hotels (p95).

2 PROMISED LAND

As you crisscross Never Never Creek, take a side trip to a pocket of the northern New South Wales hinterland (p79), hidden from the world by thick rainforest and the looming Great Dividing Range.

3 THUNDERBOLTS WAY

Roll across the New England Plateau and plummet off its southern edge as you trail in the long-gone footsteps of bushranger Captain Thunderbolt, and some of the prettiest country in New South Wales (p79).

4 LAKE BURLEY GRIFFIN BIKEPATH

On some of the greener and more remote parts of Canberra's lake bikepath (p85) it's hard to believe that you're just minutes from the engine that propels a nation. That's one of the beauties of the path – a safe sense of removal. Of course, it's also just plain beautiful.

5 BARRY WAY, KOSCIUSZKO & ALPINE NATIONAL PARKS

Eighty kilometres of dirt roads through the pulsing, gurgling and cackling heart of nature is, for some, the stuff of dreams. At times paralleling the wild Snowy River, Barry Way (p69) crosses the Victoria–NSW state line – but the flow of preserved forest is uninterrupted.

VICTORIA

1 **MURRAY TO THE MOUNTAINS RAIL TRAIL**

In summer, it's an honest–to-goodness bike highway. People of all shapes, sizes and strengths steer their way through this car-free ribbon of recreation (p129). They all want the same things: some close contact with nature and freedom from motorised mayhem.

2 **MALDON**

So little has changed here from 100 years ago that you can almost imagine what a prospector must have felt like riding into Maldon (p152) with gold nuggets in his saddlebags. What were his priorities? Maybe a beer and bath? Yours may not be so different!

3 **PORT CAMPBELL NATIONAL PARK**

Millennia of lashing winds and crashing waves have hammered Australia's southern shores, eroding inland by as much as 2km. Nature's whimsy has created sculpted rocks – and a history of deadly contact with wayward ships (p122).

4 **THE ROAD TO MT HOTHAM**

Cyclists who have tackled major climbs know that the first deep breath after cresting a hill is one of both triumph and relief. The ascent to Mt Hotham is long and tough, but of such beauty that the gasp at the top – the heart of the Alps – is also one of awe (p136).

5 **DAYBREAK AT MT ABRUPT**

Rise with the sun to watch a silent visual symphony unfold. The first rays of day reach the Grampians' Mt Abrupt as deep purples and dark reds (p120). When the pinks and yellows mellow into place, everything seems lighter – even your heart.

TASMANIA

1 COCKLE CREEK BEACHES

The southern route to Cockle Creek is lined with beaches and bays (p177). At Conningham Beach, near Snug, the brilliant water is matched only by the colours of the boathouses, gazing over the bay to Mt Wellington.

2 WORLD HERITAGE SOUTHWEST

Tasmania's true wild west is a place of impossibly thick forest, delicate waterfalls, rivers steeped in legend, and peaks that seem shaped by pencil sharpeners. Opportunities abound to walk and explore, or just pedal through and enjoy the embrace of the wilderness (p193).

3 99 BEND ROAD

Carve through Queenstown's otherworldly scenery as you ride out of town on the so-called 99 Bend Road, which coils through orange and purple rock and a curiously compelling landscape denuded by scorched-earth mining practices (p202).

4 LIFFEY FALLS

Veer off the Across the Central Plateau route to find one of Tasmania's most beautiful waterfalls cut into rainforest on the slopes of the Great Western Tiers; the ride is worth the detour alone (p188).

5 EAST COAST

Cruise on a quiet coastal highway from beach to beach to discover coastal delights such as the Bay of Fires, with its granite frame dipped in lichen as bright as the famous bay's name (p165).

SOUTH AUSTRALIA

1 MAWSON TRAIL

After looping through the famed Barossa Valley, the Wines & Climbs ride (p241) goes from red wine to red dust, hooking up with the Mawson Trail (p241). The country's premier long-distance mountain bike route, it links Adelaide to the Flinders Ranges across the Mt Lofty Ranges.

2 PORT WILLUNGA

The Fleurieu Peninsula has no lack of great beaches, but between the eroded cliffs at Port Willunga you can savour a final glimpse at the Star of Greece, one of the state's finest seafood restaurants (p238).

WESTERN AUSTRALIA

1 ROTTNEST BEACHES

A short ferry ride from Perth and Fremantle, Rottnest Island offers cycling bliss – traffic-free roads, gentle undulations and 63 beaches of brilliant colouring in less than 30km of cycling (p263). Bring a snorkel, goggles and a leisurely attitude.

2 WILDFLOWERS

Time a spring ride in Western Australia and you'll find yourself amid one of the world's great wildflower shows along the Leeuwin-Naturaliste Ridge in the country's southwest corner. The state is home to 12,000 wildflower species, including around 4000 in the southwest alone (p266).

3 WALPOLE–NORNALUP NATIONAL PARK

Shrink beneath one of Australia's great forests as you thread between the barcode-straight karri trees and the giant claw-foot buttresses of the tingle trees. For the closest look, step inside the Giant Tingle Tree or climb into the canopy on the Tree Top Walk (p275).

QUEENSLAND

1 GLASS HOUSE MOUNTAINS

Weave between the abstract peaks of the Glass House Mountains (p301) – a chain of lava plugs named by Captain Cook for their apparent likeness to glass foundries in Yorkshire – as you head for the Sunshine Coast.

2 NIMBIN

Slip into a different reality as you roll along the Queensland–New South Wales Border Loop and into an endless Age of Aquarius in a New South Wales town more colourful than a pro-rider's jersey (p343).

3 HERITAGE TOWNS OF THE ATHERTON TABLELAND

With evocative names like Herberton, Kuranda, Mareeba, Millaa Millaa and Yungaburra, these wild frontier towns are magically frozen in time. Close your eyes and you can imagine horses parked before their modest timber structures. Look again: just how different are today's weather-wearied farmers from the earth-spattered prospectors of the past (p322)?

4 SURFERS PARADISE

Groomed beaches beneath a picket of high-rises welcomes you to the state's party capital. If you are looking for a place to kick up your cleat-weary heels and indulge in a bit of Gold Coast razzle dazzle, you've come to the right place (p291).

CYCLING IN AUSTRALIA

With a little imagination, Australia can almost be seen to resemble the shape of a bicycle, with Darwin in the saddle, Cape York as the handlebars, and the bulges in the east and west coasts like the wheels that roll it around the globe. Clearly, this is a land made to be cycled.

A century ago, shearers and overland adventurers shot about the outback on bikes, darting between jobs and beating the motor car into most corners of the country. This legacy of bicycle exploration survives, with pannier-laden cyclists emerging like mirages through the heat haze of an outback highway, the salt vapour of a coastal track, or the clear fresh air of a growing network of dedicated bikepaths.

Riding in this vast and sparse country is as fulfilling as it is challenging. Distances between towns and services can be great – up to a day of riding on the east coast, up to three days on the west – but so are the rewards: flour-soft beaches whittled from granite coastlines; road-shading forests that creak with birdlife; a wombat waddling across your wheel at dawn; the contorted, colourful figure of a snow gum as you crest a High Country pass. Highways circuit Australia and minor roads radiate out like spokes, inviting cyclists to see the country as it should be seen: slowly, quietly and, like Australia's own geography, from the saddle of a bicycle.

Contents

CYCLING REGIONS - INDEX MAP

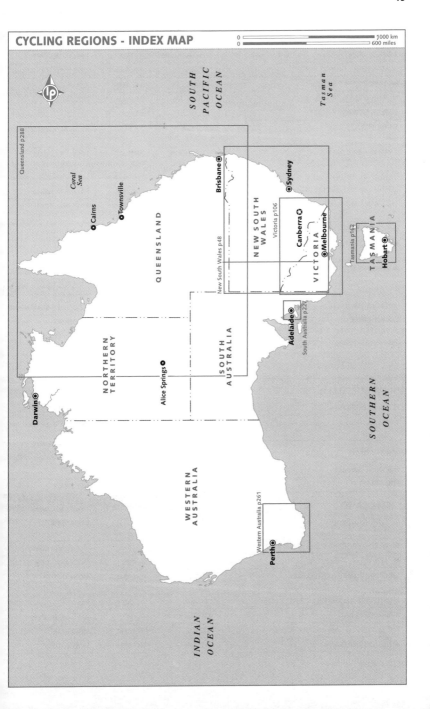

0 — 1000 km
0 — 600 miles

SOUTH PACIFIC OCEAN

Tasman Sea

Coral Sea

Queensland p288

QUEENSLAND

◉Cairns
◉Townsville

Brisbane◉

New South Wales p48

NEW SOUTH WALES

◉Sydney

Victoria p106

Canberra✪
Melbourne◉
VICTORIA

Tasmania p162
TASMANIA
Hobart◉

NORTHERN TERRITORY

Darwin◉

Alice Springs◉

SOUTH AUSTRALIA

South Australia p227
Adelaide◉

WESTERN AUSTRALIA

Western Australia p261

Perth◉

SOUTHERN OCEAN

INDIAN OCEAN

Table of Rides

NEW SOUTH WALES	DURATION	DISTANCE	DIFFICULTY
SYDNEY SURVEY	2½–4¼ HOURS	41.7KM	EASY–MODERATE
GOLD & WINE COUNTRY CIRCUIT	4 DAYS	299.5KM	MODERATE–DEMANDING
BATHURST TO THE BLUEYS	2 DAYS	147.3KM	DEMANDING
MURRAY RIVER TO ALPINE WAY	3 DAYS	256.9KM	DEMANDING
COFFS & DORRIGO CIRCUIT	2 DAYS	143.3KM	MODERATE–DEMANDING
THUNDERBOLTS WAY	3 DAYS	210KM	MODERATE–DEMANDING
CANBERRA EXPLORER	2–3½ HOURS	36.2KM	EASY–MODERATE

VICTORIA	DURATION	DISTANCE	DIFFICULTY
CENTRAL GOLD & SPA COUNTRY	5 DAYS	304.3KM	EASY–MODERATE
THE GRAMPIANS	3 DAYS	209.6KM	EASY–MODERATE
THE GREAT OCEAN ROAD	5 DAYS	281.5KM	MODERATE
RICHES OF THE NORTHEAST	3 DAYS	205.7KM	MODERATE
ACROSS THE HIGH COUNTRY	3 DAYS	240.4KM	MODERATE–DEMANDING

TASMANIA	DURATION	DISTANCE	DIFFICULTY
TASSIE'S EAST COAST	7 DAYS	499.7KM	MODERATE–DEMANDING
COCKLE CREEK	3 DAYS	216.1KM	MODERATE
ACROSS THE CENTRAL PLATEAU	5 DAYS	286.3KM	MODERATE
TASSIE'S WEST COAST	10 DAYS	661KM	DEMANDING

SOUTH AUSTRALIA	DURATION	DISTANCE	DIFFICULTY
FLEURIEU PENINSULA	5 DAYS	289KM	MODERATE
WINES & CLIMBS	6 DAYS	296.9KM	MODERATE–DEMANDING

WESTERN AUSTRALIA	DURATION	DISTANCE	DIFFICULTY
ROTTNEST ISLAND	1½–3 HOURS	289KM	EASY
SOUTHWEST FORESTS & SEAS	9 DAYS	614.1KM	MODERATE

QUEENSLAND	DURATION	DISTANCE	DIFFICULTY
BORDER LOOP	5 DAYS	325.3KM	DEMANDING
MT NEBO & BRISBANE FOREST PARK	3–5 HOURS	50.1KM	MODERATE–DEMANDING
MT MEE	4–7½ HOURS	74.8KM	MODERATE–DEMANDING
SUNSHINE COAST & HINTERLAND	4 DAYS	184.3KM	MODERATE
MT STUART & ALLIGATOR CREEK	2 DAYS	62.2KM	EASY
MAGNETIC ISLAND	1¼–2¼ HOURS	22KM	EASY–MODERATE
THE DAINTREE & CAPE TRIBULATION	3 DAYS	173.3KM	MODERATE
ATHERTON TABLELAND	5 DAYS	242.3KM	MODERATE

The Authors

ANDREW BAIN

Growing up in Adelaide, Andrew used to cycle up and down the cul-de-sac on which he lived pretending to ride around Australia. As an adult, he did it. This 20,000km journey became the book *Headwinds*. Soon, with a nagging guilt that he missed a bit, he returned to the road, riding from Cairns to the tip of Cape York in 2007. Now based in Hobart, he writes about adventure activities for a number of newspapers and magazines and is the author of Lonely Planet's *A Year of Adventures* and lead author of its *Walking in Australia* guidebook. His retirement plans don't involve a campervan, but instead a wish to cycle around Australia once more.

MY FAVOURITE RIDE

Few places in Australia can be easily cycled around in their entirety, which makes the land under Down Under – Tasmania – my choice as the country's best bike destination. The east coast of Tasmania (p165) is all about beaches that are perfect in every way (except water temperature) and, just a couple of hundred kilometres away, on the west coast (p193), you can be immersed in dense bushland and Australia's shapeliest mountains. Just as tangled, beautiful and hilly, the New South Wales Coffs & Dorrigo Circuit (p75) is my pick of the mainland rides, with its route buried deep in rainforest as you grind up the range and freewheel back to the coast.

ETHAN GELBER

An unapologetically native New Yorker, Ethan followed his heart to Australia in the year 2000, having been beguiled by a young Sydneysider's 'strine'. After almost 15 years on the road, much of this spent writing about thousands of kilometres logged on bike, he was happy to have heaved anchor for a spell. A short spell. The road is still home, the bike is still his steed and he still bends words on the matter. Now he just does it with beloved company that includes a young son. At present, his base of operations is Sydney.

MY FAVOURITE RIDE

On two wheels, I've never been particularly fast over mountains, but I love the natural, physical and mental spaces they create for me. My primordial needs are met by a buoying calm, boon on both a long uphill push in defiance of gravity and then the gleeful surrender to its downhill drive. The Across the High Country (p136) and Murray River to Alpine Way (p69) rides were my ideal retreats.

Route Descriptions, Maps & Charts

CYCLING ROUTES

This guide covers the best areas for cycle touring on roads. The rides do not traverse the country from north to south or east to west, but have been selected because they are scenic, pass through interesting towns or historic areas, are lightly used by cars and easy to reach by public transport. Rides link easily with one another, offering continuity for extended trips. Various transport options for getting to and from the rides are suggested. Rides accommodate both the novice and the experienced cyclist.

In most cases, the rides have been designed to make carrying camping gear and food optional. Each ride is broken into a set number of days, with accommodation and food options available at each day's destination. In some cases alternative destinations are offered.

Cyclists can use this book as an introduction and planning tool, as well as on the road. We hope that once cyclists become familiar with local circumstances they start planning their own routes, too.

Times & Distances

Each ride is divided into stages, and we suggest a day be spent on each stage. In some cases the distance for a particular stage is relatively short, but attractions en route, or nearby, warrant spending extra time – distance junkies may decide to condense two stages into one day.

The directions for each day's ride are given in terms of distance (in kilometres) from the starting point (specified on the cue sheets).

A suggested riding time has been given for each day's riding. Because individual riding speed varies widely, these should be used as a guide only. They only take into account actual riding time – not time taken for rest stops, taking photographs, eating or visiting a museum – and are generally based on an average riding speed of between 10km/h and 20km/h.

Ride Difficulty

Each ride is graded according to its difficulty in terms of distance, terrain, road surface and navigation. The grade appears in the Table of Rides at the beginning of the book and at the start of each ride.

Grading is unavoidably subjective and is intended as a guide only; the degree of difficulty of a particular ride may vary according to the weather, the weight in your panniers, whether children are cycling, pre-trip training or how tired and hungry you are.

Easy These rides involve no more than a few hours' riding each day, over mostly flat terrain with good, sealed surfaces. They are navigationally straightforward.

Moderate These rides present a moderate challenge to someone of average fitness; they are likely to include some hills, three to five hours of riding, and may involve some unsealed roads and/or complex navigation.

Hard These are for fit riders who want a challenge, and involve long daily distances and/or challenging climbs, may negotiate rough and remote roads, and present navigational challenges.

MAPS & PROFILES

Most rides in this book have an accompanying map that shows the route, services provided in towns en route, attractions and possible alternative routes and side trips, depending on the map scale. The maps are based on the best available references, sometimes combined with GPS data collected in the field. They are intended to show the general routes only of the rides we describe and are not detailed enough in themselves for route finding or navigation. For greater detail, we also recommend the most suitable commercial map available in the 'Maps' section of each ride.

Most chapters also have a regional map showing the gateway towns or cities, principal transport routes and other major features. Map symbols are interpreted in the legend on the inside front cover of this book.

CUE SHEETS

Route directions are given in a series of brief 'cues', which tell you at what point to change direction and point out features en route. These pages could be photocopied or cut out for on-the-road reference and used with a recommended map. The only other thing you need is a cycle computer.

To make the cue sheets as brief and simple to understand as possible, we've developed a series of symbols (see Map Legend on inside cover flap) and the following rule:

Once your route is following a particular road, continue on that road until the cue sheet tells you otherwise.

Follow the road first mentioned in the cues even though it may cross a highway, shrink to a lane, change name (we generally only include the first name, and sometimes the last), wind, duck and climb its way across the country. Rely on us to tell you when to turn off it.

Because the cue sheets rely on an accurate odometer reading we suggest you disconnect your cycle computer (pop it out of the housing or turn the magnet away from the fork-mounted sensor) whenever you deviate from the main route.

Planning

Preparing thoroughly for a cycle tour in Australia is more important than in many other parts of the world, with heat, water, distance and road trains to contemplate just for openers. That said, on most of the rides in this book you can pedal comfortably between towns and accommodation, eliminating the need to carry days' supplies of food and water.

Coastal Australia, where most of the rides are located, is a place that can be all things to all people. You can ride between secluded beach-side campsites or pedal to the doors of world-class resorts, B&Bs and restaurants, saving the panniers for a few extra items of clothing and souvenirs. Distances are sometimes large, but true mountains are few, which lets the kilometres flow comfortably past.

Cyclists should consider picking up a copy of Lonely Planet's *Australia* as an additional resource about what to see and do and where to play and stay as they ride around this ever-changing land.

WHEN TO CYCLE

As you might expect of the world's sixth-largest country, there's always somewhere in Australia that's primed for cycling at any given time of year. The trick is to be in the right place at the right time: summer (December to February) is the best time for Tasmania, the High Country of Victoria and southern New South Wales (NSW), but anywhere else it's really too hot for comfort.

For most of southern Australia, spring and autumn are the best seasons for cycling. Spring (September to November) probably sees the country at its freshest and most beautiful after winter's rains – albeit shrinking rains in recent years – though it is also the time of strongest winds across southern Australia. Spring also means copious wildflowers in Western Australia. Autumn (March to May) is the most stable season in the south, with winds at their timid best.

On the northern east coast, the warmer months (November to March) are accompanied by high humidity, and monsoonal rainfall in north Queensland. Queensland is best between July and October. Winter cycling in northern NSW is also pleasant along the coast, but it gets cold on the inland tablelands.

Of equal consideration in your planning are holiday times for the masses. In Australia the major holiday periods are the summer school holidays (mid-December to late January) and Easter, when the roads are choked with cars and, on the coast, you might even struggle to find a tent site.

Following is a general seasonal guide about where best to be, when:

December to February Tasmania, Victoria High Country, southern NSW
March to May Victoria, South Australia, Western Australia, NSW
June to August Queensland, coastal northern NSW
September to November NSW, South Australia, Victoria, Western Australia

See Climate (p353) for more information.

WHAT TO BRING

Keep the amount of gear you carry to a minimum – every gram is noticeable on a hill – but be certain to carry adequate weather protection. Cyclists planning to camp or use hostels will need more gear than those staying exclusively in hotels or B&Bs.

Clothing

When riding it's best to wear padded bike shorts or 'knicks'. These are designed to be worn without underwear to prevent chafing. If you don't fancy yourself in lycra, you can get 'shy shorts' – ordinary looking shorts with sewn-in padded knicks.

In colder weather, you'll need long knicks: lycra leg warmers, which are easily removed when things warm up, or thermal 'longs'.

Don't underestimate the seriousness of sunburn in Australia. Long sleeves provide the best protection, though to avoid overheating, you

CYCLING – THE NEW GOLF

Not too long ago the best business deals were sealed on the golf course. It was like an informal boardroom, where partnerships were formed and ideas floated. However, even before the booming world economy went theatrically bust in 2008, growing numbers of corporate high-fliers had found their way to a new sport, one liberated from manicured greens and cliché plaid plus fours hiding untoned thighs.

These business elite turned to cycling. They leaped from the fairway to the roadway and into, it must be said, much shorter pants that showed off legs of pure sinew. They have found in cycling a sport that ratchets up competitive camaraderie, and channels into reward the same drive and passion that catapulted them to success in business. On high quality machines (which they can afford), they gather regularly in bunch training rides where tenacity, vigour and – make no mistake – serious physical fitness all come into play. Oh, and they also sometimes talk shop.

The corporations for which they work have been swift, too, to support this shift from golf links to chain links. Rather than financing outings at private greens, they now sponsor cycling events, many with charitable leanings, and encourage employee participation. It all fits with corporate philanthropic giving programmes and the dynamics growing out of climate-change awareness.

Do you too maintain a seriously fast pedalling pace and have an interest in business networking? Where can you find these company pelotons? They're not at all exclusive. Just look for any capital city's main weekend morning rides (see below). But please: join the ranks primarily because you genuinely love the pedalling mateship. The connections will follow, especially during the ritual post-ride coffee.

WHERE TO RIDE

Consult your state's peak cycling organisation. They know where and when riders meet, what routes they follow and how fast they travel. Pick something that suits your form. For starters, the list below takes a shallow pass at some of the best-known up-tempo rides.

Sydney Try the blood-pumping high-octane weekend rides that begin from **Bar Coluzzi** (322 Victoria St, Darlinghurst) or from **Centennial Park** (opposite the cannons near the cnr of Grand and Parkes Drs).

Melbourne Saturday and Sunday mornings on Beach Rd is where cyclists outnumber motorists. The Hell Ride leaves **Black Rock** (7am Sat) and is need-for-speed riders only. On weekdays, gather at **Gardenvale** (6am) with the North Rd Bunch.

Brisbane A hard-core lightning-fast Sunday-morning (6.30am) ride leaves **Zupps car yard** (Gympie Rd, Aspley). Slightly slower are the daily (5.30am-6.30am) rides from **La Dolce Vita Café** (Park Rd, Milton) on bike-busy Park Rd.

Adelaide Head to **Mega Bike** (King William Rd, Hyde Park) for a very fast bunch ride. Need hills? Head to the Mt Lofty Ranges.

Perth Leaving from the **Barrack St jetty** (6.30am Sat) is one of Perth's speediest training rides. On Sunday, the group at **South Tce**, Fremantle, is a little slower.

Hobart Head south out of the city along Sandy Bay Rd, saving some puff for the final assault, the climb over **Bonnet Hill** into Kingston.

need something light and breathable. Some cycling tops are made from synthetic fabrics such as CoolMax and Intercool and are designed to keep you cool. Silk is another alternative. Cotton is cool, but dries slowly and, as a result, is useless in the cold and wet.

Sunglasses are essential cycling wear, not only to minimise exposure to UV radiation, but also to shield your eyes from insects and dirt and stones thrown up by vehicles. They also prevent your eyes from drying out in the wind. Peaked helmet covers provide a little sun protection, and a bandanna is always useful to soak up sweat.

Go for bright or light-coloured clothing, which is cooler and maximises your visibility. A fluorescent top or vest will make sure you're visible on the road.

Be aware of the dangers of exposure, especially during cooler months or in places like Tasmania or the High Country, where the weather can change rapidly. Layering (wearing several thin layers of clothing) is the most practical way to dress in cooler weather. Start with a lightweight cycling or polypropylene top, followed by a warmer insulating layer, such as a thin synthetic fleece jacket (these are lightweight and dry quickly) and a rainproof jacket. Fine wool thermal wear is an excellent alternative to synthetic fibres, as it stays warm when wet and doesn't make you itch.

Some excellent waterproof yet breathable cycling jackets are available. Gore-Tex is probably the best-known fabric used for jackets; other fabrics such as Silmond or Activent are compact, lightweight and excellent for light rain, but won't stand up to a steady downpour.

Wear fingerless cycling gloves with padded palms to reduce the impact of jarring on your hands (which can lead to nerve damage); they also prevent sunburn and protect your hands in case of a fall.

In cold weather, you may also need full-finger gloves (either thin polypropylene gloves, which can be worn with cycling gloves, or more wind- and rain-resistant ones). You can also buy thermal socks and

MAKING MONEY MATTER

There's a growing list of charitable bike events that link corporate ooh to philanthropic aah. Some limit participation to keep groups chummy and trim; many set high financial thresholds (both sign-on and charitable fundraising minimums) in keeping with riders' corporate muscle. Check out:

Chain Reaction (www.chain-reaction.org.au) A Victoria-based spin-off of Tour de Kids (see below). Their chosen charities are the Starlight Children's Foundation and the Cerebral Palsy Education Centre.

Entoure (www.entoure.com.au) Multiple annual 400km-in-three-days rides primarily benefit the Day of Difference Foundation.

Pollie Pedal (www.tonyabbott.com.au) Launched in 1998 by politicians as a way of raising money for a variety of charitable causes, it covers about 1000km in slightly more than a week.

Tour de Cure (www.tourdecure.com.au) embarks on different rides in different locations throughout Australia and raises funds for the fight against cancer.

Tour de Kids (www.tourdekids.org.au) By 2008 it had, in eight years, raised $3.2 million through a once-annual week-long 1000km-plus pedal benefiting the Starlight Children's Foundation and other charities.

Tour de NSW (www.olympicycle.com.au/Tour%20de%20NSW/charities.html) The self-proclaimed longest tour in Australia (2100km in 21 days). All monies raised from the event go to Action Foundation Incorporated.

neoprene booties to go over your shoes, so you can feel your toes on those cold mornings. A close-fitting beanie (or other winter hat) worn under your helmet will help keep you warm.

Helmets are compulsory in Australia. To fit properly the helmet should sit far enough forward that only 3cm to 4cm of your forehead is exposed. It should be firm but not tight – decent helmets have tightening mechanisms at the back – with the strap fastened. Make certain that the strap cannot pull out over your chin. If your helmet has been in a crash, replace it.

Cycling shoes are ideal footwear (or next best: stiff-soled ordinary shoes). Stiff soles transfer the power from your pedal stroke directly to the pedal. Spongy-soled running shoes are inefficient and are likely to leave your feet sore. Some Australian touring cyclists swear by cycling sandals – stiff-soled sandals with room for a pedal cleat. They're cool in summer and dry quickly in the rain; just make sure you put sunscreen on your feet.

The clothing you carry to wear off the bike depends on the type of accommodation you're planning on using. Campers need adequate clothing to protect against the cold, particularly in the southern and mountainous areas outside summer. Pack thermal underwear (tops and bottoms), a change of socks and underwear, a warm top and hat, and gloves. Take a separate pair of shoes for when you're off the bike and bring a broad-brimmed hat to wear once you remove your helmet.

Bicycle

Bikes generally come in four flavours: road bike, touring bike, hybrid bike and mountain bike. As the name on the box suggests, touring bikes are most suited to long-term travel, though you might struggle to pick one up from a shop floor as they tend to be custom made. Hybrids, which are designed for comfort, offer a good alternative, while mountain bikes will be required for some of the routes in this book. If purchasing a mountain bike, check that it has eyelets on the rear stays for attaching a rack.

For a greater rundown on the variety of bike options, see Choosing & Setting Up a Bicycle (p374).

Equipment

Most budget accommodation (hostels, cabins in caravan parks) in Australia does not supply bedding to guests (some hire it), so it's prudent to carry a sleeping bag, even if you're not camping.

If you're planning to camp, you'll need a lightweight waterproof tent, sleeping mat, warm sleeping bag, torch (flashlight) or bike light, cooking and eating utensils, and water containers. If you plan to self-cater, you'll also need a portable stove and pots.

It's illegal to carry fuel for a stove on aircraft, but it's readily available in Australia. White gas (known as Shellite or white spirits) and methylated spirits are sold at hardware shops, outdoor stores and most supermarkets. Gas cartridges can be purchased at outdoor stores in larger centres.

It is worth taking a daypack (or using a handlebar bag) for carrying valuables when you're off the bike.

Buying & Hiring Locally

Cycling has become a recreational phenomenon in Australia and bike stores have blossomed accordingly, especially in capital cities. The typical bike-shop floor will be covered in road bikes and mountain bikes, with a sprinkling of hybrids. Rarely will you find a touring bike among them.

For a decent hybrid or rigid mountain bike you'll need to pay around $800 to $1200, though you can get a cheap one for around $400. Panniers can also be found in bike stores, though you may have to trawl through a few before you find a decent selection.

Few shops stock secondhand bikes. For this you'll need to try classified ad publications such as the **Trading Post** (www.tradingpost.com.au) or **ebay** (www.ebay.com.au). The website for **Bicycling Australia** (www .bicyclingaustralia.com) magazine has a classified section, while **Bike Exchange** (www.bikeexchange.com.au) is an Australian website purely for cycling classifieds.

It's possible to hire bikes in all capital cities and a great number of regional centres, though most are geared towards day riders, so be sure to check that racks are fitted and panniers can also be hired. The longer you hire a bike the cheaper it usually becomes. Prices will vary, but expect to pay around $150 a week.

EQUIPMENT CHECKLIST

This list is a general guide to the things that might be useful on a bike tour. Don't forget to take on board enough water and food to see you safely between towns.

BIKE CLOTHING

- cycling gloves
- cycling shoes and socks
- helmet and visor
- long-sleeved shirt or cycling top
- padded cycling shorts (knicks)
- sunglasses
- T-shirt or short-sleeved cycling top
- visibility vest
- waterproof jacket and pants

OFF-BIKE CLOTHING

- change of clothing
- sandals
- swimming gear
- sunhat
- underwear and socks

EQUIPMENT

- bike lights (rear and front) with spare batteries
- elastic cord
- camera and spare film
- cooking and eating utensils
- cycle computer
- daypack
- malaria tablets
- medical kit* and toiletries
- mosquito repellent
- padlock
- panniers and waterproof liners
- pocket knife
- sewing kit
- sleeping sheet
- sleeping bag
- small handlebar bag and/or map case
- small towel
- sunscreen
- tool kit, pump and spares*
- torch (flashlight) with spare batteries and globe
- water containers
- water purification tablets, iodine or filter

* see the First Aid boxed text (p393); Spares & Tool Kit boxed text (p379)

COSTS & MONEY

Australia is affordable by Western European and American standards, but it is certainly not a budget destination compared to somewhere like Southeast Asia. The biggest cost in any trip to Australia is usually transport, simply because it is such a large country, so as a cyclist you are at an immediate advantage (until you try to carry your bike on a plane or bus).

If you're pedalling between B&Bs, doing some general sightseeing and satisfying that cycling appetite in restaurants, then $100 to $120 per day (per person travelling as a couple) should do it. If you are travelling frugally: camping or staying in hostels, cooking your own meals and limiting your entertainment to the cycling itself, you could probably eke out an existence on about $60 per day. For a budget that realistically enables you to have a good time, allow about $80 per day.

HOW MUCH?

Campsite (tent & two people) $20–30

B&B (per person sharing) $70

Road map $10

Inner tube $7–12

Coffee $3–4

BACKGROUND READING

Recent years have seen a small surge of books with stories of cycling journeys around and through Australia.

Headwinds by Andrew Bain recounts a 14-month, 20,000km ride around the country's rim, cycling into the prevailing winds as he dodges trucks and thieving marsupials. *Cold Beer and Crocodiles* by Roff Smith tells of a similar journey, spinning out of a series of National Geographic feature articles. Richard Allen's *Shimmering Spokes* is another such account. The most recent of the crop is Kate Leeming's *Out There and Back*, the story of a 25,000km journey through Australia that included the first bicycle crossing of the Canning Stock Route by a woman.

If you're heading off the well-cycled path, *Cycling Outback Australia* by Craig Bagnall and Nikki Brown provides a good, eco-focused guide of what to expect – Bagnall and Brown cycled around Australia in 1999/2000.

The Bicycle and the Bush by Jim Fitzpatrick is a fascinating work on Australian cycling history, while you might recognise a few of your own obsessions in Keith Dunstan's *Confessions of a Bicycle Nut*.

GROUP & GUIDED RIDES

If you fancy company on a ride or just somebody else cooking the dinner at night, a guided cycle tour can be just the ticket. While there isn't an abundance of companies offering guided rides in Australia, the offerings are generally pretty enticing. The following are companies that offer rides in various parts of the country – for companies that specialise in individual states or regions, see the relevant regional chapters.

Adventure Collective (☎ 1300 948 911; www.adventurecollective.com.au) Specialises in outback tours such as the Gibb River Rd and Red Centre, with some gentler options such as Kangaroo Island, Great Ocean Rd and Barossa Valley.

AllTrails (☎ 03-9645 3355; www.alltrails.com.au) Long-distance tours such as Perth to Adelaide (across the Nullarbor) and Darwin to Broome.

Cycling Tours (☎ 1800 122 504; www.cyclingtours.com.au) A range of tours, from three to 16 days, in Tasmania, Queensland and Victoria.

Cycle Across Oz (☎ 03-9583 5414; www.cycleacrossoz.com.au) Organises an annual long-distance ride across the country: the likes of Perth to Melbourne, Rockhampton to Darwin or Darwin to Adelaide.

Outdoor Travel (☎ 03-5750 1441; www.outdoortravel.com.au) Two- to 10-day tours in Victoria, South Australia and Western Australia.

TOP FIVES

So many roads, so much to see. How do you decide where to turn those pedals? Here's our pick of the best of the best if you're seeking beaches, critters, mountains, forests or just a good glass of wine.

BEACH HOPS

Australia has around 7000 beaches and they are among the country's greatest drawcards. Park up the bike and enjoy sand and surf on the following rides.

- The Great Ocean Road (p122)
- Tassie's East Coast (p165)
- Fleurieu Peninsula (p229)
- Magnetic Island (p314)
- Rottnest Island (p263)

WILDLIFE WATCHING

Australia's wildlife is as curious in design as any on earth. You'll see a few animals at the roadside but if you really want to mingle with the fauna, try the following rides.

- Tassie's West Coast (p193)
- Border Loop (p291)
- Rottnest Island (p263)
- The Grampians (p116)
- Tassie's East Coast (p165)

MOUNTAIN ASCENTS

Australia isn't mountainous but it does have mountains. The following rides will pump some lactic acid into your thighs.

- Across the High Country (p136)
- Tassie's West Coast (p193)
- Bathurst to the Blueys (p63)
- Across the Central Plateau (p183)
- Border Loop (p291)

TALL TIMBER

The outback might be Australia's most famous landscape but there's plenty of forest to counterbalance it. These rides will have you shaded, humbled and happy.

- The Daintree & Cape Tribulation (p317)
- Southwest Forests & Seas (p266)
- Coffs & Dorrigo Circuit (p75)
- Border Loop (p291)
- Mt Nebo & Brisbane Forest Park (p299)

WINERY WOBBLES

Bikes don't use fuel, but you do, and often for cyclists it's wine that propels them onward. If you want a slurp of red or white, the follow rides are worth bottling.

- Wines & Climbs (p241)
- Gold & Wine Country Circuit (p57)
- Southwest Forests & Seas (p266)
- Riches of the Northeast (p129)
- Fleurieu Peninsula (p229)

INTERNET RESOURCES

Australian Cycling Forums (www.bicycles.net.au/forums/index.php) Discussions on all aspects of cycling, including a thread on touring in Australia.

Australian Government (www.gov.au) Gateway to all federal, state, territory and local government sites.

Australian Newspapers Online (www.nla.gov.au/npapers) A National Library-maintained listing of Australian newspaper websites.

Australian Tourist Commission (www.australia.com) Government-run tourism site with nationwide information for visitors.

Bicycle Federation of Australia (www.bfa.asn.au) Peak body for Australian cycling-advocacy groups. The website has links to state organisations.

Bikely (www.bikely.com) Worldwide list and maps of cycling routes, including around 15,000 in Australia.

HISTORY OF CYCLING

In the late 19th century, bicycles were the height of fashion around the world. Boneshakers, then penny-farthings (at the time, known simply as 'high bicycles'), became popular and, in the 1890s, the modern 'safety bicycle' came into vogue, beginning the cycling craze in Australia. The safety bike was a bike for everyone: comfortable, easy, efficient and much safer than the penny-farthing.

The other popular feature of the safety was its diminishing price tag. Initially only for the wealthy, by mid-decade these bikes were more affordable. By 1897, more than 150 brands were available. Along with imports (which, at the height of the craze, could not keep up with demand) there were many local manufacturers – one of the largest, Dux Cycle Co in Melbourne, employed 150 workers.

The craze had considerable social impact. As in the USA and Europe, elements of society found cycling confronting. They said it caused havoc on the streets, and some in the clergy considered it an evil pastime – particularly if it was undertaken on Sunday. Then there was the issue of women cycling: it was said by opponents to be promiscuous or even potentially damaging to a woman's feminine health. Yet the bicycle gave women new independence, and they took to the vehicle with a passion.

The use of bicycles soon spread to rural areas, where, rather than being a plaything for the rich and fashionable, they became a tool for workers (the rural wealthy stuck with their costly horses and many despised and ridiculed bicycles).

On Western Australia's goldfields in the 1890s, cycle-messenger services were important for communication between towns; and bikes were extremely popular for transport. Elsewhere, shearers and other itinerant workers cycled hundreds of kilometres on rough roads between jobs, and used bikes for sheep mustering and boundary riding. In Melbourne, the general post office began using bicycles for mail collection.

Before motor cars, bicycles were the fastest way to travel around rural Australia: they were far more efficient than walking – even pushing a loaded bike was preferable to carrying a heavy swag (bed roll). Over distance, cyclists were – to the chagrin of horsemen – considerably faster than horses and could even beat trains. In 1937, champion cyclist Hubert Opperman rode 405km from Albany to Perth in 12 hours, 38 minutes; the train was almost three hours behind.

With the appearance of the safety bike, bicycle touring also became popular in the 1890s. The pastime effectively opened up the country as a series of incredible transcontinental journeys was made. Long-distance journeys between the eastern cities were already common when Percy Armstrong made the first north to south continental crossing in 1893, riding from Croydon in the Gulf of Carpentaria to Melbourne. Arthur Richardson was the first cyclist to cross the Nullarbor in 1896; four years later he became the first cyclist around Australia. Successful overland journeys captured public imagination and became useful marketing tools for bicycle and tyre companies. Australia became known as the long-distance cycling centre of the world.

Along with the epic transcontinental journeys, recreational bicycle touring was gaining popularity in the eastern states. The hotel industry was boosted by cycle tourists' need for food and resting places at regular intervals. And it was cycling that led to the first road maps being produced by keen riders such as George Broadbent and Joseph Pearson.

Bureau of Meteorology (www.bom.gov.au) Australia's official weather-forecasting site, featuring wind maps and rainfall radar images.
Department of the Environment & Heritage (www.deh.gov.au/parks/links/index.html) Links to information on Australia's national parks and reserves.
Lonely Planet (www.lonelyplanet.com) Get quick Australian information and inspiration from the 'Destinations' tab, a rundown of guidebooks from the bookshop, and an On Your Bike forum with cycling information on the Thorn Tree.

Touring in the Australian Alps became popular with Melbourne and Sydney cyclists. In 1897, the Austral Wheel published a special supplement, the *Austral Wheel Guide to the Victorian Alps*, detailing routes, accommodation and road conditions, and advertising accommodation and eating establishments. By 1898 the experiences of many cyclists in the Australian Alps led to the publication of detailed alpine touring guides – the area was well travelled by the time cars arrived.

Racing became popular in Australia from the early years of cycling. On a per-capita basis, Australia has been one of the most successful nations in the world – perhaps because of its ideal cycling conditions: flat, dry and rideable year-round.

In the 1890s, bike racing was a big business. Races such as the Austral Wheel Race, held at the Melbourne Cricket Ground since 1886, drew huge crowds – 32,000 (3% of the state's population) on the last day of the 1901 meet. Some of the more popular road races included Australia's longest-established road race, the Warrnambool to Melbourne, first held in 1895; and the Goulburn to Sydney ride in NSW, which began in 1902. The generous prize money offered in Australia (£250 at the 1894 Austral) attracted professional cyclists from around the world. Gambling was common and the ensuing corruption eventually led to a decline in track racing.

Australian cyclists first rode in the Tour de France in 1912. Hubert Opperman captained teams in 1928 and 1931. His fame in the 1930s saw a resurgence in racing's popularity, though it declined again during WW2 as cyclists enlisted to fight.

Although the public remained enamoured of overland cyclists and champions like Hubert Opperman, the popularity of bikes for transport declined generally after the turn of the 20th century. As Australians had embraced the new transportation technology in the 1890s, so they took to motor vehicles. After WW2, bikes all but disappeared and Australia developed one of the highest rates of car ownership in the world.

Recreational cycling made a resurgence in the 1970s, following the boom in the USA. Bicycle-touring clubs were formed around Australia. By then bicycles were 10-speed racers, which were geared too high for touring. By the early 1980s, mountain bikes arrived in Australia. Like the safety bike almost a century before, the mountain bike appealed to the masses because it was more comfortable and easier to ride than its predecessor.

In 1984, Bicycle Victoria held the Great Victorian Bike Ride: a supported, nine-day ride across the state, with 2000 participants. It was so successful it became an annual event, with other state cycling organisations copying the idea.

In 1999 a new race, the Tour Down Under (see the boxed text, p228), was established, and the sport's popularity and participation has continued to be buoyed by Australian pro successes in European races: Robbie McEwen (2002, 2004, 2006) and Baden Cooke (2003) have won the green sprinters' jersey at the Tour de France, with Cadel Evans finishing second overall in the race in 2007 and 2008. Stuart O'Grady won the infamous Paris-Roubaix – the so-called 'Hell of the North' in 2007.

Since the start of the new century, bicycle sales have exceeded sales of motor vehicles – 1.2 million bikes were sold in 2008, a year the industry was said to be worth $1 billion in Australia. The number of people using bicycles to commute to work has grown by almost one third between 2001 and 2006.

Environment

Separated from other lands for around 33 million years, Australia has been on a unique evolutionary journey, moulding wildlife as though it was an abstract art form – mammals with pouches, a pincushion that lays eggs, a monotreme with the bill of a duck – and grinding down its ancient mountains even as the rest of the world has been erecting theirs. Is it any wonder they call it the land down under?

THE LAND

Australia contains ancient rocks and evidence of the earliest life, but the landscape itself is also very old in many areas. While northern hemisphere land masses were scraped clean by glaciers during recent ice ages, this was not the case in much of Australia, which retains landscape and soil features caused by the cumulative effects of more than 100 million years of weathering.

In general, Australia has grown from west to east. The Pilbara region in Western Australia (WA) contains both Australia's oldest rocks (3.3 billion years) and evidence of stromatolites, some of the oldest known organisms (more than 2.5 billion years). Younger (600 million years) rocks in the Flinders Ranges contain fossils of jellyfish-like organisms, the first evidence of multi-celled life. Complex life burst forth worldwide soon after.

During the last billion years Australia has lain in the centre of two supercontinents, ancient Rodinia and more-recent Gondwana. The latter contained all the major southern landmasses and was assembled around 520 million years ago. During the subsequent 150 million years, warm and shallow seas covered parts of Australia, and volcanic arcs and deeper water lay to the east. Cycles of sedimentation and deformation built new crust, the present eastern Australia.

Global cooling about 330 million years ago, with Gondwana near the South Pole, plunged Australia into an extended glacial period. As the climate thawed 40 million years later, sediments, then cold peat swamps, filled subsiding basins along the east coast: Australia's future black-coal deposits. Sands that would become the cliffs of the Blue Mountains and rocks of the Sydney region were deposited subsequently in deltas and floodplains. Despite Australia's polar location, the climate continued to warm, with the development of arid inland riverine plains. Lush vegetation developed in eastern Australia when warm and humid conditions developed, and dinosaurs and early mammals roamed the land.

Crustal extension within Gondwana began about 180 million years ago, heralded by the injection of molten rock into the crust – now Tasmania's dolerite. The separation of Australia and Antarctica and the opening of the Tasman Sea both began 100 million years ago, at about the same time the first platypus appears in the fossil record. The opening of the Tasman Sea ended after less than 20 million years, but the Australian Plate has continued to move northeast by 7cm per year since, with northern Australia reaching the tropics about 25 million years ago.

The rise of Australia's Eastern Highlands, or Great Divide, and the formation of the Great Escarpment along its eastern margin were associated with the opening of the Tasman Sea. But its subsequent erosion, in particular gorge incision and valley widening along the Great Escarpment, has been remarkably slow, a reflection of the tectonic stability of this part of Australia.

Read about the 400-million-year greening of Gondwana supercontinent in Mary White's book, *The Greening of Gondwana*.

Australia and Antarctica had fully separated by 33 million years ago; Australia had finally become the island continent. The Antarctic Circumpolar Current then became established in the new Southern Ocean, triggering the refrigeration of Antarctica and increasing aridity in Australia about 15 million years ago, thus ending a 75-million-year period during which Australia and Antarctica were heavily forested and drained by abundant rivers and lakes.

Some uplift of the Central Australian mountain ranges occurred hundreds of millions of years ago. However, uplift of the Mt Lofty and Flinders Ranges has occurred over the last 50 million years, accelerating during the last 10 million, suggesting some of Australia's central mountains were formed from rejuvenated crustal activity and are not just worn down remnants of older, higher ranges. Further west, the Nullarbor Plain limestone was uplifted at the same time, facilitating the formation of one of the world's most extensive cave systems.

Australia is the only continent lacking active volcanoes, but this has not always been so and the most recent volcanic phase has barely ended. Basalt volcanoes and lava fields occurred all down the eastern margin from 70 million to just 4600 years ago, with the latter eruption near Mt Gambier probably witnessed by the local Aboriginal people. The Border Ranges in northern New South Wales (NSW) are the remnants of a 22-million-year-old basalt shield volcano, its eroded caldera being one of the largest in the world.

The gross shape of the Australian coastline reflects the Gondwana break-up fracture pattern, but at a detailed level the coast has evolved from a combination of drowning and erosion of rocky coastal areas, and recent deposition in deltas and along sandy coastlines. Sea levels rose and fell by more than 100m over the last one to two million years, with shorelines migrating in response to the waxing and waning of several ice ages; the present level was attained only 6500 years ago.

Around 1300 sq km of Tasmania's highlands was glaciated during the last ice age, peaking 18,000 years ago, but on the mainland only a small area of ice formed near Mt Kosciuszko. However, the ice ages were periods of lowered precipitation as well as temperature, and did have a dramatic continent-wide effect on the character and distribution of vegetation. Many of Australia's desert dunes are probably relict features from the last ice age.

The Australian Museum's online resource, www.amonline.net.au, links you to hundreds of fact sheets on Australia's environment.

WILDLIFE

In the main, Australia's animals are more sensible than cyclists, avoiding the heat of day and stirring only for nocturnal activity. This means your days are unlikely to be spent among warm-blooded company, though wildlife encounters during dawn starts are common. Cyclists at least have the advantage of silence, coming upon animals often before they notice you. When they do, however, expect them to run as though you're the devil.

Animals
MAMMALS

The kangaroo is as symbolically Australian as Uluru, though it comes in about 39 flavours (counting wallabies). The most majestic of these is the **red kangaroo**, standing up to 1.8m tall. Restricted to the arid inland, these bush giants are unlikely to be seen by cyclists. A more common sight is the **eastern grey kangaroo**, marginally smaller (and a lot greyer) than big red, and found throughout eastern Australia. The **western grey**

For a more complete look at Australian animals and their distribution, see Lonely Planet's *Watching Wildlife Australia*.

ROLLING LIGHTLY

The Australian bush is more fragile than its sun-hardened image indicates, and some camping and off-road cycling practices can easily upset the ecological balance. Many of the principles outlined in minimal impact bushwalking codes also apply to cycle tourers – you will find an example of a bushwalking code at the Parks Victoria {www.parkweb.vic.gov.au/1process _details.cfm?note=18). The following guidelines are based on these codes.

RUBBISH

- If cycling into a national park, take plastic bags for your rubbish and if you have carried it in, carry it out. Also carry out rubbish left by other people.
- Don't bury or burn rubbish. Burning creates pollution and buried rubbish might be dug up by animals and scattered.

HUMAN WASTE

- If there is no toilet, bury your waste by digging a hole 15cm deep and at least 100m from any watercourse and campsite. Take a trowel or large tent peg for this purpose. Cover the waste and paper with soil.
- At many national park campsites there are composting toilets. Do not place rubbish in these toilets as it can affect the composting process.

FEEDING ANIMALS

- Don't feed animals – no matter how cute they are – and secure rubbish and food away from prying paws. Feeding makes wild creatures dependent on humans for food and can cause diseases such as lumpy jaw – a fatal condition found in marsupials, causing them to starve to death.

CAMPING

- Use an existing campsite rather than creating a new one. Avoid grassed areas; choose sandy or hard surfaces.
- Don't dig trenches around your tent to divert rainwater; use a waterproof groundsheet.

WASHING

- Don't use detergents or toothpaste in or near watercourses; try to use sand or a scourer (not detergent) to clean dishes.

kangaroo, which looks very much like the eastern grey, isn't limited by its name, ranging across southern Australia.

Wallabies are classified as kangaroo species weighing less than 25kg, and there are several you might see on your journeys. The **red-necked wallaby**, with its characteristic reddish nape, is the most commonly seen along the east coast and in Tasmania, while the dark **swamp wallaby** is also a frequent sight. In Tasmania, you're also likely to see **Bennett's wallabies** and tiny **pademelons**.

If you are going to reliably see any one mammal, it will be the **brush-tail possum**, the largest and most boisterous of Australia's possums. Renowned for making a racket on suburban roofs, brushtails are no less bold in the bush, and in many campsites, especially in Tasmania, you will need to guard your food against these bushy thieves. More reticent is the **ringtail possum**, with its white-ringed prehensile tail used for climbing.

The **koala** tops everybody's list of wildlife darlings, at least until you have slept anywhere near a randy male koala grunting like a wild boar.

○ If washing with soap, use a water container at least 50m from any watercourse. Disperse the wastewater widely so it filters through the soil before it returns to the creek.

○ Strain food scraps from dishwashing water and carry them out in your rubbish.

FIRES & TOTAL FIRE BANS

○ Campfires are not allowed in fuel-stove-only areas.

○ Carry a fuel stove to avoid campfires; fires inevitably result in some scarring of the land.

○ Fires of any kind (including fuel stoves) are prohibited on days of Total Fire Ban.

○ In remote areas, regard any hot, dry, windy day as a fire ban day.

○ If having a campfire, use an existing fireplace rather than making a new one.

○ If there are multiple fireplaces, use the major one – you might even consider dismantling the others.

○ Don't surround fireplaces with rocks; instead, clear away all flammable material for at least 2m. Use the minimum of dead, fallen wood.

○ Be absolutely certain the fire is extinguished.

○ Drown the embers with water – sand and soil won't extinguish a fire. A fire is only safe to leave when you can comfortably put your hand on it.

○ Place your stove on hard, nonliving surfaces (ie not vegetation). Cooking on vegetation can cause scorching from radiant heat – you may not see the effect immediately as it can come through over subsequent days.

THERE IS ALSO A CODE SPECIFIC TO MOUNTAIN BIKING AND OFF-ROAD CYCLING

○ Ride in control at all times

○ Respect the rights of others

○ Give walkers right of way and announce your presence

○ Give horses right of way

○ Don't cut corners; stay on the track

○ Avoid skidding, which damages tracks and leads to erosion

○ Wash your tyres before riding in a different area

○ Stay on roads and obey signs

○ Don't disturb plants or animals

With tufted ears and a hard black nose, it is among the easiest marsupials to spot during the day, often resting in a low fork of a eucalypt; manna gums are a favourite. You will find koalas along much of the east coast – frequently in Port Macquarie (p49) – and also in South Australia, where they have been reintroduced after becoming extinct.

The common **wombat** is another bit of bush cuddliness that cyclists in NSW, Victoria and Tasmania might encounter. With its vaguely bear-like shape and amble, it looks cumbersome but can hit speeds of up to 40km/h, offering you a good race.

One creature you won't want to cuddle is the **echidna**. Commonly seen by cyclists nosing along bush tracks and by the road, this creature has a coat of long spines on its back and an elongated, beak-like snout perfect for catching ants and termites, its main food. If an echidna notices you, it will generally burrow frantically, leaving only its spines exposed. Echidnas are found throughout Australia.

Along with the echidna, the **platypus** is the world's last remaining monotreme, or egg-laying mammal. It is something of a jigsaw, with a

Legend suggests that 'kangaroo' is an Aboriginal word for 'don't know'. When James Cook first saw this strange creature, he supposedly asked an Aboriginal man what it was. The man answered that he didn't know…'kangaroo'.

DEVIL OF A DISEASE

Since the mid-1990s, the Tasmanian devil population has been decimated by a fatal condition known as devil facial tumour disease (DFTD). Beginning as small lesions on the face and in the mouth, DFTD develops into large and hideous cancers around the face and neck. Affected animals usually die within six months of the appearance of lesions.

First found in Tasmania's northeast in 1996, DFTD has since become prevalent throughout eastern, central and northern parts of the island – around 60% of the island. The west coast has remained steadfastly free of the disease. There has been a drastic population decline in some of these areas, with up to 95% of some populations dying from DFTD, and sightings of the animal said to have dropped by around two-thirds. Tasmanian devils were listed as an endangered species in May 2008, with the population predicted at between 20,000 and 50,000.

If you see a sick Tasmanian devil, leave it be but report it to the Save the Tasmanian Devil Program (www.tassiedevil.com.au).

duck-like bill, short legs, webbed feet and a short, beaver-like tail. It is confined to the eastern mainland and Tasmania, and you are not going to see a platypus on many rides, though it is seen at Lake St Clair (p216) and Gradys Creek (p339).

Discover the curious world of the wombat in James Woodford's *The Secret Life of Wombats*.

As the name suggests, you will find the **Tasmanian devil** only in Tasmania. As stocky as a small pig, with white stripes across its black chest, its ferocious name gives it a largely undeserved notoriety, though watch a group of devils arguing over roadkill and you will wonder. It has solitary and nocturnal habits, either scavenging or hunting vertebrates. If you hear a banshee scream in the night, it is likely to be a Tassie devil but, don't worry, it is not about to come charging through your tent.

BIRDS

Australia has around 800 recorded bird species and they are the most visible of the animals you are likely to see while cycling. They are most active in the early morning and you will have a better chance of seeing a good variety if you set off early each day.

Australia's most recognisable birds are the **emu** and the **kookaburra**. The former looks like an ostrich baked dry by the sun and is found across most of the country. When startled, it can hit speeds of 50km/h. You will almost certainly hear the loud cackling laugh of the kookaburra (the largest member of the kingfisher family) before you see it, though it is also easily spotted. Closely related is the blue-winged kookaburra, found in the tropics.

If you are cycling in spring, the **Australian magpie** will probably find you before you find it. This large black-and-white bird has one of the bush's most melodious songs, but can be highly territorial when breeding, swooping anything that comes near, including humans. Cyclists are particularly prone to swooping.

Ecotourism Australia (www.ecotourism.org.au) has an accreditation system for environmentally friendly and sustainable tourism in Australia.

Looking like a cross between a crow and a magpie, the **pied currawong** is one of the most regularly seen birds in the bush. This black bird has yellow eyes and a strip of white across its tail feathers. It is among the most gregarious of the birds you will encounter and has a piercing, almost parrot-like call.

The greatest sight you will see in the Australian skies is the freewheeling figure of a **wedge-tailed eagle**. The country's largest bird of prey has a wingspan of up to 2m and is named for the distinctive shape of its tail.

Though 'wedgies' are found across Australia, they are most commonly seen in the interior.

Just as fascinating is the sight of a male **bowerbird** at work. This stocky, stout-billed bird builds a bower that he decorates with various coloured objects: the glossy-blue male satin bowerbird will use almost anything so long as it's blue; the golden bowerbird uses pale-green moss, pale flowers and fruits; and the great bowerbird accumulates stones, shells, seeds and metallic objects.

Among the parrots and cockatoos you can expect to see, the **galah** and **sulphur-crested cockatoo** are prominent. The former is pink and grey in colour, while the latter is white and has a crest coloured like the rim of a volcano. It also has a shriek loud enough to wake the dead. The **black-cockatoo**, whether yellow-, red- or white-tailed, is another welcome sight. They can look like crows from a distance, but have a heavier, lazier wing motion and a call like a creaky door. The **crimson rosella** is a common sight – look for a flash of red through the trees – and the brilliantly coloured **rainbow lorikeet**, with its blue head, orange breast and green body, gathers in great numbers around flowering plants.

The **superb lyrebird**, which graces the Australian 10-cent coin, is a ground-dwelling bird. The male lyrebird has tail feathers that form a lyre shape when hoisted to attract a female. Its party trick is bush mimicry, copying almost any noise it has heard, from the calls of other birds to livestock and chainsaws.

Cyclists in Queensland will soon become aware of the Australian **brush-turkey**, with its bald red head and yellow wattles – it will be the bird trying to pilfer your food and rubbish bag. You might even start wishing Christmas dinner upon it.

Magpies usually swoop from behind. Painting eyes on the back of your helmet can dissuade them from attacking.

For a bird identification guide that will fit easily into a pannier, carry the *Slater Field Guide to Australian Birds* by Peter, Pat and Raoul Slater.

REPTILES

It is true that Australia has a few reptiles, but work under the assumption that they are at least as frightened of you as you are of them.

Australia has 130 species of **snake** and, despite the negative press, the majority are harmless (though it is always wise to assume otherwise). Warm, sunny conditions, such as the start of spring, are best for seeing snakes. It is difficult at a glance to tell one snake from another as most

ROADKILL

It is the great curse of the Australian highway, a thing you will smell before you see it. It varies from tiny critters to – in the country's north – enormous cattle. Ride downwind from it and you'll wonder if you're ever going to escape the stench.

Roadkill is one of the quintessential sights of the Australian road, with creatures wandering out of the bush and into the paths of cars and trucks. Most roadkill occurs at dawn and dusk as the bush stirs to life, so you're unlikely to witness the kill but you will undoubtedly smell it at some point.

Tasmania is something of an epicentre for roadkill. It's been estimated that around 300,000 animals – 34 an hour – are killed on the state's roads every year, including 4000 Tasmanian devils and 110,000 brushtail possums. It is at once a sign of the health of the state's bush, with so many creatures wandering about, and a cause of distress to numerous visitors, with some saying they would never return to the island state because of the roadside carnage. A website (www.roadkilltas.com) has been created, documenting roadkill hotspots in the state, and a movie – *Tasmania: Your Roadkill State* – made about the animal road toll. It's nothing to sniff at.

come in fetching shades of brown or black. As sealed roads are popular sunning spots for snakes expect to see at least a few on your ride.

One reptile you will want to see is the **goanna**, or monitor lizard, a primordial reptile with the swagger of a cowboy. Australia has around 25 species of goanna, which can stretch to 2.5m. Gould's goanna, with cream or yellow spots, and the lace monitor, with white, cream or yellow scales forming a lace-like pattern, are often seen ambling through camps.

Only cyclists riding in far north Queensland will need to read up on **crocodiles**. The saltwater (or estuarine) crocodile is the one that causes all the fuss. Growing to 7m, it will attack and kill humans. It lives in large numbers on mangrove-rimmed Hinchinbrook, though there have been no recorded attacks. The freshwater crocodile is smaller, not so interested in the taste of humans, and can be distinguished from 'salties' by its narrow snout (salties have wide, box-like snouts).

PLANTS & TREES
Native Grasses
Australia has more than 700 species of native grass, though the one that will be noticed most by cyclists is Tasmania's **buttongrass**. Largely confined to poorly drained plains in southwest Tasmania, it grows in tall tussocks, separated by bare patches of bog – you'll see plenty of it on the Tassie's West Coast ride (p193). Its leaves are tough and the flower for which it is named is a small cluster of white spikelets.

Shrubs & Flowers
The best known of the Australian shrubs (and among the easiest to identify) is the **bottlebrush**, or callistemon. Named for its brush-like flowers, it is found right across the country, and ranges in height from 1m to 10m. There are about 30 species with varying flower colours – red, white, pink and yellow among them – though species are difficult to distinguish. These shrubs are a favourite with some birds.

There are around 250 species of **grevillea**, of which 245 are endemic to Australia. They come in various sizes and flower colours and are found in the Australian Alps, forests, semi-arid country and near the coast. Most are small to medium in size, although the silky oak can grow to 25m and, covered with orange flowers, is one of Australia's most beautiful trees.

There are around 80 species of **tea-tree**, which are found in all states. Most species are large, dense bushes, not trees (despite the name). Early settlers gave the plant its name after trying to brew tea using the leaves. Its flowers are mainly white and stalkless, and leaves are small.

The **pandani** is the tallest heath plant in the world, and though it looks more like a tropical palm you will only find it in west and southwest Tasmania – there are a few pandani growing at Ronny Creek on the side trip to Dove Lake during the Tassie's West Coast ride (p193). It can reach a height of 12m, and has a crown of stiff leathery leaves 1.5m long, with old, dead leaves or fronds forming a huge skirt around the lower trunk.

Cycads & Ferns
The **burrawang** grows along the NSW coast on sandy soils. The 2m-long palm-like fronds grow from ground level. Its red seeds are also poisonous.

The beautifully ornate **rough tree fern** and the **soft tree fern** are found in eastern Australia's temperate rainforests. Some reach a height of 20m and all are capped by a crown of green fronds.

Trees

First among equals for Australian trees is the ubiquitous eucalyptus, or gum tree. Of the 700 species, all but about eight are endemic to Australia. Eucalypts vary in form and height from the tall, ruler-straight **karri** (confined to WA) and the towering **mountain ash** to the twisted snow gum. The latter is one of Australia's most striking trees, flourishing at higher altitudes than any other eucalyptus – up to 1700m in the High Country and also found in the Tasmanian highlands. **River red gums** typically line watercourses, permanent or ephemeral, where their deep roots tap underground water reserves. The most widespread eucalypt, these massive, spreading trees grow to 45m high and can live for hundreds of years. River red gums are notorious shedders of branches, so never camp under this tree; people have been killed by falling branches.

Australian acacias are commonly known as wattles and around 700 species have been recorded. They vary from small shrubs to the **blackwood**, which grows up to 30m. The flowers come in all shades of yellow; most species flower during late winter and spring, bringing brilliant splashes of colour to the bush.

The **golden wattle**, with its masses of bright-yellow flowers, is Australia's floral emblem. A less showy acacia is the **mulga**, found across the arid inland. Its wide, funnel-like shape acts as its own water catchment, channelling rain to its base.

Banksias take their name from Sir Joseph Banks, the botanist who accompanied James Cook on his exploration of eastern Australia. Numbering about 70 species and confined to Australia, they are common on sandy soils. Most banksias sport upright cylindrical flower spikes up to 30cm long, covered with vibrant orange, red or yellow flowers. As the flowers die, the woody fruits appear. Aboriginal people dipped the banksia spikes in water to make a sweet drink.

Casuarinas, also known as she-oaks, are hardy trees characterised by wiry 'leaves' that are actually branchlets; the true leaves are small scales clustered in whorls at intervals along the branchlets. Casuarinas produce distinctive small knobbly cones. They are widely distributed from the desert to the coast.

The **melaleuca**, also called paperbark or honey-myrtle, is easily recognised by its pale papery bark, which peels from the trunk in thin sheets. It is widespread on rocky ground, from the coast to semiarid inland areas. The flower spikes consist of many tiny filaments and range from cream through crimson to purple.

Australia has several families of native conifer, but they rarely dominate the vegetation as some pines and spruces do in the northern hemisphere. Endemic to Tasmania, the **pencil pine** is found in areas of high rainfall around the central plateau and the southwest. A graceful tree, it usually grows to a height of about 15m. Growing in coastal areas and inland semi-arid country in all states except WA, the **Oyster Bay pine** has distinctive segmented cones and reaches a height of 6m. Foliage is typical of the Callitris genus – tiny scaly leaves arranged along thin branchlets. The **cypress pine** has hard, furrowed bark and its resistance to termites has made it a favourite bush building material.

The unusual looking **grass tree** is widespread in southeastern and southwestern Australia, mainly on sandy soils. It has very thin long leaves, a short thick trunk and a distinctive flower spike up to 3m tall, with tiny flowers massed along the upper half of a long stem.

Never again will you think of the humble gum tree as just a khaki-coloured bit of stick after reading Murray Bail's beautiful *Eucalyptus*.

Australia has about 50 species of **mangrove** – trees and shrubs adapted to daily flooding by salt water. Along northern coasts and estuaries, various species grow to around 30m, while at the southern limit of their distribution, in Victoria, they rarely exceed 5m. Mangroves have various ways of coping with inundation, with some breathing through aerial roots that are exposed at low tide. Cyclists on the Daintree & Cape Tribulation ride (p317) will particularly notice mangroves.

NATIONAL PARKS & RESERVES

It is safe to suggest that Australia has more national parks than any other country on earth. While Britain has 15 and the USA has around 60, Australia has about 330 national parks.

Around 7% of Australia's land is protected as either national park or as some other form of nature conservation reserve. It doesn't sound huge, but it represents an area about twice the size of New Zealand. South Australia has the greatest amount of protected land, both in area (203,700 sq km) and as a proportion of the state (20.7%). This is followed by Tasmania (20%), Victoria (13.4%), WA (6.1%), NSW (4.8%), Queensland (3.1%) and the Northern Territory (2.8%).

ENVIRONMENTAL ISSUES

Headlining the environmental issues facing Australia's fragile landscape are climate change, water scarcity, nuclear energy and uranium mining. All are interconnected. For Australia, the warmer temperatures resulting from climate change spell disaster to an already fragile landscape. At the time of research, Australia was suffering its worst drought on record. Dams throughout the country are at record lows and mandatory water restrictions have been imposed. A 2°C climb in average temperatures on the globe's driest continent will result in an even drier southern half of the country and greater water scarcity. Scientists also agree that hotter and drier conditions will exacerbate bushfire conditions and increase cyclone intensity, two natural phenomena that regularly beset Australia – in February 2009, Australia experienced its worst-ever peacetime disaster when bushfires killed 210 people in Victoria.

Australia is a heavy greenhouse-gas emitter because it mostly relies on coal and other fossil fuels for its energy supplies. The most prominent and contentious alternative energy source is nuclear power, which creates less greenhouse gases and relies on uranium, in which Australia is rich. But the radioactive waste created by nuclear power stations can take thousands of years to become harmless. Moreover, uranium is a finite energy (as opposed to cleaner and renewable energy sources such as

WORLD HERITAGE ON WHEELS

Australia has 17 sites inscribed on the Unesco World Heritage list, including four that feature in routes in this book:

○ Gondwana Rainforests of Australia (Border Loop, p291; Coffs & Dorrigo Circuit, p75)

○ Greater Blue Mountains Area (Bathurst to the Blueys, p63)

○ Tasmanian Wilderness (Tassie's West Coast, p193; Across the Central Plateau, p183)

○ Wet Tropics of Queensland (The Daintree & Cape Tribulation, p317)

For a full list of World Heritage sites, log on to whc.unesco.org.

solar and wind power), and even if Australia were to establish sufficient nuclear power stations now to make a real reduction in coal-dependency, it would be years before the environmental and economic benefits were realised.

Uranium mining itself also produces polarised opinions. As countries around the world are also looking to nuclear energy, Australia finds itself in a position to increase exports of one of its top-dollar resources. But uranium mining in Australia has been met with fierce opposition for decades, not only because the product is a core ingredient of nuclear weapons, but also because much of Australia's uranium supplies sit beneath sacred Aboriginal land. Supporters of increased uranium mining and export suggest that the best way to police the use of uranium is to manage its entire life cycle; that is, to sell the raw product to international buyers, and then charge a fee to accept the waste and dispose of it. Both major political parties consider an expansion of Australia's $570 million-a-year uranium export industry to be inevitable for economic reasons.

Conservation groups in Australia include the following:

Australian Conservation Foundation (ACF; ☎ 1800 332 510; www .acfonline.org.au)
Foundation for National Parks & Wildlife (☎ 02-9221 1949; www .fnpw.com.au)
Friends of the Earth Australia (☎ 03-9419 8700; www.foe.org.au)
Greenpeace Australia Pacific (☎ 02-9261 4666; www.greenpeace.org.au)
Landcare Australia (☎ 1800 151 105; www.landcareonline.com)
Wilderness Society (☎ 03-6270 1701; www.wilderness.org.au)

DID YOU KNOW?

The world's first 'green' political party was formed in Australia, arising from failed efforts to stop the flooding of Lake Pedder in Tasmania's southwest in the 1960s and early 1970s.

Outback Tracks

Australia's defining landscape is the outback, the remote, drought-dry lands that make up the bulk of the country. Rides described in this book steer clear of the outback with its difficulties, demands and complicated logistics, but still it beckons like a siren call for a growing number of riders determined to test themselves against Australia's mighty elements.

Outback cycling requires meticulous preparation and planning and, yes, a decent boredom threshold – didn't you see that same tree 100km ago? But the rewards go beyond the scenery. To cross the Nullarbor or reach the tip of Cape York is about finding fulfilment in your self-sufficiency, savouring the emptiness and truly discovering the epic vastness of Australia.

This chapter provides a bare-bones look at a selection of the best outback routes. It's not intended as a guide but may inspire (or discourage) you to research further that grand outback cycling adventure.

NULLARBOR

The Australian road with the most fearsome reputation is, conversely, one of the most straightforward and manageable outback rides, with trucks and traffic being greater obstacles than distances and lack of services.

From Ceduna, at its eastern end, to Norseman, in the west, it's 1210km across the Nullarbor. Along this length there are 10 roadhouse stops, cutting the ride into manageable slices, though there are three extended gaps that might necessitate camping in the scrub and carrying extra food and water. Between Nullarbor Roadhouse and Border Village it's 186km of cycling; from Caiguna to Balladonia it's 182km; and it's a 191km stretch from Balladonia to Norseman. Otherwise, the roadhouses are in nice manageable order, giving cyclists a spot to camp and fill up with water each evening. From the east, the distances between roadhouse stops are: Ceduna to Penong, 73km; Penong to Nundroo, 74km; Nundroo to Yalata, 55km; Yalata to Nullarbor, 94km; Nullarbor to Border Village, 186km; Border Village to Eucla, 13km; Eucla to Mundrabilla, 66km; Mundrabilla to Madura Pass, 116km; Madura Pass to Cocklebiddy, 93km; Cocklebiddy to Caiguna, 65km; Caiguna to Balladonia, 182km; Balladonia to Norseman, 191km. All of the roadhouses have campsites – unattractive in the main, but serviceable – and many have motel rooms or dongas (portable buildings). Water supplies are an issue for a number of the roadhouses, so check ahead on their current mood about supplying water to cyclists.

The surprising thing about crossing the Nullarbor is that it's not the bore that the name and reputation suggest (though there is the presence of the Ninety Mile Straight out of Caiguna – 145km of unbending bitumen that forms one of the longest straight bits of road in the world). The small road section through the Nullarbor Plain is bookended by gently rolling mallee scrub, draping away in the west to the cliffs of the Great Australian Bight, which fall away 70m into the Southern Ocean and the world's second-largest marine park (after the Great Barrier Reef). At the foot of the cliffs, from July to September, you can view southern right whales as they migrate from Antarctic waters to their mating and calving grounds in the Great Australian Bight.

STUART HIGHWAY

In the minds of many foreign cyclists, the Stuart Hwy is the ultimate Australian challenge, rolling from the Top End to the bottom end at Adelaide, a 3000km journey through tropics, savannah and desert. It's a ride of discovery, both of Australia's red centre and, often, of self, with the loneliness of distance sometimes taking its toll on those who fly direct to Darwin from crowded European or Asian cities and then ride straight out into the never-never.

This highway is perhaps the most iconic in the country, passing through Katherine, Daly Waters, Alice Springs and Coober Pedy – a who's who of the outback – but distances are long and scenery often short on features.

From Darwin it's a straightforward run to Katherine (315km from Darwin), from where the towns and roadhouses begin to spread thin. From Katherine to the Northern Territory–South Australia border, it's around 1450km that's broken up by fly-speck towns, the Alice and a string of roadhouses. All up there are 17 stops to the border and the only times you really exceed 100km between services is from Katherine to Mataranka (106km), Renner Springs to Three Ways (136km), Tennant Creek to Wauchope (114km) and Aileron to Alice Springs (133km). On the Northern Territory (NT) stretch it's not distance but drivers that you need to be most cautious about. Until recently the NT section of the Stuart Hwy had open speed limits; it wasn't unusual to have vehicles racing past at 150 or 160km/h. The speed limit is now 130km/h – the highest in Australia – but there's still a sense of lawlessness about some NT drivers. It's not uncommon to have them drive close, scream, throw things…

Curiously, given that it's the NT that has Australia's remote and raw image, it's when the highway crosses into South Australia (SA) that the difficulties of distance begin. From Kulgera it's 180km to Marla; and from Cadney Homestead it's 152km to Coober Pedy, from where it's more than 250km to Glendambo. As a final stiffener, it's around 170km from Pimba to Port Augusta. It's almost inevitable that you'll need to carry water and food supplies and camp out in the bush, although actual bushes can be thin on the ground.

The Stuart Hwy ends at Port Augusta – ah, civilisation again – but most cyclists continue on the 300km to Adelaide. The Princes Hwy between Port Augusta and Adelaide is a narrow crowd of trucks, so it's better to cross low Horrocks Pass into Wilmington, from where Main North Rd travels south – and more scenically – into Adelaide.

OODNADATTA TRACK

If you want to travel through northern SA but don't want the sealed Stuart Hwy or its traffic, the bumpy Oodnadatta Track is the option of choice. This 615km dirt road links Marree to Marla via the lyrically named Oodnadatta, a classic outback town best known for its Pink Roadhouse. The road traces the route of the old Overland Telegraph Line and the Great Northern Railway, taking in ruins of railway sidings and telegraph stations.

If you're out for the long haul, a good place to start an Oodnadatta Track ride is Port Augusta, riding to Wilpena Pound and then cutting through Parachilna Gorge to the B83 and Lyndhurst and Marree, where the Oodnadatta Track kicks left as the more remote Birdsville Track turns away right.

Out of Marree it's 202km to the first services at William Creek, though there's a campsite 130km along at Coward Springs. You'll also pass the shores of Lake Eyre South, which will either be blindingly white with salt or, at rare moments, full of water. The sixth-largest lake in the world, Lake Eyre is also Australia's lowest point, at around 15m below sea level – so if you're breathing hard it's not because of lack of oxygen. It's another 203km along the track to the next town at Oodnadatta and then 212km to Marla. Across corrugated roads it's best to allow three days between each of the service stops, so you'll need to camp in the bush and carry a few days of food and water. There are coolabah-lined streams along the way, but check with the William Creek Hotel or the roadhouse in Oodnadatta as to the presence of drinking water.

A host of mud maps and brochures about the Oodnadatta Track can be downloaded from the **Pink Roadhouse** (www.pinkroadhouse.com.au).

WEST COAST

Western Australia has more coastline than Queensland, New South Wales and Victoria combined so it's to be expected that a cycle tour up these shores would be an epic journey. There's great beauty here – the Pinnacles, Shark Bay, Ningaloo Reef, Broome – but there's penance in between. To ride the west coast you must be prepared for the longest distances between services of any of the Australian highways, you must be mentally ready to face sections of bare land that out-Nullarbor the Nullarbor, and you must surrender to the frustration that some of the west coast's finest moments can only be reached on lengthy side trips – 170km or 220km into Exmouth (depending on which turning you take) and 130km into Shark Bay.

For favourable prevailing winds it's best to start in the north, at Broome, and ride the 2200km south along the coast, though this has the flipside of throwing you straight into 560km of nothingness to Port Hedland, a section of road that's been called Australia's dullest – if it's an exaggeration, it's not by much. There's a 286km section without services, so there's no time for fine-tuning your packing system. The gaps between roadhouses stay large for most of the journey so this is a trip for riders comfortable with self-sufficiency, wild camping and the maelstrom of passing road trains – traffic isn't thick on this highway but it is heavy, literally.

The road runs close to the coast though it's rarely in sight, making detours a necessity if you want to see anything more than the roadside scrub. If you're not up for the long hauls into Exmouth and Shark Bay, it's possible to touch the Indian Ocean with some shorter detours such as Ninety Mile Beach, Karratha and Kalbarri.

If you really want to add an outback, out-of-your-mind experience, turn inland at Port Hedland (if riding south) or Nanutarra Roadhouse (if riding north) and venture into Tom Price and Karijini National Park, one of the most spectacular parks in the country with a web of gorges sliced deep into the spinifex-coated Hamersley Range. It's a 290km, serviceless haul between Nanutarra and Tom Price, partly on dirt roads, and you'll need to carry plenty of water for the perpetual heat.

GIBB RIVER ROAD

If you ride out of Broome heading east instead of south, the most enticing – and difficult – route across the Kimberley is Gibb River Rd, providing around 640km of dirt road, corrugations, heat and sublime scenery. The road begins in Derby, around 220km from Broome, and bumps overland to near Kununurra. It is a destroyer of 4WDs – tyres get slashed, axles shear through – and on a bike it's also difficult as you negotiate deep sand one day, sharp stones the next and canyon-sized corrugations throughout. Carry plenty of spares and a good supply of food because

OUTBACK ENCOUNTERS WITH GREY NOMADS

Any touring cyclist venturing into the outback is likely to come across a unique genus of traveller increasingly endemic to Australia, the Grey Nomad. This species of over-50 adventurer can often be sighted, at any time of day, cruising outback roads in well-appointed rigs. While caravaners and mobile-homers are most common, 4wd-drivers are increasingly widespread.

Grey Nomads are living the dream. Visit any out-of the-way campsite or outback roadhouse and you'll encounter spry Baby Boomers who, finally unshackled from life-long responsibilities, are embracing the unequalled freedom of a life on the road. While some have acquired their homes on wheels to enjoy cheap and frequent getaways around the country, for others this is the ultimate adventure – The Great Australian Big Trip, from one corner of this vast, beautiful, rugged land to the other, and every sealed and unsealed road in between.

Like all breeds of traveller, the Grey Nomads help to support the small outback towns they visit by injecting money into the local economy. But they are possibly unique in Australia as tourists who also seek to improve these communities. It is fair to say that the Grey Nomad population has a level and range of skills unmatched by those of most other travellers, and when they work or volunteer in isolated rural towns they make a truly valuable contribution. In realising their nomadic quests, these greying tourers are also helping to strengthen the nation's future, rest stop by rest stop.

It's not only outback communities that benefit from the presence of a network of Grey Nomads on the road. Nomads are wizened counterparts of the touring cyclist. Though the rigs might differ, the mindset is the same; a thirst for local information, the best route or even just the best roadhouse burger are shared passions. So, if you happen upon a Nomad roadside or fireside, take the opportunity to consult with one of these outback oracles of the modern travel experience.

progress is slow, due to both the road surface and the certain desire to explore the various gorges that sit back from the road.

Expect the opening 215km haul from Derby to Imintji Roadhouse to take three or four days, especially if you detour away to visit Windjana Gorge or Bell Gorge (both side trips are recommended). From Imintji it's 90km to Mt Barnett Roadhouse. This is the last of the roadhouses, though there's more than 300km still to ride. There are basic supplies, however, at Jack's Waterhole and there's a slathering of outback luxury at El Questro, near the road's end, if you're up for a splurge – a double room will set you back around $1800.

The Gibb River Rd is impassable in the Wet (November to March) and while the road crosses plenty of creeks, water supplies are dependent on the previous Wet season – some years water is plentiful; others, it's like squeezing a lemon. It's worth ringing ahead to the roadhouses and stations along the road to check on water levels.

Two things add moments of discomfort to this ride. One, the road was built for cattle trucks, which still barrel up and down its length, towing storms of dust behind them, so you will finish each day powder-coated. Two, approaching the road's eastern end, you must cross the wide Pentecost River on a causeway that's often below the river's surface. This river is home to saltwater crocs, and pushing across is an enormous risk. Try instead to cadge a lift across with a 4WD. You might have to wait a while but that's far better than the possible alternative…

For a general insight into the Gibb River Rd, pick up a copy of *The Kimberley: An Adventurer's Guide* by Ron and Viv Moon.

MATILDA HIGHWAY

If it's dinky-di Australiana you want, then it's dinky-di Australiana you'll get on western Queensland's Matilda Hwy. In Longreach, there's the Stockman's Hall of Fame and the Qantas Founders Outback Museum.

Combo Waterhole is said to be the billabong in 'Waltzing Matilda' (the unofficial national anthem that had its first public reading at the North Gregory Hotel in Winton). A short distance on, the Walkabout Creek Hotel is still famous 20 years on as the pub in *Crocodile Dundee*. But as you cycle along the Matilda Hwy the thing you'll notice more than the Aussie icons is the treeless Mitchell grass plains – this is not heart-stirring country to look at, but you can smell the history almost as strongly as the roadkill.

The highway begins in Queensland's south at Cunnamulla and stretches 1700km north to the prawn-fishing centre of Karumba, on the shores of the Gulf of Carpentaria. Entirely sealed, the highway's greatest issues for a cyclist are road trains and the distances between services – get used to long days in the saddle or nights in the scrub. If you start in Cunnamulla, it's 200km to Charleville. There's then a 175km chasm between Longreach and Winton, where you gather breath ahead of the 165km leap to Kynuna. Between Cloncurry and Normanton it's almost 380km to Normanton, with just the discouragingly named Burke and Wills Roadhouse midway to break the ride.

Fiery summers – Longreach averages a maximum of almost 38°C in December – and a lack of shade on the black soil plains make winter the sensible time to ride the Matilda Hwy.

CAPE YORK

Ask any 4WDer in Australia about the ultimate outback road challenge and they're likely to answer 'Cape York', the northern tip of the country. This geographical boast has given the cape legendary status – people bring champagne to celebrate the achievement of reaching the rocky tip, though nobody has earned it more than the few cyclists who fight through the sand, bulldust and corrugations (and crocs) to get here.

Most Cape York journeys begin in Cairns, following the route of the Daintree & Cape Tribulation ride (p317) to Cape Tribulation and then ploughing north along the Bloomfield Track to Cooktown. Here, the first of the difficulties arise, with the road containing 33% gradients through the Cowie Range – an easier route to Cooktown travels inland through Mt Molloy and Lakeland but has none of the beauty of the coastal route.

The choice between beauty and expediency continues past Cooktown. As you ride north you can stick to the Peninsula Development Rd – the main drag – which beelines directly and mundanely to the tip, or you can venture through Lakefield National Park and then, later, along the Old Telegraph Track. Lakefield has the Laura River (where the crocs are rather a blight on the beauty) and a skyline of termite mounds, while the sandy Old Telegraph is the most attractive section on Cape York, with its flowering heathlands and succession of waterfalls – the campsite at Eliot Falls demands a rest day.

It's a 1200km ride from Cairns to Cape York, and it's best to allow three weeks to fight through the sand, corrugations and creek crossings. If you travel through Lakefield National Park, there's a 290km stretch between services. As most of the roadhouses don't stock groceries, it's best to post in food drops along the way – ring ahead to roadhouses and they're normally happy to hold packages of food for you.

After cycling 1200km, the bad news is that you won't be able to ride to the very tip, with the final 400m of the journey across a rocky headland. The better news is that you don't necessarily need to ride back to Cairns, with the cargo ship *Trinity Bay* – the last passenger-carrying

A basic resource for any cyclist riding to the tip is *Cape York: An Adventurer's Guide* by Ron Moon. While the entry on cycling isn't particularly useful, the remainder of the material is good.

cargo ship in Australia – making a weekly sailing from Seisia, near the tip, to Cairns. For information about the ship and sailings, see www .seaswift.com.au.

CANNING STOCK ROUTE

If Cape York has the reputation as the country's toughest road journey, the Canning Stock Route has the reality. Cutting through the desert heart of Western Australia, it's a journey attempted only by the hardiest, most driven cyclists, and usually then with 4WD support. If you want to ride it, breathe deeply, think about it for a year or two and see if the urge persists.

Covering 1700km between Wiluna and Halls Creek, the Canning is the longest stock route in the world and is a place of deep sand, intense heat and little water. There's not a single service between Wiluna and Halls Creek, so the support vehicle is usually required not only for safety but also to carry food – even 4WDs take around two weeks to cover the 1700km distance.

The Canning is a death-wish in summer – nobody travels here then – with the first travellers usually seen on the track around April or early May. The track tends to grow over with Spinifex during the summer so, unless you fancy your legs being punctured by spinifex needles with every pedal stroke, it's best to wait a couple of months, giving the 4WDs time to clear the track. The Canning season finishes up around October.

The stock route is lined with 54 wells plus a few water-bores and waterholes, but many are dry, so research into the track is as vital as fitness.

The best books on the Canning are *The Australian Geographic Book of the Canning Stock Route* by Jenny Stanton (ed) and *The Canning Stock Route: A Traveller's Guide for a Journey Through History* by Ronele and Eric Gard.

New South Wales

HIGHLIGHTS

- Floating through the heavenly **Promised Land** (p79) loop
- Riding into history in golden **Hill End** (p60)
- Savouring the view from **Carsons Pioneer Lookout** (p83) before whooshing down into it
- Losing yourself on the vast cycleways network of Australia's most bike-friendly city, **Canberra** (p85)
- Finally catching your breath at Dead Horse Gap, the highest pass of the **Alpine Way** (p74)

TERRAIN

A bit of just about everything, from flats and rolling along the coast and in the vineyards to hills and then mountains in the interior.

Telephone Code – 02	www.bicyclensw.org.au	www.visitnsw.com.au

The people of New South Wales (NSW) are passionate about their state. In pubs, sports arenas, business meetings and arts gatherings, they'll tell you in no uncertain terms just how and why it's the best in the federation. It's got the largest population, churns out the biggest bang for buck in most trades and industries, and has the kinds of A-grade cities and diversity of country that most places can only dream of.

Thrillingly for cyclists, this best-of-the-best-of-everything manifests itself as a rich choice of destinations and a fascinating range of terrain. Sydney, the state's political, economic and cultural engine, measures up again and again to visitors' high expectations, especially given its incomparable setting on Port Jackson. A sunny 2000km-long coastline is freckled with sparkling beaches and lively towns. To the west, the Great Dividing Range separates the populated ocean-front fringe from the scattered towns and villages of the interior. There are World Heritage–listed rainforests, elevated farmlands and, in the Snowy Mountains, alpine wilderness and peaks rising above 2000m. Nestled in its southern hills are the small Australian Capital Territory (ACT) and national capital, Canberra. West of the divide are grazing and farmlands, national parks showcasing Aboriginal endurance and culture, and almost unimaginable light and space.

HISTORY

Aboriginal people inhabited the land now known as NSW for over 50,000 years before the arrival of Europeans. These first custodians were thought to have included about 60 language groups comprising a total population of 300,000 to one million people.

In 1770 the young English Lieutenant (later Captain) James Cook stumbled across the east coast of Australia and landed at Botany Bay, just south of present-day central Sydney. Cook was met warily by the local people; as he noted in his journal, 'All they seemed to want was for us to be gone'. Eighteen years later, though, Arthur Phillip and the 'First Fleet' of 751 ragtag convicts and children, and around 250 soldiers, officials and their wives, landed at Port Jackson, just north, to establish the permanent British penal colony of NSW.

It's believed there were about 3000 Aboriginal people in the Sydney region at the time. They belonged to the Ku-ring-gai, Dharawal and Dharug language groups. Sydney Cove, itself, where Phillip's fleet landed, was home of the Eora people.

NSW was a harsh place in those days. Early attempts at farming were unsuccessful, so the colony bumbled through near-starvation and rum-fuelled political turmoil. As many settlers were convicts displaced from their homelands, they in turn set about dispossessing Aboriginal people, stripping them of their legal land rights and systematically subjecting them to incarceration, death or expulsion by force.

It wasn't until Lachlan Macquarie began his term as governor in 1810 that things improved, made even better by the gold-rush boom times of the 1850s. By then Sydney had been transformed into a well-planned colony, graced by fine civic architecture. It was during Macquarie's tenure, too, that colonists pushed over the Blue Mountains to the broad-acre pasture and croplands that would support the maturing colony – and make some of its settlers very rich.

Transportation of convicts to NSW ceased by 1850, but immigration was encouraged. Meanwhile, new colonies in present-day Victoria and South Australia were carving off areas of NSW, whose boundaries once covered more than half the continent.

In the 20th century post-WW2 immigration from the UK, Ireland and the Mediterranean – and more recently from Asia (especially Vietnam and China), the Middle East and Africa – brought new spirit and prosperity to NSW. The state has maintained its position as the forerunner in terms of both population and economic activity.

A long way from its colonial origins, Sydney today is a confident world city. In 2000 it welcomed the new millennium by hosting a spectacularly successful Olympic Games. Ugly race riots on Sydney's Cronulla Beach in 2005 laid bare long-simmering tensions between some old and new Australians, but overwhelmingly, the people of NSW are warm and open to travellers.

ENVIRONMENT

NSW can be roughly divided into five regions: the coastal strip; the Great Dividing Range, about 100km inland from the coast; the Blue Mountains west of Sydney; the Snowy Mountains in the south; and, west of the Great Dividing Range, farming country that dwindles into pan-flat dry plains covering two-thirds of the state and fading into the barren far-west outback.

The Great Dividing Range runs most of the length of Australia's east coast and incorporates many of the state's natural highlights. The Snowy Mountains in the south include the continent's highest peak, Mt Kosciuszko (2228m). The major rivers are the Murray and the Darling, which meander westwards across the plains and into Victoria. The eastern side of the range forms a generally steep escarpment, usually heavily forested. Most of the ancient range's peaks have been worn down to plateaus.

Despite extensive clearing for agriculture, vast areas of native vegetation remain little changed. Wollemi National Park, less than 100km northwest of Sydney, contains the state's largest officially recognised wilderness area – 3610 sq km. It's so wild that in 1994 the Wollemi pine, one of the world's oldest and rarest plants, was discovered (see boxed text The Tree that Time Forgot p63). It's just one example of the enormous floral biodiversity thriving on dry plains, coastal heath and in temperate and subtropical rainforests. Eucalypt forest is especially common, towering above banksias, grevilleas, bottlebrushes and boronias.

NEW SOUTH WALES

GOLD & WINE COUNTRY CIRCUIT p58

BATHURST TO THE BLUEYS p64

CANBERRA EXPLORER p86

MURRAY RIVER TO ALPINE WAY p70

Aborigines' land-management practices prior to European settlement – especially undergrowth burning to reduce fire risk and encourage plant regeneration and feed for mammals – gave early Sydney a park-like appearance. The dense scrub that's common today was largely absent. You could apparently gallop a horse through the bush.

Kangaroo and wallabies are common – at some picnic and campsites you sometimes have to shoo them off (but don't get aggressive – they're powerful animals!). Cheeky and nocturnal, brush-tailed possums are the great urban survivors; they're a common sight, even in cities. Koalas, echidnas and platypuses are more private, but encounters are not out of the question.

The NSW bush is home to what are surely some of the world's most raucous bird species – such as kookaburras, cockatoos, galahs and various other species of parrot. There are also the famous venomous snakes and spiders. In spite of popular perceptions, the snakes are rarely aggressive – if you do see one, simply stand back and let it pass – and the spiders are rarely seen.

CLIMATE

As a general rule, NSW gets hotter the further north you go and drier the further west. The coastal strip, especially in central and southern parts, is generally temperate, although uncomfortable midsummer heat is not uncommon, especially in the north.

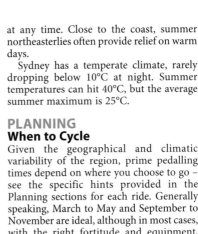

On the Great Dividing Range, expect milder summer temperatures and cool to cold winters. In winter, the Snowy Mountains live up to their name, but only for a few months of the year. West of the divide, summer days can be dangerously hot and cycling is probably best avoided, especially in the far west.

Rainfall also varies according to region, with annual averages generally highest along the coast and lowest in the far west. From February to June is the wettest period on the coastal fringe.

Prevailing winds are from the east in summer and west in winter, although the eastward march of cold fronts can produce cooler southerlies and southwesterlies at any time. Close to the coast, summer northeasterlies often provide relief on warm days.

Sydney has a temperate climate, rarely dropping below 10°C at night. Summer temperatures can hit 40°C, but the average summer maximum is 25°C.

PLANNING
When to Cycle

Given the geographical and climatic variability of the region, prime pedalling times depend on where you choose to go – see the specific hints provided in the Planning sections for each ride. Generally speaking, March to May and September to November are ideal, although in most cases, with the right fortitude and equipment, rides can be tackled at any time of year.

Bike Hire

Although Sydney may be your point of arrival and departure, long-term hire from Sydney isn't necessarily the best move. Rental rates are often higher than in regional centres and bike transport can add cost. Given the wide availability of bike hire throughout the state, especially in areas known for their tourist attractions and often in any town with a bike shop, you're best to pursue local resources – see Supplies & Equipment for each start city in Towns & Facilities at the end of this chapter.

Maps

For general road maps, NSW (and, in fact, all of Australia) is covered by Geoscience Australia's 1:250,000 scale Natmap topographical series; these have sufficient contour detail for touring and are the most practical scale. One potential drawback is the infrequency of updates, although that shouldn't have too much of an impact. The 1:100,000 Natmap series, with even more contour detail, is also available, but not as practical since you will often need multiple sheets per day. They're all available at map retailers or directly from **Geoscience Australia** (☎ 02-6249 9966, 1800 800 173; www.ga.gov.au).

For mountain bike rides, the topographic maps 1:50,000 produced by the **Department of Lands** (☎ 02-9228 6666, 13000 LANDS; www.lands.nsw.gov.au; 1 Prince Albert Rd, Queen's Sq, Sydney) are ideal.

Maps are sold over the counter or via the web, as well as through retailers.

The NSW motoring organisation **National Roads and Motoring Association** (NRMA) publishes a fine series of road-touring maps that cover the state in varying scales (but have no contour detail). Regularly updated and with a town index, they're free to NRMA members.

Cartoscope (☎ 02-9987 4533; www.cartoscope.com.au) produces a series of tourist maps that include all of the NSW rides in this book, supplemented by useful maps of many smaller town centres. They're available for free in visitors centres or as downloads. A hefty per-map postage and handling service fee is levied on mail orders.

BUYING MAPS

In Sydney, **Mapworld** (☎ 02-9261 3601; www.mapworld.com.au; 280 Pitt St, Sydney; 9am-5.30pm Mon-Fri, 10am-3.45pm Sat) is the best map shop. The **NRMA** (☎ 02-1300 762 060; www.mynrma.com.au; Touring Services, 9a York St, Sydney) has a shopfront, also in the CBD.

Books

NSW is the subject of an eye-opening variety of general guides, Lonely Planet's *Sydney & New South Wales* being one of the hot contenders and a particularly useful supplement to this guide. There are fewer NSW-specific cycling books. In concert with Bicycle NSW, the NRMA (see p370 for contact details) produces *Great Cycling Rides in NSW,* a collection of 75 short (maximum of 23km) rides throughout the state.

Although not updated since 1996, Amanda Lulham's *Discovering NSW & Canberra's Bike & Walking Paths* is still good for inspiration, looking at 1000km of shared-use paths in and around Sydney, Canberra and 11 other regional centres.

BUYING BOOKS

With a large selection of general travel books to choose from, the **Travel Bookshop** (☎ 02-9261 8200; www.travelbooks.com.au; 175 Liverpool St, Sydney; 9am-6pm Mon-Fri, 10am-5pm Sat) is an excellent place to shop for guides.

Cycling Events

Loop the Lake (www.loopthelake.com.au; Mar) is a leisurely charity ride (16km, 50km or 85km) around Lake Macquarie, attracting more than 2000 riders.

For a women-only charity ride in the Sydney area, try **Gear Up Girl Challenge** (www.gearupgirl.com.au; early Apr) with distances of 15km or 55km.

Ride for Life (www.rideforlife.org.au; Aug) combines professional racing with a family fun-day feel as part of a bike charity event in Sydney's Centennial Park.

Mudgee Bike Muster (www.bikemuster.com.au, Apr) is a family-friendly cycling weekend in the Central Ranges of NSW.

NSW Bike Week (www.rta.nsw.gov.au/usingroads/events/bikeweek/; Sep/Oct) draws attention to cycling in a statewide week-long government initiative.

Thousands take to the streets of Sydney for the **Sydney Spring Cycle** (www.sydneyspringcycle.com.au; Oct) charity ride of 7km to 55km.

Sydney to the Gong (www.gongride.org.au; Nov) is a very large charity classic covering 56km or 90km from Sydney to Wollongong.

Information Sources

Bicycle NSW (☎ 02-9218 5400; www.bicyclensw.org.au) is the state's leading cycling advocacy body, providing information on

---

BIKES ON NSW BUSES & TRAINS

On **CountryLink** (☎ 13 22 32; www.countrylink.info) regional trains, you need to box your bike. Bikes cost $12.10 on any service and must be registered as one of the three reserved spaces per service. Bike space can't be booked online. Be at the station 60 minutes in advance to request and then pack a free bike box (20kg maximum), always available at large stations but call ahead to smaller ones.

Bikes travel free on Sydney's **CityRail** (☎ 13 15 00; www.cityrail.info) service outside peak periods (weekdays 6am to 9am and 3.30pm to 7.30pm); otherwise, buy a child's fare for them. They can travel unboxed in any carriage.

Standard charges and packing conditions also apply to transporting bikes on long-haul buses; see p368.

events, routes, clubs, user groups and more. It distributes the bimonthly *Australian Cyclist* magazine (www.australiancyclist .com.au) and manages *Push On* (www .pushon.com.au), a comprehensive online resource for cyclists.

Connecting NSW (www.nsw.gov.au) is the online portal to the NSW government. It coughs up lots of boring parliamentary information, but also great leads to festivals, markets, galleries, Aboriginal heritage and more.

NSW National Parks & Wildlife Service (NPWS; ☎ 1300 361 967; www .nationalparks.nsw.gov.au; Head Office, 59–61 Goulburn St, Sydney) manages the state's 600-odd national parks and reserves, and is a useful source of information on everything from access and camping to conservation, Aboriginal heritage and more.

Roads and Traffic Authority (RTA; ☎ 13 17 82; www.rta.nsw.gov.au; Head Office, 101 Miller St, North Sydney) is the state agency for roads. Its website has loads of information for cyclists, including downloadable maps, details about routes and links to local council sites with even more.

The state's tourism body is **Tourism New South Wales** (☎ 13 20 77; www .visitnsw.com.au).

GATEWAY
See Sydney (p98).

SYDNEY SURVEY

Duration 2½–4¼ hours

Distance 41.7km

Difficulty easy–moderate

Start Pyrmont Bridge, Darling Harbour

Finish Sydney Opera House

Summary From the edge of the CBD to the surf-battered beach at Bondi, trace a broad Sydney circuit that also takes in the quirks of the unconventional inner western boroughs and smirks of the well-heeled eastern 'burbs.

Sydney does not enjoy a reputation as a bike-friendly town. Fortunately that's all about to change. A sure sign of the changing times, the city has committed to 'making cycling as attractive a choice of transport as walking or using public transport'. Its *City of Sydney Cycle Strategy and Action Plan 2007–2017* outlines major infrastructural developments, the centrepiece of which is a $70-million 245km cycle network (160km on separated paths), complete with an inner city cycleway and links to 14 neighbouring councils. In the meantime, getting around town still comes with the standard perils of urban two-wheeled commuting.

In the absence of purpose-built bikepaths, the ride described below – an extended survey of Sydney's highlights – does its best to keep to quieter byways in the entrancing inner western and eastern suburbs.

PLANNING
This ride can be enjoyed year-round, although try to avoid rush hour and midsummer weekends, when roads are crowded.

Bike Hire
The leading bike hire service in Sydney is **Centennial Park Cycles** (☎ 02-9398 5027; www.cyclehire.com.au; 50 Clovelly Rd, Randwick). For the extensive fleet of mountain bikes, hybrids, road bikes, tandems and more, rates vary from $15 to $25 per hour to between $40 and $65 for four to eight hours. Daily rates of $50 to $75 become more reasonable, with additional days for only $10 each. Centennial also has hire outlets in Centennial and Olympic Parks.

Maps
By far and away the best map for cycling around Sydney is *Bike-It! Sydney* (www .bike-it.com.au), a back-street guide and all-round resource for two-wheeling in and around town. These road details were transferred to a foldout *Bicycle Map* centred around Royal Prince Alfred Hospital and the University of Sydney but covering a 10- to 15-minute ride circuit from there, including the CBD and Balmain (north), Moore Park and Kensington (east), Marrickville (south), Summer and Drummoyne (west).

The RTA (see this page) also produces a series of cycleway maps that cover the entire extended Sydney region, as well as a fairly comprehensive *Handbook for Bicycle Riders*, all free in print or as downloads (www.rta.nsw.gov.au/usingroads/bicycle/). Also, many Sydney-area city councils and bike-user groups have created their own local bike maps.

NEW SOUTH WALES

SYDNEY SURVEY

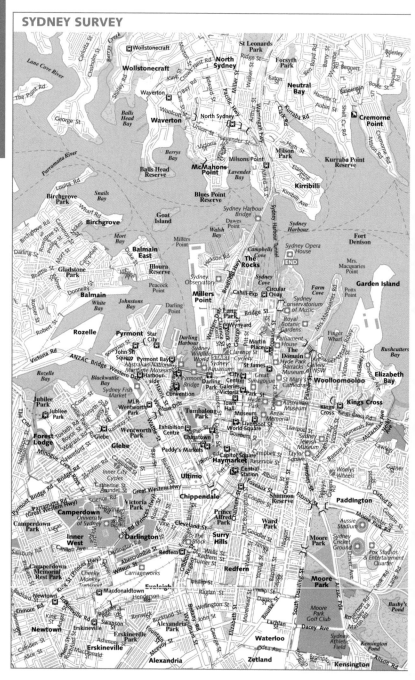

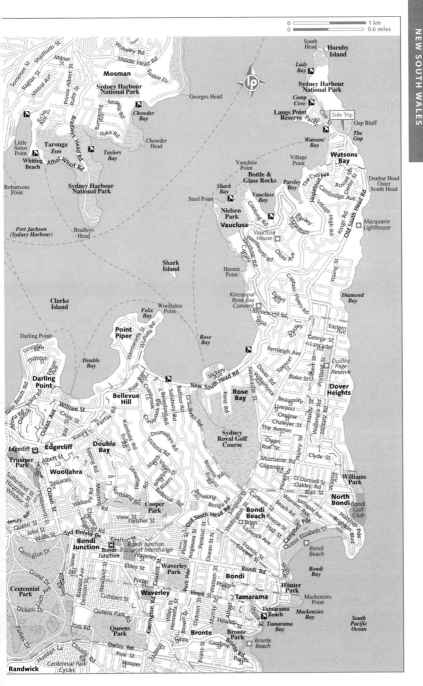

NEW SOUTH WALES

Books

Cycling Around Sydney by Bruce Ashley is now in its fourth edition and details 30 of the area's best rides. *Bike Rides Around Sydney* by Ian Connellan and Neil Irvine similarly explores the city's cycling experiences.

Information Sources

BikeSydney (☎ 0403-999 899; www.bikesydney.org) helps drive the effort to make Sydney a safer and more liveable city, in part by improving its cycling infrastructure.

The bike pages of the city's official website, **City of Sydney** (www.cityofsydney.nsw.gov.au/cycling), are refreshingly optimistic and thorough.

Try **Sydney Cyclist** (www.sydneycyclist.com) to share or read the latest news and gossip about life in the saddle in Sydney.

GETTING TO/FROM THE RIDE

For information on transport options to/from Sydney, see p101.

Eastern access to the Pyrmont Bridge in Darling Harbour is about 1km from both Central Station and Circular Quay. The best approach from the north is on Hickson Rd/Sussex St or from the east downhill on King St (walk your bike on the footpath since this is one-way traffic in the other direction).

The Sydney Opera House is within shouting distance of Circular Quay or a 2km roll from Central Station.

THE RIDE

The pedestrian **Pyrmont Bridge** spans Cockle Bay at **Darling Harbour** (www.darlingharbour.com), a rambling, purpose-built, waterfront tourist development. The beautifully restored bridge is accessible

SYDNEY SURVEY

CUE		
start		cnr Sussex & Essex Sts
0km		go W on Pyrmont Bridge access
{0.1	★	Aquarium & Wildlife World}
0.3		cross Pyrmont Bridge
{0.7	★	Maritime Museum}
0.8		Union St
1.1		Miller St
1.4		'to Fish Market', dangerous junction
{1.7	★	Sydney Fish Market}
1.9		Bridge Rd
2.4		Taylor St
2.7		Ferry Rd
	▲	300m moderate climb
3.0		Glebe Point Rd
3.6		Eglington Rd
3.7		Northcote Rd
3.8		Jubilee Park bikepath
4.1		bikepath before bridge
4.4		cross canal
5.0		dirt bikepath
5.2		Wigram Rd
	▲	200m steep climb
5.4		Upper Rd
5.5		Hereford St
		(20m) Cross St
5.8		Bridge St
		(30m) Junction St
6.0		Short St
6.1		Arundel St
6.2		Ross St
6.3		cross Parramatta Rd
		(20m) Sydney University gates

CUE CONTINUED		
{	★	Sydney University}
6.4		Western Ave
7.1		Carillon Ave
		(40m) Queen St
{	★	King St}
7.3		cross King St
7.5		Wilson St
{8.0	★	Carriageworks}
8.3		cross pedestrian area
		(20m) Little Eveleigh St
8.6		Lawson St
{	★	The Block}
8.8		Wells St bikepath
9.3		Chalmers St
		(50m) Redfern Lane
9.5		Elizabeth St bikepath
		Redfern St
9.8		Young St
{10.2	★	Danks St}
10.5		Bourke St
10.9		Thurlow St
11.1		cross little park
		(30m) South Dowling St
11.2		cross at light
		bikepath
11.3		Moore Park bikepath
11.6		Cleveland St bikepath
11.8		cross Anzac Parade
11.9		Lang Rd bikepath
12.4		Centennial Park gates
{	★	Centennial Park}
12.7		Dickens Dr

from the east via a shared pedestrian and cycle path that begins at the junction of Sussex and King Sts. Go west on this path.

Off to the right are the **Sydney Aquarium** (☎ 02-8251 7800; www.sydneyaquarium .com.au; Aquarium Pier, Darling Harbour; adult/child $30/15; 9am-10pm) and **Sydney Wildlife World** (☎ 02-9333 9288; www .sydneywildlifeworld.com.au; Aquarium Pier, Darling Harbour; adult/child $30/15; 9am-10pm). As you cross the bridge, ahead and to the right on the far shore is the **Australian National Maritime Museum** (☎ 02-9298 3777; www.anmm.gov.au; 2 Murray St, Darling Harbour; admission free, special exhibits adult/child from $10/6; 9.30am-5pm).

Once across the bridge, climb up and over the hump of Pyrmont and head straight into the **Sydney Fish Market** (☎ 02-9004 1122; www.sydneyfishmarket.com.au; cnr Pyrmont Bridge Rd & Bank St, Pyrmont; 7am-4pm), through which 15 million kilograms of seafood are shipped annually. Arrive early to check out the morning auctions or take a behind-the-scenes **auction tour** (per person $20; 6.50-8.30am Thu) – reservations aren't required.

On the far side of Blackwattle Bay, over which the fish market looks and from which there are views of the elegant Anzac Bridge, turn uphill again towards the heights of Glebe, a cosy bohemian quarter of yuppies galore. The right turn (3km) on Glebe Point Rd leads past a few cafes and gentrified workers cottages and then back down to the waterfront at **Jubilee Park**.

Turn left just before Johnstons Creek and follow it for 1km into the off-the-radar suburb of Forest Lodge, through which you

CUE CONTINUED		
13.0	↗	Parkes Dr
13.7	↑	Cross Grand Dr
	↰	(50m) Darley Rd
14.6	▲	500m moderate climb
17.3	↱	Bronte Park bikepath
17.5	▲	200m moderate climb
17.7	↱	Bronte Marine Dr
18.6	↱	Gaerloch Ave
18.8	↑	Alexander St
18.9	↰	Sandridge St
19.1	↱	Bondi Rd/Campbell Pde
{19.8	★	Bondi Beach}
20.7	↑	Military Rd
	▲	1.2km moderate climb
{23.1	★	Dudley Page Reserve}
23.6	↱	Military Rd
24.3	↱	Old South Head Rd
{25.5	★	Macquarie Lighthouse}
26.3	↰ ⊚	Hopetoun Ave
{	●● ↰	Watsons Bay 400m (↻)}
28.2	↱ ⊚	Fitzwilliam Rd
29.0	↰	Wentworth Rd
{29.5	★	Vaucluse House}
29.8	↑	Vaucluse Rd
{30.1	★	Nielsen Park}
{31.2	★	Kincoppal-Rose Bay Convent}
31.3	↱	New South Head Rd
34.9	↱	William St
35.4	↰	Ocean Ave
35.8	↱	Greenoaks Ave
	▲	500m steep climb

CUE CONTINUED		
36.3	↱	Darling Rd
	↰	(30m) Loftus Rd
	⚠	300m steep descent
36.6	↗	park bikepath
36.8	↰	away from water
37.1	↱	New South Head Rd footpath
37.2	↱	cross under overpass
37.3	↱	New South Head Rd
37.4	↰	Barcom Ave
	▲	600m moderate climb
37.8	↱	Liverpool St
38.0	↰	Victoria St
38.1	↱	Burton St
{38.2	★	Sydney Jewish Museum}
38.4	↰	Forbes St
38.6	↑	pedestrian area
{38.7	★	Taylor Sq}
{	↱★	Oxford St}
39.2	↑	go into Hyde Park
{39.4	★	Anzac Memorial}
{go NW through park}		
39.7	↑	cross Park St
{continue NE through park}		
{40.1	★	Hyde Park Fountain}
{go N to edge of park}		
40.2	↑	Macquarie St
{	★	Hyde Park Barracks}
{40.5	★	Parliament House}
{41.0	★	Sydney Conservatorium of Music}
{41.7	★	Sydney Opera House}

HARBOURSIDE RIDES & WALKS

Riding on the harbour foreshores is a mixed experience. It's very up and down, and many of the roads closest to the water are crowded. A detailed map (see p51) is essential if you're keen to ride.

The 10km Manly Scenic Walkway from Manly Cove to Spit Bridge winds past waterside reserves, quiet harbour beaches and through pretty Dobroyd Head Scenic Area, part of Sydney Harbour National Park. Travel by ferry to Manly and catch a bus back to the city centre.

The 4km walking track through Ashton Park, south of Taronga Zoo, passes Bradleys Head and Taylors Bay. West of the zoo, there's a shorter walk through Sirius Cove Reserve. Take the Taronga Zoo ferry from Circular Quay to access both walks.

The 2.6km walk from South Head to Clarke Reserve has harbour and ocean views; it passes the high cliffs at the Gap and the historic Macquarie Lighthouse. Just west, the walking track through Hermitage Foreshore Reserve runs from plush Kincoppal-Rose Bay School to Nielsen Park, giving spectacular views down the harbour to the city. Reach both walks via a Watsons Bay bus.

weave on your way to the junction (6.3km) with Parramatta Rd, a major west–east thoroughfare.

Go straight ahead and through the gates of **University of Sydney**. Continue onwards, traversing the impressive campus – the main buildings are off to the left – and into Newtown, a melting pot of social and sexual subcultures, students and edgy boutiques. **King St**, which you cross at 7.3km, is its relentlessly urban main drag, full of funky clothes shops, bookshops and cafes.

Turn left on Wilson St (7.5km) continue parallel to the rail line past **Carriageworks** (☎ 02-6871 9089; www.carriageworks. com.au; 245 Wilson St, Eveleigh), Sydney's newest performing arts centre, magnificently installed in a 19th-century Heritage-listed railway workshop complex.

Push straight across the pedestrian zone at the end of Wilson St and down quaint Little Eveleigh St. Its junction with Lawson St is one of Sydney's most infamous corners. Straight ahead, down Eveleigh St, is **the Block**, an area that more than 30 years ago was purchased by the Aboriginal Housing Company for development into Aboriginal-managed housing. It has been a political, social, cultural and racial flashpoint ever since.

Turn right on Lawson St (8.6km) and cross in front of the Redfern train station. Traverse Redfern on a series of back lanes and pleasant residential streets and then turn right (9.8km) on Young St. Follow this for 400m into the trendy suburb of Waterloo and a left on **Danks St**, one of Sydney's surprise cafe, restaurant and gallery oases.

More back-street wandering takes you to the Moore Park playing fields and a bikepath to tree-lined **Centennial Park** (12.4km; www.centennialpark.com), Sydney's biggest and most beloved urban green space. Near Moore Park, much of the former Sydney Showgrounds has been converted into the **Fox Studios** (www.foxstudiosaustralia .com), a private venture supporting Australia's film industry, and the **Entertainment Quarter** (www.entertainmentquarter.com .au), a shopping and leisure complex. Nearby are the **Aussie Stadium** and **Sydney Cricket Ground**.

Spend as much time as possible exploring **Centennial Park**. It's one of the most pleasant – and certainly one of the most popular – places in Sydney to ride a bike. When you do leave, exit on Darley Rd, which heads uphill, becomes Macpherson St and then drops straight down to **Bronte Beach**.

Go right into Bronte Park through the gates near the bus stop. Follow the path up the short rise behind the surf club and bump back onto Bronte Marine Dr, which leads through groovy Tamarama and up short, steep pinches to Bondi Rd. A stop for coffee somewhere along Campbell Pde – the beachfront boulevard that curves past famous **Bondi Beach** (19.8km) – is a must.

Campbell Pde becomes Military Rd, which proceeds up a long hill to the **Dudley Page Reserve** (23.1km) at Dover Heights, renowned as the best (public) place in eastern Sydney for city and harbour views. Further along, now on Old South Head Rd, you pass **Macquarie Lighthouse** built in 1833 and Australia's first and longest-running navigational light.

Take time for the side trip to pretty and popular **Watsons Bay** before looping back into chichi Vaucluse – shady, pretty and very, very expensive. On Wentworth Rd, Heritage-listed **Vaucluse House** (☎ 02-9388 7922; www.hht.net.au; adult/child $8/4; 9.30am-4pm Fri-Sun) is Sydney's last remaining 19th-century harbourside estate, once home to early patriot WC Wentworth.

Continue past **Nielsen Park** – a very popular harbour beach and reserve that's part of Sydney Harbour National Park, which protects scattered pockets of harbourside bushland – to **Kincoppal-Rose Bay Convent** (31.2km), a school with distracting views.

Harbour-hugging New South Head Rd rises and dips through a shimmering, conservative conglomeration of Range Rovers, skinny models and mortgage madness at Rose Bay (33.1km), Double Bay (35km) and Rushcutters Bay (36.8km) before climbing through leafy Darlinghurst back into bustling urbania. A short detour from the route at 38.2km takes in the powerfully evocative **Sydney Jewish Museum** (☎ 02-9360 7999; www.sydneyjewishmuseum .com.au; 148 Darlinghurst Rd, Darlinghurst; adult/child $10/6; 10am-4pm Sun-Thu, to 2pm Fri).

Taylor Square is the nucleus of arguably the second-largest gay community in the world. **Oxford St**, the adjacent thoroughfare, is a long string of very gay-friendly shops, cafes, bars and clubs that descends all the way to Hyde Park, on the eastern edge of the city centre. To the southwest are Sydney's teensy Spanish Quarter and thriving Chinatown, the latter clustered around Dixon St.

Formal **Hyde Park** (39.2km), the length of which you pedal, has a grand avenue of trees and delightful fountains. Wander into the dignified **Anzac Memorial** (☎ 02-9267 7668; www.rslnsw.com.au; admission free; 9am-5pm). **St Mary's Cathedral**, (www .stmaryscathedral.org.au), with its new copper spires, overlooks the park from the east, just north of the **Australian Museum** (☎ 02-9320 6000; www.amonline.net .au; 6–8 College St; adult/child/family $10/5/25; 9.30am-5pm), a natural history wonderland. The 1878 **Great Synagogue** (☎ 02-9267 2477; www.greatsynagogue .org.au; 187a Elizabeth St; adult/child $5/3; tours noon Tue & Thu) stands to the west.

Macquarie St extends north from Hyde Park all the way to the Opera House. It's flanked by a crop of early public buildings commissioned by Lachlan Macquarie, the first NSW governor. These include the **Hyde Park Barracks Museum** (☎ 02-8239 2311; www.hht.net.au; Queen's Sq, Macquarie St; adult/child $10/5; 9.30am-5pm), built in 1819; **Parliament House** (☎ 02-9230 2111; www.parliament.nsw.gov.au; Macquarie St; admission free; 9am-5pm Mon-Fri); and the **Sydney Conservatorium of Music** (02-9351 1222; www.usyd.edu.au/conmusic; Macquarie St). Behind it all is a vast swathe of green – the **Domain** in the south abutting the **Art Gallery of NSW** (☎ 02-9225 1744; www.artgallery.nsw.gov.au; Art Gallery Rd, Sydney; admission free for main exhibits; 10am-5pm Thu-Tue, to 9pm Wed), and the vast, relaxed **Royal Botanic Gardens** (☎ 02-9231 8111; www.rbgsyd.nsw.gov.au; Mrs Macquaries Rd; admission free; 7am-sunset), established in 1816 as the colony's vegetable patch.

At long last you speed down a final hill and out along Bennelong Point to the gem in Sydney's crown – the **Sydney Opera House** (41.7km; ☎ 02-9250 7111; www .sydneyoperahouse.com), Australia's most recognisable icon and the end of the ride. It's towered over by the 1932 **Sydney Harbour Bridge**. Nearby exploration should take in **the Rocks** (www.therocks.com) – the site of Sydney's first European settlement – visible across Sydney Cove.

As an add-on, if you wish to cross the harbour bridge's span on its 1.4km bridge cycleway, enter from the west via Watson Rd, near the Sydney Observatory. The views are unparalleled.

GOLD & WINE COUNTRY CIRCUIT

Duration 4 days

Distance 299.5km

Difficulty moderate–demanding

Start/Finish Bathurst

Summary Ride through some of Australia's oldest goldfields, mixing it with Mudgee wines and classic Australian countryside.

This ride showcases the best of the Central West, and though it's not a ride for seeing Australia's star attractions – there's no reef, rock or rainforest in sight – it's a great route for getting under the country's skin. Passing

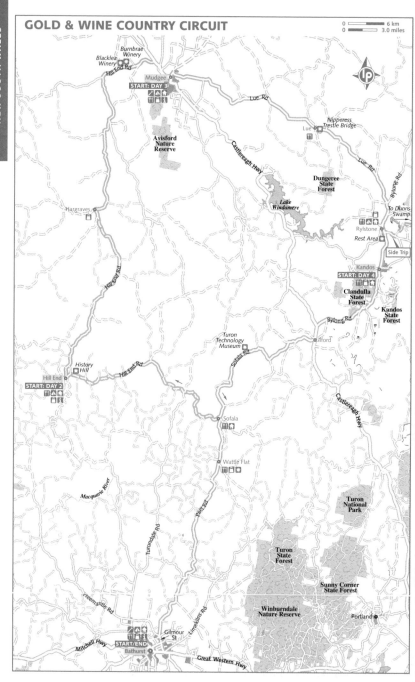

GOLD & WINE COUNTRY CIRCUIT

0 — 6 km
0 — 3.0 miles

Burnbrae Winery
Blacklea Winery
Hill End Rd
Mudgee
START: DAY 3

Lue Rd

Nipperess Trestle Bridge
Lue

Lue Rd

Bylong Rd

Avisford Nature Reserve

Castlereagh Hwy

Dungeree State Forest

Lake Windamere

Hargraves

To Dunns Swamp

Rylstone
Rest Area

Side Trip

Hillgrove Rd

Kandos
START: DAY 4

Clandulla State Forest

Kandos State Forest

Bylong Rd

Turon Technology Museum

Ilford

History Hill
Hill End
START: DAY 2

Hill End Rd

Sofala Rd

Castlereagh Hwy

Sofala

Macquarie River

Wattle Flat

Turon National Park

Turondale Rd

Pike Rd

Limekiln Rd

Turon State Forest

Sunny Corner State Forest

Freemantle Rd

Winburndale Nature Reserve

Portland

Gilmour St
START/END
Bathurst

Mitchell Hwy

Great Western Hwy

through former gold-mining towns and the emerging wine centre of Mudgee (one of the few NSW country towns still experiencing growth), the ride features pastoral expanses, bush-clad hills, wildlife and roads that are normally the sole domain of farmers and their utes. The vision of quintessential Australia will be complete when you hit the dirt roads out of Sofala.

For an extended tour, you can hook up with the Bathurst to the Blueys (p63) ride to explore the Blue Mountains and Jenolan Caves.

PLANNING
When to Cycle
Spring and autumn are the best times on this ride. The Central West can be very hot in midsummer (the average January temperature in Mudgee in January is 31°C) and, at a general elevation of around 600m above sea level, cool to cold in midwinter. March and April tend to be the driest months.

Bike Hire
Winning Edge Cycles (☎ 02-6332 4025; www.wec.net.au; 213 Howick St, Bathurst; 9am-5.30pm Mon-Fri, 9am-1pm Sat) hires out front-suspension mountain bikes for $45 a day, with discounts for longer rentals.

Maps
The NRMA's 1:550,000 NSW Touring map No 5 *Central West, New England, North West* has the most up-to-date road information. It can be purchased at the **NRMA's Bathurst office** (☎ 02-6331 8322; 209 Howick St).

GETTING TO/FROM THE RIDE
Bathurst (start/finish)
BUS
Bathurst is served by **Selwood's Coaches** (☎ 02-6362 7963), which travel daily to Orange ($9, 45 minutes) and Sydney ($30, four hours).

The **CountryLink** (☎ 13 22 32; www .countrylink.info) XPT (express train) stops here on the daily Sydney ($34, 3½ hours) to Dubbo ($31, 1½ hours) service.

BICYCLE
From Parramatta, in Sydney's western suburbs, there's a wide shoulder/bike lane most of the way along the Western Motorway and Great Western Hwy to Katoomba. From Katoomba, the most enjoyable approach is to follow the Bathurst to the Blueys (p63) ride in reverse, taking in the Jenolan Caves along the way.

THE RIDE
Day 1: Bathurst to Hill End
5½–7 hours, 79.5km

With parts of this day spent on dirt, this can be a taxing beginning. Happily, the dirt road is well maintained (it's an official NSW Tourist Drive route) and suitable even to touring bikes. Classic scenes of the Central West – cattle, dams, the distant

GOLD & WINE COUNTRY CIRCUIT – DAY 1

CUE			GPS COORDINATES
start		Bathurst visitors centre	149°34′53″E 33°25′02″S
0km		go E on Great Western Hwy	
1.6	↰	Gilmour St, 'to Sofala'	
30.3	▲	3.2km steep climb	
37.2	★	Wattle Flat	149°41′35″E 33°08′32″S
44.3	↰	Hill End Rd, Sofala	149°41′23″E 33°04′49″S
44.7	⚠	2.5km dirt road	
49.1	⚠	5.3km dirt road	
56.3	▲	3.3km steep climb	
69.3	⚠	8.8km dirt road	
{78.1	★	History Hill}	
79.3	↰	High St	
79.5		Hill End visitors centre	149°25′04″E 33°01′45″S

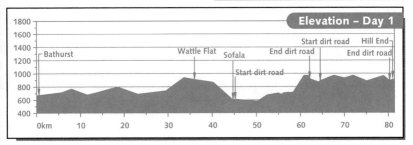

Elevation – Day 1

blue haze of hills – set the tone for the days to come. A couple of the day's climbs have some sting; the flip side is the rollicking downhill to Sofala.

The ride begins as it doesn't intend to continue, on a busy highway, though a wide shoulder makes it an easy exit from Bathurst, threading between new estates and horse paddocks as it leaves town on Sofala Rd. After around 15km, the ride enters a small range of hills, from where it's a sea of undulations until the final steep climb into Wattle Flat (37.2km). If you've come in January you might find that you're in town for the **Bronze Thong**, a classic bush race meeting with champion thong tossing thrown in to boot. At any time you can wander the **Buurree Walking Trail** past evidence of 19th-century gold mining, with some fantastic views; allow two to three hours.

Three kilometres past Wattle Flat, a glorious freewheeling descent leads to Sofala (44.3km), an 1851 gold-rush town that claims to be Australia's oldest surviving gold town. There's still liquid gold in the 1862 **Royal Hotel** or you could grab some fossicking equipment from **Sofala Souvenirs**. If you're short of time, you can just have a quiet spin around Sofala's narrow streets – it'll take no more than 10 minutes.

The dirt road begins almost immediately after Sofala, burrowing even deeper into the hills and passing beneath two hillsides of bare rock as it approaches the Turon River – watch your wheels in the grooves of the bridge across the river. The land opens out beyond the Turon, though the road narrows, so be alert for oncoming vehicles. The hills continue apace, making the night's goal of Hill End seem like an unfulfilled prophecy, though once you hit the third (and final) section of dirt road, the lay of the land does become a little kinder.

Just before Hill End, the ride passes **History Hill** (☎ 02-6337 8222; admission $10), an underground tourist mine with 175m of subterranean workings. It provides interesting insight into the area if you plan to noodle about in Hill End for a while. The official opening hours are: 'we're open when the gates are open'.

Day 2: Hill End to Mudgee
5–6 hours, 70.2km

Another day of rolling terrain and on-again, off-again dirt roads (mostly off-again thanks to recent road-sealing work). There's little of note en route, yet it's one of the classiest days of cycling in NSW's Central West, crossing three small hill ranges and offering great rural views. Keep a watch for the little things – lonely headstones, lizards (and snakes) sunning on the road, the khaki grey of the bush, and the rusted, abandoned farmhouses at the edge of the Mudgee wine region. This day of subtle charms really is one for the pure cyclist.

The ride leaves Hill End through an arch of deciduous trees, so that briefly

GOLD & WINE COUNTRY CIRCUIT – DAY 2

CUE			GPS COORDINATES
start		Hill End General Store	149°25′04″E 33°01′45″S
0km		go N on Beyers Ave	
0.5	↘	`to Mudgee'	
13.4	▲	3.3km steep uphill	
16.8	⚠	2.5km dirt road	
25.0	⚠	3.7km dirt road	
32.5		Hargraves	149°27′40″E 32°47′06″S
32.9	▲	1km moderate climb	
42.1	▲	1.3km steep climb	
(61.0	★	Blacklea Winery)	
(61.2	★	Burnbrae Winery)	
66.7	↱	`to Mudgee'	
70.2		Mudgee visitors centre	149°35′13″E 32°35′58″S

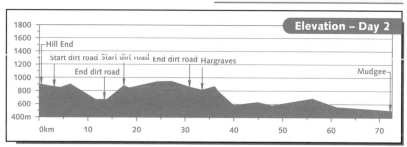

Elevation – Day 2

| 1800 |
| 1600 | Hill End
| 1400 |
| 1200 | Start dirt road Start dirt road End dirt road Hargraves
| 1000 | End dirt road   Mudgee
| 800 |
| 600 |
| 400m |

0km   10   20   30   40   50   60   70

it feels more like a French lane than the Australian bush, but quickly the eucalypts and grass take over again, resuming normal transmission. If you left Hill End mid-morning, **Hargraves** (32.5km) makes for a logical lunch stop, though the general store is a pies-only kind of place.

At 61km, you get the first taste, literally, of the Mudgee wine region, passing two wineries – **Blacklea** (☎ 02-6373 3366; blackleavineyard@bigpond.com; 10am-5pm Fri-Mon) and **Burnbrae** (☎ 02-6373 3504; www.burnbraewines.com.au; 9am-5pm) – to help lubricate your legs for the final kilometres through a flattening landscape into Mudgee.

Day 3: Mudgee to Kandos
4–5 hours, 58.2km

After a couple of days of fairly hard slog, this shorter and predominantly flat day is a welcome relief. Road surfaces are good and though the scenery is similar to Days 1 and 2 – bush-topped hills and bush-cleared valleys – it heads between the hills rather than over them. For variety, there's a smattering of vineyards and, later, the northwestern flank of rugged Wollemi National Park for company.

GOLD & WINE COUNTRY CIRCUIT – DAY 3

CUE		GPS COORDINATES	
start	Mudgee visitors centre	149°35′13″E	32°35′58″S
0km	go E on Market St		
0.3	Church St		
1.0	'to Lue'		
29.0	Lue		
{30.2	Nipperess Bridge}		
47.3	'to Rylstone'		
51.3	Rylstone	149°58′10″E	32°47′59″S
51.8	'to Kandos'		
{52.4	Dunns Swamp 46km}		
58.2	Bridge Motors, Kandos	149°58′06″E	32°51′28″S

Out of Mudgee the road seems to bounce between hillsides along Lawsons Creek. The creek was named for iconic bush poet Henry Lawson, who lived from infancy to his mid-teens in a cottage 8km north of Mudgee, at Eurunderee (then known as Pipeclay). Past the pub at **Lue**, the road dips beneath beautiful **Nipperess trestle bridge** before the ragged edge of Wollemi National Park becomes visible to the east. Its sandstone escarpments might look like the Blue Mountains, but the treasure hidden within is something truly unique (see the boxed text The Tree That Time Forgot p63).

Pass through Rylstone (if you're wanting to camp, stop here) and pick up the bikepath opposite the hospital; the path runs beside the road all the way into Kandos. Kandos' *raison d'être*, its cement works (even the town name is an acronym based on the names of the first cement company's directors), becomes visible at the foot of Coomber Melon Mountain almost as soon as you leave Rylstone. The rest area at 54.5km has a water tap.

SIDE TRIP: DUNNS SWAMP
3–4 hours, 46km

This detour will add a night to your tour but you'll get to experience one of the few easily accessible places in wild Wollemi National Park. Dunns Swamp has some wonderful camping (sites per person $5), and nearby are some striking examples of pagoda-shaped rock formations and an Aboriginal art site. There are five marked walking trails beginning from the campsite, ranging from 500m to 5.5km in length. Wildlife is also prolific, with campers frequently encountering eastern grey kangaroos, various wallaby species, wombats, possums and birdlife. Turn left at 52.4km and follow the signs.

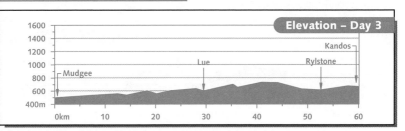

NEW SOUTH WALES

GOLDEN DAYS

Art lovers may recognise Sofala's streetscape from Russell Drysdale's painting of the same name in the Art Gallery of New South Wales, but the town's place in history was assured almost 100 years before Drysdale's 1947 visit. Sofala is the patriarch of Australian gold fields – albeit a well-faded one – with Edward Hargraves (from whom the town of Hargraves, on the Day 2 route, takes its name) discovering the precious metal in Summerhill Creek in February 1851, six months before gold was more famously found in Ballarat, Victoria.

Within months, Sofala was a campsite bordering on a metropolis, with 10,000 people, a pub and a general store sprawled around the creek's banks. The good times burned out like a firecracker, and within months most of the gold diggers were streaming back out of town.

Many headed for nearby Hill End, where gold had also been discovered in 1851, and where the alchemy would last significantly longer. Hill End was to become one of New South Wales' richest gold-mining towns and Australia's first reef-mining area. More than 50 tonnes of the metal were extracted, including, most famously, the Beyers and Holtermann nugget in 1872. Weighing 286kg, it's the world's largest nugget of reef gold, a find that sparked the region's final gold rush. Quickly, Hill End's population reached 30,000 and its pub count ballooned to 51. Today a single pub remains in the virtual ghost town.

Day 4: Kandos to Bathurst
6½–8 hours, 91.6km

A long and hilly day, with three climbs of significance (and a whole lot of lesser ascents), though any difficulties are erased by the beauty of both the riding and the country. Through the Clandulla State Forest and beyond Ilford, the route is an absolute joy for cycle touring, combining good road surfaces, manageable climbs, lively descents and wide, wide views. The short stretch on the Castlereagh Hwy to Ilford can be busy with trucks so get an early start to beat them to the road.

There's a true Kandos send-off as you leave town beneath the cement works' cable car (the bikepath continues out of Kandos but runs out after 1.5km). The route then enters the thick growth of the **Clandulla State Forest**, with some of the most beautiful forest of the ride and views that open out onto yet more shapely escarpment-rimmed peaks. Breathe in the good air before, at 15km, the country opens up into an almost treeless landscape.

Bookended by the day's two longest climbs, the **Turon Technology Museum** (☎ 02-6358 8434; www.hermes.net.au /turon; admission $8; 10am-4pm Sat & Sun, or by appointment) traces the development of the steam and internal combustion engine

GOLD & WINE COUNTRY CIRCUIT – DAY 4

CUE			GPS COORDINATES	
start		Bridge Motors, Kandos	149°58'06"E	32°51'28"S
0km		go S on Ilford Rd		
7.8	⤴	'to Ilford'		
13.0	▲	1.5km moderate climb		
16.6	⤴	'to Bathurst'		
18.8	⤵	'to Sofala', Ilford	149°51'26"E	32°57'45"S
23.4	▲	7.3km moderate climb		
{34.5	★	Turon Technology Museum}		
35.4	▲	3km demanding climb		
47.2		Sofala	149°41'23"E	33°04'49"S
	▲	4km moderate climb		
54.2		Wattle Flat	149°41'35"E	33°08'32"S
58.5	⚠	2.5km steep, winding descent		
90.0	⤵	Great Western Hwy		
91.6		Bathurst visitors centre	149°34'53"E	33°25'02"S

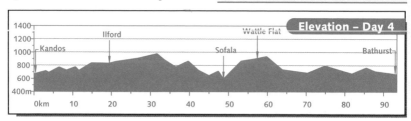

Elevation – Day 4

Kandos · Ilford · Sofala · Wattle Flat · Bathurst

THE TREE THAT TIME FORGOT

In August 1994 ranger David Noble and two friends were exploring a deep, damp and very sheltered gorge in Wollemi National Park when Noble made the discovery of a lifetime – a tree with palm frond–like leaves and bubbly looking bark, quite unlike anything he'd seen before.

Four months later, the discovery was announced: the tree, named *Wollemia nobilis* – the Wollemi pine – had previously been known only from 100-million-year-old fossils. It was placed in a genus all its own, and became the third living genus of the conifer family, Araucariaceae.

Subsequent finds in other locations within the park have shown the population of Wollemi trees in the wild to be at around 100, but a propagation programme selling pines grown from cuttings of the wild trees has seen the tree sprout around the world. The pines were first offered for sale in 2006 and have since become a popular gift and even, for some, a fair dinkum Christmas tree. In Australia alone the trees are stocked at more than 200 nurseries, and have sold in the USA through the National Geographic catalogue. They have also been offered for sale in countries as far ranging as Japan, Ukraine, Slovakia and the UK.

For further information about the tree that may once have been grazed by dinosaurs, visit the **Wollemi Australia** (www.wollemipine.com).

since the 1850s. On the first weekend of each month, the museum fires up all the steam engines.

The winding descent into Sofala offers good views of the yesteryear town, and from here the route retraces its Day 1 path – the descent you enjoyed into Sofala on Day 1 is a lot crueller in reverse.

BATHURST TO THE BLUEYS

Duration 2 days
Distance 147.3km
Difficulty demanding
Start Bathurst
Finish Katoomba
Summary Dip deep into Jenolan Caves then climb to the tops of the Blue Mountains' signature sandstone escarpment.

A ride of contrasts, this short but taxing journey heads from the agricultural patchwork around Bathurst to the intricate designs of the caves at Jenolan and the high sandstone cliffs of the World Heritage-listed Blue Mountains. While sections of the route are flat or gently undulating, the formidable climbs and descents near Jenolan Caves are best attempted only by fit and experienced riders.

The ride can be extended by appending it to the Gold & Wine Country Circuit (p57), making for a six-day tour, covering almost 450km of the finest country west of Sydney.

HISTORY

The route covers a region that extends from traditional Wiradjuri Aboriginal lands to the western lands of the Dharug people. Because of its proximity to the Sydney to Bathurst road, Europeans were exploring the area soon after the Blue Mountains were breached in 1813; the Oberon area was being settled as early as the 1820s.

The Jenolan Caves' extraordinary, open-ended Grand Arch (which you will ride through) was discovered in the late 1830s by bushranger James McKeown and first came to public attention when McKeown was tracked down. The cave system was explored further over subsequent decades and the area was declared a reserve in 1866. A cave was opened to tourists a year later.

Jenolan Caves was a popular cycling destination from Sydney in the late 19th century. Some rode the 180km as a challenge; others took the train to Mt Victoria and rode only the final 65km.

PLANNING
When to Cycle

Weekends are best avoided, with the highway section from Little Hartley to Katoomba particularly busy with weekend warriors. Spring and autumn are the best seasons to ride. Winters get cold on the plateau and in the mountains – Katoomba's average temperature in July is 9.3°C. Rainfall is consistent (between 70mm and 175mm a month), with spring drier than autumn and only marginally more windy.

BATHURST TO THE BLUEYS

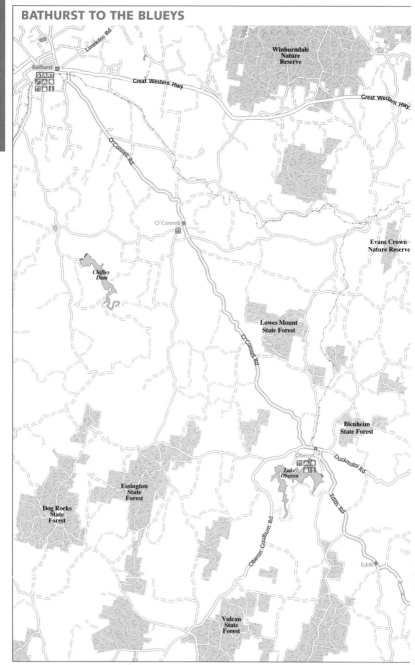

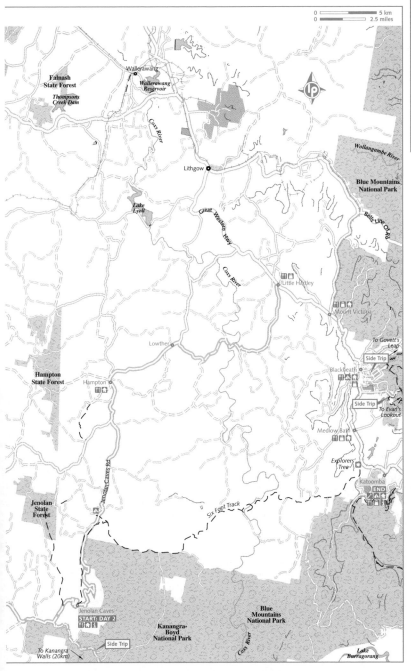

Bike Hire

Winning Edge Cycles (☎ 02-6332 4025; www.wec.net.au; 213 Howick St, Bathurst; h 9am-5.30pm Mon-Fri, 9am-1pm Sat) hires out front-suspension mountain bikes for $45 a day, with discounts for longer rentals. If riding the route in reverse, **Velo Nova** (☎ 02-4782 2800; 182 Katoomba St, Katoomba; half/full day $28/50; 9am-5pm Mon & Wed-Sat, 9.30am-4.30pm Sun) rents out mountain bikes.

Maps

The NRMA's 1:550,000 NSW Touring map No 5 *Central West, New England, North West* has the most up-to-date road information. It can be purchased at the **NRMA's Bathurst office** (☎ 02-6331 8322; 209 Howick St).

Information Sources

The **National Parks & Wildlife Service area office** (☎ 02-6335 1972; 38 Ross St) in Oberon is the place to gather information if you're detouring to the Kanangra Walls (see p67).

GETTING TO/FROM THE RIDE

Bathurst (start)

BUS

Bathurst is served daily by **Selwood's Coaches** (☎ 02-6362 7963; www.selwoods .com.au), travelling to Orange ($9, 45 minutes) and Sydney ($30, four hours).

The **CountryLink** (☎ 13 22 32; www .countrylink.info) XPT (express train) stops here on the daily Sydney ($34, 3½ hours) to Dubbo ($31, 1½ hours) service.

BICYCLE

From Parramatta, in Sydney's western suburbs, there's a wide shoulder/bike lane most of the way along the Western Motorway and Great Western Hwy to Katoomba. From Katoomba, the most enjoyable approach is to follow the Bathurst to the Blueys (p63) ride in reverse, taking in the Jenolan Caves along the way.

Katoomba (finish)

BUS

The **Blue Mountains Bus Company** (☎ 02-4751 1077; www.mountainlink.com .au) services Katoomba en route from Mt Victoria to the north ($7, 40 minutes, four

daily Monday to Friday) and Springwood to the east ($9, one hour, seven daily Monday to Saturday).

TRAIN

CityRail (☎ 13 15 00; www.cityrail.info) runs from Katoomba to Sydney's Central Station (adult/child $12/6, two hours, hourly).

BICYCLE

If you plan to cycle to Katoomba from Sydney, consider taking the train at least as far as Parramatta. From here, there's a wide shoulder/bike lane most of the way along the Western Motorway and Great Western Hwy to Katoomba (though it does narrow to almost nothing for short periods). The road climbs around 1100m but it's generally gradual. Katoomba can be reached from Sydney in a day.

THE RIDE

Day 1: Bathurst to Jenolan Caves

5½–7 hours, 73.1km

Big landscapes, big climbs and a roaring descent are the hallmarks of this tiring but satisfying day, which comes in three parts: flat, hilly then downhill. Traffic is generally light and on the plummeting Jenolan road caravans are discouraged, which is always a good thing for cyclists.

The ride leaves Bathurst through an industrial estate, and it's delightfully easy going to the village of O'Connell (21km), bobbing through gentle hills where sheep outnumber trees. Even with a cyclist's thirst, however, it might be too early in the day for a beer at the 1865 **O'Connell Hotel**.

The rise from O'Connell (about 700m above sea level) to Oberon (nearly 1100m) is like a staircase, climbing one step after another over 24km. Between Oberon and Edith there's a chance to catch your breath, with the number of downhill runs seeming to exceed the climbs (even though there's only a 30m altitude difference between the towns). On the climb out from Oberon you'll notice the wall of Oberon Dam off to the right, and there are good views back to the town if you swivel your neck. The terrain here is noticeably lumpier, with big, smooth-sided hills on which the road seems no more than a scratch.

The main climb begins just past Edith, with the route rising to its high point (above

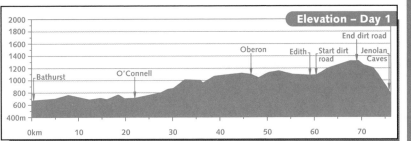

BATHURST TO THE BLUEYS – DAY 1

CUE		GPS COORDINATES	
start	Bathurst visitors centre	149°34'53"E	33°25'02"S
0km	go E on Great Western Hwy		
2.6	⬆️🔼🔁 `to Oberon'		
21.0	O'Connell	149°43'43"E	33°32'02"S
26.5	▲ 1.5km moderate climb		
29.6	▲ 1.5km steep climb		
35.1	▲ 7.7km moderate climb		
43.6	↰ Carrington Ave, `to Jenolan Caves'		
44.7	↱ Ross St, Oberon	149°51'33"E	33°42'14"S
45.1	↘ `to Jenolan Caves'		
46.2	▲ 2km moderate climb		
49.1	▲ 1.4km moderate climb		
57.3	Edith	149°55'12"E	33°47'25"S
58.5	▲ 8.5km moderate climb		
{68.8	●● ↱ Kanangra Walls 55km ↻}		
69.7	⚠️ 3.4km steep, winding descent		
73.1	Jenolan Caves	150°01'21"E	33°49'12"S

1300m) over 8.5km of ascent. Thankfully it rises moderately most of the way, just occasionally steepening.

Check your brakes by the communication towers at the top of the climb, because the writhing descent to the caves is about to begin. It's tempting to simply hare down the hill, but by going slowly you can appreciate the precipitous view into the valley, with Jenolan Caves (p95) nestled at the bottom. Stop frequently to ensure rims and brakes don't overheat.

SIDE TRIP: KANANGRA WALLS
3–5 hours, 55km

If you want to see the **Kanangra Walls**, the sandstone cliffs that form one of the most imposing sights in the region, it's a long ride, but the gravel road is usually in good condition and there's a campsite at Boyd River, a few kilometres before the walls. Take the road to the right at 68.8km.

Day 2: Jenolan Caves to Katoomba
5½–7½ hours, 74.2km

If you don't normally stretch before a ride, today might be a good day to start because the climbs are bigger (and the views are even wider) than yesterday – it's a 400m climb out from the caves alone. If you plan to duck underground into one of the Jenolan Caves this morning, be aware that a one-way system operates on the road out between 11.45am and 1.15pm – you must leave before or after these times.

Even if you haven't been into any caves during your stay, the fabulous start through the cavernous **Grand Arch** at least offers a taste: it's nearly 130m long and soars to more than 20m high.

Mercifully, the climb out from the caves is not as steep as the descent of the previous day, yet the views are somehow even more dramatic. The climbs tops out after about 16km at the crest of the Great Dividing Range (1250m above sea level), where you'll be greeted by the sight of an extensive logging operation. A few bends ahead comes the first glimpse of the Blue Mountains' sandstone escarpment, so save that celebratory chocolate bar for here.

Past the cemetery in Lowther, the route drops off the spur and down to Coxs River, one of the major feeder streams for Lake Burragorang – Sydney's main water supply reservoir. It's a gliding descent on a very smooth road, with cattle peering down on you from the boulder-studded hills above. The road surface quickly changes, first to dirt and then, across **Coxs River**, an already-difficult climb is complicated by the very rough sealed road. Atop the climb comes the best views yet, with the rim of sandstone making the Blue Mountains look more like the orange mountains.

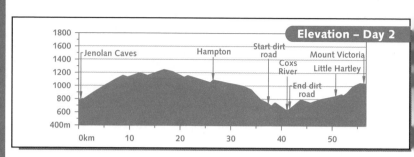

BATHURST TO THE BLUEYS –
DAY 2

CUE			GPS COORDINATES
start		Jenolan Caves House	150°01'21"E 33°49'12"S
0km		go N through Grand Arch	
0.2	↑	8km steep climb	
9.6	↑	1.4km moderate climb	
{12.8	★	campsite}	
13.2	↑	3km moderate climb	
25.7		Hampton	150°02'55"E 33°38'53"S
33.0	⌐→	Lowther Siding Rd, 'to Coxs River'	
36.3	↰	Ganbenang Rd, 'to Hartley'	
	⚠	3.2km dirt road	
36.9	↑	600m steep climb	
{39.9	★	Coxs River}	
	↑	2.7km steep climb	

CUE CONTINUED			GPS COORDINATES
44.9	↑	2.4km moderate climb	
49.2	⌐→	Great Western Hwy, Little Hartley	150°12'20"E 33°34'11"S
51.2	↑	2.5km steep climb	
54.1		Mt Victoria	150°15'19"E 33°35'28"S
56.5	↑	1.4km moderate climb	
61.2		Blackheath	150°17'11"E 33°37'57"S
{	●●↰	Govett's Leap 5.8km (↻) }	
{62.8	●●↰	Evans Lookout 8.4km (↻) }	
65.9		Medlow Bath	150°16'56"E 33°40'46"S
{69.3	★	Explorers' Tree}	
70.2	↰	Bathurst Rd, 'to Katoomba Town Centre'	
71.9	⌐→	Lurline St, 'to Echo Point'	
74.2		Echo Point, Katoomba	150°18'42"E 33°42'41"S

After rejoining the Great Western Hwy at Little Hartley (49.2km), the route climbs Victoria Pass on a road surveyed and first opened in the early 1830s; it may seem steep (it's around a 1-in-8 gradient) but it's better than the much steeper and rougher earlier routes pioneered by William Cox and William Lawson. You'll have to contend not only with the gradient but also the highway traffic. If it has you spooked (the verge between Mt Victoria and Katoomba is variable: sometimes wide, sometimes nonexistent), you can finish the ride at Mt Victoria, which has train connections to Sydney ($14, 2¼ hours), though you'll miss some of the Blue Mountains' signature scenes.

Near Blackheath there's the choice of two worthwhile side trips. **Govett's Leap** (5.8km return) is a clifftop lookout with views along the zig-zagging Grose River, dominated by the rhino-like Pulpit Rock, with feathery Bridal Veil Falls tucked into the cliffs. **Evan's Lookout** (8.4km return) is same, same but different. It also looks

across to Pulpit Rock, but the valley itself dominates, with the interlocking canyons providing a greater sense of scale – it's like looking at nature's street plan. The two lookouts are also connected by a 3km walking trail along the clifftop.

Just west of Katoomba, Wentworth, Blaxland and Lawson, the first Europeans to cross the Blue Mountains, notched the **Explorers' Tree** to mark their trail. The sad, bushfire-ravaged stump has been amputated, gored by termites and filled with concrete but it's still a major feature.

The tree stands on Pulpit Hill, named according to local knowledge, because religious ceremonies were once held here to try to save the souls of convicts working on road construction in the area.

You're likely to arrive at **Echo Point** at the best time of day, with the late-afternoon sun shining on the Three Sisters. Peer through the gap between Mt Solitary and Narrow Neck and you'll see the distant crease of Coxs River, the waterway that dominated part of your day.

MURRAY RIVER TO ALPINE WAY

Duration 3 days
Distance 256.9km
Difficulty demanding
Start Albury
Finish Thredbo
Summary From long lonely lengths of the pasture-packed upper Murray River Valley, climb through lush national park and over the highest point of the Kosciuszko Alpine Way to a triumphant finish in thin-air Thredbo.

This is a ride of glorious extremes. It begins with a marathon reach along the upper Murray River, Australia's longest waterway. It climbs towards the river's source, set in the wilds of the Snowy Mountains – the continent's highest. It follows in the footsteps of early explorers to the highest pass of the Alpine Way, arguably Australia's premier scenic mountain road. And it finishes in Thredbo alpine village, one of the names most reverently whispered by Australian snow enthusiasts when winter comes around.

HISTORY

The Murray River is a prime mover in the Murray-Darling Basin, an area that once sustained more than 30 Indigenous nations within its boundaries. The first Europeans to explore its banks were Hamilton Hume and William Hovell, who in 1824 crossed the flow near where Albury now stands. With the subsequent arrival of pastoralists, the basin became the most important agricultural region in Australia and its waters a vital transportation route. In the last 60 years, although trains and trucks have replaced steamboats, extensive irrigation projects designed to harness water from the basin's rivers have resulted in harvest returns that amount to one-third of Australia's agricultural output. See p235 for related environmental concerns.

Kosciuszko National Park (KNP) takes in the traditional lands of the Ngarigo Aboriginal people, who travelled extensively along the Monaro Tablelands (east of the park) and entered the High Country each year for ceremonial reasons and to feast on bogong moths. Polish-born adventurer/ scientist Paul Edmund de Strzelecki is credited as the first European to climb the region's (and Australia's) highest peak, which he named after the great Polish patriot Tadeusz Kosciuszko.

The Kosciuszko High Country has largely resisted permanent settlement. Rather, the plains were long used as summer pasturelands by cattlemen and are the site of the huge Snowy Mountains Hydro-Electric Scheme. KNP was gazetted (as Kosciusko State Park) in 1944 and, at more than 6700 sq km, became the state's largest national park in 1967.

ENVIRONMENT

The source of the Murray River is in the Snowy Mountains, down whose western face the waters cascade, before a long meander across inland plains. The Murray's health has been on the decline ever since European settlement. To begin with, far-reaching engineering projects completely regulated the water's flow; in 2008 the Murray had been reduced to only 36% of its natural flow. Coupled with the removal of native vegetation and increasingly poor water quality (damaged by chemical runoff), this has made it impossible for many animal and plant species to survive. Even the agricultural industries are suffering as a result of dryland salinity. A huge project involving government and communities is underway to reduce the amount of water diverted from the basin's rivers, but the recent six-year-plus spell of extreme drought and the threats of global warming are great challenges to reversing the decades of degradation.

The Kosciuszko region contains evidence of glacial activity – rare in Australia – from the most recent ice age; striking remnants of this are glacial lakes in the highest reaches of KNP, which are also the only areas of NSW that consistently see snow in winter. They consequently harbour many plants and animals found nowhere else on the continent. High-country fauna includes the rare mountain pygmy possum and the striking, black-and-yellow corroboree frog; at lower reaches wombats, wallabies, grey kangaroos and emus are commonly seen. The park includes six designated wilderness areas amounting to about 3000 sq km.

MURRAY RIVER TO ALPINE WAY

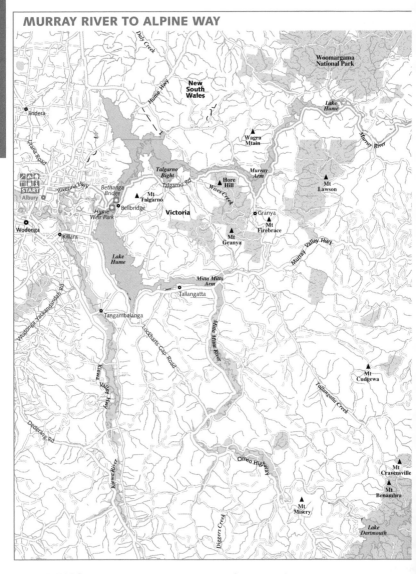

PLANNING
When to Cycle

November, December, March and April are best. Midsummer temperatures in the mountains may be tolerable, but in the valley they're intense. The higher reaches of Dead Horse Gap often see snow from late May until September or October.

What to Bring

Mountain conditions are changeable, even in summer. It always makes sense to prepare well and pack warm, windproof and waterproof clothing.

If you are planning on breaking the final day into two parts with a night at Geehi, you will need a tent and cooking and sleeping

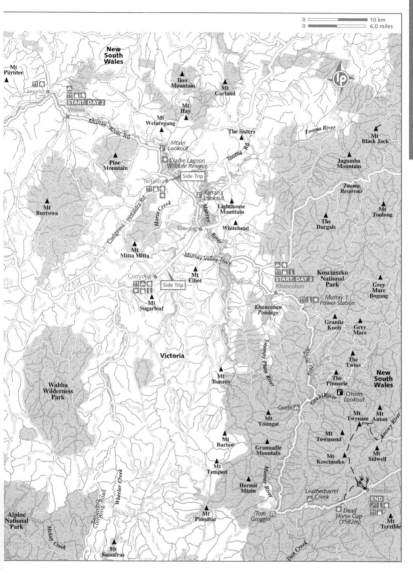

gear. Some parts of the park are fuel-stove only (as are all areas on a fire ban day), so check before departure. Your tent should be rated to four seasons. Have insect repellent on hand too.

Bike Hire

See Albury (p89).

Maps

For full coverage of the ride, in Albury pick up the free 1:588,200 *North East Victoria and the Southern Riverina of NSW* map and guide. Its major drawback is the absence of distance markings.

Cartoscope's free Snowy Mountains map gets in closer for the section from Tintaldra

NEW SOUTH WALES

MOUNTAIN BIKING IN KOSCIUSZKO NATIONAL PARK HIGH COUNTRY

If you can arrange for travel – or have the legs to bike – to the start of this ride, there's an incredible three-day mountain bike alternative trail that crosses through the heart of Kosciuszko National Park (KNP). You will need to be completely self-contained for this ride, ready to tote all-weather camping and cooking gear as well as provisions for three days. You will also need a good map that covers this ride in detail.

From Thredbo or Jindabyne, you need to book private transport to the Guthega Power Station, directly accessible on sealed road from Jindabyne (36km) or via a 10km 4WD track from Perisher Valley.

On Day 1, the 20km trail to Valentine Hut climbs to Schlink Pass (1810m) and then follows the rough Valentine Fire Trail to Valentine Hut. On Day 2, all the climbing is rewarded as most of the 51.7km to Geehi are downhill. Back at the bottom of the Valentine Fire Trail, a right turn onto the Geehi Fire Trail begins a 14km stretch of virtually uninterrupted descent on a brilliantly smooth track to the Geehi Dam. There's a bit of climbing from there on the Olsens Lookout/Geehi Reservoir Rd, but that too finds its peak and then it's a long way down to the junction with the Alpine Way. Camp at Geehi and then battle over Dead Horse Gap as described in Day 3 of the Murray River to Alpine Way ride (p74) to finish in Thredbo.

to Thredbo and includes an inset map of Thredbo village.

If you will be doing any mountain biking in the area (see boxed text above), buy Rooftop's 1:50,000 *Kosciuszko National Park Jindabyne–Khancoban* map.

Information Sources

The **Albury-Wodonga Cycling Club** (www .alburywodongacyclingclub.com). Check out the website to see how you can tap into the city's excellent cycling vibe.

Discover Murray (www.rivermurray .com) is a clearinghouse of information about travel the length of the Murray River.

For more information on the muddy Murray, try the **Murray-Darling Basin Commission** (☎ 02-6279 0100; www .mdbc.gov.au), the organisation charged with promoting and coordinating the environmental resources of the Murray-Darling Basin.

Parklands Albury-Wodonga (☎ 02-6023 6714; www.parklands-alburywodonga .org.au) is a charitable institution overseeing the regional community's parklands projects, including the High Country Rail Trail (www.highcountryrailtrail.org.au).

GETTING TO/FROM THE RIDE
Albury (start)
AIR
The airport is 10 minutes on Borella Rd. **Rex** (☎ 13 17 13; www.rex.com.au)

flies from Sydney and Melbourne, and **Brindabella Airlines** (☎ 1300 668 824; brindabellaairlines.com.au) from Canberra.

BUS
Long-distance buses running on the Hume Hwy between Sydney and Melbourne stop at the train station. **Greyhound** (☎ 13 14 99; www.greyhound.com.au) has one coach daily from from Melbourne (from $42, four hours) and Sydney (from $65, nine hours).

TRAIN
The twice-daily **CountryLink** (☎ 13 22 32; www.countrylink.info) XPTs (express trains), running between Sydney ($72) and Melbourne ($46), stop in Albury. **V/Line** (☎ 13 61 96; www.vline.com.au) runs a cheaper, daily train (from $50).

BICYCLE
Albury is roughly 45km from both Rutherglen and Beechworth, both overnight stops on the Victorian Riches of the Northeast ride (p129).

Thredbo (finish)
BUS
At the time of writing, from both Thredbo and Jindabyne there is no regularly scheduled summer transport service of any kind. **Greyhound** (☎ 13 14 99; www .greyhound.com.au) and **Transborder**

Alpine Express (☎ 02-6241 0033; www.transborder.com.au) run daily buses from Thredbo to Canberra only between May or June and October.

TAXI
Your only real option when the buses aren't running is a taxi or private car hire. As a measure of cost, **Snowy Mountains Taxi Service** (☎ 02-6457 2444) will get you to Jindabyne for around $100 (mention bikes when you call).

BICYCLE
Thredbo is a mostly 33km downhill and very pleasant ride along the Alpine Way to Jindabyne.

THE RIDE
Day 1: Albury to Walwa
6–11 hours, 110km

Today is very long, but also absolutely stunning. From a few kilometres past Albury all the way to the country town of Walwa, you roll and swerve with the meanders of the once-great Murray River. There's pretty much nothing to distract you en route – not even traffic – so pack all the water and food you will need.

Once on the Riverine Hwy and beyond Albury's industry and airport, you're utterly free of urban development. Rolling hills and a tough climb or two bridge the distance to what will guide you through the rest of the day: the **Murray River** (see p235).

At the river, two major engineering structures come into view: the Hume Weir, seen from **Hume Weir Park** (15.9km), which holds back the Murray's waters to create Lake Hume, and the nine-truss **Bethanga Bridge** (16.5km; completed in 1930), now towering over a drought-drained basin, the shallow waters of which lapped at the spans as recently as 2005.

Beyond the bridge lies 93.5km of mellow, undulating, open road with no services. Fortunately, it's gorgeous.

To the left, the waterway narrows from the lake basin to a calm river, winding across the valley. The colour combination is beguiling: the blue of the Murray irrigating a narrow strip of bright green land hemmed in by vast empty fields and mounts of seared golden earth. The withered trunks of long-dead red gum trees drowned by wetter times claw at the air, odd silhouettes interspersed with the distant dots of foraging cattle and sheep.

Walwa appears out of nowhere, a welcome manmade intrusion on the monotony of nature.

Day 2: Walwa to Khancoban
3½–6 hours, 60.3km

Picking up where you left off yesterday, you continue along the Murray River, leaving the broad basin near the end of the route to climb into the foothills of the Snowy Mountains.

Your exit from Walwa is as rapid as your entrance. Your return to the rise-and-fall rhythm of Murray River Rd is just as quick. If any change can be identified, it's the subtle

MURRAY RIVER TO ALPINE WAY – DAY 1

CUE			GPS COORDINATES
start		Albury train station	146°55′28″E 36°05′03″S
0km		go SE out of parking area	
0.1	⌐►	Young St	
1.1	⌐►	Riverine Hwy `to Lake Hume'	
10.7	▲	2.2km moderate climb	
14.0	◥⌐	`to Bellbridge'	
{15.9	★	Hume Weir Park}	
{16.5	★	700m trestle bridge}	
17.3	↑	C542 `to Walwa'	
20.7	▲	4.7km rising hills	
49.2	↘	`to Walwa'	
85.6	◥⌐	`to Walwa'	
90.4	▲	1.2km moderate climb	
104.6	↙	`to Jingelic'	
110.0		Walwa Hotel, Walwa	147°44′09″E 35°57′50″S

MURRAY RIVER TO ALPINE WAY – DAY 2

CUE			GPS COORDINATES
start		Walwa Hotel, Walwa	147°44′09″E 35°57′50″S
0km		go E on Main St/Murray River Rd	
{17.3	★	mountains lookout}	
{18.7	★	Clarke Lagoon Wildlife Reserve}	
23.3	↑	`to Corryong'	
{	●●◥⌐	Tintaldra 1km ⟳}	
{29.3	★	Farran's Lookout}	
34.3	⌐►	`to Corryong'	
39.0	◥⌐	`to Snowy Mountains Area'	
	▲	2.9km moderate climb	
{	●●↑	Corryong 12.4km ⟳}	
46.2	▲	3km hard climb	
60.1	◥⌐	`to park information office'	
60.3		Khancoban park office	148°07′20″E 36°12′57″S

increase in the number of living trees along the waterway, like the coppice at the heart of **Clarke Lagoon Wildlife Reserve** (18.7km). Pause at the **lookout** just before it (17.3km) to take in the view over this small woods to the blue-grey wall of mountain towards which your pedalling unerringly wends. The short side trip at 23.3km to Tintaldra allows the unprovisioned to pick up supplies.

Farran's Lookout (29.3km) provides stirring confirmation that the mountains are indeed getting nearer, final proof of which comes at 39km when a left turn puts you on Alpine Way, the direct road to the Snowy Mountains. Time and energy permitting, take the 12.4km side trip here to historic Corryong.

Khancoban, perched on the edge of the dam-formed Khancoban Pondage, is just two short climbs away, separated by a wide flat valley.

SIDE TRIP: TINTALDRA
5 minutes, 1km
Tintaldra offers a historic **pioneer store** (from 1864) and a memorabilia display at the **Tintaldra Hotel** (☎ 02-6077 9261), a classic country pub. Rupert Bunny (1864– 1947), the famous Australian artist, spent time here in the 1920s and painted *The Murray at Tintaldra*.

SIDE TRIP: CORRYONG
40-75 minutes, 12.4km
Corryong has long been dubbed the capital of Man from Snowy River country, a reference to Banjo Paterson's famous poem (and the film based on it). It has a lively main street with plenty of places to eat and shop. Ask at the well-stocked **information centre** (☎ 02-6076 2277; www .pureuppermurrayvalleys.com; 50 Hanson St) about the hours of the '**Man from Snowy River' Museum**, a memorabilia exhibit.

Day 3: Khancoban to Thredbo
4¾–8½ hours, 86.6km
The Kosciuszko Alpine Way is one of Australia's greatest year-round scenic roads, a spirited evocation of the early explorers who forged a path across Australia's High Country. You must tackle the Alpine Way's hardest and most glorious segment, including the long and steep climb through rugged country to its highest point, **Dead Horse Gap** (1580m) – just a few kilometres from Thredbo. There's nothing too directionally complicated about the day, you're on one road from start to finish, but it does serve up a supreme fitness challenge. From Khancoban, with the exception of a cafe at the Murray 1 Power Station, there are no services until Thredbo. Bring plenty of food and water.

The hardship begins right away. The first climb commences at Khancoban Creek (2.3km), takes you into Kosciuszko National Park (4.2km) and passes **Murray 1 Power Station**, a vital part of the Snowy Mountains Hydro-Electric Scheme. Snowy Hydro roadside information panels (8.8km) and the **visitors centre** (9.7km; ☎ 1800 623 776; www.snowyhydro .com.au; admission free; 9am-4pm Mon-Fri, 10am-4pm weekends and holidays, tours 11am, 1pm & 3pm) along an access road reveal the station's historical and industrial significance.

MURRAY RIVER TO ALPINE WAY – DAY 3

CUE		GPS COORDINATES
start	Khancoban park office	148°07'20"E 36°12'57"S
0km	go S on Scott St	
0.2	↰ Alpine Way	
2.3	Khancoban Creek	
	▲ 5.5km hard climb	
4.2	Kosciuszko National Park sign	
{8.8	★ Murray 1 Power Station}	
9.7	▲ 1.5km moderate climb	
12.3	▲ 5.3km hard climb	
17.6	⚠ 8.7km steep descent	
26.3	▲ 1.2km moderate climb	
37.4	▲ 2km moderate climb	

CUE CONTINUED		GPS COORDINATES
{41.1	★ Geehi}	
41.9	▲ 1km moderate climb	
43.9	▲ 6.5 hard climb	
62.4	Tom Groggin picnic area	
	▲ 6.7km very hard climb	
70.0	Leatherbarrel Creek	
	▲ 10.6km very hard climb	
80.6	Dead Horse Gap	
	⚠ 6km steep descent	
83.7	↘ Banjo Dr	
84.4	↰ Diggings Tce/Friday Dr	
86.6	Thredbo visitors centre	148°18'37"E 36°30'05"S

From Murray 1, more climbing (for about 8km) is followed by an ego-lifting 8.7km descent to an intermediate valley.

Geehi is a popular campsite (41.1km) and good place for a break. There are toilets, picnic tables and interpretive signs both near the Alpine Way and some historic huts, one of them about 1km west of the road. Wildlife, especially kangaroos and wallabies, are common.

The physical grind continues practically before there's been time to warm up again. From 41.9km, an ascent of nearly 8.5km through magnificent eucalypt forest takes the route towards 800m elevation followed by another superb, swooping downhill, this time down to cleared country surrounding the Murray River – the border between Victoria and NSW – in the vicinity of Tom Groggin cattle station.

The **Tom Groggin picnic area** (540m) is another good place to stop, stretch and snack in anticipation of the biggest climb yet.

The road angles up almost immediately, steepens at around 63.1km (600m), and then pushes 450m of vertical in a little over 5km. The 1km downhill breather to the **Leatherbarrel Creek** picnic and campsite (70km) may sound like a nice break but it robs you of 60m vertical. From Leatherbarrel, it's just 10.6km to the top. Most of the remaining 570m feels like it's at a gentler grade (although much of it isn't!) and the outlook is pleasant throughout.

The road crests at **Dead Horse Gap** (80.6km; 1580m), surrounded by stunted snow gums, after which it's almost all downhill to Thredbo village, with beautiful views of the Ramshead Range and Thredbo River Valley.

COFFS & DORRIGO CIRCUIT

Duration 2 days
Distance 143.3km
Difficulty moderate–demanding
Start/Finish Coffs Harbour
Summary Climb from the coast to the thick rainforest and waterfalls around World Heritage–listed Dorrigo National Park.

The rainforests of northern New South Wales are one of the country's natural treasures, thick with trees, ferns and waterfalls. From the banana plantations around Coffs Harbour, this ride journeys up through the forests on the fringe of Dorrigo National Park, hovers amid the rich volcanic country of the Dorrigo Plateau then soars downhill to the rural idylls of the Bellinger Valley. Is it any wonder they chose to name a place here Promised Land?

Take note of the weather forecast before setting out; sections of the ride are in rainforest (ergo, it rains a lot), and there are dirt sections on both days, which are not much fun in pouring rain.

PLANNING
When to Cycle
The ride is possible year-round, although autumn to spring is best. Midwinter days can be cool up at Dorrigo, but this is preferable to the steaminess of midsummer in the Bellinger Valley. Sections of dirt make riding in dry weather preferable.

Bike Hire
Bikes can be rented from **Bob Wallis Cycles** in Coffs Harbour (☎ 02-6652 5102; shop 30 Homebase Shopping Centre, 252 Pacific Hwy, Coffs Harbour). A two-day hire, with handlebar bag, helmet and lock (but not racks or panniers) costs $40.

Maps
The route straddles two 1:200,000 maps in the NRMA series: map No 1 *Lower & Mid North Coast* and map No 6 *Far North Coast*. They can be purchased at the **NRMA's Coffs Harbour office** (☎ 02-6650 0122; 30 Gordon St).

GETTING TO/FROM THE RIDE
Coffs Harbour (start/finish)
AIR
Virgin Blue (☎ 13 67 89; www.virginblue. com.au) and **Qantas** (☎ 13 13 13; www .qantas.com.au) fly to Sydney, Brisbane and Melbourne. **Brindabella Airlines** (☎ 1300 668 824; www.brindabellaairlines.com.au) flies to/from Port Macquarie.

BUS
Buses leave from the visitors centre.
Greyhound (☎ 13 14 99; www.greyhound .com.au) and **Premier Motor Service** (☎ 13 34 10; www.premierms.com.au) stop in Coffs; fares include Port Macquarie ($45, three

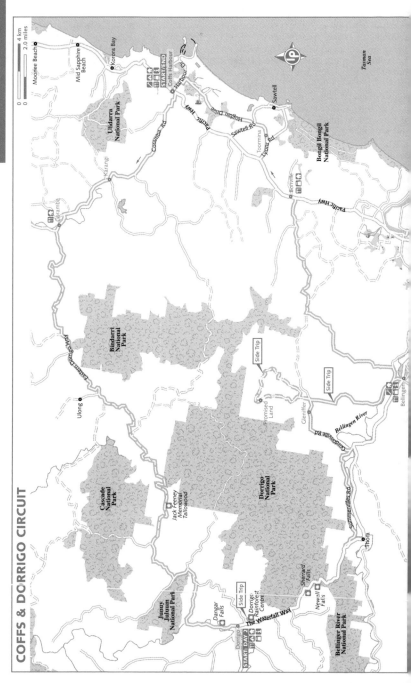

COFFS & DORRIGO CIRCUIT

hours) and Byron Bay ($55, four hours). **Keans** (☎ 02-6543 1322) has two services a week to Bellingen ($15, 40 minutes), Dorrigo ($19, 1¼ hours) and Armidale ($25, 2¾ hours). **Ryans Buses** (☎ 02-6652 3201; www.ryansbusservice.com.au) runs to Grafton ($20, 1½ hours) twice daily.

TRAIN
CountryLink (☎ 13 22 32; www.countrylink.info) trains have three daily services to Grafton ($11.30, 1½ hours), three daily to Sydney ($60, nine hours) and two daily services to Casino ($25, 3¾ hours).

BICYCLE
Coffs Harbour can be reached from Sydney or the Gold Coast.

THE RIDE
Day 1: Coffs Harbour to Dorrigo
4½–6 hours, 70.1km

A solid opening day, with the route rising from just above sea level to more than 700m elevation. Happily, the ascents (with a few exceptions) tend to be steady rather than real grinds, so that once you get your rhythm you can begin to enjoy the towering forest, which is bookended by beautiful farmland.

Banana plantations (Coffs isn't home to the Big Banana for no reason) and rolling farmlands line the roadside between Coffs and Coramba (15km), but these give way to timbered escarpment as the route climbs Eastern Dorrigo Way, rainforest at first, then the tall timber of Orara West State Forest, and some striking pockets of rainforest towards the climb's top. Following are a series of stunning rural valleys separated by more slopes of rainforest – the view over Ulong, the 'village in the valley', is particularly beautiful.

As the ride fringes Dorrigo National Park, it climbs past the 56.5m-high **Jack Feeney Memorial Tallowood** (50.5km). When the dirt roads ends, the rainforest narrows to pockets and the cows take over again.

Dangar Falls (68.1km), on Dorrigo's outskirts, cascade over a series of rocky shelves before plummeting into a pristine gorge.

There's an excellent lookout over the falls right beside the road, or you can walk to the base of the falls for a chilly dip.

COFFS & DORRIGO CIRCUIT – DAY 1

CUE			GPS COORDINATES
start		Coffs Harbour visitors centre	153°06'49"E 30°17'47"S
0km		go N on Pacific Hwy	
0.1	&#x2197;	`to Harbour Dr'	
0.3	↖①ⓞ	West High St	
1.9	↘ⓞ	Tourist Drive 14	
3.6	&#x25B2;	1.8km steep climb	
9.6		Karangi	153°02'51"E 30°15'14"S
15.0		Coramba	153°00'48"E 30°13'13"S
15.7	&#x2196;	Eastern Dorrigo Way	

CUE CONTINUED			GPS COORDINATES
	&#x25B2;	12.2km moderate climb	
29.6	&#x25B2;	30km undulating terrain	
35.7	&#x2198;	`to Dorrigo'	
36.2	&#x26A0;	20km dirt road	
{50.5	&#x2605;	Jack Feeney Memorial Tallowood}	
56.2	&#x2196;	`to Dorrigo'	
67.3	&#x25B2;	700m moderate climb	
{68.1	&#x2605;	Dangar Falls}	
70.1		Dorrigo visitors centre	152°42'50"E 30°20'28"S

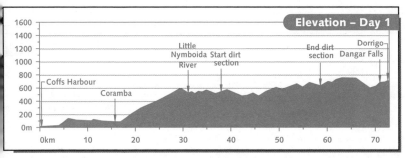

Elevation – Day 1

Little Nymboida River · Start dirt section · End dirt section · Dorrigo – Dangar Falls · Coffs Harbour · Coramba

Day 2: Dorrigo to Coffs Harbour
4½–6 hours, 73.2km

Spectacular views and charming rural lands are constant and pleasant distractions this day. The climbing from Day 1 is rewarded with an exhilarating descent early and gorgeous back roads through the Bellinger Valley. If time is short, you can beeline straight through Gleniffer to the coast (making for a 64km day) but Bellingen is one of the nicest hinterland towns in NSW.

The **Dorrigo Rainforest Centre** (☎ 02-6657 2309), a short side trip at 2km, provides the easiest access into the World Heritage–listed rainforest of Dorrigo National Park. Viewing is made simple on the Skywalk (free), a 100m-long platform above the rainforest canopy. If you're here on one of the days it's not misted in, and there are good views across the Bellinger Valley to the ocean.

The road plunges around 700m over 9km – rest tired braking hands by **Sherrard Falls** (7.1km) and **Newell Falls** (8.1km), both spilling over rock faces right beside the road. The few narrow sections on the descent are relieved by wide verges in the trickier sections; use them to enjoy the gorgeous rainforest.

It's hard to pick the prettiest spot in the Bellinger Valley, but the stretch on Gordonville Rd is in the running as the road hugs the edge of the evergreen valley with the woolly Dorrigo mountains rising above. To see another contender, take the side trip (at 28.2km) north from Gleniffer to **Promised Land** – this is truly heavenly country. Dropping down to the Bellinger River, the ride enters Bellingen, the sort of bohemian town where detox is a major industry. Here, the route U-turns back north, climbing consistently but gradually out of the valley.

The back way into Coffs Harbour avoids the busy Pacific Hwy, and from Toormina there's a pleasant bikepath to

COFFS & DORRIGO CIRCUIT – DAY 2

CUE			GPS COORDINATES
start		Dorrigo visitors centre	152°42′50″E 30°20′28″S
0km		go S on Hickory St	
0.1	↰ ◉	Cudgery St	
	▲	1.2km moderate climb	
{2.0	●● ↰	Dorrigo Rainforest Centre 3.2km (↰)}	
4.3	▲	8.7km steep, winding descent	
{7.1	★	Sherrard Falls}	
{8.1	★	Newell Falls}	
13.0	↰	Summervilles Rd	
15.0	⚠	600m dirt road	
16.7	⚠	3km dirt road	
19.5	▲	600m steep climb	
21.3	↰	Gordonville Rd (unsigned)	
25.0	↱	'to Gleniffer'	
26.5	⚠	pick-a-plank bridge	
27.3	↱	unsigned road at East Preston Reserve	
{	●● ↰	Promised Land 11.9km (↰)	

CUE CONTINUED			GPS COORDINATES
35.4	↱ ◉	Hammond St/Bridge St	
36.1		Bellingen	152°53′53″E 30°27′8″S
{(↰	north on Bridge St/Hammond St)}		
36.8	↱ ◉	'to Hydes Creek'	
37.7	↰	Hydes Creek Rd	
43.3	↗	'to Valery'	
47.3	↱	Valery Rd	
48.3	⚠	4km dirt road	
56.8	↰	Pacific Hwy	
57.8		Bonville	153°02′06″E 30°22′34″S
60.7	↰	Lyons Rd	
61.0	↱ ◉	Lyons Rd	
63.0	↰	Toormina Rd	
71.7	↰ ◉	Albany St	
73.1	↱ 🚲	Pacific Hwy	
73.2		Coffs Harbour visitors centre	
		153°06′49″E	30°17′47″S

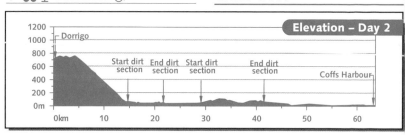

Elevation – Day 2

Dorrigo · Start dirt section · End dirt section · Start dirt section · End dirt section · Coffs Harbour

the roundabout at Albany St, giving you a traffic-free chance to scan the trees for the koalas that inhabit the area. Albany St connects directly to the visitors centre at Coffs Harbour, avoiding the town centre.

SIDE TRIP: PROMISED LAND
1–1½ hours, 11.9km
Crossing and recrossing Never Never Creek, this road burrows up to the foot of the range through farmland and forest to the biblically inspiring Promised Land. It's a must-do loop, even if it means stopping the night in Bellingen (not a bad thing in itself).

THUNDERBOLTS WAY

Duration 3 days
Distance 210km
Difficulty moderate–demanding
Start Armidale
Finish Gloucester
Summary A gentle roll along the New England tablelands ends deep within some of the east coast's most beautiful hinterland country.

Thunderbolts Way was named for the bushranger Fred Ward, aka Thunderbolt, who operated in a wide stretch of country from the Hunter River up to New England in the 1860s (see boxed text p82), and heads through some of the highest and prettiest country in NSW.

Away from major through routes, it makes for an inviting cycle, leading through wide grazing lands atop the New England plateau, before undulating through gorgeously green country around Nowendoc and Gloucester, near the spectacular Barrington Tops National Park.

PLANNING
When to Cycle
As with so much of the country, spring and autumn are the best seasons to ride. Since the route takes in both tablelands (at an elevation of around 1000m or more) and lowlands (300m or lower), winter riding will involve cold mornings up high, but ideal conditions in the lower country – for instance, the average July temperature in

Armidale is 12.2°C, while it's around 16.2°C close to Gloucester.

Maps
The route is covered in its entirety on the NRMA's 1:550,000 map No 5 *Central & North West*. It can be purchased at the **NRMA's Armidale office** (☎ 02-6771 1322; 101–103 Rusden St).

GETTING TO/FROM THE RIDE
Armidale (start)
AIR
The airport is 5km southeast of town. **QantasLink** (☎ 13 13 13; www.qantas.com.au) has three flights a day from Sydney.

BUS
Travelling by bus, **Greyhound** (☎ 13 14 99; www.greyhound.com.au) runs twice daily from Glen Innes ($55, 1½ hours) and Tamworth ($50, 1½ hours). One daily service departs Sydney for Armidale ($120, 10 hours). **Keans** (☎ 02-6545 1945) runs from Coffs Harbour ($37, 2¾ hours).

TRAIN
CountryLink (☎ 13 22 32; www.countrylink.info) trains travel daily from Tamworth ($20, two hours), Broadmeadow-Newcastle ($75, 5½ hours) and Sydney ($95, 8¼ hours).

BICYCLE
Armidale is around 120km inland from Dorrigo (p93), on the Coffs & Dorrigo Circuit. The ride is along the Waterfall Way through beautiful, undulating farmland and the Cathedral Rock National Park, and is a long but feasible day's ride.

Gloucester (finish)
TRAIN
From the end of the ride, **CountryLink** (☎ 13 22 32; www.countrylink.info) trains thrice daily travel south to Sydney ($50, 4¼ hours) and daily north to Byron Bay (adult/child $145, 9½ hours) via Casino.

BICYCLE
Gloucester is inland from Taree. At the southern end of town, near the Pacific Hwy junction, join The Bucketts Way through Tinonee and Krambach. It's a good day's

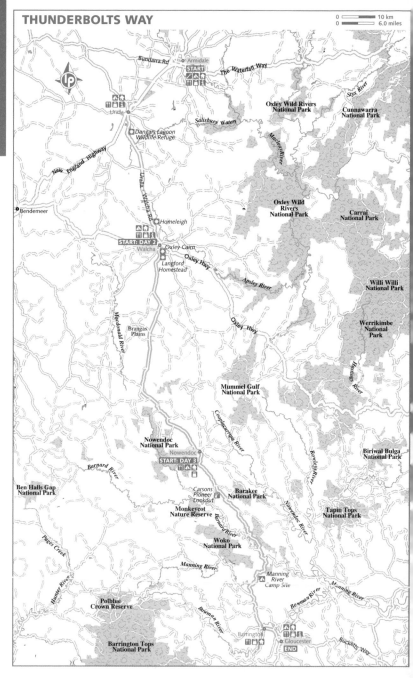

NEW SOUTH WALES

THUNDERBOLTS WAY

0 ————— 10 km
0 ————— 6.0 miles

Bundarra Rd

Armidale
START

The Waterfall Way

Styx River

Uralla

Oxley Wild Rivers
National Park

Cunnawarra
National Park

Dangars Lagoon
Wildlife Refuge

Salisbury Waters

New England Highway

Macleay River

Bendemeer

Uralla–Walcha Rd

Oxley Wild
Rivers
National Park

Carrai
National Park

Homeleigh

START: DAY 2
Walcha

Oxley Cairn

Oxley Hwy

Apsley River

Langford
Homestead

Willi Willi
National Park

Macdonald River

Brangas
Plains

Oxley Hwy

Werrikimbe
National
Park

Hastings River

Mummel Gulf
National Park

Coopbacarega River

Nowendoc
National Park

Nowendoc

Rowleys River

Biriwal Bulga
National Park

START: DAY 3

Barnard River

Ben Halls Gap
National Park

Carsons
Pioneer
Lookout

Barakee
National Park

Nowendoc River

Tapin Tops
National Park

Monkeycot
Nature Reserve

Barnard River

Woko
National Park

Pages Creek

Manning River

Manning
River
Camp Site

Hunter River

Polblue
Crown Reserve

Bowman River

Bowman River

Manning River

Barrington

Gloucester
END

Buckets Way

Barrington Tops
National Park

ride (about 75km), and while the terrain is undulating, there are no major climbs.

THE RIDE
Day 1: Armidale to Walcha
3½–5 hours, 64km

This is the first of a couple of glorious days on the high New England tablelands, gently undulating between 1000m and 1100m almost all the way to Walcha, usually under the watchful eye of cattle. The first part of the route follows the New England Hwy to Uralla, the final resting place of the bush-ranger Thunderbolt (see boxed text p82).

The route climbs out of Armidale past the airport and onto the bare plateau. Here, the stark, bleached trees stand as a sobering display of New England dieback disease, caused by a variety of natural and human pressures, including the ravages of the Christmas beetle. Recent replantings along the road show an attempt to recover some of the balance of the ecosystem. If nothing else, the skeletal trees make for easy viewing of the raptors and other birds.

To Uralla, the highway has a wide verge and there's just a gentle swell to the land. **Uralla** is central to the story of Thunderbolt:

a statue of the bushranger atop his mount marks the turn into Salisbury St (23.1km) in Uralla. Thunderbolt's grave is a bit further south, in the old cemetery at the corner of John and Roman Sts. **McCrossins Mill Museum** (☎ 02-6778 3022; Salisbury St; admission $4; noon-5pm) has displays about Thunderbolt and is worth a visit, though the opening hours can be awkward for cyclists leaving Armidale in the early morning. The mill was built in 1870, the same year Thunderbolt was killed.

The grasslands roll on south from Uralla – if this is a 'new' England, it most resembles the moors – to **Dangars Lagoon Wildlife Refuge** (27.2km). Even a glimpse of the lagoon from the road will show that it's rich in birdlife, but there's also a bird hide on its southern shore. Soon afterwards a hill crest opens up panoramic views of New England grazing country. There's far less traffic and a delightful sense of solitude grows throughout the rolling country that follows.

At 57.2km, the old settler's slab cottage at **Homeleigh** (which was, rather amazingly, lived in until the 1980s) is a remnant of a settlement known as Irish Town. Past the delightfully named Bergen op Zoom Creek, it's a gentle climb up into Walcha.

Day 2: Walcha to Nowendoc
4½–6 hours, 70.4km

Open farmland sprinkled with grizzled gum trees, light traffic and several flying descents, the longest about 8km, make this day a pleasure from start to finish. About the only blights on the day are the sections of road with more divots than a public golf course.

As you leave Walcha, stop for a moment at the **Oxley cairn** (0.6km). Explorer John Oxley camped about 1.6km southeast of here en route to Port Macquarie in 1818, after leading the first party of Europeans across the Liverpool Plains. Just 1km

THUNDERBOLTS WAY – DAY 1

CUE		GPS COORDINATES	
start	Armidale visitors centre	151°40'16"E	30°30'30"S
0km	go S on Marsh St		
0.5	Barney St/Waterfall Way		
0.9	Dangar St/Waterfall Way		
1.9	Waterfall Way		
4.5	1km moderate climb		
5.5	New England Hwy		
23.1	`to Walcha', Uralla	151°30'02"E	30°38'28"S
23.6	Duke St, `to Walcha'		
{27.2	Dangars Lagoon Wildlife Refuge}		
{57.2	Homeleigh}		
63.7	Fitzroy St, `to Tamworth'		
64.0	Walcha visitors centre	151°35'36"E	30°59'06"S

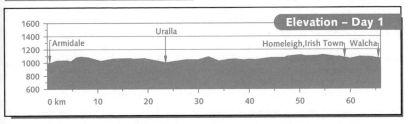

Elevation – Day 1

NEW SOUTH WALES

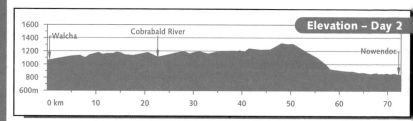

THUNDERBOLTS WAY – DAY 2

CUE		GPS COORDINATES
start	Walcha visitors centre	151°35'36"E 30°59'06"S
0km	go E on Fitzroy St	
0.2	Derby St/Thunderbolts Way, 'to Gloucester'	
{0.6	John Oxley cairn}	
{1.6	Langford Homestead}	
	46km undulating terrain	
69.5	Brackendale Rd, 'to Nowendoc'	
70.3	'to Taree'	
70.4	Nowendoc store	151°43'01"E 31°30'51"S

further on, **Langford Homestead** marks the site of the original Wolka run, established in 1832, the first landholding in the New England. Langford is a striking presence: a two-storey, red-brick Italianate mansion, sporting a central tower and decorative cast iron.

One of the prettiest stretches on the route is Brangas Plains (around 30km to 36km),

its broad undulating paddocks framed by timbered ranges. In good seasons, livestock stand in lush feed so deep it tickles their bellies – it's like riding through velvet.

At around 48km the road rises to the route's high point of about 1300m. After a dip, the first views of the steep Barrington Tops country, further south, come into view. After the long descent, it's an easy roll along the Nowendoc Valley to the fly-speck town of Nowendoc.

Day 3: Nowendoc to Gloucester
5–6½ hours, 75.6km
On a map this day looks all downhill; the map lies. Though there's a clutch of superb descents, this is the toughest physical challenge of the ride. Conversely, it is also the most spectacular, slicing through one of the east coast's most beautiful hinterland areas.

ROBIN HOOD OR A ROBBING HOOD?

In Australia, bushrangers hold a lofty perch, ranking right up there with sporting heroes for national affection. Robin Hood types (who usually didn't give to the poor), they roamed the bush, robbing mail coaches, businesses and anybody with any sniff of money. Frederick Ward, aka Thunderbolt, was one such bushranger in the mid-19th century.

Born near Windsor outside Sydney in 1836, Ward was convicted of horse stealing in 1856 and sentenced to 10 years on Cockatoo Island in Sydney Harbour. Escaping in 1863, he made up for lost time over the next seven years, robbing around 25 mail coaches and more than 30 hotels, general stores, stations and homes.

Ward relied on his ability as a horseman to evade mounted police – firing at them only as a last resort – and his time at large has yielded innumerable stories of his gentlemanly conduct. Once, while waiting to steal a racehorse he fancied, Ward is said to have bailed up a group of German musicians. After taking all their money (£16), he had them play by the roadside and, apparently pleased with the entertainment, returned some money and asked for a forwarding address. Some time later the band received a letter from Ward with £16 tucked inside.

In late May 1870 Ward robbed several individuals near Uralla, the last of whom alerted the police. Constable Walker gave chase, and shot and killed Ward at Kentucky Creek. He was buried, without religious rites, in the Uralla cemetery. Today Uralla is more enamoured of its dead 'hero': a large statue of Thunderbolt on his horse stands at the main intersection, his grave has become a tourist attraction and the highway named in his honour begins from the town.

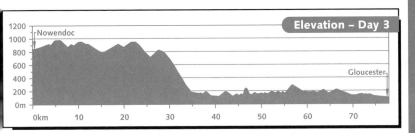

THUNDERBOLTS WAY – DAY 3

CUE		GPS COORDINATES
start	Nowendoc shop	151°43'01"E 31°30'51"S
0km	go W on Wickham St	
0.1	`to Gloucester'	
0.8	Thunderbolts Way	
1.7	1.7km moderate climb	
3.8	2km moderate climb	
7.4	700m steep climb	
8.8	600m steep climb	
15.0	3km moderate climb	
19.3	1.7km moderate climb	
{20.3	Carsons Pioneer Lookout}	
25.1	1.7km steep climb	
27.5	5.5km steep, winding descent	
36.0	30km undulating terrain	
67.6	`to Gloucester'	
69.2	Barrington	151°54'37"E 31°58'28"S
75.4	Church St	
75.5	Denison St	
75.6	Gloucester visitors centre	151°57'48"E 32°00'28"S

The rippling farmland of the first two days is quickly forgotten as the route rolls out through a range of thickly forested hills in a series of steep pinches. At 20.3km, **Carsons Pioneer Lookout** offers one of the best vantage points in northern NSW, staring south over the agricultural Barnard Valley to a line of sharply folded hills; behind are the Barrington Tops, one of NSW's finest wilderness areas.

The climb ends abruptly at 27.5km with a roaring (and, at times, bumpy) descent, plunging 600m in 5.5km. Suddenly you're in the Barnard Valley, looking up at the hills you were just looking down on – easy come, easy go.

Following the descent is about 30km of up-and-down that might break your heart if it didn't cross such lovely country. Several river crossings, of the Barnard, Manning and Bowman Rivers, provide cool, shady spots to rest; in between, the road rolls and winds through beautiful farming country. The **camping and picnic area** on the Manning's banks has grassy sites sheltered by healthy eucalypt trees within crawling distance of a casuarina-lined river.

The final run through Barrington into Gloucester includes some flat sections – absolute bliss!

AUSTRALIAN CAPITAL TERRITORY

The people of the ACT declaim often. It is after all the job of politicians to try to make people listen. However, there seems to be a lot of fact supporting ACT's declaration that it's the best place in Australia for cycling. If it isn't the best, it's certainly one of them. Its only city (civic) and the national capital, Canberra, has a dazzling web of bikepaths, a large part of it away from traffic. Once beyond the urban confines, the pedalling is even better – on quiet secondary roads for pavement pelotons and through extensive forest and reserves for dirt demons.

HISTORY

For over 20,000 years the nomadic Ngunnawal Aboriginal people have called this country home. Throughout the ACT, especially in places like Namadgi National Park, you can see evidence of their presence. In long-ago days, the seasonal food cycles of bush tucker staples like the yam daisies of the plains and the bogong moths of the High Country dictated their movements. Occasional large gatherings of people resulted; 'Canberra' or 'Kanberra' is believed to be an Aboriginal term for 'meeting place'.

European settlement began in the 1820s, and pastoralists had moved onto the grasslands of the Limestone Plains before the decade was out, often employing the Ngunnawal people on expansive sheep stations. There was a small community in the area of modern-day Canberra by the 1840s, and the region was widely settled by the 1870s.

When Australia's separate colonies were federated in 1901, the notion of an ACT and Canberra was floated as a compromise between colonial rivals NSW and Victoria. In 1908 the site was selected, and in 1911 the Commonwealth government created the Federal Capital Territory (changed to the Australian Capital Territory in 1938). A competition to design a city for 25,000 people was launched the same year and won by American architect Walter Burley Griffin.

Although the foundation stones were laid on 12 March 1913, Federal Parliament didn't sit in Canberra until 1927, and the departmental main offices were slowly moved to the city over several decades, followed by other institutions, including the High Court of Australia, and the various galleries and attractions that continue to grow in number.

ENVIRONMENT

The early establishment of European farmers had a profound effect on the land. While pockets of eucalyptus woodland remain around Canberra – particularly near Black Mountain, Mt Ainslie and Mt Majura – the clearing of native plant communities is still being felt. The best examples of surviving native vegetation are found in Namadgi National Park and the Tidbinbilla Nature Reserve, which together cover most of southwestern ACT. Nearer to Canberra are large tracts of introduced pine forest, and in the city itself there's been considerable alteration to the natural order. Both the Molonglo River and Ginninderra Creek have been dammed (to create lakes Burley Griffin and Ginninderra), and widespread plantings of introduced, mostly deciduous, trees in older parts of the city give it an appearance that's both very pretty in autumn and rather European.

CLIMATE

Built on undulating terrain at about 550m to 700m above sea level, Canberra enjoys low humidity, a moderate rainfall (evenly spread throughout the year) and plenty of sunshine (an average of more than seven hours a day). With midsummer mean temperatures of 13°C to 28°C, days across the ACT range from comfortably warm to uncomfortably hot, though the thermometer rarely tops 40°C. Winter days are invariably cool, with little winds and sometimes glorious sunshine. Midwinter temperature means run from 0°C to 11°C, so snowfalls are rare.

PLANNING
When to Cycle

Given the clement climate, riding is possible at any time of year, although certainly best enjoyed during the warmer days of mid-September through May.

MOUNTAIN BIKING IN THE ACT

The cycle buzz about the ACT is for more than just its road routes and bikepaths. It's also got some of Australia's best mountain biking. **Stromlo Forest Park** (☎ 02-6256 6700; www .stromloforestpark.com.au; Uriarra Rd, Stromlo; 6am-9pm daylight savings, 6am-6pm otherwise) is the focus of most of the recent chatter, its trails having only been inaugurated in January 2007. The world-class facility has a purpose-built pavilion, fantastic 1.2km criterium cycling circuit, cross-country running tracks and the kinds of mountain bike trails that bring the experts back again and again and again. How good is it? Well, it hosts the world's largest 24-hour mountain bike race, the annual October **Australian 24-Hour Mountain Bike Championships** (www.corc24hour.com.au). It has also opened its gates to the **Australian Mountain Bike Championships** (www.mtbnationals .com.au; late Jan) run by the MTBA (Mountain Bike Australia). In 2009 it even hosted the Union Cycliste Internationale (UCI) Mountain Bike and Trials World Championships. There's obviously good dirt in those hills! Many of the trails were built and are maintained by volunteers from **Canberra Off-road Cyclists** (CORC; www.corc.asn.au), Canberra's leading MTB organisation.

Bike Hire

Mr Spokes Bike Hire (☎ 02-6257 1188; www.mrspokes.com.au; Barrine Dr, Acton; 9am-5pm daily according to weather) is near the Acton wharf, thus perfectly situated for a pedal around Lake Burley Griffin (hour/day $15/35). Alternatively, **Real Fun** (☎ 1800 637 486; www.realfun .com.au; half/full day/weekend $30/39/65) delivers a range of hire bicycles directly to your door.

Canberra Youth Hostel Australia (YHA; p352) and **Victor Lodge** (p91) also rent out bikes.

Maps

For most of the ACT, the only map you need is TravelSmart's *The Canberra & Queanbeyan Cycling & Walking Map* ($6). It's waterproof, durable, very thorough, and available from the Canberra visitors centre (see this page) and most bike shops. However, for the Canberra Explorer ride, all you need is the free *See Yourself Cycling Around the Lake* and *Lakeside Self-Guided Walking Tour* brochures with maps.

For other maps, check out **Mapworld** (☎ 02-6230 4097; www.mapworld.com .au; Jolimont Centre, 65 Northbourne Ave, Civic) and **NRMA** (☎ 02-6222 7000; Canberra Centre, City Walk, Civic).

Cycling Events

For mountain bike events, see boxed text p84.

Organised as part of the Canberra Festival, the **Australian Ethical Big Canberra Bike Ride** (www.pedalpower.org.au/bcbr; early Mar) is a fun ride around the streets of Canberra on the morning of Canberra Day.

On a Gear Up Girl Challenge (www .gearupgirl.com.au; early Apr) is a women-only charity ride of 20km to 60km.

With 2009 its 23rd year, **Fitz's Challenge** (www.canberracyclingclub.org.au; first Sun in Nov) is Canberra's biggest and best-known one-day cycling event (and challenge, not a race!) with distances of 50km, 105km, 165km or 207km.

Another women-only event, **Tour de Femme** (www.canberracyclingclub.com.au; mid-Nov) is an easy 20km ride for the racers as well as the cruisers.

In a weekend cycling extravaganza, the **Brindabella Challenge** (www.rinda bellachallenge.com.au; early Dec) offers road racing open to anyone with a Cycling Australia licence (day licences are available on-site).

Information Sources

Canberra and Region Visitors Centre (☎ 1300 554 114; www.visitcanberra.com .au; 330 Northbourne Ave, Dickson; 9am-5pm Mon-Fri, 9am-4pm Sat & Sun) is the primary source of information about everything in the ACT and Canberra.

One of the oldest and largest cycling clubs in Australia, the **Canberra Cycling Club** (www.canberracyclingclub.org.au) is a leading force in the ACT, with an emphasis on racing and group training.

The very active **Pedal Power ACT** (☎ 02-6248 7995; www.pedalpower.org. au; 2nd Floor, Room 10, Griffin Centre, 20 Genge St, Civic; noon-2pm Tue-Fri) is the region's leading bicycle advocacy group.

GATEWAY

See Canberra (p91).

CANBERRA EXPLORER

Duration 2–3½ hours

Distance 36.2km

Difficulty easy–moderate

Start/Finish Acton Wharf

Summary Take in the best of Canberra – its glistening central lake, monumental structures to culture and politics, its green parks – almost entirely from the safety of dedicated paths off limits to motorised vehicles.

Canberra is justly proud of its bikepath networks, arguably the best and most extensive of any Australian city. This planned city seemingly had the bike rider in mind when the blueprints were submitted. Dedicated routes make it almost possible to tour the entire city without touching a road. One of the most beautiful paths circles Lake Burley Griffin. This route mainly follows the lake path, taking in the majority of the most important national museums and key buildings of the state. Two key additions are an out-and-back trip to the top of Mt Ainslie (for superb views of Canberra) and another to Parliament House.

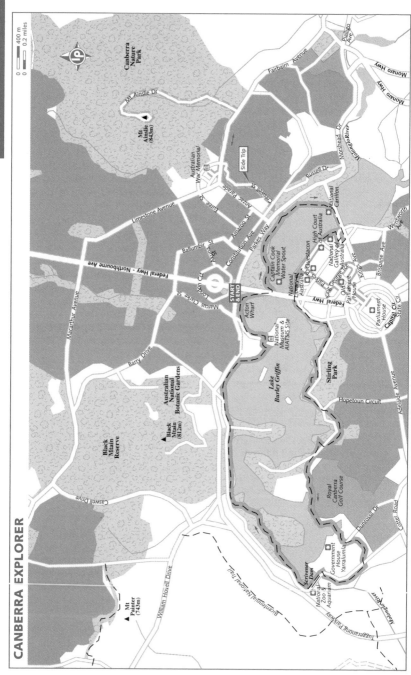

THE RIDE

A quick glide from Civic, the old Acton ferry wharf is a convenient spot to start your ride on the Lake Burley Griffin bikepath, although anywhere you choose is just as good. The ride is predominantly flat around the more urban central basin, but there are some low rollers when you get out to the wilds of the west. The climb to Mt Ainslie, however, is the only genuine ascent of the day.

Inside 1km the route passes the **Captain Cook Memorial Water Jet**, which shoots water more than 100m above the lake (and all over lakeside viewers, if there's a southerly blowing) from 2pm to 4pm daily.

The Mt Ainslie side trip leaves from the northern side of the lake.

Continue eastwards, passing the **National Carillon** (www.natcap.gov.au), with recitals on Wednesday and Sunday from 12.30pm to 1.20pm.

This route crosses the Kings Ave Bridge; although there is an additional 13km extension around the lake's east basin should you wish to extend your ride.

After the bridge and looping back to the lake, you pass the **National Gallery of Australia** (☎ 02-6240 6502; www.nga.gov .au; Parkes Place, Parkes; free admission; 10am-5pm), which has a fine permanent collection and visiting exhibitions (for

CANBERRA EXPLORER

CUE			GPS COORDINATES	
start		Acton wharf	149°07'31"E	35°17'12"S
0km		go E on lakeside bikepath		
2.2	⬑	Wendouree Dr		
2.5	⬐	Constitution Ave		
2.6	⬑	Creswell St		
3.9	⬐◎	Fairbairn Ave		
{	●●⬑	Australian War Memorial 600m ⟲}		
4.9	⬑	Mount Ainslie Dr		
	▲	3km steep climb		
7.9		Mt Ainslie (843m)	149°09'30"E	35°16'12"S
{retrace outward route to bikepath}				
13.6	⬑	rejoin lakeside bikepath		
{14.3	★	National Carillon}		
14.6	↘	Kings Ave bridge		
15.1	⤢	`to City'		
15.4	⬑	rejoin lakeside bikepath		
{15.7	★	National Gallery of Australia}		
{15.9	★	High Court of Australia}		
16.3	⬑	Parkes Place West		
{16.6	★	National Library of Australia}		

CUE CONTINUED			GPS COORDINATES	
{	★	Questacon}		
17.0	⬑	King George Tce		
{17.3	★	Old Parliament House}		
17.5	⤢	Rte 7/Queen Victoria Tce		
18.0	⬑	Federation Mall		
18.4	⬐	Parliament House concourse		
{18.5	★	Parliament House}		
18.6	⬐	Federation Mall		
19.0	⬑	Queen Victoria Tce		
19.2	⬐	Magna Carta Place		
19.3	↑	Parkes Place West		
20.0	⬑	rejoin lakeside bikepath		
21.5	⤢	bikepath beside Alexandrina Dr		
{26.9	★	Government House Yarralumla}		
{29.1	★	National Zoo & Aquarium}		
33.9	↘	bridge beside Parkes Way		
34.5	⤢	towards Acton Peninsula		
35.0	↘	beside Lawson Crescent		
{	★	National Museum & AIATSIS site}		
36.2		Acton wharf	149°07'31"E	35°17'12"S

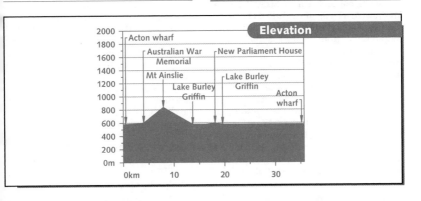

Elevation

which an entry fee is charged); and the **High Court** (☎ 02-6270 6811; www.hcourt.gov .au; Parkes Place, Parkes; 9.45am-4.30pm Mon-Fri), Australia's highest venue for legal appeal. Visitors are welcome to sit in on cases but most are fairly dry.

A 3.7km detour from the lake at 16.3km takes the route past the **National Science and Technology Centre/Questacon** (☎ 1800 020 603; www.questacon.edu.au; Parkes Place, Parkes; adult/concession/child $18/13/11.50; 9am-5pm), a hands-on science museum; the **National Library** (☎ 02-6262 1111; www .nla.gov.au; Parkes Place, Parkes; 9am-9pm Mon-Thu, 9am-5pm Fri & Sat, 1.30-5pm Sun), which also has regular exhibitions, usually of a literary or historical theme; **Old Parliament House** (☎ 02-6270 8222; www .oph.gov.au; King George Tce, Parkes; adult/ concession/child $2/1/1; 9am-5pm daily), the seat of Federal Parliament from 1927 to 1988; and **Parliament House** (☎ 02-6277 5399; www.aph.gov.au; 9am-5pm daily), on Capital Hill, the federal law–makers' permanent home since 1988.

From about 26.9km, the bikepath rolls past the extensive grounds of **Government House Yarralumla**, home of the Governor-General (not open to the public), en route to Scrivener Dam, which holds back the waters of Lake Burley Griffin. On the western side of the dam is the **National Zoo & Aquarium** (☎ 02-6287 8400; www .nationalzoo.com.au; adult/concession/child $26.50/21.50/14.50; 10am-5pm daily).

The complex housing the collection of the **National Museum** (☎ 1800 026 132; www.nma.gov.au; free admission; 9am-5pm daily) and the **Australian Institute of Aboriginal and Torres Strait Islander Studies** (AIATSIS; ☎ 02-6246 1111; www .aiatsis.gov.au) is further east at 34.5km, just a short distance from the finish at the wharf.

Think twice about skipping the side-trip climb to **Mt Ainslie lookout** (7.9km). Although steep over the second half, the ascent is not a punishing one and the views from the top really help you get oriented. If the full hill is out of the question, at least go to the **Australian War Memorial** (☎ 02-6243 4211; www.awm.gov.au), where sobering light is cast on the conflicts in which Australians have fought; the Roll of Honour lists 102,000 Australians who have died at war.

MOUNTAIN BIKE RIDES

Manly Dam

One of Sydney's popular mountain biking track loops around the edges of the Manly Dam Reserve and the Manly Golf Course. The circuit covers around 11km and has some steep and rocky sections, nicely compensated for by the views over Manly and the coast. There are plenty of singletracks, planks and some jumps, making this a true mountain biker's playground. Parts of the track go to mush after heavy rain, so it's worth avoiding at these times.

The Oaks & St Helena Trail

This long downhill run – one of the best mountain bike rides in the country – rolls off the Blue Mountains to near the edge of Sydney's western suburbs. The Oaks trail begins at Woodford train station and branches off onto the St Helena Trail after 5km, descending around 450m to Glenbrook train station. St Helena is the more technical of the two trails, and you should probably steel yourself to push your bike up the stiff final climb from Glenbrook Creek.

Kosciuszko National Park

For a description of mountain biking in the High Country, see boxed text p72.

Thredbo

When the snow melts at one of Australia's major ski fields it is a run of a different type, the Cannonball Run, that comes to the fore. Descending 600m from the top of the Kosciuszko Express chairlift to the ski village of Thredbo, the 4.2km singletrack trail has ladders, rock gardens and an extreme run called Snakes and Ladders that can be dodged by taking the more leisurely Village Trail instead. To gain chairlift access you'll need to complete the Thredbo Downhill Initiation, a 3 hours instruction on using the chairlift, trail access and technical skills for riding down a mountain safely.

Australian Capital Territory

For a description of the ACT's state-of-the-art MTB trails in Stromlo Forest Park, see boxed text p84.

TOWNS & FACILITIES

ALBURY

☎ 02 / pop 42,000

Albury is a major regional centre on the Murray River, just below the big Hume Weir. Outsiders often refer to it as Albury-Wodonga because its Victorian neighbour is just across the river, but a healthy dose of cross-border snobbery will have New South Wales locals putting you straight: 'the former is all that's required'.

Information

The **Gateway visitors centre** (☎ 1300 796 222; www.destinationalburywodonga.com .au; Lincoln Causeway) is part of a large 'island' complex on the Victorian side of the river. Stock up on all the details you will need for the road ahead, including maps and information about the Murray River and Snowy Mountains. If you have extra time in Albury, ask for the *High Country Rail Trail* brochure and consider a spin out to Lake Hume for a swim. For getting around town, the *Albury City Trails* and *Wodonga Pathways* booklets show how cycle-friendly both cities are.

Supplies & Equipment

For a bike check before hitting the road, stop in at the **Full Cycle** (☎ 02-6041 4181; www .fullcycle.com.au; 523 Macauley St; 8.30am-5.30pm Mon-Fri, 8.30am-2pm Sat), a big and relatively central shop that also rents hybrid/mountain bikes for $20/30 per day.

Sleeping & Eating

Albury Motor Village & Tourist Park (☎ 1800 624 520, 6040 2999; www.albury motorvillage.com.au; 372 Wagga Rd; sites from $25, cabins $71-150) A tidy park with a range of campsites, cabins, vans and dorm beds about 4.5km north of the centre.

Albury Motor Village YHA (☎ 02-6040 2999; www.yha.com.au; dm/d from $28/58) On the grounds of the Motor Village.

Sodens Hotel (☎ 02-6021 2400; www .sodens.com.au; cnr David & Wilson Sts; r $45-60) A large old-style pub (established in 1854) with a grand veranda and 50 rooms within easy reach of the beer garden.

Winsor Park Motor Inn (☎ 02-6021 8800; www.winsorpark.com.au; 471 Young St; s $75, d $85-90) A standard but welcoming motel just minutes from the train station. There are more than two dozen other motel-style accommodation scattered around the city centre.

Coffee Mamma (☎ 02-6041 2600; www.coffeemamma.com.au; 5/501 Olive St; breakfast & lunch, closed Sun) Does the best coffee in town and has a handy footpath takeaway service area.

Star Hotel (☎ 02-6021 2745; 502 Guinea St) A local favourite with a huge beer garden out the back and a front bar with pool tables. It's a little off the main drag but worth the walk down Olive St.

Green Zebra (☎ 02-6023 1100; www .greenzebra.com.au; 484 Dean St; breakfast & lunch) For homemade pasta.

Zen X (☎ 02-6023 6455; 467 Dean St; mains from $15; lunch & dinner) Does excellent sushi and teppanyaki.

For food supplies, visit **Centrepoint Shopping Centre** (526 Olive St). There lots of local colour at the **Farmers Market**, held every second Saturday near the visitors centre – just a small taste of what the **Albury-Wodonga Food & Wine Festival** (www .hmfb.org; late Sep/early Oct) must be like.

ARMIDALE

☎ 02 / pop 25,000

Famed for its spectacular autumn foliage and heritage buildings, Armidale also claims to be Australia's highest city, which makes it the perfect point to start a tour as everything is downhill from here.

The **visitors centre** (☎ 1800 627 736, 02-6772 4655; www.armidaletourism.com.au; 82 Marsh St) is at the bus station.

Supplies & Equipment

Jock Bullen's Armidale Bicycle Centre (☎ 02-6772 3718; 244 Beardy St), opposite Woolworths, is extremely well stocked. The New England Bicycle Users Group runs a social ride from the shop at 9am Sunday if you want to warm up your legs before your tour.

Sleeping & Eating

There are motels around the visitors centre and on Barney St. Head out of town on the Glen Innes Rd to find doubles under $60.

Pembroke Tourist & Leisure Park (☎ 02-6772 6470; 39 Waterfall Way; unpowered/powered sites $22/27, dm $26, cabins $62-98) Doubling as the YHA hostel, this leafy park just east of town has a spacious, grassy tent area plus a kitchen, recreation room, tennis courts, mini-golf and TV lounge. The office stocks a small range of groceries.

Cameron Lodge Motor Inn (☎ 02-6772 2351; cnr Dangar & Barney Sts; s/d $65/72) Conveniently located just one block from the main strip, this spot offers good value and faux-fur bedspreads – very Miami Vice.

Quality Inn Regency Hallmark (☎ 02-6772 9800; 208 Dangar St; r $105-130, ste $175) A touch of luxury, this hotel has bland but very comfortable rooms and a confused French restaurant featuring overpriced French cuisine and Asian dishes.

Lindsay House (☎ 02-6771 4554; www .lindsayhouse.com.au; 128 Faulkner St; d incl breakfast from $165) The antique-filled rooms here house lavish four-poster beds, and some overlook the immaculate gardens and Central Park. It's beautifully cosy on a cold winter's day.

Goldfish Bowl (☎ 02-6771 3271; Dangar St; mains $6-9; breakfast & lunch) The baristas here make the best coffee in town.

Red Grapevine Restaurant & Bar (☎ 02-6772 2822; 1st fl, 113 Jessie St; mains $19-26; dinner Tue-Sat) It arrives hot, hearty, rich and filling – chorizo, tomato and cannellini bean is what soup was always meant to be. This restaurant is simply a fantastic Italian dining experience.

Wicklow Hotel (☎ 02-6772 2421; cnr Marsh & Dumaresq Sts; mains $15-30; lunch & dinner) The Wicklow is about as Irish as Vegemite but the turreted dining room, with its wraparound windows, is a fantastic spot when the sun is shining (the 16 beers on tap also help).

Woolworths (cnr Jessie & Beardy Sts) and **Bi-Lo** (104 Dangar St) are in side-by-side shopping centres, while **Coles** (cnr Marsh & Dumaresq Sts) is near the visitors centre.

BATHURST

☎ 02 / pop 37,100

Bathurst may have Australia's only complete Tyrannosaurus rex skeleton, but even though it's Australia's oldest inland settlement, it's no dinosaur of a town.

Boasting European trees, a cool climate, formidable Victorian buildings and leafy, manicured parks, it also happens to be Australia's major motor-sports town. It is more common to see V8s than V-brakes here.

The **visitors centre** (☎ 02-6332 1444; www.bathurst.nsw.gov.au; Kendall Ave) is particularly helpful.

Supplies & Equipment

Winning Edge Cycles (☎ 02-6332 4025; www.wec.net.au; 213 Howick St; 9am-5.30pm Mon-Fri, 9am-1pm Sat), next to the NRMA, has a good range of spares and clothing. The shop's website has details on a selection of other rides around the town – follow the 'Local Rides' link.

Sleeping & Eating

Commercial Hotel (☎ 02-6331 2712; 135 George St; www.geocities.com/com mercialhotelbathurst; dm/s/d $20/29/49) This quaint old pub has a cosy downstairs bar and small but inviting rooms upstairs, opening onto a veranda.

Bathurst Panorama Holiday Park (☎ 02-6331 8286; www.bathurstholidaypark .com.au; Great Western Hwy; unpowered/ powered sites $25/29, cabins from $65) Around 3.5km east of the visitors centre, this well-spaced park is sprinkled with Aussie kitsch, from the wooden outdoor dunny to the top-of-the-range miners' huts. The grassed tent area is a little too close to the highway but the adjoining kitchen has a stove, BBQs, microwave and fridge, with outdoor tables overlooking the pool and waterslide.

Accommodation Warehouse (☎ 02-6332 2801; www.accomwarehouse.com.au; 121a Keppel St; s/d $80/116) This soaring brick building with its arched windows and Juliet balconies has lovely self-contained apartments.

Blackdown Estate (☎ 02-6331 7121; www.blackdownestate.com.au; 90 Eleven Mile Dr; d/ste $150/170) The majestic rooms at this dreamy retreat have claw-foot bathtubs and views across the historic outbuildings and lakes to the low ranges.

Guan Yin Vegetarian (☎ 02-6332 5388; 166a William St; mains $10-14; lunch Mon-Fri, dinner Wed-Fri) This cosy restaurant serves I-can't-believe-it's-not-meat dishes where vegetarian Mongolian beef is the order of the day.

Ellie's Café (☎ 02-6332 1707; 108 William St; mains $11-15; breakfast & lunch Sun-Wed, dinner Thu-Sat) Ellie's has a popular courtyard and serves a great range of hot meals, such as fish with tomato-and-olive tapenade, or delicious crepes.

Crowded House (☎ 02-6334 2300; www .crowdedhousecafe.com.au; 1 Ribbon Gang Lane; mains $16-30; lunch & dinner Tue-Sat) From a restored 1850s church with soaring ceilings, the restaurant spills out onto a medieval-style courtyard off William St and serves fabulously elegant fare.

The **Coles** (47 William St) and **Wool-worths** (William St) supermarkets stare across the street at each other. There's a **Foodworks** (Gilmour St) supermarket on the Day 1 route out of town on the Gold & Wine Country Circuit.

CANBERRA
☎ 02 / pop 339,000

Too many people dismiss Canberra too easily. Sure, it isn't Sydney or Melbourne, but nor was it meant to be. After the colonies of Australia were federated in 1901, the decision to build the national capital on this site diplomatically placed it between the two rival cities. Not coincidentally, the name Canberra is derived from an Aboriginal term for 'meeting place'. Today, although still a city dominated by federal public servants and their various service providers, Canberra isn't without an impressive character all its own.

Information

The **Canberra and Region Visitors Centre** (☎ 1300 554 114; www.visitcanberra.com .au; 330 Northbourne Ave, Dickson; 9am-5pm Mon-Fri, 9am-4pm Sat & Sun) is about 2km north of Civic (the city centre), on the main north-south artery through Dickson. It has a tremendous range of maps and information. For more information on available maps, see p85.

Supplies & Equipment

Centrally situated Lonsdale St, just north of Civic and a few streets east of Northbourne Ave, hosts a small cluster of bike shops. The **Bike Shed** (☎ 02-6257 2171; www .bikeshed.com.au; 28 Lonsdale St, Braddon;

8.30am-6pm Mon-Fri, 9am-4pm Sat, 10am-3pm Sun) is one large, well-stocked and reliably staffed choice for sales, supplies and repair. For bike hire, see p85.

Not too far away, turn to **Kathmandu** (☎ 02-6257 5926; www.kathmandu.co.nz; 20 Allara St, Braddon; 8.30am-6pm Mon-Fri, 9am-4pm Sat, 10am-3pm Sun) for general camping supplies and outdoor equipment.

Sleeping

This is a government town. There are very few bargains and your options are limited when Parliament is sitting. It pays to book ahead or seek assistance through the visitors centre.

Canberra Motor Village (☎ 02-6247 5466; www.canberravillage.com; Kunzea St, O'Connor; sites $16-29, cabins $125-215) Dozes in a peaceful bush setting 6km northwest of the centre.

Canberra City YHA (☎ 02-6248 9155; www.yha.com.au; 7 Akuna St, Civic; dm $26.50-35.50, d $83-93) A large, bright complex with a rooftop BBQ area, bar, indoor swimming pool, spa, pool tables and comfy lounge.

Dickson Backpackers (☎ 1300 734 911; www.dicksonbackpackers.com.au; 4/14 Woolley St, Dickson; dm from $35, r from $88) Canberra's newest backpackers, in the heart of Dickson. It has a distinctly boutique feel.

Victor Lodge (☎ 02-6295 7777; www .victorlodge.com.au; 29 Dawes St, Kingston; s/d $75/92) On the south side of the lake, this large house may be far from flash, but offers clean rooms with shared facilities, a communal kitchen and a free all-you-can-eat breakfast.

Blue & White Lodge (☎ 02-6248 0498; www.blueandwhitelodge.com.au; 524 Northbourne Ave, Downer; s/d $95/100) A family-run B&B that offers cooked breakfasts and comfortable, clean rooms.

Eating

Canberra is full of reasonably priced eateries. If you're staying on the north side, head to Civic, where West Row and Garema Pl are the happiest hunting grounds for tucker. On the south side, Manuka and Kingston are the best places to troll. There's a fantastic Asian strip in Dickson and many other possibilities scattered throughout the suburbs.

Silo Bakery (02-6260 6060; 36 Giles St, Kingston; mains $3-15; 7am-4pm Tue-Sat) Popular to the point of insanity, a legendary bakery and cheese shop with cafe seating and an excellent breakfast menu.

Milk & Honey (02-6247 7722; Garema Pl, Civic; breakfast $5-16, lunch $11-22, dinner $18-29) The newcomer standout on this alley of longstanding cafes.

Pizzazz Café (02-6239 6200; cnr Kennedy & Eyre Sts, Kingston; mains $10-19; breakfast & lunch Tue-Sun) It may sound like a dodgy 1980s hairdresser, but it offers an interesting take on cafe fare with a vaguely Mexican bent.

Ginseng Restaurant (02-6260 8346; 15 Flinders Way, Manuka; lunch mains $11-26; lunch & dinner) Makes up for its shoebox size by spilling onto the street. Its modern Chinese dishes include lots of vegetarian options.

Ottoman (02-6273 6111; cnr Broughton & Blackall Sts, Barton; mains $29-35; lunch Tue-Fri, dinner Tue-Sat) Has a real sense-of-occasion flair. Ottoman is to Turkish what Mod Oz is to meat and two veg.

For all other fare, including food supplies, try the **Canberra Centre** (02-6247 5611; Bunda St, Civic), the city's biggest shopping centre, whose food hall offers a multicultural cornucopia of sushi, kebabs, burgers, laksa, gourmet rolls and smoothies.

GETTING THERE & AWAY
AIR
Canberra International Airport is 7km southeast of the city. A taxi to Civic costs around $30. **Deane's Buslines** (02-6299 3722; www.deanesbuslines.com.au) operates the frequent AirLiner shuttle bus alternative (one way/return $9/15, 20 minutes). Using your own wheels, from the airport go west on Pialligo Ave, Morshead Dr and Parkes Way as the most direct way to Civic.

BUS
The interstate bus terminal is the **Jolimont Centre** (Northbourne Ave, Civic), which has free phone lines to the visitors centre. It's served by **Greyhound** (13 14 99; www .greyhound.com.au), with frequent services to Sydney ($36, 3½ hours) and Melbourne ($70, nine hours); and **Murrays** (13 22

51; www.murrays.com.au), with daily buses to Sydney ($36, 3½ hours), Batemans Bay ($22, 2½ hours), Narooma ($33, 4½ hours) and Wollongong ($33, 3½ hours).

For Greyhound bike transport policies, see p369. For Murrays, bikes must be boxed and cost $18.70 extra.

TRAIN
Kingston train station (02-6295 1198; Wentworth Ave, Kingston) is the railway terminus, where you can book tickets and seats at the **CountryLink travel centre** (13 22 32; www.countrylink.info; 6am-4.45pm Mon-Fri). Trains run direct to/from Sydney ($40, 4½ hours, two daily), but for Melbourne you must catch a CountryLink coach to Yass and transfer to a train there (which takes a couple of hours longer than the direct bus).

Take note of CountryLink's prohibitive bike transport policies in the boxed text on p50.

BICYCLE
By the most direct routes, Canberra is about 280km southwest of central Sydney; 145km west of Batemans Bay, which is close to Thredbo, the finish of the Murray River to Alpine Way ride (p69).

COFFS HARBOUR
 02 / pop 68,400
With a string of fabulous beaches, Coffs Harbour has been working hard to tart up its image and capitalise on its seaside location. Consequently, attractions swing heavily in favour of water-based fun, action sports, unabashed kitsch, encounters with soft, fuzzy wildlife and, most noticeably, bananas.

According to one website, the CSIRO has somehow scientifically declared Coffs Harbour's climate the best in Australia.

The **visitors centre** (1300 369 070, 02-6652 1522; www.coffscoast.com.au; Pacific Hwy) offers comprehensive information.

Supplies & Equipment
For spares or repairs, try **Bob Wallis Cycles** (02-6652 5102; Shop 30 Homebase Shopping Centre, 252 Pacific Hwy) or **Ventoux Cycles** (02-6651 3355; 27 Park Beach Rd). Bob Wallis also hires out bikes (see Bike Hire p75 for more details).

Sleeping & Eating

Park Beach (☎ 1800 200 111; Ocean Pde; unpowered sites $26-28, powered sites $29-36, cabins & villas $61-185) Coffs has the unmistakable scent of holidays, and this mega-park, about the length of a banana from the beach, confirms it with more than 250 sites plus a host of villas, water slides and a tennis court.

Aussitel Backpackers Hostel (☎ 1800 330 335, 02-6651 1871; www.aussitel .com; 312 Harbour Dr; dm/d $22/60) This capacious brick house has a relaxed ambience, homey dorms and a shady courtyard. By night it brews a party atmosphere. Diving is offered (PADI courses from $245), as well as kayaking, skydiving and rafting.

Pacific Property & Management (☎ 1800 658 569, 02-6652 1466; www.coffs holidayrentals.com.au; 101 Park Beach Rd) Has holiday-rental listings.

Coffs Harbour YHA (☎ 02-6652 6462; www.yha.com.au; 51 Collingwood St; dm/d from $24/70; is) Kudos to this hostel, it's a cut above. The staff are like family, dorms and en suite doubles are spacious and modern, and the TV lounge and kitchen are immaculate. You can hire surf boards as well.

Observatory Holiday Apartments (☎ 1300 302 776, 02-6650 0462; www .theobservatory.com.au; 30–36 Camperdown St; apt from $140) Some have window spas with ocean views, some have balconies and some sleep up to six, but all the apartments at this quiet, compact block are bright and airy with sunny decor.

Aanuka Beach Resort (☎ 02-6652 7555; www.aanuka.com.au; 11 Firman Dr; r $170, apt incl breakfast from $215) Planted in luscious foliage, this classy resort has excellent studios and apartments, all with spas and dishy interiors. It sits right on a quiet neck of Diggers Beach and has a restaurant and tennis courts.

The Jetty and Marina boast the best dining options and at night there's no point eating elsewhere; most of the CBD closes down around 6pm.

Fisherman's Co-op (☎ 02-6652 2811; 69 Marina Dr; meals $7-10) The place to head for grilled or battered catch of the day in a cardboard box. You can also buy the goods uncooked.

Crying Tiger (☎ 02-6650 0195; 384 Harbour Dr; mains $10-20; dinner) Swimming in ambience and fragrant smells, the Crying Tiger keeps inquisitive diners happy with red-duck curry, and king prawns in lime leaf and coconut. You can turn the chilli gauge as high or low as you like.

Vibes at the Jetty (☎ 02-6651 1544; 382 Harbour Dr; mains $15-25; Tue-Sun) This trendy restaurant nails Mod Oz, serving salt and pepper squid with raspberry vinaigrette and double-roasted duck with cumin and orange cognac glaze. The back courtyard is bliss on balmy evenings.

Tide & Pilot (☎ 02-6651 6888; Marina Dr; mains cafe $6-12, restaurant $20-30) This cosmopolitan institution sizzles the who's who of the deep with finesse, herb and goat cheese–crusted swordfish on roast garlic for example. The casual 'lower deck' specialises in unfussy fish and chips.

Coles (Palms Shopping Centre, Harbour Dr) is open seven days a week.

DORRIGO
☎ 02 / pop 1000

Dorrigo is in the midst of farms and forest, but there's no doubting which comes first – Dorrigo is a farming town right down to its wellies. From the war memorial at the main intersection to the veranda-wrapped pub, it's an authentic slice of rural Australia that also just happens to be on the edge of World Heritage–listed rainforest.

Preserved beautifully by cool air and affable locals, Dorrigo is perched on the edge of the New England escarpment. It's geared for tourists but that detracts little from its easygoing charm.

The **visitors centre** (☎ 02-6657 2486; 36 Hickory St; 10am-4pm) is run by helpful volunteers.

Sleeping & Eating

Dorrigo Mountain Resort (☎ 02-6657 2564; www.dorrigomountainresort.com .au; 3991 Waterfall Way; sites $15-20, cabin per person $55-70) On the way out of town (towards Bellingen), with good grassy sites and valley views. The cabins offer the chance to stay in the likes of the bakehouse, bank or blacksmith, though the theme extends only to the sign on the roof. Inside, they're all as basic as trappers' huts.

Dorrigo Hotel (☎ 02-6657 2016; fax 6657 2059; cnr Cudgery & Hickory Sts; r hotel/motel $55/65) The charm of this almighty pub's exterior is somewhat withered on the inside, and the hotel rooms with shared bathrooms have a slightly smoky ambience. But no one's arguing with the price. The bistro (mains $16 to $26; open lunch and dinner) spruiks 'traditional country meals', which means standard pub nosh.

Gracemere Grange (☎ 02-6657 2630; www.dorrigo.com/gracemere; 325 Dome Rd; s/tw/d incl breakfast from $35/70/80) Oz hospitality doesn't get any warmer. Cosy bedrooms upstairs have slanted, attic-style roofs, and the en suite double has a skylight for views of the twinkling canopy. The owner is a gem.

Lick the Spoon (☎ 02-6657 1373; 51-53 Hickory St; breakfast & lunch Mon-Fri, breakfast Sat) For a gourmand's start to the day, try this cafe-winery-distillery. The coffee and cakes are the best in town, and it makes its own chutneys, jams and sauces plus wines made from local fruits such as quince, lemon myrtle and Dorrigo pepper. It also produces Australia's only commercial potato vodka.

Tallowood Cafe (☎ 02-6657 2427; 17 Cudgery St; breakfast $7-14, mains $7-12) Fry-up breakfasts, and sandwiches, burgers, nuggets and fish and chips throughout the day and evening, with the occasional surprise such as the sweet potato and lentil burger.

Misty's (☎ 02-6657 2855; www.dorrigo.com/mistys; 33 Hickory St; r incl breakfast $95) Misty's self-contained cottage dates from the 1920s and has a gorgeous antique kitchen and bedroom. Breakfast comes in the form of a generous hamper. The main event, however, is Misty's restaurant (mains $26; open for lunch on Sun and dinner Wed to Sun), where culinary delights such as grilled salmon with saffron and vanilla cream are matched by flawless presentation and service. Even more impressive is the fact that it's a two-person show – one's front of house and the other does all the cooking.

The **Spar** (Hickory St) supermarket is beside Misty's and is open seven days a week, as is the **IGA** (Cudgery St).

GLOUCESTER
☎ 02 / pop 2500

A churchy town at the base of the Barrington Tops, Gloucester is a peaceful place where farmers still do business at the end of the bar in the local pub. The town is just east of the striking rocky hills called The Bucketts (the name is said to come from the Aboriginal word *buccans,* meaning 'big rocks'), which give their name to the main road through the region.

The **visitors centre** (☎ 02-6558 1408; www.gloucester.org.au; 27 Denison St) is just off the main street.

Supplies & Equipment

Base Camp Warehouse (☎ 6558 1444; 36 Church St) has a small selection of bike spares.

Sleeping & Eating

Gloucester Holiday Park (☎ 02-6558 1720; Denison St; unpowered/powered sites $24/27, dm $20, cabins $40-70) Riverside park at the foot of the Bucketts that's both spacious and shady. It's right beside the town pool, which has a 34°C hydrotherapy pool – the perfect finish to a ride.

Gloucester Country Lodge Motel (☎ 02-6558 1812; www.gloucestercountrylodge.com.au; The Bucketts Way; s/d $76/90 Sun-Thu, $80/98 Fri & Sat). The best accommodation, albeit in the paddocks at the far edge of town. You'll need to cycle into town for dinner, but the views of the Bucketts make the inconvenience forgivable.

Bucketts Way Motel (☎ 02-6558 2588; www.bucketts.com; 19 Church St; s $76-80, d $88-92) Past the faux-tropical entrance, this motel is 50m from the main roundabout – just far enough to feel isolated. The cafeteria-like dining room (mains $18 to $32) is open to nonguests and has an imaginative menu featuring the likes of asparagus and sundried tomato omelette, or chicken saltimbocco on mushroom risotto.

Perenti (☎ 02-6558 9219; 69 Church St; breakfast $8-15; breakfast & lunch Mon-Sat) After a breakfast of macadamia nut muesli or sourdough fruit and nut loaf, fill the panniers with local produce from the shelves: wines, fish, cheese and herbs.

Roundabout Inn (☎ 02-6558 1816; cnr Bucketts Way & Church St; pizza $16-24, mains $16-26; lunch & dinner) Good pub meals (and good old-fashioned sticky pub floors), with a menu that favours pizza and seafood. You're unlikely to need the 'buy nine meals, get one free' card.

Stock up on groceries at **Garners IGA** (cnr Bucketts Way & Church St).

HILL END
☎ 02 / pop 80

Pretty Hill End was a gold-rush boomtown in the 1870s, briefly becoming the largest inland town in NSW, with a mile-long strip of shops. Today it's a faded beauty managed by the National Parks and Wildlife Service (NPWS). It has an authentic and irresistible charm, with just about every building oozing history and interpretive plaques every few metres.

The **visitors centre** (☎ 02-6337 8206; hill.end@npws.nsw.gov.au), also run by the NPWS, is on the approach to town in the restored hospital.

Sleeping & Eating

Village and Glendora camping grounds (powered sites per adult/child $7.50/4, unpowered sites $5/3) Run by the NPWS and handy to the town centre (Village is on the banks of Hill End Creek, a few hundred metres from town); bookings should be made at the visitors centre.

Royal Hotel (☎ 02-6337 8261; Beyers Ave; r $35-90) The last remaining pub of the 28 that once served and watered the town. It doubles as Hill End's only real dining option (mains $10-26) with standard SOS (Steak Or Schnitzel) pub meals served in the rear courtyard.

Hosies B&B (☎ 02-6337 8347; Clarke St; d $132) Upstairs in the old Hosies General Store building with poplars for a view and geese for a soundtrack.

Cooke's Cottage (☎ 02-6332 4410; www.printsandimages.com.au; Lees Lane; d incl breakfast provisions $135) Two-bedroom cottage as authentic as grandad's farm – think rusted bull-nose veranda, fruit trees in the yard and the requisite macrocarpa. Take the first road on the right past the Mudgee turn-off.

The **general store** (☎ 02-6337 8237; 9am-5.30pm Mon-Thu, 9am-6.30pm Fri & Sat, 9am-3pm Sun) stocks groceries and drinking water, while its 111 Restaurant

dishes out hot chips, burgers and other typical country cafe fare.

JENOLAN CAVES
☎ 02

Deep in a steep-sided valley, **Jenolan Caves** (☎ 02-6359 3911; www.jenolancaves.org.au; Jenolan Caves Rd; admission with tour from $17; 9.30am-5.30pm) is one of the most extensive and complex limestone cave systems in the world. It has 10 show caves, which can only be entered on a tour. There's a trio of cave passes ($25/33/38), each allowing entry into one cave. If you arrive on a Saturday you've a chance to witness a **classical concert** (☎ 1300 763 311; www.georgcello.com; adult/child $38/20) in the caves. Concerts are held twice monthly at 4pm. There's also an Opera in the Caves event in mid-February.

Sleeping & Eating

There's no camping at the caves, unless you're prepared to plough up the hill again at day's end. Here, there are two options: 10.6km past the caves you can turn off right onto the Six Foot Track (one of Australia's most popular bushwalks) and bump along the trail for 3km to the **Black Range campsite** (with toilets and shelter); or at 12.8km, a **roadside rest area** (with toilets) has become a de facto campsite.

Jenolan Caves House (☎ 02-6359 3322; www.jenolancaves.house.com.au; Jenolan Caves Rd; dm $25, motel d $95-185, guestroom d $65-295) Fabulously eerie, and catering to all wallets and tastes. Dinner, bed and breakfast packages are available.

Jenolan Caves Cottages (☎ 02-6359 3911; www.jenolancaves.org.au; Jenolan Caves Rd; cottages $90-125) Four comfortable, self-contained cottages about 8km north of (and 400m above) the caves, on the ride out towards Katoomba. The cottages sleep six to eight people and there's a $35 supplement for single-night stays.

Eating options begin and end at Jenolan Caves House. If you're early enough (and cheap enough) the **cafeteria** (mains $10-16; 8.30am-5pm) churns out sandwiches, coffee and basic meals such as lasagne and chicken curry. **Chisholm's Restaurant** (bar mains $16-22, restaurant mains $26-30) is the flasher option, with the likes of roasted organic lamb rack and Black Angus striploin.

KANDOS
☎ 02 / pop 1800

Perched beside Coomber Melon Mountain, Kandos is strangely likeable for a place obsessed with cement. Founded in the early 20th century, it's a classic company town, yet it has arguably the finest setting of any town on the Gold and Wine Country Circuit ride. If you hope to fit in, wear an orange shirt like the cement workers. From Kandos, it's about 25km to the western fringe of Wollemi National Park, the hidden home of one of Australia's most remarkable trees (see boxed text p63).

The local information outlet is the **Bridge Motors** (☎ 02-6379 4004; Ilford Rd) service station. The **Rylstone visitors centre** (☎ 02-6379 1132) has more tourist information.

Sleeping & Eating

Rylstone Caravan Park (Carwell St; unpowered/powered sites $17/20), About 7km north along the Day 3 cycling route, this is the nearest camping option. It's basic but the grass is as manicured as the greens on the golf course behind. There's a good laundry if the knicks are in need of some treatment.

Fairways Motel (☎ 02-6379 4406; www.kandosfairwaysmotel.com.au; cnr Ilford Rd & Henbury Ave; s/d $66/88) Overlooking the golf course and opposite the town swimming pool, the Fairways offers DVD players (but not DVDs) and microwaves in its 14 rooms, which are otherwise unremarkable. Consider that encouragement to sit outside and watch the sunset light across the golf course.

Kandos Motel (☎ 02-6379 6507; www.kandosmotel.com.au; 4 Angus Ave; s/d $75/100) Neater, more stylish rooms than the Fairways, though the view is limited to an aviary of crimson rosellas and the back of the Kandos Hotel.

Henbury Recreation Club (Henbury Ave; mains around $16; dinner Fri & Sat) Great reputation – 'the standards with sizzle', described one local – and it's a two-minute stroll if you're staying at Fairways Motel.

Kandos Hotel (☎ 02-6379 6507; 2 Angus Ave; mains $9-18; lunch & dinner) Calls itself the Kandos Steak House, which is obviously a local translation for 'front-bar meals'.

Gourmet Pizza (☎ 02-6379 4300; Angus Ave; pizza $15-20; 5-9pm, Wed-Sun)

Simple name, cosmopolitan idea for a town as workaday as Kandos.

Kandos IGA (Angus Ave) and **5-Star Handimarket** (Angus Ave) are both open every day.

KATOOMBA
☎ 02 / pop 18,000

Outdoorsy and opulent at once, Katoomba is about the point at which the city decides to surrender to nature. It has an undeniably beautiful setting, with astonishing valley views from within town. The best (and most popular) view is from Echo Point, where a series of sensational viewing platforms gaze out over the Jamison Valley, dominated by the trident of rocks that form the impressive Three Sisters.

Information

Taking some time out for a bushwalk is all but mandatory in Katoomba, and the **Echo Point visitors centre** (☎ 02-4782 9865, 1300 653 408; www.australiabluemountains.com.au; Echo Point; 9am-5pm) has information on short and day walks.

The **Blue Mountains Heritage Centre** (02-4787 8877; Govetts Leap Rd, Blackheath; 9.30am-5pm) in nearby Blackheath can help with details on overnight jaunts.

Supplies & Equipment

For bike repairs and parts, try **Velo Nova** (☎ 02-4782 2800; 182 Katoomba St; 9am-5pm Mon & Wed-Sat, 9.30am-4.30pm Sun).

Sleeping

Blue Mountains Accommodation Booking Service (☎ 02-4782 2857; www.bluemountainsbudget.com; 157 Lurline St; 10.30am-5.30pm) This helpful service can book your bed at no charge.

Katoomba Mountain Lodge (☎ 02-4782 3933; www.katoombamountainlodge.com.au; 31 Lurline St; dm/s/d from $18/42/58) Hysterically uncool wallpaper and naff timber panelling are the prices you'll pay for the best-value rooms in town. It's a cheerily run, 90-year-old house right in the middle of town, with astounding views from some of the top-floor rooms.

Katoomba Falls Caravan Park (☎ 02-4782 1835; www.bmcc.nsw.gov.au; Katoomba Falls Rd; unpowered/powered sites $25/32, cabins from $75) This park lacks atmosphere and gets mixed reviews from travellers, but it's Katoomba's only camping option.

Blue Mountains YHA (☎ 02-4782 1416; www.yha.com.au; 207 Katoomba St; dm/d/f from $24/73/116) The austere Art Deco exterior of this much-lauded hostel belies its cavernous, sparkling innards. Dorms and family rooms are spotlessly bright, and common areas have more beanbags than bottoms. Highlights include a pinball machine, pool tables, open fires, a giant chess set, central heating, BBQs and curry nights. Hard to fault.

Clarendon Guesthouse (☎ 02-4782 1322; www.clarendonguesthouse.com.au; 68 Lurline St; s with/without bathroom from $65/45, d from $90/130) The rambling old Clarendon is light on ceremony and heavy on character. Original rooms (with shared bathrooms) are charmingly old school; the newer motel extension is snazzier than its exterior suggests.

Carrington Hotel (☎ 02-4782 1111; www.thecarrington.com.au; 15–47 Katoomba St; d incl breakfast $190-485) Katoomba's social and architectural high-water mark, the Carrington has been accommodating road-weary travellers since 1880. Every inch has been refurbished, but its historical character remains intact. The rooms are truly indulgent; the dining room and ballroom are utterly opulent.

Eating

Most of Katoomba's eateries charge an extra 10% on Sunday.

Paragon Café (☎ 02-4782 2928; 65 Katoomba St; mains $10-20; breakfast & lunch) The heritage-listed 1916 Paragon is Katoomba's undisputed Art Deco masterpiece. Sampling coffee and chocolates in the salubrious surrounds is a compulsory Blue Mountains experience.

Niagara (☎ 02-4782 4001; 92 Bathurst Rd; mains $13-26; lunch & dinner) High ceilings with ornate cornices, oversized tiles underfoot and large wooden booths embellish this vegetarian-friendly diner. The food is fab too: gourmet burgers, pastas and salads with a twist during the day, scrumptious steaks and fish at night.

IsoBar Café (☎ 02-4782 4063; 40 Katoomba St; mains $17-23) This cafe hums with chilled vibes, ambient tunes and moody lighting – about as funky as Katoomba gets. Tasty staples include Turkish toasties, burgers, stir-fries and salads.

Solitary (☎ 02-4782 1164; 90 Cliff Dr; mains $26-33; lunch Sat & Sun, dinner Wed-Sun) To-die-for views, sublime food and inescapable romance are Solitary's stock in trade. Mains such as venison and juniper sausages, and scallop and Moreton Bay bug ravioli are inventive; desserts are downright sexy. Reservations essential.

Coles (Waratah St) is at the southern end of Katoomba St (the main street).

KHANCOBAN
☎ 02 / pop 300

Originally constructed by the Snowy Mountains Hydro-Electric Scheme to house 7000 construction workers, Khancoban is now a sleepy lakeside hollow with good facilities (like a public pool) and a pleasant vibe.

Information

The **shopping centre** (Mitchell Ave) houses the post office, which also serves as a basic **visitors centre** (☎ 02-6076 9440). The **NPWS office and information centre** (☎ 02-6076 9373; Scott St; 8.30am-noon & 1-4pm) has better maps and materials covering Kosciuszko National Park. It's also where you can buy park entry permits.

There are no banks in Khancoban, and the ATM in the Country Club is only available to customers. Eftpos capability, however, is fairly widespread.

Sleeping & Eating

Lakeside Caravan Resort (☎ 02-6076 9488; www.klcr.com.au; Alpine Way; unpowered/powered sites $19/27.50, vans $53, cabins $64-120) A well-equipped place with an unbeatable outlook over the Khancoban Dam.

Rose Garden Holiday Units (☎ 02-6076 9530; www.khancobanroseholidayunits.com.au; Mitchell Ave; s/d $70/80) A cluster of self-contained cabins directly across a quiet side street from Khancoban's rose garden.

Queens Cottage B&B (☎ 02-6076 9033; www.queenscottage.com.au; Pendergast Rd; s $105-115, d $115-130) Modern and tasteful hillside cabins with awesome views across the beautiful valley.

Pickled Parrot Restaurant (☎ 02-6076 9471; Alpine Inn, Alpine Way; lunch & dinner) Serves bistro food in a retro decor.

Khancoban Country Club (☎ 02-6076 9468; Mitchell St; mains $17-23; dinner Thu-Sat) has a good specials board in addition to classic Australian tucker.

If you are in search of food supplies, try the **general store** (☎ 02-6076 9559; Mitchell Ave). It also has good-value takeaway food, including a monstrous chicken schnitzel.

MUDGEE
☎ **02 / pop 8500**
Mudgee, an Aboriginal word for 'nest in the hills', is the centre for the new regional gourmet food and wine industries. It's a popular weekend getaway, combining attractive natural surroundings with gastronomic exploration.

Information
The **visitors centre** (☎ 1800 816 304, 02-6372 1020; www.visitmudgeeregion.com .au; 84 Market St), near the post office, can clue you up on wine-tasting opportunities; they're well located for a day of cycling, with most sprinkled around the town's northern edge.

Supplies & Equipment
Even in a town of this size, there's a bike shop. **Mudgee Cycles** (☎ 02-6372 4000; 92 Church St) should be able to get you out of most fixes.

Sleeping & Eating
Mudgee Riverside Caravan & Tourist Park (☎ 02-6372 2531; www.mudgeeriverside .com.au; 22 Short St; unpowered/powered sites $20/25, cabins & villas $70-85) Central and leafy, this pleasant park has an aviary and self-contained cabins.

Mudgee Vineyard Motor Inn (☎ 02-6372 1022; 252 Henry Lawson Dr; s/d/f $75/85/120) A short distance from town, this is an attractive place in the heart of the vineyards, with pretty rooms and great views.

Bleak House (☎ 02-6372 4888; www.geo cities.com/bleakhousemudgee; 7 Lawson St; d incl breakfast $165) Built in 1860, this place is anything but bleak, with gracious verandas, soaring ceilings and pretty

gardens. The rooms are tasteful and the breakfasts scrumptious.

Butcher Shop Café (☎ 02-6372 7373; 49 Church St; mains $7-15; breakfast & lunch daily, dinner Fri & Sat) A hip eatery in an old butchery, with stained glass, interesting artwork and the best scrambled eggs and smoked salmon for miles. Dinner is well-presented Mod Oz.

Blue Wren Wines Café & Restaurant (☎ 02-6372 6205; Cassilis Rd; mains $24-29; lunch daily, dinner Wed-Sat) An exceptional restaurant in an interesting space, this winery is the place to indulge in dishes such as Moroccan spiced lamb tagine.

Roth's Wine Bar (☎ 02-6372 1222; 30 Market St; noon-6.30pm Mon-Fri, 10am-noon Sat) Roth's is the oldest wine bar in NSW, and the atmosphere is still there.

Coles (Mortimer St) and **Woolworths** (Mortimer St) sit like bookends to central Church St.

NOWENDOC
Nowendoc's name is just about as long as the town itself, which pretty much consists of a shop, a hall, a tennis court, a cop shop and, thankfully, a motel. Sunsets over the escarpment to the west are magical.

Sleeping & Eating
You can camp (free) in the grounds of the Nowendoc Memorial Hall. It has toilets and tables, but no showers.

Nowendoc Country Motel (☎ 02-6777 0952; Wingham Rd; s/d $45/70) Expect a fine country welcome; this place may have the quietest setting of any motel in the country. Rooms are old-fashioned and basic (much like Nowendoc itself). The owner also allows cyclists to pitch tents in the grounds, charging around $5 for a shower.

You will need to self-cater, or grab a burger at the **Nowendoc Store** (7.30am-8.30pm), which also sells basic foodstuffs and grog. If you want anything more than tinned food, bring it from Walcha.

SYDNEY
☎ **02 / pop 3.27 million**
Australia's oldest and largest settlement is a vibrant and progressive city built around one of the world's most spectacular

harbours, Port Jackson. Outwardly Sydney is a welcoming place, with strong gay and lesbian and many ethnic communities lending the city a diverse and tolerant air. This isn't an illusion; it is an easygoing place. The worst visiting cyclists will have to contend with is the ratbag drivers – and they're definitely not an illusion.

Sydney sprawls, but is nevertheless quite manageable, especially for those on two wheels. If you think of the downtown area's Hyde Park as your own Ground Zero, you're rarely more than 15 minutes from the best on offer: the edgy vibe of Newtown, the suddenly-in-Asia feel of Chinatown, the finally-seeing-it-with-your-own-eyes marvels of the Opera House and Harbour Bridge, the rough edges of Kings Cross, the hip lifestyles in Darlinghurst and the top noshes in Surry Hills. Further afield are Sydney's famous beaches and superb national parks. It's all there, if you know where to look.

Information

Start at one of the **Sydney visitors centres** (☎ 02-9240 8788; www.sydneyvisitorcentre .com; 9.30am-5.30pm) either at the Rocks (cnr Argyle & Playfair Sts); or at Darling Harbour (Palm Grove), behind Imax. There is also the **Sydney Harbour National Parks Information Centre** (☎ 02-9247 5033; Cadman's Cottage, 110 George St, The Rocks; 9.30am-4.30pm Mon-Fri, 10am-4.30pm Sat & Sun), which has maps of park walks and information on tours of the harbour islands.

If you are travelling in high season, you may also wish to stop by the **YHA Membership & Travel Centre** (☎ 02-9261 1111; www.yha.com.au; 422 Kent St; 9am-5pm Mon-Wed & Fri, to 6pm Thu, 10am-2pm Sat) for information and advance bookings.

At the airport pick up a free copy of *Sydney, the Official Guide,* which combines maps and places of interest with what's-on listings and coupons for reduced entry to most major attractions in Sydney and environs.

For a comprehensive list of activities, get a copy of Lonely Planet's *Sydney,* which works well with Lonely Planet's *Sydney City Map.* Weekly entertainment listings are in *Time Out Sydney* and the Metro lift-out of

Friday's *Sydney Morning Herald,* as well as free music and entertainment newspapers such as *Drum Media, Revolver, 3D World* and *Sydney City Hub.* The *Sydney Star Observer* covers the gay and lesbian scene.

Supplies & Equipment

In the city centre, **Clarence St. Cyclery** (☎ 02-9299 4962; www.cyclery.com .au; 104 Clarence St, Sydney) has an enormous range of services and products, knowledgeable and friendly staff and a very devoted customer base. Further south, turn to **Inner City Cycles** (☎ 02-9660 6605; www.innercitycycles.com .au; 151 Glebe Point Rd, Glebe), and to the east, aim for **Woolys Wheels** (☎ 02-9331 2671; www.woolyswheels.com; 82 Oxford St, Paddington). **Cheeky Monkey Transport** (☎ 02-9557 5424; www.cheeky transport.com.au; 3a Georgina St, Newtown) is Sydney's commuting and touring specialist shop.

Choose general-purpose outdoor and camping equipment by comparing prices in the row of about a dozen travel and outdoor gear shops on Kent St. For places to buy maps and books, see p49.

Sleeping

Sheralee Tourist Caravan Park (☎ 02-9567 7161; www.sydneycaravanpark.com .au; 88 Bryant St, Rockdale; unpowered/powered sites $30/35) With no campsites close to central Sydney, the Sheralee, just west of General Holmes Dr before the airport, is probably your best camping bet. It is about 13km to the southwest of the city centre.

Sydney Lakeside Holiday Park (☎ 02-9913 7845; www.sydneylakeside.com .au; Lake Park Rd, North Narrabeen; unpowered/powered sites from $35/45) Occupying prime real estate around the northern beaches, this camping alternative is 26km north of Sydney.

Sydney Central YHA (☎ 02-9218 9000; www.yha.com.au; 11 Rawson Pl; dm/d $30/90) Near Central Station, this is the largest and most modern of Sydney's backpackers. This 1913 heritage-listed 556-bed monolith has been massively renovated and now has its own supermarket, cinema, rooftop pool and more. Bikes are stored indoors but bring a lock.

Glebe Point YHA (☎ 02-9692 8418; www.yha.com.au; 262-264 Glebe Point Rd, Glebe; dm $25-40, r $70-120) Ideal for those seeking a quiet and leafy inner-city suburb to park their bikes. As well as its proximity to a mouth-watering range of cafes and restaurants, the other main lure is the rooftop on BBQ nights. Warn ahead about your bike.

Billabong Gardens (☎ 02-9550 3236; www.billabonggardens.com.au; 5-11 Egan St, Newtown; dm from $25, r $50-100) Further out (but still handy to the city), Billabong Gardens offers a richer experience than most similar accommodation. Bike parking is secure but limited.

Bondi Beachouse YHA (☎ 02-9365 2088; www.bondibeachouse.com.au; 63 Fletcher St; dm/r from $25/55) This is where you'll want to be if the sound of surf is essential. The Art Deco, 94-bed Bondi Beachouse has a pool table, TV rooms, a BBQ, free play stuff and Tamarama Beach views from the rooftop spa.

Australian Sunrise Lodge (☎ 02-9550 4999; www.australiansunriselodge.com; 485 King St, Newtown; s $79-99, d $99-119) A neat establishment in Newtown, with no objection to bicycles in rooms.

Haven Inn (☎ 02-9660 6655; www .haveninnsydney.com.au; 196 Glebe Point Rd, Glebe; r from $109) A lovely Glebe-based lodging with a large pool, attached Oasis Restaurant and secure bike parking.

Lord Nelson Brewery Hotel (☎ 02-9251 4044; www.lordnelson.com.au; 19 Kent St, The Rocks; d $130-180) Built in 1841, the Lord Nelson is a sandstone pub with its own brewery and just far enough from the Rocks' tourist mobs. Bikes are welcome in the rooms, but it's a tough climb up several flights of steps to get there.

Eating

If you plan to do some serious eating, pick up Lonely Planet's *Sydney;* the Good Living lift-out in Tuesday's *Sydney Morning Herald* reviews the latest and grooviest places.

CITY CENTRE, THE ROCKS & CIRCULAR QUAY

The mix of dining options in Sydney's urban core ranges from frenetic lunchtime cafes to some fine establishments. In the centre, weekday lunchtime pleasures

abound in mall and arcade food courts along George St.

La Renaissance (☎ 02-9241 4878; 47 Argyle St; meals $6-14; breakfast & lunch) An authentic French bakery hidden in a maze of inner courtyards at the heart of the Rocks.

Spice I Am (☎ 02-9280 0928; 90 Wentworth Ave; mains $8-26; lunch & dinner Tue-Sun) Welcomes legions of Thai cuisine aficionados in search of an authentic taste of Southeast Asia.

One Alfred Street (☎ 02-9241 4636; 1 Alfred St; mains $16-20) A better restaurant than its fast-food neon sign might lead you to believe. Australian cuisine gets star treatment morning, noon and night.

CHINATOWN & DARLING HARBOUR

Chinatown is flush with spicy nooks dishing up cheap and scrumptious fare, especially around Dixon St. Darling Harbour's developments place an emphasis on seeing and being seen.

Marigold Restaurant (☎ 02-9281 3388; Level 5, 683 George St, Haymarket; four to five serves of yum cha $15-25; 10am-3pm & 5.30pm-midnight) A vast yum cha palace so popular it has an extra floor (4th) just for Sunday.

Zaaffran (☎ 02-9211 8900; Level 2, 345 Harbourside, Darling Harbour; mains $17-38; lunch & dinner) One of those rare waterside restaurants where the food will divert you from the view. Vegetarians will beam at the creative takes on Indian cuisine.

KINGS CROSS, POTTS POINT & DARLINGHURST

The Cross has a good mixture of tiny cafes, swanky eateries and greasy fast-food joints.

Harry's Café de Wheels (☎ 02-9357 3074; Cowper Wharf Roadway, Woolloomooloo; mains $5-10) With pea and pie floaters at the top of the menu, for decades this has been the chosen retreat of cab drivers, sailors and boozed-up nocturnals.

Bar Coluzzi (☎ 02-9380 5420; 322 Victoria St, Darlinghurst; meals $5-10; 5am-7pm) Where cyclists go for their coffee injection after the weekend morning rides.

Dov@Delectica (☎ 02-9368 0600; 130 Victoria St, Potts Point; mains $17-24; 7.30am-3pm Sun-Tue, 7.30am-10pm Wed-

Sat) Opens onto the nicest part of leafy Victoria St. Its foods vary throughout the day on an ever-changing blackboard menu.

SURRY HILLS & PADDINGTON
Sydney's trendiest neighbourhoods reward culinary explorations. Restaurants and cafes line Crown St north of Cleveland to Oxford St with many more on parallel Bourke St.

Bourke Street Bakery (☎ 02-9669 1011; 633 Bourke St, Surry Hills; mains $3-7; 7am-4pm Mon-Fri, 8am-4pm Sat) Has impeccable baked goods, particularly the sourdough bread.

Arthur's Pizza (☎ 02-9332 2220; 260 Oxford St, Paddington; mains $10-25; lunch Sat & Sun, dinner daily) Continues to draw the masses for the crispy cheesy goodness.

Tabou (☎ 02-9319 5682; 527 Crown St; mains $14-25; lunch Mon-Fri, dinner daily) Settles you into *belle époque* France. The steak *frites* always rewards.

GLEBE & NEWTOWN
The inner west is one of Sydney's most condensed melting pots, and global ethnic treats beckon from the main strips.

Taste (☎ 02-9519 7944; 235 King St; meals $5-8; lunch & dinner) Has Middle Eastern food so fresh it almost crackles.

Café Otto (☎ 02-9552 1519; 79 Glebe Point Rd, Glebe; mains $15-20; lunch & dinner) Lets you dine under trees or inside the airy, woodsy main room. Plough through the long menu of burgers, pizza, pasta and salads.

Getting There & Away
AIR
Only 10km south of the city centre. **Sydney's Kingsford Smith Airport** (SYD; ☎ 02-9667 9111; www.sydneyairport.com .au) is Australia's busiest airport.

One of the easiest ways to/from it is with a shuttle company such as **Kingsford Smith Transport** (☎ 02-9666 9988; www .kst.com.au), which services central Sydney hotels between 5am and 11pm (one way/ return $13/22). Book ahead.

Airport Link (☎ 13 15 00; www .airportlink.com.au) has services from Central Station to the domestic terminal (one way/return $14.60/22.20) and international terminal (one way/return $14.80/22.60) between 5am and midnight.

You pay through the nose to use the airport stations on a normal commuter line. Bikes travel free outside peak period (see boxed text p50). Taxi fares between the airport and Circular Quay are approximately $30 to $40.

The pedal from the airport is an uncomfortable one for anyone lacking experience in heavy traffic. Go via O'Riordan, Bourke, Elizabeth, Redfern and Chalmers Sts.

BUS
All private interstate and regional bus travellers pass through the **Sydney Coach Terminal** (☎ 02-9281 9366; Central Station, Eddy Ave, Redfern; 6am-10.30pm). There are lots of discounted fares – if you hold a VIP or YHA discount card – and rules about bikes vary from company to company, so shop around (see p368).

CountryLink (☎ 13 22 32; www .countrylink.info), the state railway network, is also complemented by coaches, although they don't officially take bikes.

TRAIN
Sydney's main railway terminus is the huge **Central Station** (Eddy Ave, Redfern) It has staffed ticket booths open from 6am to 10pm, and 24-hour ticket machines. **CountryLink** (☎ 13 22 32; www.country link.info) discounts often nudge 40% on economy fares – sometimes cheaper than buses. Unfortunately it's also very bicycle-unfriendly (see boxed text p50).

CityRail (☎ 13 15 00; www.cityrail.info), the Sydney metropolitan service, is more bike-friendly (see boxed text p50), and the network is big enough to get you into some great cycling country – Newcastle in the north, Katoomba in the west, through Wollongong to Bomaderry in the south, or Goulburn in the southwest. For train information, visit the **CityRail Information Booth** (www.131500.com.au; Circular Quay, Sydney; 9.05am-4.50pm).

THREDBO
☎ 02 / pop 300
Finishing your ride here is doing it in style. Thredbo claims to be the country's premier alpine resort, and its unusual-for-Australia high-elevation location is just breathtaking. Built on a human scale and with facilities

NEW SOUTH WALES

that blend well with the surrounding snow gums and alpine flora, it's worth a day or two of exploration, especially given an enticing range of activities and ease of access to the Kosciuszko High Country, capped by the highest point in Australia, Mt Kosciuszko itself.

Information

The **visitors centre** (☎ 1300 020 589; www .thredbo.com.au; Friday Dr) is across from the bridge leading to Valley Terminal. It has limited resources, but can help with organising transport and accommodation.

For activities, drop by **Thredbo Sports** (☎ 02-6459 4119), at the bottom of the Kosciuszko Express chairlift, which, among other things, has a free map of area rides and walks.

There are ATMs dotted about Thredbo and most businesses have Eftpos and accept credit cards. The post office is in the **Thredbo Supermarket**, which is under Mowamba Apartments.

Supplies & Equipment

Southeast MTB Co (☎ 02-6457 6282; www.mountainbikingco.com.au; Thredbo Service Station, 51 Friday Dr) is the right stuff for parts and repairs in Thredbo. It is also the prime point of contact for tackling the famed **Cannonball Run**, an adrenaline-pumping 6.2km downhill plummet. Southeast MTB Co will provide all you need (bike, body armour, lift ticket) and the required orientation. Regular mountain bike hire is also available.

Sleeping & Eating

Summer accommodation rates (listed here) rise during Christmas and Easter, but are nothing compared to midwinter prices. There's no camping in Thredbo; **Ngarigo campsite** is about 10km down the Alpine Way and **Thredbo Diggings** a few kilometres further. Both are managed by the NPWS and free if you have paid your park-use fee.

Thredbo YHA Lodge (☎ 02-6457 6376; www.yha.com.au; 8 Jack Adams Path; dm/d/r incl bathroom $30/69/80) A well-appointed ski lodge, with great common areas, a good kitchen and a balcony.

Aneeki Lodge (☎ 0417-479 581; www .aneeki.com.au; 9 Bobuck Lane; d incl

breakfast $95-130) One of the cheapest lodges on the mountain.

Candlelight Lodge (☎ 1800 020 900; www.candlelightlodge.com.au; 32 Diggings Tce; s/d from $95/125) Has large and well-appointed rooms, all with balconies for taking in the Thredbo views.

Thredbo Alpine Hotel (☎ 1800 026 333, bistro ☎ 02-6459 4200; Friday Dr; r incl breakfast from $165) The only hotel on the mountain, Thredbo Alpine has flash rooms, a summer pool and a full buffet breakfast. Its bistro has good dinner standards.

Bernti's (☎ 02-6457 6332; www.berntis .com.au; 4 Mowomba Pl; dishes $10-14; dinner) A lively place with an evening tapas bar menu. Prices are in keeping with the medium-sized servings.

Al Fresco Pizzeria (☎ 02-6457 6327; Alpine Hotel Complex; pizzas $14-22) Lives up to its reputation as a Thredbo tradition for pizza and pasta.

Altitude 1380 (☎ 02-6457 6190; www.altitude1380.com; Shop 5, Upper Concourse, Alpine Hotel; breakfast & lunch daily, dinner Wed-Sat) A BYO with great food at prices that don't bite. Cash only.

T-Bar Restaurant (☎ 02-6457 6355; 1 Mowamba Pl; mains $20; dinner) A long-time locals' dinner favourite.

Credo (☎ 02-6457 6844; www.credo .com.au; 2 Diggings Tce; mains $28-32; dinner) Brings the Mediterranean to the mountains, just a five-minute walk from the village centre.

WALCHA
☎ 02 / pop 1800

Behind its Art Deco façade, Walcha is a surprisingly chic and artsy country town; hunt around and you will find 27 open-air sculptures, including one at each of the town's entrances. There's not a lot here but it's all done well.

The **visitors centre** (☎ 02-6774 2460; www.walchansw.com.au; 51W Fitzroy St) is on the corner of South St.

Sleeping & Eating

Walcha Caravan Park (☎ 02-6777 2501; 113 Middle St; unpowered/powered sites $18/25, cabins $39-89) If you're a neat freak, this park lays claim to have the cleanest amenities in the country. The office is like a general store: newspapers, magazines, groceries, smokes. It's an easy wander into town along the levee of the Apsley River.

Apsley Arms Hotel (☎ 02-6777 2502; 33N Derby St; www.walchapubs.com.au; s without bathroom $55, d with/without bathroom $85/65) More like the wing of a country house, with above average, stylishly rustic pub rooms. Those without bathrooms are a tad spartan – nothing but beds. Set back from the main pub area, the noise of bar banter is kept to a minimum. The bistro speciality is pizza (pizzas $9 to $16).

Walcha Motel (☎ 02-6777 2599, 31W Fitzroy St; www.walchamotel.com.au; d/tw $87/89, deluxe d $97) has neat, quiet rooms. The deluxe rooms are newer and large enough to subdivide. If you don't want to step out for dinner, there's room service (mains $12 to $24; Sun-Thu).

Anglea House B&B (☎ 02-6777 2187; cnr Thunderbolts Way & Hill St; r $100) A detached cottage with full kitchen, washing machine and a lounge room stocked with DVDs and books. Look for the yolk-yellow house as you ride into town.

Cafe Graze (☎ 02-6777 2409; 21N Derby St; breakfast $5-14; 8.30am-4.30pm Mon-Fri, 8.30am-1pm Sat) Part cafe, part jewellery and homeware shop. The cafe design is as much a feature as the food, with the dining area wrapped around the open stainless-steel kitchen.

Walcha Royal Cafe (☎ 02-6777 1117; 26E Fitzroy St; meals $6-15; breakfast & lunch) Inside a former hotel but styled like an American diner. Sandwiches, burgers and salads are the foundation of the menu, while the fad for all-day breakfast has reached even this far.

Foodworks and **IGA** eyeball each other across Fitzroy St.

WALWA
☎ 02 / pop 270

As the first settlement of any real size on the road east of Albury, Walwa is also a

lovely place to pause. Its name means 'a meeting of waters'. Once a substantial town with a butter factory and tin-mining industry, it has always relied heavily on the nearby Murray River (back when it was more than its presently reduced trickle). Today, with little more than the wide main road remaining (along which all its services are set), it's got a wild-frontier feel to it, as if a posse will gallop into town at any moment.

There is no visitors centre or bank, but the Walwa Hotel does have Eftpos capability.

In a mechanical pinch, ask at the Walwa General Store for Andrew, who once ran a bike shop and definitely knows his way around two wheels.

Sleeping & Eating

Walwa Riverside Caravan Park (☎ 02-6037 1388; 110 River Rd; unpowered/powered sites $20/25, s unpowered/powered cabins $40/55, d unpowered/powered cabins $65/80) Pleasantly placed right on the banks of the Murray River, this camping retreat maintains a casual air.

Walwa Hotel (☎ 02-6037 1310; Murray River Rd; r per person incl breakfast $30) It has the rough edges one would expect in a remote outpost, but its clean, rudimentary rooms are a welcome retreat, as is the comfy beer garden in which the pub food (mains $16 to $24, dinner Monday to Saturday) can be enjoyed.

Upper Murray Resort (☎ 1800 800 780, 02-6037 1226; www.uppermurrayresort .com.au; Murray River Rd; d $92-100, cottage $195) The resort's upscale motel units and self-contained cabins find ample privacy on 180 acres that include pools, a spa and a very good restaurant (dinner mains $22 to $29). It is 3.5km before town.

The **Walwa General Store** (☎ 02-6037 1291; 48 Main St; 8am-6pm Mon-Sat, 9am-4pm Sun) stocks the essentials for self-caterers, but also has a cafe (eat in or take away).

Victoria

HIGHLIGHTS

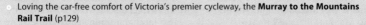

- Loving the car-free comfort of Victoria's premier cycleway, the **Murray to the Mountains Rail Trail** (p129)
- Rolling into a historic gold-rush town like **Maldon** (p152) and trying to imagine it in its heyday
- Setting your cadence to the wave-against-rock rhythm in **Port Campbell National Park** (p122) on the Great Ocean Road
- Breathing that deep sigh of relief when you crest the climb to **Mt Hotham** (p136)
- Waking at sunrise to watch Mt Sturgeon changing colour as daylight arrives in **Dunkeld** (p120)

TERRAIN

It's all there: fertile flood plains, river valleys, rolling hills, tablelands and mountains worthy of their European namesake Alps.

| Telephone Code – 03 | www.bv.com.au | www.visitvictoria.com |

Some people look at Victoria through the spinning wheel of a bicycle. What they see is paradise: a slim state, easily traversed by regional transport, but with as much variety, wilderness, remoteness, pluck and urban oomph as its more portly neighbours. From what many claim is the most spectacular coastline in the world to a High Country that rivals its European-namesake Alps, the Great Ocean and Great Alpine Rds bracket a land of many marvels that draw in visitors by the millions.

Cyclists have been turning to Victoria in larger and larger numbers. Whether to tour great roads, slip between the historic towns of the central goldfields, sample the wares of gourmet producers, singletrack the trails of extensive state and national parks, or just meander along any of the numerous rail trails, cyclists in Victoria are satisfied. So too are the communities that cater to them, some at last seeing the commercial viability of a cycle-friendly salute.

No, the boasts are not off base; Victoria really does have something to suit all cycling speeds. And unlike elsewhere in Australia, where the more ground you cover the more you realise how far you still have to go, in Victoria the banks of nearly every billabong have some new historical titbit to take in. That's why Victorians themselves never tire of their own state. They know they'll never exhaust the supply of things they haven't seen, usually just a couple of hours from home.

HISTORY

Estimates of the number of Aborigines in Victoria at the time of European colonisation vary between 15,000 and 100,000. What is known is that in 1803 a small party of convicts, soldiers and settlers arrived at Sorrento (on Port Phillip Bay) but abandoned the settlement within a year. It wasn't until 1824 that explorers Hume and Hovell made the first overland journey south from Sydney to Port Phillip Bay.

The first permanent European settlement in Victoria was established in 1834 at Portland (in the Western District) by the Henty family from Van Diemen's Land (Tasmania), some 46 years after Sydney was colonised. In 1851 Victoria won separation from New South Wales (NSW), and in that same year the rich Victorian goldfields were discovered, attracting immigrants from around the world. Towns like Beechworth and Ballarat boomed during the gold rush, and are veritable museum pieces today. Melbourne was founded in 1835 by another enterprising Tasmanian, John Batman, and to this day it retains much Victorian-era charm and gold-boom 1880s architecture.

Melbourne, on Port Phillip Bay, was a natural attraction for free settlers, and by the 1860s, squatters had settled much of the state's extensive lightly wooded areas, which were pronounced ideal for grazing. By this time, the colonisers' violence, land clearing and introduced diseases had reduced the Indigenous Koorie population to less than 2000.

The gold rush saw hundreds of thousands of miners flock to the goldfields. By the 1870s much of the surface gold had run out, although reef mining continued until the 1890s. By then a rich centre, Melbourne became Australia's premier bicycling city (see boxed text p154).

In the 1890s the property market collapsed and left Melbourne in a depression, from which it did not recover until the 1920s, with the establishment of coal, dairy and manufacturing industries. The latter suffered greatly during the Great Depression, when more than one-third of Victoria's workforce became unemployed.

The latter half of the 20th century saw a huge influx of immigrants. As a result, Melbourne today is widely regarded as Australia's most multicultural city. The 1990s witnessed another period of ferocious development – a process that, with an ever-growing population, continues today.

ENVIRONMENT

Victoria has vastly contrasting geographical regions. In fact, Victoria is like greater Australia in microcosm: desert-like landscapes in its west, extensive stands of temperate rainforest in the east, mountains in between and strings of beaches along the coast. The Great Dividing Range runs east to west and includes Victoria's highest peaks. It buffers the north of the state from rain and cold southerly winds, producing drier and warmer conditions. The hottest and driest areas are the northern Wimmera and Mallee regions, which make up the Victorian section of the Murray-Darling Basin. Coal is mined at Gippsland (in the southeast), which also has fertile dairy country and vast forests. The coast varies from seemingly endless sandy beaches to imposing rocky headlands.

Approximately 65% of the state has been deforested but the diversity of Victoria's vegetation is still apparent, with 16 landform and vegetation regions on register. Eucalypts – including the hardy Mallee scrub, towering mountain ashes and twisted High Country snow gums – and acacias (wattles) are the most common trees. Wild flowers abound, especially in the Grampians and coastal regions.

Native fauna (pretty much all of the 'pin-up' species) is concentrated in protected areas, although possums and honeyeaters are common in urban climes too. Kangaroos, wallabies, emus, wombats, koalas, cockatoos, galahs and rosellas are often seen on the roads.

CLIMATE

Victoria has a temperate four seasons climate and three climatic regions. The southern and coastal areas are subject to changeable weather patterns associated with frequent cold fronts and southwesterly winds.

The alpine areas have the most unpredictable conditions, dominated by weather extremes like winter (and sometimes even summer) snow.

The weather is generally more stable north of the Great Dividing Range, where the Mallee of the northwest is hot and dry.

VICTORIA

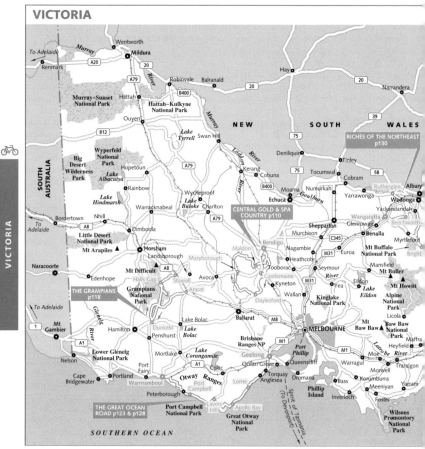

In summer the average daily maximum temperatures are around 25°C along the coast, around 20°C in alpine areas, and up to 35°C in the northwest. Winter averages are around 13°C along the coast, between 3°C and 10°C in the alpine areas and 17°C in the northwest.

Rainfall, which has been in short supply for several years, is spread fairly evenly throughout the year. The wettest areas are the Otway Ranges and the High Country, and the driest the northwest corner.

PLANNING
Bike Hire
Although each ride presents options for local hire, **St Kilda Cycles** (☎ 03-9534 3074; www.stkildacycles.com.au; 150 Barkly St, St Kilda) in Melbourne changes everything. With very good touring bikes and all equipment available at advantageous long-term hire rates ($150 per week for a bike) and free bike transport on regional trains (see boxed text p108), hiring in Melbourne is a smart economical option.

Maps
Some of the best maps for cycle touring are the **Royal Automobile Club of Victoria** (RACV) 1:350,000 regional maps, available at the club's office in Melbourne and elsewhere throughout the state. Where there's coverage, **Hema** maps are also usually good.

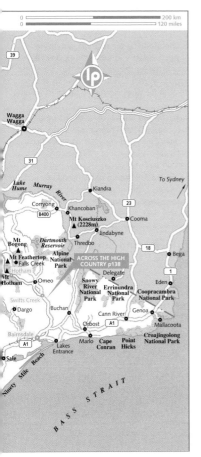

are the most practical scale. One potential drawback is the infrequency of updates, although that shouldn't have too much of an impact. The 1:100,000 Natmap series, with even more contour detail, are also available, but not as practical since you will often need multiple sheets per day. They're all available at map retailers or directly from **Geoscience Australia** (☎ 1800 800 173, 02-6249 9966; www.ga.gov.au).

BUYING MAPS

One of the best shops for maps is **Information Victoria** (☎ 1300 366 356; www .information.vic.gov.au; 356 Collins St, Melbourne). The shopfront of the **RACV** (☎ 131 111; www.racv.com.au; 438 Little Collins St, Melbourne) is just a few doors down.

In a less central location, **Mapland** (☎ 03-9557 8555; www.mapland.com .au; 408 Centre Rd, Bentleigh) is one of Melbourne's oldest travel guide and map specialists, with an impressive range of guides and maps.

Books

From the pool of scores of regional guides, Lonely Planet's *Melbourne & Victoria* is a good companion to this volume.

Cycling guides to the state include *Bike Paths Victoria,* covering more than 2800km of bikepath; *Rail Trails of Victoria and South Australia* by Alexander McCooke et al (see www.railtrails.org.au for purchase details); *Bike Tours Around Victoria*, 25 rides presented by Julia Blunden; and, for mountain bikers, Kieren Ryan's *Off Road Cycling Adventures.*

BUYING BOOKS

Mapland (see Buying Maps above) is the first place to look for cycling guides. Books can be purchased online if pre-planning a trip from outside Victoria.

Cycling Events

Audax Alpine Classic (www.audax.org .au; Jan), celebrating its 25th anniversary in 2010, offers a 70km to 250km day ride with a lot of climbing in the Alps. Drawing thousands to the picturesque town of Bright for the Australia Day weekend, this is a perennial favourite on the Victorian cycle calendar.

During pre-trip planning, use the superb online resource of **Vic Roads** (www.vicroads.vic.gov.au), the state's road authority. Bike maps at all scales are available for download, but, even better, there's an interactive facility.

In 2009 **Explore Australia** released a six-in-one *Bike Riding in Victoria* map folder of the state's best bike trails, created in cooperation with **Bicycle Victoria** (see p108) and available for purchase on its website.

For general road maps, Victoria (and, in fact, all of Australia) is covered by Geoscience Australia's 1:250,000 scale Natmap topographical series; these have sufficient contour detail for touring and

BIKES ON VICTORIAN BUSES & TRAINS

Although **V/Line** (☎ 13 61 96; www.vline.com.au) is one of the better state rail systems for bikes, it's got its limitations. The big plus: bikes are carried (intact and unswaddled) anywhere for free, subject to space availability, a decision usually made by the conductor. The minus: the space available can be very limited and there's no way to reserve it. You just show up at the station and hope for the best. On reserved trains, check-in for bikes is possible up to 30 minutes prior to departure.

V/Line buses (which have replaced some rail services) do not carry bikes at all. However, until the Albury line upgrades are complete in 2010, exceptions have been made in Northeast Victoria. **Wangaratta Coachlines** (☎ 03-5722 1843), which manages the V/Line replacement service, is taking bikes when possible. Call ahead. More generally, even in other regions, bike acceptance is at the discretion of the driver – travel at off-peak times.

In the Melbourne metropolitan area, bikes may be carried for free on trains outside peak periods (7am-9am and 4pm-6pm), when a concession fare is charged. They cannot, however, be carried on buses or trams. Contact the **Metlink Information Centre** (☎ 13 16 38; www.met linkmelbourne.com.au) for routes, timetables and fares.

Capped at 3000 riders, the **Alpine Attack** (www.bv.com.au; Labour Day weekend) features a one-day 230km challenge along the newly paved Bogong High Plains Rd. Organised by the Melbourne Bicycle Touring Club, the **MAD Ride** (www.mbtc .org.au; Apr), aka Melbourne Autumn Day Tour, covers 60km or 110km of road or 65km of dirt in the Macedon Ranges region one hour northwest of Melbourne.

The **Fruit Loops Ride** (www.fruit loopshepparton.com; Sep) is the first endurance ride of the season – 50km, 100km or 200km around Shepparton, known for its stone fruits.

Around the Bay in a Day (www .aroundthebay.com.au; Oct) is Australia's largest single-day bike ride, with 16,000 participants in 2009 donating to charity for the right to ride 50km to 250km around Port Phillip. Held the same weekend as the three-day **Melbourne Cycling Festival/Go Bike Expo**, it's a celebration of all things cycling.

The popularity of Rutherglen as a destination for wine lovers has led to the establishment of the **Tour de Rutherglen**, a fundraising bike tour held the first weekend in October. See the visitors centre for details (p157).

For details of Bendigo's **Cyclismo** (Nov), see p145.

During the **Great Victorian Bike Ride** (www.greatvic.com.au; Dec), 5000 cyclists take to the road for nine days in a new Victorian destination every year.

Information Sources

Bicycle Victoria (☎ 03-8636 8800; www .bv.com.au; Level 10, 446 Collins St, Melbourne) is the state's peak cycling organisation, with 40,000 members, and by far the best source of information about biking in Victoria. Bicycle Victoria publishes the monthly bike-centric *Ride On* magazine.

Parks Victoria (☎ 131 963; www .parkweb.vic.gov.au; Head Office, Level 10, 535 Bourke St, Melbourne) manages Victoria's national parks.

Railtrails Australia (☎ 03-9306 4846; www.railtrails.org.au) promotes alternative public uses of old rail corridors. Its website contains a description of established rail trails across Victoria – a rapidly growing number. Copies of the *Rail Trails of Victoria and South Australia* guide can also be purchased here.

Royal Automobile Club of Victoria (RACV; ☎ 131 111; www.racv.com.au; 438 Little Collins St, Melbourne) produces maps and guides with loads of accommodation and touring information.

Tourism Victoria (☎ 13 28 42; www .tourism.vic.gov.au) is Victoria's state tourism body. The **Visit Victoria** website (www.visitvictoria.com.au) is a great first reference for general travel information. See p107 for details of the Information Victoria bookshop.

Vic Roads (☎ 131 171; www.vicroads .vic.gov.au), with offices throughout the state, maintains comprehensive online resources for cyclists, including maps, road rules, safety tips and planning.

GATEWAY

See Melbourne (p154).

CENTRAL GOLD & SPA COUNTRY

Duration 5 days

Distance 304.3km

Difficulty easy–moderate

Start/Finish Bendigo

Summary Be seduced by a blend of quaint townships, impressive regional centres and rolling countryside, all tinged with ever-present reminders of the gold-rush days. Along the way, indulge yourself at the spa centre of Victoria.

Central Victoria has a lot of appeal, but for many the goldfields are the most interesting area. Even small towns boast impressive Victorian architecture, the legacy of the enormous prosperity mined from the earth during the 19th century. Hopeful prospectors, including thousands of Chinese immigrants, flooded the region and many towns burst into being. Though some are now little more than quiet villages, each has plenty of character and historical lore.

Around Daylesford, other mineral riches bubble from underground springs. Marketed as Victoria's spa centre, the region has become a massage and alternative-therapy hub, and foodies will have a field day.

HISTORY

In 1850, at Clunes, on land once inhabited by the Jaara Jaara Indigenous people, Australia's first significant payable gold deposit was uncovered. It was a watershed moment in the history of Victoria. When word reached the public in 1851, people couldn't move fast enough to claim their pieces of the pie. Tens of thousands of starry-eyed miners joined the rush, many from all around the world. By the end of 1852, 90,000 new arrivals had swelled the population of Victoria, most of them settling around mining centres.

By the 1860s central Victoria's surface gold was running out. To get at deeper deposits, mining companies with expensive heavy machinery replaced independent diggers. The resulting reef-mining boom produced enormous wealth. It was during this period that many of the towns' impressive structures were built.

When profits from reef mining dwindled, new industries arrived, turning some towns, like Maryborough and Bendigo, into important regional centres and all but abandoning others. A more recent boom has been in wine production and tourism. Praised as early as the late 19th century, the region's wines didn't find a strong market until the last quarter of the 20th century.

ENVIRONMENT

Central Victoria was once largely covered in relatively open box-ironbark forest, but today 83% of this has been cleared. What survives helps support a variety of other plants including wattles, orchids and wild flowers. The deforestation (due to mining and clearing for animal grazing) as well as the introduction of rabbits and salinity from heavy irrigation have all contributed to serious land degradation in some areas.

Eastern grey kangaroos and wallabies are common, as are possums. Koalas can be seen in the Leanganook Koala Sanctuary (see p112). Other fauna includes snakes, echidnas, eagles, kookaburras, cockatoos and galahs.

PLANNING
When to Cycle

The best seasons for this ride are March to May, when days can be still and clear, and September to November, at the height of the wattle bloom. Try to avoid Easter and festivals, when accommodation is tight and expensive, especially in Daylesford and Maldon, where even low-season weekends are a challenge.

Maps

If you can get it, the discontinued VicRoads 1:250,000 No 05 *Bendigo* map is ideal. If not, the RACV 1:350,000 *Goldfields* regional map is very good, and the approximately 1:500,000 *Goldfields Official Touring Map* a tolerable free option. Both are available at the visitors centre in Bendigo.

Information Sources

Victoria's **Goldfields website** (www.visit goldfields.com.au) is a good place to start

VICTORIA

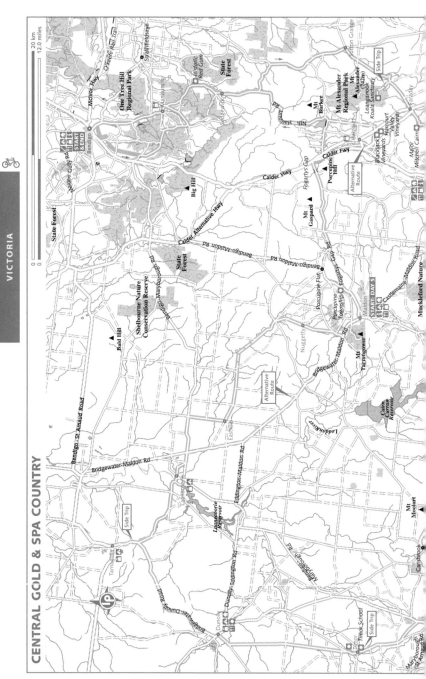

CENTRAL GOLD & SPA COUNTRY

VICTORIA

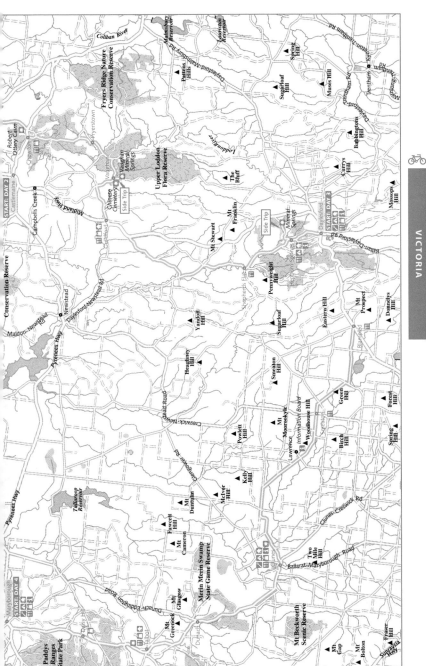

for general inquiry. Especially interesting for cyclists is the **Cycling the Golden Trail website** (www.thegoldentrail .com), which follows in the footsteps of Chinese gold seekers who trod the 500km from the South Australian coast to Bendigo. The route passes through many of the towns described in this guide.

GETTING TO/FROM THE RIDE
Bendigo (start/finish)
BUS
Bendigo Airport Service (☎ 03-5444 3939; www.bendigoairportservice.com.au) moves three to four minibuses a day between the Bendigo train station and Melbourne airport ($38, two hours). Bikes must be wrapped and pre-announced.

TRAIN
V/Line (☎ 13 61 96; www.vline.com.au) runs regular trains between Melbourne and Bendigo ($22.50, two hours).

BICYCLE
From Maryborough, this ride connects to The Grampians ride (p116), though the connecting route is fairly exposed and uninteresting. Take the Pyrenees Hwy to Avoca, head northwest on the Sunraysia Hwy for 13km, continue on the C221 past the wineries to Landsborough and then go west to Stawell (121km).

THE RIDE
Day 1: Bendigo to Castlemaine
3¼–5¾ hours, 58.4km
Leaving Bendigo, you head out along a railway line on quiet roads through box-ironbark forest and open farmland. The most significant climb is a steep grunt over the shoulder of Mt Alexander (742m).

Given its size, the ease and speed with which you quit Bendigo is quite satisfying. You're into the wilds before you know it, gazing contentedly at classic grazing-land vistas. One particular roadside **red gum tree** (20.7km), thought to be more than 700 years old, is where the rescue party of ill-fated explorers Burke and Wills camped in 1862. You can't help but imagine what the land was like only 150 years ago – a seemingly endless woodland expanse. Don't miss the **Leanganook Koala Sanctuary** turn-off (44km).

A thankfully short (400m) spin on the Calder Hwy is a jolting reminder that you can't really appreciate the Australian bush unless you get off the main roads. This you do, paralleling a delightful creek.

Towards Castlemaine the ride passes evidence of the area's gold-mining past, along with monuments to 1830s explorer Major Mitchell (49.7km) and to Robert Ottery (53.4km), who found the first gold in the area after walking barefoot from the Melbourne suburb of Williamstown.

SIDE TRIP: LEANGANOOK KOALA SANCTUARY
15–20 minutes, 4km
The Leanganook Koala Sanctuary is a 2km detour up Mt Alexander (at 44km). It's not touristy and koalas are often seen in the manna gums from the walking trails through the sanctuary. The basic picnic area has toilets and water.

You're also likely to see Black-tailed Wallabies, Eastern Grey Kangaroos, echidnas, Possums, and sugar gliders.

CENTRAL GOLD & SPA COUNTRY – DAY 1

CUE		GPS COORDINATES
start	Bendigo visitors centre	144°16′52″E 36°45′34″S
0km	go SE on Williamson St	
0.5	⌐ Myers St	
0.6	⌐⌐ Wills St (dogleg)	
1.5	⌐ Russell St	
1.8	⌐ Breen St	
13.3	⌐ Nankervis Rd	
16.3	⌐ Sedgewick Rd 'to Sedgewick'	
{20.7	★ historic red gum tree}	
26.7	↘ 'to Sutton Grange'	
29.9	↗ 'to Sutton Grange'	

CUE CONTINUED		GPS COORDINATES
38.1	⌐ 'to Faraday', Sutton Grange	144°21′31″E 36°59′22″S
42.8	▲ 1.2km steep climb	
{44.0	●●⌐ Leanganook Koala Sanctuary 4km ↺}	
47.5	⌐ A79 'to Melbourne'	
47.9	⌐ Golden Point Rd 'to Chewton'	
{49.7	★ Major Mitchell cairn}	
53.2	⌐ B180 'to Castlemaine'	
{53.4	★ Robert Ottery cairn (RHS)}	
58.3	⌐ 'to visitors centre'	
58.4	Castlemaine visitors centre 144°13′13″E 37°03′57″S	

Day 2: Castlemaine to Daylesford
2¾–4¾ hours, 48.1km

From mining gold to mineral springs, today's ride undulates along generally quiet roads, before becoming busier and hillier over the final 15km to the 'Spa Centre' of Victoria. If you're planning to take advantage of the facilities, put in a little extra effort. It'll get you there earlier.

Though the gold rush ended well over a century ago, the road between Castlemaine and Vaughan is littered with relics of the frenzy. Keep your eyes peeled for the abandoned poppet head (5.6km), engine house (10.2km) and degraded digging sites. Some place names, like Irishtown – a settlement without a village – mark long-gone mining communities.

Even the next town, Vaughan (15.4km), which still exists, is but a whimper compared to the force of 13,000 said to have lived in the area during its heyday. The 1850s **Chinese Cemetery** at the Vaughan Springs side-trip turn-off commemorates the large number of Chinese buried there.

Vaughan Springs, one of 14 discovered by miners in 1852, is smaller and less touristy than famous **Hepburn Springs**, also a side trip at 44.1km. Both are well worth the detour, especially for a gurgle of the goods.

Blink and you'll miss Shepherds Flat, set amidst rolling farmland. It has a **cafe with cricket memorabilia** (39km). Just beyond it are the fragrant fields of the **Lavendula Swiss Italian Farm** (☎ 03-5476 4393; www.lavandula.com.au; adult/student $3.50/1; 10.30am-5.30pm, closed Wed), its shop and cafe. It's a good break before the short but steep climbs ahead.

Attractive urban sprawl, dozens of B&Bs and one final hill connect the twin spa towns of Hepburn Springs and Daylesford.

Day 3: Daylesford to Maryborough
4–7¼ hours, 72.3km

After a scenic 11km (and the day's main climb) on the Midland Hwy, it's an easy, quiet ride to Clunes. Traffic increases a little on the Maryborough Rd, which undulates gently through attractive box-ironbark forest. Make sure you carry enough water today. If the hotel at Smeaton is closed, it's a long dry road to Clunes.

CENTRAL GOLD & SPA COUNTRY – DAY 2

CUE			GPS COORDINATES
start		Castlemaine visitors centre	144°13'13"E 37°03'57"S
0km		go E on Forest St/B180	
4.0		Fryers Rd, Chewton	144°15'21"E 37°04'53"S
13.6		`to Vaughan'	
{15.4 ●●		Vaughan mineral springs 800m	
{	★	Chinese Cemetery}	
17.8		`to Guildford'	
21.9		Templeton St/A300, Guildford S	144°09'44"E 37°09'04"
24.4		Limestone Rd `to Yandoit'	
31.3		Daylesford-Newstead Rd	

CUE CONTINUED			GPS COORDINATES
	▲	2.3km gradual climb	
34.0		`to Hepburn'	
38.4	★	Shepherds Flat	144°06'31"E 37°16'17"S
38.8	▲	500m moderate climb	
40.0	▲	600m steep climb	
41.4	▲	300m steep climb	
44.1		`to Daylesford', Hepburn Springs	144°08'18"E 37°18'55"S
{	●●	mineral springs 1km }	
44.9	▲	3.2km gradual climb	
48.1		Daylesford visitors centre	144°08'31"E 37°20'39"S

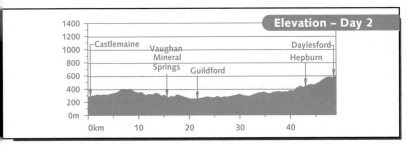

Elevation – Day 2

Castlemaine · Vaughan Mineral Springs · Guildford · Daylesford · Hepburn

CENTRAL GOLD & SPA COUNTRY – DAY 3

CUE			GPS COORDINATES
start		Daylesford visitors centre	144°08'31"E 37°20'39"S
0km		go N on Vincent St	
0.3	↰	Albert St/A300	
2.5	▲	2.2km moderate climb	
11.3	↙	'to Clunes', Blampied	144°03'22"E 37°21'37"S
17.0	↱	'to Clunes'	
17.4	↰	'to Clunes'	
21.7		Smeaton	143°56'58"E 37°18'45"S
{27.3	★	information board (RHS)}	
31.2	↘	'to Clunes'	
39.1	↱	Ligar St 'to Town Centre'	

CUE CONTINUED			GPS COORDINATES
31.3	↰	Daylesford-Newstead Rd	
39.4	↰	'to Town Centre'	
39.7	↱★	'to Talbot', Clunes	143°47'12"E 37°17'42"S
56.5	↱	'to Talbot'	
57.4	↰	Scandinavian Cres 'to M'borough'	
57.8	↰★	'to Maryborough', Talbot	143°41'53"E 37°10'17"S
57.8	↱	(40m) Ballarat St 'to M'borough'	
58.3	↱	'to Maryborough'	
71.0	↱	Napier St 'to Visitors centre'	
72.1	↰	Nolan St 'to Visitors centre'	
72.3	↰	'to Visitors centre'	
72.3		(50m) Maryborough visitors centre	143°44'15"E

Lead mine by-products, called mullock heaps, litter the paddocks between Blampied and Clunes. After surface gold ran out, many such mines operated well into the 20th century. Along with gold, these diggings turned up fossils. Look for the **information board** (27.3km).

The tiny hamlet of Smeaton (21.7km) is just a crossroads with shops. On one corner stands the **Cumberland Hotel** (☎ 03-5345 6205), a welcome oasis halfway between Daylesford and Clunes.

The population of **Clunes** (39.7km) skyrocketed to 30,000 with the discovery of Victoria's first payable gold. Today, it's a pint-sized town (population 1600) of gallon-sized buildings, many of which have changed little since its halcyon days. Fortunately there's a **cafe-bakery**, **IGA supermarket** and more. The **visitors centre** (☎ 03-5345 3896; 70 Bailey St) can fill you in on the large number of interesting sights.

Talbot (57.8km) is another old gold town, again with some magnificent architecture. Don't miss 'the most intact block of gold-era government buildings in Australia' or the bluestone **Chesterfield House** (☎ 03-5463 2002; www.chesterfieldhousebandb.com; 2 Ballarat St North), now a well-regarded B&B. This is a lively little place, especially during the annual yabbie festival (Easter Sunday; www.talbottourism.org).

Day 4: Maryborough to Maldon
4¼–7½ hours, 75.2km

With a good thing going, why change your speed? Today you glide through more classic gold country on quiet, relatively easy, rolling roads through farmland, old mining towns and even some box-ironbark forest. With few services past Dunolly, stock up on water and food.

Timor (8.3km) is now an oops-there-it-was locality. The **general store** (closed) is

CENTRAL GOLD & SPA COUNTRY – DAY 4

CUE			GPS COORDINATES
start		Maryborough visitors centre	143°44'15"E 37°02'53"S
0km	↰	(50m) Nolan St	
0.2	↱	High St/Park Rd	
0.8	↰	Wills St 'to Timor'	
0.9	↱	'to Timor/Goldfields Route'	
1.0	↘	Dundas St	
{8.2	●●↱	Timor School 300m (♪)}	
{8.3		Timor}	
21.1	★	'to Dunolly'	
22.5	★	Dunolly	143°43'55"E 36°51'38"S
	↰	'to Tarnagulla'	
22.9	↱	C274 'to Bridgewater'	

CUE CONTINUED			GPS COORDINATES
35.7	↱	Tarnagulla-Laanecoorie Rd	
{	●●↑	Tarnagulla 5.2km (♪)	
43.2		Laanecoorie	143°54'16"E 36°49'38"S
{46.4		alt route: Maldon 20km	
49.9	↱	Eastville Rd 'to Shelbourne Silo'	
50.7	↰	'to Bendigo'	
53.6	↰	Shelbourne Rd	
58.9	⚠	3.5km dirt road	
72.4	↰	Bridgewater–Maldon Rd	
{		alt route rejoins (continue)}	
75.2		Maldon visitors centre	144°04'06"E 36°59'47"S

full of character and the lovely old **school** (300m side trip) is typical of the era.

Dunolly (22.5km) and the rich alluvial goldfields to its north were known as the 'Golden Triangle', yielding more shiny nuggets than any other area in the country. There's a replica of the world's largest pure gold hunk – the 65kg Welcome Stranger, found here in 1869 – at both Dunolly's **Goldfields Historical Museum** (☎ 03-5468 1516; 77 Broadway; 1.30-4.30pm Sat & Sun) and the Maryborough visitors centre (p153).

For a small town, Dunolly's not bad on food. Although it's probably too early for lunch, the **Dunolly Bakery** (97 Broadway) has got some real treats. Pack in food and water for the road ahead; supplies are hit and miss until Maldon. Take the side trip turn-off to **Tarnagulla** at 35.7km.

The road from Dunolly to Laanecoorie (note the alternative route available here) brings welcome change when you dip into a long and lovely section of box-ironbark forest. Imagine: this is what the whole region used to be like!

SIDE TRIP: TARNAGULLA
20–30 minutes, 5.2km
Tarnagulla is worth a visit for more gold-rush architecture, which includes multiple **churches** and the **Victoria Theatre**, a former dance hall and vaudeville theatre. The sleepy, pretty village also has a small shop and pub.

ALTERNATIVE ROUTE: VIA BRIDGEWATER–MALDON RD
1–2 hours, 20km
Shortly after Laanecoorie, this paved alternative bypasses a short 3.5km dirt section (58.9km), although you end up on the busier Bridgewater–Maldon Rd rather than on back lanes all the way to Maldon.

Day 5: Maldon to Bendigo
2¾–5 hours, 50.3km
A very gradual climb through Fogarty's Gap is followed by some rolls through pretty Harcourt and a relaxed climb over Mt Alexander's other shoulder (22.5km) before an easy run back to Bendigo. The plus: the country is attractive, lightly wooded and there are very few cars. The minus: pack food and drink for the whole

CENTRAL GOLD & SPA COUNTRY – DAY 5

CUE			GPS COORDINATES	
start		Maldon visitors centre	144°04'06"E	36°59'47"S
0km		go S on High St		
0.1	↰	Main St/C283		
{2.7	★	Porcupine Township}		
3.9	↗	Fogartys Gap Rd 'to Harcourt'		
10.0	▲	5.4km gradual climb		
{16.5	↱	alt route: vineyards 14.8km}		
16.6	↑	cross Calder Hwy		
16.8	↱	unsigned road (after Calder Hwy)		
18.3	↑	McIvor Rd (cross Calder Hwy)		
{21.7		alt route rejoins (turn right)}		
31.3	↰	Sedgewick Rd 'to Bendigo'		
47.5	↱	Carpenter St		
49.7	↱	Myers St		
49.8	↰	Williamson St		
50.3		Bendigo visitors centre	144°16'52"E	36°45'34"S

day, since there are no services until Bendigo.

The **Porcupine Township** (2.7km; ☎ 03-5475 1000; www.porcupinetownship.com.au; adult/concession/child $10/8/6) is an award-winning re-creation of gold-rush living conditions in the 1850s.

The alternative route to the celebrated **Harcourt Valley vineyards** leaves the main route at 16.5km.

The day ends as you retrace part of the Day 1 route (at 31.3km) through the Sedgwick district before heading back to Bendigo.

ALTERNATIVE ROUTE: VIA BLACKJACK & HARCOURT VALLEY VINEYARDS
1–1½ hours, 14.8km
Enjoy this deeper dip into the fruit-growing Harcourt Valley via two wineries: **Blackjack Vineyards** (☎ 03-5474 2355; www.blackjackwines.net.au) and **Harcourt Valley Vineyards** (☎ 03-5474 2223; www.harcourtvalley.com.au), where the Bendigo Wine Festival is held each Easter. Turn right (unsigned) just before the Calder Hwy.

Turn left at the first junction and pass beneath the highway. Go right again on Symes Rd to the Midland Hwy, where you head left and then right onto Coolstore Rd. After 1.5km turn left onto Black Rd. Turn right on the old Calder Hwy for the wineries. Otherwise, continue on Blackjack and Danns/Reservoir Rds to McIvor Rd.

THE GRAMPIANS

Duration 3 days
Distance 209.6km
Difficulty easy–moderate
Start Stawell
Finish Ararat
Summary Marvel at the Grampians' stunning views, spectacular waterfalls, rock formations, Aboriginal rock art and, in spring, magnificent wild flower display.

The Grampians' 1680-sq-km national park, surrounded by the Wimmera, a seemingly endless expanse of wheat fields and sheep properties, has been a popular tourist destination since the early 1900s. This ride revels in its outstanding natural features, with a rich diversity of flora and fauna, unique rock formations and Aboriginal rock art. While the route focuses on sealed roads, opportunities abound for dirt-road riding and trail tramping throughout the park, equally well supplied with basic campsites in idyllic locations.

HISTORY

Gariwerd, as the Grampians were originally known, is an area of immense cultural significance to Jardwadjali and Djab Wurrung Aboriginal people, evident in the more than 100 rock-art sites among the escarpments. In 1836 Major Thomas Mitchell called Gariwerd 'the Grampians' after the Scottish ranges and promoted European settlement of the rich grazing land. Within 10 years the Aboriginal population had dwindled. By 1857, long before the 1887 discovery of gold in Stony Creek, there were only 900 of the original inhabitants left.

While the mountains themselves were unsuited to agriculture or grazing, timber was extracted and water dammed to supply the growing towns. In 1984, after a lengthy campaign, the Grampians became a national park. Recognising the land's traditional custodians the name Gariwerd was adopted in 1991, but a change of state government led to its revocation in 1994.

In January 2006 a lightning strike on Mt Lubra, 15km south of Halls Gap, ignited a bushfire that burned around 1300 sq km, including almost half of the national park. The regrowth has been phenomenal.

ENVIRONMENT

The Grampians are the western extremity of the Great Dividing Range. They comprise a clustered series of mountain ranges, 80km north–south and 50km east–west, with sandstone escarpments that rise above the Wimmera Plain. Mt William (1167m) is the highest summit.

The ranges are composed of 500-million-year-old layers of sandstone and shale. The hard, quartz-rich and erosion-resistant sandstones form the ridges of the Serra and Mt William Ranges. The gentle western slope and steep eastern escarpment are typical of cuesta landforms, formed by the uneven erosion of strata. River valleys have formed in the more easily eroded shales. The rounded outcrops of granite are most obvious as narrow bands in the Wonderland area, where vegetation is taller and relatively luxuriant.

The Grampians region is renowned for its flora, especially spring wild flowers. More than 970 native plant species have been identified (20 of them endemic), including 85-plus that burst into bloom. The diversity of the vegetation means a great array of habitats, from wet heathlands to woodlands on rocky outcrops, and a corresponding range of animal communities. Mammals are particularly easy to spot in the Grampians, though it will be some time before the full effect of the bushfires is known.

PLANNING
When to Cycle

The mountains are at their best from September to November, when the wild flowers peak. In April and May the mornings are cool and the days warm. At other times, summer is hot and winter can be cold and wet, with snow on the Major Mitchell Plateau. The Grampians are off-puttingly busy during school holidays, especially at Easter.

Maps & Books

The free *Wilkins Tourist Map of Stawell* includes a Grampians National Park Area Map on the back with distance markings and secondary-road quality and names, as well as a Halls Gap inset. Detailed walking maps are widely available.

Discovering Grampians–Gariwerd by Alistair and Bruce Paton is an all-round resource, featuring colour plates of wild flowers and details of 48 walks. It can be ordered from the **Victorian National Parks Association** (www.vnpa.org.au).

Information Sources

The Halls Gap national park office and the visitors centres at Stawell (p158) and Halls Gap (p149) are all good first points of contact. Secure your useful copies of the *Northern Grampians Official Visitors' Guide* and its accompanying map. Parks Victoria's *Grampian National Park Visitor Guide* is also important.

Other information can be gleaned from the **Friends of Grampians Gariwerd** (www .foggs-online.org), who work to conserve the park. You can also try **Visit Grampians** (www.visitgrampians.com.au), the regional tourism body.

Permits & Regulations

There are no entry fees to the park. Mountain biking is permitted on fire and four-wheel-drive trails but not on walking tracks. The 11 park campsites cost $13 for two people. Bush camping is permitted anywhere except in the Wonderland Range, around Lake Wartook, in Victoria Valley and in parts of the Serra, Mt William and Victoria Ranges. Permits are available at or by calling Brambuk Centre (see p120), the national park and cultural centre.

GETTING TO/FROM THE RIDE

For a circuit of western Victoria, bracket the Grampians ride with those of the Central Gold & Spa Country (p109) and the Great Ocean Rd (p122). From Maryborough (Day 4 of Central Gold & Spa Country), it's 121km on quiet roads to Stawell via Avoca and Landsborough.

Link to Warrnambool (121km) on The Great Ocean Rd ride from Dunkeld (Day 2) by heading down the C178 through Penshurst to Port Fairy and then turning east. Work on the Port Fairy to Warrnambool Rail Trail should be complete by the end of 2009.

Stawell (start)
BUS/TRAIN
V/Line (☎ 13 61 96; www.vline.com.au) runs trains to Ararat, with connecting coaches to Stawell ($23.90, three hours, three or four daily weekdays, two daily weekends). If you can't convince the bus driver to take your bike, pedal the mostly flat 32km direct road separating the two towns.

Ararat (finish)
TRAIN
V/Line (☎ 13 61 96; www.vline.com.au) trains run to Melbourne ($20.40, 2¼ hours, three or four daily weekdays, two daily weekends).

THE RIDE
Day 1: Stawell to Halls Gap
3–5¼ hours, 53.7km

It's a short ride from Stawell to Halls Gap through open farmland, with expansive views of the Mt William Range. Organise accommodation (and leave your bags) in Halls Gap before setting off on the second part of the ride, a circuit through the Wonderland Range.

Although the wide, flat, tree-lined pastures of the first 20km are beautiful – textbook images of the Australian bush – the monotony makes other distractions memorable. At 3.5km **Blue Moon Alpacas** (☎ 03-5358 2581; 340 Pomonal Rd; 10am-5pm Tue-Sun) puts you face to face with these Peruvian imports, whose fleece has contributed to products for sale on-site. A dirt access road at 5.7km leads to **Bunjil's Cave** rock art site.

Pomonal (21.4km) has the **Grampians Store** (☎ 03-5356 6294), a friendly and exemplary all-in-one country outpost, the only one between Stawell and Halls Gap.

As the road after Pomonal edges closer to the park, the increasing density of trees brings welcome shade. At 28km, **Halls Gap Zoo** (☎ 03-5356 4668; www .hallsgapwildlife.com; 4061 Ararat Halls Gap Rd; adult/child $16/8; 10am-5pm, closed Tue) can introduce you to the native animals you may not see in the park.

The afternoon route looping through the Wonderland Range features some of the national park's highlights. Heading uphill at first, you are exposed to rock formations, such as the **Elephants Hide** (36km), that are good examples of the cuesta landform. The short, 2km-return side trip (at 35.8km) leads to the **Wonderland Turntable**. Here, erosion of the sandstone has created deep

VICTORIA

THE GRAMPIANS

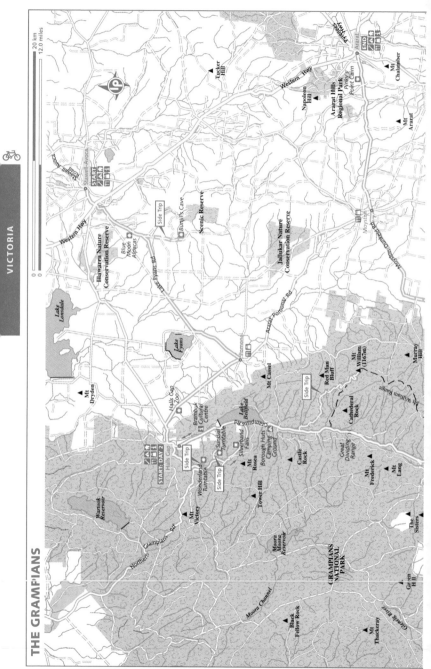

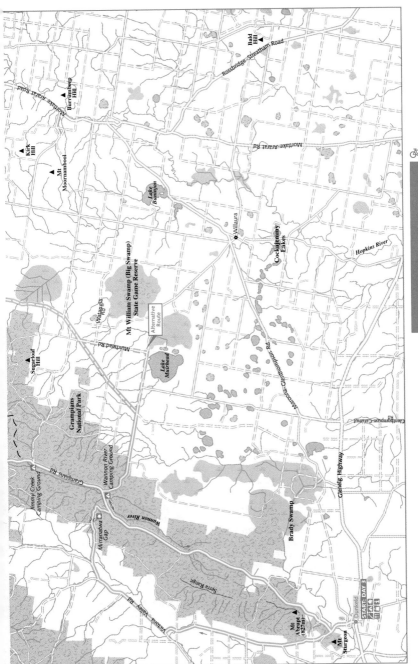

VICTORIA

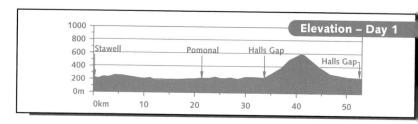

Elevation – Day 1

THE GRAMPIANS – DAY 1

CUE		GPS COORDINATES
start	Stawell visitors centre	142°45'52"E 37°03'51"S
0km	go SE on Western Hwy	
0.1	Seaby St `to Pomonal'	
{3.5	Blue Moon Alpacas}	
{5.7	Bunjil's Cave 7km }	
21.4	`to Halls Gap' Pomonal	142°36'33"E 37°11'32"S
{28.0	Halls Gap Zoo}	
30.9	Grampians Rd/111 `to Halls Gap'	
33.4	Mt Victory Rd, Halls Gap	142°31'11"E 37°08'12"S

CUE CONTINUED		GPS COORDINATES
33.6	4.8km hard climb	
{35.8	Wonderland Turntable 2km }	
38.4	`to Sundial Turntable'	
{41.0	Sundial Turntable 2.3km }	
{44.3	Silverband Falls}	
45.6	`to Halls Gap'	
{51.7	Brambuk Centre}	
53.7	Halls Gap visitors centre	142°31'31"E 37°09'02"S

canyons and formations, like the Grand Canyon and Silent St, which can be reached along walking tracks. Several walks have trailheads at **Sundial Turntable**, another short side trip (at 41km). The circuit to Lakeview Lookout and Devils Gap boasts stunning views.

Dry sclerophyll forest, in which flowers abound in spring, is prominent after the Sundial Turntable turn-off. So too are the scars of the 2006 fires. It's eerie how the green living foliage emerges from the blackened tree trunks.

From the Sundial Turntable, the road descends past the **Silverband Falls** (44.3km) and emerges at Lake Bellfield. On the way back to Halls Gap, be sure to visit **Brambuk Centre** (51.7km; ☎ 03-5361 4000; www.brambuk.com.au; 277 Grampian Tourist Rd; 9am-5pm daily), owned and operated by five Aboriginal communities. The award-winning building incorporates elements of cultural significance and the cafe (p150) incorporates bush food ingredients. The Parks Victoria centre, part of the complex, has excellent natural history interpretive displays and recreational information.

SIDE TRIP: BUNJIL'S CAVE
25–40 minutes, 7km
Bunjil's Cave is one of the state's most important Aboriginal art sites. It contains a rare depiction of Bunjil, the creator spirit of the region. The 3.5km access road is corrugated and, unfortunately, the rock art is now behind a protective wire cage.

Day 2: Halls Gap to Dunkeld
3½–6½ hours, 64.7km
Today it's just you and the Grampians, often without a car in sight. Once beyond Brambuk, there's nothing but glorious nature until Dunkeld. There's not much around in terms of civilisation or supplies so you'll need to bring food and water.

Grampians Rd follows Fyans Creek up to the Great Dividing Range and then descends along the Wannon River valley. At all times it allows spectacular views of the Serra Range (to the west) and the Mt William Range (east). The road has some steep stretches crossing the foothills of Mt Abrupt. You can see it coming for kilometres, but the reality is easier than the built-up anticipation. Campsites along the route are in quiet, beautiful bush settings.

SIDE TRIP: MT WILLIAM
1¼–2 hours, 20km
The road to **Mt William** is a steep 10km grunter, rewarded by jaw-dropping views across the Major Mitchell Plateau. Of course, the descent is as good as it gets.

VICTORIA

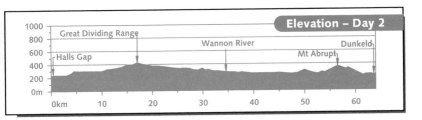

THE GRAMPIANS – DAY 2

CUE			GPS COORDINATES
start		Halls Gap visitors centre	142°31'31"E 37°09'02"S
0km		go S towards Dunkeld	
10.0	▲	7km gradual climb	
{12.3	●●⤴⌐	Mt William 20km (🚲)}	
54.5	▲	3.3km moderate climb	
61.9	⤴⌐	`to Dunkeld'	
62.1		600m moderate climb	
64.5	⌐→	Glenelg Hwy/B160 `to Hamilton'	
64.7		Dunkeld visitors centre	142°20'30"E 37°38'58"S

Day 3: Dunkeld to Ararat
5–9 hours, 91.2km

This long, easy ride puts the parklands (and views) behind you for a traverse of the Wimmera to Ararat. A small shop at Moyston (75.1km) is the only shop on the route.

From Dunkeld, the road today passes to the west of the Serra Range, keeping to the flat, rural landscape of the Victoria Valley.

Views over the sheep and red gums are now bounded to the west by the Victoria Range. But it's the **Mirranatwa Gap** (34.2km) in the Serra that you must cross, the climb to which thrusts you into the heart of the hills. Stop at the lookout for expansive views.

About 9.1km before Ararat the terrain hiccups. A couple of short but surprisingly steep climbs flank the strangely named **Pinky's Point cairn** (84.8km), marking the place where Joseph Pollard found the first gold in the district in 1854.

ALTERNATIVE ROUTE: VIA LAKE MUIRHEAD
45–75 minutes, 12.7km

A slightly longer route bypasses the roughest sections of the 18.7km of unsealed road before Moyston. You're still left with 10.1km of dirt, but it's well tended and sees regular use.

THE GRAMPIANS – DAY 3

CUE			GPS COORDINATES
start		Dunkeld visitors centre	142°20'30"E 37°38'58"S
0km		go E on Glenelg Hwy	
0.2	⤴⌐	C216/Templeton St	
0.4	↘	Victoria Valley Rd	
2.8	↑	C217 `to Halls Gap'	
27.4	↙	`to Halls Gap'	
28.6	↙	`to Halls Gap'	
31.5	▲	2.7km moderate climb	
{34.2	★	Mirranatwa Gap}	
	⚠	2.3km narrow twisting descent	
36.6	⤴⌐	`to Halls Gap'	
38.5	⌐→	`to Willaura'	

CUE CONTINUED			GPS COORDINATES
47.2	⤴⌐	unsigned road at Stop sign	
	⚠	18.7km dirt road	
{		alt route: sealed road 12.7km}	
{55.8		alt route rejoins (turn right)}	
75.1	⌐→	`to Ararat', Moyston	142°46'02"E 37°18'03"S
82.1	▲	1.6km very steep climb	
{84.8	★	Pinky's Point cairn}	
87.2	▲	1km steep climb	
90.6	⤴⌐🚦	Vincent St/B180 `to Avoca'	
90.7	⌐→🚦	High St/Western Hwy	
91.2		Ararat visitors centre	142°56'09"E 37°16'57"S

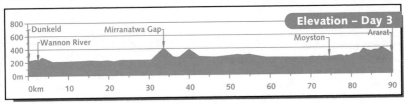

THE GREAT OCEAN ROAD

Duration 5 days

Distance 281.5km

Difficulty moderate

Start Warrnambool

Finish Geelong

Summary Discover the highs – cliffs, lighthouse, vista-rich coastal climbs – and superlative lows – ports, villages, beaches, limestone stacks – of Australia's most famous scenic drive. All at a human speed.

The aptly named Great Ocean Road (GOR) is Australia's, and one of the world's, most spectacular seaside routes. The landscape ranges from stunning coastal cliffs to beautiful, sandy beach fringes where steep green hills meet the azure sea. Add to this some challenging climbs and exhilarating descents through the Otway Ranges and you have a real coastal adventure. The road's attraction to motorists means the perfumed mix of bush, beach, gums and saltwater is often tainted by exhaust, but there's no denying the beauty of this long reach of wind- and wave-swept shoreline.

HISTORY

In 1859, during construction of the telegraph line between Victoria and Tasmania, a track was cut along the coast. As the area's population grew, so did the demand for a road linking settlements. The idea for the GOR was finally floated in 1917 as a way to employ soldiers returning from WW1. The following year the first surveys were completed. Construction began near Lorne in September 1919. It would take 13 years to complete the road and require the labour of around 3000 workers using shovels and crowbars. The GOR was officially opened on 26 November 1932 and ran from Eastern View to Apollo Bay. The later extension of the road across the Otways to Port Campbell was called merely the 'Ocean Rd'.

ENVIRONMENT

The GOR is a tale of two coasts. To the west, the broad plateau around Port Campbell consists of limestone laid down about 50 million years ago. The relentless tides have worn away at this land, leaving limestone cliffs and stacks such as the Twelve Apostles. Heavy clearing has left only remnant heath adapted to dryness and sea spray. There is little wildlife.

In marked contrast is the steep Otway coast of folded and faulted sandstones and mudstones blanketed in thick forest and drained by waterfalls. The Otways' western side is exposed to storm waves; on the more protected eastern coast an extensive shore platform abuts the ranges.

The Otway Ranges' high rainfall has led to deeply cut valleys and healthy soils. Wetter areas have ferns, myrtle beech and mosses, while eucalypt forests dominate higher land. Ironbark forests and heathlands occur in the rain shadow of the Otways between Anglesea and Geelong.

The ranges are home to a variety of animal and bird life. Cockatoos shriek high above the canopy and koalas are common in the manna gums near Cape Otway.

In December 2005 the former Otway National Park and Angahook–Lorne, Carlisle and Melba Gully State Parks, as well as areas of state forest, were incorporated into the 1030-sq-km Great Otway National Park, making it the largest coastal national park in the state.

PLANNING

When to Cycle

Although you can pedal at any time of year, late spring, summer and autumn are the best; only mid-May to mid-September is cold and wet. Try to avoid travel during the January school holidays, when road traffic is heavy and accommodation can be scarce. Most weekends (particularly at Easter) are also busy between Lorne and Torquay.

THE SHIPWRECK COAST

The coast from Port Fairy to Apollo Bay is justly called the Shipwreck Coast. In sailing's golden age, ships crossing the Bass Strait faced treacherous waters largely without navigational aids. Fierce winds often drove them off course and onto limestone reefs close to shore. More than 160 ships have been wrecked, giving names to such localities as Childers Cove (after the barque *Children*), Halladale Cove (after the *Falls of Halladale*) and Loch Ard Gorge (after the clipper *Loch Ard*).

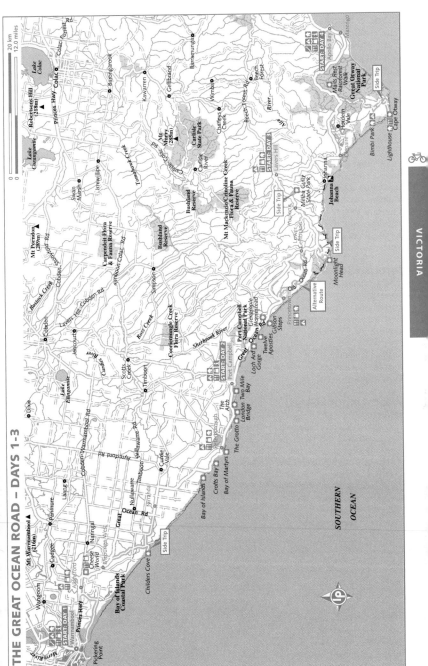

THE GREAT OCEAN ROAD – DAYS 1-3

VICTORIA

SOUTHERN
OCEAN

Maps & Books

The free *Great Ocean Road Official Touring Map* provides a pretty good overview. Combine it with the free *Otways Official Touring Map* and *Surf Coast Official Touring Map* and all you're missing is the first part of Day 1. None provide road distances, which the RACV *Great Ocean Road* regional map does. Vicmap's 1:50,000 *The Otways & the Shipwreck Coast* map provides detailed topographic information from Port Campbell to Anglesea. Tourist offices are the best sources for all maps and guides.

The Great Ocean Road Cycling Guide is ridiculously hard to come by. Produced by Geelong Otway Tourism, it places greater emphasis on the eastern half of the ride, although it's not without value starting wherever you secure a copy.

Information Sources

The **Official Great Ocean Road website** (www.greatoceanroad.org) has clear and entrancing presentations of the area by destination, but almost nothing about cycling.

GETTING TO/FROM THE RIDE

Precede the Great Ocean Road ride with the Grampians ride (p116).

Warrnambool (start)
TRAIN

There are daily **V/Line** (☎ 13 61 96; www .vline.com.au) trains from Melbourne's Southern Cross station to Warrnambool ($26, 2¼ hours, three daily Monday to Saturday, two Sunday), with a train change at Geelong. Warrnambool's **train station** (Merri St) is about 1km west of the visitors centre.

Geelong (finish)
TRAIN

V/Line (☎ 13 61 96; www.vline.com.au) trains run frequently from **Geelong train station** (☎ 03-5226 6525; Railway Tce, Geelong) to Melbourne's Southern Cross station ($9.20, one hour).

THE RIDE
Day 1: Warrnambool to Port Campbell
3¾–6¾ hours, 68.2km

The ride advances and retreats along the coast in an easy first-day introduction. The hardest parts are the few short and low hills and the extended stretches with little shade. If the wind is southwesterly, you'll barely notice either. Allansford and Peterborough have shops, but take food and water for the picnic spots along the way.

After a pleasant push east out of the Warrnambool suburbs, your first taste of the GOR comes after Allansford. The uninspiring building of **Cheese World** (☎ 5565 3130; www.cheeseworld.com.au; tastings every hour on the half-hour 9.30am-4.30pm) hides an interesting dairy museum, supermarket and restaurant serving fittingly great ice creams and milkshakes.

THE GREAT OCEAN ROAD – DAY 1

CUE			GPS COORDINATES
start		Warrnambool visitors centre	
142°28'50"E		38°23'13"S	
0km		go SE on Merri St	
1.4	⬏	Nicholson St	
1.6	⬏	Flaxman St	
2.4	⬏	Hopkins Rd	
2.9	⬑	Marfells Rd/Hopkins Point Rd	
10.0	⬑	'to Allansford'	
13.2	⬏	'to Great Ocean Rd'	
14.4		Allansford	142°35'37"E 38°23'09"S
16.2	⬏	B100/Great Ocean Rd	
{16.9	★	Cheese World}	
22.4	⬏	'to Childers Cove'	
28.9	⬑	'to Peterborough'	
{	●●↑	Childers Cove 3.4km (⟳)}	

CUE CONTINUED			GPS COORDINATES
31.0	⬏	'to Peterborough'	
35.0	↑	B100/Great Ocean Rd	
39.6	⬏	B100/Great Ocean Rd	
45.5	⬏	B100/Great Ocean Rd	
{49.9	●●⬏	Bay of Islands 500m (⟳)}	
{53.6	●●⬏	Bay of Martyrs 200m (⟳)}	
55.1		Peterborough	142°52'37"E 38°36'18"S
{59.2	●●⬏	The Grotto 400m (⟳)}	
{60.8	●●⬏	London Bridge 400m (⟳)}	
{61.8	●●⬏	The Arch 300m (⟳)}	
{65.0	●●⬏	Two Mile Bay 1.7km (⟳)}	
67.2	⬏	B100 'to Port Campbell'	
68.1	⬏	Morris St	
68.2		Port Campbell visitor centre	142°59'46"E 38°37'08"S

The first opportunity to view the coast is on the side trip to **Childers Cove** (22.4km), where the barque *Children* was wrecked in 1839. You'll have to wait another 20km before the main road finally rubs up against the shore, and where walking tracks explore the promontories and rock stacks of the **Bay of Islands** (49.9km) and **Bay of Martyrs** (53.6km), the latter where a group of Koorie men were driven to their deaths off the cliff. The wide **Crofts Bay** that separates the two has water access.

Peterborough, which also has a fine beachfront, is a welcome opportunity to restock. The general store is off the main road, but the **Schomberg Inn Hotel** (☎ 03-5598 5285; Great Ocean Rd; r $79) is right on it with good counter meals and, if necessary, reasonably priced rooms.

Numerous sights in the final 12km – all within Port Campbell National Park – show the extent of erosion along the coast, including **The Grotto** (59.2km); **London Bridge** (60.8km), which fell down in 1990; and **The Arch** (61.8km).

Evidence of a previous shoreline exists at **Two Mile Bay** (65km), where a broad natural platform protects the receding beach.

Day 2: Port Campbell to Lavers Hill

2¾–5 hours, 49.1km

The morning is for sightseeing, but the afternoon a blinding slog: after following the cliffs of Port Campbell National Park past one of the greatest sights of the Southern Ocean shore – the Twelve Apostles – the route launches into the Otway Ranges. The short distance allows ample time to explore the coast (with its numerous small side trips) and adjust to climbing hills. Princetown has the only shop (a small one) on the way to Lavers Hill (which has an even smaller one).

It's easy to spend a couple of hours exploring the trails around **Loch Ard Gorge**

(7.7km), where the *Loch Ard* was wrecked in 1878 (see boxed text p122).

The **Twelve Apostles** (11.2km), the GOR's most iconic wonder, are best in the early morning light. Park off to the left and then walk under the road to the oceanside cliffs.

Gibson Steps (12.2km) allows rare (for these parts) access to the beach and a different view of a couple of the Apostles.

As the place to which the survivors of the *Loch Ard* wreck were brought, **Glenample Homestead** (12.6km), a quarried sandstone structure from 1869, has been restored with a picnic area and excellent *Loch Ard* museum.

The short detour to Princetown (17.6km) climbs easily up to the **Twelve Apostles Tavern** (☎ 03-5598 8288; www .twelveapostlestavern.com.au), also known as the Talk of the Town, where the extensive Gellibrand River wetlands can be admired over coffee. Before you leave, make sure you've got snacks for the climb ahead.

From back at the bottom of the Princetown hill, the quiet, unsealed Old Ocean

THE GREAT OCEAN ROAD – DAY 2

CUE		GPS COORDINATES
start	Port Campbell visitors centre	142°59'46"E 38°37'08"S
0km	go E on Morris St	
0.4	B100 'to Lavers Hill'	
{7.7	Loch Ard Gorge 900m	}
{11.2	Twelve Apostles 400m	}
{12.2	Gibson Steps 150m	}
{12.6	Glenample Homestead 1.4km	}
{17.6	Princetown 800m	}
{	alt route: Old Ocean Rd 12.8km}	
	700m steep climb	
29.5	1.8km steep descent	
{30.4	alt route rejoins (turn right)}	
30.5	18.6km very hard, steep climb	
{33.5	Moonlight Head 8km	}
{46.4	Melba Gully walk 2.2km	}
49.1	YatZies Café, Lavers Hill	143°23'29"E 38°40'50"S

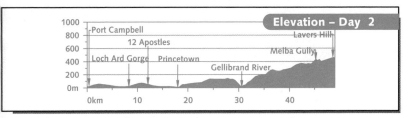

Elevation – Day 2

Port Campbell · 12 Apostles · Loch Ard Gorge · Princetown · Gellibrand River · Melba Gully · Lavers Hill

Rd is a short alternative flat route that follows the Gellibrand River for 12.8km. Right where the two roads come together, the push against gravity commences. It's a pretty relentless 19km test of mettle, but the road is shaded and generously engineered with pullouts for rest.

Moonlight Head (at 33.5km), an 8km return side trip on an unsealed road, is finally reached by a short walk to the headland, which affords spectacular views of 100m-high cliffs.

The jewel of the Otways rainforest is **Melba Gully**, now part of Great Otway National Park. It's one of the wettest places in Victoria and a walk through its dense rainforest, featuring a 300-year-old messmate tree, is a delightful side trip at 46.4km.

Day 3: Lavers Hill to Apollo Bay
2¾–5 hours, 48.4km

Although short, Day 3 is tough. You've got two long downhills but they're split by a wicked climb at the halfway point. As there are no shops en route make sure you leave Lavers Hill with adequate food and water.

After a long descent from Lavers Hill, past the Johanna Beach turn-off (10km return) and the **Castle Cove Lookout** (15km), both with spectacular views, the route reaches the pancake-flat floodplain of the Aire and Calder Rivers. A long and, at times, steep climb leads through

THE GREAT OCEAN ROAD – DAY 3

CUE		GPS COORDINATES	
start	YatZies Café, Lavers Hill	143°23'29"E	38°40'50"S
0km	go S on B100 'to Apollo Bay'		
{15.0 ★	Castle Cove Lookout}		
24.1 ▲	2.1km steep climb		
{27.5 ●● ⌐	Cape Otway 24km (↺)}		
{31.3 ★	Maits Rest rainforest walk}		
45.7	Marengo	143°39'48"E	38°46'35"S
48.4	Apollo Bay visitors centre	143°40'10"E	38°45'22"S

the spectacular tall timbers of the Great Otway National Park and past the side-trip turn-off to **Cape Otway** (27.5km) to the **Maits Rest Rainforest Walk** (31.3km), a signposted boardwalk through spectacular surviving rainforest.

The ride is capped off with another long descent (and more spectacular views) to the coast.

SIDE TRIP: CAPE OTWAY LIGHTHOUSE
1½–2½ hours, 24km

Built in 1848, Cape Otway Lighthouse is Australia's second-oldest lighthouse, its light still in continuous operation. Self-guided tours (adult $14.50) take in the whole of the **Cape Otway Lightstation** (☎ 03-5237 9240; www.lightstation.com), including its historic buildings and the lighthouse. The grounds include a cafe and expensive accommodation. Alternative lodging is available at **Bimbi Park** (☎ 03-5237 9246; www.bimbipark.com.au; unpowered/ powered sites from $17/20, dm/r/van/cabin from $20/45/40/60) under a canopy of manna gums full of birds and koalas.

The road to Cape Otway winds through the tall eucalypts of the national park before it emerges into coastal farming country.

Day 4: Apollo Bay to Lorne
2½–4½ hours, 45.3km

This is the most spectacular section of the GOR, where the route has been carved into the seaside cliffs. The narrow road, which can be busy, winds around the coastline, passing small towns whose populations explode with tourists in summer. Allow plenty of time to enjoy the views or swim at the beautiful beaches.

The short, steep climb up to **Cape Patton Lookout** (17km) is rewarded by expansive coast views in both directions.

From Kennett River (22.6km), the hills are covered by the wide-ranging eucalypts

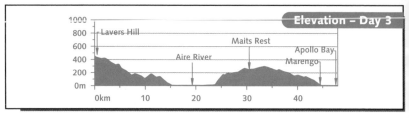

Elevation – Day 3

THE GREAT OCEAN ROAD – DAY 4

CUE			GPS COORDINATES
start		Apollo Bay visitors centre	143°40'10"E 38°45'22"S
0km		go N on B100	
5.3		Skenes Creek	143°42'42"E 38°43'27"S
15.6	▲	1.4km moderate climb	
{17.0	★	Cape Patton Lookout}	
22.6		Kennett River	143°51'44"E 38°39'60"S
27.9		Wye River	143°53'27"E 38°38'06"S
{35.4	★	Mt Defiance Lookout}	
37.5		Cumberland River campsite	
45.3		Lorne visitors centre	143°58'27"E 38°32'12"S

of the national park. Soon after is the **Mt Defiance Lookout** (35.4km), where you can see as far as the Aireys Inlet lighthouse, almost 30km away by road.

At the beautiful **Cumberland River campsite** (37.5km), a steep gorge has been chiselled out of the sandstone. There is a sheltered BBQ area and some lovely walks into the forest.

Day 5: Lorne to Geelong
4–7 hours, 70.5km

As you push east on today's ride the shift from coastal calm to urban energy is palpable. The least enjoyable part of the change is the increase in traffic intensity, although most of the route has a good shoulder. Between Lorne and Anglesea the road hugs the coast, with a climb over Big Hill. The **Memorial Arch**, spanning the road at 12.4km, commemorates the 1932 completion of the original GOR.

In Anglesea, the **Trailhead Bike Co** (☎ 03-5263 3251; www.trailhead.com.au;

67 Great Ocean Rd) is the first real bike shop since Day 1.

Bells Beach (40.4km), home of Australia's largest surfing competition, provides a final view west along the spectacular southern coastline.

Bell's Beach is an icon among Australia's surfing fraternity. Its breaks are recognised as some of the best in Australia, but the manner in which Bells rose to prominence also became part of the trailblazing mythology of the surfing culture. Though Bells has been visited by surfers from nearby Torquay since 1939, it was remote from main roads and very difficult to access. It wasn't until a local surfer, tired of having to hike through thick bush to get to the beach, hired a bulldozer and chewed a path through the scrub in 1960 that the beach opened up to the outside world.

Torquay (46.7km) is quiet during the week but hectic with weekend day-trippers. It's also your last look at the Southern Ocean before turning inland to Geelong. Head to the Esplanade, which follows the city beach and its parade of huge Norfolk pines. The cafes and shops are set back a bit.

SIDE TRIP: POINT ADDIS
15-20 minutes, 3.8km

The side trip at 36.2km to **Point Addis** winds through box-ironbark forest before descending to a car park where a track leads to the expansive swimming beach, backed by huge cliffs. From this track a 1km **interpretative trail** leads through the Ironbark Basin, explaining the traditional lifestyle of local Koorie people.

THE GREAT OCEAN ROAD – DAY 5

CUE			GPS COORDINATES
start		Lorne visitors centre	143°58'27"E 38°32'12"S
0km		go E on Mountjoy Pde/B100	
5.4	▲	2.8km hard climb	
10.0	▲	700m moderate climb	
{12.4	★	Memorial Arch}	
17.5		Aireys Inlet	144°06'25"E 38°27'32"S
17.7	▲	700m steep climb	
29.3		Anglesea	144°11'22"E 38°24'18"S
31.5	▲	800m moderate climbs	
{36.2 ●●	⌐	Point Addis 3.8km ⟲}	
36.5	⌐	Jarosite Rd `to Bells Beach'	
{40.4	★	Bells Beach}	

CUE CONTINUED			GPS COORDINATES
41.6	⌐	C132 `to Torquay'	
42.4	▲	1.5km of steep climbs	
43.9	⌐	B100 `to Torquay'	
46.7	⌐◎	Bell St `to surf beach', Torquay	144°19'02"E 38°20'15"S
47.4	⌐◎	Esplande	
50.0	⌐◎	Horseshoe Bend Rd	
63.0	⌐⌐	Reserve Rd/Horshoe Bend Rd (dogleg)	
63.1	⌐	C121 `to Geelong'	
64.2	⌐目	M1 `to city centre'	
67.0	⌐	`to Belmont'	
67.1	⌐目	Moorabool St `to city centre'	
70.5		Geelong visitors centre	144°21'34"E 38°09'01"S

THE GREAT OCEAN ROAD – DAYS 4-5

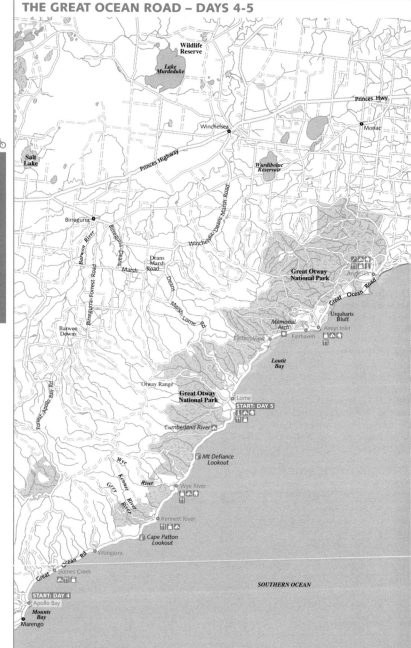

VICTORIA

Wildlife Reserve

Lake Murdeduke

Salt Lake

Princes Hwy

Winchelsea

Moriac

Princes Highway

Wurdiboluc Reservoir

Birregurra

Barwon River

Birregurra-Deans Marsh

Deans Marsh

Winchelsea-Deans Marsh Road

Deans Marsh Road

Birregurra-Forrest Road

Deans Marsh-Lorne Rd

Great Otway National Park

Anglesea

Barwon Downs

Urquharts Bluff

Memorial Arch

Aireys Inlet

Fairhaven

Eastern View

Loutit Bay

Otway Range

Great Otway National Park

Forrest-Apollo Bay Rd

Lorne

START: DAY 5

Cumberland River

Mt Defiance Lookout

Wye River

Kennett River

Grey River

Wye River

Kennett River

Cape Patton Lookout

Great Ocean Rd

Wongarra

Skenes Creek

START: DAY 4

Apollo Bay

Mounts Bay

Marengo

SOUTHERN OCEAN

RICHES OF THE NORTHEAST

Duration 3 days
Distance 205.7km
Difficulty moderate
Start Rutherglen
Finish Bright
Summary From a glass of shiraz to mountain pizzazz you take in Rutherglen wines, Milawa foods, historic gold towns and inspiring high-peak sightings at the gateway to the Alps.

Flat riding along the floodplains of the Murray and Ovens Rivers is combined with some climbs to the notable gold towns of Beechworth and Yackandandah and a finish at the entrance to the Alps. Along the way, it takes in some of the best wine and food the state has to offer and takes advantage of Victoria's – and perhaps Australia's – greatest bikeway: the Murray to the Mountains Rail Trail.

HISTORY

Although barely recognisable from pre-European days, the hill country of northeastern Victoria is sacred to the Aboriginal groups who settled in the lowland areas thousands of years ago. Europeans, following the explorations of Hume and Hovell, took up residence in the early 1840s, but the discovery of gold in the 1850s brought about the first real wave of significant change. Beechworth, from which 85 tonnes of gold were extracted, was one of the region's richest goldfields and thousands of prospectors flocked to the area.

Small mining settlements spread but, with the decline of gold, the area reverted to grazing and, on the lower slopes, forestry. Wine making, first established in the 19th century but decimated by a root disease, was restabilised in the 1960s and soon the northeast was placed firmly on the map as a premier tourist attraction.

ENVIRONMENT

Northeastern Victoria's High Country foothills are largely composed of folded and faulted sedimentary rock. With erosion, granite intrusions seamed with alluvial gold were made evident in and around

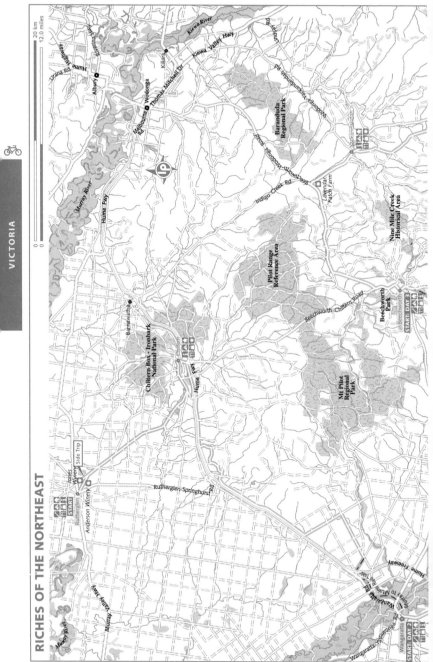

RICHES OF THE NORTHEAST

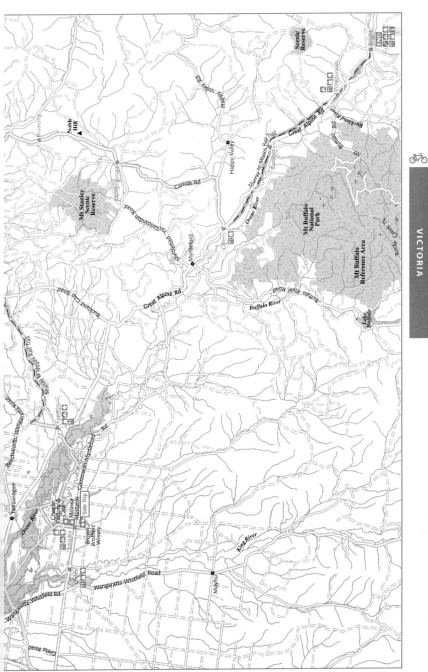

VICTORIA

the Ovens, Goulburn, Kiewa and Murray Rivers. Since European settlement, most of the land has been cleared for grazing and agriculture or mined for gold. The pockets of forest surviving in the river valleys and adjacent floodplains are dominated by red gums, while on higher drier land, like Chiltern–Mt Pilot National Park, box-ironbark woodlands rule the day. In these latter areas spring brings shows of wild flowers, especially orchids, and chirping choruses of honeyeaters, parrots and cockatoos. The granite country around Beechworth stars red gum, endemic black cypress pine and, in spring, a magnificent display of wattles.

PLANNING

Although presented as a three-day ride, this could easily be extended to five or six, depending on how deeply you wish to indulge yourself. From Rutherglen, the wineries merit an entire day (see boxed text below), which you could take before you begin this route. If the distance covered on Day 3 looks too daunting, break the ride in Yackandandah or Myrtleford (a quick backtrack from Ovens). And, for the stout of thigh, the climb from Bright to Mt Buffalo makes for a brilliant day in the mountains.

When to Cycle

This part of Australia has four distinct seasons, each of which brings different colours and fragrance to the land, for the ride can be done at any time of the year. Wine and food festivals are held all year, but particularly in early autumn and spring. Holiday periods, especially Christmas and Easter, are the busiest times (albeit quieter than coastal areas). Summers can be hot, especially down by the Murray.

Maps & Books

The Rooftop 1:100,000 *Beechworth–Albury–Wangaratta Adventure* map provides excellent coverage of all but the rail-trail section south of Ovens. It even has a 1:50,000 enlargement of the extended forests around Beechworth. For the rail trail, the free *Murray to the Mountains Rail Trail* brochure is best by far. Another worthwhile free map is the Demap approximately 1:400,000 *Victoria's Alpine High Country*.

The free *Ride Guide 2009 Cyclists Guide to North East Victoria* is an indispensable tool for taking advantage of cycle resources and programs (see boxed text p135) and identifying trails throughout the region. For foodies, don't hit the road without the free *Seasonal Indulgence Food and Wine Guide*

WINERIES OF THE RUTHERGLEN REGION

More than 20 wineries are within easy striking distance of Rutherglen. With nice, flat terrain to navigate, it's perfect for a day (or two) of bike-and-wine touring. Hire bikes suitable for the area's unsealed roads are available from the visitors centre (p157), which also has excellent free bike maps and supporting brochures. By the end of 2009 a new rail trail linking Rutherglen to Wahgunyah should be in place, making access to the area's vintners both easier and more enjoyable.

The cellar of **Jones Winery** (see p133), off Chiltern Rd, 3.4km southeast of Rutherglen, has a unique bark-lined ceiling; try the vintage port. Nearby, the tin shed of **Anderson Winery** (p133) houses some of the state's best sparkling wine. **Chambers Rosewood** winery, 1km northwest on Corowa Rd, is full of character and history and well known for fortified wines. The first winery west of Rutherglen is **Campbells Wines**, a modern complex with the sloping roof featured on its label. Across the road is the **Stanton and Killeen** vineyard; try the reds from the little-grown durif grapes. Further along, on the corner of Three Chain Rd, is **Buller's Calliope Winery**, which has some great aged fortified and shiraz wines, a picnic area and an interesting aviary.

South of Wahgunyah is **Pfeiffer Wines'** rustic old winery complex. St Leonard's vineyard, 1km northeast of Wahgunyah, has a delightful picnic area overlooking the river and an excellent bistro.

East of Rutherglen, on Gooramadda Rd, **Mt Prior** vineyard has outstanding accommodation and a restaurant. Nearby is the famous **Morris Wines**, renowned for its fortified wines, in particular its muscats. At the edge of the district on the Murray Valley Hwy is **Gehrig Estate Winery**, Victoria's oldest, set around the historic Barnawartha Homestead (1870). It has picnic facilities.

With a couple of exceptions, the wineries in the area open daily from 9am to 5pm (from 10am on Sunday). Most will freight wine and some will deliver to Rutherglen.

prepared by North East Valley Victoria (www.northeastvalleys.com.au).

GETTING TO/FROM THE RIDE
To link with the Central Gold & Spa Country ride (p109), travel for two days between Wangaratta and Bendigo via Rushworth and Murchison. Alternatively, the route between Bendigo and Seymour is shorter. Seymour, is on the train line (bus route until track work is completed in 2010) to Wangaratta.

Rutherglen (start)
BUS/TRAIN
Until track work is complete in 2010, there's only one **CountryLink** (☎ 13 22 32; www.countrylink.info) XPT train per day operating in each direction on the V/Line corridor between Wangaratta and Melbourne ($22.20, 2¼ hours). With limited seats at the V/Line fare class, book early. If you don't want a layover in Wangaratta, you may need to switch to a V/Line bus at Seymour with timed direct connections in Wangaratta for the once- or twice-a-day (except Saturday) V/Line bus service to Rutherglen ($3.40, 30 minutes).

Bright (finish)
BUS
To get between Bright and Wangaratta ($7, 1½ hours, two or three daily weekdays, daily weekends), **V/Line** (☎ 13 61 96; www.vline.com.au) buses *do* take bikes, despite a policy to the contrary.

TAXI
There's a **Bus-a-Bike** (☎ 03-5752 1394, 0409-806 458; geoffs@internode.on.net; Ardens Caravan Park, Myrtleford) taxi

service specially designed for you and your bike. The minimum fare (based on six people) is $140.

BICYCLE
Of course, this distance could be pedalled – 98km the length of the Murray to the Mountains Rail Trail (www.murraytomountains.com.au). Bright is also the start of the Across the High Country ride (p136).

THE RIDE
Day 1: Rutherglen to Wangaratta
3½–6¼ hours, 62km
This first day sits prettily in easy floodplain surroundings; there's little to challenge gravity. You pull away from the Murray for a visit to cinematic Chiltern and then parallel the Hume Fwy through farm and cattle country. The ride enters Wangaratta on a first pass of Victoria's premier rail trail.

The day begins in the tranquil rural landscape of the Rutherglen Wine District. It initially looks more like grazing country than one of the state's premier wine-growing areas (see the boxed text p132). If you haven't tasted any local nectar, don't miss your only two chances: **Anderson Winery** (1.8km; ☎ 03-6032 8111; www.andersonwinery.com.au; 10am-5pm) and **Jones Winery** (☎ 03-6032 8496; www.joneswinery.com; 11am-4pm Mon, Tue & Fri, 10am-5pm Sat & Sun), a 2km side trip at 2km.

Historic **Chiltern** (19.1km) is a bit worn around the edges, but people love it that way – so much so that the main street lined with historic buildings has often been used in films. The old **Bank of Australasia** is now

RICHES OF THE NORTHEAST – DAY 1

CUE			GPS COORDINATES
start		Rutherglen visitors centre	146°27'33"E 36°03'13"S
0km		go SE on Main St/Chiltern Valley Rd	
{1.8	★	Anderson Winery}	
{2.0	●● ↰	Jones Winery 2km (↺)}	
5.4	↗	'to Chiltern Valley'	
15.8	↱	T-junction (no sign)	
18.6	↱	'to Town Centre'	
19.1	↰★	'to Beechworth', Chiltern	146°36'37"E 36°08'54"S
19.7	↱	Railway Access Rd	
23.4	↰	'to Old Cemetery Rd'	

CUE CONTINUED			GPS COORDINATES
23.7	↑	cross Hume Hwy	
23.8	↱	Gayfer Rd	
33.0	↱	Benton Rd	
36.4	↑	Benton Rd	
43.9	↰	'to Tarrawingee'	
48.6	↱	Byawatha Rd	
53.7	↱	Murray to the Mts Rail Trail	
61.1	↱	B500/Great Alpine Rd	
61.4	↖	Parfitt Rd	
62.0		Wangaratta visitors centre	146°19'41"E 36°21'16"S

a cafe-restaurant and B&B. The **museum** in the Star Theatre has old photographs of the town and a giant grapevine in the courtyard.

In all honesty, the next 30km or so are a little tedious. There are no services, no distractions and the whoosh of traffic from the nearby Hume Hwy breaks the bush spell.

The final 8.3km, though, are on the Murray to the Mountains Rail Trail, once a disused and derelict railway line .

Day 2: Wangaratta to Beechworth
3–5½ hours, 55.2km

Food glorious food. Don't deny it; you love it. And along the Gourmet Food and Wine Drive to Milawa, today is a day to indulge in it. Views of Mt Buffalo dominate the horizon and your second serving of rail trail awaits, although this time up a long slow hill. Be sure to carry adequate water after Everton.

Red gums on the Ovens River floodplain provide some shade on the relatively flat road to Milawa (17.5km). The town is synonymous with gourmet food. **Milawa Mustards** (☎ 03-5727 3202 www.milawa mustard.com.au), at the town crossroads, serves samples of mustard flavoured with local herbs. Detour to **Brown Brothers Winery** (☎ 03-5720 5500; www .brownbrothers.com.au; Epicurean Centre 11am-4pm, cellar door 9am-5pm), which has tastings in the cool cellars. Lunch at its Epicurean Centre includes a glass of wine that complements the meal. Finally, on the way out of town sample unusual cheeses at the **Milawa Cheese Factory** (19.3km, ☎ 03-5727 3589; www.milawacheese. com.au), which also sells coffee and light lunches.

Alternatively, bread, cheese, mustard and wine can be enjoyed at the beautiful **picnic area** beside the Ovens River at 32km.

Everton (33.5km) has a general store, campsite and pub. Stock up on anything you may need for the final 20km. Shortly after Everton, you hop on to a very scenic section of the Murray to the Mountains Rail Trail. It gains about 200 vertical metres in a gentle 16km ascent to Beechworth.

Day 3: Beechworth to Bright
5–8¾ hours, 88.5km

Surrounded by stunning, ever-changing high-country scenery, today is relatively easy despite the length. The morning pedal through highland hills weaves through storied Yackandandah and then down into

RICHES OF THE NORTHEAST – DAY 2

CUE		GPS COORDINATES
start	Wangaratta visitors centre	146°19'41"E 36°21'16"S
0km	go SW on Murphy St	
0.7	Warby St/C521 `to King Valley'	
11.1	C522 bikepath `to Milawa'	
13.0	Oxley	
17.5	at Milawa Hotel, Milawa	146°25'52"E 36°26'58"S
{19.3	Milawa Cheese Factory & Cafe}	
19.5	angled T-junction (no sign)	
20.0	`to Beechworth'	
22.6	T-junction (no sign)	
28.9	`to Everton'	

CUE CONTINUED		GPS COORDINATES
32.0	Ovens River picnic area	
32.9	B500 `to Bright'	
33.5	Everton	146°32'29"E 36°25'59"S
33.6	White Post Rd `to Beechworth'	
36.5	Boundary Rd	
36.6	Murray to the Mts Rail Trail	
37.0	rail trail `to Beechworth'	
	15km moderate climb	
53.7	Albert Rd, end of bikepath	
54.7	Ford St	
55.2	Beechworth visitors centre	146°41'16"E 36°21'30"S

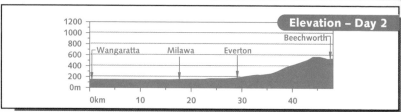

WHEELIE GOOD BUSINESSES

Two Northeast Victoria initiatives have helped spur the development of cycle-friendly business networks catering to the growing two-wheeling market. Linked inextricably to the popularity of the Murray to the Mountain Rail Trail, they've added tremendously to pedallers' pleasure in the region.

Wheelie Good Businesses will soon be identified by a logo (and in the Towns & Facilities section of this guide by the initials WGB). WGBs value cyclists' business by promising four things: availability of drinking water, knowledge of where mechanical support can be found, a readiness to share details about local cycling routes and a secure bike storage area.

Pedal to Produce (www.pedaltoproduce.com.au) lets cyclists experience the fruit (sometimes literally) of local agricultural labour. Maps of eight areas identify producers who have agreed to welcome cyclists with something more than their already warm smiles. Vouchers printed with each map let you know what special treats await. Just ride from reward to reward. Better yet, rent a Pedal to Produce Bike Basket ($25) and there's an additional voucher booklet valued at $400.

the Ovens Valley. From there to Bright the route follows the Murray to the Mountains Rail Trail, now a welcome friend.

From Beechworth, the ride undulates through gentle hills,. The vista alternates between open fields and pleasantly shady forest.

Drop in at the shop of the **Lavender Patch Farm** (17.6km), which has an amazing array of lavender products and serves Devonshire tea overlooking the Kiewa Valley. From there, the downhill run into Yackandandah through more forest and farmland is exhilarating.

Yackandandah (22.3km) is quiet and picturesque, little more than its tree-lined Main St flanked by 19th-century buildings. The discovery of alluvial gold nearby in 1852 saw a sudden influx of miners. Yackandandah survived as a major town, although after the rush it fell into decline. It now prospers through tourism.

The farming country continues, although as you turn southwest, views open to the High Country and the Kiewa and Ovens Valleys. Passing the granite tors of Nobb Hill, the panorama expands to include Mt Buffalo, a towering granite massif south of

RICHES OF THE NORTHEAST – DAY 3

CUE		GPS COORDINATES
start	Beechworth visitors centre	146°41'16"E 36°21'30"S
0km	go NE on Ford St	
2.7	C315 'to Wadonga'	
16.8	C53 'to Yackananda'	
{17.6	Lavender Patch Farm}	
22.3	Yackananda	146°50'17"E 36°18'47"S
22.5	C527 'to Myrtleford'	
23.3	Back Creek Rd	
32.4	C527 'to Myrtleford'	
33.7	5km gentle climb	
45.1	Mudgegonga	146°50'16"E 36°29'23"S
45.3	cross bridge	

CUE CONTINUED		GPS COORDINATES
45.5	Carrolls Rd	
55.3	1.2km steep descent	
57.3	C534 'to Ovens'	
62.3	cross B500, Ovens	146°45'40"E 36°35'18"S
	Murray to the Mts Rail Trail	
73.5	Eurobin train station	
81.0	Porepunkah	146°54'31"E 36°42'00"S
87.4	Railway Av (end of trail)	
87.8	Irving St	
88.3	Gavan St	
88.5	Bright visitors centre	146°57'33"E 36°43'41"S

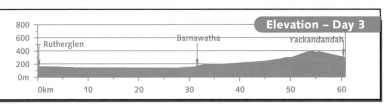

Elevation – Day 3

the Ovens River, which waits in the valley below. Scorched-earth reminders of the deadly 2009 bushfires along this road.

The **Happy Valley Hotel** (☎ 03-5751 1628; www.ovenshappyvalleyhotel.com.au) at Ovens (62.3km) serves the only rations between Yackandandah and Porepunkah, although water is available at the old Eurobin train station (73.5km). All three of these towns are on or near the Murray to the Mountains Rail Trail, your constant guide up the lengthy but very slight valley incline to Bright.

ACROSS THE HIGH COUNTRY

Duration 3 days
Distance 240.4km
Difficulty moderate–demanding
Start Bright
Finish Bairnsdale
Summary Strike out across dazzling contrasts on the Great Alpine Road, a lengthy traverse from the Ovens River valley to the vista-rich coast via Alpine High Country.

The addition, in 1998, of 'Great' to the name of the now-sealed Alpine Road between Wangaratta and Bairnsdale is apt; and this ride truly is a great one. Cyclists lured into conquering the steep but rewarding climb up Mt Hotham will experience the quiet majesty of the mountain. The route passes through the largest cattle station in Victoria and dabbles with the eastern Gippsland towns of Omeo, Swifts Creek and Ensay. Following the Tambo River to Bruthen, it ends along a rail trail from Bruthen all the way to Bairnsdale.

HISTORY
Koorie people have been visiting the high plains area for more than 5000 years. Traditionally, they travelled to the Alps during summer for ceremonial reasons and to feast on the large bogong moths. Later, European cattlemen used the High Country for summer grazing.

From the 1850s onwards, gold mining, particularly around Omeo, triggered the construction of major supply routes. In the 1880s a route from the Ovens Valley to Omeo (the present GAR) was built. Extensive

bush fires around Melbourne in 1939 and the post-WW2 building boom prompted increased demand for Alpine timber and the expansion and improvement of the high-country roads. This really opened the Alps to recreational users.

The battle over land use in the High Country raged for many years between supporters of a national park and cattlemen wanting grazing access to the high plains. Alpine National Park, Victoria's largest, was declared in 1989, ensuring protection of the unique alpine environment. While land management plans are in place, the increase in year-round tourism and resort development have still not exactly always been low impact.

ENVIRONMENT
The Victorian High Country is an uplifted plateau extending from NSW to Gippsland and well above the winter snow line. Mt Feathertop, the Queen of the Alps, is the only significant peak.

Eucalypts predominate in the lower climes, from the dry stringybarks and box forest through to stands of towering mountain ash. In colder regions, mountain gums and white sallees – the beautiful twisted snow gums – occur. Above the tree line, alpine grasses, herbs and shrubs grow in wind-scoured hollows, and boggy pools are surrounded by sphagnum moss. More than 1100 plant species have been recorded in the park, including 12 that are unique to Australia.

Echidnas and wombats live in the alpine areas throughout the year and the endemic mountain pygmy-possum is recovering (see boxed text p137). Cockatoos, pipits, honeyeaters and robins frequent the Alps during the brief summer flowering period.

Devastating bushfires in 2003 and then again in the summer of 2006–2007 tore through the park, the effects of which can still be seen in many places.

PLANNING
When to Cycle
The best time to ride is from early October (spring) to the end of April. In summer the ski resorts are deserted, the roads are quiet and the weather is cool. The road, though open in winter, can be snowed in and very tough on thin tyres.

What to Bring

Be warned: it can snow at Mt Hotham in summer, so pack at least a couple of layers of warm clothing into your panniers. Also, whether or not the sun is shining it is important to wear sunglasses and high-strength sunscreen, as the Victorian sun is strong, and especially so at high altitudes.

Carry spares, as the route has only one bike pit stop in Dinner Plain. Between Bright and Omeo, other than what's at Hotham, there are few facilities; it's important to pack sufficient food and drink.

Maps

The Hema 1:200,000 *High Country Victoria* regional map is perfect for this ride, although the Cartoscope 1:500,000 *East Gippsland* map is a tolerable free option (without distance markings). The map-brochure of the *East Gippsland Rail Trail* will also be useful for the end of Day 3. Check at the visitors centre in Bright.

Information Sources

The best place for regional information is the visitors centre in Bright (p146). The **Australian Alps National Parks** (www .australianalps.deh.gov.au) website is useful for background detail about the Alps region. For an overview of the GAR, turn to www.greatalpineroad.info, a print version of which is the *Great Alpine Road Touring Guide* brochure.

GETTING TO/FROM THE RIDE

The Riches of the Northeast ride (p129) ends at Bright.

Bright (start)

See p146.

Bairnsdale (finish)

TRAIN

V/Line (☎ 13 61 96; www.vline.com.au) trains connect directly to Melbourne ($26, 3¾ hours, three daily Monday to Saturday, two on Sunday).

THE RIDE

Day 1: Bright to Hotham

3–5½ hours, 55km

The first 24km to Harrietville give you a chance to warm up for the boil-over steep and demanding climb to Mt Hotham – one of beauty and challenge that rivals climbs in the European Alps. With no shops after Harrietville, leave Bright prepared or make a supply stop in Harrietville. Have waterproof and warm clothes at the ready. Although the ride ends at Hotham, camping is possible at JB Plain, 10km on; Dinner Plain, after a further 1.5km, has more accommodation (see p150).

The lazy lope up the Ovens Valley is dominated by views of Mt Feathertop and the surrounding mountains. The **Lavender Hue Farm** (22.3km) is a good place for morning tea accompanied by lavender-flavoured everything!

Small Harrietville (24km) has accommodation, a **shop** and the last toilets before Hotham. In preparation for the climb ahead, stop at the **cafe** just past the bridge and sample one of their homemade gelati. Then the climbing really begins: 31km and nearly 1300m to Hotham.

The first 10km past Harrietville average about 6.6% but lurch to as much as 9% for 400m on the hairpin bend called the Meg (29.5km). Stay within your reserves, since the hardest is yet to come. Rather, appreciate the changes in vegetation, from stringy bark

THE TUNNEL OF LOVE

Australia's mammals are often small and usually nocturnal, so seeing them is a rare treat. They nevertheless play an important role in the Australian ecology and their protection is vital. One habitat-protection story tells of the mountain pygmy-possum of the Australian Alps. This tiny mammal (it fits in your palm) lives among the rock-stream habitats in alpine and subalpine regions, particularly in the Mt Hotham region. When not breeding, adult males disperse to low-lying areas. They reascend during the rutting season to the females, who remain at high elevations. Construction of the Alpine Way through Mt Hotham disrupted the route used by the males during the breeding season. The solution: build a boulder tunnel under the road. Today, when on the GAR on your way to Omeo, spare a thought for the male pygmy-possum, protected below, heading to a long-awaited high-slopes tryst.

VICTORIA

ACROSS THE HIGH COUNTRY

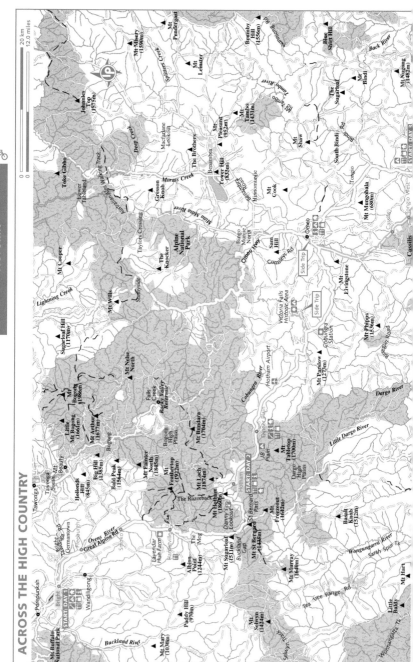

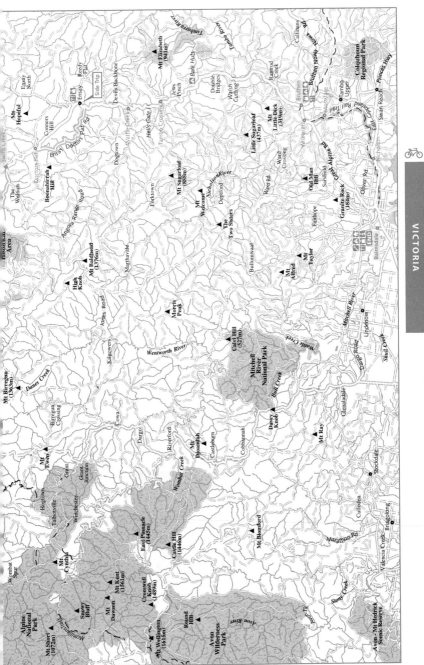

VICTORIA

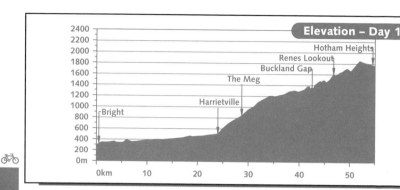

Elevation – Day 1

ACROSS THE HIGH COUNTRY – DAY 1

CUE		GPS COORDINATES	
start	Bright visitors centre	146°57′37″E	36°43′37″S
0km	go E along Gavan St/B500		
{22.3 ★	Lavender Hue farm}		
24.0	Harrietville	147°03′51″E	36°53′31″S
24.5 ▲	28km very hard, steep climb		
45.2	St Bernards Pass		
53.4	Mt Hotham		
54.5 ⚠	200m tunnel		
55.0	Hotham Resort Mgmt, Hotham	147°08′54″E	36°59′28″S

and box in the valleys to towering mountain ash and finally, beautiful snow gums, the scars of recent bushfires eerily evident.

From the picnic area at 34.5km, the next 10km are mostly a false flat with an incline of 1.8%.

Soon after St Bernard Pass (45.2km), from which Hotham is visible, the hurt begins. With about 10km to go, the average gradient is a mild 4.9%, but there are sections of 7% for 750m, CRB Hill's 10% for 1.1km and, just before the peak, the Djamantina rise of 9.7% for 850m. In between there are a couple of fiery descents.

In good weather, the views from Danny's Lookout (50.4km) west across the High Plains to Mt Buffalo are stupendous.

The road into Hotham descends through the garish tunnel under a ski run to the Hotham Resort Management office.

Day 2: Hotham to Swifts Creek
4½–8 hours, 81.2km
Descend to the quiet, isolated towns of East Gippsland, steeped in the legends of pioneer pastoralists and gold seekers. With

the exception of Dinner Plain, there are no facilities between Hotham and Omeo, an alternative stopover point, reached on a side trip at 52.3km. The route continues to Swifts Creek to ensure a comfortable distance for the last day (Omeo to Bairnsdale is 130km, although mostly downhill).

The Dinner Plain ski resort (11.5km) has won architectural awards for its tasteful planning and architecture. Detour in to see the town and pause at the **supermarket-cafe** for any final needs.

Just beyond it, Flourbag Plain was the original site of the Alpine Lodge, a vital overnight stop for travellers on the old Alpine Way until it, like many others, burned down in 1928.

As you whizz down the hill towards the Victoria River, the country opens up to the winter grazing areas of the 400-sq-km

ACROSS THE HIGH COUNTRY – DAY 2

CUE		GPS COORDINATES	
start	Hotham Resort Mgmt, Hotham	147°08′54″E	36°59′28″S
0km	go E on B500/Great Alpine Rd		
11.5	Dinner Plain	147°16′31″E	37°02′00″S
27.0 ⚠	4.5km steep twisting descent		
{34.2 ●●⤴	Victoria Falls 9km ↺}		
{34.6 ★	Cobungra Station}		
41.8 ▲	3.3km steep climb		
46.3 ⚠	6km steep twisting descent		
52.3 ⌐	`to Swifts Creek'		
▲	4km moderate climb		
{ ●●↑	Omeo 6km ↺}		
59.5 ⚠	15m pick-a-plank bridge		
62.7 ⚠	1.4km steep descent		
74.4 ⚠	15m pick-a-plank bridge		
81.2	Swifts Creek general store	147°42′44″E	37°15′00″S

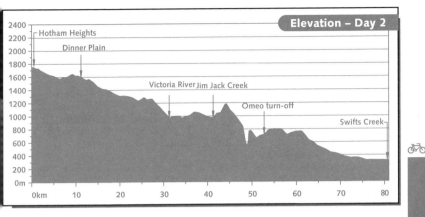

Elevation – Day 2

VICTORIA

Cobungra Station (34.6km). Much of the cleared area on the plateau is part of this, Victoria's largest cattle station.

There are two short side-trip possibilities for the day: **Victoria Falls** (34.2km) and **Omeo** (52.3km). The final gentle back road follows Swifts Creek to its eponymous town through the **Cassilis Historic Area** (see the roadside signs at 67.9km).

SIDE TRIP: VICTORIA FALLS
30-60 minutes, 9km

Turn off to the Victoria Falls and follow the Victoria River to a beautiful picnic area and camping site.

SIDE TRIP: OMEO
20–40 minutes, 6km

Detour (at 52.3km) along Livingstone Creek to Omeo, which is steeped in frontier town history. The grassy plains were used for cattle grazing before alluvial gold was discovered in 1851, when the town was settled. It's worth a longer linger. Ask at the **visitors centre** (☎ 03-5159 1679; www .omeoregion.com.au; 152 Day Ave) about accommodation and eating options both here and at Swifts Creek.

Day 3: Swifts Creek to Bairnsdale
5¾–10½ hours, 104.2km

For the most part you follow the Tambo River as it winds downstream towards the Gippsland Lakes. The cycling is easy and the climb to Walsh Cutting (58.7km) precedes a great descent into Bruthen.

ACROSS THE HIGH COUNTRY – DAY 3

CUE			GPS COORDINATES	
start		Swifts Creek general store	147°42'44"E	37°15'00"S
0km		go SE on B500		
7.1	⌐	Ensay-Doctors Flat Rd		
11.9	⚠	10m pick-a-plank bridge		
23.1	⌐	B500 'to Bairnsdale'		
{	●● ⌐	Ensay 1.8km (↺)}		
47.7	▲	11km gradual climb		
50.0		Bark Huts		
58.7		Walsh Cutting		
73.9	⌐	B500 'to Bairnsdale', Bruthen	147°49'53"E	37°42'29"S
75.7	↖	East Gippsland Rail Trail		
93.5		Nicholson		
102.9	↑	cross bridge on main road		
104.1	⌐	'to information'		
104.2		Bairnsdale visitors centre	147°37'40"E	37°49'36"S

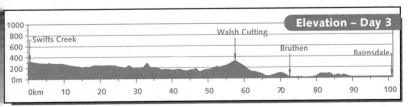

Elevation – Day 3

Ensay, reached on a side trip at 23.1km, has the only shop until Bruthen.

The route passes through beautiful forests and, although on the main highway, is quiet. In an emergency, there's a shelter and a camping site at the **Bark Huts** (50km), but by then you should be able to carry on at least to Bruthen.

Signs such as £1000 Bend and Battle Point add interest to a day with nothing but nature to distract you. The unusual names' origins are explained by the information board at Bruthen (73.9km). Take advantage of the village pub, shop and bakery before jumping on the mellow East Gippsland Rail Trail through Nicholson River and on to Bairnsdale.

MOUNTAIN BIKE RIDES

It's here to stay, and well it should be, for the mountain biking in Victoria is superb. Not only is the current infrastructure already outstanding, it looks like there's lots more on the way. Listen carefully in any town adjacent to state forests or national parks and someone always seems to think a bike park is a priority.

For lots more about trails and access, contact the **Mountain Biking Association of Australia** (www.mtba.asn.au). Parks Victoria, which has played a lead role in the development and maintenance of these sites, is also a primary resource. Kieren Ryan's *Off Road Cycling Adventures* guide to mountain biking in Victoria is another key link in the information chain.

A couple of leading annual mountain-biking events worth knowing about are the February **Otway Odyssey Mountain Bike Challenge** (www.rapidascent.com .au/OtwaOdyssey) and the **Terra Australis Mountain Bike Epic** (see p151).

Beechworth Mountain Bike Park

For knobbies only! It's a dedicated mountain bike park with an inspiring mix of moderate and advanced trails, including jumps and ramps. Access is easiest from Beechworth (p145), home of the Beechworth Chain Gang and the terminus of one spur on the Murray to the Mountains Rail Trail.

Forrest Mountain Bike Trails

There's no better showcase of the beauty of the Otway Ranges. Fifteen signposted purpose-built and sustainable mountain bike trails cater to all levels. The town of Forrest, at the heart of the zone, is 35km north of Apollo Bay (p122) on the Great Ocean Road ride.

Lysterfield Park Mountain Bike Trails & State Mountain Bike Course

Lysterfield's 20km of trails were designed with an eye on long-term environmental sustainability. The 2006 Commonwealth Games mountain bike events were held here, so test yourself against winning times. Lysterfield is 35km southeast of Melbourne.

You Yangs Regional Park

The 50km of track designed specifically for fire tyres will put everyone to the test, regardless of skill level. Trails are signposted with names and difficulty. Check Park Victoria's online You Yangs park notes since trail redevelopment has meant changes to access. The You Yangs are between Melbourne and Geelong, just west of Little River.

TOWNS & FACILITIES

APOLLO BAY

☎ 03 / pop 1800

Once a fishing town, beautiful Apollo Bay was never going to be a secret for long. At the base of the Otway Ranges, with a backdrop of steep, cleared hills, the crayfish port is reminiscent of seaside villages of Scotland and Wales. Fortunately, despite creeping development and the now-famous **Apollo Bay Music Festival** (www .apollobaymusicfestival.com.au) that attracts thousands over a weekend in March/April, it has kept its charm.

Apollo Bay is the closest point along the GOR to the town of Forrest, synonymous in Victoria with quality mountain biking in Great Otway National Park (see p142).

Information

The **visitors centre** (☎ 1300 689 297; www .visitapollobay.com; 100 Great Ocean Rd) is right on the foreshore and has displays on Aboriginal history, rainforests, shipwrecks and the building of the GOR.

Banks with ATMs are alll along Great Ocean Rd.

Supplies & Equipment

Basic bike parts are sold at **Apollo Bay Sports Store** (☎ 03-5237 6434, 39 Great Ocean Rd); but you're on your own for repairs.

If you want to head into the hills, for convenient rentals, try **Apollo Bay Surf & Kayak** (☎ 0405-495 909; www .apollobaysurfkayak.com.au; 157 Great Ocean Rd; two/five/eight hours $10/18/30, two days $45), almost directly opposite the visitors centre.

Otway Eco Tours (☎ 03-5236 6345; www.platypustours.net.au) has gear more specifically attuned to Forrest MTB forays (half/full day hire $30/50) and can supply transport for a $5 charge to the top of Mount Sabine.

Sleeping & Eating

Marengo Holiday Park (☎ 03-5237 6162; www.marengopark.com.au; unpowered/powered sites from $24/25, d on-site caravans/cabins from $70/93) Just 2km west of town by the beach, this campsite is meticulously run and has good facilities.

Eco Beach YHA (☎ 03-5237 7899; www .yha.com.au; 5 Pascoe St; dm/r from $32/88) Fits into its natural surroundings with every ecological care.

Iluka Motel (☎ 03-5237 6531; 65–71 Great Ocean Rd; s/d from $80/100) The most economical motel in town, Iluka is all the better for its central location and attached restaurant (mains $15 to $20).

Buffs Bistro & Bar (☎ 03-5237 6403; 51 Great Ocean Rd; lunch & dinner) May be small but boasts delicious Asian-style dishes.

Café Nautigals (57 Great Ocean Rd; mains $12-20) This cafe has been a local hero, pleasing punters with its Asian grub for years.

Craypot Bistro (☎ 03-5237 6250; www .apollobayhotel.com.au; 95_101 Great Ocean Rd; mains $20-31; lunch & dinner) Tucked away in the Apollo Bay Hotel, the Craypot satisfies that seafood urge.

The **bakery** (125–129 Great Ocean Rd) opens from 7am and the **IGA supermarket** (77 Great Ocean Rd) is licensed.

ARARAT
☎ 03 / pop 8215

This agricultural town lies between the Grampians and the Pyrenees Ranges. The squatter Horatio Wills camped on the Black Range and named the peak Mt Ararat, because 'like the Ark, we have rested here'. With the discovery of the world's richest shallow alluvial goldfields in 1857, the town, founded by Chinese prospectors, prospered. As the centre of a rich pastoral region, it continued to grow even after the boom went bust. Ararat is still a rural service centre, although it also depends on tourism.

Information

The **visitors centre** (☎ 1800 657 158; www .ararat.vic.gov.au; 91 High St) is in the train station and has an excellent panorama of the region's attractions, including a brief presentation on recommended cycling routes in the district and lots about the surrounding Grampian wine region.

Most banks can be found in Barkly St, the main commercial strip.

Supplies & Equipment

The friendly staff at **Lardner Bros** (☎ 03-5253 1074; www.lardnerbros.com.au; 2 Ingor St) offer a range of bike parts and full repair service.

Sleeping & Eating

At **Green Hill Lake**, 2.5km east of town on Western Hwy, there's free camping with access to an amenities block.

Acacia Caravan Park (☎ 03-5352 2994; www.acaciatouristpark.com; 6 Acacia Ave; unpowered/powered sites from $20/24, cabins from $70) Offers a serviced shady space in a relaxed setting. There's even a solar-heated swimming pool.

Shire Hall Hotel (☎ 03-5352 1280; www .shirehallhotel.com.au; 240 Barkly St; s/d $30/40) Has traditional but comfy pub-style rooms with shared lounge and bathroom. See Namaskaar Restaurant on p144 for a review of the hotel's restaurant.

Ararat Hotel (☎ 03-5352 2477; 130 Barkly St; s/d $40/55) Serves the busiest part of Barkly St. Its rooms are pleasant and you couldn't be closer to the best bistro (mains around $17) in town.

Waack's Bakery (☎ 03-5352 1744; 74 Barkly St; mains $12-20; breakfast & lunch Thu-Mon) Crowned the 2008 winner of Australia's best vanilla slice, this high-achieving bakery also has gold-medal meat pies.

Fish on Barkly (☎ 03-5352 7358; 262 Barkly St; mains $12-20; lunch & dinner) This is quality takeaway, especially the fish 'n' chips cooked in cholesterol-free oil.

Ararat Golden Dragon (☎ 03-5352 3311; 190 Barkly St; mains $12-17; closed lunch & dinner Wed-Mon) Serving good takeaway and eat-in Chinese meals.

Namaskaar Restaurant (☎ 03-5352 7766; mains $14 to $20) The Shire Hall Hotel's restaurant whips up very tasty Indian dinners.

There are **Coles** and **Aldi** supermarkets near the intersection of Vincent and Moore Sts. For daily fresh local produce, also try **Ararat Fruit Basket** (☎ 03-5352 1001; 234–238 Barky St).

BAIRNSDALE
☎ 03 / pop 11,300
On the banks of the Mitchell River, Bairnsdale is East Gippsland's commercial hub. Here also you'll find the MacLeod Morass wetlands, a reminder of what existed before European settlement. Cattle, gold, then crops (hops and grains) and, later, dairying, have profoundly altered the natural landscape since the 19th century.

Information
The **visitors centre** (☎ 1800 637 060, 03-5152 3444; www.discovereastgippsland .com.au; 240 Main St) is well stocked for general information, but has few resources for cyclists.

Given the remote roads ahead, you may wish to visit **Parks Victoria** for more information (☎ 03-5152 0600; 73 Calvert St; 8.30am-5pm Mon-Fri).

A block down Main St are the major banks (with ATMs).

Supplies & Equipment
Riviera Cycles (☎ 03-5152 1886; www .rivieracycles.com.au; 193 Main St) isn't far from the visitors centre. **Rawsons Bikes** (☎ 03-5152 3333; www.rawsonsbikes

.bikeit.com.au; 157 Main St) is just a few doors down. Between the two of them, you parts and repair needs can be met. Rawsons may have hire bikes, but only in very small numbers.

Sleeping & Eating
Mitchell Gardens Holiday Park (☎ 03-5152 4654; www.mitchellgardens.com.au; unpowered/powered sites $21/24, cabins $52-144) A friendly park with plenty of shade, it's east of the centre on the banks of the Mitchell River.

Grand Terminus Hotel (☎ 03-5152 4040; www.grandterminus.com.au; cnr MacLeod & Service Sts; s/d $50/60) A welcome surprise, the Grand Terminus puts clean and comfortable rooms into circulation at real budget rates. The bustling bistro (mains $14 to $30) churns out sizable dishes from a menu with considerable choice.

Travellers Rest Motel (☎ 03-5152 3200; www.travellersrestmotel.com.au; 49 Main St; s/d $69/79) Family-owned, this place has a real motel feel to it, but lies conveniently within a stone's throw of the town centre.

Riversleigh Country Hotel (☎ 03-5152 6966; www.riversleigh.info; 1 Nicholson St; s/d incl breakfast from $125/130) A heritage-listed Victorian-era boutique hotel. Its formal restaurant (mains $25 to $33), open lunch and dinner Monday to Saturday, champions the use of local ingredients.

AJ's Pizza (☎ 03-5152 4845; 87 Main St) One among the dozens of fast-food places around town, AJ's serves pasta as well as the requisite pizza.

Georges (229 Main St) Has good burgers and souvlaki.

Peppers (☎ 03-5152 3217; 222 Main St) Perfects the contemporary fish and chip by adding flair to the usual offerings.

Gourmet Deli (☎ 03-5152 1544; 144 Main St; dishes $6-10; lunch Mon-Fri) This deli takes coffee seriously, and you're encouraged to specify precisely how you like it. Gourmet sandwich ingredients are served up in thick crusty bread.

To stock up on supplies try the **Coles** (96–118 Main St) or **Aldi** (132 Nicholson St) supermarket, the latter visible behind the visitors centre.

BEECHWORTH
☎ 03 / pop 3250

Beechworth is a living legacy of the 1860s gold-rush era. Once the administrative centre of the Northeast's lucrative mining areas, Beechworth prospers today as a tourist town with a distinctive heritage-listed historic and cultural precinct (www .beechworthprecinct.com.au). Among the town's historic buildings are the courthouse and jail where Ned Kelly was charged and remanded for murder.

Information
The **visitors centre** (☎ 1300 366 321; www .beechworthonline.com.au; 103 Ford St), in the Old Shire Hall, has lots of information on hand and can book accommodation and activities.

Westpac and the **newsagent**, both in Ford St, have the town's ATMs.

Supplies & Equipment
Beechworth Cycles & Saws (☎ 03-5728 1402; 17 Camp St; WGB) has a subtly serious supply of bike parts and the wherewithal to use them. Bike hire is also possible ($20/30 per half/full day).

Now that you've got knobbies, want to find some dirt? The **Beechworth Chain Gang** (www.beechworthchaingang.com) is one of the largest mountain bike clubs in the region and looks after the Beechworth Mountain Bike Park (see p142).

Sleeping & Eating
Lake Sambell Caravan Park (☎ 03-5728 1421; www.caravanparkbeechworth.com.au; Peach Dr; unpowered/powered sites from $11/21, on-site caravans/cabins from $70; WGB) Occupies a shady park with great facilities next to beautiful Lake Sambell.

Old Priory (☎ 03-5728 1024; www .oldpriory.com.au; 8 Priory Lane; dm/s/d $40/50/80, cottages incl breakfast $115; WGB) In a converted historic convent, these are the cheapest digs in Beechworth. Its lovely gardens and rooms are often overrun by school groups.

Tanswells Commercial Hotel (☎ 03-5728 1480; 50 Ford St; s/d incl breakfast $50/70) Tanswells opened its doors in 1852 and now boasts cosy, comfortable rooms (with shared bathroom facilities) and a great community vibe. It has a

seasonal bistro menu that uses local produce (mains $16 to $26), open for lunch and dinner.

Beechworth Bakery (☎ 03-5728 1132; 27 Camp St; 6am-7pm) Famous and worthy of its reputation; the beestings (yeasted, almond-topped custard cakes) are a knockout.

Beechworth Pizza (☎ 03-5728 1062; 3 Camp St; large $12-15; dinner) A pizza in this establishment shouldn't make you smirk. Like everything else in town, it's gourmet.

Gigi's (☎ 03-5728 2575; www .gigisofbeechworth.com; 69 Ford St; mains $30-34; Fri-Wed) A restaurant that is Italian by name but Mod Oz by nature. It's top-notch stuff, with a hint of attitude.

The **IGA** supermarket (Ford St) is open daily, as is **Beechworth Provender** (☎ 03-5728 2650; 18 Camp St), a gourmet deli specialising in local produce.

BENDIGO
☎ 03 / pop 94,000

This lively provincial centre was once one of Australia's richest gold-mining towns. From 1851 onwards, thousands converged on the bountiful diggings, and mining companies poured money into the town, resulting in the Victorian architecture that graces it today. By the 1860s diggers were no longer tripping over surface nuggets and deep mining began. Local legend has it that you can walk underground from one side of the town to the other.

Now a self-declared Centre of Cycling, Bendigo is a cyclist's city, crisscrossed by paths that lead to great trails in the surrounding bush. The city also hosts several major annual cycling events. **Cyclismo** (www.cyclismo.com.au), held in November, takes over the town for two days of professional road races, challenge rides open to enthusiasts, inner-city MTB heats and a bike festival. The **Bendigo International Madison** (www.madison.org.au), on the Labour Day weekend, is one of Australia's biggest cycling events, focusing on the bewildering Madison race but also including community rides.

Information
The **visitors centre** (☎ 1800 813 153, 03-5434 6060; www.bendigotourism.com; 51

Pall Mall) is a large facility with informative dioramas, on the ground floor of the historic former post office. The mere mentioning of cycling elicits an excited response from staff, now that Bendigo is the self-declared Centre of Cycling. Check out the city-sanctioned www.cyclingbendigo.com.au. The best bike map of town is TravelSmart's *City of Greater Bendigo*. Also good are the two *Experience Bendigo Outdoors* maps, one for the city and the other for the surrounding parks and forests.

Mitchell St is the site of several banks with ATMs.

Supplies & Equipment

Bendigo's four bike shops are neighbours in the CBD. Try **Moroni's Bikes** (☎ 03-5443 9644; 104 Mitchell St), which can handle all needs, including bike hire (about $25 per day).

Sleeping & Eating

There's an accommodation booking service at the visitors centre.

Central City Caravan Park (☎ 1800 500 475; www.centralcitycaravanpark.com .au; 362 High St, Golden Sq; unpowered/ powered sites from $21/26, cabins from $62) This is the closest campsite to town, 2.5km northeast of the centre.

Bendigo Backpackers (☎ 03-5443 7680; 33 Creek St South; dm/s/d $27/46/64) A small, homey YHA-affiliated hostel in a weatherboard cottage. The interior has been opened up to make bright cheery rooms.

Fleece Inn (☎ 03-5443 3086; www .thefleeceinn.com.au; 139 Charleston Rd; dm/s/d incl breakfast $33/50/75) This may be a 140-year-old ex-pub, but the refurbished interior and huge back courtyard with lounge area are as contemporary as can be.

Gillies' (Hargreaves St Mall) The pies from Gillies' are a Bendigo institution and among the best in Australia.

Clogs (☎ 03-5443 0077; www .clogsrestaurant.com.au; 106 Pall Mall; pizzas $12-22, mains $16-29; dinner) A long-time local favourite, it's a licensed restaurant open late.

Typhoon Café-Restaurant (☎ 03-5443 3111; 95 Mitchell St; mains $16-22; dinner) Serving contemporary Thai and Asian cuisine, Typhoon is modern yet relaxed and informal.

Bridge Bendigo (☎ 03-5443 7811 www.thebridgebendigo.com.au; 49 Bridge St; bistro mains $16-24; lunch & dinner) Perhaps the best restaurant in Bendigo. The bistro prices are half those in the restaurant but the food is just as good.

For food and other supplies, the **Coles** (cnr Williamson & Myers Sts) is across the street from **Bendigo Wholefoods**.

BRIGHT
☎ 03 / pop 2700

In the upper reaches of the Ovens River and surrounded by the foothills of the High Country, the pretty, leafy town of Bright thrives as a centre for outdoor activity, including cycling. It's busy year-round, but particularly in autumn when the deciduous trees paint the country dazzling shades of red, orange and yellow.

Bright is the base for Audax Australia's **Alpine Classic** (see p107), held in January every year. If around in December, watch the **Tour of Bright** (www.tourofbright .com.au) speed by.

Information

Bright's accredited **visitors centre** (☎ 1800 111 885; www.visitalpinevictoria.com .au; 119 Gavan St) has a wide range of printed material, as well as Parks Victoria information. If you're commencing the Across the High Country ride (p136), get your maps here.

There are a number of banks in Gavan St, most of which have ATM's.

Supplies & Equipment

CyclePath (☎ 03-5750 1442; www .cyclepath.com.au; 74 Gavan St) does repairs, spares, tours and bike hire (from $16/28 per hour/day, depending on the bike). Bright is surrounded by forest, with myriad dirt paths open to mountain bikes. The board on the front of the shop details regular rides open to all. For a real workout head, up Mt Buffalo.

Bright Disposals & Outdoor Centre (☎ 03-5755 1818; 9 Ireland St) sells a variety of outdoor and camping equipment.

Sleeping & Eating

Bright Escapes (☎ 03-5755 2275; www .brightescapes.com.au; 76a Gavan St) If a bed is eluding you, Bright Escapes can help.

Bright Caravan Park (☎ 03-5755 1141; www.brightcaravanpark.com.au; 1 Cherry Ave; unpowered/powered sites from $24/28, cabins from $65) Occupies a shady location beside Morses Creek only three minutes' walk from the shops.

Bright Hikers Backpackers' Hostel (☎ 03-5750 1244; www.brighthikers.com .au; 4 Ireland St; dm/s/d $25/38/60) Budget accommodation with a cosy atmosphere and great veranda overlooking the main shopping street.

Elm Lodge Motel (☎ 03-5755 1144; www.elmlodge.com.au; 2 Wood St; s/d from $70/75; WGB) In a restored 1950s pine mill amid pleasant gardens.

Bright Bakery (☎ 03-5750 1128; 80 Gavan St) Sells a huge range of breads, and wonderful pies and pasties.

Jackie's (☎ 03-5750 1303; 6 Ireland St; breakfasts $4-15, mains $5-15; breakfast & lunch) Serves delicious breakfasts and cakes, and fabulous damper.

Tin Dog Café & Pizzeria (☎ 03-5755 1526; cnr Gavan & Barnard Sts; pizzas $14-20, mains $18-25; breakfast, lunch & dinner) Popular with outdoor enthusiasts at any time of year, but particularly in summer.

Cosy Kangaroo (☎ 03-5750 1838; 96 Gavan St; mains $18-25) A great place for burgers, pancakes and lime-spiders.

For food and other provisions, the **IGA** (16 Ireland St) is open until 9pm.

CASTLEMAINE
☎ 03 / pop 7300

The area around Castlemaine and Chewton was one of the world's richest shallow alluvial goldfields. The discovery of the gold in 1851 unleashed a flood of 30,000 diggers. The town grew up around the government camp and soon became the marketplace for all the goldfields of central Victoria. Today Castlemaine's a relaxed country town with other riches: a significant arts community, several galleries and, in odd-numbered years, the **Castlemaine State Festival** (www.castle mainefestival.com.au), a leading arts festival held in March or April. Less widely known is the wealth of mountain biking opportunities in the region's state forests. For more on this, contact the **Rocky Riders Mountain Bike Club** (www.rocky riders.com).

Information

The **visitors centre** (☎ 1800 171 888, 03-5470 6200; www.maldoncastlemaine .com; Mostyn St) occupies the stunning Castle-maine market building. It has a whole rack of suggested walks but little about cycling.

Banks with ATMs are on Barker and Mostyn Sts.

Supplies & Equipment

Castlemaine Cycles (☎ 03-5470 5868; 28 Hargraves St) and the **Bike Vault** (☎ 03-5470 6333; 220 Barker St) both have parts. repairs and mountain-biking advice, but neither has hires available.

Sleeping & Eating

Mount Alexander Shire Council provides a free **accommodation booking service** (☎ 1800 171 888).

Castlemaine Gardens Caravan Park (☎ 03-5472 1125; www.cgcp.com.au; 18 Walker St; unpowered/powered sites $22/25, cabins from $55) Ideally situated in a leafy park next to the Botanic Gardens and public swimming pool.

Northern Hotel (☎ 03-5472 1102; 359 Barker St; d $60) One kilometre north of Castlemaine's centre, the Northern has the cheapest rooms in town – basic and clean with shared bathrooms.

Campbell Street Motor Lodge (☎ 03-5472 3477; www.campbellstlodge.com. au; 33 Campbell St; s/d from $75/95) A National Trust–classified building, it wraps modern comforts in the charm of the old world.

Theatre Royal (☎ 03-5472 3913; www .theatreroyal.info; 28 Hargreaves St; mains $18-30; lunch Wed-Fri, dinner Wed-Sat) Set in one of Australia's oldest theatres.

Saff's Café (☎ 03-5470 6722; 64 Mostyn St; mains $12-26) Serves excellent homemade bread, cakes and savouries, the best coffee in town and interesting meals.

Papas Fish Shop (☎ 03-5472 2974; 99 Moyston St) and **Blue Sea Fish Shop** (☎ 03-5472 1194; 91 Moyston St) are almost next door to each other, both serving good fish and chips, and hamburgers.

The **IGA supermarket** (cnr Mostyn & Hargraves Sts) is the place to go for ride supplies.

VICTORIA

DAYLESFORD
☎ 03 / pop 2100

Set among the idyllic hills, lakes and forests of the central highlands, delightful Daylesford's prosperous past is evident in its well-preserved architecture. The Hepburn mineral springs, discovered (before gold) in 1836, made the area a popular health resort by the 1870s. Today Daylesford and neighbouring Hepburn Springs are still the 'Spa Centre of Victoria', attracting droves of fashionable Melburnians. If you need a soak or a massage, this is the place to get it – ask the visitors centre for a list of practitioners.

Information
The staff at the **visitors centre** (☎ 03-5321 6100; www.visitdaylesford.com; 98 Vincent St) are both knowledgeable and helpful, even though there are no cycling-specific resources. Banks with ATMs are on Vincent St.

Sleeping & Eating
It's best to book ahead, but if you're caught short, the **Daylesford Accommodation Booking Service** (☎ 03-5348 1448; www.escapesdaylesford.com.au; 94 Vincent St) is open until about 6pm most nights.

Daylesford Victoria Caravan Park (☎ 03-5348 3821; www.familyparks.com.au; Ballan Rd; unpowered/powered sites from $25/27, cabins $65-160) Daylesford's closest campsite, 1.7km south of town, is in a quiet botanical parkland setting.

Wildwood Youth Hostel (☎ 03-5348 4435; www.yha.com.au; 42 Main Rd, Hepburn Springs; dm/s/d from $27/40/64) A charming cottage with a homey lounge room and garden views. You'd never know it was a youth hostel.

Continental House (☎ 03-5348 2005; www.continentalhouse.com.au; 9 Lone Pine Ave, Hepburn Springs; s/d incl breakfast $45/80) A rambling, timber 'vegan life sanctuary' with a laid-back alternative vibe and a cafe (mains $20). Choose between a room and a more exotic teepee.

Daylesford Hotel (☎ 03-5348 2335; www.daylesfordhotel.com.au; cnr Albert & Howe Sts; d $66) Standing grandly in the centre of town, the old pub has small neat rooms and a cosy common area. The bar and restaurant (mains $16 to $27) are frequented by locals and visitors alike.

Himalaya Bakery (☎ 03-5348 1267; www.himalayabakery.com; 73 Vincent St) A standout for its healthy, organic breads – even by Daylesford standards, which has the highest concentration of good bakeries for miles.

Harvest Café (☎ 03-5348 4022; 29 Albert St; mains $25-35; breakfast & lunch daily, dinner Sat) Enjoy the fantastic retro feel, good music, blackboard specials and excellent food, with good vegetarian options.

Koukla Café (☎ 03-5348 2363; www.frangosandfrangos.com; 82 Vincent St; mains $18-30) Ensconced in a corner building that's had a groovy refit, the cafe serves light meals next door to the Frangos & Frangos main dining room.

The central **IGA** supermarket has entrances on Vincent and Albert Sts.

DUNKELD
☎ 03 / pop 450

Idling contentedly at the southern tip of the Grampians and the Great Dividing Range is this tiny country town. It has dreamy views of Mt Sturgeon and Mt Abrupt – best beheld at sunrise or sunset, when they're practically aglow – and a reputation for friendly welcome that has created a faithful following. Dunkeld sheds its reserve the second Saturday of each November, when the Dunkeld Races gallop into town.

Information
The **visitors centre** (☎ 03-5577 2558; Glenelg Hwy) is a friendly community-run clearinghouse of local information. The post office, also a Commonwealth Bank agent, is on Wills St. There's an ATM at the Royal Mail Hotel.

Sleeping & Eating
Dunkeld Caravan Park (☎ 03-5577 2578; cnr Glenelg Hwy & Victoria Valley Rd; unpowered/powered sites from $15/22, on-site caravans from $30, cabins from $75) A community-managed facility on the trail to the town's awesome arboretum.

Dunkeld Bunkhouse (☎ 03-9561 6863; off William St; dm $25) A cosy backpacker option off the main drag. Its views of the mountains are arresting.

Southern Grampians Cottages (☎ 03-5577 2457; www.grampianscottages.

.au; Victoria Valley Rd; d $110-190) Spend the night in lovely stand-alone cottages grouped around a shaded bush garden.

Royal Mail Hotel (☎ 03-5577 2241; www .royalmail.com.au; Glenelg Hwy; r $140-290) It ain't cheap, but the Royal Mail is one of a kind, especially its multiple-award-winning restaurant (fixed-price gourmet meals for vegetarians $110, carnivores $150) with one of Australia's best wine cellars. The bistro (mains $22 to $30) serves substantial meals as well.

The **general store** and **Mountain View Café** (for takeaway) close at 7pm.

GEELONG
☎ 03 / pop 209,000

Geelong, on Corio Bay, is Victoria's largest provincial city. Much like nearby Melbourne, Geelong boomed during the gold rush. Its fortunes then shifted to wool and giant wool stores – many, now converted to offices, still line Eastern Beach. After WW1, automotive, aluminium and chemical industries established a strong industrial base. The town suffered a major financial collapse in the late 1980s but is slowly recovering. It is now the state's busiest port and attracts heavy industry. Even with recent beautification along Corio Bay designed to boost tourism, smokestacks loom over Geelong's otherwise attractive beaches.

Geelong was the first Victorian town to produce a bike plan (in 1978) and places a strong emphasis on ensuring cycling is feasible and safe. The Industrial Heritage Track along the Barwon River is a recommended ride. Brochures are available from the visitors centre.

Information

The most convenient of four **visitors centres** (☎ 1800 620 888, 03-5222 2900; www.visitgeelong.org; 26 Moorabool St) is in the National Wool Museum, located in the restored Dennys Lascelles Wool Store. It has a comprehensive range of maps (get the free and indispensable *Geelong Official Tourist Map*) and brochures, notably cycling guides. Ask for the *Walk or Ride the City of Greater Geelong* map.

In November the Geelong Touring Cyclists group runs the 160km **Otway Classic**, a fund-raising circuit ride through the Otway Ranges via Lorne.

Supplies & Equipment

The **Bicycle Factory** (☎ 03-5222 1363; 380a Latrobe Tce) isn't far from the visitors centre and has accessories, repair and advice for touring cyclists. For bike hire, **Future Rentals** (☎ 03-5221 0100; www.futurerentals.com.au; 42–46 Autumn St; $15 per day) will deliver and pick up anywhere in the Geelong area.

Sleeping & Eating

National Hotel Backpackers (☎ 03-5229 1211; www.nationalhotel.com.au; 191 Moorabool St; dm/d $22/50) This is central Geelong's only backpacker accommodation, with live bands providing a taste of the city's music scene.

Riverglen Holiday Park (☎ 03-5243 3788; www.riverglenhp.com.au; 87 Barrabool Rd; unpowered/powered sites from $24/32, cottages $70-125) Right on the banks of the Barwon River.

Gatehouse on Ryrie (☎ 0417-545 196; www.bol.com.au/gatehouse/g.html; 83 Yarra St; incl breakfast s $80, d $95-120) A central, rambling guesthouse with a shared kitchen and sitting room.

Irrewarra Sourdough Café (☎ 03-5221 3909; www.irrewarra.com.au; 10 James St; mains $10-18; breakfast & lunch Mon-Fri) Makes some of the best bread in town and serves it up in wholesome sandwiches or as delicious breakfast toast.

Lamby's (☎ 03-5223 2536; www.lambys .com.au; cnr Moorabool & Brougham Sts; mains $17-29; breakfast & lunch daily, dinner Thu-Sat) Upstairs at the National Wool Museum, Lamby's has a tranquil atmosphere, in contrast with the downstairs bar.

Wharf Shed Café (☎ 03-5221 6645; www .wharfshedcafe.com.au; 15 Eastern Beach St; mains $18-28) Right on the waterfront, the Wharf Shed attracts a large passing crowd (and seagulls) with reasonable fare and the odd surprise.

The closest and most central supermarkets are the **Coles** (cnr Moorabool & Brougham Sts), in the Bay City Plaza Shopping Centre, and **Foodworks** (259 Myers St).

HALLS GAP
☎ 03 / pop 300

Pinched between the Wonderland Range and the northern tail of the Mt William

VICTORIA

Range, pretty Halls Gap is a popular base for exploring the Grampians. So popular, in fact, that Halls Gap and its environs host more overnight visitors than any other Victorian destination. Only the Great Ocean Rd (p122) sees more visitors (day-trippers). It's named after Charles Hall, a squatter who explored tracks through the gap where Fyans Creek emerges from the Mt William Range. Now a singular tourist town, Halls Gap is unobtrusive and likeable. The January 2006 bushfires that devastated the Grampians nearly engulfed the town too.

Information

The **visitors centre** (☎ 1800 065 599; www.visithallsgap.com.au; Grampians Rd) has lots of printed information and a free accommodation booking service. A Parks Victoria visitors centre is in the **Brambuk Cultural Centre** (☎ 03-5361 4000; www.brambuk.com.au; 277 Grampians Rd; 9am-5pm daily), 2.5km south of Halls Gap, and can provide additional details and maps for mountain biking (which is permitted, but only on certain roads).

There's an ANZ ATM right on Grampians Rd.

Supplies & Equipment

Absolute Outdoors (☎ 03-5356 4556; www.absoluteoutdoors.com.au; 105 Grampians Rd) hires mountain bikes (half/full day $25/40) and may be able to help with mechanical needs if you're in a bind. The **general store** (☎ 03-5356 4247; Grampians Rd; 7am-10pm) has a modicum of camping gear.

Sleeping & Eating

Halls Gap Caravan Park (☎ 03-5356 4251; www.hallsgapcaravanpark.com.au; Grampians Tourist Rd; unpowered/powered sites from $20/25; on-site caravans $50-70, cabins $80-129) As central as a GPO but a little spartan.

Grampians YHA Eco-Hostel (☎ 03-5356 4544; www.yha.com.au; cnr Buckler St & Grampians Rd; dm/s/d $30/64/78) Counted among the best YHA hostels in Australia – purpose-built, architecturally designed and eco-friendly.

Pinnacle Holiday Lodge (☎ 03-5356 4249; www.pinnacleholiday.com.au; 21–45 Heath St; r from $95) The Pinnacle has the wonderful knack of being both central and well hidden, tucked away behind Stony Creek Stores. The indoor pool's a big bonus.

Halls Gap Hotel (☎ 03-5356 4566; 2262 Grampians Rd; mains $15-25; lunch & dinner) Serves generous portions of well-prepared pub food. It's about the best value in town, so book ahead.

Kookaburra Restaurant (☎ 03-5356 4222; www.kookarest.com.au; 125–127 Grampians Rd; mains $18-31; lunch Sat & Sun, dinner Tue-Sun) You'll need to reserve a table at this restaurant, which favours local produce to create a popular and extensive menu.

Quarry Restaurant (☎ 03-5356 4858; www.quarryrestaurant.com.au; Shop 10, Stony Creek Shops, Grampians Rd; mains $16-35; brunch Sun, dinner Wed-Mon) Offers excellent cuisine that ranges the globe.

Brambuk Bush Tucker Cafe (☎ 03-5361 4057; Brambuk Cultural Centre, 277 Grampians Rd; mains $8-19; breakfast & lunch until 5pm) This is the place for kangaroo steak sandwiches, emu kebabs and other bush treats.

The **bakery** (☎ 03-5356 4439; Shop 3, Stony Creek Shops, Grampians Rd) opens from 7am. The licensed **general store** (☎ 03-5356 4247; Grampians Rd; 7am-10pm) has a good range of groceries.

HOTHAM
☎ 03 / pop 100

Hotham is Victoria's highest Alpine village, a ski resort spread along 5km of the GAR and surrounded by Alpine National Park. While the original lodges are eyesores, recent ones are more in keeping with a contemporary sense of environmental sensitivity. The 1986 development of Dinner Plain – a stylish purpose-built resort village 11.5km beyond Hotham – was designed to blend in with the surrounding snow gums and high plains backdrop. Outside the ski season, Hotham and Dinner Plain are very quiet. Day-trippers from Bright come here to walk, but at night it's blissfully serene.

Information

The **Mount Hotham Alpine Resort Management Board** (☎ 03-5759 3550; www.mthotham.com.au; 8am-4.30pm Mon-Fri) has a public office that serves as a visitors centre with brochures, maps, guidebooks and friendly staff. Information is also available at the **Dinner Plain visitors centre** (☎ 1300 734 365; www .visitdinnerplain.com).

Cycling is an increasingly popular activity at Hotham. Dinner Plain hosts the three-day **DP Festival of Cycling** (www .hotham.com.au/cycling; Mar), a celebration of high-country pedalling; and **Terra Australia** (www.terraaustralismtbepic .com.au; Mar/Apr), the seven-day, 550km mountain bike epic.

If you're after a more private buzz, **Adventures with Altitude** (☎ 03-5159 6608; www.adventureswithaltitude.com .au; Dinner Plain) can help arrange rides in the area – mountain and downhill biking. It rents all the required equipment (per hour/half day/full day $15/40/60), sells spare parts and does repairs.

Sleeping & Eating

Camping is not permitted at the ski-resort towns of Mt Hotham or Dinner Plain. The nearest option is the bush camp at **JB Plain** on Day 2 of the Across the High Country ride (p136).

Hotham accommodation and restaurant options in summer are a bit limited, although there are additional options at Dinner Plain. On the plus side, the room rates are relatively cheap. Contact **Hotham Holidays** (☎ 1800 HOTHAM; www .hotham.com.au) to confirm availability. If reserving directly with a lodge, always call ahead to provide an estimated time of arrival.

Leeton Lodge (☎ 0407-765 952; www .leetonlodge.com; Dargo Court; r per person $40) Managed by a nonprofit organisation, it provides a very comfortable, friendly, affordable option just five minutes from The General.

Currawong Lodge (☎ 03-5159 6452; www.currawonglodge.com.au; Dinner Plain; s/tw $75/120) About as budget as Dinner Plain gets in summer. There's a huge communal lounge and kitchen area, laundry and a spa for those aching thighs.

Zirky's (☎ 03-5759 4482; www.zirkys. com.au; r $130-150) A step upscale, with luxury apartments built with comfort and views in mind. The Zirky's cafe (mains $10 to $15) is open for breakfast and lunch.

Brandy Creek Café & Supermarket (☎ 03-5159 6488; www.brandycreek.net; cafe 8.30am-4pm, supermarket to 6pm) A self-caterer's resource for a night in Dinner Plain or in anticipation of the Day 2 ride.

The General (☎ 03-5759; www .thegeneral.com.au; 1 Great Alpine Rd; mains $18-28; lunch & dinner) This is Hotham's only reliable bet – and a good one at that – for summer meals and supplies on the mountain. This general shop–cum–pub does tasty pizzas and counter fare, and is a popular watering hole.

Dinner Plain Hotel (☎ 03-5159 6462; www.dinnerplainhotel.com.au; mains $18-27.50; lunch & dinner) Looks somewhat like an overgrown mountain hut, with its split-level interior of huge timber poles and slabs, but the bistro serves good pub grub.

LAVERS HILL
☎ 03 / pop 200

High in the Otway Ranges, Lavers Hill is at the junction of roads to Colac, Apollo Bay and Port Campbell. It's the highest point of the GOR, commanding views of the Southern Ocean towards Johanna. Although once a busy timber town, it is now very, very quiet and has few facilities.

YatZies (☎ 03-5237 3215; yatzie @hotmail.com; Great Ocean Rd; 8.30am-5.30pm Mon-Sat, 9am-5pm Sun) runs the post office, has an ATM, cooks solid breakfasts and takeaway, sells basic groceries and even has a stand with a few brochures about town. Try www .lavershillanddistrict.org too.

Sleeping & Eating

Lavers Hill Roadhouse Caravan Park & Tavern (☎ 03-5237 3251; Great Ocean Rd; sites $15, d $50) It might scare a few people away but really shouldn't. The friendly staff also run a cafe, takeaway and the Foggy Hill Bistro (see p152).

Otway Junction Motor Inn (☎ 03-5237 3295; 4730 Great Ocean Rd; s $89-120, d $98-150) Perched at the edge of the best views of the ride.

Blackwood Gully (☎ 03-5237 3290; www.blackwoodgully.com; 1–15 Great Ocean Rd; mains $13-16; breakfast & lunch) Combines terrace views with tasty home cooking.

VICTORIA

Foggy Hill Bistro (☎ 03-5237 3251; Great Ocean Rd; mains $17-20; lunch & dinner) Try this place for recommended traditional eats.

Otway Junction Bistro ((☎ 03-5237 3295; 4730 Great Ocean Rd; mains $16-33) Adjacent to the Otway Junction Motor Inn, another establishment taking full advantage of the vista.

LORNE
☎ 03 / pop 1200

Approaching Lorne from the south, with views of Loutit Bay framed by the tall eucalypts of the Otways, it's easy to understand why it has always been the most popular holiday destination on this coast. The regular population swells on weekends and during holidays. Most of the action is along Mountjoy Pde, where cafe tables and chairs spill over the footpath.

Information
The **visitors centre** (☎ 03-5289 1152; www.visitlorne.org; 15 Mountjoy Pde) has lots of information about accommodation (necessary in peak season), maps of nearby Great Otway National Park and the free *Cycling the Surf Coast Shire* brochure.

Both **Westpac** (Mountjoy Pde) and **Commonwealth** (Mountjoy Pde) have ATMs.

Supplies & Equipment
There is no bike shop in Lorne, but several companies hire out mountain bikes. You may be able to ask them for some help. Try **Otway Eco Tours** (☎ 03-5236 6345; www .platypustours.net.au; half/full day $30/50), which offers guided tours and can supply transport to the top of Mount Sabine for a $5 charge.

Sleeping & Eating
If without a bed, consult with the visitors centre for frank advice on places around town.

Great Ocean Road Cottages & Back-packers YHA (☎ 03-5289 1070; www.great oceanroadcottages.com, www.yha.com.au; 10 Erskine Ave; on-site tents $20, dm/d from $25/65, cottages from $130) Based around a two-storey timber lodge snuggled into the bush.

Lorne Foreshore Caravan Park (☎ 1300 736 533, 03-5289 1382; www.gorcc.com.au; 2 Great Ocean Rd; unpowered/powered sites from $25/30, on-site caravans/cabins from $50/60) With gum tree–bordered sites by the banks of the river, this is a popular budget choice handy to town and the beach.

Erskine River Backpackers (☎ 03-5289 1496; 6 Mountjoy Pde; dm/d $25/70) With beautiful verandas wrapped around a classic old building just steps from town and on the river.

Loutit Bay Bakery (☎ 03-5289 1207; 46b Mountjoy Pde) Has a fabulous range of breads and pies.

Arab (☎ 03-5289 1435; 94 Mountjoy Pde; mains $10-25) Arab has been the spot for coffee and breakfast since it opened in 1956. There's no fussing with food, just classics like its famous apple crumble.

Lorne Hotel (☎ 03-5289 1409; www .lornehotel.com.au; cnr Mountjoy Pde & Bay St; mains $20-40; lunch & dinner) A refitted pub that serves good bistro meals and occasionally has weekend live music.

For food needs, try **Foodworks** (1 Great Ocean Rd; 8am-7pm).

MALDON
☎ 03 / pop 1600

Declared by the National Trust to be Australia's first 'Notable Town' in 1965, Maldon is a well-preserved relic of the gold-mining era. It certainly makes the most of its old-world charm – much of its historic architecture remains intact – while minimising tackiness. Its population is a fraction of the 20,000 reached during boom times. The tourist town is virtually closed on Monday and Tuesday, since traders work their 'olde worlde' shops over the busy weekend.

Information
In the Shire Gardens, the **visitors centre** (☎ 03-5475 2768; www.maldon castlemaine.com; 93 High St) stocks lots of useful free literature. Ask about trails open to mountain bikes in the adjacent Maldon Historic Reserve. For more information, Maldon Inc's website (www.maldon.org.au) is arguably a better online resource.

Next door to the visitors centre is a Bendigo Bank with ATM. There's another ATM at the newsagent, although Eftpos is possible at the milk bar and Maldon Pharmacy, both on Main St.

Supplies & Equipment

A limited but helpful supply of bike parts is available at the **Central Service Station** (see Sleeping & Eating).

Sleeping & Eating

The Mount Alexander Shire Council provides a free **accommodation booking service** (☎ 1800 171 888), useful during weekends and festivals.

Maldon Camping & Caravan Park (☎ 03-5475 2344; www.mtalexander.com /maldonpark.htm; Hospital St; unpowered/ powered sites from $21/24, on-site caravans from $50, cabins from $70) Straggles up through the bush at the foot of Mt Tarrengower, a short distance from town. It's friendly, homey and has a swimming pool next door.

Central Service Station (☎ 03-5475 2216; 1 Main St; r $88) Also known as **Mrs Gilmore's**, this is an excellent budget option in the unlikely setting of a former garage (the pumps are still out the front).

Maldon's Eaglehawk (☎ 1800 801 017, 03-5475 2750; www.maldoneaglehawk .com; 35 Reef St; s/d from $85/95) Beautiful heritage units are set in delightful grounds with little alcoves overlooking a pool and BBQ nooks. This place has loads of appeal.

Maldon Milk Bar (☎ 03-5475 2282; 27 Main St; mains $6-10) Very affordable takeaway nosh.

Tucci's Pizza (☎ 03-5475 2104; 18 High St; pizzas $9-19; dinner Thu-Mon) Just what the carbo-loader ordered: piping hot pizza and fresh pasta with the choice of dining in.

Two Fat Men (☎ 03-5475 2504; www .twofatmen.com.au; 24 High St; mains $18-29; lunch Thu-Sun, dinner Wed-Sun) Dishes up European-inspired cuisine in light and welcome digs.

For food needs, head to the **IGA** (Main Street) and the nearby **Maldon Historic Bakery** (☎ 03-5475 2713; 51 Main St), which crams fresh goodies into a tiny space.

MARYBOROUGH

☎ 03 / pop 7400

Gold was discovered here in 1854. A police camp at the diggings, named Maryborough after the police commissioner, kept watch over the population of 40,000 at the height of the rush. Today Maryborough has some fine Victorian architecture – its disproportionately massive and magnificent train station is particularly famous – but on the whole it is less of a tourist town than a bustling small city.

Maryborough's annual events include the November **RACV Energy Breakthrough** (www.racvenergybreakthrough.net), which boasts a Human-Powered Vehicle Grand Prix.

Information

The **visitors centre** (☎ 1800 356 511, 03-5460 4511; www.visitmaryborough.com .au; cnr Alma & Nolan Sts) has loads of helpful maps and friendly staff. There is also a **Parks Victoria office** (☎ 03-5461 0800; Office 2, 82 Alma St).

The major banks (with ATMs) are represented in High St, as is **Dragon Cycles** (☎ 03-5460 4854; www.dragoncycles.com .au; 89–91 High St), a full-service bike shop.

Sleeping & Eating

Maryborough Caravan Park (☎ 03-5460 4848; www.maryboroughcaravanpark.com .au; 7 Holyrood St; unpowered/powered sites from $20/24, cabins $60-95) Right in town by Lake Victoria, this is a well-equipped and bike-friendly campsite.

Albion Hotel Motel (☎ 03-5461 1035; 57 High St; s/d from $55/70) Perhaps less noisy than the others, the Albion has motor inn–style units and a family-style bistro (mains $10 to $20), open lunch and dinner.

Wattle Grove Motel (☎ 03-5461 1877; 65 Derby Rd; s/d $75/80) A friendly place with pleasant enough units.

Bull & Mouth Hotel (☎ 03-5461 3636; cnr High & Nolan Sts; d $100) Has a magnificent staircase to match the newly renovated rooms.

Station Café (☎ 03-5461 4683; mains $15-25; lunch Wed-Mon, dinner Thu-Sat) Right at the train station, the Station dishes up generous pasta servings, plus cakes and snacks.

VICTORIA

VICTORIA

CYCLING IN THE CITY

More and more Melburnians are commuting by bike. And well they should. Melbourne has almost 1000km of bikepaths, many following rivers, the bay and disused railway lines that serve as scenic, quiet recreational escapes (although they can be congested at weekends). In the inner city, there's even an excellent network of roads with designated bike lanes. To cap it all off, Melbourne is relatively flat.

Free maps highlighting specific trails can be obtained from Bicycle Victoria (www.bv.com.au), the state's peak cycling body, or sometimes the visitors centre (see Information). The best are the TravelSmart *Walking, Cycling & Public Transport* maps, of which the purple *National Ride to Work Melbourne* folio is the most useful. Three good cycling guides that provide even more direction are: the ubiquitous *Bike Paths Victoria* by Sabey et al; *Where to Ride in Melbourne*, 40 on- and off-road rides reviewed by David Russell; and *Bike Rides Around Melbourne*, 37 routes presented by Julia Blunden.

Inner-city rides include the 30km Capital City Trail and the Anniversary Outer Circle Loop. Melbourne's extended leafy suburbs are traversed by the Main Yarra Trail, Melbourne's premier bikepath and a 33km spin along the Yarra River to Westerfolds Park; and the 28km Maribyrnong River Trail to Brimbank Park (about 28km). Alternatively, bike the Bay Trail, roughly 60km of path along Port Phillip Bay. All of these trails are described in detail on the Bicycle Victoria website (www.bv.com.au). The Main Yarra and Bay Trails are included in the *Bike Riding in Victoria* map folder (see p107), also available on the Bicycle Victoria website.

Access to the hills east of Melbourne is easy using the suburban railway network. Hurstbridge train station is the start of rides to Kinglake, Yarra Glen and Whittlesea. Lilydale and Belgrave train stations give access to the Dandenong Ranges, which have some exciting mountain bike tracks. The popular 40km Warburton Rail Trail starts at Lilydale and follows the Yarra Valley to the foothills of the Yarra Ranges.

Peppa's Restaurant (☎ 03-5461 3833; 1 High St; mains $23-33; dinner Tue-Sat) A carnivore's delight.

Safeway (Tuaggra St) is opposite the **Parkview Bakery & Café** (☎ 03-5461 4655; 21 Tuaggra St), which serves breakfast from 7.30am.

MELBOURNE

☎ 03 / pop 3.806 million

Melbourne keeps some people at arm's length; others it draws in. It's a hot-and-cold thing that extends to the seasons, something even locals love to complain about. Whether it's working with you or against, eating at you or letting you eat at its dazzling diversity of restaurants, playing you or letting you barrack for one its high-loyalty football teams, one thing is certain: Melbourne's a city of cyclists. They're everywhere. And you'll revel in joining the parade.

If you have the time, and it's definitely worth taking it, try out the varied and continuously expanding network of bikepaths that crisscross the city. For more details, see the boxed text above.

Information

The visitors centre (☎ 03-9658 9658; www .visitmelbourne.com; Federation Sq; 9am-6pm) is a superb source of information on Melbourne and the surrounding area. **Best of Victoria** (☎ 03-9928 0000; www.bestof.com .au) has operators on-site to help with bookings of all kinds. There's also a small **visitors booth** (Bourke St Mall, Bourke St; 9am-5pm Mon-Fri, 10am-5pm Sat & Sun) for those wandering the city's maze of laneways.

For sightseeing purposes, choose the *Melbourne Official Visitors' Guide* for its overview of town and the coupons lift-out. For a comprehensive list of activities, get a copy of Lonely Planet's *Melbourne & Victoria*, or its *Melbourne Encounter*. Or try the Friday lift-out Entertainment Guide in *The Age*.

Supplies & Equipment

Abbotsford Cycles (☎ 03-9429 6889; www.abbotsfordcycles.com.au; 27 Swan St, Richmond) prides itself on old-fashioned service and specialises in repairs of any kind to any bike – no hard sell.

For bike purchases, equipment, touring accessories and **rentals**, head to **St Kilda Cycles** (☎ 03-9534 3074; www.stkildacycles .com.au; 150 Barkly St, St Kilda). Bike hires cost $35 to $60 per day or $120 to $200 per week, depending on the steed.

Most of Melbourne's **outdoor equipment shops** are conveniently clustered on Little Bourke St, between Elizabeth and Queen Sts. You'll definitely find what you need if you take a little time to compare quality and price.

Sleeping

Melbourne Connection Travellers Hostel (☎ 03-9642 4464; www.melbourne connection.com; 205 King St; dm $22-28, d $67-80) Follows the small-is-better principle. It's simple, clean, uncluttered and with modern facilities.

Greenhouse Backpacker (☎ 03-9639 6400; www.friendlygroup.com.au; 6/228 Flinders La; dm/s/d incl breakfast $30/65/80) Has a low-key, relaxed vibe. Freebies include pancakes on Sunday, rooftop BBQs and luggage storage.

Olembia Guesthouse (☎ 03-9537 1412; www.olembia.com.au; 96 Barkly St, St Kilda; dm/s/d $30/80/100) Offers impeccably presented rooms at backpacker prices. It's a small, elegant old house with a leafy courtyard out front and a secure bike shed too.

Ashley Gardens Big 4 Holiday Village (☎ 1800 061 444; http://ashley-gardens .vic.big4.com.au; 129 Ashley St, Braybrook; sites $36-47, cabins $55-175) On spacious grounds 9km northwest of the city. Take the Footscray bikepath to the Maribyrnong bikepath. Turn left on Mitchell and then left on Ashley.

City Centre Hotel (☎ 03-9654 5401; www.citycentrebudgethotel.com.au; 22 Little Collins St; r from $90) An intimate, independent and inconspicuous find. All rooms share bathroom facilities, a roof lounge and friendly service.

Jasper Hotel (☎ 03-8327 2777; www .jasperhotel.com.au; 489 Elizabeth St; d from $125) Managed by the YWCA but rebranded and renovated, this is comfortable and chic accommodation – a top mid-range option. Guests get free gym and pool access at the Melbourne City Baths.

Alto Hotel on Bourke (☎ 03-9606 0585; www.altohotel.com.au; 636 Bourke St; r/apt from $155/165) An award-winning, purpose-built 'green' hotel. Rooms are well equipped and light.

Eating

Melbourne's ethnic diversity is reflected in the exhaustive variety of its cuisines. Food is such a local obsession that many believe Melbourne is one of world's great eating cities. Interestingly, some of the best options are away from the centre, but the CBD is certainly spoiled for choice.

The Queen Victoria Market (☎ 03-9320 5822; cnr Victoria & Elizabeth Sts; 6am-2pm Tue-Thu, 6am-6pm Fri, 6am-3pm Sat & 9am-4pm Sun) A self-caterer's slam dunk, with a food hall for breakfast and lunch on-site.

Invita Café (☎ 03-9329 1267; 76 Therry St; mains $10-13; breakfast & lunch) Specialises in organic vegetarian – try the brown rice balls and vegetarian lasagne.

Journal Canteen (☎ 03-9650 4399; 253 Flinders La; mains $15-25; lunch Mon-Fri) Although tucked away up an obscure

CYCLING TO/FROM THE AIRPORT

The 25km between the airport and city are made easy by a quiet bikepath along Moonee Ponds Creek. Leaving the airport, at the first set of lights turn right on Centre Rd (signed 'Tullamarine Precinct'). After two sets of lights take the left ('Airline Maintenance, Keilor') exit of a roundabout onto Melrose Dr, which you follow for about 5.2km. At a roundabout over a railway line, turn left into Mascoma St and then straight into Boeing Dr at the next roundabout. Continue to the car park and rotunda at Moonee Ponds Creek. The bikepath here (turn right) runs south along the west side of the waterway.

At the Flemington Bridge train station, access to North Melbourne is easiest along the bike lane on Flemington Rd. Otherwise the bikepath continues under the City Link freeway to Footscray Rd, where a left onto the Capital City Trail bikepath goes through Docklands, with easy connection to Southern Cross Station and the CBD.

flight of stairs off the CAE building foyer, the Canteen is packed with diners happy to choose from a few fresh and seasonal offerings.

Supper Inn (☎ 03-9663 4759; 15 Celestial Ave; mains $15-30; dinner) This is where the chefs eat when they finish a shift. It's open very late (2.30am) and serves congee, noodles, dumplings and other yummies that really hit the spot.

Mecca Bah (☎ 03-9642 1300; 55a New Quay Promenade, Docklands; mains $17-21; lunch & dinner) To sample Melbourne's Middle East, head west to the Docklands precinct. The Mecca Bah is all warm tagines and Turkish pizzas.

Chocolate Buddha (Federation Sq; mains $15-25; lunch & dinner) Specialises in noodles not chocolate, and appeals for its communal Japanese-style dining room.

Galleon (☎ 03-9534 8934; 9 Carlisle St, St Kilda; meals $7-16; breakfast, lunch & dinner) A local institution just off Acland St, the Galleon has fuelled the creative juices of St Kilda's arts community for years with simple and inexpensive cafe-style food.

Getting There & Away
AIR
Direct domestic and international flights operate out of **Melbourne Airport** (www.melair.com.au; Tullamarine Fwy) in Tullamarine, 22km northwest of the city centre. Some interstate flights use **Avalon Airport** (☎ 1800 282 566; www.avalonairport.com.au; 80 Beach Rd, Lara), 55km southwest.

From Tullamarine the pleasant ride to the city is mainly along bikepaths (see boxed text p155). A toll-inclusive taxi fare over the same ground costs around $50, or $100 from Avalon (taxi vans take boxed bikes).

Skybus (☎ 03-9335 2811; www.skybus.com.au) operates a 24-hour shuttle bus between Tullamarine and Southern Cross (one way $16; 20 minutes; frequent departures).

From Avalon, **Avalon Airport Transfer** (☎ 03-9689 7999; www.sitacoaches.com.au) runs to Southern Cross (one way $20, 50 minutes, meeting every flight). In both cases, space permitting, bagged or boxed bikes travel for free.

BOAT
The overnight **Spirit of Tasmania** (☎ 1800 634 906; www.spiritoftasmania.com.au) crosses the Bass Strait between Port Melbourne and Tasmania's Devonport at 8pm nightly year-round. A bikepath covers the ground between Port Melbourne's Station Pier, Waterfront Place, and the city centre.

BUS
The long-distance bus terminal is at the **Southern Cross Railway Station** (☎ 03-9619 2587; Spencer St, Melbourne). **Greyhound** (☎ 13 14 99; www.greyhound.com.au) and **Premier** (☎ 13 34 10; www.premierms.com.au) both have daily services throughout the state and to other capital cities.

TRAIN
Southern Cross is the main hub for interstate rail travel and Victoria's **V/Line** (☎ 13 61 96; www.vline.com.au), which runs train services between Melbourne and regional Victoria. For bike transport on V/Line trains see boxed text p108.

PORT CAMPBELL
☎ 03 / pop 600
Nestled beneath steep cliffs along Campbells Creek is mild-mannered Port Campbell. Whalers used the bay during the early 19th century, as it was the only coastal shelter between Warrnambool and Apollo Bay. A township was finally established in the 1870s, at first as a fishing village but, with transport connections to Timboon and the opening of the new Ocean Rd, it quickly became a holiday destination. The town's population swells during summer.

Information
The **visitors centre** (☎ 03-5598 6089; www.visit12apostles.com; 26 Morris St) and **Parks Victoria** (☎ 03-5558 6333) share a building.

The **general store** (Lord St) houses the post office, which is a Commonwealth Bank agency. There's also an ATM.

Supplies & Equipment
Although there's no bike shop, **Crater to Coast Bicycle Hire** (☎ 0438-407 777; timboontaxi@reachnet.com.au), run by Timboon Taxi, offers rentals (half/full day

$20/30). It delivers and picks up anywhere in the Camperdown Timboon Rail Trail local area, including Port Campbell.

Sleeping & Eating

Port Campbell Holiday Park (☎ 03-5598 6492; www.pchp.com.au; 1 Morris St; unpowered/powered sites from $22/27, cabins from $80) Neat, small and a two-minute walk to the beach and bottom end of town. The preference is for two-night stays.

Port Campbell Hostel (☎ 03-5598 6305; www.portcampbellhostel.com.au; 18 Tregea St; dm $23) A rustic-looking hostel with good dorms. It's in a central spot and has a huge communal area. Bookings are essential.

Port Campbell Guesthouse (☎ 0407-696 559; 54 Lord St; s $40, d $70-80 incl breakfast) A convivial place just a hop from the centre with a comfortable common room and full kitchen.

Craypot Bistro (☎ 03-5598 6320; 40 Lord St; mains $18-30; lunch & dinner) Inside the Port Campbell Hotel, the Craypot serves excellent bistro meals in a busy, all-welcome kind of way.

Splash (☎ 03-5598 6408; 26 Lord St; mains $19-22; breakfast & dinner) Upstairs from Koo-Ahh Café, Splash prepares delicious vegetarian curries.

Waves (☎ 03-5598 6111; www.wavesportcampbell.com.au; 29 Lord St; mains $21-30) This just may be the town's best eatery. It excels at seafood and meat, but doesn't have much for vegetarians.

RUTHERGLEN

☎ 02 / pop 2500

On the floodplains of the Murray River and dating from gold-rush days, Rutherglen is at the centre of one of the oldest wine-growing areas in Australia. Famous for big red wines, it also produces a range of quality table wines. There is perhaps no better way to enjoy them than by bike. The region is relatively flat, the roads quiet and fresh air does wonders for a fuddled brain. Some lovely picnic areas have been created among the red gums on the Murray River floodplains.

The popularity of Rutherglen as a destination for wine lovers has resulted in, among other activities, the **Tour de Rutherglen**, a fundraising bike tour held the first weekend in October (contact the visitors centre for details).

Information

The **visitors centre** (☎ 1800 622 871, 03-6033 6300; www.rutherglenvic.com; 57 Main St) offers an accommodation referral service and hires bikes (half/full day $25/35). As a wine experience centre, it also provides information about Rutherglen's wineries. For inspiration (see boxed text p132), ask to look at the set of Rutherglen Cycle Routes or download them in advance (www.rutherglenvic.com/visitorinfo/default.asp).

There's an ATM on the corner of High and Main Sts, as well as others in pubs.

Basic spares and a hand with simple bike repairs are available at the **BP Service Station** (☎ 03-6032 8663; Main St).

Sleeping & Eating

Rutherglen Caravan & Tourist Park (☎ 03-6032 8577; www.rutherglencaravanandtouristpark.com; 72 Murray St; unpowered/powered sites from $17.50/24, d cabins $51-115) A well-serviced park on the banks of Lake King.

Victoria Hotel (☎ 03-6032 8610; www.victoriahotelrutherglen.com.au; 90 Main St; s/d incl breakfast from $35/60; WGB) This beautiful old National Trust–classified place doesn't show its age. Dinner mains cost around $20 in the hotel restaurant. If you're planning to stay in Rutherglen for a couple of nights, try the Cycle Special Accommodation Package and ask about the Cycle Concierge program.

Wine Village Motor Inn (☎ 03-6032 9900; www.winevillagemotorinn.com.au; 217 Main St; s/d $85/89; WGB) Management is ready to help you with cycling plans and repairs, and even provides a breakdown service within 35km.

Parker Pies (☎ 03-6032 9605; www.parkerpies.com.au; 86–88 Main St) Arguably Australia's best, with the awards to prove it.

Star Hotel (☎ 03-6032 9625; 105 Main St; mains $18-28) Good bistro meals in a family-friendly environment. There are also budget motel rooms available (singles/doubles $45/75).

Forks & Corks (☎ 03-6032 7662; 82 Main St; mains $18-30; lunch daily, dinner

Fri & Sat) A bright, airy place that serves simple, well-prepared favourites – fish and chips, curries and pastas.

The **IGA** supermarket (95 Main St) stocks most groceries, while the **Rutherglen Bakery** (137 Main St; from 7am) has a great range of breads, cakes and quiches.

STAWELL
☎ 03 / pop 6000

Stawell is a gateway to the Grampians and the closest major town to the tourist hub of Halls Gap (p158). A former gold-mining town, its prosperity saw construction of fine buildings, many made of Grampians sandstone. Its main industries today lie in the lustreless areas of brick-production and farming. Stawell is most famous for the Stawell Gift (www.stawellgift.com), a 120m foot race run every Easter Monday since 1878 and attracting up to 20,000 spectators.

Information
The **visitors centre** (☎ 1800 330 080; www .grampianstravel.com; 50–52 Western Hwy) is about 1.5km southwest of the centre, near the bottom of Seaby St (the extension of Main St). Pick up the Wilkins *Tourist Map of Stawell,* which has a Halls Gap inset and a regional map on the back with distance markings and secondary road names.

Between Stawell and Ararat, there is limited access to cash. Stock up at banks (with ATMs) on the mall.

Supplies & Equipment
Pyke's Pets & Cycles (☎ 03-5358 3133; 57 Main St) is the only bike shop until Ararat. See to any parts or repair needs here.

Sleeping & Eating
Stawell Park Caravan Park (☎ 03-5358 2709; www.stawellcaravanpark.com.au; Western Hwy; unpowered/powered sites $18/20, d cabins from $54) On 48 hectares of attractive bushland about 2km southeast of the centre. Try the pool and recreation room for relaxation at the end of a long day.

Central Park Motel (☎ 03-5358 2417; www.centralparkmotel.com; 3 Seaby St; s $50-55, d $60-80) A recently refurbished classic motel closer to the centre than most others and sporting its own restaurant, the Stone Grill.

Magdala Motor Lodge (☎ 03-5358 3877; www.magdalamotorlodge.com.au; Western Hwy; s $99/112, d with/without spa $105/135) Magdala is just outside town in a bush setting overlooking a small private lake (free canoes). The motel's restaurant (mains $15 to $25), open for dinner Monday to Saturday, gets good reviews.

Chris 'n' Di's Bakery (☎ 03-5358 5255; 76 Main St) Opens from 7am and is very popular.

New Hong Kong Restaurant (☎ 03-5358 1005; 96 Main St; mains around $15; closed Mon) A good Asian-food standby.

Brix Hotel (☎ 03-5358 1058; 39 Barnes St; mains $15-23; lunch Mon-Fri, dinner Fri-Sun) Nothing fussy here, just cheap, straightforward pub grub.

Town Hall Hotel (☎ 03-5358 1059; 62 Main St; mains $18-25.50) A grand old pub with commendable bistro meals.

Stawell's supermarkets include an **IGA** (126–130 Gold Reef Mall) and **Safeway** (26–32 Scallan St).

SWIFTS CREEK
☎ 03 / pop 281

Swifts Creek was once a timber town en route to the Omeo goldfields. Later it provided sheep and cattle to markets for the surrounding Tambo Valley. Today it's an extended crossroads, very small and quiet, home to many artists and writers. The large numbers of eastern grey kangaroos that feed along the road, especially at night, give truth to the site's original name, Jirrah Gingee Munjie, which is said to mean 'big kangaroo go that place'.

The **IGA general store** (☎ 03-5159 4272; 7am-7pm) has Eftpos facilities and some information about town.

Sleeping & Eating
Swifts Creek Caravan Park (unpowered/powered sites $8/12.50) A council property with basic facilities on the Tambo River. Check in at the general store.

Albion Hotel (☎ 03-5159 4211; d $60-85) Offers comfortable self-contained units in a small house near the pub, open for lunch and dinner, which also has an excellent range of meals (mains $16 to $20).

Bella Vita B&B Retreat (☎ 03-5159 4231; 7020 Great Alpine Rd; s/d $88/99) A mellow lifestyle getaway with opportunities for therapeutic wraps, mud treatments and facials.

Miner's Cottage (d $130) 5km before town, the Miner's cottage offers a fully and tastefully furnished country retreat immersed in the bush. Register at the general store.

Creekers Café (☎ 03-5159 4272; 6864 Great Alpine Rd; meals $5-$15; 7.30am-8pm Mon-Fri, 7.30am-4pm Sat & Sun) Whips up reliable takeaway grub, although you can dine in too.

For self-caterers, there's a popular **bakery** (☎ 03-5159 4208; 9 McMillan Ave; 7am-5pm Mon-Fri, to 3pm Sat).

WANGARATTA
☎ 03 / pop 18,000

At the confluence of the Ovens and King Rivers, Wangaratta (also known as 'Wang' – its name comes from two local Aboriginal words meaning 'resting place of cormorants') grew during the gold rush as a stopover point for travellers. Still an important junction, Wangaratta is now mainly a rural and commercial town.

It has a strong racing fraternity and is the home town of several prominent cyclists: Dean Woods, a three-time Olympian (winner of gold, silver and bronze medals); Damian McDonald, who raced at two Olympics; and veteran legend Barry Burns. The active **Wangaratta Bicycle Users Group** (www.wangarattabug.org.au) runs regular rides.

Information
The **visitors centre** (☎ 1800 801 065, 03-5721 5711; www.visitwangaratta.com.au; 100–104 Murphy St) is in the old library and has extensive information for cyclists and an excellent display about the **Murray to the Mountains Rail Trail** (www.murraytomountains.com.au), of which Wangaratta is a major supporter and hub. In particular, pick up the *Murray to the Mountains Rail Trail map,* the *Ride Guide 2009 Cyclists Guide to North East Victoria* and read about Pedal to Produce (see boxed text p135), all of which might influence what you do with your days.

Most banks are in Murphy and Reid Sts; all have ATMs.

Supplies & Equipment
Wang has three full-service bike shops, all of which also have hire fleets. Try **Dean Woods Cycles** (☎ 1800 353 123; www.deanwoods.com.au; 6–8 Handley St; daily rate for one/three/five days $29/27/25; WGB).

Sleeping & Eating
Painters Island Caravan Park (☎ 03-5721 3380; www.paintersislandcaravanpark.com.au; Pinkerton Cres; sites from $26, d cabins $60-125; WGB) Claims 10 hectares on the banks of the Ovens River, just two minutes from town.

Pinsent Hotel (☎ 03-5721 2183; 20 Reid St; s/d $40/70) A completely refurbished country pub with comfortable rooms upstairs and bistro below.

Wangaratta Motor Inn (☎ 1800 811 049, 03-5721 5488; www.wangarattamotorinn.com.au; cnr Ovens St & Roy St East; s $75-85, d $78-88) Conveniently close to the train station, its Oasis Bar & Grill Restaurant (mains $15 to $25) puts out hearty budget meals.

Scribblers Coffee Lounge (☎ 03-5721 3945; 66 Reid St; meals $8-16; breakfast & lunch) Has a varied menu including pasta and interesting quiches, pies and cakes.

Vine Hotel (☎ 03-5721 2605; www.thevinehotel.com.au; Detour Rd; mains $13-23; lunch daily, dinner Mon-Sat) This charming old pub (circa 1895) on the rail trail north of town hasn't changed much since Ned Kelly drank here (check out the history museum in the basement). The bar menu ($12) is a bargain.

Café Martini (☎ 03-5721 9020; 87 Murphy St; mains $13-30; dinner daily, lunch Mon-Sat) A big and bustling family bistro known for its Italian food and wood-fired pizzas.

For picnic supplies go to the **Coles** (cnr Ryley St & Greta Rd) supermarket and **Monty's Bakery** (☎ 03-5722 3377; 58 Reid St).

WARRNAMBOOL
☎ 03 / pop 31,000

On the protected Lady Bay, Warrnambool is the largest city in Victoria's southwest. Originally a whaling and sealing station, the town was settled following the growth of harbour facilities. The main town is on a cliff overlooking Lake Pertobe, its historic buildings, waterways and tree-lined streets a playground for a large student population. Between June and September, southern right whales still return to local waters to calve. They're often visible from a viewing platform at Logan's Beach.

The town is the end point of the 299km **Melbourne to Warrnambool Cycling Classic** (www.melbournetowarrnambool. com), held every October. It's the longest one-day competitive pedal in the world. First run in 1895, it's also the second oldest.

Information

The **visitors centre** (☎ 03-5559 4620; www.warrnamboolinfo.com.au; Flagstaff Hill, 89 Merri St) overlooks Lady Bay. It distributes the handy *Warrnambool Official Visitors' Guide*, a map of local cycling routes and lots of information about the long road ahead. **Parks Victoria** (☎ 03-5561 9900; 78 Henna St) also has an office here, near the train station.

The major banks (with ATMs) are in Liebig and Koroit Sts.

Supplies & Equipment

Bicycle Superstore (☎ 03-5561 5225; www.bicyclesuperstore.com.au; 184 Fairy St) has got your spares and repairs. Bike hire ($30 per day) is also an option, but only through the visitors centre, to which they provide the material.

Sleeping & Eating

Surfside Holiday Park (☎ 03-5559 4700; www.surfsidepark.com.au; Pertobe Rd; unpowered/powered sites from $28/37, cabins from $84) One of several caravan parks in town, Surfside is perfectly situated between the town and the beach.

Warrnambool Beach Backpackers (☎ 03-5562 4874; www.beachbackpackers.com.au; 17 Stanley St; dm/d $23/70) Occupies a former museum close to the sea. It's got a huge living area and free use of mountain bikes and canoes.

Atwood Motor Inn (☎ 03-5562 7144; www.atwoodmotorinn.com.au; 8 Spence St; d from $85) Maintains small but attractive doubles in a quiet side street only three minutes' walk from the centre.

Fishtales Café (☎ 03-5561 2957; 63 Liebig St; mains $7-24) An upbeat, friendly eatery and takeaway with a cheery courtyard.

Bojangles (☎ 03-5562 8751; www.bojanglespizza.com; 61 Liebig St; mains $11-20; lunch & dinner) Presses fresh pasta and wood-fires pizza in its upmarket digs. There's an excellent wine list too. Highly recommended.

Whaler's Inn (☎ 03-5562 8391; www.whalersinn.com.au; cnr Liebig & Timor Sts; dinner mains $15-28; lunch & dinner Mon-Sat) A family-friendly bistro with tasty and generous meals that include an all-you-can-eat salad bar.

For self-caterers, a **Coles** (Lava St) supermarket is close to the centre.

Tasmania

HIGHLIGHTS

- Rolling into **Coles Bay** (p171) in view of the musk-tinted Hazards
- Beach-hopping south from Hobart to **Cockle Creek** (p177)
- Burrowing through rainforest on a detour to **Liffey Falls** (p188)
- Rising out of Queenstown through an otherworldly landscape on the **99 Bend Road** (p202)
- Cruising through World Heritage wilderness amid the forest, waterfalls, peaks and rivers of Tasmania's **Southwest** (p193)

TERRAIN

Hilly throughout the island, switching from wild and mountainous in the west to hill-ribbed coast in the east.

| Telephone code – 03 | www.biketas.org.au | www.discovertasmania.com |

In so many ways Australia's island state is often an afterthought, but not among cyclists. The smallest of Australia's states, Tasmania is arguably the country's best region for cycle touring, offering achievable goals – east coast, west coast, the full circuit – in realistic time frames, cool summer cycling and some of Australia's most striking landscapes.

Tasmania is always beautiful and often demanding – flat, here, is a relative term – with most cyclists migrating to the east coast in search of the fewest bumps and the finest coastal scenery along stretches of beach that might embarrass the rest of the nation if they had the heat to match. Riders who prefer mountains will find one of the country's best highland routes along Tasmania's west coast, with views of shapely peaks such as Cradle Mountain and Frenchmans Cap and brief coastal respite in Strahan.

If you've arrived on the ferry in Devonport, you might prefer to ride straight on down through Tasmania's heart on the Across the Central Plateau ride. Less popular than the coasts, it is far from the second-cousin option. The climb up through the Great Western Tiers, past Liffey Falls, is one of the great sections of riding in the state, while the plateau is a multi-speckled land of lakes and isolation; bring a rod and reel if you're the least bit inclined to angling.

Heading to the last stop before Antarctica, the Cockle Creek ride hugs Tasmania's southern shores. Here, in an area often overlooked by cyclists, you'll find some of that elusive flat riding in combination with beaches, island views, caves and hot springs.

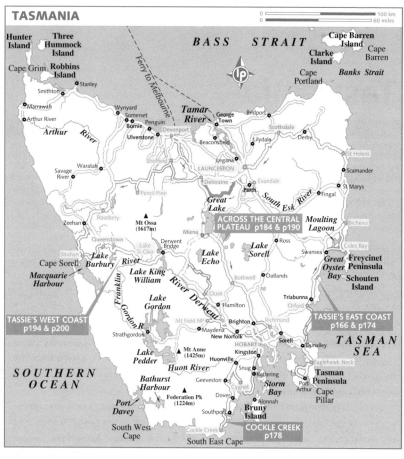

TASMANIA

0   100 km
0   60 miles

BASS STRAIT

ENVIRONMENT

Tasmania separated from mainland Australia between 12,000 and 10,000 years ago when rising seas created stormy Bass Strait. Its highest mountain, Mt Ossa, reaches only 1617m but much of the interior is extremely rugged. The coasts' shallow bays and broad estuaries derive from postglacial flooding of river valleys. The Central Plateau, which was covered by a single ice sheet, is a sometimes bleak environment dotted with thousands of lakes. Most of the island's western half is a maze of mountainous ridges bearing signs of recent glaciation. The major environmental differences across the state are largely due to the interaction of prevailing moist westerly winds with these mountains; the rainforest

valleys and sometimes snow-capped western mountains contrasting with the mild climate of the eastern 'sun coast'.

The diverse flora ranges from the dry forests of the east, to the alpine moorlands of the centre and the rainforests of the west. Many of the state's plants are unlike those found in the rest of Australia and have ties with species that grew more than 50 million years ago, when the southern continents were joined as Gondwana. Tasmania's eucalyptus trees range from the swamp gum, which is the tallest flowering plant in the world (growing to 100m), to the small, shrubby alpine varnished gum. The famous Huon pine can live for thousands of years. Others, such as King Billy, pencil and celery-top pines, common in higher regions, live for 500 years. Myrtle beech, similar to European beeches, favours wetter forests. In autumn, deciduous beech, Australia's only deciduous native, adds a splash of gold and red to the forests.

Tasmania's fauna is not as varied as that of the rest of Australia and there are relatively few large mammals, with its largest marsupial, the Tasmanian tiger (thylacine), extinct for more than 70 years. Nevertheless, Tasmania is the final refuge of a number of species that have vanished from the mainland (the eastern quoll and pademelon, for example). The carnivorous Tasmanian devil is endemic (and under threat; see p34), wallabies, wombats and possums are common, and there's a wide variety of seabirds, parrots, cockatoos, honeyeaters and wrens. Birds of prey such as falcons and eagles are also readily seen.

About a quarter of the state is national park, with 20% of the state having World Heritage status.

CLIMATE

Tasmania has four distinct seasons but, lying in the path of the Roaring Forties, it can experience wintry conditions at any time of year. As a general rule, however, summer days are generally warm, with mild nights. Ultra-violet radiation can be intense in the middle of the day. Hobart's average January maximum is 21.6°C while in Launceston it's around 24°C.

Pleasant conditions continue into autumn – Hobart's March temperatures are generally comfortable, averaging a maximum of 20°C. From April, temperatures plunge and by July, Hobart's average maximum is just 11.6°C (12.5°C in Launceston).

Frequent wet weather is a fact of life, especially in the west, where the prevailing west–east airflow delivers 3000mm of rain annually (compared to around 600mm on the east coast). The east coast is warmer and milder than elsewhere in the state and boasts the most hours of sunshine of any part of the Australian coast.

PLANNING
Bike Hire

In Hobart, **Derwent Bike Hire** (☎ 0428 899 169; www.derwentbikehire.com; touring bike per 1/2/3/4 weeks $140/250/340/410) has a full species list of bikes for rent: mountain bikes, tourers, recumbents, tandems and child trailers. Touring bikes come with racks and panniers. In Launceston, try **Rent a Cycle Tasmania** (☎ 03-6334 9779; www.tasequiphire.com.au; 4 Penquite Rd, Newstead; bikes per week $160).

Maps

Tasmania is covered in detail in an excellent series of four 1:250,000 maps – *South East, South West, North East* and *North West* – produced by the state government's Information and Land Services Division. Some features are a little out of date but they include contours and are excellent cycling maps.

Books

Lonely Planet's *Tasmania* guide is an excellent in-depth supplement to this book.

THE DOUGHNUT

Few places in Australia are small enough to ride around in their entirety, but Tasmania is that place. Each summer, swarms of cyclists descend on the state, most heading for the flatter east coast but a hardy few intent on circling the island.

By combining the East Coast and West Coast rides in this chapter you can all but piece together an 18-day loop of the island, covering around 1250km. There are two gaps between the East Coast and West Coast rides as described here, which are easily and pleasantly plugged. To reach Eaglehawk Neck from Hobart, ride out across the Tasman Bridge on the narrow roadside path, following the Tasman Hwy through Sorell to the Lewisham turn-off. This road passes through Dodges Ferry and Carlton, joining the Arthur Hwy at Dunalley, near to Eaglehawk Neck. It's a ride of around 75km, so allow a full day.

To reach Evandale from Launceston, head out of town along the bike lane on Elphin Rd, staying with the road as it becomes Penquite Rd and then Glenwood Rd, passing through the Relbia wine region and joining the C412 to Evandale. The ride is around 25km in length.

Where to Ride Tasmania has 45 day rides around the state. Two of Australia's classic historical tales are set in Tasmania: Robert Hughes' *The Fatal Shore* and Marcus Clarke's *For the Term of His Natural Life*.

Cycling Events

Penny Farthing Championships (www .evandalevillagefair.com; Feb) Penny farthings trundle through the streets of Evandale in northern Tasmania.

Fleche Opperman All Day Trial (www. audax.org.au; Mar) Teams of three to five cyclists ride a 360km course, finishing in Hobart.

Great Western Tiers Cycling Challenge (www.tas.cyclechallenge.org.au; Mar) Charity ride from Prospect along the foot of the Great Western Tiers; distances are 24km, 52km, 76km, 100km and 160km.

The BIG Ride (www.biketas.org.au; Nov) Bicycle Tasmania event, departing from Margate, with a 106km Around the Channel ride or a 35km Tinderbox loop.

ASH Dash (www.audax.org.au; Dec) Seven hill climbs south of Hobart and 210km makes for a big day out.

Information Sources

For general tourist information, contact **Tourism Tasmania** (☎ 03-6230 8235, 1300 733 258; www.discovertasmania.com; GPO Box 399, Hobart 7001).

Bicycle Tasmania (www.biketas.org .au) is Tasmania's cycling advocacy group.

Cycling South (www.cyclingsouth.org) is a great resource for cycling information about the south of the state.

Parks & Wildlife Service (☎ 1300 135 513; www.parks.tas.gov.au) has national park information.

Cycle Tours

Green Island Tours (☎ 03-6376 3080; www .cycling-tasmania.com) offers a nine-day west-coast and an 11-day east-coast tour.

Island Cycle Tours (☎ 03-6228 0126; www.islandcycletours.com) runs a selection of tours around the state, from the half-day Mt Wellington Descent to a 13-day loop of the island.

True Tasmania Cycling Tours (☎ 03-6427 3157; www.truetasmania.com.au) offers three main tours: island loop, a west-coast ride similar to Tassie's West Coast described in this chapter, and a five-day circuit around the northeast.

World Expeditions (☎ 1300 720 000; www.worldexpeditions.com.au) runs a selection of rides, from the single-day Ben Lomond descent to combination walk-cycle journeys.

GETTING AROUND

Buses are about the only feasible public transport option in Tasmania. The two

---

CYCLING MT WELLINGTON

For any cyclist who's ever coveted a polka-dot jersey, Mt Wellington sits like a siren behind Hobart. From the city to the summit it's a fairly relentless 22km ride, beginning near sea level and topping out at the Pinnacle Shelter at 1270m. You might even start out in sun and finish in fog – things change quickly on this mountain. The best route to the mountain is to head for Molle St and take the Hobart Rivulet Track from the car park at the end of Collins St – there's an almighty lump of hill in the middle of the track, which is easily skirted by heading out onto the roads. By the Cascade Brewery join Strickland Ave and wind gently uphill to Huon Rd.

About 10km from the city, turn right from Huon Rd onto Pillinger Dr, which climbs relentlessly for 12km, zig-zagging across the face of the mountain. The average gradient is 7.6% – it's a gentle climb to the Springs but ramps up slightly beyond.

On a clear day, there's a great view over Hobart and the Derwent estuary from the summit, as well as across parts of the Southwest Tasmania Wilderness World Heritage Area.

In 1895 weather watcher Clement Wragge (unsurprisingly nicknamed 'Inclement') established the first staffed meteorological station on the summit. It now operates automatically. Unfortunately, there is nowhere to get food or drinks.

The descent is almost pedal free. If you prefer to do only the downhill, **Island Cycle Tours** (☎ 03-6228 0126; www.islandcycletours.com) runs a tour, driving participants to the summit and then letting them roll back into the city. The descent costs $75.

main operators are **TassieLink** (☎ 1300 300 520; www.tassielink.com.au) and **Redline Coaches** (☎ 1300 360 000; www.tasredline .com.au). It costs $10 to transport a bike with TassieLink and the front wheel must be removed (book ahead as buses have space for only two bikes); it costs $15 with Redline (bikes do not need to be disassembled).

GATEWAYS
See Hobart (p215), Launceston (p217) and Devonport (p212).

TASSIE'S EAST COAST

Duration 7 days

Distance 499.7km

Difficulty moderate–demanding

Start Eaglehawk Neck

Finish Launceston

Summary Probably the nation's most popular cycle-touring route, clinging to the relentlessly beautiful east coast, where the only thing more brilliant than the ocean is the white sand and the orange lichen on the granite boulders.

Welcome to the sunny side. Sitting in the rain shadow of the western mountains, Tasmania's east coast is dry, clear and – in summer – warm; everything a coastal destination should be. But what draws most cyclists here is the beauty of the coast, with its long, sandy beaches split by colourful granite headlands, and its perceived flatness…at least in comparison to the mountainous west.

This ride is not flat, with the Day 2 section to Orford as testing as any road in the state, but along the main stretch of coast it's pleasantly easy going ahead of another taxing climb overland towards Launceston. This ride uses the A3 highway as its guiding line but veers away at several opportunities to indulge in the coast.

You can just about expect to see as many bikes as cars on this popular route.

PLANNING
When to Cycle
A popular holiday destination, the east coast is best avoided at Easter and late December through January, when accommodation and the roads are most crowded. On Day

3, the route requires that cyclists use a ferry service that only operates between October and late April – be prepared for a 52km detour if riding outside these months.

Maps
The route is covered by the 1:250,000 *South East* and *North East* maps produced by the Information and Land Services Division.

Permits & Regulations
The ride passes several national parks – Maria Island, Freycinet, Douglas-Apsley – so it's best to carry a national-parks pass. A daily pass costs $11 per person, or you can purchase an eight-week holiday pass for $28. Passes can be bought at visitors centres and national park offices.

GETTING TO/FROM THE RIDE
Eaglehawk Neck (start)
BUS
The **Tassielink** (☎ 1300 300 520, 03-6230 8900; 64 Brisbane St, Hobart; www .tassielink.com.au) Tasman Peninsula service from Hobart stops at Eaglehawk Neck ($23, 1½ hours, departs 4pm).

BICYCLE
To ride from Hobart, head out across the Tasman Bridge and along the Tasman Hwy to Sorell – it's not the world's greatest cycling road but there are bike paths on the bridge crossings. Take the Lewisham Scenic Dr turning shortly after Sorell, passing through Dodges Ferry and Carlton to Dunalley. Cross over the canal onto Forestier Peninsula and follow the Arthur Hwy to Eaglehawk Neck. It's about a 75km ride from Hobart.

Launceston (finish)
AIR
There are regular flights between Launceston and both Melbourne and Sydney, connecting with other Australian cities. For flight details see **Qantas** (☎ 13 13 13; www.qantas.com.au), **Jetstar** (☎ 13 15 38; www.jetstar.com), **Virgin Blue** (☎ 13 67 89; www.virginblue.com.au) or **Tiger Airways** (☎ 03-9335 3033; www .tigerairways.com).

Launceston airport is 15km south of the city. A **shuttle bus** (☎ 03-6343 6677) runs a door-to-door airport service costing $14 per adult. You must notify the service

TASMANIA

TASSIE'S EAST COAST – DAYS 1-4

TASMANIA

Nature World

Bicheno

START DAY 5

Friendly
Beaches

Side Trip

Mt Peter
(20m)

Freycinet
National
Park

Coles Bay

The
Nuggets

START DAY 4

Wineglass Bay

Lemon
Rock

Refuge
Island

Schouten
Island

Taillefer
Rocks

Ile Des
Phoques

Moulting
Lagoon

Swanwick

Swan River

Swansea

Spiky Bridge

Mayfield Bay

Tasman Hwy

Little Swanport

Buxton

Cranbrook

Snowy River

Lake
Leake

Elizabeth River

Macquarie River

Town
Lake

Little Swanport
River

Bluff River

Coal River

Midland Hwy

Oatlands

Lake
Tiberias

Mud Walls Rd

Macquarie
River

Lower
Marshes

Lake
Sorell

Lake
Crescent

0   10 km
0   6.0 miles

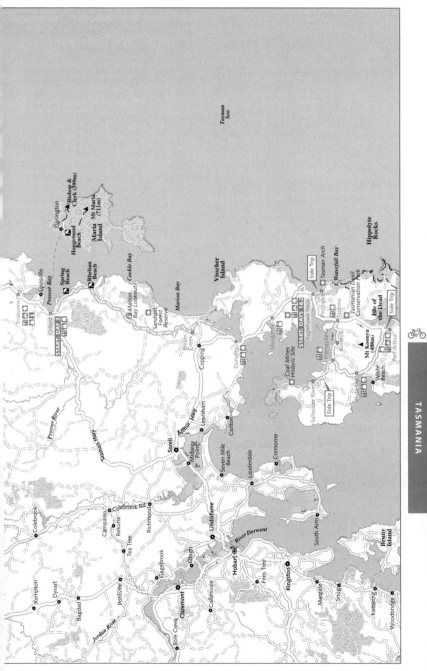

ahead of time that you'll have a bike; boxed bikes cost $5.

A taxi to the city costs about $40.

BUS

Redline Coaches (☎ 1300 360 000; www .tasredline.com.au) and **Tassielink** (☎ 1300 300 520; www.tassielink.com.au) operate out of Launceston to points around the state. The depot for services is at **Cornwall Square Transit Centre** (cnr St John & Cimitiere Sts), behind the visitors centre.

BICYCLE

Roads approach Launceston from all directions. If coming from Devonport, avoid the main highway, taking the minor roads through Frankford and Exeter to the West Tamar Hwy. The Midland Hwy from Hobart has good verges into Launceston.

CAR

Many of the major car rental firms have desks at the airport or in town. There's **Europcar** (☎ 13 13 90, 03-6331 8200; 112 George St) and **Thrifty** (☎ 03-6333 0911, 1300 367 227; 151 St John St) and cheaper operators like **Economy Car Rentals** (☎ 03-6334 3299; 27 William St), with prices starting at $37 per day (older cars and rentals of at least seven days). **Lo-Cost Auto Rent** (☎ 03-6334 3437, 1800 647 060; www.rentforless.com .au; 80 Tamar St) has starting rates from $30 daily for multiday hire.

THE RIDE
Day 1: Tasman Peninsula Circuit
3–6 hours, 56km

Like a fish hook hanging off the line of Tasmania's east coast, the Tasman Peninsula is a quite remarkable filament of land, and the chance to start your tour unladen is another enticement onto the peninsula, which is home to Australia's most famous convict prison and the highest sea cliffs in the country. There are a number of hill climbs so you'll appreciate the lack of baggage on your bike.

The ride begins along the rocky shores of Norfolk Bay, looking across to the wooded slopes of the Forestier Peninsula. **Taranna** (8.1km) is a sprawling town of B&Bs, gingerbread cottages and one of the finest nooks of Norfolk Bay coastline. Just past town is the **Tasmanian Devil Conservation Park**

TASSIE'S EAST COAST – DAY 1

CUE		GPS COORDINATES
start	Eaglehawk Cafè & Guesthouse, Eaglehawk Neck	147°55'11"E 43°01'08"S
0km	go W on Arthur Hwy	
8.1	Taranna	147°51'54"E 43°03'23"S
{8.7 ★	Tasmanian Devil Conservation Park}	
11.3 ▲	1.2km moderate	
15.1 ▲	700m moderate	
{18.7 ●● ↰	Port Arthur 1.4km ↻}	
20.1 ▲	1.5km steep	
30.6 ↰	B37, `to Taranna', Nubeena	147°44'33"N 43°05'55"S
32.3 ▲	2.2km moderate	
37.7	Premaydena	147°46'20"E 43°03'20"S
{ ●● ↰	Coal Mines Historic Site 24km ↻}	
47.0 ↰	A9, `to Eaglehawk Neck'	
47.9	Taranna	147°51'54"E 43°03'23"S
56.0	Eaglehawk Cafè & Guesthouse, Eaglehawk Neck	147°55'11"E 43°01'08"S

(☎ 03-6250 3230; www.tasmaniandevilpark .com; Arthur Hwy; admission $24; 9am-6pm), which functions as a quarantined breeding centre for devils to help protect against DFTD (see boxed text p34). It's also a breeding centre for endangered birds of prey. There are plenty of other native species here too, with feedings throughout the day: devils at 10am, 11am, 1.30pm and 5pm (4.30pm in winter), and kangaroos at 2.30pm. There's also a sea eagle show at 11.15am and 3.30pm.

The highway cuts overland, through forest and gentle undulations, to **Port Arthur** – there are more postcard-perfect coastal glimpses as you approach the town – where you can make a short side trip into the historic site, which is Tasmania's most popular tourist attraction.

Your own punishment begins just beyond the convict prison, with the road crossing back over the peninsula, this time steeply, descending through an apple orchard into **Nubeena** (30.6km), the largest town on the peninsula, fanned out along the shore of Wedge Bay.

The hill beyond town offers fine views over Norfolk Bay, Forestier Peninsula and the 'mainland', with the descent passing through a small but beautiful stand of tall gums. At Premaydena you can head west on the side trip or continue straight on for the undulating run back across the peninsula, rejoining the outward route near the Tasmanian Devil Conservation Park.

SIDE TRIP: COAL MINES HISTORIC SITE
1½–2½ hours, 24km

The C341, signed to Saltwater River and Coal Mines Historic Site, runs north from Premaydena store, hugging the Norfolk Bay coast for most of its run to the Coal Mines Historic Site. Tasmania's first operational **mine** opened here in 1834, and it also served as penal station from 1833 to 1848. The car park is 500m past the historic site's entrance, and from here a series of walks radiates out among the mine and prison detritus buried among the bush – walks range from 500m to 5km in length.

Return to Premaydena via the outward route.

Day 2: Eaglehawk Neck to Orford
4½–7½ hours, 75.1km

If you chose to ride the east coast because it's Tasmania's flatter side, today will be a surprise. This is a rough and tough day with hills that are further complicated by rough dirt roads. On the plus side (and they are huge pluses), the ride takes the closest possible course to the coast, the day is feature packed and you're likely to see very few vehicles once you leave the Arthur Hwy near Dunalley.

The day begins across the narrow isthmus of Eaglehawk Neck, where chained dogs once stood guard to prevent prisoners escaping from Port Arthur – look to the right as you cycle across and you'll see a statue of a frothing guard dog. Also here, right by the turning onto Pirates Bay Dr, is the only remaining structure from the convict days, the 1832 **Officers Quarters** (admission free; 9am-4.30pm), also the oldest wooden military building in Australia.

The long climb on Pirates Bay Dr is moderated by stops at the **Tessellated Pavement** (1.6km), where a rock shelf is sliced into unnaturally perfect sections, and at a **lookout** (4.7km) with a magnificent view over Pirates Bay to the sea stacks at Cape Hauy.

TASSIE'S EAST COAST – DAY 2

CUE			GPS COORDINATES
start		Eaglehawk Cafè & Guesthouse, Eaglehawk Neck	147°55'11"E 43°01'08"S
0km		go E on Arthur Hwy	
0.3	●● ⌐	Tasmans Arch 8.6km	147°57'02"N 43°02'31"S
0.9	⌐	Pirates Bay Dr	
{	★	Officers Quarters}	
1.0	▲	3.7km moderate	
1.6	★	Tessellated Pavement	
{4.7	★	lookout}	
5.5	⌐	A9, 'to Dunalley'	
13.2		Murdunna	147°52'01"N 42°56'53"S
14.8	▲	700m moderate	
22.0	⌐	A9, 'to Sorell', Dunalley"	
24.4	⌐	C337, 'to Marion Bay'	
26.0	⚠	200m dirt road	
26.9	⚠	39.7km dirt road	
31.9	↖	C337, 'to Copping'	
32.3	⌐	Burnt Hill Rd	

CUE CONTINUED			GPS COORDINATES
33.5	▲	1.6km moderate	
34.0	↰	Burnt Hill Rd	
35.1	⌐	C336, 'to Bream Creek'	
37.5	▲	700m moderate	
38.9	▲	800m steep	
41.3	⌐	Wielangta Forest Dr	
41.6	▲	2km steep	
43.7	★	Marion Bay lookout	147°51'35"N 42°49'32"S
{50.1	★	Sandspit Forest Reserve}	
50.3	▲	1.4km steep	
51.7	⚠	1.7km steep descent	
60.5	⤢	C320 (unsigned)	
63.4	★	Rheban beach	147°55'28"N 42°37'55"S
65.5	▲	800m steep climb	
70.7	⚠	pick-a-plank bridge	
70.8	★	Spring Beach	147°54'30"N 42°34'44"S
75.1		Orford IGA supermarket	147°52'34"N 42°33'09"S

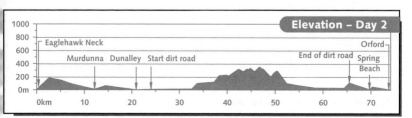

Elevation – Day 2

EAST COAST BY ROAD BIKE

If your vehicle of choice along the east coast is a road bike, you will need to vary your route from that described here, as the dirt section from Eaglehawk Neck to Orford (Day 2) will be unpassable. Begin instead in Hobart, from where you'll have sealed roads across to Orford, joining this ride on Day 3.

Head out of Hobart on the Tasman Hwy to Sorell, following the A3 from here on its hilly crossing to the east coast at Orford. The highway climbs through the delightfully(?) named Bust-Me-Gall Hill and Break-Me-Neck Hill and past the church at Buckland, where legend suggests the stained-glass window comes from Battle Abbey in England.

From Hobart, it's 79km to Orford.

Approaching Dunalley across the suitably forested Forestier Peninsula, the ride skirts the brilliant colours of **Sunset Beach** and crosses the **Denison Canal**, Australia's only purpose-built sea canal, into Dunalley (22km). Beyond Dunalley the C337 starts out wide and smooth but quickly turns to dirt, first hugging swan-stacked Blackman Bay then grinding up into the cleared hills for a bit of very rural, very remote riding.

At the crest of the first main climb (41.3km), the ride turns into Wietlanga Forest Dr, where the road roughens and the second big climb begins immediately. It will be a joy, at least, to enter the forest, while there's further comfort at the top where **Marion Bay lookout** (43.7km) stares down onto the northern tips of the Forestier Peninsula.

At 50.1km **Sandspit Forest Reserve** protects a valley of tall eucalypt forest and a patch of rainforest. The reserve's picnic area is the best place for a lunch break. The climb out of the valley is very steep and rough, topping out amid a stand of blue gums that glisten in the wet.

At around 63km the ride returns to the coast where Maria Island, crowned by Mt Maria, rises across Mercury Passage. On a fine day the beach at **Rheban** (63.4km) is the perfect grandstand onto the island. The day's final sting comes just before Spring Beach with an 800m climb that also signals the end of the dirt road – there are things you'll miss about this day but the road surface is not one of them.

Bone-white **Spring Beach** (70.8km) is a taster of the beaches to come and from here it's a gentle ride into Orford.

SIDE TRIP: TASMANS ARCH
¼–1 hour, 8.6km

From the southern edge of the Eaglehawk Neck isthmus, a side road runs down the coast to the collapsed sea cave at Tasmans Arch. From the turning the road climbs fairly relentlessly for 600m, with views

MARIA ISLAND

Afloat offshore from Orford, Maria Island offers a tempting diversion for east-coast cyclists. Between 1969 and 1971, the island was chosen as a virtual ark, with animals such as forester kangaroos, Bennetts wallabies, eastern barred bandicoots, brown bandicoots, wombats and Cape Barren geese introduced to the former prison island to help protect them from extinction. The project succeeded beyond imagination, and today the island is one of the surest places in the country to view critters such as wombats and Cape Barren geese.

Entirely national park, the island is vehicle-free with its main tracks open to bikes. **Ferries** (☎ 03-6257 0239; www.mariaislandferry.com.au) to Maria Island leave from Triabunna, 7km north of Orford. Between October and March they depart Triabunna at 9.30am and 4pm, returning from Darlington at 10.30am and 5pm; between April and September they leave Triabunna at 10.30am and 3pm, leaving the island at 11.30am and 4pm. Return fare is $50, with bikes costing an additional $10. There is camping in the former convict prison grounds at Darlington.

For an overview of cycling policy and possibilities on the island, visit the **Maria Island National Park website** (www.parks.tas.gov.au/index.aspx?base=3495) – click on the 'Maria Island by Bike' link.

emerging behind of curvaceous Pirates Bay. In Doo Town, where each home has been christened with a daft 'Doo' name, turn right for a second steep climb up to **Tasmans Arch** and **Devil's Kitchen**. The impressive arch is right beside the car park, while it's a 15-minute return walk to Devil's Kitchen, slotted into the cliffs.

Day 3: Orford to Coles Bay
4½–8 hours, 85.4km

In contrast to Day 2, this is a ride without hills, it's almost dead flat from Triabunna to Swansea, while an informal ferry service also means that cyclists are saved a 52km ride around Moulting Lagoon to get to Coles Bay. The highway is wide for 30km, then narrow for the next 30km. After that it doesn't really matter because it's unlikely that you'll see more than a vehicle or two on the road to Point Bagot.

Expect a few log trucks for the 7km between Orford and Triabunna, but beyond this mill town the traffic thins to holidaymakers on a highway that's wide with a small verge. At 27.8km there's the momentary distraction of hundreds of shoes strung along a fence, but more compelling is the triceratops of bridges, **Spiky Bridge** (50.5km), built by convicts in the 1840s. The mortarless bridge was built using thousands of fieldstones, but the reason for the spikes is unknown.

Just before Swansea, at 55.7km, **Kate's Berry Farm** (☎ 03-6257 8428; teas & desserts $4-9; 10am-4.30pm) is worth building a day around. Overlooking Great Oyster Bay, the berries here are conjured into a range of ice creams, jams, sauces and a handmade berry chocolate.

On the other side of Swansea, the road to Point Bagot cuts through a seemingly endless line of holiday homes, with the musk-tinted Hazards drawing ever nearer. The beach at road's end is a popular campsite (free); there's a basic long-drop toilet. From here, there's an informal **boat service** (☎ 03-6257 0239) to Swanwick for cyclists. It operates between October and April, weather permitting. Phone from Swansea to arrange the dinghy, which costs $15 per person.

From Swanwick it's a short ride into Coles Bay, one of the most beautifully positioned towns in Tasmania.

Day 4: Coles Bay to Bicheno
2½–3½ hours, 41.1km

A flat, straightforward day – between the town limits of Coles Bay and Bicheno it turns one corner. The short ride will allow time to explore Freycinet National Park in the morning, as it's possible to walk to Wineglass Bay in the morning and then ride to Bicheno in the afternoon. There's time also to explore the northern end of the park at the Friendly Beaches.

Take the scenic route out from Coles Bay by ringing the lichen-splashed shores on Jetty Rd before joining the C302, skirting Ramsar-listed Moulting Lagoon and passing the turning into the Friendly Beaches (see the side trip, p172).

Shortly after crossing the stout-black Apsley River the ride turns right onto the coastal A3 highway, which pushes through gorse-choked farmland and across the lyrical Lilla Villa Bridge to the fishing town of Bicheno. Finish the day here with another scenic loop around the Bicheno coast, past the Blowhole and along the granite-studded shores. In the evenings, little penguins shuffle ashore along this bit of coast.

TASSIE'S EAST COAST – DAY 3

CUE		GPS COORDINATES
start	Orford IGA supermarket	147°52'34"N 42°33'09"S
0km	go N on A3	
2.1	1.2km moderate climb	
2.57	Triabunna	147°54'42"N 42°30'29"S
44.2	1km moderate climb	
(50.5	Spiky Bridge)	
(55.7	Kate's Berry Farm)	
58.1	Swansea	148°04'26"N 42°07'23"S
62.3	Swan River Rd, 'to Nine Mile Beach'	
63.8	Dolphin Sands Rd	

CUE CONTINUED		GPS COORDINATES
76.3	unsigned road	
(77.8	Bagot stream)	
	catch dinghy across river	
77.8	go S on pier	
77.9	unsigned road	
78.1	unsigned road	
78.9	C302	
85.0	Jetty Rd	
85.3	Garnet Ave	
85.4	Coles Bay Trading Company	148°17'25"N 42°07'33"S

TASMANIA

TASMANIA'S FRIENDLY BEACHES

The 140-hectare Friendly Beaches Reserve is a protected area. Unlike most environmental reserves, its protection status has not been declared by the government but rather has been purchased by a private organisation. In an example of a new direction in conservation, organisations such as Bush Heritage Australia, which manages the Friendly Beaches Reserve, privately purchases land of high conservation value where it feels governments lack the resources or the will to take action themselves.

TASSIE'S EAST COAST – DAY 4

CUE		GPS COORDINATES
start		Coles Bay Trading Company 148°17′25″N 42°07′33″S
0km		go NW on Garnet Ave
1.0	⬑	Jetty Rd
1.6	⬑	C302
{19.5 ●●⌐		Friendly Beaches 8km ↺}
28.0	⌐	A3, 'to Bicheno'
39.0	⌐	Douglas St
39.4	⬑	The Esplanade
40.9	⌐	Foster St East
41.1		Bicheno visitors centre 148°18′17″N 41°52′27″S

SIDE TRIP: FRIENDLY BEACHES
½–1 hour, 8km
North of the Hazards and Wineglass Bay, the Friendly Beaches are a less visited but no less beautiful section of Freycinet National Park, thought to have been named after a friendly encounter between explorers and Aboriginal people. The dirt access road travels 3km to a lookout with a view along the gleaming white beaches and translucent waters, with the Hazards peeping over the land to the south. From here the road dips steeply to the coast, where you can idle away time on the sand or set up camp in the free campsite that stretches away to the north.

Day 5: Bicheno to St Helens
5–7 hours, 77.6km
This day is spent rarely out of sight or scent of the coast – unless you take the pancake-and-passes alternative route – following sand and headlands along a gentle, enjoyable swell of road. There are no facilities until Scamander so stock up in Bicheno.

Leaving Bicheno the road overlooks the town's fishing fleet and the pretty nature reserve of Diamond Island, looking within swimming distance of shore. At 4.6km the route passes the turning into Douglas Apsley National Park, with the access road climbing to Apsley Waterhole. The star attraction at **Natureworld** (☎ 03-6375 1311; www

.natureworld.com.au; admission $16; 9am–5pm) is the Tasmanian devil. There are devil feedings daily at 4pm, and a devil house where you can get up close to these creatures. Other animals, such as wallabies, quolls, wombats and enormous roos, are fed at 10am. In the lagoon behind the sanctuary, swans flock in seagull-like quantities.

The highway forks at 28.1km, with the alternative route heading off left and the main route continuing straight ahead. There's wild **camping** on the coast at Lagoons Beach at 30km.

Past the junction, the hills press close to the coast bringing more climbs, though few of any significance. At 39km, White Sands Estate, a resort that may be of interest if only for the presence of the **Ironhouse Brewery** (www.ironhouse.com.au). Beer tastings can be had at the resort restaurant (open for lunch and dinner), though it may take more than a beer to get you back up the hill to the highway.

After hugging the granite-rimmed coast past Four Mile Creek, the road turns briefly inland, hooking up with the alternative route at 50.6km to Scamander. The town slipped into Tasmanian history in January 2009 when it recorded the state's hottest

TASSIE'S EAST COAST – DAY 5

CUE		GPS COORDINATES
start		Bicheno visitors centre 148°18′17″N 41°52′27″S
0km		go N on A3
6.7	★	Nature World 148°15′20″N 41°50′17″S
28.1	⬑	alt route: St Marys 27.3km
30.9	▲	1.2km moderate
33.3	▲	700m moderate
38.2	▲	500m moderate
39.0	★	IronHouse Brewery 148°18′21″N 41°34′47″S
50.6	⌐	A3, 'to Scamander'
58.5		Scamander 148°15′45″N 41°27′28″S
64.1		Beaumaris 148°16′33″N 41°25′11″S
{77.4 ●●⬑		Binalong Bay 25km ↺}
77.6		St Helens visitors centre 148°14′56″N 41°19′14″S

emperature on record: 42.2°C. From the own, lovely beaches stretch north before the road arcs around Dianas Basin and climbs through a low lump of land into St Helens.

ALTERNATIVE ROUTE: VIA ST MARYS
2–3½ hours, 27.3km

How much do you love a good pancake? Enough to cycle over two passes? The inland chicane through St Marys leaves the main route just beyond Chain of Lagoons, climbing immediately towards 400m Elephant Pass, just beyond which you'll find isolated Tassie institution, the **Mt Elephant Pancake Barn** (☎ 03-6372 2263; savoury pancakes $15-20, sweet pancakes $8-10; 8am-6pm). From here it's 9km into St Marys, where the highway turns back towards the coast, crossing St Marys Pass and cruising downhill for 5km to rejoin the main route.

SIDE TRIP: BINALONG BAY
2–3 hours, 25km

This moderately difficult ride heads north from St Helens to the holiday settlement of Binalong Bay, which is the southern full stop to the gorgeous Bay of Fires, featuring a sweep of white sand, orange granite boulders and views of the bay stepping away to the north. The return route is through coastal forest, partly on a hard-packed dirt road (a mountain bike is not essential).

Ride east from the centre of St Helens along Quail St, which zings left to become Binalong Bay Rd. Follow this road into Binalong Bay, which has a general store and, next door, little **Angasi** (☎ 03-6376 8222; www.angasi.com.au; Main Rd; mains $27-38) restaurant, which is making a name for itself as one of the best eateries in the state.

Continue through Binalong Bay, veering left onto the dirt Dora Point Rd just before Binalong Bay Rd swings up the hill. The dirt road climbs over Humbug Hill, and near the top there's a view over St Helens Point. Turn left when you return to Binalong Bay Rd, retracing your route into St Helens.

Day 6: St Helens to Scottsdale
5½–9 hours, 102km

Heading inland anywhere in Tasmania means hills, and today the ride leaves the coast for the forested (and deforested) northeast hinterland. It's a long day in the saddle but it can be broken at Weldborough, Derby or Branxholm.

TASSIE'S EAST COAST – DAY 6

CUE			GPS COORDINATES
start		St Helens visitors centre	148°14'56"N 41°19'14"S
0km		go NW on A3	
2.2	▲	1.2km moderate	
6.7	★	Shop in the Bush	
26.0	●●↰	Pub in the Paddock, Pyengana 5km ↺	148°00'17"N 41°17'18"S
{26.5	★	Willows Roadhouse Tearoom}	
30.0	▲	8km moderate	
{37.8	★	Weldborough Pass Little Plains lookout}	
{40.4	★	Weldborough Pass Rainforest Walk}	
44.5		Weldborough	148°57'05"N 41°12'11"S
54.8		Moorina	147°52'11"N 41°07'36"S

CUE CONTINUED			GPS COORDINATES
56.6	▲	1km moderate	
60.9	▲	800m moderate	
67.2	▲	Derby	147°48'05"N 41°08'51"S
75.3		Branxholm	147°44'19"N 41°10'06"S
	▲	600m steep	
76.9	▲	600m moderate	
81.5	▲	600m moderate	
98.0	▲	1.2km moderate	
100.0	▲	1km steep	
100.7	↰	A3, `to Launceston'	
102.0		Scottsdale visitors centre	147°30'24"N 41°10'00"S

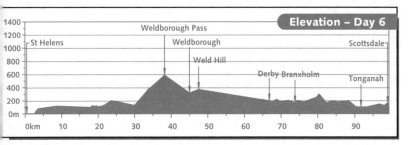

Elevation – Day 6

TASSIE'S EAST COAST – DAYS 5-7

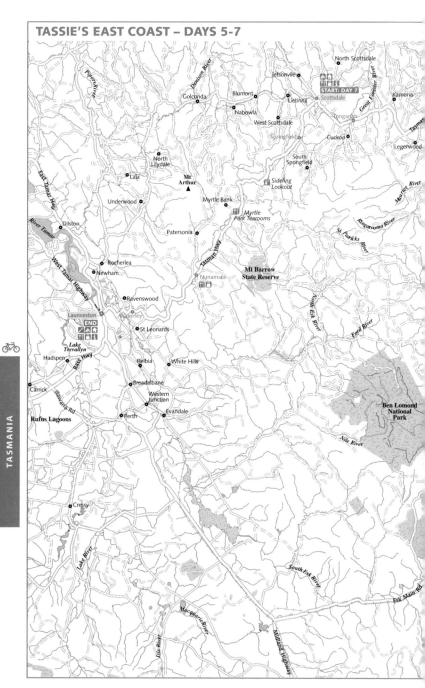

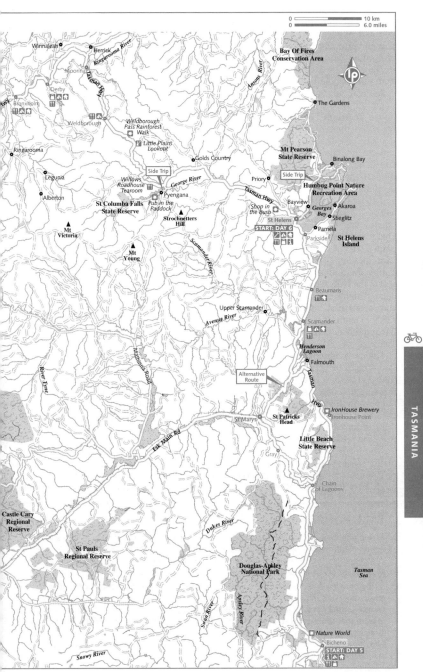

The climb starts pretty much the moment you exit St Helens town limits, elevating you up into the hills. If you've run out of reading matter, the **Shop in the Bush** (6.7km), billing itself as Tassie's best bric-a-brac store, isn't a bad option for books.

As the route continues to creep higher you might appreciate a stop at **Willows Roadhouse Tearoom** (26.5km), though its less tea room than roadhouse. For something quirkier take the side trip at 26km to the isolated, heritage-listed **Pub in the Paddock** (☎ 03-6373 6121; mains $11-25; lunch & dinner) and enjoy a lager next to the beer-drinking pig. Food is on all day at the pub and there's accommodation (single/double $40/55) if you want to stick around and (ahem) pig out on the swine's performances. On the way back to the highway, stop at **Pyengana Dairy Company** (☎ 03-6373 6157; 9am-5pm Sep-May, 10am-4pm Jun-Aug) to sample the clothbound cheddars, then take a seat in the **Holy Cow! Café** (meals $8-30) for dairy delights such as ploughman's lunch, cheese on toast, milkshakes and heavenly, rich ice creams. Try the pepperberry version, flavoured with berries from the nearby Blue Tier plateau.

The *real* climbing begins at 30km in two steep stages to Weldborough Pass. The tall timber at the base of the pass might have you thinking it will be a shaded, forested climb, but beyond this belt of trees it's back up into pasture. At the pass, veer away 100m to the right to look back over the morning's ride from the **Little Plain lookout** (37.8km)…at least until the plantation gums around the platform eclipse the view.

The descent whizzes past the **Weldborough Pass Rainforest Walk**, a 15-minute stroll through myrtle forest, and drops into **Weldborough** (44.5km), the kind of town where the locals sit jawing on porches. The Weldborough Hotel offers free camping on its lawns on the assumption that you'll dine in the pub.

It's gently back skyward for the climb over 373m-high Weldborough Hill before a long, gradual descent through pockets of rainforest to Moorina (54.8km), which is a golf course masquerading as a town. The road dives down through a gully into **Derby** (67.2km), an old tin-mining town that now has a bit of an artsy-cafe thing happening. There's free camping in Derby Park at the west end of town.

In **Branxholm** (75.3km) the hop fields behind the pub look like an effort to cut out the middle man, while the run into Scottsdale passes crops of both hops and opium poppies; name your vice. After 100km the last thing you'll want is the final grind up the hill into Scottsdale.

Day 7: Scottsdale to Launceston
3½–5½ hours, 62.5km

This marvellous day's ride has just one climb and a long descent. The countryside is agricultural until the tough climb of the celebrated Sideling where native forest dominates. The Tasman Hwy is wide enough for comfort and usually has moderate traffic. Despite the fact that it's so close to Tasmania's second city, there are no real towns en route, but there are two food stops: Myrtle Park Tearooms (29.5km) and Nunamara Store (40.7km).

The logging sculpture on the tree stump in Springfield (5.6km) is fairly heroic, as is the tour's final big climb, beginning at 9.3km

---

TALL POPPIES

As you ride through the hills around Scottsdale, and other agricultural areas in Tasmania, you will no doubt notice the tall, purple poppies – yes, they are opium poppies; no, you're not in Afghanistan. Tasmania grows 40% of the world's legal poppy crop and extracts the opiate alkaloids for use in the production of painkillers and other medicines.

The growing and harvesting of poppies in Tasmania is strictly controlled by the state government and the Poppy Advisory and Control Board, but because poppies are grown in rotation with a range of farm crops, accidents can happen. A local horse trainer was surprised to learn that some of his steeds had ingested poppy seeds that had stowed away in horse feed, disqualifying three from racing after testing positive for opium 'use'. Never try to enter a poppy field; it's illegal and most are protected by electric fences. Believe the warning signs on fences: the unrefined sap from opium poppies can kill.

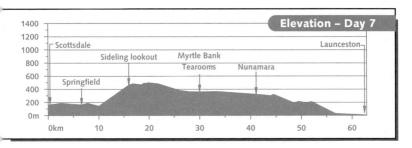

TASSIE'S EAST COAST – DAY 7

CUE		GPS COORDINATES
start	Scottsdale visitors centre	147°30'24"N 41°10'00"S
0km	go SW on A3	
0.5	▲ 700m moderate	
5.6	Springfield	147°29'10"N 41°12'38"S
9.3	▲ 6.2km steep	
{15.5	★ Sideling lookout}	
{29.5	★ Myrtle Park tea rooms}	
40.7	★ Nunamara	147°18'10"N 41°23'18"S
48.2	▲ 800m moderate	
57.8	↱⊙ Tasman Hwy, 'to Launceston'	
59.5	↱⊙ Elphin Rd	
61.5	↱⊙ Lawrence St	
61.7	↰⬆🏠 Cimitiere St	
62.5	Launceston visitors centre	147°08'14"N 41°21'06"S

and fluctuating between steep and moderate. From **Sideling lookout** (15.5km), Scottsdale fills the centre of the view with Bridport away to the northwest. The road climbs gradually on for another 4km before contouring across the range. Then the fun begins as it unfurls down through the forest and past a fleeting view of Ben Lomond at 24km.

There's a lovely roller-coaster descent into Launceston's suburbs, with your arrival into the city eased by a cycleway on Elphin Rd.

COCKLE CREEK

Duration 3 days

Distance 216.1km

Difficulty moderate

Start Hobart

Finish Cockle Creek

Summary Coast-hugging ride to the southernmost road-end in Tasmania, looping around bays and headlands as you meander along the Derwent and Huon Rivers and the D'Entrecasteaux Channel.

Most cyclists come to Tasmania to ride the east or west coasts (or both), overlooking a ride that showcases more coastline than either of these routes; it's also one of the least hilly rides possible in the island state. The ride heads south from Hobart towards the southern extremes of travel in Australia, staring out most of the way at Bruny Island and petering away into dirt roads as it nears what feels like the end of the world. There's also the chance to savour a soak in some hot springs near the ride's end.

PLANNING
What to Bring
Unless planning to loop out from Dover to Cockle Creek and return in a day, cyclists will need to carry camping and cooking equipment for the final night at Cockle Creek, where there are no services (but campsites are plentiful).

Maps
The Information and Land Services Division 1:250,000 *South East* map covers the route.

Permits & Regulations
To camp at Cockle Creek you will need a national-parks pass, which is best picked up at the Hobart visitors centre at the start of the ride. A daily pass costs $11 per person, or you can purchase an eight-week holiday pass for $28.

GETTING TO/FROM THE RIDE
Hobart (start)
AIR
Hobart Airport (☎ 03-6216 1600; www.hiapl .com.au) is at Cambridge, 16km east of town. **Qantas** (☎ 13 13 13; www.qantas.com .au), **Virgin Blue** (☎ 13 67 89; www.virgin blue.com.au) and **Jetstar** (☎ 13 15 38;

TASMANIA

COCKLE CREEK

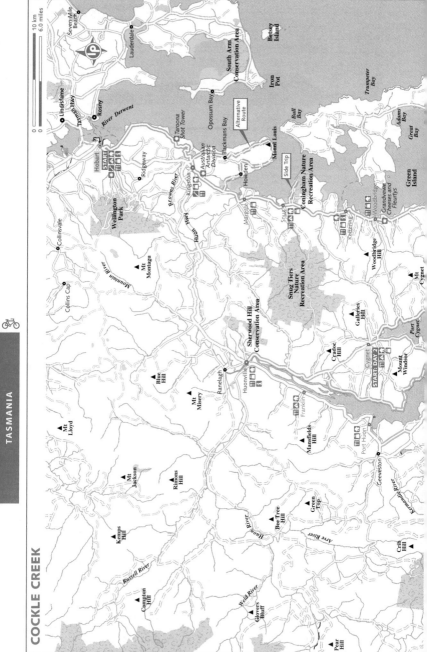

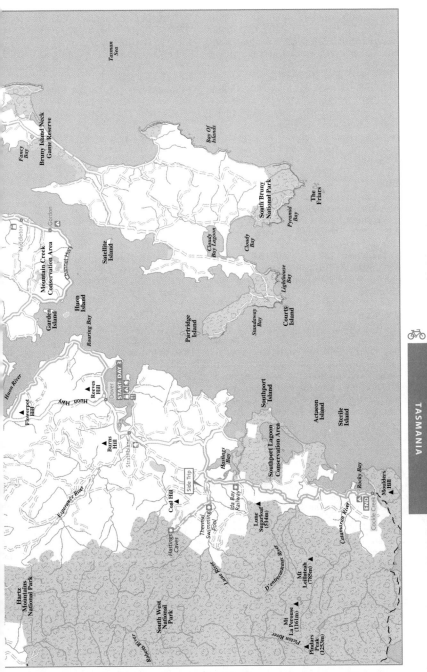

Tasman Sea

Fancy Bay

Bruny Island Neck Game Reserve

Bay Of Islands

Gordon

Middleton

Channel Hwy

Mountain Creek Conservation Area

South Bruny National Park

The Friars

Pyramid Bay

Satellite Island

Cloudy Bay Lagoon

Cloudy Bay

Garden Island

Huon Island

Roaring Bay

Lighthouse Bay

Huon River

Partridge Island

Standaway Bay

Courts Island

▲ Flowerpot Hill

Reeves Hill ▲

Dover

START DAY 3

Huon Hwy

Southport Island

Actaeon Island

Sterile Island

Burns Hill ▲

Strathblane

Esperance River

Side Trip

Southport Lagoon Conservation Area

Hastings Bay

Coal Hill ▲

Thermal Swimming Pool

Ida Bay Railway

Rocky Bay

END

Cockle Creek

Moulders Hill ▲

Hastings Caves

Lune River

Lune Sugarloaf (54m) ▲

D'entrecasteaux Rd

Catamaran River

Hartz Mountains National Park

South West National Park

Mt Leillateah (785m) ▲

Mt La Perouse (1161m) ▲

Picton River

Pindars Peak (1253m) ▲

Huon River

TASMANIA

www.jetstar.com.au) operate flights between Hobart and mainland Australia. **Tasair** (☎ 03-6248 5088; www.tasair.com.au) flies between Hobart and Devonport and Burnie.

The **Airporter Shuttle Bus** (☎ 1300 385 511; www.tasredline.com.au; 199 Collins St; adult/concession $15/6) scoots between the airport and CBD, connecting with all flights. Bookings are essential and when travelling from the city to the airport you must let the operator know that you'll have a bike. Bikes cost $7 to transport.

BUS
There are two main intrastate bus companies operating to/from Hobart:

Redline Coaches (☎ 1300 360 000, 03-6336 1446; 199 Collins St; www.tasredline.com.au) operates from the Transit Centre.

Tassielink (☎ 1300 300 320, ☎ 03-6230 8900; 64 Brisbane St; www.tassielink.com.au) operates from the Hobart Bus Terminal.

BICYCLE
Cyclists riding from the east coast enter Hobart across the Tasman Bridge, which has narrow bike/footpaths at its edges (and a nuisance set of stairs at its western end). If coming from the west coast or the Midland Hwy you enter suburban Hobart at Granton, by the Bridgewater Causeway. Swing left onto Main Rd, following this into Claremont, where you can join the Intercity Cycleway (at Box Hill Rd), which runs for 16km into the city centre.

CAR
The big-boy rental firms have airport desks and city offices as follows:

AutoRent-Hertz (☎ 03-6237 1111; www.autorent.com.au; cnr Bathurst & Harrington Sts)

Avis (☎ 03-6234 4222; www.avis.com.au; 125 Bathurst St)

Budget (☎ 03-6234 5222, 13 27 27; www.budget.com.au; 96 Harrington St)

Europcar (☎ 03-6231 1077, 1800 030 118; www.europcar.com.au; 112 Harrington St)

Thrifty (☎ 03-6234 1341, 1300 367 227; www.thrifty.com.au; 11-17 Argyle St)

Cheaper local firms offer daily rental rates from as low as $25:

Bargain Car Rentals (☎ 03-6234 6959, 1300 729 230; www.bargaincarrentals.com.au; 173 Harrington St)

Lo-Cost Auto Rent (☎ 03-6231 0550, 1800 647 060; www.locostautorent.com; 105 Murray St)

Rent-a-Bug (☎ 03-6231 0300, 1800 647 060; www.rentabug.com.au; 105 Murray St)

Rent For Less (☎ 03-6231 6844; www.rentforless.com.au; 92 Harrington St)

Selective Car Rentals (☎ 03-6234 3311, 1800 300 102; www.selectivecarrentals.com.au; 47 Bathurst St)

Cockle Creek (finish)
BUS
Tassielink (☎ 1300 300 520; www.tassielink.com.au) buses arrive at and depart from the Cockle Creek ranger station. The service runs three times a week (Mon, Wed and Fri) from December through March. The bus departs Cockle Creek at 11.45am for the 3½-hour trip to Hobart ($71).

THE RIDE
Day 1: Hobart to Cygnet
5–7 hours, 82.6km
A constantly undulating run south from the capital, with near-constant views across the D'Entrecasteaux Channel to Bruny Island. The looping route means you won't get far on the map, but you should have fun getting there.

The route begins by passing through a couple of Hobart's icons: the sandstone warehouses along **Salamanca Place** and ye-olde-Englande **Arthur Circus**.

There are good river views through Lower Sandy Bay, and as the ride heads up and over Bonnet Hill, the 48m-high **Taroona Shot Tower** (☎ 03-6227 8885; fax 6227 8643; admission $5.50; 9am-5pm) forms a sandstone spike beside the road. The tower was built in 1870 to make lead shot for firearms. Molten lead was dribbled from the top, forming perfect spheres on its way down to a cooling vat of water at the bottom. The river views from atop the 318 steps are wondrous. The tower is surrounded by leafy grounds and has a snug **tea room** (light meals $4-8; 11am-3pm) downstairs. At the foot of the hill, Kingston marks the southern limit of Hobart's suburbs; the alternative route departs from here.

COCKLE CREEK – DAY 1

CUE			GPS COORDINATES
start		Hobart visitors centre	147°19'54"N 42°52'59"S
0km		go SE on Elizabeth St	
0.1		Morrison St	
0.4		Montpellier Retreat	
0.5		Salamanca Place	
0.7		200m steep	
0.8		Runnymede St	
1.1		Hampden Rd	
(50m)		Colville St	
1.4		Trumpeter St	
1.5		Napoleon St	
1.8		cross footbridge to Marieville Esp	
2.4		Sandy Bay Rd	
10.0		2.3km moderate	
{11.2	★	Taroona Shot Tower}	

CUE CONTINUED			GPS COORDINATES
15.7		Kingston	147°18'30"N 42°58'36"S
		alt route: Tinderbox 26km	
16.4		B68, `to Margate'	
{18.0	★	Australian Antarctic Division}	
23.6		Margate	147°15'35"N 43°01'26"S
29.0		Snug	147°15'17"N 43°03'56"S
{29.9		Conningham 6km }	
36.7		Kettering	147°14'52"N 43°07'46"S
41.1		Woodbridge	147°14'18"N 43°09'38"S
{44.3	★	Grandvewe Cheesery}	
{45.4	★	Fleurtys}	
50.9		Middleton	147°15'14"N 43°13'54"S
55.4		Gordon	147°14'27"N 43°15'41"S
68.9		2.3km moderate	
82.3		B68, `to Huonville'	
82.6		Cygnet hall	147°04'29"N 43°09'29"S

On Kingston's outskirts the Channel Hwy (B68) – the ride's guiding line for the day – passes the **Australian Antarctic Division** (☎ 03-6232 3209; www.aad.gov .au; 203 Channel Hwy; admission free; 8.30am-5pm Mon-Fri) headquarters. The Division administers Australia's 42% wedge of the frozen continent and visitors can check out displays that feature Antarctic equipment, clothing and scientific vehicles, plus ecological information and some brilliant photographs. The centre's cafeteria is open to the public.

The alternative route returns at 21km, and as you enter Margate (23.6km) you'll pass the **Margate Train** (☎ 03-6267 1020; www.view.com.au/margatetrain; admission free; 9am-4.30pm), the last passenger train used in Tasmania, standing idly on a redundant section of track, its carriages now transformed into marketlike stores. Behind it is **Inverawe Native Gardens** (☎ 03-6267 2020; www.inverawe.com.au; admission $8; 9.30am-sunset Sep-May), a private 9.5-hectare property with landscaped native gardens, trails and water views.

Through Snug there's a nice side trip out to **Conningham Beach** (6km return), one of the most beautiful coastal spots in southern Tasmania. The road to Conningham hugs the water's edge – this is not the place to drift off line – then climbs through low hills to the beach, it's bush-backed sands and colourful boatsheds looking across North West Bay to Mt Wellington and Cathedral Rock.

Out of Kettering the road rises to overlook Bruny Island, a short distance across the D'Entrecasteaux Channel. The flash establishment by the jetty in Woodbridge (41.1km) is **Peppermint Bay** (☎ 03-6267 4088; www.peppermintbay.com.au; 3435 Channel Hwy), housing a provedore, an art gallery, an upmarket restaurant (mains $25 to $30; open daily for lunch, and for dinner on Saturday) and a casual bar (mains $15 to $20; open daily for lunch, dinner Tuesday to Saturday). The emphasis is on local produce: seafood, fruits, meats and cheeses, used to fantastic effect. South of town the gourmet cycling continues at **Grandvewe Cheeses** (44.3km; ☎ 03-6267 4099; 59 Devlyns Rd, Birchs Bay; tastings free; 10am-5pm Sep-Jun, 10am-4pm Wed-Mon Jul & Aug), a farm churning out organic cheese from both sheep and cows' milk; and **Fleurtys** (45.4km; ☎ 03-6267 4078; www.fleurtys.com.au; 3866 Channel Hwy, Birchs Bay; 11am-4pm daily), a cool little glass-fronted provedore in the trees where you can take a bushwalk, inspect the essential-oil distillery and stock up on homemade jam, vinegar, honey, chutney, herbs, fudge and oils. The cafe (mains $10 to $16) here is great for lunch.

The land opens up a little beyond Middleton as farms squeeze themselves between the hills and the channel, the road running along a sea wall through Gordon, where Bruny Island seems even closer. The road swings west around the frayed coast, passing through **Verona Sands** (63.7km), a lovely sandy nick in the shoreline, and saving the day's toughest climb until near the end as it chugs over hills to Port Cygnet and, on its shores, the town of Cygnet. The **lookout** at the top of the climb has a view south along the coastline that you'll be following for the next two days.

ALTERNATIVE ROUTE: TINDERBOX
1½–2½ hours, 28km

If you want to keep the coastal theme going out of Kingston, it's a good loop ride through isolated Tinderbox. Take the C623 down to Kingston Beach, crossing the headland to Blackmans Bay – Blowhole Rd is the best entry into the bay. From here the road heads across wooded slopes to the **Tinderbox Marine Nature Reserve**, where there's a 100m snorkelling trail along the edge of rock shelf. Turning back north, the route passes through Howden to rejoin the main ride between Kingston and Margate.

Day 2: Cygnet to Dover
5–7½ hours, 90.7km

Another day of million-dollar views, wrapping around the Huon estuary and continuing the meander down the D'Entrecasteaux Channel, rarely more than a few hundred metres from the shore. The ride is mostly flat until Geeveston, beyond which it's lined with small (and a couple of not-so-small) climbs.

For cyclists in a hurry it's 17km straight across to Huonville from Cygnet, but the more leisurely, more scenic route is through Lymington and Petcheys Bay along the shores of the Huon estuary. The road has about 9km of dirt but it's smooth and

hard-packed and is a favourite with local cyclists. It hovers near the coast most of its length, looking onto rocky coast and fish farms, with little traffic. All in all, it's a perfect cycling section.

The road heads out past Cygnet's yacht moorings, the road all but nailed to the coast until Lymington. Near Beaupre Point it passes through some **blueberry farms**; you can pick your own in January and February. When you return to the coast the land you can see immediately across the water is that through which you'll ride later in the day. After following the Huon River upstream beside the grassed Egg Islands, the route heads south, crossing the river at Huonville and heading back downstream. Out of Huonville there are plenty of **stalls** selling apples and other fruit, while the star feature in Franklin (45.8km) is the **Wooden Boat Centre** (☎ 03-6266 3586; www.woodenboatcentre.com; Huon Hwy; admission $6; 9.30am-5pm), which is part of the School of Wooden Boatbuilding, a unique school running accredited 12-month courses in traditional boat-building using Tasmanian timbers. Stick your head in the door to learn about boat-building and watch boats being cobbled together.

Tunnelling through apple orchards, Scotts Rd (59.2km) adds a couple of climbs to the day but also provides a welcome breather from the highway, which the route leaves again at Surges Bay (67.4km). This road undulates around Flowerpot Hill and down through Brooks Bay, at about the point where the Huon empties into the channel. Along the way, you can wave to your morning's route across the river.

COCKLE CREEK – DAY 2

CUE			GPS COORDINATES
start		Cygnet town hall	147°04'29"N 43°09'29"S
0km		go S on Mary St (B68)	
5.5		Lymington	147°04'18"N 43°11'56"S
7.7	⚠	600m dirt road	
8.9	⚠	8.3km dirt road	
27.7	↰	B68, `to Huonville'	
38.5		A6, `to Geeveston', Huonville"	
45.8		Franklin	147°00'38"N 43°05'23"S
56.8		Port Huon	146°57'48"N 43°09'19"S
59.2	↰	Scotts Rd (C634)	
59.7	▲	1.4km moderate	

CUE CONTINUED			GPS COORDINATES
62.7	▲	600m steep	
63.4	↰	A6, `to Dover'	
67.4	↰	C638, `to Police	
71.1	▲	500m moderate	
74.9	▲	500m moderate	
77.5	▲	900m steep	
81.8	▲	500m moderate	
83.1	▲	1.5km moderate	
87.7	⚠	pick-a-plank bridge	
89.9	↱	Station Rd (unsigned)	
90.7		Dover Grocer & Newsagency	147°00'54"N 43°18'50"S

After the longest climb of the day, the road drops to the coast and follows the curve of Kent Beach into Dover.

Day 3: Dover to Cockle Creek
3–4 hours, 42.8km

If you've developed the taste for coastline, you might pine for it today with the route hanging back just out of sight of the shoreline – hang in there; the coast around Recherche Bay is pretty special. There's no store at Cockle Creek, although there's a cafe at Ida Bay, so stock up in Dover or Southport, which is 3km off the route.

The perfect pyramid of **Adamson's Peak** dominates the view as the ride heads south out of Dover, climbing – mostly gradually – for the first 14km over forested Tylers Hill and then dropping more quickly towards Southport.

At Lune River, **Ida Bay Railway** (☎ 03-6298 3110; www.idabayrailway.com.au; rides $25; 9am-5pm daily Oct-Apr, Wed, Sat & Sun only May-Sep) tracks a scenic 14km, 1½-hour narrow-gauge course through native bush to Deep Hole Bay. It is Australia's southernmost railway and, shortly after, you leave Australia's southernmost bit of bitumen road – there are all sorts of southernmost claims down here; you're likely to be Australia's southernmost cyclist.

With its stony base, the dirt road offers a rock 'n' roll sort of finish to your tour. Encased in bush, the views are narrow until the road pops out on the shores of **Recherche Bay** – if this is the end of the world there are worse places to be. There are a number of basic campsites along the bay's shores, the largest of which is at Cockle Creek.

COCKLE CREEK – DAY 3

CUE		GPS COORDINATES
start	Dover Grocer & Newsagency	147°00′54″N 43°18′50″S
0km	go S on Huon Hwy	
5.0	▲ 800m moderate	
16.0	↗ C635, 'to Ida Bay'	
19.3	▲ 600m moderate	
{20.2 ●● ⌐ Hastings Caves & Thermal Springs 16km ↻}		
23.5	★ Ida Bay Railway	146°54′15″N 43°26′38″s
23.7	⚠ dirt road	
35.1	↘ C686, 'to Catamaran'	
42.8	Cockle Creek campsite	146°53′11″N 43°34′41″S

SIDE TRIP: HASTINGS CAVES & THERMAL SPRINGS
1½–2 hours, 16km

Near Lune River a dirt road heads west through thickening forest. After 3.5km, it pops out at the Hastings visitors centre and, 100m behind it, a **thermal swimming pool** (admission $5) filled with 28°C water from hot springs. There's a decent **cafe** (light meals $6-15; breakfast & lunch) at the visitors centre.

The road burrows on through the rainforest for another 4.5km to the road end, from where it's a five-minute walk to the **Hastings Caves** (☎ 03-6298 3209; www.parks.tas.gov.au/reserves/hastings; admission incl thermal pool $22; 9am-5pm Mar, Apr & Sep-Dec, 9am-6pm Jan & Feb, 10am-4pm May-Aug). Tours leave on the hour and admission includes a 45-minute tour of the amazing dolomite Newdegate Cave; tickets need to be purchased at the Hastings visitors centre.

ACROSS THE CENTRAL PLATEAU

Duration 5 days
Distance 286.3km
Difficulty moderate
Start Devonport
Finish Hobart
Summary An island traverse through the haunting, lake-splattered Central Plateau, crossing from the ferry terminal in the north to the capital city in the south.

Almost a diagonal crossing of the island, this ride traverses a variety of terrain from fertile coastal plains to the rainforested slopes of the Great Western Tiers; from the barren and wild Central Plateau to the heritage towns of the grassed Midlands.

The highlight of the journey, in more ways than one, is the climb to and descent from the plateau, passing an option into Liffey Falls and rising beneath the rippled escarpments of the Great Western Tiers. Day 2 has an epic climb but otherwise it's pretty straightforward terrain. Towns are few, as are vehicles and, on the plateau, trees; this is as close to outback riding as Tasmania can offer.

TASMANIA

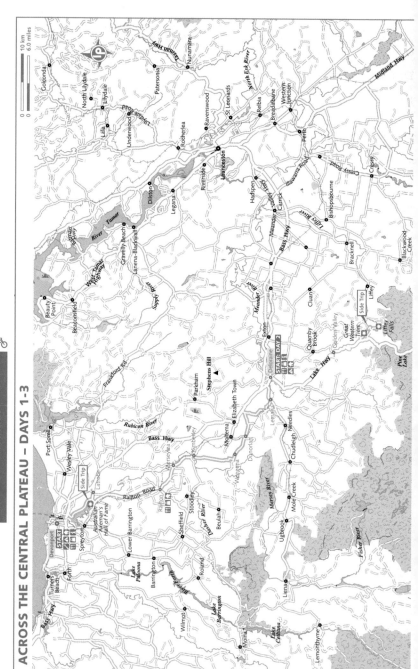

ACROSS THE CENTRAL PLATEAU – DAYS 1-3

TASMANIA

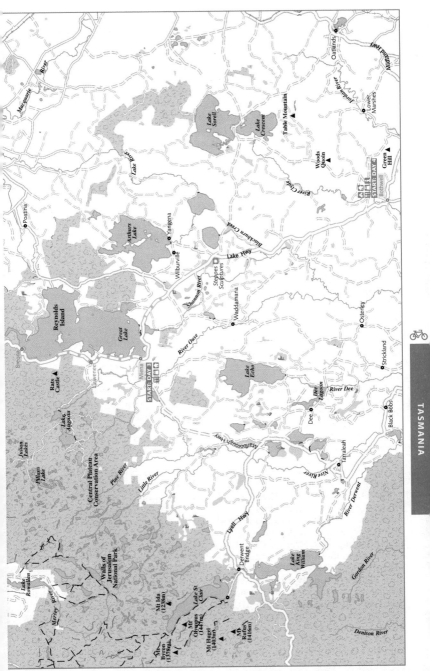

PLANNING
When to Cycle
Though it's exposed to the conditions, this ride is best in summer. The altitude – the ride reaches 1210m and coasts along the plateau at around 800m to 1000m – sees average temperatures drop to around 5.5°C in winter. Even in October, average temperatures reach only around 12°C.

What to Bring
The treeless Central Plateau is particularly exposed, so carry plenty of sun protection and, on the flip side, a stock of warm clothes.

Maps
The ride is covered on the 1:250,000 *North West*, *North East* and *South East* maps in the Information and Land Services Division series.

GETTING TO/FROM THE RIDE
Devonport (start)
AIR
Qantas Link (☎ 13 13 13; www.qantas .com.au) connects Devonport to Melbourne. **Tasair** (☎ 03-6248 5088; www.tasair.com .au) flies between Hobart and Devonport.

BUS
Redline Coaches (☎ 1300 360 000, 03-6336 1446; www.tasredline.com.au) services the north and northwest coasts daily, with buses from Launceston to Devonport ($25, 2½ hours) via Deloraine and Latrobe. This service picks up passengers at the Spirit of Tasmania ferry terminal. From Devonport, buses continue west along the Bass Hwy to Smithton ($32, 2½ hours).

Tassielink Coaches (☎ 1300 300 520, 03-6336 9500; www.tassielink.com.au) work their way west from Launceston two to three times a week, depending on the season, ending up in Strahan. These buses stop in Devonport, Sheffield and Cradle Mountain ($54, three hours). Tassielink also operates a daily express service, picking up passengers from Devonport's Spirit of Tasmania ferry terminal and running them to Launceston ($22, 1½ hours) and Hobart ($52, four hours). This service also runs daily in reverse from Hobart, reaching Devonport in time for the nightly ferry sailing.

BICYCLE
The main (A1) route west from Launceston is best avoided due to heavy traffic. Instead, head north from Launceston on the West Tamar Hwy, turning west at Exeter through Frankford towards Devonport.

Hobart (finish)
See p215.

THE RIDE
Day 1: Devonport to Deloraine
3½–5 hours, 59.1km

A pleasant, reasonably easy day begins beside the lazy Mersey River, gradually getting hillier as the day progresses. There's only one climb of note, as you leave Kimberley, but it's a doozy. The countryside is mostly grazing land, though plantation blue gums are reclaiming large sections of the landscape.

The route description assumes you will arrive on the morning ferry and ride straight out of town. If you are staying in Devonport, begin at the visitors centre and ride south on Formby Rd, crossing the Mersey River on the roadside bikepath and looping back under the bridge onto River Rd, joining the described route at 1.9km.

River Rd does exactly as the name suggests, heading along the bank of the Mersey, offering good (if sometimes industrial) views across the wide waterway.

Near Latrobe, the **Australian Axeman's Hall of Fame** (☎ 03-6426 2099; Bell's Pde; 9am-5pm) is considered the birthplace

---

TASMANIAN TRAIL

Those tempting red-and-yellow signs you're passing as you ride refer to the island-long, 480km Tasmanian Trail. Stretching from Devonport to Dover, the multi-use trail is mostly used by cyclists and follows quiet roads, fire trails and forestry tracks, sometimes circuitously. It's not an easy trail – a mountain bike is definitely required – but if you're looking to cross the island away from the highways it's a decent option.

The trail is managed by the **Tasmanian Trail Association** (www.tasmaniantrail .com.au), and the Tasmanian Trail guidebook can be purchased through the website.

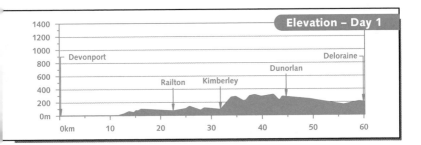

ACROSS THE CENTRAL PLATEAU – DAY 1

CUE		GPS COORDINATES
start	Spirit of Tasmania ferry terminal	
0km	go E on Murray St	
0.3	Tarleton St	
1.9	River Rd	
3.4	River Rd	
{7.8	Australian Axeman's Hall of Fame}	
8.3	B19, 'to Spreyton'	
{	Latrobe 600m	
9.1	B13, 'to Railton'	
12.3	900m moderate	
14.2	500m moderate	
22.0	Kimberley Rd (B13), Railton	

CUE CONTINUED		GPS COORDINATES
24.8	700m moderate	
31.3	C160, Kimberley, 'to Weegena'	
	2km steep	
36.5	300m steep	
39.1	C160, 'to Dunorlan'	
43.8	Dunorlan	146°33'10"N 41°29'18"S
48.3	C163, 'to Red Hills'	
52.8	Lemana Rd	
55.0	B12 (unsigned)	
57.9	Deloraine	
59.1	Great Western Tiers visitors centre	146°39'04"N 41°31'24"S

of one of Tassie's favourite sports, wood chopping, and the site of the first wood-chopping world championship in 1891. The Hall of Fame charts wood-chopping's role in the pioneering of Australia plus its development as a sport. Included in the entry fee here is the **Platypus & Trout Experience**, which sheds much light on the breeding life and habits of the platypus and has live trout in display tanks. A cafe-restaurant serves light snacks and refreshments.

Characterful **Latrobe** (side trip at 8.3km) is a well-preserved historic town with 75 National Trust–registered buildings on its main street alone. The town bills itself as the 'platypus capital of the world', and the best place to spot the shy monotreme is the **Warawee Forest Reserve**. Dawn and dusk **platypus-spotting tours** ($10) are organised through the visitors centre; be sure to book ahead. Pick-up is from the visitors centre. Each Boxing Day, Latrobe attracts professional cyclists from all over Australia for the **Latrobe Wheel Race**.

Rural Tasmania (and the truck traffic) begins on the B13 (9.1km), with crops, cows and sheep at the roadside. This road then undulates through plantation forest to Railton, where the local idea of a good time is fashioning hedges into the shapes of critters such as elephants, crocodiles and wallabies. In Railton the route briefly joins the Tasmanian Trail (see boxed text p186) before it ducks away into the scrub. Stock up on lunch items in Railton as it's the last food stop before Deloraine.

Blue gums dominate the scene past Railton, swarming over former grazing lands, while the Gog Range's **Alum Cliffs** rear from the horizon at the top of the climb out of Kimberley. Escarpment views continue on the way to Dunorlan (43.8km); then the route rolls, mostly downwards, in the lee of the **Great Western Tiers**, which rise up to the Central Plateau – there's a lookout and relief map of the Tiers as you enter Deloraine.

Day 2: Deloraine to Miena
4½–6 hours, 68.7km
This ride includes one of the longest climbs possible in Tasmania, up through the Great Western Tiers to 1210m, just 400m shy of

TASMANIA

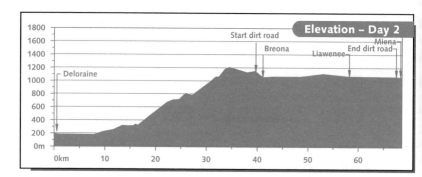

ACROSS THE CENTRAL PLATEAU – DAY 2

CUE			GPS COORDINATES
start		Great Western Tiers visitors centre	146°39'04"N 41°31'24"S
0km		go S on Emu Bay Rd	
0.1	⌐→⊙	Emu ay Rd	
0.6	⌐→⊙	unsigned road across bridge	
0.8	⌐→	A5, 'to Meander'	
8.0	↰	A5, 'to Miena'	
16.7	▲	5.8km steep	
24.3	●●↰	Liffey Falls 12km ⟳	146°45'52"N 41°41'52"S
24.7	▲	1km steep	

CUE CONTINUED			GPS COORDINATES
27.3	▲	4.7km steep	
{30.6	★	lookout}	
32.4	▲	2.1km steep	
35.3	★	Pine Lake	146°42'22"N 41°44'28"S
39.8	⚠	8.8km intermittent dirt road	
48.6	⚠	19.7km dirt road	
51.9	▲	1.1km moderate	
68.6	⌐→	B11, 'to Bronte Park'	
68.7		Great Lake General Store	146°42'58"N 41°59'03"S

the island's highest point. The climb is through damp, forest-clad slopes, topping out in alpinelike bareness atop the Tiers.

The route heads out of Deloraine through irrigated lands, which end abruptly at 8km as the ride enters forest and slowly begins the climb into the **Great Western Tiers**. The ascent begins in earnest at 16.7km, just beyond Golden Valley township – switch down into a granny gear and settle in for the long haul. The climb is through thickening bush, except for a spot of farmland atop the ridge at the end of the first pull.

About 4km before the top of the escarpment, a viewpoint (30.6km) provides a panorama through a narrow gap to the lowlands eastwards, though the view is dominated by the crenellated bluffs overlooking nearer to hand.

The road continues its twisting climb, passing beneath the dolerite neck of **Projection Bluff** and reaching the highway's highest point (1210m) at a barren pass of stunted shrubs and fractured rock. Immediately below you're welcomed into the Central Lakes area by **Pine Lake**, surrounded by pencil pines. If you want

a break of sorts, there's a good 30-minute walk by the lake.

At 39.6km, the enormous puddle of **Great Lake** comes in to view, heralding the beginning of the dirt road that coils down to the lake, the site of the first dam in Australia's largest hydroelectric power system in 1911. It's also been a trout-fishing area since the release of brown trout here in 1870.

From Great Lake it's on-again, off-again dirt and bitumen for almost 9km before dirt road wins the battle. Tiny Liawenee has the feel of a Nevada ghost town – there's a ranger station and a cop shop and that's about it – and there's little shade for most of the plateau stretch to Miena, putting cyclists at the mercy of sun and wind.

SIDE TRIP: LIFFEY FALLS
1–2 hours, 12km
A delightful forest road turns left from Lake Hwy at 24.3km, contouring across the slopes through forested areas. The final descent through World Heritage–listed rainforest is sheer magnificence; even the climb back out is to be enjoyed in forest this awesome. From the car park a walking

track descends beneath tall tree ferns and beside a series of cascades to tuck in under moss-covered **Liffey Falls**, one of the state's most beautiful waterfalls. The walk takes around 40 minutes return.

Day 3: Miena to Bothwell
3½–5½ hours, 62.9km

An easy day's ride as a reward for yesterday's big climb, with the route dropping more than 600m with only a few small rises to interrupt the downward flow. There's little in particular to see en route except the country unfold in its various nuances: heathlands, dry eucalypt forest, pasture. There are no towns or shops before Bothwell.

At the start of the day the route follows the Tasmanian Trail, continuing around the shores of Great Lake and then beneath the dam wall at pretty Shannon Lagoon.

Across St Patrick Plains, at around 22km, there are some rocks that half resemble standing stones. At 27.2km, after dipping through a section of eucalypt forest, you can see the real thing at the middle-of-nowhere Steppes, where artist Stephen Walker has created a Stonehenge of bronze artworks at the unusual **Steppes Sculptures**.

ACROSS THE CENTRAL PLATEAU – DAY 3

CUE			GPS COORDINATES
start		Great Lake General Store	146°42'58"N 41°59'03"S
0km		go SE on B11	
0.2	↱	A5, `to Bothwell'	
2.1	▲	500m moderate	
{27.2	★	Steppes Sculptures}	
41.6	▲	1.4km moderate	
62.4	↰	Alexander St	
62.8	↱	Deniston St	
62.9		Bothwell visitors centre	147°00'28"N 42°22'58"S

There's a rollicking little descent at 39km into a fertile bowl of farmland, followed immediately by the day's most significant climb. As you approach Bothwell the route skirts the **Bothwell Golf Course**, the oldest golf course in the southern hemisphere, its square greens fenced off to keep out the sheep. Cross the murky Clyde River to enter historic Bothwell, where the tartan road signs would have you believe you've just arrived in Scotland, though the parched earth is purely Australian.

Day 4: Bothwell to Richmond
3½–6 hours, 65.6km

If you're feeling fit and pressed for time it's easy enough to barrel straight to Hobart this day, but twee Richmond is worth a stop. The downhill trend continues with this day finishing virtually at sea level.

After contouring and climbing around on hillsides out of Bothwell, the ride descends tortuously for 5km into the Jordan River valley, joining the Midland Hwy at Melton Mowbray (20.6km). This is Tasmania's busiest highway, connecting Hobart and Launceston, but the verge here makes the section between Melton Mowbray and Pontville one of the more pleasant stretches. That said, it's still worth ducking away from the highway at 26.4km into **Kempton**, its handsome main street lined with old Georgian houses and coach stables. The town is named after Anthony Kemp, a name that will be familiar to anybody who's read Nicholas Shakespeare's *In Tasmania*.

Back on the highway the ride climbs gradually over 322m-high Constitution Hill; on the descent you'll get your first glimpse of Mt Wellington, Hobart's great sentinel. By the time you scoot down the

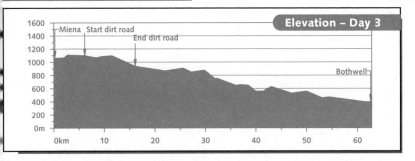

Elevation – Day 3

Miena Start dirt road
End dirt road
Bothwell

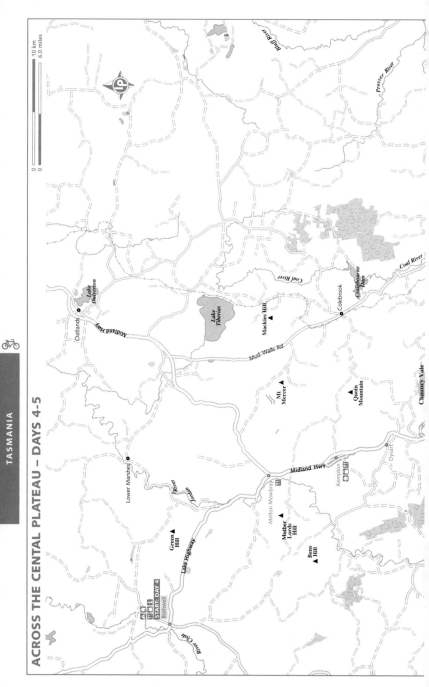

ACROSS THE CENTAL PLATEAU – DAYS 4-5

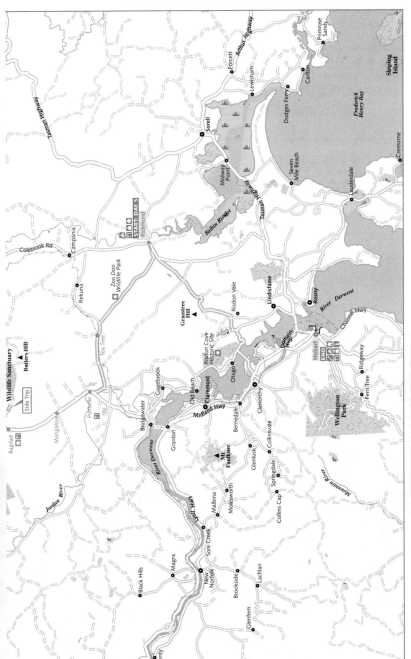

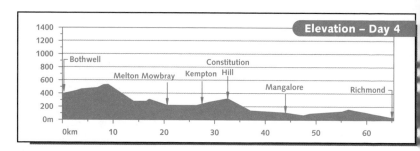

ACROSS THE CENTRAL PLATEAU – DAY 4

CUE		GPS COORDINATES
start	Bothwell visitors centre	147°00′28″N 42°22′58″S
0km	go S on Market Place	
0.1	↰ A5, 'to Melton Mowbray'	
6.8	▲ 2.1km moderate	
16.5	▲ 500m moderate	
20.6	↱ Midland Hwy, 'to Hobart', Melton Mowbray"	
26.4	↱ C194, 'to Kempton'	
27.4	Kempton	147°12′00″N 42°31′48″
29.1	↱ Midland Hwy, 'to Hobart'	
	▲ 3.5km moderate	

CUE CONTINUED		GPS COORDINATES
37.1	Bagdad	147°13′19″N 42°37′37″S
[37.7 ●● ↰	Chauncy Vale Wildlife Sanctuary 7km ↺]	
47.4		147°15′56″N 42°41′04″S
47.7	↰ Ford Rd, 'to Tea Tree'	
48.2	▲ 800m moderate	
49.0	↰ C321, 'to Tea Tree'	
55.3	↱ C322, 'to Richmond'	
58.7	★ Zoo Doo Wildlife Park	147°22′32″N 42°42′22″S
64.9	↰ B31, 'to Richmond'	
65.6	Richmond post office	147°26′18″N 42°44′06″S

hill into Pontville, where the route turns off the highway, you can see not only Mt Wellington but the city suburbs also.

At around 54km, in Tea Tree, look up to the hill of houses to the right and be grateful you're not cycling that road. The final stretch into Richmond cuts past several Coal Valley vineyards and the **Zoo Doo Wildlife Park** (☎ 03-6260 2444; www.zoodoo.com.au; 620 Middle Tea Tree Rd; admission $16; 9am-5pm), which has 'safari bus' rides, picnic areas and the sort of captive wildlife – miniature horses, wallabies and a nursery farm – that's perhaps best left to the kids.

SIDE TRIP: CHAUNCY VALE WILDLIFE SANCTUARY
½–1 hour, 7km

At the southern edge of Bagdad, take Chauncy Vale Rd, which climbs gently up a valley on a hard-packed dirt road to Chauncy Vale Wildlife Sanctuary, the 400-hectare former property of author Nan Chauncy (1900–70) that now preserves a valley of eucalypt woodland endemic to the Southern Midlands – the remainder of which is now bare. It costs $2 to visit the sanctuary, which is home to a large

population of wallabies, birds and snakes. Interpretive panels explain features of the vegetation, wildlife and geology, and marked walks visit places of interest like the caves that inspired Chauncy's children's stories.

Day Dawn, the house where all her books were written, was built between 1916 and 1918 and is preserved as it was when Chauncy and husband Anton occupied it. Admission into the house is $2.

Day 5: Richmond to Hobart
2–3 hours, 30km

It's a short ride to complete this island crossing, heading up and over Grasstree Hill to finish on Hobart's main dedicated cycle path.

The narrow, lightly trafficked C324 beelines straight across the agricultural valley to the Meehan Range, then widens as it twists its way up the dry slopes.

Beyond the crest on Grasstree Hill (9.3km) the road unwinds down onto Hobart's eastern shore, passing **Risdon Cove Historic Site** (16.1km), where the first European settlers pitched their tents in 1803. The spot became the site of the first massacre of Tasmanian Aboriginal

lonelyplanet.com

Tassie's West Coast · TASMANIA · **193**

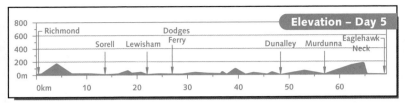

ACROSS THE CENTRAL PLATEAU – DAY 5

CUE		GPS COORDINATES
start	Richmond post office	147°26'18"N 42°44'06"S
0km	go SW on Bridge St	
1.7	C324, 'to Risdon Vale'	
5.0	4.3km moderate	
14.8	B32, 'to Bridgewater'	
16.1	Risdon Cove Historic Site	147°19'09"N 42°49'22"S
20.4	Brooker Hwy	
20.5	Elwick Rd	
21.2	Intercity Cycleway	
30.0	Hobart visitors centre	147°19'55"N 42°52'56"S

people – Risdon Cove was returned to the Aboriginal community by the state government in 1995.

Across Bowen Bridge, zig-zag briefly onto Brooker Hwy before joining up with the Intercity Cycleway, which will guide you all the way into Hobart; the visitors centre is 100m straight ahead from Mawson Place, at the end of the cycleway.

TASSIE'S WEST COAST

Duration 10 days

Distance 661km

Difficulty demanding

Start Evandale

Finish Hobart

Summary A ride on the wild side through Tasmania's spectacular western mountains, dropping to the coast at Strahan before climbing back through World Heritage–listed wilderness.

By rights, Tasmania should be too small to have huge pockets of wilderness, but untouched and untamed lands stretch along its fierce west coast. Land this wild should not come easily and it doesn't, with the hill climbs queuing up one after the other – you will notice them but not as much as the scenery, which takes

in Tasmania's most famous mountain (Cradle Mountain), its cutest coastal town (Strahan), its highest waterfall (Montezuma Falls) and its most beautiful lake (Lake St Clair), all on highways that feel at times like back roads.

The ride is written up as a 10-day outing but it's recommended that you factor in extra days for stops at places such as Cradle Mountain, Strahan and Lake St Clair.

PLANNING
When to Cycle
The best times for this ride are late October to mid-December and February to mid-April. Winter (and sometimes summer) snows on the highlands and extreme wind/rain on the west coast limit good riding times. January school holidays may make roads busier and fill accommodation.

What to Bring
Be prepared for wet and cold weather even in summer; waterproof panniers are highly recommended. Walking opportunities abound at Mt Roland, Cradle Mountain and Lake St Clair so it's worth trying to squeeze in a decent pair of hiking boots.

Maps
The best coverage of the areas is given on the Information and Land Services Division's 1:250,000 series, though you'll need all four of the maps: *South East, South West, North East* and *North West*. If you prefer to carry a single map, try Hema's 1:650,000 *Tasmania Handy Map*.

Permits & Regulations
It will be necessary to purchase a national-parks pass for this ride as this route cuts through the Franklin-Gordon Wild Rivers National Park into the Cradle Mountain–Lake St Clair National Park on Day 7 (it's also needed for the side trips to Cradle Mountain and the Mole Creek Caves). A

TASSIE'S WEST COAST – DAYS 1-4

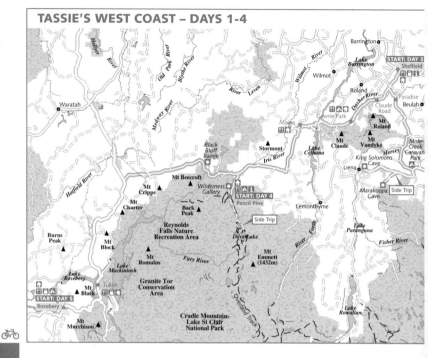

daily pass costs $11 per person, or you can purchase an eight-week holiday pass for $28; it can be purchased in Mole Creek or at either of the two visitors centres in Cradle Mountain.

GETTING TO/FROM THE RIDE
Evandale (start)
To reach Evandale you'll need to cycle from Launceston. The best route is along the bike lane on Elphin Rd, staying with the road as it becomes Penquite Rd and then Glenwood Rd. This road travels through the Relbia wine region, joining the C412 to Evandale; the ride is around 25km in length.

Hobart (finish)
See p215.

THE RIDE
Day 1: Evandale to Deloraine
4½–6 hours, 81.3km
The ride begins through the dry grazing lands of the rain shadow that is the Midlands, the cleared earth invariably as bare as the cliffs of the Great Western Tiers

visible ahead. After Bracknell, the route heads for the hills and there's a long climb on dirt, eventually reaching a high point just above 600m. The route descends for the final 20km to Deloraine.

Out of Evandale there's a 2km stretch on the Midland Hwy, Tassie's major highway, though there's a good verge. Through the sort of bare landscapes more associated with central New South Wales than central Tasmania, the ride enters **Longford** through a sprawl of suburbia that belies the presence of a beautifully preserved historic town, one of the few of its era not established by convicts.

Tiny **Bracknell** is the day's logical stop, though if you want something other than a pub counter meal you'll need to carry it in from Longford. The Great Western Tiers loom large above Bracknell, and they continue to edge nearer until the ride passes directly below their escarpment at Liffey. Here, the Midland plains end, which is a double-edged sword. Forest replaces agriculture, but the climbs (and dirt road) are also about to begin.

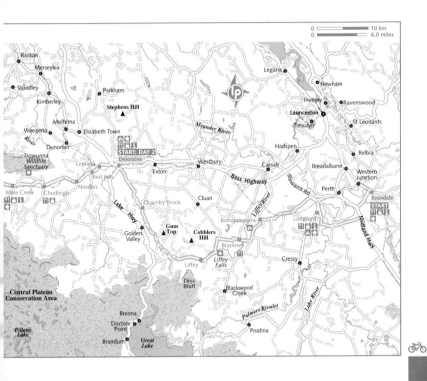

TASSIE'S WEST COAST – DAY 1

CUE			GPS COORDINATES
start		Evandale visitors centre	147°14'38"N 41°34'09"S
0km		go NW on High St	
0.4		B41	
4.7		Hwy 1, 'to Hobart'	
6.7		C521, 'to Longford'	
13.5		pick-a-plank bridge	
18.8		B51, Longford"	147°07'18"N 41°35'44"S
20.0		B52, 'to Burnie'	
21.3		Bishopsbourne Rd	
32.8		Bishopsbourne	146°59'11"N 41°37'06"S
37.7		C513, 'to Bracknell'	
39.8		Bracknell	146°56'15"N 41°39'07"S
47.3		C513, 'to Liffey'	

CUE CONTINUED			GPS COORDINATES
54.5		1km moderate	
54.8		12.2km dirt road	
{57.1		Liffey Falls Lower Track}	
		1.8km steep	
58.8		C513, 'to A5'	
60.6		C504, 'to Exton'	
70.5		C503, 'to Deloraine'	
80.4		A5, 'to town centre'	
80.5		to Devonport'	
80.6		Emu Bay Rd	
81.2		Emu Bay Rd	
81.3		Great Western Tiers visitors centre, Deloraine	146°39'04"N 41°31'24"S

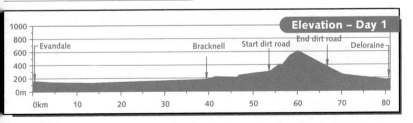

Elevation – Day 1

IN A LAND FAR, FAR AWAY

Unfold a map of Tasmania and it's a little like leafing through the index of a world atlas. Approaching Hobart on the Across the Central Plateau ride you pedal through the Jordan Valley to reach Bagdad. From here it's a step backwards into more holy lands in the Walls of Jerusalem, where feature names include King Solomon's Throne, the Wailing Wall and Damascus Gate.

It's a state where the Promised Land is offset by the Styx, and where the towns of Grindelwald and Interlaken seem to explain why Tasmania was once billed as the Switzerland of the South.

The world tour of Tasmania continues through Swansea, Sheffield, Mangalore and Dover, or as you cross the Mersey or Liffey Rivers. By the time you hit Launceston, and ponder why it's pronounced 'Lonceston' rather than 'Lonson', you may have forgotten that you're in Tasmania at all.

Beyond a bridge (57.1km) is the access track to **Liffey Falls** lower car park, from where a one-hour uphill walk leads to the impressive falls. If you're hooking up with the Across the Central Plateau ride, there's easier access to the falls on Day 2 of that route.

From here the route funnels up beside the Liffey River towards the delightfully named Bogan Gap, from where there are views to **Drys Bluff** (1298m), the highest point in the Great Western Tiers. The gap marks the start of the long, leisurely descent to Deloraine.

Day 2: Deloraine to Sheffield
3–5½ hours, 53.6km

Like Day 1, the Great Western Tiers start out distant this day and draw nearer as the first half of the ride progresses. A short ride, it can be turned into a full day by taking the side trip to the Mole Creek Caves, the major natural feature of the area.

There's an early chance to cool down at the **Honey Farm** (☎ 03-6363 6160; 39 Sorell St; www.thehoneyfarm.com.au; 9am-5pm Sun-Fri) in Chudleigh (16.5km), where you can watch the workers through a glass-fronted beehive before sampling your way through 30 honeys, including a honey chocolate paste. The honey ice cream is the real star.

Almost 3km west of Chudleigh is the **Trowunna Wildlife Sanctuary** (☎ 03-6363 6162; admission $16; 9am-5pm Feb-Dec, 9am-8pm Jan), which specialises in Tasmanian devils, wombats and koalas. The park operates an informative 75-minute tour where you get to pat, feed

TASSIE'S WEST COAST – DAY 2

CUE			GPS COORDINATES
start		Great Western Tiers visitors centre, Deloraine	146°39'04"N 41°31'24"S
0km		go NW on Emu Bay Rd	
1.1	◜◉	B12, 'to Mole Creek'	
16.5	◜	B12, 'to Mole Creek', Chudleigh	
19.6	★	Trowunna Wildife Sanctuary	146°27'06"N 41°33'21"S
23.5		Mole Creek	146°24'05"N 41°33'21"S
28.0	◜	C137, 'to Paradise'	
{	●● ◜	Mole Creek Caves, 30.7km (↻)}	
34.4	▲	2.3km steep	
42.6	▲	1km steep	
47.4	⚠	pick-a-plank bridge	
48.6	◜	C136, 'to Sheffield'	
50.3	▲	800m moderate	
53.0	◜	B14, 'to town centre'	
53.5	◜	Pioneer Crescent	
53.6		Kentish visitors centre, Sheffield	146°19'29"N 41°22'55"S

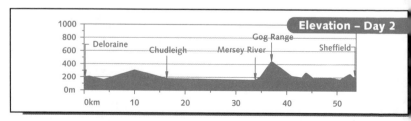

Elevation – Day 2

and hold the critters. Tours start at 11am, 1pm and 3pm. The 400m-long, dirt access road is steep.

Mole Creek is the service town for the outlying caves that dot the Mole Creek Karst National Park (see the side trip, below). At the turning to the caves (28km) is **Mole Creek Caravan Park** (☎ 03-6363 1150; unpowered/powered sites per two adults $17/20, on-site van $50, cabin $75), set down on the banks of Sassafras Creek with little shade but a nice feeling of isolation.

A few hundred metres across the black Mersey River, the ascent begins through the Gog Range. It's a tough climb through dry eucalypt forest but it provides keyhole views across the blue-gum-carpeted Mersey Valley to the Great Western Tiers.

The village of Paradise (46km) is less milk-and-honey than it sounds but it precedes a heavenly sort of descent with the ride's first views of lumpy, rocky, 1234m-high Mt Roland, one of northern Tasmania's most striking peaks. On the C136 there's one final climb before the route rolls into mural-fixated Sheffield.

SIDE TRIP: MOLE CREEK CAVES
2–3 hours, 30.7km

The Mole Creek area contains over 300 known caves and sinkholes, and it's quite feasible this day to branch away to the park's two public show caves: King Solomons Cave and Marakoopa Cave. Compact King Solomons Cave has lavish colours and formations, while Marakoopa, which is tucked under the rocky escarpment of the Great Western Tiers, has two tour options. On the first you visit underground rivers and an incredible display of glowworms, as well as sparkling crystals and beautiful reflective pools; while the second tour

involves climbing a steep stairway to the Great Cathedral with delicate limestone gardens of shawls and straws and glow-worm clusters. Admission to each cave is $15; check at the Mole Creek visitors centre for tour times.

If you wish to visit only Marakoopa it's a 20km return ride, while King Solomons Cave alone is a 24km round trip.

Day 3: Sheffield to Cradle Mountain
3½–6 hours, 54.5km

This day leaps between two pictures of mountain beauty: Mt Roland and famed, fabulous Cradle Mountain, dipping deep to Lake Cethana and crawling out through forest and alpinelike plains.

Mt Roland dominates the early part of the day, its furrowed escarpment resembling one of Sheffield's famous scones – with a backdrop like this it's easy to see why the towns around it took names such as Paradise and Promised Land. If you fancy

TASSIE'S WEST COAST – DAY 3

CUE			GPS COORDINATES	
start		Kentish visitors centre, Sheffield"	146°19'29"N	41°22'55"S
0km		go NE on Pioneer Cres		
0.1	┌→	Main St		
0.6	┌→	C136, 'to Gowrie Park'		
15.5		Gowrie Park	146°12'4"N	41°28'14"S
18.7	▲	2km moderate		
24.5	▲	5.5km steep		
30.0	←┐	C132, 'to Cradle Mountain', Moina	146°06'03"N	41°28'41"S
	▲	3km moderate		
51.2	←┐	C132, 'to Cradle Mountain'		
{53.4	★	Wilderness Gallery}		
54.5	end	Cradle Mountain visitors centre	145°55'51"N	41°35'45"S
	●●	Dove Lake 18km ↻	145°57'40"N	41°39'02"S

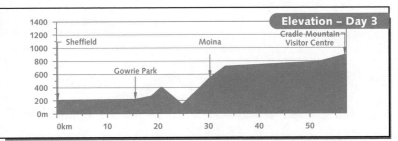

Elevation – Day 3

climbing the mountain, the walking track begins 100m past O'Neil's Creek Picnic Reserve in Gowrie Park; allow about four hours for the return hike.

From Gowrie Park, which has caught some of Sheffield's mural zeal, it's a wonderful descent to the River Forth, crossing just below the dam wall of Lake Cethana, with a gruelling climb back out. As you pop over the crest of into Moina, **Cradle Chalet** (☎ 03-6492 1401; www .cradlechalet.com.au; ste from $175, chalets from $195) stares back across the road at you. The chalet has luxury accommodation and a restaurant (open lunch and dinner) that is the last food stop before Cradle Mountain.

The climbing continues past Moina, though the sting has now gone from the hill. From about 37km look out for the various views at various angles of Cradle Mountain, like a cupped pair of hands on the horizon, before the road undulates through the subalpine Middlesex Plains to the Cradle Mountain turn-off. Two kilometres down this road you'll pass the entrance to Cradle Mountain Chateau – it's worth ducking in to visit the **Wilderness Gallery** (☎ 03-6492 1404; www.wildernessgallery.com .au; Cradle Mountain Rd; admission $5; 10am-5pm), which showcases incredible environmental photography.

SIDE TRIP: DOVE LAKE
1½–2 hours, 18km
If ever a side trip was compulsory, this is it, because Cradle Mountain is hardly Cradle Mountain until you've seen it from the shores of Dove Lake. The park road is a single lane but accommodates two-way traffic, so ride with care as it undulates along the Cradle Valley to the northern shores of the lake. Here, you can walk around the lake in a couple of hours or, if you have more time and sure hands and feet, you can scramble to the summit of Cradle Mountain.

Day 4: Cradle Mountain to Rosebery
4–7 hours, 68.5km
The trend today is down, 750m down, but there are times that you won't believe it, with three decent climbs to confuse your inner altimeter. Despite the descent, it is a day of highs: the tour's highest point atop the Black Bluff Range, and a crossing of the Murchison Hwy's highest section of road. It will pay to stock up on food before setting out, with Tullah (53.7km) the only food stop.

Out of Cradle Mountain, the route crosses the exposed Vale of Belvoir plains to the zig-zagging climb up **Black Bluff Range** (if coming from the other direction, watch for the cattle grid at the base of the descent; hitting it at 70km/h is not a lot of fun). The climb starts out gently enough but is lung-tearingly steep by the top. Glance back from the crest for a last look at Tassie's most famous mountain, almost

TASSIE'S WEST COAST – DAY 4

CUE			GPS COORDINATES
start		Cradle Mountain visitors centre	145°55'51"N 41°35'45"S
0km		go N on C132	
3.1	◤	C132, `to Waratah'	
10.1	▲	2.1km steep	
{12.2	★	Black Bluff Range}	
29.6	◤	A10, `to Tullah'	
31.1	▲	1.2km moderate	
34.0	▲	1.6km moderate	
53.7		Tullah	145°37'07"N 41°44'15"S
59.5	▲	4.3km moderate	
68.5		Rosebery post office	145°32'19"N 41°46'47"S

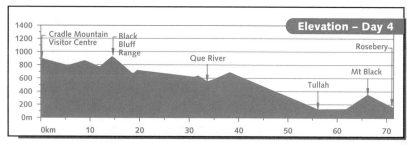

Elevation – Day 4

unrecognisable in shape from this angle, before enjoying the 10% descent.

The road undulates along the First of May Plains (yes, the name is a misnomer) past Hellyer mine to the Murchison Hwy (29.6km), which is a highway in name only. Lightly trafficked, it's narrow, twisting and full of climbs – everything a good cycling road should be. When you reach the highway's highest point (690m), give only a muted cheer because it's not all downhill from here. The road continues to undulate before flattening out through buttongrass plains at around 41km, soon descending into Tullah (53.7km), crossing Lake Rosebery near the entrance to town – look right as you cross the bridge and there's a good view up a rocky gorge. In town, the **Tullah Tavern Museum & Café** (☎ 03-6473 4141; Murchison Hwy; apt $110) has two spacious self-contained apartments with lovely mountain views. In the bright and welcoming cafe (mains $3 to $10, open 9am to 5pm) you can grab a light meal, sup on some of the on-tap beers or warm up by the log fire. At least take a rest, as the day's toughest climb is about to begin.

Mt Murchison dominates the view on the ride out from Tullah, but it's Mt Black that you'll have to overcome. The climb up the fern-lined hillside begins soon after you recross Lake Rosebery, rising 355m up the 929m-high mountain before a headlong dive into Rosebery.

Day 5: Rosebery to Strahan
4–7 hours, 72.2km

This relatively easy ride heads through isolated, wild terrain, providing a day of true contrasts, from the heavy tree cover out of Rosebery to the treeless expanses beyond Zeehan; from the rough diamond of Rosebery to the polished diamond of Strahan. Zeehan is the only town en route. Three short climbs, two of them steep, punctuate the first third of the ride but,

after leaving the highway, there are just two moderate climbs into Strahan.

The first steep climb (10.6km) rises to the **Renison tin mine**, which isn't pretty but it did revitalise the Zeehan economy when it reopened in the late 1960s. As the ride enters Zeehan (28.2km), it crosses Pea Soup Creek, which aptly describes west-coast weather in Tasmania – Zeehan gets 2.5m of rain a year.

Head out of Zeehan past more mine tailings, skirting Mt Zeehan (702m) and climbing through the bare, apocalyptic Professor Range, which is a beautiful place in its own bleak way. At 50.4km, near the top of the second climb, there's a roadside **lookout** where, on a clear day, the views extend to the restless Southern Ocean. South along the coast you can see the sandy tips of the Henty Dunes.

Rolling down to the Henty River (52.6km) and close behind the **Henty Dunes** – at 58.2km there's a turn-off into a picnic area by the dunes, which are a popular sandboarding destination – the route trails along the coast into Strahan, where the avenues of trees are suddenly replaced by avenues of holiday units…welcome to one of Tasmania's major tourist towns.

TASSIE'S WEST COAST – DAY 5

CUE			GPS COORDINATES
start		Rosebery post office	145°32'19"N 41°46'47"S
0km		go S on Murchison Hwy	
0.6	▲	1.2km moderate	
1.9	●●	Montezuma Falls, 22km ↰	
10.6	▲	1.1km steep	
11.7	★	Renison tin mine	145°26'02"N 41°46'54"S
15.4	▲	1.2km moderate	
23.4	⌐→	B27, 'to Zeehan'	
28.2	↰	B27, 'to Strahan', Zeehan"	
38.7	▲	500m moderate	
47.4	▲	2.8km moderate	
50.4	★	lookout	
71.0	↘	Innes St	
72.2		Strahan visitors centre	145°19'52"N 42°09'09"S

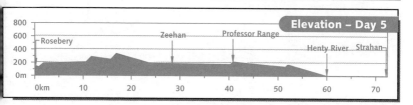

Elevation – Day 5

Rosebery — Zeehan — Professor Range — Henty River — Strahan

TASSIE'S WEST COAST – DAYS 5-10

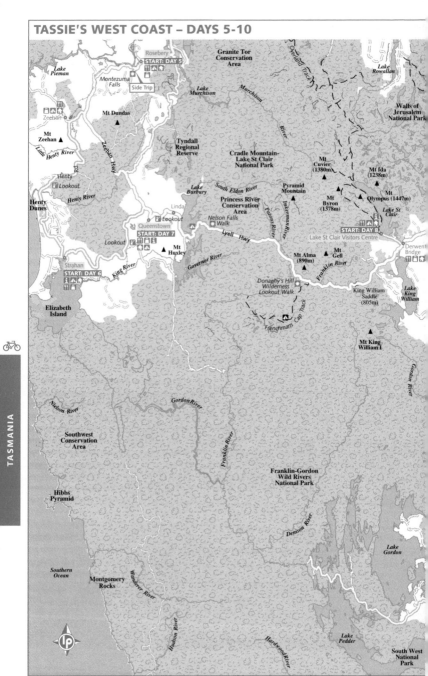

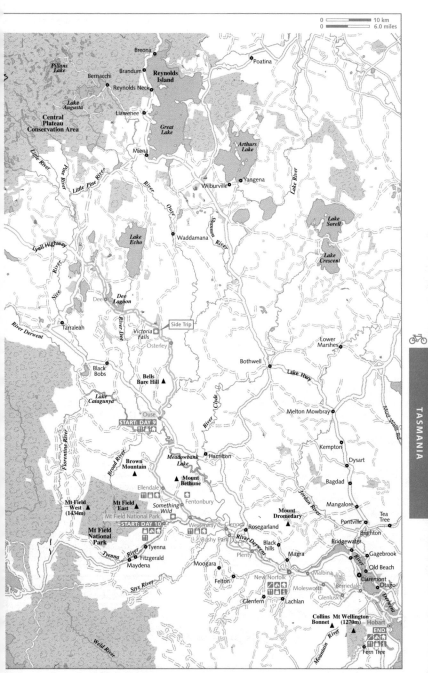

TASMANIA

SIDE TRIP: MONTEZUMA FALLS
2–3 hours, 22km
If you're taking a day off in Rosebery, this ride up to Tasmania's tallest waterfall is well worth consideration for it can be done without panniers and offers the rare chance to ride off-road – you will need to be on a mountain bike. Out of Rosebery, follow the Murchison Hwy south for 1.9km, turning onto Williamsford Rd, which climbs to the Montezuma Falls car park, the road turning to rough dirt and stone over the last 1km. From here a shared walking track, one of the Tasmania's listed 60 Great Short Walks, heads 4.4km along an old tramway to the base of the 104m-high falls.

Day 6: Strahan to Queenstown
2½–4 hours, 41.3km
This short day allows time to explore Strahan before you set out for Queenstown, but don't underestimate the workload – the road climbs more than 300m over the first 25km, ascending a ridge that separates the northwest-flowing tributaries of the Henty River from the south-flowing tributaries of the King River – before winding down to otherworldly Queenstown. The route is lightly trafficked outside school-holiday times, and there are no services on the way.

It's a fairly constant stepladder up to the **lookout** (23.2km), though the greatest

TASSIE'S WEST COAST – DAY 6

CUE		GPS COORDINATES
start	Strahan visitors centre	145°19′52″N 42°09′09″S
0km	go NE on the Esplanade	
0.1	●● ↰ B24, 'to Queenstown'	
▲	5.5km moderate	
0.3	↱ B24, 'to Queenstown'	
20.1	▲ 2.5km moderate	
{23.2	★ lookout}	
37.7	↱ A10, 'to Queenstown'	
41.2	↱ Driffield St, 'to town centre'	
41.3	Queenstown visitors centre	145°33′22″N 4204′47″S°

sting is in the first 5km and the final 5km. Most of the climb is hemmed in by bush. Enjoy it, for by the day's end you'll be scratching to find a tree. The lookout stares across to the bone-coloured tops of the West Coast Range. Crouched below are Queenstown's denuded hills with their orange and purple hues.

There are more good mountain and mine views as the Lyell Hwy coasts down towards Queenstown; the final descent on the A10 is slippery-slide quick.

Day 7: Queenstown to Lake St Clair
5–9½ hours, 92.6km
There's so much to like about this day: the so-called 99 Bend Rd; the World Heritage area; the waterfalls and walks; the views of Frenchmans Cap, one of Tasmania's pin-up mountains. It's packed with climbing, though after the early steep grind most of it is moderate.

The writhing climb out of Queenstown is known affectionately as the **99 Bend Rd** and is one of the best bits of cycling road in the state – granted it's better downhill but it's still a fantastic ride in this direction. Climbing through the barren landscape, amid orange and purple rocks, you might feel more like a Mars space probe than a cyclist.

The bends keep coming as the road descends through ghost-town-like Gormanston but it flattens out and straightens beyond Linda, passing beneath bare hills still dappled with colour. The sight of **Lake Burbury** (11km) is unexpected after the desertlike scenes around Queenstown. As you approach the bridge over the lake, look east for a glimpse of the quartzite peak of Frenchmans Cap.

At 24.7km the road enters the World Heritage area, where the only things that disturb the landscape are the road and the apiarists' hives. A 20-minute return walk

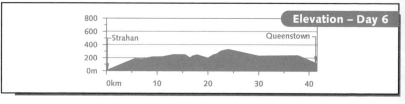

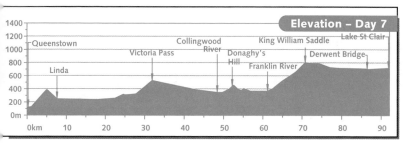

TASSIE'S WEST COAST – DAY 7

CUE		GPS COORDINATES
start	Queenstown visitors centre	145°33'22"N 42°04'47"S°
0km	go NE on Driffield St	
0.1	⌐ A10, 'to Lake St Clair'	
1.4	▲ 3.5km steep	
{3.9	★ lookout over Queenstown}	
7.5	Linda	145°36'05"N 42°03'48"S
27.5	★ Nelson Falls walk	145°44'09"N 42°06'14"S
27.7	▲ 3.7km moderate	
49.2	▲ 2.8km moderate	
{51.8	★ Donaghy's Hill Wilderness Lookout walk}	
61.3	★ Franklin River	146°01'10"N 42°12'55"S
62.8	▲ 8.4km moderate	
{71.2	★ King William Saddle]	
87.2	⌐ C193, 'to Lake St Clair National Park', Derwent Bridge	146°13'44"N 42°08'13"S
92.6	Lake St Clair visitors centre	146°11'40"N 42°07'22"S

to **Nelson Falls** (27.5km) starts at the base of the climb up 530m-high Victoria Pass. The forest breaks open beyond the pass, widening the view. Look down as you cross the Collingwood River (47.9km) and you may see rafters preparing to set out down the pristine Franklin River.

Donaghy's Hill Wilderness Lookout walk (40 minutes return) ambles out to a viewpoint across to Frenchmans Cap. Four kilometres on you'll pass the trailhead for the walking track into Frenchmans, a route infamous for the depth of its mud in the so-called Sodden Loddon plains.

The **Franklin River** is crossed at 61.3km, which is a brush with river royalty. Plans to dam this river were toppled by protests in the early 1980s, an event that played a part in electing the Labor government in 1983 and all but heralded the start of Australia's major green movement.

The climb to King William Saddle starts 1km past the Franklin River, just beyond a buttongrass plain offering a lovely view

onto 1422m-high Mt Gell. The climb is through a tunnel of forest, which thins to reveal views over the final couple of kilometres before all but disappearing at the alpinelike saddle. **King William Saddle** is the watershed between east and west Tasmania.

The gradual descent to Derwent Bridge flickers between forest and buttongrass moorland. Here, you leave the World Heritage area, turning back into it at **Derwent Bridge** (87.2km), from where the road climbs almost imperceptibly beside the embryonic Derwent River to Lake St Clair.

Day 8: Lake St Clair to Ouse
5–8½ hours, 86.5km

The general trend this day is downhill with no major climbs, though the bulk of the small ascents are, of course, rudely packed together on the long dirt section. The terrain is still easier, and the traffic far lighter, than on the sealed Lyell Hwy. There are no services after Derwent Bridge, so carry plenty of water and food.

In Derwent Bridge, rejoin the Lyell Hwy, crossing the Derwent River, which is more like a mountain stream here than the grand estuary it becomes in Hobart. At 7.1km the highway passes one of Tasmania's newest attractions, the **Wall in the Wilderness** (☎ 03-6289 1134; www.thewalltasmania .com; admission $7.50; 9am-5pm Sep-May, 9am-4pm Jun-Aug), an amazing work in progress by wood sculptor Greg Duncan, who is carving a panorama in wood panels depicting the history of the Tasmanian highlands. The scale is incredible: when it's finished the scene will be 100m long, and it will take an estimated 10 years to complete. Though the tableau is large scale, it's carved with breathtaking skill

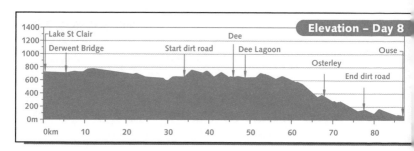

Elevation – Day 8

TASSIE'S WEST COAST – DAY 8

CUE			GPS COORDINATES
start		Lake St Clair visitors centre	146°11'40"N 42°07'22"S
0km		go SE on C193	
5.4	↰	A10, 'to Hobart', Derwent Bridge"	146°13'44"N 42°08'13"S
7.1	★	Wall in the Wilderness	146°14'50"N 42°07'07"S
29.5	⚠	one-lane bridge	
	▲	1.2km moderate	
33.7	↰	C173, 'to Lake Echo'	
	⚠	43.5km dirt road	
	▲	1.7km moderate	

CUE			GPS COORDINATES
41.1	↙	C173, 'to Ouse'	
45.7		Dee	146°34'11"N 42°15'34"S
51.1	▲	1km steep	
61.8	▲	3.7km steep winding descent	
{62.7	●●↰	Victoria Falls 400m (↻)}	
67.5		Osterley	146°44'24"N 42°20'39"S
79.5	▲	1km moderate	
86.3	↰	A10, 'to Hobart'	
86.5		Ouse Roadhouse	146°30'00"N 42°23'21"S

and detail, from the veins in the workers' hands, to the creases in their shirts, to the hair of their beards.

Open woodland accompanies the highway for 20km then, for the first time in days, it's into open farmland. The road passes within sight of Bronte Lagoon and, soon after, the ride leaves it, turning onto the dirt C173 and joins the Tasmania Trail (see boxed text, p186). The road is momentarily sealed through the collection of shacks that is Dee (45.7km) before it banks around Dee Lagoon. Crossing the dam wall, the ride climbs steeply into thicker, more enclosed forest that ends abruptly in a swathe of farmland.

The Tasmania Trail turns away by the side trip to **Victoria Falls** (62.7km), which certainly isn't Niagara but does offer a chance to wander off the bike for a few minutes. Equally, Osterley is not exactly Manhattan, the 'town' consisting of three buildings (only one of which is lived in) and three chimney stacks from fallen buildings.

The sealed road returns at around 77km in the midst of the manmade Nullarbor of grass and bare earth. Still, the downhill run into Ouse makes the landscape rather superfluous anyway.

Day 9: Ouse to Mt Field National Park

2–4 hours, 38.7km

The short, mostly easy ride undulates through agricultural land with two steep climbs before Ellendale. You can pick up lunch in Ellendale though it's just as likely that you'll be at Mt Field by lunch since there's little in Ouse to hold you through the morning.

From the highway, 7.1km south of Ouse, the C608 drops down to **Meadowbank Lake**, a widening of the Derwent River and a popular water-sports playground. The road crosses the lake on a levee and then a one-lane bridge – there's a pull-out halfway across the bridge if you encounter oncoming traffic.

From the crest of the first steep climb (12km), Mt Field rises straight ahead; the second climb follows in rapid succession, with the Tasmanian Trail reappearing part way up the second climb. There's a feet-up-on-the-panniers descent into Fentonbury. As it drops into Westerway, the road passes beneath a line of hops kilns, turning here along the Tyenna Valley towards Mt Field National Park. Just before the park you can visit **Something Wild** (☎ 03-6288 1013; www.somethingwild.com.au; admission

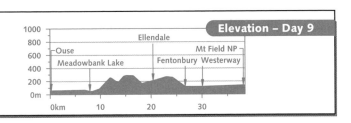

TASSIE'S WEST COAST – DAY 9

CUE			GPS COORDINATES
start		Ouse Roadhouse	146°30'00"N 42°23'21"S
0km		go SE on A10	
7.1	⌐	C608, `to Ellendale'	
8.7	⚠	one-lane bridge	
8.9	▲	300m moderate	
10.0	▲	2km steep	
13.6	▲	1.1km steep	
21.0		Ellendale	146°42'24"N 42°36'31"S
27.2		Fentonbury	146°46'00"N 42°38'55"S
30.4	⌐	B61, `to Mt Field National Park', Westerway"	146°47'26"N 42°40'27"S
{36.2	★	Something Wild wildlife sanctuary}	
38.1	⌐	C609, `to Mt Field National Park'	
38.7		Mt Field National Park visitors centre	146°43'14"N 42°41'02"S

$13; 10am-5pm), a wildlife sanctuary that rehabilitates orphaned and injured wildlife, and provides a home for animals unable to be released. It has an animal nursery and residents such as Tassie devils, wombats, quolls and platypuses.

Day 10: Mt Field National Park to Hobart

4–6 hours, 71.9km

This ride eases back to the Derwent River, following it for almost 16km before settling on the lesser of two evils: a steep climb over the Wellington Range instead of heavy highway traffic, finishing with a bike-path cruise into the city.

Return to Westerway and head out of town past pine plantations and farmland. At 17km the ride pops out above Glenora, the valley around it filled with hops. In New Norfolk (38.9km), which is the logical lunch stop, the route description weaves up through the town. If you want to plough

TASSIE'S WEST COAST – DAY 10

CUE			GPS COORDINATES
start		Mt Field National Park visitors centre	146°43'14"N 42°41'02"S
0km		go SE on C609	
0.7	↰	B61, `to A10'	
8.3	⌐	B61, `to New Norfolk', Westerway	146°47'26"N 42°40'27"S
19.0		Bushy Park	146°53'53"N 42°42'32"S
19.6	⌐	B62, `to New Norfolk'	
24.5	▲	1km moderate	
27.6		Plenty	146°56'57"N 42°44'18"S
38.3	⌐ ⊙	Blair St	
38.6	↰	Richmond St	
38.9	↰	High St, New Norfolk	
39.3	↰	Bathurst St	
39.4	⌐	Pioneer Ave	
39.8	⌐ ⊙	A10, `to Hobart'	
43.3	⌐	C165, `to Molesworth'	
45.3	⚠	pick-a-plank bridge	
48.8	⌐	to Collinsvale', Molesworth"	147°08'49"N 42°48'10"S
49.0	▲	5.1km steep	
54.6	↰	C615, `to Berriedale'	
60.1	⌐	Intercity Cycleway	
71.9		Hobart visitors centre	147°19'54"N 42°52'59"S

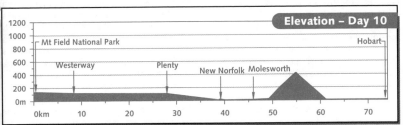

on through, go straight ahead at the roundabout at 38.3km.

The route leaves the highway at 43.3km, riding towards the hills and then onto them. There are some steep pinches but, hidden within the bushy folds of the range, with occasional glimpses of dolerite columns, it's hard to believe that you're at the very edge of a capital city. From the top of the climb there's a brief look at the Derwent River, then it's down, down, down – be sure to check your brakes at the top. Approaching the river, the ride hooks onto the Intercity Cycleway, following beside the railway into Hobart.

MOUNTAIN BIKE RIDES

For information about the Tasmanian Trail, see boxed text p186.

HOBART
North South Track
Opened in 2008, this purpose-designed track cuts a groove across the slopes of Mt Wellington, departing from Shoobridge Bend on Pinnacle Road (halfway up Mt Wellington) and contouring for 2.8km to Junction Cabin. Sections of the track are rocky, particularly on the short, bumpy crossing of a boulder field, and there's a selection of log rides and jumps if you really want to up the skills ante. Plans are to eventually extend the track to the Springs and the Glenorchy Mountain Bike Park.

Glenorchy Mountain Bike Park
At Hobart's edge, on the lower slopes of Mt Wellington, this **mountain bike park** (www.tasbikepark.com), designed by Glen Jacobs (the designer of the Sydney Olympic course and the North South Track) has a variety of trails for downhill, mountain cross, cross-country and jumps riders. Created in 2005, it's hosted national championships and has a reputation – enhanced by an overhaul in early 2009 – as one of the finest mountain bike parks in the country. Access is from Tolosa St or, if coming off the mountain, from the Knights Creek Track.

LAUNCESTON
Youngtown Regional Park
Easy mountain biking trails through eucalypt forest and grasslands in Launceston's southern suburbs. There are a few steep grades but the tracks are well formed. Parking is on Poplar Parade, and if you want to keep riding out of the city, you can connect onto the Glenwood Trail towards Relbia.

TOWNS & FACILITIES

BICHENO
☎ 03 / pop 750
Bicheno is blessed with the kind of idyllic coastal scenery that was always going to make it a hit with seaside holidaymakers. The Gulch, Bicheno's curvaceous natural harbour, is filled with water of the clearest blue, its foreshore is edged with granite and fine white beaches, and the whole town is fringed with the startling green of eucalypts under an often deep-blue sky. The fishing boats that shelter in the harbour are this town's mainstay – as are the tourists in the summer-holiday season. The style here is buckets and spades, but it's still a hugely popular holiday spot.

Information
Book accommodation ahead if you're cycling through in summer – the helpful volunteers at the **Bicheno visitors centre** (☎ 03-6375 1500; 69 Burgess St; 9am-5pm Mon-Fri, 9am-1pm Sat, 11am-4pm Sun, winter hr vary, closed Sun in winter) can assist.

Sleeping & Eating
Bicheno East Coast Holiday Park (☎ 03-6375 1999; www.bichenoholidaypark.com.au; 4 Champ St; unpowered/powered sites $20/25, d $85, d cabin $98-108) This neat, friendly park with plenty of green grass and shady tent spots is centrally located and has a BBQ, camp kitchen and laundry facilities. It also has showers for nonguests for $2.

Bicheno Backpackers (☎ 03-6375 1651; www.bichenobackpackers.com; 11 Morrison St; dm $23-25, d $60-70) This friendly backpackers stretches across two mural-painted buildings. The double rooms are quite plush (the sea-view room is the pick) and there's a good communal kitchen. While here you can rent kayaks, surf boards, boogie boards, fishing rods and tennis gear.

Old Tram Road B&B (☎ 03-6375 1298; www.oldtramroad.com.au; 3 Old Tram Rd; d $150-160) An old-world B&B set in pretty gardens with a private track to Waubs Beach. There are just two rooms, both with sparkling en suites. The gourmet breakfasts should keep you going for the ride ahead.

Bicheno by the Bay (☎ 03-6375 1171; www.bichenobythebay.com.au; cnr Foster & Fraser Sts; 1-bedroom apt $140-175, 2-bedroom $170-210) There are 20 cabins in a bushland setting, some of which sleep up to six people and some with sea views. Facilities include an outdoor heated pool, a tennis court and communal fire pit. The on-site restaurant, Seasons (open for dinner), is probably the best in Bicheno. Predictably, marine fare heads the menu, but if you're over seafood, try the finger-licking honey and soy–coated pork cutlets.

Blue Edge Café (☎ 03-6375 1972; 55 Burgess St; meals $3-10, 7am-5.30pm) Good sandwiches, wraps, pies, cakes and salads, and you can enjoy the aromas of the freshly made breads, all baked on the premises. The Tasmanian smoked-salmon pie is heavenly.

Sea Life Centre Restaurant (☎ 03-6375 1121; 1 Tasman Hwy; meals $13-30; lunch & dinner Sep-Jul) The best thing about the restaurant is the view over the startlingly blue waters of the Gulch. The menu offers a variety of sea morsels (choose your crayfish fresh from the tanks – natural, chargrilled or mornay) as well as steaks, and even a good vegetarian lasagne.

Beachfront at Bicheno (☎ 03-6375 1111; Tasman Hwy) This crowd-pleasing complex has two eateries: Delmare's (mains $16 to $30; open for dinner October to April), offering Mediterranean fare such as pizza, pasta, seafood and salads; and the laid-back Beachfront Tavern (mains $14 to $25; open for lunch and dinner), which serves standard pub fare – lots of grilled meats, plus fish of the day, schnitzels and salads.

Festival IGA (cnr Foster & Burgess Sts) Supermarket beside the visitors centre.

BOTHWELL
☎ 03 / pop 340

Encircling a village green, Bothwell is a low-key (some would say catatonic) historic town in the Clyde River Valley. The town lays claim to Australia's oldest golf course, the **Ratho golf links** (☎ 0409 595 702; www.rathogolf.com; Highland Lakes Rd; green fees $15; 8am-dusk), laid out in 1822.

Information
The **Bothwell visitors centre** (☎ 03-6259 4033; www.bothwell.com.au; Market Pl; 10am-4pm Sep-May, 11am-3pm Jun-Aug) doubles as the Australasian Golf Museum.

Sleeping & Eating
Bothwell Caravan Park (☎ 03-6259 5503; http://bothwell.50webs.com/caravanpg .htm; Market Pl; unpowered/powered sites $10/15) Not exactly a park, but more a small patch of gravel behind the visitors centre. Check in at the Central Highlands Council on Alexander St, or after hours at the Bothwell Garage on Patrick St.

Park House (☎/fax 03-6259 5676; 25 Alexander St; d $80, extra person $20) On Alexander St there are a couple of decent, self-contained houses for rent. An unremarkable 1950s red-brick number, this one sleeps six; inquire at 28 Elizabeth St.

Batt's Cottage (☎ 03-6265 9481, 0409 659 480; 23 Alexander St; d $115, extra person $20) Next door to Park House and the far more appealing (and more expensive), this National Trust–registered cottage has warped brick walls, dating from 1840.

Bothwell Grange (☎ 03-6259 5556; bothwell_grange@skyoptic.com.au; 15 Alexander St; d incl breakfast $99) A highway hotel built in 1836, the once-grandiose Grange has a snug Georgian atmosphere and comfortable B&B accommodation. There are six rooms, all with antique beds and timber ceilings. Evening meals by arrangement. Mind your head – the doorways were built for diminutive 19th-century folk.

Castle Hotel (☎ 03-6259 5502; 14 Patrick St; mains $14-19; lunch daily, dinner Fri & Sat) The affable, country-aired Castle has been continually licensed since 1829 and continues to serve up better-than-average meals (heavy on the meat and local produce). There are a couple of surprisingly good rooms upstairs (d $90), with bathrooms, TVs and DVDs.

Fat Doe Bakery & Coffee Shop (☎ 03-6259 5551; 12 Patrick St; breakfast & lunch Mon-Fri) Fuel up for a day in the saddle with sandwiches, lamingtons, fresh-from-the-oven cakes or something from the tasty range of pies.

Bothwell Super Store (cnr Patrick & William Sts) Has a decent range of groceries and is open seven days a week.

COCKLE CREEK
☎ 03

Welcome to the southernmost road end in Australia. A grand grid of streets was once planned for Cockle Creek, but dwindling coal seams and whale numbers scotched that idea. Expect to see plenty more walkers than cyclists, for the great South Coast Track starts here – if you're not cleaned up, you might want to hike the first stretch out to South Cape Bay.

There are some brilliant free campsites along Recherche Bay, including at Gilhams Beach, just before Catamaran. You can also camp for free at Cockle Creek itself, but national-park fees apply as soon as you cross the bridge. If you plan to stay overnight and not head straight out on the bus, you'll need to bring all your own provisions, including a stove. There are pit toilets (no showers) and some tank water (boil before drinking).

COLES BAY
☎ 03 / pop 150

Set on a beautiful sweep of sand and clear sea at the foot of the dramatic granite peaks of the Hazards, Coles Bay is a laid-back, salt-tousled holiday town at the edge of magnificent Freycinet National Park, which is famed for the perfect curve of Wineglass Bay. Like most visitors, you'll probably want to work in a stroll to Wineglass Bay while you're here; it's about 3 hours on foot there and back and the trailhead is about a 7km ride out of town.

Green to its core, Coles Bay was the first town in Australia to ban plastic bags.

Information
If you're going to wander into the park, information is available from the helpful

National Park Visitors Centre (☎ 03-6256 7000; freycinet@parks.tas.gov.au; 8am-5pm May-Oct, 8am-6pm Nov-Apr), just past Coles Bay. General tourist information is available from most stores in town.

Sleeping & Eating
Accommodation is at a premium at Christmas, in January and at Easter, and prices climb accordingly.

Richardsons Beach (☎ 03-6256 7000; freycinet@parks.tas.gov.au; unpowered/powered sites $12/15). Camping here is deservedly popular, especially during the summer-holiday period. Between 1 December and Easter, allocation of sites is by a ballot system. Applications must be made on a form downloadable from the national parks website (www.parks.tas.gov .au) or by calling the park visitors centre (☎ 03-6256 7000), and must be submitted by 31 October. There's sometimes the odd tent spot left over, even during peak season – vacancies are posted outside the visitors centre in the evening.

Iluka Holiday Centre (☎ 03-6257 0115; 1800 786 512; www.ilukaholidaycentre .com.au; Coles Bay Esplanade; unpowered/powered site $23/28, dm $27, on-site van $65, d cabin & apt $95-160) A large, friendly holiday park that's a favourite with local holidaymakers, so book well ahead during peak times. There's a shop, bakery and pub-bistro adjacent.

Coles Bay Youth Hostel (dm $12-15, r $50-70) This place will only do if you're riding with company, as there's a two-person minimum booking. Right on the waterfront at Parson's Cove, it's a rustic, unstaffed hostel with two basic five-person cabins and a kitchen area with fridge and stove. There are pit toilets and only cold water on tap. Entire cabins can be rented for $50 ($70 for non-YHA members) via a ballot system from mid-December to mid-February and at Easter (call before mid-September to register for the summer ballot, and by mid-January for the Easter ballot). Book through Tasmania's **YHA head office** (☎ 03-6234 9617; yhatas@ yhatas.org.au); keys and bed linen are obtained from the Iluka Holiday Centre.

Hubie's Hideaway (☎ 0419 255 604; 33 Coles Bay Esplanade; d $120-160, extra person $25) At this cute timber cabin, close to the shops and bakery, you'll fall asleep to the sound of the sea. Sleeps up to seven.

Freycinet Rentals (☎ 03-6257 0320; www.freycinetrentals.com; 5 Garnet Ave) has a range of good holiday cottages in Coles Bay. Prices vary from $130 to $170 in summer for two people (extra person $15), with the price for doubles about $20 lower in winter. Minimum stays apply for long weekends and Christmas holidays.

Freycinet Lodge (☎ 03-6257 0101; www .freycinetlodge.com.au; d cabin $182-319, extra person $55, 2-bedroom cabins $214-384) The quintessential Coles Bay stay, Freycinet Lodge is in a gorgeous location right in the national park. It has smart cabins, some with enormous spas and enticing views. There are two restaurants on-site.

Freycinet Bakery & Café (☎ 03-6257 0272; Shop 2, Coles Bay Esplanade; meals $3-15, 8am-5pm) Pick up hearty sandwiches or enjoy a lazy all-day breakfast outside.

Oystercatcher (☎ 03-6257 0033; 6 Garnet Ave; meals $6-15; lunch & dinner Nov-Apr) You can sit on the deck here or grab a quick takeaway. It serves excellent fish and chips, wraps, salads and rolls.

Iluka Tavern (☎ 03-6257 0429; Coles Bay Esplanade; mains $18-29; lunch & dinner) This popular, friendly pub gets packed with both tourists and locals. It offers excellent pub nosh: look past the beef 'n' reef and the ubiquitous chicken parmigiana and you'll find concoctions such as Thai green prawn curry and seafood linguine.

Madge Malloys (☎ 03-6257 0399; 7 Garnet Ave, Coles Bay; mains $28-33; dinner Tue-Sat) At Madge's, the menu depends on what the fishing fleet plucks from the sea each day. That might mean steam-baked bastard trumpeter, wrasse with crab stuffing, or poached calamari that melts in the mouth. Bookings essential.

Coles Bay Trading Company (1 Garnet Ave; 8am-6pm Mar-Nov, 7am-7pm Dec-Feb) is the general store, and there's also a mini-market at the Iluka Holiday Centre.

CRADLE MOUNTAIN
☎ 03 / pop 330

Along with Wineglass Bay, Cradle Mountain is the pin-up rock star of natural Tasmania, its sagging profile as recognisable as Uluru or the Pinnacles. Visitor services are concentrated at Pencil Pine, so you'll have to ride an extra 9km (see the side trip, p198) if you want a close look at the famed mountain and its front-yard pond, Dove Lake, or you can jump on the bus shuttle that leaves from the **Cradle Mountain visitors centre** (☎ 03-6492 1110; Cradle Mountain Rd; 8.30am-4.30pm). The bus (adult $7.50, free if you have a national-parks pass) leaves at around 20-minute intervals from mid-September to mid-May, with less-frequent departures through winter. There may be substantial queues at peak times.

Information
There's a second **Cradle Mountain visitors centre** (☎ 03-6492 1133; www.parks .tas.gov.au; 8am-5pm Jun-Aug, 8am-6pm Dec-Mar), where rangers provide detailed bushwalking information and weather updates. There's also an interpretative display here on the flora, fauna and history of the park. Both centres have small shops, though choices are subsistence-level so carry food in if you plan to self-cater.

Sleeping & Eating
Discovery Holiday Parks Cradle Mountain (☎ 03-6492 1395, 1800 068 574; Cradle Mountain Rd; unpowered/powered sites $25/35, dm $30, cabins $112-175) This is a bushland complex situated 2.5km outside the national park. It has well-separated sites, a YHA-affiliated hostel, a camp kitchen and laundry and self-contained cabins. There's a reasonable range of groceries in the reception store.

Waldheim Chalet & Cabins (☎ 03-6492 1110; cradle@depha.tas.gov.au; cabins from $70) If you want to be near to the mountain, these rustic cabins are set in forest just a few kilometres before Dove Lake. Each hut has bunks and kitchen facilities and there's a shared shower and toilet. Bookings are handled by Cradle Mountain visitors centre (see above).

Cradle Mountain Highlanders Cottages (☎ 03-6492 1116; www.cradlehighlander .com.au; Cradle Mountain Rd; cabins $115-290) This genuinely hospitable place has a charming collection of self-contained, timber cottages with wood or gas fires, queen-sized beds, electric blankets and hearty continental-breakfast provisions. Three cabins include a spa, and all include

TASMANIA

linen. The surrounding bush is peaceful and wildlife-filled.

Cradle Mountain Wilderness Village (☎ 03-6492 1500; www.cradlevillage.com.au; Cradle Mountain Rd; cottages d $180, 4-person chalets & villas $260) When you walk into the reception here on a clear day, you'll be treated to some exceptional views of Cradle Mountain. There are some quite luxurious chalets and cabins set peacefully in the trees, but they're painted in such perfect eucalypt greys and greens that it feels almost like camo.

Cradle Mountain Lodge (☎ 03-6492 2100, 1300 134 044; www.voyages.com.au; Cradle Mountain Rd; d $260-620) There are various standards of cabin at the lodge – the most luxurious are the King Billy Suites, privately secluded in the forest and with hot tubs on their decks. There is a little lake to fish in and plenty of short walks nearby, and the lodge puts on a plethora of guided activities to keep you busy if you're staying on a day or two. You can also have the knots kneaded out of your thighs and back at the **Waldheim Alpine Spa** (☎ 03-6492 2133). Good, casual mountain fare is served in the Tavern (mains $8 to $24, open lunch and dinner), but the **Highland Restaurant** (two/three courses $55/64, open for dinner only) is the real culinary experience here, serving the likes of prosciutto-wrapped wild rabbit saddle with mustard potato gnocchi – all accompanied by fine Tasmanian wines.

Cradle Wilderness Cafe (☎ 03-6492 1400; Cradle Mountain Rd; mains $7-20; 8am-5pm Mar-Nov, 9am-8pm Dec-Feb) This cafe at the Cradle Mountain Transit Terminal is welcomingly warm and has a good range of drinks and snacks, and you can also pick up sandwiches for the day's ride.

CYGNET

☎ 03 / pop 930

Groovy Cygnet was originally named Port de Cygne Noir (Port of the Black Swan) by Bruni D'Entrecasteaux, and it's easy to see why with the proliferation of swans on the bay. Youthfully reincarnated as Cygnet, the town has evolved into a dreadlocked, artsy enclave while still functioning as a major fruit-producing centre. Weathered farmers and banjo-carrying hippies chat amiably in the main street and prop up the bars of the town's three pubs.

Sleeping & Eating

Cygnet Holiday Park (☎ 03-6295 1267; contact@cygnettophotel.com.au; 3 Mary St; unpowered/powered sites $15/25) A bog-basic campsite overlooking the town oval. Check in at the Cygnet Hotel, across the road.

Huon Valley (Balfes Hill) Backpackers (☎ 03-6295 1551; www.balfeshill.alltasmanian.com; 4 Sandhill Rd, Cradoc; unpowered sites $15, dm/d/f $25/50/75) Off the Channel Hwy, 4.5km north of town, with decent rooms, good facilities, extensive grounds and super views from the large communal area. It's especially busy from November to May, when the host helps backpackers find fruit-picking work.

Commercial Hotel (☎ 03-6295 1296; 2 Mary St; s/d with shared bathroom $45/60) Upstairs at the rambling old Commercial are decent pub rooms, though the bathrooms could use an overhaul.

Cygnet Hotel (☎ 03-6295 1267; www.cygnethotel.com.au; 77 Mary St; dm/s/d $30/90/95) The big, red-brick 'Top Pub' on the upper slopes of Cygnet's main drag has lifted its game to provide heritage pub accommodation that's a rung or two above the rest. Budget bunk rooms serve as two-bed dorms. Downstairs you can grab dinner at the bar, bistro or more upmarket Black Swan Restaurant.

Cygnet Bay Waterfront Retreat (☎ 03-6295 0980; www.cygnetbay.com.au; 11 Crooked Tree Point; 2-person apt $150, extra person $30) Occupying the ground floor of a fairly bland-looking house is this self-contained apartment, 3km south of town. But forget the architecture: this is absolute waterfront, with a private entry, terrace, BBQ area and lawns rolling down to the bay.

School House Coffee Shop (☎ 03-6295 1206; 23a Mary St; meals $5-16; breakfast & lunch Tue-Sun) Cute coffee shop with geranium-filled window boxes, serving hefty homemade pies, Turkish-bread sandwiches, pasta, soups, all-day breakfasts and tempting cakes.

Red Velvet Lounge (☎ 03-6295 0466; 24 Mary St; mains $8-12; breakfast & lunch) A new breed of hip cafes populates Cygnet's main street, the best of which is this funky wholefood store and coffeehouse serving deliciously healthy meals (asparagus, olive and goats' cheese tart; beef rendang curry).

Cygnet Central Hotel (☎ 03-6295 1244; cnr Mary St & Garthfield Ave; mains $12-21; lunch & dinner) Behind Cygnet's newest pub is a vast dining room overlooking a paddock. There's veal schnitzels, beer-battered scallops, disquieting carpet design and little joy for vegetarians.

Cygnet has a pigeon pair of **IGA** supermarkets on Mary Street (the B68).

DELORAINE
☎ **03 / pop 2500**
At the foot of the Great Western Tiers, Deloraine has wonderful views just about wherever you look. The pretty town has an artsy, vibrant feel, with several cool little eateries, some bohemian boutiques and second-hand shops. The strong artistic community here celebrates annually with the Tasmanian Craft Fair, drawing tens of thousands of visitors in late October/early November: bear in mind that accommodation is tight if you're cycling through at this time.

Information
The **Great Western Tiers Visitors Centre** (☎ 03-6362 3471; 98-100 Emu Bay Rd; 9am-5pm) can help with local information.

Sleeping & Eating
Deloraine Apex Caravan Park (☎ 03-6362 2345; West Pde; unpowered/powered sites $11/14) At the bottom of the main street and on the banks of the Meander River, is this simple camping spot with basic facilities. In typical campsite placement, there are train tracks right beside the park. Just block your ears as the freight train rolls through in the night.

Highview Lodge Youth Hostel (☎ 03-6362 2996; 8 Blake St; dm/d from $21/49, f $49-84) It's a bit of a steep climb up to this hilltop YHA, but you'll be rewarded by the expansive views over the Great Western Tiers. It has a cosy, homely atmosphere, and when the wood heater is roaring, you could just imagine you're out in a wilderness hut.

Tierview Twin Cottages (☎ 03-6362 2377; 125 Emu Bay Rd; 4-person cottage $115, 6-person cottage $135, extra person $20) These identical twin cottages are just off the main street, and offer comfortable self-contained accommodation. The four-person cottage has an open fire, while the six-person has a spa bathroom. Get your keys from the Shell service station opposite.

Bowerbank Mill (☎ 03-6362 2628; www.bowerbankmill.com.au; 4455 Bass Hwy; s/d without bathroom $125/155, cottage $195) This fantastic B&B is set in a historic 1853 flour mill around 2km east of the town centre. It's thoughtfully furnished, with beautiful antiques throughout, and the cottage has an amazing six-storey-high bluestone chimney and a great fireplace. Substantial continental breakfasts are provided and there are reduced rates for longer stays.

Bonney's Inn (☎ 03-6362 2974; www.bonneys-inn.com; 19 West Pde; s/d/tw $120/148/168) Built by John Bonney, son of a convict, in the 1830s this was Deloraine's original coaching inn: horses were tied up out the back, and servants camped in the garden. Inside, travellers still stay in an old-world atmosphere in attractively modernised rooms. The days begin with hearty cooked breakfasts, including homemade pastries and fresh, local fruit.

Deloraine Delicatessen & Gourmet Foods (☎ 03-6362 2127; 36 Emu Bay Rd; mains $6-12; breakfast & lunch Mon-Sat) A fine place for morning baguettes, bagels and focaccias, with a variety of tasty fillings. Its coffee is pungently superb, and it also does dairy- and gluten-free meals.

Empire Hotel & Thai Restaurant (☎ 03-6362 2075; 19 Emu Bay Rd; mains $10-20; breakfast, lunch & dinner summer, lunch & dinner winter) The renovated cafe in this heritage hotel serves breakfasts, cakes and coffees, while the adjacent Thai restaurant serves up fine lunches and dinners. There's also a bar next door that has live entertainment a few nights a week.

There's a large **Woolworths** (Emu Bay Rd) supermarket just down the hill from the visitors centre.

DEVONPORT
☎ **03 / pop 25,122**
Devonport is a waterside city: it straddles the Mersey River and seascapes stretch out from its either side. Many cyclists get off the ferry in Devonport, jump on their bikes and

scoot. This quiet little port town is possibly not the most glamorous spot in the state, but take your time to ground your feet on Tasmanian soil here.

Information

The **visitors centre** (☎ 03-6424 4466; tourism@devonport.tas.gov.au; 92 Formby Rd; 7.30am-5pm or 9pm) has smiling faces to meet all ferry arrivals – the 9pm closure is on days when the ferry makes day crossings, arriving at 7pm.

Supplies & Equipment

Spares and repairs can be found at **Noel von Bibra Cycles** (☎ 03-6424 7778; 142 William St).

Sleeping & Eating

Mersey Bluff Caravan Park (☎ 03-6424 8655; mbcp1@bigpond.net.au; Bluff Rd; unpowered/powered sites $15/18, on-site vans $40, cabins from $62) In a seaside setting on Mersey Bluff, this pleasantly tree-filled park is just steps from the beach. There's a campers' kitchen and BBQ facilities, a takeaway shop on-site and walks nearby.

Tasman Backpackers (☎ 03-6423 2335; www.tasmanbackpackers.com.au; 114 Tasman St; dm/tw per person $16/18, d with/without bathroom $50/40) This recently renovated hostel was once a sprawling nurses' quarters but it's now a friendly place to stay with a great international feel. The en suite doubles all have TV and DVD player, and there's an in-house movie theatre for the rest.

Alice Beside the Sea (☎/fax 03-6427 8605; www.alicebesidethesea.com; 1 Wright St; d $99-130) Located close to the ferry terminals, this compact B&B offers comfortable, two-bedroom, self-contained accommodation across the road from the beach and close to supermarkets.

MacFie Manor (☎ 03-6424 1719; www.macfiemanor.com.au 44 MacFie St; s $100, d $110-130) The beautiful wrought-iron tracery on this handsome Federation home tells you you've found one of Devonport's nicest places to stay. The comely decoration continues inside, with four-poster beds, carved timber fireplaces and a Scottish theme: you can choose from the Edinburgh, Kilmarnock or Stewart rooms. Fully cooked breakfasts are part of the deal.

Cameo Cottage (☎ 03-6427 0991, 0439 658 503; www.devonportbedandbreakfast .com; 27 Victoria Pde; d $140-160, extra person $30) Tucked away in quiet backstreets, this ultra-neat two-bedroom cottage was built in 1914, but is now thoroughly up-to-date. It's got a well-equipped kitchen, cosy lounge where you can watch DVDs to your heart's content, a laundry, and a quiet garden where you can cook up a storm on the BBQ.

All Things Nice (☎ 03-6427 0028; 175 Tarleton St; 24hr) This bakery and cafe is located near the ferry terminal. It offers all manner of bakery items: gourmet chunky pies, including that Tassie icon, scallop pie; cakes and other sweets; and a good strong cuppa.

Renusha's (☎ 03-6424 2293; 132 William St; mains $9-18; lunch Wed-Fri, dinner Tue-Sat) The gaudy decor here may be what first catches your attention, and you'll be glad it did: the food is sensational. It serves superb Indian food and a fine Italian pasta too, and has earned a local reputation for being consistently great.

Twist (☎ 03-6423 2033; 5 Rooke St; mains $22-27; lunch Tue-Fri & Sun, dinner Tue-Sat) This smart new restaurant with a lime green 'twist' to its decor is getting rave reviews from locals. Try the pan-fried wallaby sirloin served with pepperberry sauce.

There's a **Foodworks** (Tarleton St, East Devonport) store about 1km along the route out of Devonport towards Deloraine, and a **Woolworths** (74 Best St) in town.

DOVER
☎ 03 / pop 570

Dozy Dover – a Port Esperance fishing town with a pub, a beach and a pier to dangle a line from – is a chilled-out kind of place, as reflected by the names of the three small islands afloat in the bay: Faith, Hope and Charity. In the 19th century, this was timber territory.

Huon pine and local hardwoods were milled and shipped from here (and also nearby Strathblane and Raminea) to China, India and Germany for use as railway sleepers. Today, the major industries are fruit-growing and fish farming, harvesting Atlantic salmon for export throughout Asia.

Sleeping & Eating

Dover Beachside Tourist Park (☎ 03-6298 1301; www.dovercaravanpark.com.au; 27 Kent Beach Rd; unpowered/powered sites $20/28, on-site caravans/cabins from $45/85) Passed as you ride into town, this proudly maintained park features spotless cabins, a bookshelf full of beachy novels and actual grass (the drought hasn't made it this far south).

Anne's Old Rectory B&B (☎ 03-6298 1222; www.annesoldrectory.com.au; 6961 Huon Hwy; s $70-90, d $90-100) North of town with two uber-floral B&B rooms, each with private bathroom down the hall, in a 1901 rectory surrounded by colourful gardens.

Smuggler's Rest (☎ 03-6298 1396; www.smugglersrest.info; Station Rd; d $85-105) Immaculate self-contained studios and two-bedroom units with fishing rods and old golf clubs to play with.

Driftwood Holiday Cottages (☎ 1800 353 983; www.driftwoodcottages.com.au; 51 Bayview Rd; d $160-220) Offers modern, self-contained studio-style units and two large houses sleeping four to eight people. Sit on your veranda, sip something chilly and watch fishermen rowing out to their boats on Port Esperance.

Gingerbreadhouse Bakery (☎ 03-6298 1502; Main Rd; items $4-13; breakfast & lunch) On the town's main corner, this small Germanic bakery dishes out cooked breakfasts, stuffed croissants, homemade pies and tasty cakes, all made on-site.

Dover Woodfired Pizza (☎ 03-6298 1905; Main Rd; mains $9-19; lunch & dinner Wed-Sun) A snug, wood-panelled eatery offering traditional and gourmet wood-fired pizzas, baked spuds and filling pasta dishes. Eat in or takeaway.

Dover Hotel (☎ 03-6298 1210; Huon Hwy; mains $16-22; lunch & dinner) This far-flung pub makes a real effort to depart from the deep fries, schnitzels and steaks omnipresent on Tasmanian pub menus. Nigh-on-gourmet selections include Hastings oysters, Huon Valley honeybrown mushrooms, local scallops and the fresh catch of the day from the local fishing fleet.

Self-caterers can stock up at the **Dover Grocer & Newsagency** (☎ 03-6298 1201; Main Rd; 6.30am-6.30pm Mon-Fri, 7am-6.30pm Sat, 7am-6pm Sun), which is fully stocked with beaut deli produce, Tassie wines and fresh fruit and veg. There's a **Festival IGA** (Southgate Shopping Centre, Huon Hwy) just across the road.

EAGLEHAWK NECK

☎ 03 / pop 100

Eaglehawk Neck is a narrow isthmus connecting the Forestier Peninsula to the Tasman Peninsula. In Port Arthur's convict days, the 100m-wide Neck had a row of ornery dogs chained across it to prevent escape – the infamous Dogline. Timber platforms were also built in narrow Eaglehawk Bay to the west, and stocked with yet more ferocious dogs to prevent convicts from wading around the Dogline. Rumours were circulated that the waters were shark-infested to discourage swimming. Today, the place is somewhat more welcoming.

Sleeping & Eating

Eaglehawk Neck Backpackers (☎ 03-6250 3248; 94 Old Jetty Rd; unpowered sites $16, dm $20) A very simple, family-run hostel in a peaceful location signposted west of the isthmus. There are just four beds in the dorm, plus a couple of tent spots on the back lawn and a camp kitchen.

Eaglehawk Café & Guesthouse (☎ 03-6250 3331; www.theneck.com.au; 5131 Arthur Hwy; d incl breakfast $110-130) Upstairs at this artsy little cafe (built in 1929) are three lovely B&B rooms, taking up the spaces once occupied by slumbering shipwrights. Two of the rooms have beaut French doors opening onto a balcony overlooking Eaglehawk Bay. The cafe (mains $10 to $23; open for breakfast and lunch year-round, dinner Fri to Sun from Dec to Feb) is arguably the peninsula's best dining option. Breakfast runs until midday if you're off to a lazy start.

Eaglehawk Hideaway (☎ 03-6250 3513; www.eaglehawkhideaway.com; 40 Ferntree Rd; s/d $120/140) About 1km beyond Eaglehawk Neck is the turn off to this big brick house, the ground floor of which is given over to guests. The bloom-filled gardens are great, but the house itself is nothing to write home about – stay for the location not the accommodation. Breakfast costs an extra $20, and dinner can be organised by arrangement.

Lufra Hotel (☎ 03-6250 3262; 380 Pirates Bay Dr; mains $15-34) This hefty hotel aims to please all comers with its bistro serving fine local produce (seafood, quail, wallaby), and its public bar where you can get traditional pub grub for a few dollars less.

There is no supermarket, so carry in supplies if you're self-catering.

EVANDALE
☎ 03 / pop 1035

National Trust–classified Evandale is known to cyclists as the venue for the National Penny-Farthing Championships, part of the February Evandale Village Fair. For the rest of the year, its narrow streets, flanked by quaint 19th-century buildings and cottage gardens, give it the atmosphere of an English village. Penny-farthings lean nonchalantly against shop doorways and murals depict cycling amid a variety of village activities.

Information
The informative **visitors centre** (☎ 03-6391 8128; 18 High St; 10am-3pm) contains a history room with a display on famous locals including painter John Glover and decorated WW1 soldier Harry Murray.

Sleeping & Eating
Riverside Caravan Park (☎ 03-6391 1470; www.longfordriversidecaravanpark .com; 2a Archer St; unpowered/powered sites $20/25, on-site vans $60; tw $40) In Longford, 19km along the Day 1 route of the Tassie's West Coast ride. Beautifully positioned on the banks of the Macquarie River, it's spacious, grassy and shady, a surprising spot of green in the brown Norfolk Plains. There's no campsite in Evandale itself, but this is the best nearby option.

Solomon Cottage (☎ 03-6391 8331; 1 High St; s/d $100/130) This cottage was built in 1838 as a bakery, and Joseph Solomon would never have envisaged his oven taken up by a queen-sized bed (note the brick-vaulted ceiling). The cottage has two bedrooms and the price includes a cooked breakfast with fresh croissants and fruit.

Arendon Cottage (☎ 03-6391 8093; 30 Russell St; d $120, extra person $10) You can sit out on the veranda here and watch the world go by through the white roses. The beautifully kitted-out cottage sleeps up to four. You can get cosy by the wood-burning stove. The breakfast provisions are abundant for a good start to the ride.

Wesleyan Chapel (☎ 03-6331 9337; 28 Russell St; d apt $120) Built in 1836, this tiny brick chapel has been used as a Druids hall, an RSL hall and a meeting place for scouts. Now, under the high-pitched ceiling, it's eminently stylish accommodation for two.

Muse Coffee Bar (☎ 03-6391 8552; 14 Russell St; mains $7-18; 10am-5pm daily, 6-8pm Fri & Sat) This cool little eatery does morning and afternoon teas and delicious lunches using plenty of fresh local produce. Try the Tasmanian smoked salmon on sourdough with figs. Friday and Saturday are pizza nights.

Ingleside Bakery Café (☎ 03-6391 8682; 4 Russell St; mains $15-20; breakfast & lunch) Sit in the beautiful walled courtyard or under the high ceiling inside these atmospheric former council chambers. Fresh baking smells waft from the wood oven, making the bakery wares quite irresistible. It does delectable pies and pasties, a swagman's lunch for the hungry ($20) and all manner of sweet treats.

Clarendon Arms Hotel (☎ 03-6391 8181; 11 Russell St; mains $13-20; lunch & dinner) This pub serves commendable bistro meals and has an outdoor beer garden where you can dine under the trees. Try the homemade beef-and-Guinness pie.

The **Evandale General Store** (Russell St) is open seven days a week.

HOBART
☎ 03 / pop 203,600

Australia's second-oldest city may also be its most beautiful, pinched between the wide Derwent River and the ruffled dolerite collar of 1270m-high Mt Wellington. With scant flat land along its narrow line of suburbs, it's a perfect warm-up for cyclists venturing into the mountainous hinterland.

Information
The **Hobart visitors centre** (☎ 03-6230 8233; www.hobarttravelcentre.com.au; cnr Davey & Elizabeth Sts; 8.30am-5.30pm Mon-Fri, 9am-5pm Sat, Sun & public holidays) has city and state information.

Supplies & Equipment

There's a cluster of good bike stores around a two-block section of Elizabeth St, between Liverpool and Melville Sts, in central Hobart: **Ken Self Cycles** (☎ 03-6234 4175; 124 Elizabeth St), **Bike Ride** (☎ 03-6231 6202; www.bikeride.com.au; 74a Liverpool St) and **Appleby Cycles** (☎ 03-6234 7644; http://applebycycles.com.au; 109 Elizabeth St). For bike rentals, see p163.

The **Tasmanian Map Centre** (☎ 03-6231 9043; www.map-centre.com.au; 100 Elizabeth St) stocks all the maps you will require.

Sleeping & Eating

Elwick Cabin & Tourist Park (☎ 03-6272 7115; www.islandcabins.com.au; 19 Goodwood Rd, Glenorchy; unpowered/powered sites $20/30, cabins $90-115, 3-bedroom house per d $130) The nearest campsite to town (about 8km north of the centre), with a range of cabins but limited campsites (book ahead). The park can be reached from the city centre along the Intercity Cycleway; pick the path up along Davey St at Sullivans Cove.

Central City Backpackers (☎ 03-6224 2404, 1800 811 507; www.centralcityhobart .com; 138 Collins St; dm $23-27, s/d $55/69) Smack-bang in the middle of the city, this mazelike hostel has loads of communal space, a great kitchen, OK rooms, friendly staff and extras such as baggage storage and tour desk. Bathrooms are a tad shabby.

Astor Private Hotel (☎ 03-6234 6611; www.astorprivatehotel.com.au; 157 Macquarie St; s with/without bathroom $115/75, d $150/89) A rambling, downtown, 1920s charmer, the Astor retains much of its character: stained-glass windows, old furniture, ceiling roses and the irrepressible Tildy at the helm. Older-style rooms have shared facilities; newer en suite rooms top the price range. Breakfast is included.

Graham Court Apartments (☎ 03-6278 1333, 1800 811 915; www.grahamcourt .com.au; 15 Pirie St, New Town; d $145-170, extra person $25) Probably Hobart's best-value self-contained option, this block of 23 well-maintained apartments sits amid established gardens in the northern suburbs, not far from North Hobart's buzzing Elizabeth St strip. Units range from one to three bedrooms (decor from '70s to '90s). Located near the Intercity Cycleway.

Henry Jones Art Hotel (☎ 03-6210 7700; www.thehenryjones.com; 25 Hunter St; d $290-390, ste $390-850) For a pre- or post-tour treat, check in to super-swish HJs. Absolute waterfront in a restored jam factory, it oozes class. Modern art enlivens the walls, and facilities are world class. The hotel also makes smart use of recycled materials.

The waterfront and North Hobart offer the city's best dining options. Salamanca Pl is an almost unbroken string of excellent cafes and restaurants, while Elizabeth St in North Hobart has evolved into a diverse collation of cosmopolitan cafes, multicultural eateries and improving pubs.

Flippers Fish Punt (☎ 03-6234 3101; Constitution Dock; meals $5-12; lunch & dinner) With its voluptuous fish-shaped profile and alluring sea-blue paint job, floating Flippers is both a Hobart institution and an awesome fish and chippery. Fillets of flathead and curls of calamari come straight from the deep blue sea and into the deep fryer.

Annapurna (☎ 03-6236 9500; 305 Elizabeth St, North Hobart; mains $14-17; lunch & dinner) It seems like half of Hobart lists Annapurna as their favourite eatery (bookings advised). Northern and southern Indian options served with absolute proficiency – the best Indian meal you'll have on the island, guaranteed! The *masala dosa* (south Indian crepe filled with curried potato) is a crowd favourite. BYO; takeaway available. Also at 93 Salamanca Pl.

Sirens (☎ 03-6234 2634; 6 Victoria St; mains $18-20; dinner Mon-Sat) Sirens serves up creative vegetarian and vegan food in a warm, welcoming space, offset by excellent service and impeccable ethics. But it's not all earnest long-hairs stirring lentils – there's some sophisticated cooking going on in the kitchen! Try the three-cheese beetroot ravioli in champagne, dill and pink peppercorn cream.

The most central self-catering option is **City Supermarket** (☎ 03-6234 4003; 148 Liverpool St; 8am-7pm Mon-Fri, 9am-5pm Sat, noon-5pm Sun). Those with a gourmet bent should head to **Wursthaus** (☎ 03-6224 0644; www.wursthaus.com.au; 1 Montpelier Retreat, Battery Point; 8am-

6pm Mon-Fri, to 5pm Sat, 9.30am-4pm Sun) for deli produce, or the **Salamanca Fresh Fruit Market** (☎ 03-6223 2700; 41 Salamanca Pl; 7am-7pm) for fruit and groceries.

LAKE ST CLAIR
☎ 03

Australia's deepest freshwater lake is best known as the southern terminus of the Overland Track, though it's a destination in its own right. Dramatic dolerite peaks rise up to 700m above its shores, and the waters are home to platypuses. After a week in the saddle, it's a restive (or active) place to stop for a day.

Information
The **Lake St Clair visitors centre** (☎ 03-6289 1172; 8am-6pm Dec & Jan, to 8pm Feb, to 5pm Mar-Nov) provides information on the Cradle Mountain–Lake St Clair National Park and has displays on the area's geology, flora and fauna, bushwalking and Aboriginal heritage.

Sleeping & Eating
Lake St Clair Wilderness Resort (☎ 03-6289 1137; www.lakestclairresort.com. au; unpowered/powered sites $20/25, dm $28, cabins d $130-190, extra person $25) Campsites on the lakeshore, a backpackers lodge with two- to four-bunk rooms and kitchen facilities, and comfortably upmarket self-contained alpine cabins. In the main building opposite the Lake St Clair visitors centre there's a great cafe (mains $8 to $26, open 7.30am to 9pm summer, 10am to 3pm winter) serving a hearty menu, light snacks and coffee that's been voted the best in Tasmania. There are a few basic food supplies and some outdoor gear in the shop.

Derwent Bridge Wilderness Hotel (☎ 03-6289 1144; dm $25, d with/without bathroom $115/95) This chalet-style pub has a high-beamed roof and a pleasant country feel. The lounge bar is warm and expansive, making it a great place in which to enjoy a beer and a meal in front of a massive log fire. The hostel and hotel accommodation is plain but comfortable, and the restaurant (mains $18 to $39.50) serves commendable pub fare, including excellent roasts, pasta dishes, steaks and daily fresh soups. Derwent Bridge is just 5.5km from Lake St Clair, back on the Lyell Hwy – you will pass through it as you ride both in and out of Lake St Clair.

Derwent Bridge Chalets & Studios (☎ 03-6289 1000; www.derwent-bridge .com; Lyell Hwy; d $155-230) Five hundred metres east of the Lake St Clair turn-off, this place has one-, two- and three-bedroom self-contained roomy cabins, some with spa but all with full kitchen and laundry facilities and back-porch bush views.

Hungry Wombat Café (☎ 03-6289 1125; Lyell Hwy; mains $5-11; 8am-6pm summer, 9am-5pm winter) Part of the Caltex service station, this cafe is well placed to feed the famished, serving breakfasts to keep you going all day. Everything's homemade and good. There's also a small grocery section.

LAUNCESTON
☎ 03 / pop 71,000

Tasmania's second city has shed its former stolid, country-bumpkin air and it's now surprisingly artsy and sophisticated. It's still got a relaxed, rural sort of feel – rush hour lasts barely 10 minutes – and remarkable Cataract Gorge brings the wilds into the heart of town. It's said that the city has more cafes per head than any other Australian city. If you want a brush with Tassie cycling stardom, head a few kilometres out of town to **Velo Wines** (West Tamar Hwy, Legana; cellar door 10am-5pm), owned by former Tour de France cyclist Michael Wilson.

Information
The **visitors centre** (☎ 1800 651 827, 6336 3133; www.ltvtasmania.com.au; cnr St John & Cimitiere Sts) has racks of pamphlets, and handles statewide accommodation, tour and transport bookings.

Supplies & Equipment
There's a pair of good bike stores on Wellington St, south of the city centre: **Kinnane Cycles** (☎ 03-6331 9880; 187 Wellington St), which is crammed full of with bikes; and **Geard Cycles** (☎ 03-6344 9154; www.geardcycles.com; 335 Wellington St), which has an excellent range of spares. For bike hire, see p163.

Topographic maps can be bought at **Service Tasmania** (☎ 1300 13 55 13;

www.service.tas.gov.au; Henty House, 1 Civic Sq).

Sleeping & Eating

Treasure Island Caravan Park (☎ 03-6344 2600; treasureislandlaunceston@netspace .net.au; 94 Glen Dhu St; unpowered/ powered sites $22/26, on-site vans $50, cabins $75-82) A stiff cycle up the highway and you could forget that the city is so close (2.5km) – you won't be able to ignore the highway noise, however, though this does die down at night. There are pretty camping spots among the trees.

Lloyds Hotel Backpackers (☎ 1300 858 861; www.backpackers-accommodation .com.au; 23 George St; dm $22, s/d $55/70) Lloyds stakes a claim as Launceston's happening-est pub. Downstairs the place goes nuts, but above, things remain relatively calm, with clean en suite rooms, kitchen, capacious communal areas and wi-fi.

Arthouse Backpacker Hostel (☎ 03-6333 0222; www.arthousehostel.com.au; 20 Lindsay St, 4-/6-/8-bed dm $27/25/23) Housed in a beautiful old heritage home, the Arthouse has spacious, airy dorms, a welcoming sitting room with a huge plasma TV, a wide upstairs veranda for shooting the breeze on, and a courtyard with BBQ out back. You can also hire bikes or camping equipment, store gear…and the young owners are friendly to boot. It's also Australia's first carbon-neutral backpackers.

Old Bakery Inn (☎ 1800 641 264, 03-6331 7900; www.oldbakeryinn.com.au; cnr York & Margaret Sts; d $90-135) You can almost smell the freshly baked bread coming from the ovens that are still a feature of this 130-year-old building. There are 24 appealingly decorated rooms here with mod cons like minibars and electric blankets. Rates don't include breakfast.

Lido Boutique Apartments (☎ 03-6334 5988; www.thelido.com.au; 47-49 Elphin Rd; apt $190-420) For self-catering with style, the eight spacious and wonderfully decorated apartments here exude 1930s style. They all have the most comfortable queen-sized beds and expansive living areas. For pure indulgence, reserve the exotic three-bedroom 'Japanese Imperial' suite with an enormous spa and every imaginable mod con.

Three Steps on George (☎ 03-6334 2084; 158 George St; mains $17-26; dinner) Part of the Colonial on Elizabeth complex, this wonderful restaurant–wine bar not only has great decor (check out the convict bricks), but friendly service and slap-up bistro fare. There's plenty to keep meat-eaters happy, including the aged Fillet Wellington and the Three Steps Burger.

Flavours on Charles (☎ 03-6331 3968; 252 Charles St; mains $17.50-26-50; Tue-Sun) If it's pub grub you crave, this restaurant in the Sportsmans Hall Hotel does great bistro fare: hearty staples like thick beef sausages with creamy herb mashed potato. Leave room for a wicked liquid-centre chocolate pudding afterwards.

Luck's (☎ 03-6334 8596; 70 George St; mains $24-37; lunch Tue-Fri, dinner) This classy restaurant was once a butcher's shop, but now it's all ornate gilded wallpaper, spanking white tablecloths and a definite air of retro-cool. Luck's serves fancy food in a French-bistro atmosphere. There's chateaubriand with chasseur sauce, or closer to home, a Flinders Island lamb rack. For afters try the dark chocolate and Turkish-delight tart.

Gather groceries at **Coles** (Wellington St), just south of the city centre.

MIENA
☎ 03 / pop 100

Wrapped around the southern shore of Great Lake, Miena is a motley collection of shacks posing as the largest town on the central plateau. Yours may be the only vehicle in town not towing a boat.

Sleeping & Eating

Campsite (sites $20) The roadhouse-style ground is basically an extension of the dusty car park between the general store and the hotel; check in at the hotel.

Great Lake Hotel (☎ 03-6259 8163; www.greatlakehotel.com.au; Swan Bay, Miena; dm $35, d from $95, f $135) This small-town pub offers accommodation from bog-basic anglers' cabins with shared facilities to self-contained motel-style units. The flesh-filled bar meals (mains $10 to $23; open lunch and dinner) will reduce vegetarians to tears.

Central Highlands Lodge (☎ 03-6259 8179; www.centralhighlandslodge.com.au;

Haddens Bay, Miena; s/d $108/136) On the highway, 3.5km south of Miena, this jaunty, rough-sawn timber lodge offers clean, comfortable cabins. The lodge restaurant (mains $13 to $26; open lunch and dinner) is a great place to rejuvenate with a cold beer and a hot meal (try the venison hot pot).

The **Great Lake General Store** (☎ 03-6259 8149; Swan Bay, Miena; 8am-5pm Sun-Thu, to 7pm Fri & Sat), next door to the Great Lake Hotel, sells pies, pasties and filled rocks plus a basic range of groceries (there's a far more extensive line of fishing tackle).

MT FIELD NATIONAL PARK
☎ 03

Mt Field was declared a national park in 1916 and is famed for its mountain scenery, alpine moorlands, lakes, rainforest, waterfalls and abundant wildlife. As a cyclist you're unlikely to make it past Russell Falls (it's an 850m climb to Lake Dobson if you do want to experience the mountain), at the foot of the mountain, but the waterfall alone is good reason to stay.

Unless you're staying in the town of National Park, bring in your own food or ride hungry the next day.

Information
The **Mt Field National Park visitors centre** (☎ 03-6288 1149; www.parks.tas.gov.au; 66 Lake Dobson Rd; 8.30am-5pm Nov-Apr, 9am-4pm May-Oct) houses a cafe and displays on the park's origins.

Sleeping & Eating
Land of the Giants Campground (☎ 03-6288 1526; unpowered/powered sites $16/25) A privately run, self-registration campsite with adequate facilities (toilets, showers, laundry and free BBQs) just inside the park gates. Camp prices are additional to national-park entry fees.

Russell Falls Holiday Cottages (☎ 03-6288 1198; 40 Lake Dobson Rd; d $140, extra person $20) In a super location next to the park entrance, these spotless, self-contained cottages have been the happy recipient of a slick makeover.

Celtic Dawn (☎ 03-6288 1058; www.celticdawn.com.au; 2400 Gordon River Rd; light meals $5-10; lunch Sat & Sun)

About 600m west of the national park turn-off is this kooky little octagonal cafe with only a couple of tables. Tacos, soups, filo pastries and great coffee are the order of the day. There are also a couple of great-value rooms: one double ($70) and one room with two single beds ($50). Both have bathrooms and a shared outdoor kitchen.

Waterfalls Café (☎ 03-6288 1516; 66 Lake Dobson Rd; meals $8-15; lunch) Simple eatery next to the visitors centre, serving up reasonable cafe fare (burgers, nachos, soup and schnitzels).

National Park Hotel (☎ 03-6288 1103; Gordon River Rd; mains $15-27; dinner) This relaxed rural pub, 300m past the park turn-off, cooks up mixed grills, chicken dishes and steaks. Skip the ordinary pub accommodation (s/d $50/85) unless you're desperate.

ORFORD
☎ 03 / pop 500

The low-key seaside village of Orford was once a seaport for the East Coast whaling fleet, and the convict and military settlement on Maria Island, just across Mercury Passage. Today, it's mostly a summer-holiday village where Hobartians have their seaside shacks.

Sleeping & Eating
Triabunna Cabin & Caravan Park (☎ 03-6257 3575; www.mariagateway.com; 4 Vicary St; unpowered/powered site $16/19, on-site van $44-54, cabin $77-110) Orford's campsite at Raspins Beach has closed. The handiest camping now is this small, cheek-by-jowl compound opposite the sports fields in Triabunna, 7km north of Orford.

Prosser Holiday Units (☎ 03-6257 1427; cnr Tasman Hwy & Charles St; d $95, extra person $20) Self-contained units opposite the IGA supermarket, on the bank of the Prosser River; the two-storey units have views of the water, and accommodate up to five.

Sanda House (☎ 03-6257 1527; www.orfordsandahouse.com.au; 33 Walpole St; d $100-120) A colonial B&B occupying Orford's oldest house, this pretty 1840s stone cottage on the south side of the river is surrounded by lovingly tended gardens. Continental breakfasts are served in front of the fire in the dining room.

Orford Riverside Cottages (☎ 03-6257 1655; www.riversidecottages.com.au; Old Convict Rd; d $150-190, extra person $40) These pretty timber cottages are set in trees overlooking the Prosser River and have spas, fully equipped kitchens and an extensive DVD library. You can borrow a fishing line and catch your dinner from the deck.

Scorchers on the River (☎ 03-6257 1033; 1 Esplanade; mains $11-23; 11am-8pm Thu-Tue) Known for superior wood-fired pizzas, including such creations as garlic prawn and Spring Bay seafood. There's also good lasagne and salads.

Gateway Café (☎ 03-6257 1539; 1 Charles St; lunch mains $7.50-15.50, dinner mains $15-22; 7am-9pm summer, 7am-6pm winter) By the bridge over the Prosser River, this excellent cafe also sells Tasmanian gourmet provisions.

Blue Waters Motor Inn (☎ 03-6257 1102; Tasman Hwy; mains $16-26; lunch & dinner) The dining room has wide river views and the cooks serve up large meals that are better-than-pub: try the bourbon-marinated T-bone or the wallaby schnitzel.

The **IGA** (Charles St) supermarket is almost on the banks of the Prosser River.

OUSE

☎ 03 / pop 160

Ouse was proclaimed early in Tassie's colonial saga, but has little of the historic charm – more just a collection of weatherboard houses bisected by the highway.

Sleeping & Eating

Ouse has no camping, but there's a free campsite just on the first rise out of Meadowbank Lake, 9km along the Day 9 route of the Tassie's West Coast ride. It has toilets but it's dusty, unshaded and not enticing.

Lachlan Hotel (☎ 03-6287 1215; ousepub@bigpond.com; Lyell Hwy; s/d $45/65) The rough-as-guts Lachlan offers serviceable, sunny pub rooms with shared facilities, plus bar lunches and dinners daily (mains $12 to $19).

Sassa-del-Gallo (☎ 03-6287 1289; cnr Ticknell St & Lyell Hwy; d $90, extra person $25) Shamelessly suburban, Sassa-del-Gallo fails to deliver the Mediterranean flair

suggested by its name. Still, it's clean and serviceable.

If you want to ride on 21km to Ellendale, **Hopfield Country Cottages** (☎ 03-6228 1223; www.hopfield.com.au; 990 Ellendale Rd; d $140) are a pair of connected cottages. The detached Possum Shed is prime platypus-spotting real estate. The tariff includes breakfast provisions.

There's a **Value Plus** (Main St) supermarket that's open seven days a week, while **Ouse Roadhouse** (☎ 03-6287 1281; Main St) does burgers and other fried goodies.

QUEENSTOWN

☎ 03 / pop 3400

The hillsides around Queenstown are unforgettable for their moonscape of bare, dusty hills and eroded gullies, where once there was rainforest. The area is the clearest testimony anywhere to the scarification of the west coast's environment by mining. Copper was discovered here in the 1890s and mining has continued ever since, but today pollution is closely monitored and sulphur emissions controlled. Ironically, when green started to creep back to these barren hills, Queenstown residents were perplexed: they felt the town's identity was so closely tied to the surrounding barrenness that hills covered in green simply wouldn't do. Although Queenstown is now getting in on the tourism trend, unlike overcommercialised Strahan it's still got that authentic, rough-and-ready pioneer town feel.

Information

The **Queenstown visitors centre** (☎ 03-6471 1483; 1-7 Driffield St), in the Eric Thomas Galley Museum, is run by volunteers with comprehensive information on the region.

Sleeping & Eating

Queenstown Cabin & Tourist Park (☎ 03-6471 1332; 17 Grafton St; unpowered/powered sites $25/30, on-site vans d $50, cabins d $70-90, extra person $10-15) Set on gravel and a bit bare, though it has clean vans and cabins, a communal kitchen and a sheltered BBQ area. There's more appealing, lakeside camping 22km out of town, along the Day 7 route of the Tassie's West Coast ride,

THE BALD HILL OF QUEENSTOWN

It's a peculiarly Tasmanian oddity that a town's identity both externally and within its own psyche is rooted in the unambiguous visible evidence of overwhelming environmental damage. In a stark counterpoint to the emerging global consciousness on ecological preservation and rehabilitation, Queenstown's ring of hills, stripped bare by over a century of logging to feed it's copper smelters have become ingrained in the cultural memory of its population. Their connection with the profound desolation of their impacted environment has become a kind of sentimental link with a past they have been reluctant to relinquish. In what would strike many outsiders as perplexing, since the 1980's some local residents have been voicing opposition the limited environmental recovery seen in some parts of Queenstown, fearing that a greening of Queenstown would strip it of its defining character.

Balancing the relatively recent push to try to start to reverse man's impact on the environment with the sensibilities of a population that has only known one way of relating to its land is a conundrum and in some ways, one has to at least consider their perspective. Founded, like so many Australian towns, initially on the promise of its gold deposits, copper eventually replaced gold as the town's lifeblood, and to this day, employs the bulk of its working population. At one time, Queenstown supported 11 copper smelters, and those not working in the mines or the smelters, were employed as timber cutters to feed the smelter furnaces. At the height of this activity, over 2000 tonnes of timber went to the furnaces every week. The mines and the forests fed Queenstown's families, built their schools and churches and shaped the region.

As far-flung and isolated as Queenstown may be in more ways than one, the traveller will always find a way to any destination, however and tourism is inevitably starting to become a significant contributor to the Queenstown economy As tourism grows, so does the imperative to become more open to a range of views on the environment and its role in ongoing ecological and economic sustainability. In a wryly ironic evolution, one of Queenstown's premier attractions these days is the West Coast Wilderness Railway. Not only does it signify Queenstown's recognition that its environment is actually one of its key assets, the restored tourism railway which carries between 60 and 100,000 tourists per year into the surrounding wilderness once carted copper ore from the mines originally responsible for the bald hills of Queenstown.

at Lake Burbury (per tent $5). The basic campsite has toilets, drinking water and a BBQ shelter. The ground is mossy and soft, so best avoided when it's wet (or when it's been wet).

Queenstown Copper Country Cabins (☎ 0417 398 343; 13 Austin St; s $70-80, d $80-100, extra person $15) A compact collection of modern, self-contained timber cabins. They are incredibly neat and tidy and there are laundry facilities nearby.

Comstock Cottage (☎ 03-6471 1200, 0409 711 614; 5 McNamara St; d $130-140, extra person $40) This pretty miner's cottage set in attractive gardens has its original pressed-tin ceilings and sleeps up to four. The master bedroom has a four-poster bed and the house is decorated with antiques throughout. The price includes breakfast provisions so you can cook up a morning protein fix.

Penghana (☎ 03-6471 2560; www .penghana.com.au; 32 The Esplanade; d

with/without bathroom from $150/140, ste $175 This National Trust–listed mansion was built in 1898 for the first general manager of the Mt Lyell Mining and Railway Company and, as befits its managerial stature, is located on a hill above town amid a rare number of trees. The B&B accommodation here is first-rate and includes a billiards room and a grand dining room for enjoying chef-prepared à la carte meals nightly. Packed lunches on request. Access via Preston St.

Dotties Coffeeshop (☎ 03-6471 1700; Queenstown Station, Driffield St; breakfast & lunch) Have breakfast alfresco on the train platform. There's smooth, creamy coffee and a selection of cafe delights, such as gourmet pies, pastries, cakes and biscuits.

Filis Pizza (☎ 03-6471 2006; 21 Orr St; pizzas $9-24; lunch & dinner) This friendly place suggests over 40 different takes on the humble pizza – if you need a filling meal you can't go wrong with this fab option. Try the roast garlic and olive supreme with roasted chicken. It does good roast dinners ($10) at Sunday lunchtime also.

Maloney's Restaurant (☎ 03-6471 1866; 54-58 Orr St; mains $22-24; dinner Mon-Sat) Who would expect such good food in a small-town motel? You can order the likes of garlic-infused chicken breast stuffed with roasted pine nuts, pesto and semidried tomatoes. There's also good steak, lamb, pork and seafood all cooked fresh to order.

The **Railway Express General Store** (cnr Ord & Strict Sts) has a good range of supplies.

RICHMOND
☎ 03 / pop 750

Straddling the Coal River 27km northeast of Hobart, historic Richmond was once a strategic military post and convict station on the road to Port Arthur. Riddled with 19th-century buildings, it's arguably Tasmania's premier historic town, centred on the 1823 convict-built Richmond Bridge, the oldest road bridge in Australia. See www.richmondvillage.com.au for more town information.

Sleeping & Eating

Richmond Cabin & Tourist Park (☎ 03-6260 2192, 1800 116 699; www .richmondcabins.com; 48 Middle Tea Tree Rd; unpowered/powered sites $18/24, cabins $60-110) This park is 1km south of town and has neat, no-frills cabins alongside the tent sites.

Richmond Cottages (☎ 03-6260 2561; www.richmondcottages.com; 12 Bridge St; d $125-165) Just can't get enough colonial accommodation? On offer here are two fully self-contained abodes: Ivy Cottage, a family-friendly, three-bedroom home, complete with claw-foot bath; and behind it the Stables, a rustic one-bedroom cottage with spa. Breakfast provisions provided.

Richmond Colonial Accommodation (☎ 03-6260 2570; www.richmondcolonial .com; 4 Percy St; d $140-160) Manages three (Willow, Bridge and Poplar) well-equipped, historic cottages around town. All are self-contained with a roll call of colonial touches.

Prospect House (☎ 03-6260 2207; www.prospect-house.com.au; 1384 Richmond Rd; d $160-180 About 1km west of Richmond is this haughty Georgian mansion, built in 1830, offering heritage-style guest rooms in converted outbuildings. The grounds evoke an old-money rural splendour, and there's an upmarket restaurant (mains $27 to $30; open for dinner). Dinner, bed and breakfast costs $249 for two.

Richmond Wine Centre (☎ 03-6260 2619; 27 Bridge St; mains $12-25; breakfast & lunch daily, dinner Wed-Sat) Don't be duped by the name, this place dedicates itself to fine food as well as wine. Tassie produce reigns supreme.

Ashmore on Bridge Street (☎ 03-6260 2238; 34 Bridge St; mains $13-18; breakfast & lunch daily, dinner Tue) Cheery corner food room with the sun streaming in through small-paned windows. Order up a big breakfast (scrambled eggs, cinnamon French toast with berry compote) and the best coffee in town.

Richmond Arms Hotel (☎ 03-6260 2109; 42 Bridge St; mains $13-22; lunch & dinner) This laid-back sandstone pub, popular with bikers of the petrol variety, has an uncreative but reliable pub-grub menu. Coal River Valley wines available.

Self-caterers can stock up at the **Bridge St Cafe and Supermarket** (Bridge St), on the main road.

ROSEBERY
☎ 03 / pop 1500

Rosebery might be something of a rough diamond, but it sure has a beautiful location, nestled in a valley of temperate rainforest with Mt Murchison to the east, imposing Mt Black (950m) to the north, and Mt Read (which has Tasmania's highest rainfall) to the south. Carry your raincoat at the top of your pannier, Rosebery itself gets an average 3.5m of rainfall a year.

Sleeping & Eating

Rosebery Caravan Park (☎ 03-6473 1366; Park Rd; unpowered/powered sites $20/25, cabins $50-90) This park is surrounded by hills and has a small, grassy campsite, a gravel caravan area and basic cabins. It's so shady it can get quite cool once it loses the sun.

Rosebery Top Pub (☎ 03-6473 1351; Agnes St; s with/without bathroom $65/40, d $80/60, extra person $20) Right in the centre of town, this pub has clean and quiet budget rooms over a friendly bar where you're sure to get chatting with locals. Counter meals are served in the restaurant nightly (mains $18 to $28).

Mount Black Lodge (☎ 03-6473 1039; www.mountblacklodge.com; Hospital Rd; d $110-130) This cosy and rustic lodge, run by friendly owners, looks towards Mt Murchison and Mt Read, so ask for a mountain-view room. There's an appealing lounge where you can stay warm by the wood heater. The lodge also features the Blue Moon Restaurant & Gallery (mains $19 to $28; open for dinner), serving excellent home-cooked food including such enticing dishes as Blue Moon beef with strawberry chilli jus, and fantastic fresh lasagne and ravioli.

Rosebery Bakehouse (Agnes St; breakfast & lunch) It's basic – pies and lamingtons – but the coffee's good and it's the best choice in town for breakfast.

The **Value Plus Supermarket** (Agnes St) likes to claim city prices and country service. It's open every day of the week.

SCOTTSDALE
☎ 03 / pop 2000
Scottsdale is the largest town in Tasmania's northeast and services the farming communities that work the rich agricultural here. Potato, poppy (see boxed text p176) and dairy farming are now mainstays, as are forestry operations.

Information
The **Scottsdale visitors centre** (☎ 03-6352 6520; scottsdale@tasvisinfo.com.au; King St) shares a building with the **Forest EcoCentre** (☎ 03-6352 6466; admission free; 9am-5pm), run by Forestry Tasmania, which may say something about priorities hereabouts.

Sleeping & Eating
On the highway southeast of town, there's free camping at Northeast Park; the price you pay is the traffic noise. It has clean toilets and showers.

Lords Hotel (☎ 03-6352 2319; 2 King St; s/d $30/50; lunch & dinner) Lord's has been a Scottsdale landmark since 1911 and is still known for better-than-average pub meals (mains $10 to $24), such as its signature chicken Oscar, as well as good roasts and steaks. The refurbished accommodation has shared facilities.

Willow Lodge (☎ 03-6352 2552; 119 King St; s $70-90, d $90-125, extra person $30) One of the most lovely places to stay in the northeast, this wonderful B&B in a Federation home is presented with absolute attention to detail. The bright, colourful rooms look over lovely gardens, and you'll be spoiled with a Devonshire tea on arrival and after-dinner liqueurs.

Anabel's of Scottsdale (☎ 03-6352 3277; www.vision.net.au/~anabels; 46 King St; s/d $110/130, extra person $15; dinner Tue-Sat) Anabel's is a National Trust–classified home with accommodation in spacious, modern motel-style units (some with cooking facilities) overlooking a woodland garden. There's relaxed fine dining in the restaurant (mains $20 to $28) with seafood, game, great eye fillet and quality Tasmanian wines.

Cottage Bakery (☎ 03-6352 2273; 9 Victoria St; 6am-5.30pm Mon-Fri) Brekky or pies for the pannier.

Stock up on groceries at **Tony and Wendy's Value Plus** (6 George St) supermarket.

SHEFFIELD
☎ 03 / pop 1020
Self-created as the 'Town of Murals' in a deliberate attempt to woo tourists (it worked), Sheffield is a veritable outdoor art gallery with more than 50 fantastic large-scale murals.

Mural Fest, Sheffield's celebration of the outdoor art, is held late March to early April each year (nine new murals earn a place in town each festival). Book ahead if you'll be arriving at festival time.

Information
ou can grab a headset from the **visitors centre** (☎ 03-6491 1036; 5 Pioneer Cres; 9am-5pm) and take an informative audio tour of the alfresco art – the tour takes about 90 minutes.

Sleeping & Eating
O'Neill's Creek Picnic Reserve (C136; free) In Gowrie Park, 15.5km along the Day

3 route of the Tassie's West Coast ride, this is the nearest campsite. It has toilets and views onto the pewter-like escarpment of Mt Roland.

Sheffield Country Motor Inn (☎ 03-6491 1800; 49-53 Main St; s/d $85/95, apt $90-100) Neat and well-equipped motel rooms (one with three bedrooms), set just back off Main St. Some of the town's best murals are immediately adjacent.

Tanglewood (☎ 03-6491 1854; www .tanglewoodtasmania.com; 25 High St; s from $90, d $95-110, extra person $10) There are three large bedrooms here, all with en suites, feather doonas, electric blankets and a great sense of old-world style. You can sip port in front of the open fire in the guest lounge, or stroll the English gardens. Evening meals are available by arrangement if you just want to hang out in the evening.

Acacia (☎ 03-6491 2482; www .acaciabbtas.com.au; 113 High St; s from $80, d $110-135 This welcoming B&B is set in a 1906 home surrounded by attractive gardens and has appealing guest rooms, excellent breakfasts and friendly hosts. You can make yourself tea or coffee and grab a homemade biscuit, or relax in the guest lounge by the cosy fire with a board game or a DVD.

Platypus Valley B&B (☎ 03-6491 2260; www.platypusvalley.com.au; 10 Billing Rd; s $99-130, d $110-150, extra person $60) A short ride out of town (off the C141; take the turn-off onto the B141 about 1km outside town), this beautiful spot is worth the extra pedalling if you're keen to see a platypus in the wild. This is a beautiful timber home with attractive guest rooms, in an environment where the key ingredient is peace.

Bossimi's Bakery (☎ 03-6491 1298; 44 Main St; breakfast & lunch Mon-Fri) This bakery does the industry proud with lots of speciality pastries, cakes and bread.

Hotel Sheffield (☎ 03-6491 1130; 38 Main St; mains; $10-16; lunch & dinner) Good-value counter meals and a lively local atmosphere to boot.

Highlander Restaurant & Scottish Scone Shoppe (☎ 03-6491 1077; 60 Main St; mains $18-20; Wed-Sun) A delightful place serving delicious pumpkin scones (the grand dame of pumpkin scones, Flo Bjelke-Petersen, once ran this restaurant) and hearty cafe fare such as homemade pies and desserts by day, and an à la carte menu, including traditional roasts, by night.

The **Sheffield IGA** (Main St) is about 50m from the visitors centre.

ST HELENS
☎ 03 / pop 2000
Set on the wide and protected sweep of Georges Bay, St Helens began life as a whaling and sealing settlement in the 1830s and still today harbours the state's largest fishing fleet. For landlubbers this sweet little town is a lively holiday spot, with good beaches nearby.

Information
The **St Helens visitors centre** (☎ 03-6376 1744; 61 Cecilia St), just off the main street behind the library, can make accommodation bookings. It also houses the town's interesting History Room, which gives a good insight into St Helens' past.

Supplies & Equipment
East Lines (☎ 03-6376 1720; Cecilia St) has a small range of bike spares (tyres, tubes, pedals, seats) and does repairs.

Sleeping & Eating
St Helens Youth Hostel (☎ 03-6376 1661; 5 Cameron St; dm $22-27, d $55-70) This YHA has bunk and double rooms, but the highlight here is all the gear for hire, including bikes ($25 per day) if yours has broken down. There's even camping gear for rent if you want to try roughing it or head up into the Bay of Fires.

St Helens Caravan Park (☎ 03-6376 1290; http://sthelenscp.com.au; 2 Penelope St; sites $25-31, cabin $75-125, villa $110-160) Quiet, neat-as-a-pin park at the southern edge of town. The pinball machine and jumping pillow will help unearth your inner child.

Kellraine Units (☎ 03-6376 1169; 72 Tully St; 2-person apt $70, extra person $40) Just north of the town centre, these spick-and-span units are incredibly good value. Each has a full kitchen, laundry and spacious living area. The friendly owners also tend a good video library.

Artnor Lodge (☎ 03-6376 1234; 71 Cecilia St; s with/without bathroom $85/65, d $95/75) Just off St Helens' leafy main street, this neat little complex has off-street parking, clean rooms and shared laundry and kitchen facilities.

Old Headmaster's House (☎ 03-6376 1125; www.theoldheadmastershouse .com.au; 74 Cecilia St; r $115-125) You'll get a real Tassie welcome in this slightly eccentric household. Don't expect this to be your blandly anonymous motel-room experience, and embrace the owners' quirks. The rooms are prettily antique-decorated, and breakfasts are cooked to order.

Village Store & More (☎ 03-6376 1666; 55 Cecilia St; meals $7.90-15; breakfast & lunch This great deli-cafe serves what it calls 'peasant food' on big wooden tables among funky decor. There are wood-fired organic breads and gourmet Tassie titbits to take away; scrumptious breakfasts; and lunch items such as focaccias, rotis and homemade meat pies.

Pasta Resistance (☎ 03-6376 2074; 22 Cecilia St; mains $5-16; 8am-9pm summer, 11am-7pm winter) This little eatery serves cyclist-sized dishes of freshly made pasta. It does a killer chilli gnocchi, carbonara that'll have you ordering seconds, and there's gelato to finish.

Salty Seas (☎ 03-6376 1252; 16 Medeas Cove Esplanade; mussels/crayfish per kg $7/50) Crayfish are the special here – you can choose them right out of the tanks – but there also oysters, mussels and fish fresh off the boat. You can feast on this marine abundance on the deck overlooking a bird sanctuary.

The **Supa IGA** (Cecilia St) supermarket is passed as you ride into town from Scamander.

STRAHAN

☎ 03 / pop 700

Strahan's tourist reputation is bigger than the town itself, nestled between the waters of Macquarie Harbour and the rainforest. With these faultless natural assets, it's no surprise that it magnetically draws west just about every tourist who sets foot on Tasmania, though you may well love or loathe Strahan for it. If you're planning a rest day, it's all but compulsory in Strahan to take a boat across the harbour and onto the mercury-smooth Gordon River – for details and other assistance, visit the

Strahan visitors centre (☎ 03-6472 6800; wcvibcs@westcoast.tas.gov.au; Esplanade; 10am-8pm summer, 9am-6pm winter).

Sleeping & Eating

Strahan Village (☎ 03-6471 4200, 1800 628 286; www.puretasmania.com.au; 7am-7pm May-Oct, 7am-9pm Nov-Apr) Much of the accommodation in the centre of town is run by Pure Tasmania under the banner of Strahan Village, which has its booking office under the clock tower on the Esplanade.

Discovery Holiday Parks Strahan (☎ 03-6471 7239; cnr Andrew & Innes Sts; unpowered sites $20-35, cabins $95-150 Right on Strahan's West Beach, this neat and friendly park has good facilities including a kiosk, camp kitchen and BBQs.

Strahan Wilderness Lodge (☎ 03-6471 7142; www.bayviewcottages-cabins.com.au; Ocean Beach Rd; d without bathroom $70, tw with bathroom $80) A kilometre or two north of town, you can hear nothing but birdsong among 11 peaceful hectares of coastal vegetation. This old-style, laid-back place has spacious rooms and great views of gardens and harbour; prices include continental breakfast.

Cedar Heights (☎ 03-6471 7717; cedarheights@vision.net.au; 7 Meredith St; d $100-120) These timber cabins with private courtyards are set back in a quiet street away from the hustle and bustle; the most you'll hear are the sounds of a golf ball being thwacked at the nearby golf course or a game of footy at the oval opposite. One apartment has a spa.

Ormiston House (☎ 03-6471 7077; www .ormistonhouse.com.au; Esplanade; d $130-230 This grand but informal historic house is the pick of the accommodation in Strahan. Built in 1899 by Frederick Ormiston, Strahan's founder, it's a stately home, now beautifully refurbished and gracefully attended as a top-notch B&B. There are just five rooms, furnished in Queen Anne style. Climb up to the widow's walk for some of the best harbour views in town.

Schwoch Seafoods (☎ 03-6471 7157; Esplanade; mains $8-15; 9am-9pm) Run by a local cray fisherman, this little eatery serves up the freshest fish and seafood in town. Come for eat-in or takeaway and savour fish encrusted in light, golden batter that melts in the mouth, or oysters split fresh to order. Does a fine gourmet pizza, too.

Hamer's Hotel (☎ 03-6471 7191; Esplanade; lunch mains $8-17, dinner mains $17-27; lunch & dinner) This renovated historic pub is now the casual eating hub in Strahan and serves a commendable menu of better-than-pub fare. Forget soggy pub roasts: starters here include such delicacies as grilled haloumi cheese with macadamia, rocket and zucchini salad; followed by steaming piles of black-lipped mussels. It is deservedly popular and often packed.

Risby Cove (☎ 03-6471 7572; Esplanade; mains $22-33; dinner) People come from all over to dine at the Cove. The menu features such local delights as myrtle-infused blue-eye trevalla. It's all classy here with good, unpretentious service and consistently praiseworthy food. Perhaps the best place to dine in Strahan.

Azza's General Store (Innes St; 6.30am-9pm) Basic food supplies and takeaways.

South Australia

- Watching for whales as you cycle past **The Bluff** (p235)
- Riding atop the eroded cliffs at **Port Willunga** (p238)
- Sampling the **Mawson Trail** (p241) on the Wines & Climbs ride
- Whooshing down **Gorge Rd** (p251) as you descend back towards Adelaide from Birdwood
- Swapping wheels for wines through **Seppeltsfield** (p249)

TERRAIN

Most of the state is undulating, with few mountains of any note. There are short, sharp climbs through the Mt Lofty Ranges, draping down into gentle valleys and coastal plains.

Telephone code – 08	www.bikesa.asn.au	www.southaustralia.com

In some ways, South Australia (SA) is the country's cycling heartland. Home to Australia's only Pro Tour event and the finest long-distance mountain biking route in the country, it's a state that could have been created by a cycling god. Why else the pancake-flat plains of Adelaide and its suburbs?

In Australia's driest state you don't have to ride far from the capital city to get the sense that you're flirting with the outback, though you don't have to endure desert deprivations to experience it. The rides detailed in this chapter loop out from Adelaide into the Barossa Valley and around the Fleurieu Peninsula, taking cyclists past wines, waves and whales while showcasing the best (and, at times, the hilliest) of the land surrounding the capital. As a bonus, both cycling tours intersect with sections of the Tour Down Under, the bike race that opens the Pro Tour season each January; with panniers on, time trial yourself up Menglers Hill or Sellicks Hill at your peril.

The Wines & Climbs route through the Barossa Valley also offers a lingering glimpse of the Mawson Trail, the mountain biking route that connects Adelaide to the glorious Flinders Ranges, South Australia's outback treasure, in the state's midnorth. One of the longest signposted cycling routes in the country, and arguably the most challenging, it is another reason to stay and play a while longer in the state where bikes could be king.

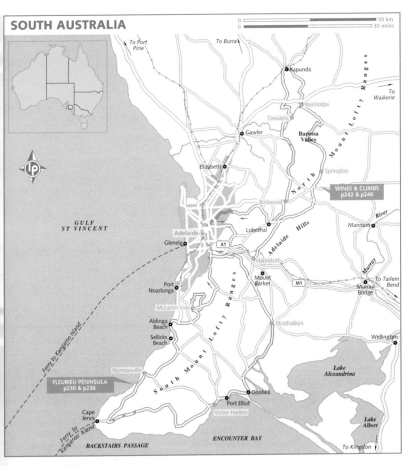

WINES & CLIMBS
p242 & p246

FLEURIEU PENINSULA
p230 & p236

ENVIRONMENT

Covering 12.8% of the country, South Australia (SA) is Australia's fourth-largest state and its lands are the most protected in the country – more than 20% of the state is covered by conservation parks of some sort. The Great Victoria, Simpson, Strzelecki and Sturt Stony Deserts form a cap across the north and west of the state, seemingly held aloft by a mountain range that runs from the Strzelecki Desert south to Cape Jervis – both rides in this chapter cross this range at its lower, less-dramatic southern end.

As you ride you will see plenty of SA's bird emblem, the magpie, but not its mammal emblem, the southern hairy-nosed wombat. The state is home to four species of kangaroo: red, western grey, eastern grey and the euro, while koalas are easily sighted in the Mt Lofty Ranges.

The landscape is dominated by fire- and drought-tolerant plants such as acacias (wattles), eucalypts and saltbush. Most obvious are the larger eucalypts, especially the river red gums that grow along watercourses throughout the state, the blue gums and candlebarks of the Mt Lofty Ranges, and the sugar gums of Kangaroo Island. There is a distinct boundary between the eucalypt-dominated communities of the south and the acacia communities further north. The massed, rich purple flowers of Salvation Jane (also known as Patterson's curse) are a stunning feature of the Mt Lofty Ranges in early spring. Although apiarists love them, they can be poisonous to stock.

CLIMATE

With its Mediterranean climate of hot, dry summers and cool winters, SA's weather is generally reliable and temperate. It is Australia's driest state, where Adelaide averages 565mm of rain a year, with most rain falling between May and October. Winters are short and temperatures are rarely below freezing, although maximum temperatures can be as low as 12°C between June and September.

The main climatic consideration for cyclists is the heat, with summer (January, February and occasionally March) temperatures often prohibitively high for cycling. Daily maximums of 40°C or more are not uncommon in Adelaide and, generally, the further north you go, the hotter the weather gets. Cyclists will also need to watch out for 'northerlies', blisteringly hot winds from the north. These winds are about the most uncomfortable in Australia and riding on days of summer northerlies should be avoided.

The best seasons for cycling in SA are autumn and spring. In April and October the average temperature in Adelaide is around 22°C, with around 40mm of rainfall. October is the windiest month, however, with March and May the least blowy.

PLANNING
Maps

The best maps for cycle touring are the 1:200,000 regional maps published by the **Royal Automobile Association** (RAA; ☎ 08-8202 4600; 55 Hindmarsh Sq), showing all roads, distances, tourist attractions and even accommodation options.

The Map Shop (p252) in Adelaide is the best place to purchase any other maps.

Books

Lonely Planet's *Central Australia* is an excellent supplement to the information provided in this chapter. For a light-

TOUR DOWN UNDER

Australian cycling had never seen anything like it. January 2009 and a fellow named Lance Armstrong, seven-time winner of the Tour de France, jetted into Adelaide for his comeback to professional road racing. Bodyguards, escorts, media scrums. Cycling royalty was in town and the **Tour Down Under** (www.tourdownunder.com.au) was well and truly etched onto the world cycling map.

First staged in 1999 as the brainchild of Olympic gold-medallist Mike Turtur, the Tour Down Under was awarded Pro Tour status in 2008, making it the only Pro Tour event to be held outside of Europe. The race follows a similar format to that of the biggest European races such as the Tour de France. It is contested over six days, beginning with a criterium (circuit race) through the streets of Adelaide. From here, the tour heads out into the Adelaide Hills, Barossa Valley and Fleurieu Peninsula. Befitting Adelaide's landscape, the terrain is comparatively flat when compared with the towering French Alps or the Pyrenees, but the infamous Willunga Hill, to the south of Adelaide, and Menglers Hill, in the Barossa Valley, certainly sift the sprinters from the climbers. Past winners of the race have included Stuart O'Grady (1999 and 2001), Michael Rogers (2002) and Simon Gerrans (2006).

The race uses a jersey system similar to the Tour de France. At the end of each stage, the overall leader gets to wear the coveted yellow jersey. The best sprinter is awarded a green jersey, while the best climber wears the blue King of the Mountains jersey. There are also jerseys for most aggressive rider and best-placed rider aged under 23.

Highlights for spectators include the Tour Village in central Victoria Square, which opens each evening, allowing visitors to mingle with riders, mechanics and team staff; and the Breakaway Series, in which you can ride a full stage of the event in the hours before the pros whiz through. There's also a Fun Tour (a ride of around 12km) and a special 'mini tour' for children between the ages of eight and 14.

As for Lance Armstrong…in 2009 he finished 29th, 49 seconds behind the winner, Australian Allan Davis.

hearted, home-spun look at pioneering in the SA outback, pick up any of Len Beadell's books, recounting tales of bulldozing roads through the state's northwest.

You might have to trawl online or through second-hand bookstores to find Jim Daly's *Cycling in the Adelaide Parklands.*

Cycling Events

Tour Down Under (see text box p228).

Coast to Coast (www.bikesa.asn.au; Mar) Either 100km or 120km ride from Glenelg to Victor Harbor, along the Fleurieu Peninsula.

Dirty Weekend (www.bikesa.asn.au; May) A 24-hour mountain bike endurance challenge in the Cudlee Creek forest.

Outback Odyssey (www.bikesa.asn.au; May) Bike SA–run cycle tour that heads into a different outback destination each year.

Melrose Fat Tyre Festival (www .otesports.com.au; Jun) Mountain bike gathering over the June long weekend, featuring rides, skills sessions and maintenance courses at the foot of the Southern Flinders Ranges.

Simpson Desert Bike Challenge (www .sdcc.org.au; Sep) Five-day, 590km mountain bike event across the myriad dunes of the Simpson Desert from Purnie Bore to a welcome beer at Birdsville.

Amy's Ride (www.amygillett.org.au; Nov) The Southern Expressway is closed to vehicles and open to bikes to promote cycling safety and raise money for the Amy Gillett Foundation. Ride 100km, 60km or 30km.

Information Sources

For general state-wide information there are several good starting points. Try **South Australian Visitor and Travel Centre** (☎ 1300 655 276; www.southaustralia .com)

Bed & Breakfast Booking Service South Australia (☎ 1800 227 677; www .bnbbookings.com) has an online booking service for about 100 B&Bs around the state.

Bicycle SA (☎ 08-8168 9999; www .bikesa.asn.au; 111 Franklin St, Adelaide) is SA's peak cycling organisation, providing information on all aspects of cycling as well as sales of some maps.

Department for Environment and Heritage (DEH; ☎ 08-8204 1910; www .parks.sa.gov.au) is the national parks authority; the website contains pages on all national parks in this chapter.

Trails SA (www.southaustraliantrails .com) is a government-run website to promote trails around the state, including cycling routes such as the Mawson Trail (p241), Riesling Trail and Kidman Trail (p239).

Cycle Tours

Barossa Classic Cycle Tours (☎ 0427 000 957; www.bccycletours.com.au) offers a tour looping out through the Flinders Ranges from the Barossa Valley, and another that follows the Tour Down Under.

Cycling Tours Australia (☎ 0411 256 908; www.cyclingtoursaustralia.com.au) runs three-, four- and five-day tours around the Fleurieu Peninsula.

GETTING AROUND

Most of SA's bus routes are operated by **Premier Stateliner** (☎ 08-8415 5555; www.premierstateliner.com.au). Carriage of disassembled bicycles costs between $7 and $15, and for assembled bikes, $12 to $25, depending on the destination.

GATEWAY

See Adelaide (p251).

FLEURIEU PENINSULA

Duration 5 days
Distance 289km
Difficulty moderate
Start/Finish Adelaide
Summary Roll between waves and wine as you circuit through one of South Australia's major holiday regions.

The ever-undulating Fleurieu Peninsula incorporates wild stretches of protected coast, pretty seaside hamlets, a fine wine region and one of SA's finest stretches of sand and sea, from Normanville to Port Willunga.

This ride loops through all of it, taking in the superb coastal scenery, surf beaches, rolling hills, historic townships and the vineyards. It is a reasonably tough stretch

SOUTH AUSTRALIA

FLEURIEU PENINSULA – DAYS 1&5

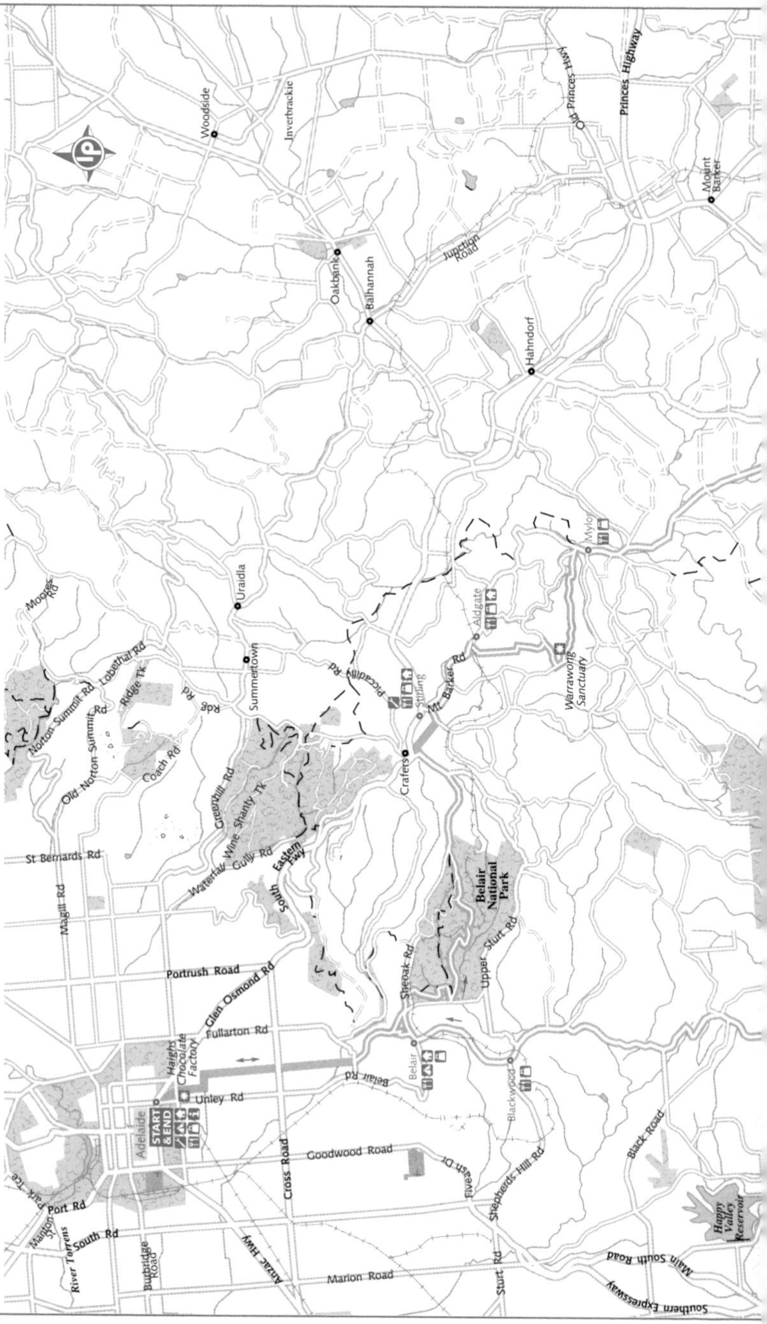

SOUTH AUSTRALIA

4 km
2.0 miles

Woodside

Inverbrackie

Princes Hwy

Princes Hwy

Mount Barker

Oakbank

Balhannah

Junction Road

Hahndorf

Mylor

Uraidla

Adgate

Warrawong Sanctuary

Summertown

Piccadilly Rd

Stirling

Mt Barker Rd

Norton Summit Rd

Lobethal Rd

Ridge Tk

Rd

Coach Rd

Old Norton Summit Rd

Greenhill Rd

Crafers

St Bernards Rd

Waterfall Gully Rd

Wine Shanty Tk

South Eastern Fwy

Belair National Park

Magill Rd

Sheoak Rd

Upper Sturt Rd

Portrush Road

Glen Osmond Rd

Fullarton Rd

Heights Chocolate Factory

Belair Rd

Belair

Blackwood

Adelaide

START & END

Unley Rd

Goodwood Road

Black Road

Cross Road

Shepherds Hill Rd

Fiveash Dr

Happy Valley Reservoir

Old Port Rd

River Torrons

South Rd

Marion Rd

Sir Donald Bradman Dr

Anzac Hwy

Bundridge Road

Marion Road

Sturt Rd

Main South Road

Southern Expressway

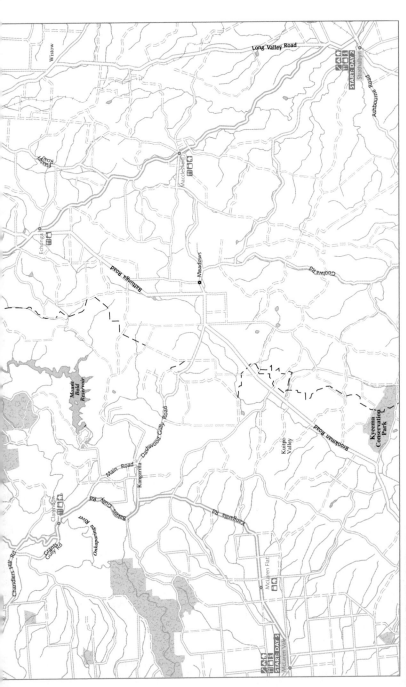

Wistow

Long Valley Road

START: DAY 2
Strathalbyn

Ashbourne Road

Paris Creek Road

Macclefield

Echunga

Bathinga Road

Meadows

Goolwa Rd

Mount Bold Reservoir

Dashwood Gully Road

Kuitpo Valley

Kyeema Conservation Park

Brookman Road

Main Road

Kangarilla

Baker Gully Rd

Clarendon

Onkaparinga River

Granite Gully Rd

Chandlers Hill Rd

Kangarilla Rd

McLaren Flat

START: DAY 5
McLaren Vale

SOUTH AUSTRALIA

in the saddle, particularly the hilly, exposed section from Victor Harbor to Normanville, but the rewards are plentiful.

HISTORY

In 1802 the Fleurieu Peninsula was first sighted by Europeans, with Baudin's French expedition naming the peninsula after Charles Pierre Claret, Comte de Fleurieu, an eminent 19th-century French explorer. Baudin met a more famous explorer, Matthew Flinders, in the waters off Victor Harbor, and Encounter Bay was named to commemorate the meeting.

In 1837 whalers set up stations at Encounter Bay to hunt southern right whales. From the 1850s until the 1880s, Goolwa, at the Murray mouth, was SA's major port. In the 1880s, however, a new railway line linking Adelaide and Melbourne via Murray Bridge was established, consigning Goolwa to its status as simple country town.

The first winery in the region was established in 1838 by John Reynell at Reynella, now part of Adelaide's southern suburban sprawl. These days, most of the Peninsula's 70 or so wineries are concentrated around McLaren Vale.

PLANNING
When to Cycle

There are few bad times for riding through the Fleurieu, although accommodation can be extremely hard to find around Christmas and January. In summer the peninsula is cooled by sea breezes, and in winter (June to September) it has the attraction of a passing parade of southern right whales, which come in close to shore to breed. The flipside is that this is the wettest (around 70mm of rain a month) and coldest (around 16°C average maximum) time of year. January, February and March are the windiest months on the peninsula.

Bike Hire

Bicycle SA (☎ 08-8168 9999; www.bikesa .asn.au; 111 Franklin St) has a range o f bikes available for hire, including hybrids ($25/98 per day/week) and mountain bikes ($50/245 per day/week). Lock and helmet are included. **Victor Harbor Cycle & Skate** (☎ 08-8552 1417; vhcycle@bigpond.com; 73 Victoria St; day hire $45, 2 days $50, per extra day $20) also has bikes for hire.

Maps

The RAA's 1:200,000 *Fleurieu Peninsula* map provides good coverage of the route at a workable scale. The route out of Adelaide is shown in detail on Bikedirect map 9, while parts of the route back into Adelaide from Aldinga Beach are on maps 13, 12 and 9. These maps can be downloaded free at www.transport.sa.gov.au/personal_ transport/bike_direct/maps.asp.

GETTING TO/FROM THE RIDE
Adelaide (start/finish)
AIR

Adelaide airport (☎ 08-8308 9211; www .aal.com.au) is 7km west of the city. **Qantas** (☎ 13 13 13; www.qantas.com.au), **Virgin Blue** (☎ 13 67 89; www.virginblue.com .au), **Jetstar** (☎ 13 15 38; www.jetstar .com.au) and **Tiger Airways** (☎ 03-9335 3033; www.tigerairways.com) operate flights between Adelaide and other capital cities as well as major centres such as Alice Springs, the Gold Coast, Cairns and Canberra. **Skylink** (☎ 08-8413 6196; www .skylinkadelaide.com; adult $8.50) runs shuttles between the city and the airport (via the Keswick interstate train terminal). Bikes can be carried and there's no extra charge. If travelling from the city to the airport, bookings are essential.

If riding into the city, join the bikepath along the River Torrens by taking Sir Donald Bradman Dr left (west) out of the airport, then turning right (north) onto Tapleys Hill Rd.

BUS

Adelaide's central **bus station** (☎ 08-8415 5533; 105-111 Franklin St) has terminals and ticket offices for all major interstate and statewide services. For bus timetables see www.bussa.com.au. **Greyhound Australia** (☎ 1300 473 946; www.greyhound.com .au) has direct services to Melbourne ($70, 11 hours), Sydney ($155, 23 hours) and Alice Springs ($280, 19½ hours), while **Firefly Express** (☎ 1300 730 740; www .fireflyexpress.com.au) operates services to/ from Melbourne ($55, 11 hours) that travel onto Sydney ($125, 23½ hours).

TRAIN

The **interstate train terminal** (Railway Tce, Keswick) is just southwest of the city centre.

Great Southern Railway (☎ 13 21 47; www.trainways.com.au; 7.30am-8pm Mon-Fri, 8am-6pm Sat, 9am-5pm Sun) operates all train services in and out of SA. The following trains depart from Adelaide regularly:

Ghan To Alice Springs (economy seat/twin-berth sleeper $335/685, 19 hours)
Ghan To Darwin ($690/1390, 47 hours)
Indian Pacific To Perth ($395/1005, 39 hours)
Indian Pacific To Sydney ($285/485, 25 hours)
Overland To Melbourne ($90/150, 11 hours)

BICYCLE
Adelaide is almost 800km from the nearest capital city (Melbourne). 2700km to the west (across the Nullarbor), and Darwin, 3000km to the north (along the outback Stuart Hwy). The most popular cycling approach is from Melbourne along the Great Ocean Rd (p122) and Coorong.

CAR
Airport Rent-A-Car (☎ 1800 331 033; www.airportrentacar.com.au) has its office at the airport.

The following companies, except Apex, also have offices at the airport:

Apex (☎ 1800 804 392; www.apexrent acar.com.au; 969 Port Rd, Cheltenham)
Avis (☎ 08-8410 5727; www.avis.com .au; 136 North Tce)
Budget (☎ 08 8418 7300; www.budget .com.au; 274 North Tce)
Europcar (☎ 08-8114 6350; www .europcar.com.au; 142 North Tce)
Hertz (☎ 08-8231 2856; www.hertz .com.au; 233 Morphett St)
Thrifty (☎ 08-8410 8977; www.thrifty .com.au; 23 Hindley St)

THE RIDE
Day 1: Adelaide to Strathalbyn
3½–5 hours, 61.5km

This scenic and challenging first day winds gently through the back streets of Adelaide's southeastern suburbs before climbing into the Adelaide Hills and descending for much of the day to Strathalbyn.

The climb begins on Old Belair Rd before following an avenue of gorgeous sugar gums into **Belair National Park**, South Australia's first national park. The bird life in the park is exceptional, though you may stop noticing it as you struggle up the climb

FLEURIEU PENINSULA – DAY 1

CUE			GPS COORDINATES
start		Victoria Sq, Adelaide	138°35′59″N 34°55′42″S
0km		go E on Wakefield St	
0.5	⬏	Pulteney St	
1.3	⬈	bikepath across south parklands	
2.0	⬆	Porter St	
2.7	⬑	Maud St	
3.1	⬏	Duthy St	
5.8	⬏	Hillview Rd	
6.0	⬑	East Pde	
6.9	⬏	Barrelder Rd	
7.0	⬑	Carruth Rd	
7.4	⬑	Blythewood Rd	
7.9	⬏ ◉	Old Belair Rd	
8.1	▲	2km steep	
10.2	⬑	Sheoak Rd (hard ⬑ at crest)	
10.7	⬏ ⬑	Sheoak Rd (dogleg)	
11.2	⬏	Sir Edwin Ave (over train lines)	
12.7	⬑	Gooch Rd (beside Playford Lake)	
12.8	⬋	'to exit'	
13.2	⬈	The Valley Rd	
15.1	⬈	Saddle Hill Rd	
16.0	▲	1.5km steep	

CUE CONTINUED			GPS COORDINATES
17.7	⬏	Sheoak Rd (exit Belair National Park)	
18.9	▲	800m steep climb	
19.7	⬑	Waverley Ridge Rd	
20.4	⬏	Waverley Ridge Rd	
20.7	⬏ ◉	Ayers Hill Rd	
21.1	⬑ ◉	Ayers Hill Rd	
21.6	⬑	Avenue Rd	
21.9	⬏	Mt Barker Rd, Stirling	138°43′04″N 35°00′22″S
24.6	⬏	Kingsland Rd, Aldgate	138°44′10″N 35°00′54″S
26.2	⬈	Edgeware Rd	
27.0	⬏	Williams Rd (unsigned)	
27.7	⬑	Stock Rd (unsigned)	
	★	Warrawong Sanctuary	138°44′04″N 35°02′15″S
30.3	⬏	Macclesfield Rd (unsigned), Mylor	138°45′36″N 35°02′33″S
38.7	⬋	Angas River Scenic Dr, Echunga	138°47′46″N 35°06′13″S
48.5		Macclesfield	138°50′09″N 35°10′17″S
59.2	⬏	'to Strathalbyn'	
61.2	⬑	Rankine St	
61.4	⬏	South Tce	
61.5		Strathalbyn visitors centre	138°53′30″N 35°15′40″S

SOUTH AUSTRALIA

on Saddle Hill Rd towards the park exit at Waverley Gate.

The bulk of the day's climbing ends just outside the national park before the route winds through the forested Hills' suburbs.

Shortly before reaching Mylor, the ride passes by the **Warrawong Sanctuary** (☎ 08-8370 9179; www.warrawong .com; Stock Rd; admission after 4pm $5; 9am-9pm), just look for the feral-animal-proof fence to your left. Covering 35 acres, the sanctuary is a former dairy farm replanted with native fauna and now home to kangaroos, wallabies, platypuses, bandicoots, eastern quolls and other native animals, which roam freely. If you fancy an early stop there's accommodation in tentlike bush cabins (per person $75). The night walks ($25) offered by the sanctuary are one of the best ways to spot wildlife. If you're just passing through, the Bilby Cafe can help keep your legs fuelled.

From Mylor, a pretty stretch follows the **Angas River Scenic Dr** to Strathalbyn. At around 55km the ride approaches the end of the foothills, with views that give a preview of the flatness of the next day's route.

Day 2: Strathalbyn to Victor Harbor

3-4 hours, 53.4km

Today the ride heads for the coast and Adelaide's favourite seaside playgrounds. The early section travels along an unsealed road, where the gravel can be a little loose in places, though you won't see more than a handful of vehicles. Along the way you'll pass a couple of abandoned **stone homesteads** and a forlorn windmill, giving it a classic country-Australia appearance. The short second section of dirt near Finniss

is particularly enjoyable, winding downhill through a small gully.

Immediately across the Finniss River, the route passes two **scar trees** (19.7km) – one partly obscured by bush and the other all but in the middle of the road – from which canoes and other implements have been carved.

The short grind out from Tookayerta Creek will ready you for a quick swill at **Currency Creek Wines** (☎ 08-8555 4013; www.currencycreekwines.com.au; Winery Rd; d $115-130, mains $20-25; lunch daily, dinner Fri & Sat), before rolling on into the former river-port town of **Goolwa** (34.8km), situated at the point where Australia's largest river meets the ocean… at least for the time being (see boxed text p235). The blink-and-you-miss-it township of **Currency Creek**, a short distance on, was once slated to be the SA capital.

About 6km out of Goolwa the ride swings onto the **Encounter Bikeway**, a 30km bikepath that follows the frayed coast to Victor Harbor. Along the way it passes some of the finest surf beaches in easy reach of Adelaide – you'll find board hire in Port Elliot and Victor Harbor if you want to swap the wheels for waves for a couple of hours. The bikeway is clearly marked and easy to follow. Should you lose your way, head towards the beach and you'll soon find the next sign.

A couple of derelict buildings either side of the bikeway at 44.5km are the remains of **Pleasant Banks Homestead**, an old homestead owned by the Basham family, one of the region's first settlers.

Further along the coast, **Port Elliot** (46.5km) is the most charming of the towns along this stretch. The cliffs along

FLEURIEU PENINSULA – DAY 2

CUE			GPS COORDINATES
start		Strathalbyn visitors centre	138°53'30"N 35°15'40"S
0km		go W on South Tce	
0.2	↰⊙	Milnes Rd	
4.3	⚠	10.1km dirt road	
7.7	⌐→	Dry Plains Rd	
14.4	⌐→	Finniss-Milang Rd	
18.2	↰⊙	Barn Hill Rd	
18.3	⚠	1km dirt road	
19.4	⌐→	Winery Rd (unsigned)	
19.7	★	Aboriginal scar trees	138°49'32"N 35°23'59"S
23.1	★	Currency Creek Wines	138°47'57"N 35°25'02"S

CUE CONTINUED			GPS COORDINATES
26.0	↘	B37 (unsigned)	
34.8		Goolwa	138°47'04"N 35°30'09"S
39.5	↱	Boettcher Rd	
40.5	⌐→	unsigned road	
follow bike route to cnr Hayward Court & A13			
{44.5	★	Pleasant Banks Homestead)	
46.5	⌐→	Port Elliot	138°40'55"N 35°31'48"S
51.2	⌐→	A13 (unsigned)	
52.5	⌐↱	Bridge Tce (dogleg)	
53.4		Victor Harbor visitors centre	138°37'27"N 35°33'25"S

THE DYING MURRAY

Australia's mightiest river is also one of its sickliest. The Murray River begins as a trickle on the slopes of Mt Pilot, near Mt Kosciuszko, and in recent years it has also ended as a trickle near Goolwa. The artery of the nation is dying a dry death, with flows at record low levels. Drought and over-allocation of water have seen flows dwindle by more than 35% since the end of the 1990s.

Since 2002, only dredging has kept open the mouth of the Murray River, with the surface of Lake Alexandrina falling to around 50cm below sea level at the start of 2009 (it usually sits at around 80cm above sea level). The lake is shrinking, exposing the acid-sulphate bed to the air, turning it toxic. In 2008 a report suggested that at least 450 gigalitres of fresh water needed to be flushed down the Murray to refill the lakes. In the absence of that water, the South Australian government hatched a plan to open the barrages that currently hold back the salt waters of the Coorong, letting this water flood into the lakes to prevent acidification if the surface level of Lake Alexandrina fell to 1.5m below sea level. Other scientists argue that it could be a greater environmental disaster to allow in the salt water.

The debate is about as clear as the Murray's muddy waters.

Horseshoe Bay are great for spying whales in season as you head for Victor Harbor (p259).

Day 3: Victor Harbor to Normanville

4–5 hours, 74.8km

A coast-to-coast ride as the route switches from the surf coast to the more sheltered beaches along Gulf St Vincent. In between it climbs up and over the spine of the Fleurieu Peninsula, affording great coastal views. There are very few services en route, and the ridge between Parawa (34km) and Delamere (54.9km) is exposed, so carry enough food and water for a few hot hours in the saddle.

The day begins by hugging the coast of Encounter Bay, one of the state's prime whale-watching locations. The spectacular headland known as **The Bluff**, where a whaling station was established in 1837, makes the best vantage point if you're here during the winter migration season (June to September).

A dirt-road shortcut, past a mass of grass trees, leads to Waitpinga Rd where, at 15.3km, there's a side trip to spectacular

FLEURIEU PENINSULA – DAY 3

CUE			GPS COORDINATES
start		Victor Harbor visitors centre	138°37'27"N 35°33'25"S
0km		go W on Esplanade/Inman St	
1	↘	bikepath (beside caravan park)	
4.6		merge onto Franklin Pde	
4.9	↗	Jagger Rd	
{	●● ↰	The Bluff 1.6km (↺)}	
6.1	↰	Three Gullies Rd	
6.2	↗	Three Gullies Rd	
7.4	⚠	2.1km unsealed road	

CUE CONTINUED			GPS COORDINATES
9.5	↰	Waitpinga Rd	
15.3	●● ↰	Waitpinga Beach 7.6km (↺)	138°29'38"N 35°37'59"S
24.8	↰	Range Rd, `to Cape Jervis'	
{29.1	●● ↘	`to Cape Jervis'}	
32.0	▲	2km steep climb	
54.9	↰	B23, `to Adelaide', Delamere	135°11'58"N 35°34'06"S
{60.8	●● ↰	Second Valley 4.2km (↺)}	
74.6	↰	Main South Rd, `to town centre'	
74.8		Court House Cafe, Normanville	138°19'06"N 35°26'51"S

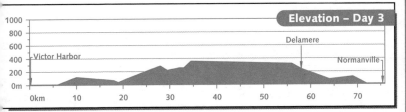

Elevation – Day 3

Victor Harbor ... Delamere ... Normanville

(1000, 800, 600, 400, 200, 0m elevation; 0km, 10, 20, 30, 40, 50, 60, 70)

FLEURIEU PENINSULA – DAYS 2-4

START: DAY 5
McLaren Vale
Tatachilla Rd
Maslin Beach
Old Coach Road
South Rd
Main Rd
Willunga
Port Willunga
Aldinga Reef
Aquatic Reserve
Aldinga
Little Road
Aldinga Beach
Delabole
Hill
Southern
Ocean
Silver Sands
Sellicks Beach
Sellicks
Hill
Pages Flat Rd
Heatherdale
Hill
Hindmarsh Tiers Rd
Myponga
Myponga
Reservoir
Carrickalinga
Main South Rd
START: DAY 4
Normanville
Yankalilla
Moon
Hill
Strangways
Hill
Yankalilla River
Second
Valley
Side Trip
Baker
Nob
Range Rd
Cole Road
Delamere
Range Rd
Deep Creek
Conservation
Park
Arthur
Hill
Side Trip
Newland Head
Conservation Park
Waitpinga
Beach

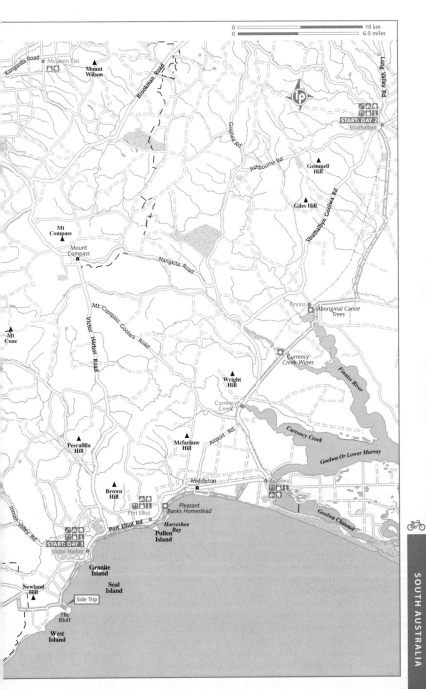

Waitpinga Beach in the Newland Head Conservation Park.

After a roller-coaster run across the hinterland, it's possible to hook left at Delamere to Cape Jervis, from where the ferry runs to Kangaroo Island (see boxed text below).

After the hilly run you may not have the legs to ride into Rapid Bay (a 10km return ride with a 250m climb back out), but it's worth the shorter detour (4.2km; 70m climb) to **Second Valley**, a small rocky cove with an unusual lagoonlike pool cradled between the jetty and the cliffs.

From the Second Valley turn-off, the route rounds Yankalilla Hill, with the road almost eating into the seaweed-crusted beach as it follows a line of Norfolk pines into Normanville.

SIDE TRIP: WAITPINGA BEACH
7.6km

This route has a steep descent (ergo, a very steep climb back out) but it's a wild and beautiful stretch of coast with humpback hills arching into the sea. The ferocious surf makes it unsuitable for swimming but it's a popular fishing spot. There's a campsite near the beach if you want to put off the climb out for another day.

Day 4: Normanville to McLaren Vale
3–4 hours, 50.5km

This day offers a pleasant surprise with the discovery that the beauty of the peninsula does not end where the suburbs begin. After heading inland the route returns to the coast, following it to the gorgeous cliff-backed bay of Port Willunga before detouring into the McLaren Vale wine district.

Normanville merges seamlessly into Yankalilla (there's a bikepath beside the road as far as the Yankalilla school) before the road climbs slowly to reach **Myponga** (17.2km). Surrounded by lush hills, this is prime dairy land, and until 1980 produced most of the milk consumed in SA – the town's dairy is now a weekend **market** (10am-4pm).

The road hugs the slopes as it wraps around **Sellicks Hill**, of Tour Down Under fame, where there are spectacular views of the azure waters of Gulf St Vincent.

The ride joins the coast at Silver Sands, trailing along beside Aldinga Beach, where

---

KANGAROO ISLAND

The third-largest island off Australia's shores, Kangaroo Island may be the most appropriately named place in the country. Chosen early last century as something of an ark on which to protect threatened animal species, the island abounds in wildlife – few places in Australia offer such easy wildlife viewing.

It also makes an ideal destination for a few extra days of touring from the Fleurieu Peninsula. From Cape Jervis, 15km from Delamere, **SeaLink** (☎ 13 13 01; www.sealink.com.au) operates a ferry to Penneshaw (45 minutes). From Penneshaw it's a good day's ride into Kingscote, the island's main town, from where you can set out on a loop of the island. There are no real towns beyond Kingscote so be sure to stock up here.

The main loop heads along the north coast to the lighthouse at Cape Borda, before dropping down to Flinders Chase National Park, which is like an open menagerie. At Rocky River, kangaroos and Cape Barren geese graze in the open, while there's a walking track to Platypus Waterholes, where you may well see platypus. Look up into the forks of trees at any time and chances are there's a slumbering koala. The park is also home to the, er, remarkable Remarkable Rocks, which resemble broken egg shells.

Heading back along the south coast there are plenty of treats. Duck into beautiful Hanson Bay or Vivonne Bay, the latter once judged Australia's best beach in an academic study, and wander among one of the country's largest colonies of Australian sea lions on Seal Bay. As a fond farewell from Penneshaw, fairy penguins wander ashore through the town's streets each evening.

A straightforward loop of the island from Penneshaw, not including side trips to the major attractions, will cover around 300km. Allow a week to really soak in the island.

For information about the island known simply as 'KI', contact the **Kangaroo Island Gateway visitors centre** (☎ 08-8553 1185; www.tourkangarooisland.com.au).

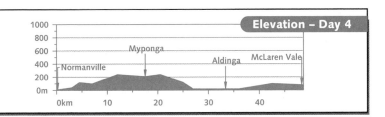

FLEURIEU PENINSULA – DAY 4

CUE			GPS COORDINATES	
start		Court House Cafe, Normanville	138°19'06	35°26'51"
0km		go E on Main South Rd		
3.1		Yankalilla	138°20'08"N	35°27'17"N
3.3	↰	B23, 'to Adelaide'		
17.2		Myponga	138°27'44"N	35°23'44"N
18.0	↘	B23, 'to Noarlunga'		
21.3	★	Sellicks Hill	138°29'11"N	35°20'49"N
24.2	↰	Justs Rd (at parking bay)		
25.5	↰↱	Sellicks Beach Rd/Justs Rd (dogleg)		

CUE CONTINUED			GPS COORDINATES	
28.0	↰	unsigned road		
28.9	↱	Esplanade, Silver Sands	138°26'58"N	35°18'30"S
35.4	↗	Jetty Rd/Port Rd		
37.0	↰	Port Rd		
37.8	↑	Aldinga Rd (cross Main South Rd)		
39.9	↱	Bayliss Rd		
40.6	↰	Aldinga Rd		
44.6	↰	Main Rd, 'to McLaren Vale'		
50.5		cnr Main Rd & Kangarila Rd, McLaren Vale	138°32'42"N	35°13'09"S

Aldinga Reef Aquatic Reserve protects a are reef formation – yours may be the only vehicle on the road rather than the beach. You might want a rear-view mirror along this section because the views back along the peninsula are spectacular, especially late in the day.

At the protected beach of **Port Willunga**, pinched between eroded cliffs, the simple kiosk-style exterior of the **Star of Greece** (☎ 08-8557 7420; The Esplanade, Port Willunga; mains $20-35; lunch), which overlooks the wreck of the same name, belies its reputation as one of the Fleurieu's finest eateries. The position is unequalled,

especially at sunset, and the seafood equally so.

If the weather's fine, join the beachgoers for a swim, or if you want to shed the knickers, detour north to **Maslins nudist beach**, 12km further north.

The road heads inland from Port Willunga through the vineyards to reach the outskirts of the pretty town of **Willunga**. Slate was discovered here in 1840 – check out the slate footpaths, gutters, roofs, bridges and even fence posts that adorn the town. If you're here in February you might even catch one of the country's more unusual events, the

---

KIDMAN TRAIL

If you're in South Australia and your intention is to simply pedal, you might want to consider linking the two rides described in this chapter, taking in both the Fleurieu Peninsula and the Barossa Valley. This can be done by returning to Adelaide, but they can also be joined along the Kidman Trail.

A 255km shared route (with horseback riders), the Kidman Trail stretches between Willunga (day 4 of the Fleurieu Peninsula ride) and Kapunda (day 4 of the Wines & Climbs ride), crossing through the Adelaide Hills where, at Nairne, you can turn east to join the Wines & Climbs ride at the end of its first day at Hahndorf. Allow two days of reasonably tough (but not long) riding between Willunga and Nairne.

The trail is covered in a series of five dedicated maps, which are available from **Bicycle SA** (☎ 8168 9999; www.bikesa.asn.au; 111 Franklin St, Adelaide). If riding from Willunga to Nairne, you will need the first two maps in the series: *Willunga to Echunga* and *Echunga to Nairne*.

For more information about the Kidman Trail, visit www.kidmantrail.org.au.

SOUTH AUSTRALIA

Mt Compass Cup, a cow race 9km from Willunga.

From Willunga, Main Rd leads north into McLaren Vale, one of SA's premier wine-making districts – a bikepath about 400m along Main Rd makes a lengthier, if more relaxed, approach, following a disused railway line to McLaren Vale.

Day 5: McLaren Vale to Adelaide
3–4 hours, 48.8km

Work off the indulgences of the Southern Vales with a climb through the southern Mt Lofty Ranges. You can delay the moment with stops at cellar doors along Kangarilla Rd, where **Tinlins Wines** (2.8km) will even fill your bidons with wine if that's your fancy.

From McLaren Vale, the vineyards slowly peter out as the route climbs towards Bakers Gully and the pretty little town of **Clarendon**, which has more stone houses than an episode of the *Flintstones*.

Another long climb to the top of Chandlers Hill is rewarded by a sweeping descent though Coromandel Valley and the start of Adelaide's suburban sprawl, it's a lovely run though there's little margin for error so free-wheel with caution. The ride reconnects with Old Belair Rd, to retrace the outward route along the bike route.

Where the bikepath leaves Porter St to cross the southern parklands, treat yourself with a detour to **Haighs chocolate factory** (☎ 08-8372 7077; 154 Greenhill Rd, Parkside; tours 11am, 1pm & 2pm Mon-Sat) – what cyclist isn't fuelled by chocolate? This manufacturer proudly claim to be the oldest family-owned chocolate maker in Australia. Alfred E. Haig started the business in 1905 where he opened a confectionery shop and introduced the town to ice cream and silent movies – a combination he thought might catch on! Turn left into Greenhill Rd; the factory is about 20m further along. Bookings are essential to join the factory tours.

FLEURIEU PENINSULA – DAY 5

CUE		GPS COORDINATES
start	cnr Main Rd & Kangarilla Rd, McLaren Vale	138°32'42"N 35°13'09"S
0km	go E on Kangarilla Rd	
4.4	McLaren Flat	138°35'20"N 35°12'23"S
14.1	⬑ Bakers Gully Rd	
15.4	⤷ Bakers Gully Rd	
18.0	⬑ unsigned road	
20.1	Clarendon	138°37'47"N 35°06'33"S
20.9	⤷ Clarendon Rd, `to Blackwood'	
	▲ 3.5km moderate	
24.4	⤧ Main Rd, `to Blackwood'	
27.2	⚠ 2.6km steep, twisting descent	
29.8	⬑ Black Rd	
30.0	⤷ Murrays Hill Rd	
32.6	⤷ Coromandel Pde	
33.5	⤷◉ Diosma Dr	

CUE CONTINUED		GPS COORDINATES
35.5	Blackwood	138°37'00"N 35°01'16"S
38.4	⤷ Russell St/Sheoak Rd, Belair	138°37'27"N 35°59'52"S
38.6	⤦ Old Belair Rd	
40.9	⬑◉ Blythewood Rd	
41.4	⤷ Carruth Rd	
41.8	⤷ Barrelder Rd	
41.9	⬑ Lochwinnoch Rd	
42.8	⤷ Hillview Pde	
43.0	⬑ Duthy St	
45.7	⬑ Maud St	
46.1	⤷ Porter St	
46.8	↑ bikepath across south parklands	
47.5	⤧ Pulteney St	
48.3	⬑ Wakefield St	
48.8	⤷◉ Victoria Sq, Adelaide	138°35'59"N 34°55'42"S

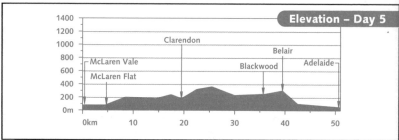

Elevation – Day 5

WINES & CLIMBS

Duration 6 days
Distance 289km
Difficulty moderate–demanding
Start/Finish Adelaide
Summary Cross through the Adelaide Hills into Australia's most famous wine-producing region, sampling both wines and one of the country's finest long-distance mountain biking trails.

Mention the words 'Australia' and 'wine' in the same sentence and it's likely that the Barossa Valley will follow in the next breath. The pin-up child of the Australian wine industry, the Barossa is a wine-drinker's paradise, and it's pretty good for cyclists also, even if it involves some testing climbing, especially along the Mawson Trail sections, to get in and out from Adelaide.

On this ride you might find yourself wondering whether you're in Germany rather than South Australia, as you pass through the historic German township of Hahndorf and then around the Barossa, with its rich German heritage. *Prost.*

HISTORY

Named by the surveyor-general William Light after a battlefield in Spain, the wide Barossa Valley was settled in 1842 by 25 German families in the town of Bethany. The following year, more families moved into Langmeil (now Tanunda), creating something of a German heartland in SA.

The soil and climate of the region was considered similar to the wine-growing areas of Germany and, in 1838, Johann Menge, the German mineralogist charged with surveying the area, had prophesised that 'I am quite certain we shall see vineyards and orchards and immense fields that are matchless in this colony'. In 1847 Johann Gramp planted the first vines at Jacob Creek, giving birth to the SA wine industry.

PLANNING
When to Cycle

There are two times *not* to ride this route: summer, when days can hit 40°C in the Barossa Valley; and Easter, when the Oakbank racing carnival crowds the roads with vehicles. Spring and autumn are far and away the best times to cycle,

THE MAWSON TRAIL

The undisputed head of South Australia's impressive list of bike routes is the Mawson Trail, an 800km-long marked route between Adelaide and the Flinders Ranges.

Named after Sir Douglas Mawson, the British-born geographer, geologist and Antarctic explorer who led the first expedition to reach the south magnetic pole (1907–09), as well as the first Australian Antarctic expedition (1911–14), the Mawson Trail covers much of the land that Mawson explored, largely on his trusty bicycle, when teaching in the Department of Mineralogy at the University of Adelaide.

Flirting with the outback for much of its route, it also dips through two of the country's premier wine regions – the Barossa Valley and Clare Valley – and passes South Australia's signature natural feature, Wilpena Pound.

The trail is an arduous but rewarding cycling undertaking. Completing the full Mawson Trail would take around a fortnight, and much of the route is very remote. You're likely to encounter few people or facilities along the way, and bush camping is the order of the day. It is possible to restock food supplies every few days. The trail can be very rugged and also steep in places. Be prepared to push your bike on the climb from Castambul, near Adelaide, and up onto the southern Flinders Ranges in the Wirrabara Forest.

The route is along minor roads, fire trails, farm tracks and road reserves and is marked with Mawson Trail signs at 1km intervals and at intersections and turn-offs. While a touring bike could possibly negotiate the full trail, a mountain bike is by far your best option.

Information about the Mawson Trail can be found at www.southaustraliantrails.com/top _trails.asp?mawson. **Bicycle SA** (☎ 08-8168 9999; www.bikesa.asn.au; 111 Franklin St, Adelaide) has produced a series of nine 1:75,000 maps covering the entire route. They can be purchased through the website.

WINES & CLIMBS – DAYS 1, 2 & 6

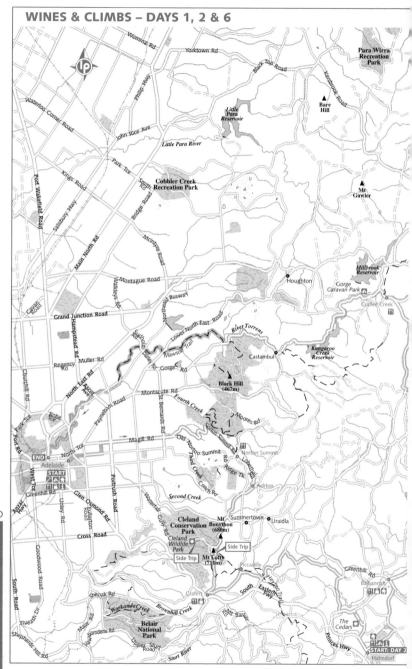

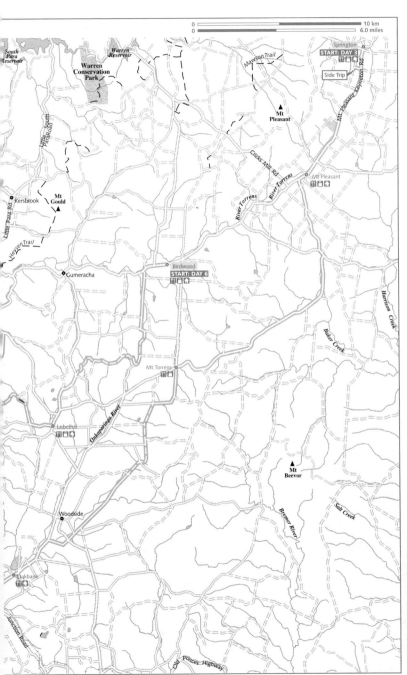

> **WARNING**
>
> Some care will need to be taken between Tanunda and Adelaide (Days 5 and 6), where the ride at times follows the unsealed Mawson Trail. A touring bike should have no problems negotiating the surface, but carry at least one spare tube.

with the best of the winds in autumn, while windier spring has the **Barossa Music Festival** (www.barossa.org).

Bike Hire

Bicycle SA (☎ 08-8168 9999; www.bikesa .asn.au; 111 Franklin St) has a range of bikes available for hire, including hybrids ($25/98 per day/week) and mountain bikes ($50/245 per day/week). Lock and helmet are included. The **Barossa Visitors Centre** (☎ 08-8563 0600; www.barossa-region .org; 66-68 Murray St) in Tanunda also has quality mountain bikes for hire. It charges $44 per day but this may be reduced to around $30 for a multiday hire.

Maps

The RAA's *Adelaide Hills* and *Barossa Valley* maps 1:200,000 cover the bulk of the route adequately. The first part of the ride out of Adelaide is shown on Bikedirect map 9, while the return along Gorge Rd and the River Torrens is covered by maps 7 and 6. These maps can be downloaded at www

.transport.sa.gov.au/personal_transport /bike_direct/maps.asp.

GETTING TO/FROM THE RIDE
Adelaide (start/finish)
See p251.

THE RIDE
Day 1: Adelaide to Hahndorf
3–4 hours, 44.2km

What may seem a short day on a map is lengthened by the climb into the Adelaide Hills. Nothing about this day is flat, in the first 23km the route climbs around 700m. Fortunately, there are plenty of places that warrant a stop and stretch. The ride fringes a number of the Mt Lofty Ranges' parklands so you will spend the day among a variety of trees.

The ride follows bike lanes (narrow at times along Magill Rd) out of the city to the foot of the Adelaide Hills. From the end of Magill Rd it makes a corkscrewing climb along the western slopes of the Mt Lofty Ranges (the beautiful Morialta gorges are tucked away to the left of the road) to reach **Norton Summit**, a popular training run for Adelaide's lycra brigade.

From here the route rolls across the top of the Mt Lofty Ranges, at the end of the steep pinch on Woods Hill Rd it intersects with the Heysen Trail, one of Australia's great long-distance bushwalking tracks. You can hike it all the way into the Flinders Ranges if you have a spare two months.

WINES & CLIMBS – DAY 1

CUE			GPS COORDINATES	
start		cnr Rundle St & East Tce, Adelaide	138°36'39"	34°55'20"S
0km		go E on Rundle Rd		
0.8	⬆	The Parade West		
1.7	⬆	Sydenham Rd		
2.3	⬆	Magill Rd		
7.3	⬆	Norton Summit Rd, 'to Lobethal'		
	▲	4.6km steep		
14.7	↘	'to Lobethal', Norton Summit	138°43'29"N	34°55'21"S
15.7	⬆	Woods Hill Rd, 'to Uraidla'		
	▲	600m steep		
17.6	⬆	Woods Hill Rd, Ashton	138°44'14"N	34°56'23"S
19.7	⬆	'to Cleland'		
20.0	⬆	Summit Rd, 'to Cleland'		
22.2	●● ⬆	Cleland Wildlife Park 3.4km ↻	138°42'49"N	35°58'00"S

CUE CONTINUED			GPS COORDINATES	
23.2	●● ⬆	Mt Lofty summit 800m ↻	138°42'32"N	34°58'26"S
24.5	●● ⬆	Mt Lofty Botanic Gardens 600m ↻	138°42'36"N	34°59'21"S
25.9	⬆ ⊙	'to Stirling via M1', Crafers	138°42'13"N	34°59'50"S
26.1		'to Piccadilly'	138°43'49"N	34°58'44"S
27.3	⬆ ⊙	'to Summertown'		
28.7	⬆	Spring Gully Rd, Piccadilly		
30.2	⬆	Old Carey Gully Rd		
33.2	⬆	Bridgewater-Carey Gully Rd		
34.3	⬆	Gum Flat Rd		
37.8	⬆	Beaumonts Rd		
40.1	⬆	Onkaparinga Valley Rd		
41.1	⬆	Heysen Rd		
41.8	★	The Cedars	138°48'17"N	35°00'46"S
42.2	⬆	unsigned road		
43.2	⬆	'to Beerenberg Strawberry Farm'		
44.2		Hahndorf visitors centre	138°48'34"N	35°01'44"S

At 22.2km there's an option to veer away into **Cleland Wildlife Park** (☎ 08-8339 2444; admission $14; 9.30am-5pm, last admission 4.30pm), though the road in has a gradient of around 12% (the ascent is on the return leg) so consider carefully how much you want to pat that koala. The two side trips that follow into **Mt Lofty Summit** (23.2km) and the **Mt Lofty Botanic Gardens** (24.5km) are kinder.

The day tops out at Mt Lofty Summit and begins a long, sweeping descent through Crafers and Piccadilly, but the climbing begins again after you pass the Mt Lofty Golf Club.

As the ride approaches Hahndorf it crosses the Onkaparinga River and then, if the Heysen Trail encounter has piqued your interest, pay a visit to **The Cedars** (41.8km; ☎ 08-8388 7277; admission $10; 10am-4.30pm Tue-Sun), the original house and studio of the eponymous artist Hans Heysen.

Day 2: Hahndorf to Springton
2½–4 hours, 53.4km

Today the hills flatten out into undulations as the ride slips east into agricultural country: livestock and grapes will be your companions along the Onkaparinga River.

To exit Hahndorf, double back 200m on the previous day's ride and head out of town on Balhannah Rd. It's a short ride into pretty Balhannah, which merges seamlessly with **Oakbank**, the most famous place in the state at Easter when it hosts a popular horse-racing carnival.

The day's most pleasant section is suitably that from Mt Torrens into Mt Pleasant. The wide, eucalypt-lined roads has little traffic and a few sweeping descents. You may even see kangaroos grazing among the sheep and cattle.

A 'false flat' will make the run into Springton tougher than it appears.

Day 3: Springton to Nuriootpa
3–4 hours, 42.6km

A short day in the saddle, Day 3 descends from the hills into Australia's premier wine-making valley, winding through Eden Valley (which is somewhat browner than the name might suggest) to reach Nuriootpa, in the Barossa Valley. There are more direct routes to 'Nuri' but the ride described here reveals more of the Barossa than just its wines.

Kaiserstuhl Conservation Park is a short, but worthwhile side trip at 17.3km. The Stringybark Loop Trail (2.4km) and Wallowa Loop Trail (6.5km) start from the Tanunda

WINES & CLIMBS – DAY 2

CUE		GPS COORDINATES
start	Hahndorf visitors centre	138°48'34"N 35°01'44"S
0km	go NW on Main Rd	
0.2	Balhannah Rd	
2.4	Jones Rd	
5.3	'to Balhannah'	
6.2	'to Oakbank', Balhannah	
8.0	Oakbank	138°50'41"N 34°58'59"S
11.3	Riverview Rd	
18.1	1km dirt road	
19.1	Teakles Rd	

CUE CONTINUED		GPS COORDINATES
19.2	Lewis Rd	
	3.9km dirt road	
23.1	Springhead Rd (unsigned)	
26.3	'to Tungkillo', Mt Torrens	138°57'32"N 34°52'32"S
26.5	1.3km moderate	
39.4	'to Mt Pleasant'	
44.3	'to Angaston'	
44.9	Mt Pleasant	139°02'37"N 34°46'32"S
53.4	Springton General Store	139°05'18"N 34°42'32"S

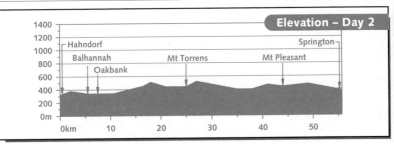

Elevation – Day 2

SOUTH AUSTRALIA

WINES & CLIMBS – DAYS 3-5

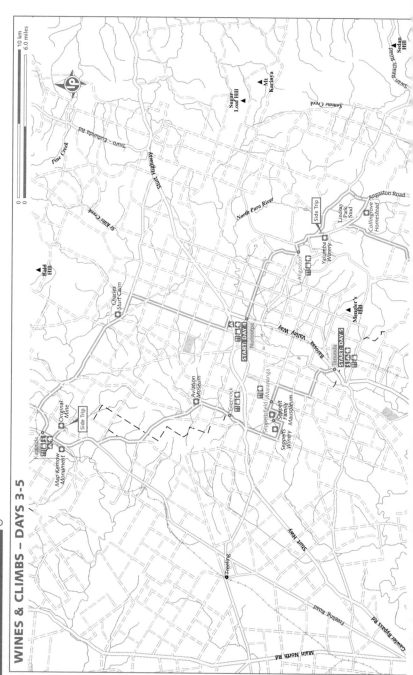

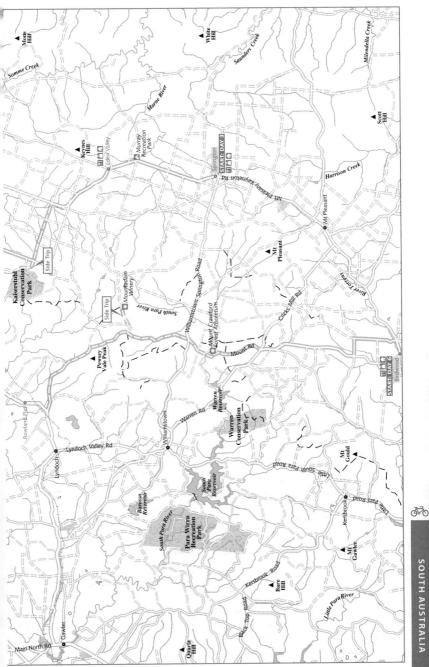

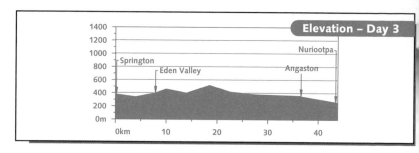

WINES & CLIMBS – DAY 3

CUE			GPS COORDINATES
start		Springton General Store	139°05'18"N 34°42'32"S
0km		go N on Miller St	
7.9		Eden Valley	139°07'48"N 34°40'02"S
13.2	↰	Mirooloo Rd	
	⚠	4.1km dirt road	
17.3	↱	Flaxmans Valley Rd (unsigned)	
{	●● ↰	Kaiserstuhl Conservation Park 2.6km 3.4km ⟲}	
24.9	↱	Angaston Rd, `to Eden Valley'	
26.7	★	Collingrove Homestead	

CUE CONTINUED			GPS COORDINATES
27.3	↰	Collingrove Rd	
27.7	⚠	1.2km dirt road	
28.9	↰	Keyneton Rd	
33.4	↱	Angaston Rd, `to Eden Valley'	
{	●● ↰	Yalumba Winery 800m ⟲}	
34.5	↰	Murray St, `to town centre'	
35.3	↱	Penrice Rd, Angaston	139°02'48"N 34°30'04"S
42.0	↰	Murray St	
42.6		Nuriootpa post office	138°59'44"N 34°28'22"S

Creek Rd park entrance, offering fantastic views from the top of the Barossa Ranges. At 19.6km the route passes a junction with Stone Chimney Creek Rd, which leads up to **Mengler's Hill**, a some-time King of the Mountain stage in the Tour Down Under with sweeping views across the Barossa.

Collingrove Homestead (26.7km; ☎ 08-8564 2061; www.collingrovehomestead .com.au; tours $7.50; 1-4.30pm Mon-Fri, noon-4.30pm Sat & Sun), built in 1856, comes after a sweeping descent through Flaxmans Valley. Once the home of George Fife Angas, the founder of Angaston, it's now owned by the National Trust, and is furnished with many of George's original antiques. The homestead is also a **B&B** (d $210-250) and whips up Devonshire teas.

The route from Collingrove passes through the middle of **Lindsay Park Stud**, home of the Hayes horse-racing dynasty, winners (so far) of three Melbourne Cups. At around 32km the route passes right beside the stud's lush-green training track. Just after is the **Yalumba Winery** (34.7km). **Angaston** (35.3km) is a thriving little town with quaint shops with crafts, antiques and bric-a-brac lining its main street (Murray St). Visit the **Angas Park Factory** (☎ 08-8561 0830; 3 Murray St; 9am-5pm Mon-Sat, 10am-5pm Sun) for dried fruit.

As the route descends Penrice Rd towards Nuriootpa you'll be greeted by a view of a sea of vines across the valley floor: welcome to the Barossa.

Day 4: Nuriootpa to Tanunda
3½–4½ hours, 51.8km

Tanunda is just 7km from Nuriootpa but today is the day to explore the Barossa and sample a few wines, the first cellar door is not until 42km so there's plenty of time to work up a thirst. The terrain is undulating, but there are no climbs of any real note. There are also a couple of nice free-wheeling descents into Greenock and Tanunda.

At the southern ends of the route there are very few moments when vines don't form at least a part of the view, usually in stark contrast to the brown pasture around them, but in the north the wines turn into mines around Kapunda, giving the day plenty of variety.

A **cairn** at 11.6km marks the spot where Captain Charles Sturt's party rested in 1844 on its central Australian expedition.

Around the former copper-mining town of **Kapunda** (22km) the reds are not the wines but the soil. In 1842, a rich copper deposit was found here and, at its peak in 1861, the town was the colony's largest commercial centre outside Adelaide. A side

WINES & CLIMBS – DAY 4

CUE			GPS COORDINATES
start		Nurioootpa post office	138°59'44"N 34°28'22"S
0km		go N on Murray St	
1.8	↰	Kalimna Rd	
2.0	↑	through walkway (cross Sturt Hwy)	
2.8	↱	Belvidere Rd	
9.8	↰	'to Kapunda'	
11.6	★	Charles Sturt cairn	
20.2	↰	B81, 'to Kapunda'	
22.0	↰	'to Gawler', Kapunda	138°54'53"N 34°20'29"S
{22.9 ●● ↰		Kapunda mine 900m (⟲)}	
23.7	★	Map Kernow monument	
26.2	↰	'to Greenock'	
35.4	★	Aviation Museum	

CUE CONTINUED			GPS COORDINATES
36.7		Greenock	138°55'55"N 34°27'32"S
42.1	★	Seppelts Winery, Seppeltsfield	138°55'15"N 34°29'22"S
43.2	↱	to Tanunda'	
{43.6	★	Seppelt family mausoleum}	
43.8	↰	to Tanunda'	
45.1		Marananga	138°55'58"N 34°28'57"S
46.2	↱	Stonewell Rd	
48.5	↰	Smyth Rd, 'to Tanunda'	
50.6	↱	Lamgmeil Rd	
51.0	↘	Elizabeth St	
51.6	↱	Murray St	
51.8		Tanunda visitors centre	138°57'32"N 34°31'30"S

trip at 22.9km marks the location of the **original mine**. A statue of **Map Kernow** ('Son of Cornwall' in the Cornish dialect) at 23.7km commemorates the area's Cornish miners, and the Kapunda Bakery can fix you up with a Cornish pasty to complete the experience.

The vines come back into view as you glide down towards Greenock. Plane buffs can pause at the **Aviation Museum** (35.4km) to ogle a Rolls Royce Merlin and a selection of other historic aircraft.

As the ride leaves Greenock, the Mawson Trail crosses its path, but continue on the road to reach the turreted Seppelts Winery… let the tastings begin. Along a corridor of

date palms through **Seppeltsfield**, the ride passes six cellar doors – Seppelts, Barossa Valley Estate (43.8km), Viking Wines (44.6km), Gnadenfrei Estate (44.6km), Two Hands Wines (45km) and Heritage Wines (45.6km) – in quick succession as well as the **Seppelt family mausoleum** (43.6km), where generations of this famous wine-making family have been buried. From here it's a nice back-roads ride into Tanunda.

Day 5: Tanunda to Birdwood
2½–3½ hours, 41.2km
There are a few more cellar doors to sample on the ride out of Tanunda, including famous labels such as Jacob's Creek and

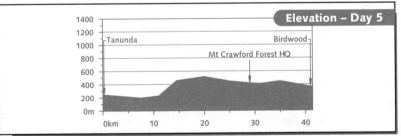

Elevation – Day 5

WINES & CLIMBS – DAY 5

CUE			GPS COORDINATES
start		Tanunda visitors centre	138°57'32"N 34°31'30"S
0km		go S on Murray St	
1.5	↙	Barossa Valley Way, 'to Gawler'	
7.5		Rowland Flat	138°55'37"N 34°34'58"S
9.5	↰	Trial Hill Rd	
10.1	⚠	2.6km dirt road	
11.0	▲	500m moderate	
12.7	▲	700m steep	

CUE			GPS COORDINATES
13.4	⚠	15.7km dirt road	
{18.5 ●● ↰		Mountadam Winery 4km (⟲)}	
{25.4	★	Mt Crawford Forest Arboretum}	
29.1	↱↰	Cricks Mill Rd/Birdwood Rd (dogleg)	
35.9	↰	Lucky Hit Rd	
37.1	↱	Cromer Rd	
40.2	↱	Shannon St	
41.2		Birdwood visitors centre	138°57'14"N 34°48'13"S

Grant Burge, but the day's real treat is in getting acquainted with the Mawson Trail. The ride follows it out of the Barossa and into Mt Crawford Forest, with lots of short (and some not so short), steep climbs on unsealed roads.

The dirt-tracking begins 3km past Rowland Flat. It is hard-packed and bikes on semi-slick tyres should be fine, with the tranquillity and solitude of pedalling almost car-free through thick forest more than compensating for the bumps.

The climb at 12.8km will test most cyclists' legs, but it does offer good views back over the Barossa. Soon after, the route links up with the Mawson Trail for the climb back into the Mt Lofty Ranges. If you want a farewell Barossa tipple, **Mountadam Winery** (☎ 08-8564 1900, High Eden Rd, Eden Valley) is a 4km side trip off the route at 18.5km. Its chardonnay is highly regarded and the cellar door is open only by appointment so call ahead.

Mt Crawford Forest is a popular recreation and picnic area that feels remote despite its proximity to Adelaide, though you'll have to excuse the heavy logging. The picnic tables at Mt Crawford's **arboretum** (25.4km) make for a good lunch stop if you've packed food from Tanunda.

A fringe of beautiful native forest (including a vibrant stand of sugar gums when the route first returns to the sealed road at 29.1km) speckled with banksias leads part of the way into Birdwood…until the vines return.

Day 6: Birdwood to Adelaide
3–4 hours, 63.7km
Return to the Adelaide plain in more rugged style than you left it, continuing to flirt with the Mawson Trail through steeply undulating terrain. Try not to leave the final descent from Cudlee Creek Rd until too late in the day as Gorge Rd is narrow and the setting sun can blind vehicles to your presence.

After an undulating journey out of Birdwood, the ride rejoins the Mawson Trail on unsealed Turner Rd (hard-packed again). The dirt roads present a real

WINES & CLIMBS – DAY 6

CUE			GPS COORDINATES
start		Birdwood visitors centre	138°57′14″N 34°48′13″S
0km		go W on Shannon St	
1.6	⬑	Angas Creek Rd	
5.1	⬑	Burford Hill Rd (unsigned)	
5.3	⬏	Turner Rd/Mawson Trail	
	⚠	6.7km dirt road	
7.5	⬏	Maidment Rd	
8.5	⬑	Maidment Rd	
10.6	⬑	Lihou Rd	
11.5	⬏	Lihou Rd (unsigned)	
12.0	⬏	Schubert Rd (unsigned)	
12.5	⬑	Gumeracha Rd (unsigned)	
15.1	⬏	'to centre'	
16.2	⬏	Post Office Rd, Lobethal	138°52′28″N 34°54′15″

CUE CONTINUED			GPS COORDINATES	
16.3	▲	400m steep		
17.5	⬏	Neudorf Rd		
18.8	⬈	Klopsch Rd		
	⚠	3.2km dirt road		
19.4	▲	1km steep		
20.7	⬋	Croft Rd		
21.0	⬏	Fox Creek Rd		
25.6	⬑	Cudlee Creek Rd		
27.4	⬑	Cudlee Creek Rd, 'to Campbell'		
27.7		Cudlee Creek	138°4′3″N	34°50′28″S
45.0	⬋	Linear Park		
follow bikepath to city				
63.7		Elder Park, Adelaide	138°35′54″N	34°55′06″S

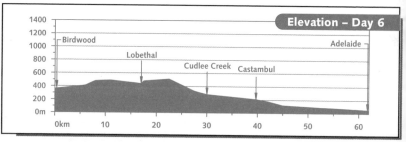

Elevation – Day 6

Birdwood · Lobethal · Cudlee Creek · Castambul · Adelaide

roller-coaster ride, with the short, sharp pinches out of Lobethal particularly hard on the legs – this is truly the spirit of the Mawson Trail.

Lobethal (16.2km) is a town straight off the chocolate box; one of the Hills' prettiest. If you happen to be here around Christmas, consider staying the night as it's famed for its Christmas lights.

The route leaves the Mawson Trail at Fox Creek Rd (from where the Mawson gets very rough) coiling down **Gorge Rd** to the plain beside the **River Torrens** – you can just about put your feet up on your front panniers from here. The ride through the gorge is the certainly most dramatic section of the entire route so take the time to savour it.

From the River Torrens Linear Park (45km), a dual bikepath follows the River Torrens into the centre of Adelaide. It's not very well signposted, but if you keep the river in sight (except for a short section beside the bus route) and to your left you shouldn't have any problems.

MOUNTAIN BIKE RIDES

For information about the Mawson Trail, see p241, and for details on the Kidman Trail, see p239.

ADELAIDE
Eagle Mountain Bike Park
Beside the freeway at Eagle on the Hill, this purpose-built mountain bike park has 21km of dirt road and single track, with a skills development course at its heart. It caters to all skill levels, with highlights including the coiling Overlocker, the screaming downhill on the Mixer and the airy Blue Gums.

At the time of writing major upgrade works were due to begin at the park in preparation for hosting the Australian MTB Championships.

Cudlee Creek Mountain Bike Park
In the Adelaide Hills (by the Day 6 route of the Wines & Climbs ride), this mountain bike park offers a great variety of rides in easy reach of the city. Novices can find

their dusty feet on the 10km Beginner Trail, while you can piece together a variety of rides on the intermediate tracks that branch out from the park entrance on Croft Rd. For a true challenge, try the advanced Goat Track along Fox Creek.

Kuitpo Forest
A short distance from McLaren Vale, this state forest has a selection of fire trail and singletrack riding. The 10km Onkeeta Trail, in the park's central area, offers a good loop through gum and pine forest. To its south, the 12km Tingella Trail circles out from Kuitpo Hall through pine plantation, while there's good singletrack riding around the northern Rocky Creek Hut area. For forest information, see www.forestry.sa.gov.au.

MELROSE
At the foot of Mt Remarkable in the Southern Flinders Ranges, this farming town has also become a bit of a mountain bikers playground. In June it hosts the Fat Tyre Festival, and at any time of year there's kilometres of single track pressed between the town and Mt Remarkable National Park. Beginners can trundle about on the Showgrounds Loop, while experienced riders will enjoy local favourites Hellrose and Greener Pastures. For the full rundown on Melrose's mountain-biking opportunities, visit the website for local bike store **Over the Edge** (www.otesports.com.au).

TOWNS & FACILITIES

ADELAIDE
☎ 08 / pop 1,467,300

As flat as a slice of Fritz, and laced with bike paths, Adelaide is truly a cycling kind of city. Having shrugged off its reputation as a large country town, the parkland-ringed city has one of Australia's busiest cultural calendars and a thriving wine-and-dine scene, making it more than just a departure point for this chapter's two rides.

If you're looking to ride in and around Adelaide, the series of 13 Bikedirect maps, covering the city from Gawler in the north to Aldinga in the south, is downloadable at www.transport.sa.gov.au/personal_transport/bike_direct/maps.asp.

Information

Bicycle SA (☎ 08-8168 9999; www.bikesa.asn.au; 111 Franklin St) is the representative body for cyclists in SA; offers information on all aspects of cycling as well as some maps and free bike hire for trundling about the city. **South Australian Visitor and Travel Centre** (☎ 1300 655 276, 08-8303 2220; www.southaustralia.com; 18 King William St) has general information on Adelaide and SA.

Supplies & Equipment

JT Cycles (☎ 08-8359 2755; www.jtcycles.com.au; 266-274 Pulteney St) and **Super Elliots** (☎ 08-8223 3946; 200 Rundle St) offer bicycle sales and repairs. For camping and other travel gear, there's a gaggle of outdoor stores on Rundle St. **The Map Shop** (☎ 08-8231 2033; www.mapshop.net.au; 6 Peel St) stocks a range of SA maps.

Sleeping & Eating

Pick up a **South Australian B&B** (www.bandbfsa.com.au) brochure for details of private B&Bs in and around the city.

Adelaide Caravan Park (☎ 08-8363 1566; www.adelaidecaravanpark.com.au/adelaide.html; 46 Richmond St, Hackney; powered sites $30-32, cabins $85-147; 🖭) On the banks of the River Torrens, 2km northeast of the city centre, with plenty of grass, though not for camping on…that's what the gravel is for.

My Place (☎ 08-8221 5299; www.adelaidehostel.com.au; 257 Waymouth St; dm incl breakfast $23, d incl breakfast & TV $60) Expect a wonderfully welcoming, personal atmosphere just a stumble away from pubs and Light Sq nightspots, a cosy TV room and a sauna in which to sweat out those cycling aches. There are six-bed dorms available and note there are no doubles in summer. Bike hire is $10 per day.

Adelaide Central YHA (☎ 08-8414 3010; www.yha.com.au; 135 Waymouth St; dm

---

SEEING RED…& WHITE

Australia may have been born a beer nation, but it's grown up into a well-rounded land of wine. From a small vineyard at the foot of the Sydney Harbour Bridge, the industry has grown to the point that vines now cover about 1700 sq km of the country, an area almost as large as Adelaide. Exports in 2008 equated to around $5.5 billion, with Aussie wine poured in more than 100 countries around the world.

Many of Australia's best cycling routes pass through wine regions – around 25 wine regions are visited on rides in this book, including six in South Australia alone. The following is a quick guide to some of the main wine regions along routes in this book.

Barossa Valley (SA) Australia's best-known wine region was settled by German families, with the first vineyards planted in 1842. Today, there are more than 100 wineries in the valley. Shiraz is its most famous wine style, and the valley is home to Australia's oldest shiraz vines, with semillon considered by many to be the Barossa's best drop.

McLaren Vale (SA) Adelaide prides itself on a Mediterranean climate, which has helped this southern wine region bloom into a wonderful wine-making area with more than 60 wineries. Soil types vary throughout the region, producing a range of wine styles, but it's best known for its dark shiraz and its cabernet sauvignon.

Adelaide Hills (SA) Pinched between the Barossa and McLaren Vale, the Adelaide Hills region might lack the media of its neighbours, but it doesn't lack for wine. The hills are home to around 50 wineries, with its cool, elevated climate well suited to pinot noir, chardonnay and its signature drop, sauvignon blanc.

Mudgee (NSW) An elevated region of volcanic soils with more than 35 cellar doors. It's best known for cabernet sauvignon, while the chardonnay is also highly regarded.

New England (NSW) Though New England only came into being as a wine region in 2008, it has impeccable wine credentials – in the 1880s, in a previous wine-making incarnation, it was described by one newspaper as 'one of the foremost wine-producing regions in the colonies'.

$27, d with/without bathroom $83/70) This is a seriously shmick hostel with key-card security on the rooms, spacious kitchen and lounge area (which has newish couches, an organ and balcony overlooking bustling Light Sq) and immaculate bathrooms. It's a real step up from the average backpackers and is surrounded by great bars and nightspots.

Festival City Motel (☎ 08-8212 7877; ecfestival@chariot.net.au; 140 North Tce; s/d/tr incl breakfast $90/110/135) The rooms might be furnished a little like a retirement home but they're immaculately clean and directly across from the train station.

Royal Coach Motor Inn (☎ 1800 882 082, 08-8362 5676; www.royalcoach.com.au; 24 Dequetteville Tce, Kent Town; s/d $115/130) Just a stroll through Rymill Park from the East End and CBD, these bright rooms have a queen-sized bed and a sofa. There's a Grecian-like indoor pool, spa and sauna. Exec rooms and spa suites face the front of the building and have better views (request when you book).

Amalfi Pizzeria Ristorante (☎ 08-8223 1948; 29 Frome St; mains $18-22; lunch Mon-Fri, dinner Mon-Sat) This Adelaide institution, just off Rundle St, seems perpetually buzzing with contented diners munching their way through piping-hot pizzas and al-dente pasta. It's often difficult to get in, but hang around because it's worth the wait.

Botanic Café (☎ 08-8232 0626; 4 East Tce; mains $22-30; lunch & dinner) Order from a seasonal menu styled from the best regional produce in this swish, contemporary hot spot opposite the Botanic Gardens. Offerings include chargrilled spatchcock with salsa verde and roast chat spuds. The lunch special (two courses and a glass of wine for $21) is a bargain.

Nu Thai (☎ 08-8410 2288; 117 Gouger St; mains $14-19; lunch Fri, dinner Tue-Sun) Tuck into dishes such as crispy chilli barramundi and scallops with wild asparagus at this contemporary Thai restaurant regarded as the best in town.

The cool climate and elevation – Australia's highest winery is here at 1320m – mean that the best tipples are chardonnay, sauvignon blanc and riesling.

Rutherglen (Vic) Hanging below the Murray River, Rutherglen is the country's undisputed champion of fortified wines. Many of the wineries here were established in the 19th century, plonked down on the rich Rutherglen loam. Come for muscat, tokay or, if you must have a table wine, shiraz.

Alpine Valleys (Vic) If the name hasn't yet given it away, this is a cool-climate region, sprawled over four valleys and making crisp chardonnays and pinot noirs.

King Valley (Vic) The King Valley is touched in this book at Milawa, and is a region that was settled by many Italian migrants, which is now reflected in the range of experimental grapes: pinot grigio, barbera, sangiovese dolcetto and nebbiolo, among others.

Tasmania Tassie is lumped into one wine region, although vines are grown in several areas. Most famous is the Tamar Valley, north of Launceston, but it's smaller areas such as the Coal Valley, East Coast, Derwent Valley and Huon Channel that are passed through in this book. Tasmania produces only 1% of Australian wine but is well known for its pinot noir and sparkling wine.

Margaret River (WA) The first vines were planted at Margaret River in the 1960s, with the region becoming one of the country's fastest growing wine areas – in the last 20 years the number of wineries has grown from around 20 to more than 100. Cabernet sauvignon is the region's star red (though the Evans & Tate 1999 shiraz was awarded best red wine at the 2000 International Wine Challenge), while the chardonnay and semillon sauvignon blanc head the list of whites.

Great Southern (WA) The bulk of the Great Southern wine region is centred around Mt Barker and Porongurup, away from the rides in this book, but the Denmark subregion is worth a wine stop. The town's best drops are its pinot noirs and chardonnays.

If you do go tasting while you're riding, remember that about five standard 20ml tastes within an hour puts you close to the legal blood-alcohol limit (0.05%).

Woolworths (86 Rundle Mall) is the most central supermarket, while the wonderful **Central Market** (Gouger St; 7am-5.30pm Mon-Thu, 7am-9pm Fri, 7am-3pm Sat) is good for ride snacks.

Getting There & Away

AIR

Adelaide airport (☎ 08-8308 9211; www .aal.com.au) is 7km west of the city. **Qantas** (☎ 13 13 13; www.qantas.com.au), **Virgin Blue** (☎ 13 67 89; www.virginblue.com .au), **Jetstar** (☎ 13 15 38; www.jetstar .com.au) and **Tiger Airways** (☎ 03-9335 3033; www.tigerairways.com) operate flights between Adelaide and other capital cities as well as major centres such as Alice Springs, the Gold Coast, Cairns and Canberra. **Skylink** (☎ 08-8413 6196; www .skylinkadelaide.com; adult $8.50) runs shuttles between the city and the airport (via the Keswick interstate train terminal). Bikes can be carried and there's no extra charge. If travelling from the city to the airport, bookings are essential.

If riding into the city, join the bikepath along the River Torrens by taking Sir Donald Bradman Dr left (west) out of the airport, then turning right (north) onto Tapleys Hill Rd.

BUS

Adelaide's central **bus station** (☎ 08-8415 5533; 105-111 Franklin St) has terminals and ticket offices for all major interstate and statewide services. For bus timetables see www.bussa.com.au. **Greyhound Australia** (☎ 1300 473 946; www.greyhound.com .au) has direct services to Melbourne ($70, 11 hours), Sydney ($155, 23 hours) and Alice Springs ($280, 19½ hours), while **Firefly Express** (☎ 1300 730 740; www .fireflyexpress.com.au) operates services to/ from Melbourne ($55, 11 hours) that travel onto Sydney ($125, 23½ hours).

TRAIN

The **interstate train terminal** (Railway Tce, Keswick) is just southwest of the city centre.

Great Southern Railway (☎ 13 21 47; www.trainways.com.au; 7.30am-8pm Mon-Fri, 8am-6pm Sat, 9am-5pm Sun) operates all train services in and out of SA. The following trains depart from Adelaide regularly:

Ghan To Alice Springs (economy seat/ twin-berth sleeper $335/685, 19 hours)
Ghan To Darwin ($690/1390, 47 hours)
Indian Pacific To Perth ($395/1005, 39 hours)
Indian Pacific To Sydney ($285/485, 25 hours)
Overland To Melbourne ($90/150, 11 hours)

BICYCLE

Adelaide is almost 800km from the nearest capital city (Melbourne), so it's a long and lonely approach from any direction, especially from Perth, 2700km to the west (across the Nullarbor), and Darwin, 3000km to the north (along the outback Stuart Hwy). The most popular cycling approach is from Melbourne along the Great Ocean Rd (p122) and Coorong.

CAR

Airport Rent-A-Car (☎ 1800 331 033; www.airportrentacar.com.au) has its office at the airport.

The following companies, except Apex, also have offices at the airport.

Apex (☎ 1800 804 392; www.apexrent acar.com.au; 969 Port Rd, Cheltenham)
Avis (☎ 08-8410 5727; www.avis.com.au ; 136 North Tce)
Budget (☎ 08-8418 7300; www.budget .com.au; 274 North Tce)
Europcar (☎ 08-8114 6350; www.europ car.com.au; 142 North Tce)
Hertz (☎ 08-8231 2856; www.hertz.com .au; 233 Morphett St)
Thrifty (☎ 08-8410 8977; www.thrifty .com.au; 23 Hindley St)

BIRDWOOD
☎ 08 / pop 724

National Trus-classified buildings and quality craft and antique shops line Birdwood's attractive main street. Originally called Blumberg (the hill of flowers), this pretty town was founded by German settlers in 1848. During WW1 it was renamed after the commander of the Australian forces, Field Marshall Lord Birdwood. Today it's most famous as the home of the **National Motor Museum** (☎ 08-8568 5006; Shannon St; www.history.sa.gov.au; adult $9; 9am-5pm).

Sleeping & Eating

Birdwood Inn B&B (☎ 08-8568 5212; 31 Shannon St; d $100) This restored cottage has tasteful home-style rooms and a lounge with garden views and plenty of comforts.

Birdwood B&B Cottages (☎ 08-8568 5444, 38 Olivedale Rd; d $145-160) Three separate cottages present different variations on the B&B theme, from the colourfully rustic mud-brick studio to the chintzy homestead with two four-poster beds.

Blumberg Tavern (☎ 08-8568 5243; 24 Shannon St; mains $12-18) A popular pub with an old truck jutting out of its 2nd-floor vertanda.

Pick up a picnic hamper (two/four people $25/45) at the **Birdwood Wine & Cheese Centre** (☎ 08-8568 5067; 22 Shannon St) or order a cheese platter with olives and crackers (three/six cheeses $3/6) to eat while tasting wines (three/six wines $3/6); half of the boutique producers featured don't have their own cellar door. For more basic fare, head to **Foodland** (Shannon St).

HAHNDORF

☎ 08 / pop 1842

You could be forgiven for thinking you've arrived at a German theme park when you reach Hahndorf, the oldest surviving German settlement in Australia. Settled in 1839 by Lutherans who left Prussia to escape religious persecution, the main street is an avenue of deciduous trees, trinkets, cafes and ye olde Deutschland.

Information

The **visitors centre** (☎ 1800 353 323; 41 Main St) has oodles of info and can assist with B&B accommodation.

Sleeping & Eating

Hahndorf Resort (☎ 1800 350 143, 8388 7921; www.hahndorfresort.com.au; 145 Main St, Hahndorf; powered/unpowered sites $29/25, cabins from $59, motel d $99, chalets $125-195) In keeping with the local theme, Bavarian-style chalets encircle this sprawling resort, complete with tennis courts and fauna park. The tidy budget cabins come with queen-size beds but no kitchen, and tents get the shelter of huge gums. It's located 1.5km north of town.

Hahndorf Inn Motor Lodge (☎ 08-8388 1000; 35 Main St; d $110, d poolside/with spa $120/140, Sat night extra $10) Behind the Hahndorf Inn, in the centre of town, you'll find comfortable motel rooms of the exposed-brick era. Poolside rooms are the best and apartments are also available. Facilities include an indoor pool, BBQ and laundry.

Elderberry Cottage B&B (☎ 08-8388 7997; tvgauld@internode.on.net; Tyntagyll Farm, Mt Barker Rd; cottage weekdays/weekends $120/140) On a farm 1km past Beerenberg, this is a lovely, self-contained, stone cottage on a historic property. You have your own private garden overlooking a creek and surrounded by birdsong and the rustling of trees. Inside there's a fireplace, queen-size bed and a cosy atmosphere.

Unsurprisingly, wurst, sauerkraut, pretzels, strudel and German beer abound in Hahndorf.

Pot Belly Pies (37A Main Rd) The wood-fired pies here have earned Pot Belly the title of SA's best pie-maker.

Hahndorf Inn (☎ 08-8388 7063; 35a Main St; mains $12-28) Fancy a meal of cheese kransky, Vienna sausage, sauerkraut and apple strudel? Gather around a wine barrel with a stein of German beer (on tap) and soak up the friendly buzz. There's a great outdoor area for dining and watching the passing trade down the main drag.

Casalinga (☎ 08-8388 7877; 49 Main St; mains $15-20; dinner Wed-Sun) This place specialises in pasta and pizza dishes using fresh local produce. The servings are generous are the pizzas are possibly the best you'll taste in this part of the world. Eat in or takeaway.

MCLAREN VALE

☎ 08 / pop 2000

Nestled in a valley of the Mt Lofty Ranges, and surrounded by vineyards, McLaren Vale has a superb setting, with most of its 48 wineries with cellar-door sales within a short ride of the town centre. If you're here in late October or early November, the Wine Bushing Festival is a grand feast of wine, food, art and music to celebrate the new vintage.

Information

McLaren Vale & Fleurieu visitors centre (☎ 08-8323 9944; www.mclarenvale.info; Main Rd; 9am-5pm Mon-Fri, 10am-5pm Sat & Sun), at the northern end of town, can assist with accommodation and shares space with **Stump Hill Café & Wine Bar** (☎ 08-8323 8999), which offers tastings from local wineries with no cellar door.

Supplies & Equipment

Oxygen Cycles (☎ 08-8323 7345; oxygencycles@gmail.com; 143 Main Rd) can make running repairs to your machine.

Sleeping & Eating

There are numerous B&Bs in McLaren Vale, with doubles starting at around $120; the visitors centre can arrange bookings.

McLaren Vale Lakeside Caravan Park (☎ 08-8323 9255; www.mclarenvale .net; Field St; unpowered/powered sites $19/23, caravans/cabins with bathroom from $50/80) In a pretty rural setting by a creek close to town, this pristine place provides the only budget accommodation in McLaren Vale.

McLaren Vale Motel (☎ 1800 631 817, 08-8323 8265; www.mclarenvalemotel.com. au; Caffrey St; s/d from $95/110) Near the visitors centre, with spacious units and complimentary laundry facilities to wash out four days of road grime.

Oscar's Diner (☎ 08-8323 8707; 201 Main Rd; dishes $12-18; lunch & dinner) A reliable favourite with delicious gourmet pizza, a sunny courtyard and a crackling open fire in winter.

Marienberg Limeburners (☎ 08-8323 8599; Main Rd; mains $16-25; lunch & dinner) Blondewood brightens this bastion of fine European-based Mod Oz cuisine on even the woolliest of days.

Salopian Inn (☎ 08-8323 8769; cnr McMurtrie & Main Rds; mains $26-30; lunch Thu-Tue, dinner Fri & Sat) Just out of town, this serious foodie haunt has a not-to-be-missed reputation. Head down the stone stairs to the cellar to choose your own bottle of wine.

You can pick up groceries at **Coles** (130 Main Rd).

NORMANVILLE

☎ 08 / pop 1100

For a holiday town, Normanville has a fairly workaday town centre, but head to the beach and its attraction is clear – unbroken kilometres of sand and 600-year-old vegetated dunes. It's a beach that invites

exploration if you arrive with some time left in the day.

The **Court House Cafe** (☎ 08-8558 3532) serves as the town's information centre.

Sleeping & Eating

Jetty Caravan Park (☎ 08-8558 2038; Jetty Rd; unpowered/powered sites $21/25, apt $55, cabin/villa $84/99) About 2km towards Cape Jervis from Normanville, and on the beachfront.

Beachside Caravan Park (☎ 08-8558 2458; www.beachside.com.au; Cape Jervis Rd; unpowered/powered sites $20/23, cabins & villas $75-90) Not far from Jetty Caravan Park.

Sunset Cove Resort (☎ 1800 083 111; www.sunset-cove.com.au; Willis Dr; unpowered/powered sites $20/25, cabins $80, d from $135; 🐾) You'll hardly need to leave this resort, 12km south of Normanville, which comes complete with a cafe, restaurant and almost any type of activity you could wish for.

Normanville Hotel (☎ 08-8558 3200; www.normanvillehotel.com.au; 46 Main Rd, Normanville; mains $12-28; lunch & dinner) Self-contained cabins ($90) and counter meals.

The **Normanville Beach Cafe** (☎ 08-8558 2575; Jetty Rd; mains $16-27) is the place for dinner, even if just to watch the sun set into the Gulf. Try the King George whiting if you want to feel like a local.

You can fill up the nose bag at **Foodland** (85 Main St).

NURIOOTPA

☎ 08 / pop 3490

Even the best tourist regions need a service centre, and in the Barossa it's 'Nuri'. The Barossa Visitors Centre (p239) in Tanunda can provide information about Nuriootpa.

Sleeping & Eating

Barossa Bunkhaus Travellers Hostel (☎ 08-8562 2260; Barossa Valley Way; dm $17, cottage d $50) This pleasant and clean hostel is about 1km from town and there are great views over the surrounding vineyards. However, there's no heating or air-con, and the dorms are a bit basic. Bicycles can be hired here ($10 per day).

Barossa Valley SA Tourist Park (☎ 08-8562 2615; Penrice Rd; unpowered/powered sites $19/22, cabins with/without bathroom from $62/55) A green, peaceful and shady park, close to the river. There are walking tracks, tennis courts, barbecue areas and playgrounds. The cabins have small balconies and a central grassed oval that just calls out for a game of cricket.

Doubles d'vine (☎ 08-8562 2260; www .doublesdvine.com.au; Barossa Valley Way; d from $60) This refurbished backpackers provides excellent budget accommodation 1km south of town. There's a self-contained cottage as well as a separate 'lodge' with two doubles with bathrooms, which share a lounge and kitchen. Surrounded by vines, the cosy rooms boast BBQs and wood fires.

Nuriootpa Vine Inn (☎ 08-8562 2133; www.vineinn.com.au; 14 Murray St; d $95-120) A standard, central motel where, despite the name, the palms are more noticeable than the vines. To save weary legs, it has a restaurant (mains $10 to $23; open for lunch and dinner) and serves counter meals in the bar.

Linke's Bakery & Tearooms (☎ 08-8562 1129; 40 Murray St; light meals $5-10; breakfast & lunch Mon-Sat) A visit to Linke's is a Nuri tradition, especially for the Nuriootpa Pasty.

Maggie Beer's Farm Shop & Restaurant (☎ 08-8562 4477; www.maggiebeer .com.au; Pheasant Farm Rd; mains $12-15; 10.30am-5pm) Culinary magic is dished up in celebrity-gourmet Maggie's kitchen – she's famous for her pheasant products. Picnic fare is served all day in the small restaurant and alfresco garden overlooking the dam. Hot terrines and tarts feature the Beer farm produce and you can finish off with a range of signature ice creams.

For groceries, head to the **Community Store Foodland** (1 Murray St).

SPRINGTON
☎ 08 / pop 500
At the top of the River Torrens, Springton is a quintessential bush town, with a general store, petrol bowser, pub and little else. The town's main attraction is the **Herbig Tree**, a river red gum that Frederich and Caroline Herbig used as their home for two years in the late 1850s. It looks a little like

Derby's prison tree without the history of imprisonment.

Sleeping & Eating
The nearest camping is at **Murray Recreation Park** (☎ 08-8564 1069; site $10) as you ride towards Eden Valley. If you are camping, the Eden Valley Hotel, 2km away, does meals on Wednesday and Saturday night.

Hillbrook Cottage (☎ 08-8568 2920; 50 Miller St; d from $120), as you leave town, has self-contained cabins, which is just as well because dining options are few. The **Springton Hotel** (☎ 08-8568 2290, cnr Miller & Main St) is your best bet.

STRATHALBYN
☎ 08 / pop 2600
Established in 1839 by Scottish immigrants, much of Strathalbyn's streetscape and its impressive buildings have been preserved, making it one of the Adelaide Hills' most appealing towns. Manicured gardens flank the Angas River as it flows through the picturesque town, overlooked by the turreted St Andrew's Church, while antique, bric-a-brac and New Age stores line High St.

Information
Strathalbyn visitors centre (☎ 08-8536 3212; South Tce; 9am-5pm Mon-Fri, 10am-4pm Sat, Sun & public holidays), in the train station, has oodles of information on 'Strath' and its surrounds, and walking-tour maps with detailed heritage information.

Sleeping & Eating
Strathalbyn Caravan Park (☎ 08-8536 3681; Ashbourne Rd; unpowered/powered sites $14/18, cabins with bathroom $75) This modest spot off West Tce has shady sites, a couple of cabins, barbecues and tennis courts.

Victoria Hotel (☎ 08-8536 2202; www .victoriahotelstrathalbyn.com.au; 16 Albyn Tce; d incl breakfast without spa $100-120, with spa $110-140) This stylish country hotel, opposite the Angas River parkland, has comfortable rooms and a great vertanda for lunch or dinner (mains $13 to $22), a beer and a bit of Strath people-watching.

Watervilla House (☎ 08-8536 4099; www.watervillahouse.com; 2 Mill St; d without/with breakfast $140/160) This grand 1840s residence in the heart of Strathalbyn will transport you back in time with its antique Victorian decor.

Gasworks B&B (☎ 08-8536 4291; 12 South Tce; d $160) Stay in one of the beautifully restored residences of the old gasworks, with terraced gardens overlooking a sweep of the river. Each cottage has a spa and kitchen for cooking up bumper breakfast provisions.

Argus House Patisserie (Dawson St; meals $8-10; breakfast & lunch) Locals huddle over papers at this wholesome cafe in the old Argus press building. There's a good mix, including pizzas, laksa, pad thai and homemade cakes.

Jack's Café & Bakery (☎ 08-8536 4147; 24 High St; sandwiches $4-7.50) Tasty cakes, pies and gourmet fare are the go at this large spot in the centre of historic High St. Nab a kerbside table.

Pick up provisions at **Woolworths** (cnr Dawson & Donald Sts) or **IGA** (24 Dawson St).

TANUNDA
☎ 08 / pop 3600

Tanunda puts the oompah into the Barossa…it's the major tourist town and is home to some of the largest wine labels in the country. The most Germanic of the Barossa towns, it's worth a stroll around town to see old Lutheran churches and the delightful cottages around Goat Sq on John St.

Information

The **Barossa Visitors Centre** (☎ 08-8563 0600; www.barossa-region.org; 66-68 Murray St, Tanunda) includes the Barossa Wine Centre and also hires out bikes (see p244).

Sleeping & Eating

Tanunda Caravan & Tourist Park (☎ 08-8563 2784; www.tanundacaravan touristpark.com.au; Barossa Valley Way; unpowered/powered sites $20/25, caravans from $49, cabins from $59) Just a short walk from town, this park has excellent facilities, including a camp kitchen and recreation hall with activities. The park has some excellent deluxe cabins.

Tanunda Hotel (☎ 08-8563 2030; 51 Murray St; s/d $70/80) This boisterous

hotel in the centre of town has adequate rooms and a typical pub-grub menu (mains $12 to $25; open for lunch and dinner). The rooms are not for light sleepers, particularly towards the end of the week.

Valley Hotel & Motel (☎ 08-8563 2039; 73 Murray St; s $85, d $100-120) The refurbished rooms have bathrooms and are in a separate building at the rear of this family-run hotel so they don't suffer from pub noise. A room with a spa is available and there's an outdoor, streetside bistro to enjoy a beer and inexpensive meal (mains $10 to $25; open for lunch and dinner).

Stonewell Cottages (☎ 08-8563 2019; www.stonewellcottages.com.au; Stonewell Rd; cottages $205-255) These waterfront spa retreats are on the cycling route, 3km before you reach Tanunda. Tucked into a vineyard with exemplary privacy, comfort and serenity, they also have generous offerings of wine, port and edible goodies.

Fig (☎ 08-8563 0405; 90 Murray St; mains $6-14; breakfast & lunch) Fig is cool, clean and uncluttered with a select offering of light meals (toasted sandwiches, baguettes etc) as well as breakfasts and excellent coffee. The weekend breakfasts are cranked up a notch, which should suit hungry cyclists.

Die Barossa Wurst Haus & Bakery (☎ 08-8563 3598; 86a Murray St; breakfast $4-12, mains $7-15; 7.30am-5pm Mon-Fri, 7.30am-4pm Sat & Sun) This deli-cum-bakery boasts metwurst (Bavarian sausage) and cheeses, pies, cakes, strudel and value-packed all-day breakfasts. Delve into the region's heritage with a traditional German roll of kransky sausage, sauerkraut and mustard or the Bayern Schmaus, Bavarian Feast meal.

1918 Bistro & Grill (☎ 08-8563 0405; 94 Murray St; mains $20-29; lunch & dinner) This casual restaurant set in an old cottage serves a generous and always changing (predominantly meaty) menu.

Fill your cycling larder at **Foodland** (119 Murray St).

VICTOR HARBOR
☎ 08 / pop 8968

South Australia's Blackpool has a long foreshore adorned with towering pines and kitsch attractions. It's designed for kids and ice creams but it also has a great location overlooking Granite Island and Encounter Bay – if you're riding in winter keep a watch for southern right whales in the bay. To learn more about the ocean giants it's worth visiting the **South Australian Whale Centre** (☎ 08-8552 5644; www.sawhalecentre.com; 2 Railway Tce; adult/student $6/4.50; 11am-4.30pm), opposite the causeway.

Information

The **Victor Harbor visitors centre** (☎ 08-8552 5738; www.tourismvictorharbor.com.au) is at the mainland end of the Granite Island causeway.

Supplies & Equipment

For bike repairs, head to **Victor Harbor Cycle & Skate** (☎ 08-8552 1417; vhcycle @bigpond.com; 73 Victoria St).

Sleeping & Eating

Victor Harbor Holiday & Cabin Park (☎ 08-8552 1949; www.victorharborholiday.com.au; Bay Rd; powered/unpowered sites $28/24, vans/cabins from $45/70) Runs rings around other caravan parks in Victor, with tidy facilities, free BBQs and a large grassed area with a few trees.

Grosvenor Junction Hotel (☎ 08-8552 1011; www.grosvenorvictor.com.au; 40 Ocean St; dm $30, s/d $35/70) Reasonable rooms, some with balconies, share sex-segregated bathrooms. The backpacker rooms are twin share. Continental breakfast is included.

Anchorage (☎ 08-8552 5970; www.anchorageseafronthotel.com; cnr Coral St & Flinders Pde; s/d incl breakfast from $40/70) This grand seaside villa has most of its comfortable rooms on the beach-side, some with balconies overlooking the bay. The attached cafe is a salties' lair with a bar hewn from the hull of an old wooden whaling boat. There's a seafood-dominated, Mediterranean-Greek meets mod-Oz menu, and hotel guests earn 10% off menu prices (mains $22 to $30).

Whalers Inn Resort (☎ 08-8552 4400; www.whalersinnresort.com.au; 121 Franklin Pde; 1-/2-/3-bedroom apt $220/290/350) Out under the Bluff, this upmarket spot has sublime views, a restaurant, cocktail bar, a croquet lawn and tennis courts.

Red Orchid (☎ 08-8552 8488; 2 The Esplanade; mains $14-20; lunch & dinner) For a dose of good-value, wok-fried Asian cooking and smiling waiters, head here. Some dishes are given an Aussie twist, with chargrilled roo on offer.

Fish and chips under the foreshore Norfolk pines is the quintessential Victor eating experience, and the **Original Victor Harbor Fish Shop** (☎ 08-8552 1273; 20 Ocean St; fish & chips $6; lunch & dinner) was once named SA's second-best fish and chippery.

Stock up on groceries at **Woolworths** (27 Torrens Rd) or **Coles** (cnr Torrens & Seaview Rds).

SOUTH AUSTRALIA

Western Australia

HIGHLIGHTS

- Swapping cleats for flippers to float through the **Little Salmon Bay snorkel trail** (p265)
- Wine crawling along **Caves Rd** (p270)
- Scaling the **Dave Evans Bicentennial Tree** (p274)
- Parking up inside the **Giant Tingle Tree** (p275)
- Discovering beach perfection at **Greens Pool** (p275)

TERRAIN

Low, heavily forested hills through the southwest corner. Flat limestone and gentle dunes on Rottnest Island.

Telephone code – 08	www.dpi.wa.gov.au/cycling/1515.asp	www.westernaustralia.com

For cyclists, Western Australia (WA) can be unnervingly large. Covering one-third of Australia's land mass, the state is 10 times the size of the UK and almost as large as Argentina, with settlement pressed hard against the coast by the large deserts at its back. Riding here, however, doesn't need be all about big distances and complicated logistics. The southwest corner of the state is as enticing, and as manageable, as anything in the eastern states, and usually with a whole lot less traffic to worry about. Here, you can have green forests, white beaches and blue seas by day and reds and whites from the celebrated Margaret River wine region by night. Your rides will indeed be colourful, especially if you visit during spring, when the southwest turns on Australia's finest wildflower display.

This chapter includes descriptions of two rides, one long and one short. On Rottnest Island bicycles share the road only with the island bus service, and whether you use Rottnest as a warm-up to longer things or simply a day ride of its own merit, you'll appreciate all the things that have made it such a popular cycling destination, from the traffic-free roads to the endless succession of beaches. The Southwest Forests & Seas ride ranges through most of southern WA's major attractions, passing caves, beaches and vineyards and breezing beneath some of the world's tallest forests. You may not know about karri and tingle trees now, but you soon will.

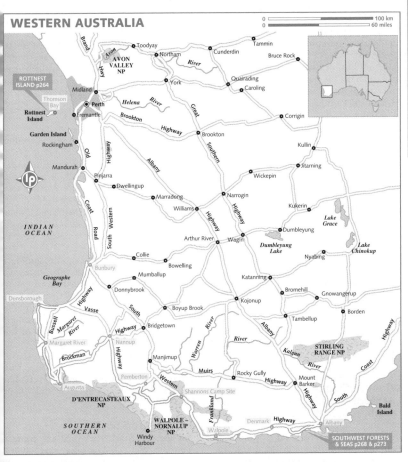

ENVIRONMENT

Western Australia's southern forests are of a type found nowhere else on earth, with the magnificent karri, jarrah and tingle trees endemic to this part of the state. Karri trees will be the most noticeable as you ride, their salmon-pink, ruler-straight trunks making them among the most beautiful eucalyptuses in the country, right up there with the snow and ghost gums. For more detailed information about karri and tingle trees, see p276.

Western Australia's most striking natural sight is its spring wildflowers, with the state having more than 12,000 recorded types of wildflower, including around 4000 in the southwest. A couple of good wildflower websites, if you want to study up, are CALM's **FloraBase** (http://florabase.calm .wa.gov.au) and the **Wildflower Society of Western Australia** (http://members .ozemail.com.au/~wildflowers/manydays .htm). The latter has special sections on the Leeuwin-Naturaliste Ridge, Pemberton region and Albany region.

Cyclists following the ride descriptions in this chapter have a great chance to see one of WA's iconic mammals, the quokka (see boxed text p266) and an armada of whales. Humpback whales frequent the waters off the Leeuwin-Naturalise coast (near Margaret River) from around October to December, while southern right whales can be seen between June and September.

CLIMATE

Western Australia is large enough to straddle several climate zones, but in the southwest, where this chapter focuses, there are hot, dry summers and cool, wet winters. Little rain falls between November and March; most falls between May and September. Perth's average annual rainfall is 975mm.

In Perth the average maximum temperature is above 30°C in summer, February being the hottest month. It's generally warmer further inland (the Avon Valley reaches 40°C) and several degrees cooler in the southwest; Albany's maximum during January and February averages 25°C.

Perth's winds are predictable from late spring to mid-autumn. Morning winds are easterly, with the westerly sea breeze, the 'Fremantle Doctor' blowing during the afternoon.

Afternoon sea breezes are common down the coast to Cape Naturaliste. Further south, southwesterly winds predominate during winter and spring, but during summer and autumn they're more likely to be southeasterly. Autumn is generally calmest.

PLANNING
When to Cycle

Like much of southern Australia, autumn (March to May) brings the most stable conditions to the southwest, with winds at their gentle best. That said, spring is *the* best time to be riding in the southwest, with masses of wildflowers colouring the landscape. For seasonal factors affecting the individual rides, see the relevant When to Cycle sections.

Maps

Perth-based **Quality Publishing** (☎ 08-9387 1279; www.qualitypublishing.com.au) produces the most useful and interesting maps of the state, featuring a wealth of side information. It publishes regional maps and both a large and compact state map.

The **RAC** (☎ 13 17 03; http://rac .com.au; 832 Wellington St, West Perth) publishes a series of regional maps, which can be purchased online, at RAC stores or downloaded (free) as PDFs from the website – the PDFs show only major routes,

however, and not the side roads you'll probably be seeking.

In Perth, **Bikewest** (www.dpi.wa.gov.au /cycling), a division of WA's Department for Planning and Infrastructure, has produced five printed maps and has eight maps covering most of the city and suburbs available for download.

Books

For a good selection of rides in and around Perth, grab a copy of *Where to Ride Perth*. Lonely Planet's *Perth & Western Australia* guide provides general detail.

Cycling Events

Fleche Opperman All Day Trial (www .audax.org.au; Mar) Teams of three to five cyclists riding over a 360km course, finishing in Fremantle.

Karri Cup (www.karricup.com.au; Mar) Two-day, 100km mountain bike stage race in the forests around Northcliffe.

On Your Bike (www.ctawa.asn.au; Oct) Supported nine-day tour organised by the Cycle Touring Association of Western Australia; riders must be members of the CTAWA.

Great Bike Ride (www.greatbikeride .com.au; Nov) Fund-raising loop ride around the Swan River; choose from 106km (two laps), 53km (one lap) or a family 10km route.

Information Sources

For general tourist information, contact **Tourism Western Australia** (☎ 1300 361 351; www.westernaustralia.net; cnr Forrest Pl & Wellington St, Perth). Its website has a dedicated cycling page – follow the link to 'Things to See & Do/People & Lifestyle/ Cycling in Western Australia'.

Bicycle Transportation Alliance (☎ 08-9420 7210; www.btawa.org.au; 2 Delhi St, West Perth) is a cycling-advocacy group; the website has links to bicycle user groups (BUGs) around the state.

Bikewest (☎ 08-9216 8000, www.dpi .wa.gov.au/cycling) is the bike-dedicated section of the Department for Planning and Infrastructure. The website is a good source of cycling info, especially for around Perth.

Cycle Touring Association of Western Australia (www.ctawa.asn.au) is a recreational group with a social ride every

Sunday. It also runs the annual On Your Bike tour (see p262). See also **Conservation and Land Managment** (CALM; www.calm .wa.gov.au)

Cycle Tours

Dirty Detours (☎ 0417 998 816; www .dirty detours.com) runs mountain bikes tours in the Boranup forest near Margaret River. **Pedal Oz** (☎ 1300 784 864; www .pedaloz.com.au) offers self-guided tours around Margaret River and on the Munda Biddi Trail, plus one-day guided rides near to Perth.

GETTING AROUND

Transwa (☎ 1300 662 205; www.transwa .wa.gov.au) operates bus routes around WA's southwest. Bicycles cost $10 and you should book ahead as they can only be carried if space permits. **South West Coach Lines** (☎ 08-9324 2333) buses also zip about the southwest; bikes cost $15.

The one train service (of the state's four services) of use to cyclists is Transwa's Perth-Bunbury *Australind* train. Bikes can be taken ($10), though bookings are essential.

GATEWAY

See Perth p283.

ROTTNEST ISLAND

Duration 1½–3 hours
Distance 28.5km
Difficulty easy
Start/Finish Thomson Bay
Summary Circuit WA's most famous and most cycle-friendly island, with no traffic, myriad beaches and plentiful wildlife.

Afloat off the shores of Perth, Rottnest Island has long been a WA summer-holiday tradition. Its second tradition is cycling, with private cars banned on the island and all visitors shooting about on bicycles, flitting between Rottnest's 63 beaches on the island-wide road system.

Less than 30 minutes by ferry from Fremantle, the island has no traffic, few real hills and a rim of gorgeous beaches, making it about as perfect as a day ride gets. The route described here circuits the drumstick-shaped island, with the option of a climb at the end to one of the taller hills. Maps are posted regularly along the roads and there are bike racks at every beach – the greatest difficulty of the day may be finding your treddly amid the crowds of parked bikes.

The unmarked streets around the Settlement can make for difficult navigation, but all roads eventually join up so just keep pedalling.

PLANNING
When to Cycle

Rottnest is a good destination year-round. In summer, temperatures are generally a couple of degrees lower than in Perth because every wind here is a sea breeze. The summer and Easter school-holiday periods, when the island becomes as crowded as a lifeboat, are best avoided, if you do plan to ride during the summer holidays, accommodation is so heavily booked up that a ballot system applies. The one time to especially avoid is the end-of-year schoolies week (usually late November), when revved-up school-leavers invade the island for a week of drinking and debauchery.

What to Bring

Once you leave the Thomson Bay/Geordie Bay area there is no drinking water on the island, so carry enough to last the ride.

Bike Hire

Rottnest Island Bike Hire (☎ 08-9292 5015; cnr Bedford Ave & Welsh Rd; bike hire per hour/day $12/26) also rents out helmets (per hour/day $2.50/3), child or cargo trailers (per hour/day $10/22) and even gel seat covers (per hour/day $2.50/3) if you haven't yet developed elephant skin on your butt.

Hire bikes are also available through each of the ferry services (see below) to the island.

Maps

There is pretty much the one road for looping around Rotto, with roadside maps sprinkled around the island, making the free map available at the Rottnest Island visitors centre sufficient for navigation. The map can also be downloaded at www .rottnestisland.com, just follow the Useful Information/Maps link.

ROTTNEST ISLAND

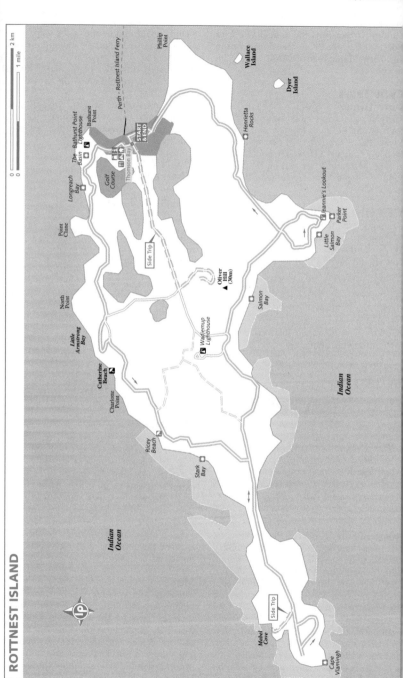

0   1 mile
0   2 km

Phillip Point

Wallace Island

Dyer Island

Henrietta Rocks

Perth – Rottnest Island Ferry

Bathurst Point Lighthouse
Bathurst Point

The Basin

START & END

Thomson Bay

Longreach Bay

Golf Course

Jeannie's Lookout

Point Clune

Parker Point

Little Salmon Bay

Side Trip

North Point

Oliver Hill (30m)

Salmon Bay

Little Armstrong Bay

Wadjemup Lighthouse

Catherine Beach
Charlotte Point

Indian Ocean

Ricey Beach

Stark Bay

Indian Ocean

Side Trip

Mabel Cove

Cape Vlamingh

GETTING TO/FROM THE RIDE
Rottnest Island (start/finish)

Rottnest Island is a half-hour ferry ride from Perth, making it an ideal day trip from the capital. If you do wish to stay on the island, see p285 for accommodation info.

FERRY

Besides points of departure, all the ferry services to Rottnest Island are basically the same. Return trips start at $51 from Fremantle (25 minutes) and $66 from Perth (1½ hours), with bikes costing around $13 extra. There's an extra evening service on Friday. Check the websites for exact departure times, as these change seasonally.

Rottnest Express (☎ 1300 467 688; www.rottnestexpress.com.au) departs Fremantle (C Shed, Victoria Quay) about five times daily; and Northport terminal, Fremantle, about four times daily. There's a thrice-daily service from Perth. It also hires out bikes.

Oceanic Cruises (☎ 08-9325 1191; www.oceaniccruises.com.au) departs Perth about three times daily. From Fremantle, there's a single morning service from the East St jetty and four daily boats from the B Shed.

Rottnest Fast Ferries (☎ 08-9246 1039; www.rottnestfastferries.com.au) runs trips from Hillarys Boat Harbour three times daily from September to June.

Rottnest Air-Taxi (☎ 1800 500 006; www.rottnest.de) has a same-day return fare from Jandakot airport in Perth starting at $240.

Extended return is $300. This price is for a four-seat plane (three passengers), so it can be a good deal, but is only useful if you plan to hire a bike once you're on the island.

THE RIDE

When you step off the ferry, head up the stairs to the right of the visitors centre. The ride description begins from here, heading through the barracks-like cottages, rounding the oval and heading away from the holiday hovel on Thomson Bay.

It's just a few minutes to the beach at **The Basin**, where a rock platform plunges into a gorgeous aquamarine pool. Pinched between the island's main holiday centres, it's a popular beach but there are about 20 beaches to come if you think it's a little too crowded.

A dedicated bikepath (what's the need on a traffic-free island?) heads along the perfect curve of **Longreach Bay** before the route joins the main road around the island. Along the north coast, there are almost constant water views as you thread between lakes and coast, with the views unimpeded by any real tree growth. There are regular opportunities to duck away to beaches such as Little Parakeet Bay and City of York Bay.

Bike traffic thins considerably, and if you come outside of holiday periods you may score sandy treasures such as **Ricey Beach** and **Stark Bay** (which has arguably the finest setting of all the island's beaches) to yourself. At

ROTTNEST ISLAND

CUE			GPS COORDINATES	
start		Rottnest Island visitors centre, Thomson Bay	115°32′27″N	31°57′49″S
0km		go N on Vincent Way		
0.4	↰	Raven Rd (unsigned)		
0.5	↗	Raven Rd (unsigned)		
1.0	★	The Basin	115°32′09″	31°59′21″S
1.9	★	Longreach Bay	115°31′47″	31°59′24″S
1.9	↰	Katemeraire Rd (unsigned)		
2.4	↱	unsigned road		
3.8	↱	'to Little Armstrong Bay'		
4.6	↱	Bovell Rd		
6.5	★	Ricey Beach	115°29′25″N	31°59′56″S
7.6	★	Stark Bay	115°29′10″N	32°00′22″S
8.6	↱	Digby Dr, 'to Cape Vlamingh'		
11.4	●● ↱	Mabel Cove 1km ↺	115°27′23″N	32°01′00″S
12.3	★	Cape Vlamingh	115°26′54″N	32°01′32″S
12.6	↱	Radar Hill Rd		

CUE CONTINUED			GPS COORDINATES	
13.0	▲	300m moderate		
13.7	↱	Digby Dr		
18.9	↱	Digby Dr		
19.3	↱	Parker Point Rd		
21.3	↱	Parker Point Rd (unsigned)		
21.7	★	Salmon Bay	115°30′23″N	32°00′41″S
22.3	★	Little Salmon Bay	115°31′27″N	32°01′26″S
22.6	★	Jeannie's Lookout	115°31′42″N	32°01′22″S
23.3	★	Parker Point	115°31′45″N	32°01′35″S
23.8	↱	'to Thomson Bay'		
25.7	★	Henrietta Rocks	115°32′28″N	32°00′48″S
28.0	↱	McCallum Ave (unsigned)		
28.1	↰	bikepath		
28.5		Rottnest Island visitors centre , Thomson Bay	15°32′27″N	31°57′49″S
	●● ↰	Oliver Hill 7.7km ↺	115°30′47″N	32°00′26″S

QUOKKAS

The quokka, which looks like something midway between a kangaroo and a rat, was known to the Aborigines as the quak-a, which was heard by Europeans as 'quokka'. Quokkas were once found throughout the southwest but are now confined to forest on the mainland and a population of 8000 to 12,000 on Rottnest Island. You will quite likely see quokkas while you're riding on the island. If not, stop in at the **Geordie Bay General Store** (8am-7pm). The presence of the attached cafe has made this a popular gathering/begging spot for quokkas. They're likely to come sniffing around for a titbit, but don't feed them, as this can make them sick, and hot chips don't make for a very well-rounded diet.

8.6km you can turn back (left) for a shorter loop of the island but to really feel a bit of Rotto solitude, cross through Narrow Neck and out to Cape Vlamingh. For a beach with more of a growl, take the short side trip out to wild and wave-beaten **Mabel Cove**, where the full fury of the Indian Ocean beats onto its reef. From **Cape Vlamingh,** the next landfall west is South Africa. Look north along the reef and you may spy some surfers riding their good fortune near Cathedral Rocks.

After looping over Radar Hill, which has views across the island to the jagged teeth of Perth's CBD, the return route trails along Rottnest's south coast, the lean of the trees giving a fair indication about the prevailing winds. The most beautiful stretch of the ride is out and around Parker Point, through bone-white dunes and views over the gin-clear waters of Salmon Bay. At **Little Salmon Bay** there's a different kind of tour, with a snorkel trail (bring your own snorkel) over the reef taking in 10 underwater plaques.

The short climb to **Jeannie's Lookout** presents views along the crinkle-cut coast to Cape Vlamingh, while the turning into **Parker Point** reveals yet another view of yet another beautiful, reef-protected beach. The return to Thomsons Bay passes **Henrietta Rocks**, where three ships came to grief on the reef – the twisted hull of one of the ships is still poking out from the water.

SIDE TRIP: OLIVER HILL
½–1 hour, 7.7km
To see Rottnest's version of hilltop lookout, head directly inland from behind the visitors centre, crossing a causeway between Herschel and Government House Lakes (look for nesting fairy terns on a sandbank in Government House Lake) and climbing to gun-crowned **Oliver Hill**. The climb begins immediately after the lakes, though it really only becomes steep at the final pinch – there are bike racks at the base of this final climb if you lack the puff.

The view from the hill is bookended by the island's two lighthouses, and includes the lakes, airstrip and Parker Point. The 9.2-inch gun on the summit was built in WW2 to protect Fremantle port, and is the only one of its type remaining in Australia.

SOUTHWEST FORESTS & SEAS

Duration 9 days
Distance 614.1km
Difficulty moderate
Start Bunbury
Finish Albany
Summary An extended idyllic tour that takes in some of Australia's mightiest forests, sections of castaway coast and the wine capital of the west.

Think of great Australian forests and it might be the Daintree that springs to mind, but in the southwest corner of Western Australia there's a swathe of forest to at least rival the mighty rainforest of the north. Highlighted by a trio of jolly green giants endemic to the region, including one of the world's tallest trees and the only buttressed eucalyptus, it's a unique forest that rings with names like harmonies: karri, marri, tingle, jarrah. Couple this with one of Australia's prime wine-making regions, the best wildflowers display in the land and a coast where deep caves meet high waves, and this is one of the most enticing corners of the country. And, with quiet roads throughout, it's best explored by bike.

PLANNING
When to Cycle
This ride is good at any time of year but the best months are March and April,

when the weather is calm, or October and November, when the spring wildflowers carpet the land. Rainfall is highest between May and August; summer is dry. Avoid holiday periods (mid-December to the end of January, and Easter).

What to Bring

While you can get by without camping gear for most of the ride, it is required for Day 6, unless you alter the timetable described here (for options, see p274). Between Margaret River and Albany, there are no bike stores so be sure to have a decent supply of spares.

Bike Hire

You can easily hire a bike in Perth at **About Bike Hire** (☎ 08-9221 2665; www .aboutbikehire.com.au; Point Fraser Reserve, 1-7 Riverside Dr; bike hire per day/week $33/70) and take it on the *Australind* train to Bunbury, returning by coach from Albany. If riding in reverse, try **Albany Bicycle Hire** (☎ 08-9842 2468; www.albanybicyclehire .com; 1-/4-/7-day hire $18/45/50).

Maps

Quality Publishing Australia produces the most useful maps for cyclists, featuring extensive detail, including all wineries and most of the tourist attractions along the route. This ride (barring a short stretch out of Bunbury) is covered by two maps in the series: the 1:170,000 *South West Corner* and the 1:268,000 *South Coast West Australia*. Both maps are on sale at the Bunbury visitors centre.

Permits & Regulations

This ride passes through a number of national parks, which charge an entry fee. The best-value pass is the Holiday Parks Pass ($35), which allows entry to any park in the state for four weeks. An annual All Parks Pass costs $75. Passes can be obtained at major visitors centres.

GETTING TO/FROM THE RIDE

Bunbury (start)
TRAIN
Transwa (☎ 1300 662 205; www.transwa .gov.wa.au) and **South West Coach Lines** (☎ in Perth 08-9324 2333, in Bunbury 08-9791 1955) run daily bus services from Perth to Bunbury ($25, three hours). Transwa's

Australind train service travels from Perth to Bunbury ($23.90, 2½ hours) twice daily. Bikes can be carried on both buses and train, though you should book them ahead.

BICYCLE
There's little to recommend about cycling from Perth to Bunbury – it's two days with lots of traffic and little to see. If you do plan to ride, there are two passable routes out of Perth: along the bikepath beside the Kwinana Fwy to Mandurah; or along Cockburn Rd from Fremantle, onto Rockingham Rd and Ennis Ave through Mandurah and on towards Bunbury. Around 22km from Bunbury, turn right onto the Australind-Bunbury Tourist Dr, following this into the town – there's a bikepath beside the road between Australind and Bunbury.

Albany (finish)
AIR
SkyWest (☎ 1300 660 088; www.skywest .com.au) flies daily from Perth to Albany ($230, 1¼ hours).

BUS
Transwa (☎ 1300 662 205; www.transwa .wa.gov.au) runs bus services between Perth and Albany ($48, six hours); bikes are permitted in baggage though you should book them ahead.

BICYCLE
If you are cycling beyond Albany be prepared for greater distances between services. To head east you can follow the Chester Pass Rd through the spectacular, sharp-tipped Stirling Range, or continue along the South Coast Hwy towards the gleaming white beaches around Esperance.

THE RIDE
Day 1: Bunbury to Dunsborough
4–5 hours, 89.2km
The **lighthouse** on McCarthy Point is Bunbury's most prominent landmark and an appropriate chequered flag for the start of this tour. The ride begins along the sand dunes that separate Bunbury from the sea (there's a bikepath on the sea side of Ocean Dr), with good views across Geographe Bay.

From the sea to waves of traffic, the route travels for 16km along the bustling Bussell Hwy, which has a good shoulder,

SOUTHWEST FORESTS & SEAS – DAYS 1-4

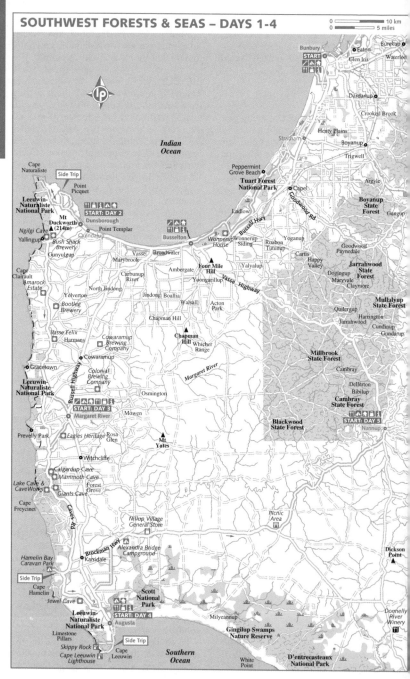

0 ─────── 10 km
0 ─────── 5 miles

Indian Ocean

Bunbury **START** · Eaton · Burekup
Glen Iris · Waterloo

Dardanup

Crooked Brook

Henty Plains

Stratham · Boyanup

Trigwell

Cape Naturaliste

Side Trip

Point Picquet

Peppermint Grove Beach
Tuart Forest National Park · Capel · Argyle

Leeuwin-Naturaliste National Park

START: DAY 2
Dunsborough

Mt Duckworth ▲ (214m)

Ngilgi Cave
Yallingup

Point Templar

Ludlow

Goodwood Rd

Boyanup State Forest · Gungup

Busselton · Bussell Hwy

Wonnerup House · Wonnerup Siding

Ruabon · Tutunup

Yoganup

Cartis

Happy Valley

Goodwood
Paynedale

Jarrahwood State Forest

Quindalup

Bush Shack Brewery

Gunyulgup

Vasse

Marybrook

Maryvale

Dogingup

Claymore

Broadwater

Four Mile Hill ▲

Ambergate

Yoongarillup · Vasse Highway

Yalyalup

Mullalyup State Forest

Carbunup River

North Jindong

Quilergup

Jindong · Boallia

Harrington
Jarrahwood

Cundinup

Gundarup

Cape Clairault

Amarock Estate

Yelverton

Bootleg Brewery

Walsall

Acton Park

Chapman Hill

Millbrook State Forest

Vasse Felix

Harmans

Cowaramup Brewing Company

Chapman Hill ▲

Whicher Range

Cambray

Gracetown

Cowaramup

Dellerton
Bibilup

Cambray State Forest

Leeuwin-Naturaliste National Park

Bussell Highway

Colonial Brewing Company

Margaret River

Blackwood State Forest

START: DAY 5
Nannup

START: DAY 3
Margaret River

Osmington

Möwen

Prevelly Park

Eagles Heritage

Rosa Glen

Mt Yates ▲

Witchcliffe

Calgardup Cave

Mammoth Cave

Lake Cave & CaveWorks

Forest Grove

Giants Cave

Cape Freycinet

Nillup Village General Store

Picnic Area

Dickson Point ▲

Hamelin Bay Caravan Park

Brockman Hwy

Karridale

Alexandra Bridge Campground

Side Trip

Cape Hamelin

Jewel Cave

Pa-Sanp

Scott National Park

START: DAY 4
Augusta

Leeuwin-Naturaliste National Park

Milyeannup

Donnelly River Winery

Limestone Pillars

Skippy Rock

Cape Leeuwin Lighthouse

Side Trip

Cape Leeuwin

Southern Ocean

White Point

Gingilup Swamps Nature Reserve

D'entrecasteaux National Park

SOUTHWEST FORESTS & SEAS – DAY 1

CUE			GPS COORDINATES
start	★	McCarthy lighthouse, Bunbury	115°37'55"N 33°19'16"S
0km		go S on Ocean Dr	
0.4	↱ ⊙	Ocean Dr	
7.3	↰ ⊙	Washington Ave, 'to Busselton'	
9.3	↱	Bussell Hwy	
27.2	↱	Roberts Rd	
31.5	↰	Mallokup Rd	
35.3	↱	Ludlow North Rd	
47.3	↱	Tuart Dr, 'to Busselton'	
53.0	↱ ⊙	Layman Rd	
{54.0	★	Wonnerup House}	
65.1	↰ ⊙	Bussell Hwy, Busselton	
89.0	↱ ⊙	'to centre'	
	●●↑ ↻	Cape Naturaliste, 33km	115°01'03"N 33°32'03"S
89.2		Dunsborough visitors centre	115°20'40"N 33°39'16"S

before heading for the almost-traffic-free roads between it and the sea – you'll see more horses than horsepower for a while. If you've already worked up a sweat, you can make the short detour to **Peppermint Grove Beach** (38km), a name that might alert you to the peppermint gums that line much of the day's ride.

Tuart Dr leads through the lovely tuart forest, a tree that grows only on the coastal limestone 200km either side of Perth. The forest ends at **Wonnerup House** (☎ 08-9752 2039; admission $5; 10am-4pm Wed-Sun), a lovingly restored colonial homestead built in 1859, crossing through marshy country between a pair of estuaries. This is a great section for birdlife, with the numbers of swans, pelicans, ibis and cormorants rivalled only by the number of homes springing up in new seaside developments.

At Busselton, be wowed by what's said to be the longest wooden jetty in the southern hemisphere, all 2km of it, and if you're tired choose from the town's 12 camp grounds. Welcome to the holiday coast. **South West Cycles** (☎ 08-9752 3892; 7-9 Bussell Hwy; 9am-5pm Mon-Fri, 9am-noon Sat) has a huge range of equipment if you've overlooked any of the essentials.

It's a suburban kind of run out of Busselton, until you join Caves Rd, where the homes fade into peppermint gums and church camps before you arrive in Dunsborough.

SIDE TRIP: CAPE NATURALISTE
2–3½ hours, 33km

The length of this ride, and the lure of Meelup Beach and Eagle Bay, make this side trip most suited to the short second day. You could even leave your gear in Dunsborough and collect it on the way back through.

From the town centre, take Dunn Bay Rd, which quickly meets Cape Naturaliste Rd. Looping out past Meelup Beach, it's a glorious winding descent to the coast, though its ugly sister, the climb back out, starts immediately beyond Eagle Bay. Take the time to enjoy this section of coast, which is as colourful as any in the country. And it's not just humans who appreciate it – humpback whales frequent the Geographe Bay area from around October to December, while southern right whales can be seen between June and September.

Back on Cape Naturaliste Rd, the route undulates west before the final climb to the lighthouse, where there are tours, drinks and ice creams, though of most interest is the 600m walking trail out to a cliff-top whale lookout.

Return via the outward route, skipping the detour to Meelup Beach.

Day 2: Dunsborough to Margaret River
2½–3½ hours, 46.6km

This day is a taster on two fronts: there are the Margaret River wines to quaff, and there's Ngilgi Cave, a precursor to an ellipsis of caves on Day 3. The dominant feature of the Capes region is the Leeuwin–Naturaliste Ridge, composed of 600-million-year-old granite overlaid with relatively new limestone (about two million years old) and punctured by around 300 caves. The ridge parallels the coast, rising up to 200m, and this day's ride climbs up, down and around the ridge, though never too steeply. It's a lovely, undulating ride, the forest interchanging with vineyards throughout.

Mystical **Ngilgi Cave** (☎ 08-9755 1288; ngilgi@geographebay.com; adult/child $15.50/6.50; 9.30am-4.30pm, last entry 3.30pm) is just before the Yallingup turn off, and there's all manner of distraction to keep you busy (or not busy) through the day: art studios, microbreweries (see

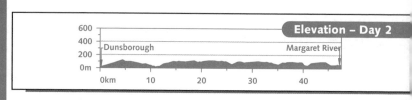

SOUTHWEST FORESTS & SEAS – DAY 2

CUE		GPS COORDINATES
start	Dunsborough visitors centre	115°20′40″N 33°39′16″S
0km	go S on Seymoure Blvd	
0.1	Caves Rd, `to Augusta'	
7.4	Ngilgi Cave 2km	
8.1	Caves Rd	
18.0	Amarok Estate	115°02′02″N 33°46′35″S
28.8	Vasse Felix	115°02′15″N 33°49′28″S
39.9	Carters Rd	
	800m moderate	
45.8	Bussell Hwy	
46.6	Margaret River visitors centre	115°04′26″N 33°56′56″S

boxed text p271), an Aboriginal culture centre and, of course, wineries in WA's most famous wine-making region. The first vineyards begin about 3km past Ngilgi Cave, and you ride past around 23 wineries. If you want tastings with a view, stop in at **Amarok Estate** (18km; ☎ 08-9756 6888; www.amarok.com.au), beside WA's most northerly stand of karri trees; if you want the whole wine-and-dine package, **Vasse Felix** (28.8km; ☎ 08-9756 5000; www .vassefelix.com.au; mains $30; lunch to 3pm), which was the first vineyard established in Margaret River, is considered by many to have the finest restaurant in the area. It also has an art display from the Holmes à Court Gallery collection. Or you could just pick a road, any road, to the west and veer away to check out the wild, wave-beaten coast. Author favourites along this coast include Quininup Falls (take Quininup Rd), Injidup Beach (Wyadup Rd) and the Wilyabrup cliffs (Wilyabrup Rd), popular with rock climbers.

Vasse Felix marks the virtual end of the vineyards, and as you drop off the ridge into Margaret River, the karri forest grows in height accordingly. It is yet another taster, this time of the grand forests still ahead on this tour.

Day 3: Margaret River to Augusta
2½–3½ hours, 55km

Another day in which you might spend more time out of the saddle than in, as you head south along the gently undulating scenic Caves Rd. Parts of the day are spent beneath an umbrella of trees, and there are some truly wonderful stands of karri, most spectacularly after Giants Cave.

Out of Margaret River the ride re-enters vine country, passing also **Eagles Heritage** (5km; ☎ 08-9757 2960; www.eaglesheritage .com.au; admission $10; 10am-5pm), which rehabilitates many birds of prey each year. There are free-flight displays at 11am and 1.30pm.

Back on Caves Rd, you will be immediately (if briefly) encased by karri forest before entering Leeuwin-Naturaliste National park, which you've been skirting since Dunsborough. If you're cycling in spring you may notice the change by the sudden profusion of wildflowers.

The national park also heralds the start of the caves. **Calgardup Cave** (admission $10; 9am-4.15pm) is a self-guided cave, with an underground lake. You can also enter **Mammoth Cave** (admission $16.50; 9am-4pm) by yourself, while there are guided tours of **Lake Cave** (admission $16.50; 9.30am-4.30pm). Entry to any of the caves also includes admission to the **Caveworks visitors centre** (☎ 08-9757 7411; 9am-5pm), which has excellent screen displays about caves and cave conservation, an authentic model cave, a 'cave crawl' experience and displays on fossils found in the area. **Giants Cave** (admission $10; 9.30-3.30 school & public holidays only) is another self-guided hole, with some steep ladders and scrambles. The day's cave crawl saves the best for last: spectacular **Jewel Cave** (admission $16.50; 9.30am-4pm) contains one of the longest known straw stalactites in the world, at 5.4m in length.

The side trip to Hamelin Bay heads through an alley of peppermint gums to

REDS, WHITES & AMBERS

Since the 1960s, when its first vines were planted at Vasse Felix (p270), Margaret River has been famed as a wine-making region, with almost 100 wineries now splashed around the town. But there's a new drink on the block in Margaret River, where four boutique breweries now operate.

In Yallingup, you could be excused for thinking you'd walked into a liquid grocery store rather than **Bush Shack Brewery** (☎ 08-9755 2848; www.bushshackbrewery.com.au; Hemsley Rd; 10am-5pm Sun-Thu, 10am-6pm Fri & Sat), where the brews include a chocolate beer, chilli beer and, on tap, a strawberry and lavender beer.

Down the coast, in Wilyabrup, **Bootleg Brewery** (☎ 08-9755 6300; www.bootlegbrewery .com.au; Puzey Rd) was the original Margaret River microbrewery (it opened in 1994) and bills itself as 'an oasis of beer in a desert of wine'. The Wils Pils has won multiple awards, including best Australian draught lager, while if you're pedalling on, it may be best to avoid the 7.1% dark Raging Bull, though it can be soaked up in the brewery restaurant.

The **Cowararamup Brewing Company** (☎ 08-9755 5822; www.cowaramupbrewing.com.au; North Treeton Rd; 10am-6pm) is a pup in comparison, having opened at the end of 2006. The four brews include an Indian pale ale, a pilsener, and an unfiltered Bavarian-style Hefeweizen wheat beer. The brewery's restaurant goes hard on beer-and-food matching.

Closest to Margaret River is the **Colonial Brewing Company** (☎ 08-9758 8177; www .colonialbrewingco.com.au; Osmington Rd), named the champion small brewery in Australasia in 2006 and 2007 at the Australian International Beer Awards. In the huge beer garden you can sip samples or quaff pints, or just enjoy a beer with lunch.

The microbrewery craze doesn't end at Margaret River. Ahead on the ride, at Pemberton, **Jarrah Jacks** (☎ 08-9776 1333; www.jarrahjacks.com.au; Kemp Rd) is a fantastic craft brewery, though the hill climb (and the potholes) to get here may not be worth any amount of beer.

---

bone-white Boranup Beach. It's a gorgeous stretch of sand, while the water holds another treat: 'friendly' stingrays that come in by the boat ramp to eat the scraps from anglers. You can stand in the water and watch them swim about you. Right beside the beach a few kilometres north of Augusta, **Hamelin Bay Caravan Park** (☎ 08-9758 5540; hamelinbay@bordernet.com.au; unpowered sites $18-20, cabins $90-110) has one of the best locations in the southwest, though you might feel like the odd person out since you're not towing a boat. Bring your own provisions if staying the night. If not, continue south to likeable Augusta.

SIDE TRIP: CAPE LEEUWIN
1–2 hours, 20.5km

Australia's most southwesterly point marks the line where the Indian Ocean meets the Southern Ocean, the lighthouse-tipped cape parting the seas like a comb. To reach Cape Leeuwin, follow the main road through Augusta and the fast-dwindling scrub to the shore of Flinders Bay. At the road's end is the **lighthouse** and a sprinkling of lighthouse-keepers' cottages, standing guard over an invariably wild sea.

SOUTHWEST FORESTS & SEAS – DAY 3

CUE			GPS COORDINATES
start		Margaret River visitors centre	115°04'26"N 33°56'56"S
0km		go S on Bussell Hwy	
1.4	⌐►⊙	Boodjidup Rd	
5.0	★	Eagles Heritage	115°03'44"N 33°58'38"S
8.4	▲	300m moderate	
8.9	⬑	Caves Rd	
14.1	★	Calgardup Cave	115°02'14"N 34°01'02"S
14.9	★	Mammoth Cave	
{17.9	●●⌐►	Caveworks & Lake Cave}	
19.6	★	Giants Cave	
38.0	⬑	Caves Rd, 'to Augusta'	
{	●●⌐►	Hamelin Bay 5.5km (🚴)}	
{46.3	★	Jewel Cave}	
51.3	⌐►	Bussell Hwy	
55.0		Augusta visitors centre	115°09'28"N 34°18'59"S
	●● ↟	Cape Leeuwin 20.5km (🚴)	115°08'10"N 34°22'30"S

About 1km back along the road from the lighthouse, turn left onto an unsigned dirt road and veer down to **Quarry Bay**. At the northern end of the beach is a small set of orange **tufa cliffs**, created by a combination of spring water, algae and bacteria, and looking like wax melting down from the

WESTERN AUSTRALIA

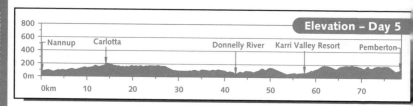

land. Further along the road you can also detour down to **Skippy Rock** for a wide-angle view of the coast.

Continue around on the dirt road, which loops back to the Cape Leeuwin road, but be cautious on the descent as the surface can be a little sandy. Turn left and follow the Cape Leeuwin road back into town.

Day 4: Augusta to Nannup
4–6½ hours, 88.1km

Today's ride has no particular attractions of note; it's a day to sit back and smell the jarrah. There are also no services en route other than the small Nillup Village General Store (27km), which has the usual eats and drinks and a basic line of groceries – tuna, coffee, pasta and the like (plus homemade salami). If you pick up lunch supplies here, there's a picnic area (with toilets but no water) about 26km further on.

The short cut across to the Brockman Hwy on Kudarup and Glenarty Rds, through farmland and blue-gum plantations, offers plenty of short, sharp rises, creating the feeling that you're riding against the grain of the land. The lumps flatten out on the Brockman Hwy, making for a pleasant ride through jarrah forest sprinkled with grass trees and a spring coating of wildflowers.

In Nannup the day ends where it began, on the banks of the Blackwood River.

SOUTHWEST FORESTS & SEAS – DAY 4

CUE			GPS COORDINATES
start		Augusta visitors centre	115°09'28"N 34°18'59"N
0km		go NW on Blackwood Ave	
6.8	↱	Kudarup Rd	
18.3	↱	Brockman Hwy	
22.7		Alexandra Bridge camp ground	
27.0		Nillup Village General Store	
{53.7	★	picnic area}	
70.0	▲	900m moderate climb	
88.0	⌐L	Brockman St	
88.1		Nannup visitors centre	115°45'53"N 33°58'35"S

SOUTHWEST FORESTS & SEAS – DAY 5

CUE			GPS COORDINATES
start		Nannup visitors centre	115°45'53"N 33°58'35"S
0km		go E on Brockman St	
0.1	↱	Warren Rd	
2.7	⌐L	Vasse Hwy, 'to Pemberton'	
41.6	★	Donnelly River Winery	
58.1	●●⌐L	Beedelup Falls 3.8km (↻)	
74.4	⌐L	Vasse Hwy, 'to Pemberton'	
77.1		Pemberton visitors centre	116°02'05"N 34°26'40"S

Day 5: Nannup to Pemberton
4–6 hours, 77.1km

Today's ride is almost entirely on the Vasse Hwy, which rolls south like a gentle swell…rarely flat, rarely too hilly. Add all the undulations together, however, and it makes for quite a taxing day, though there's the compensation of re-entering karri forest.

Until you near Pemberton there's little to break the day. The main point of interest is **Donnelly River Winery** (41.6km; ☎ 08-9405 3455; 10am-5pm), perfectly positioned for a civilised lunch stop. It has a picnic table, or you can sit out on its delightful balcony, overlooking the dam, and graze through a platter of cheese, olives and a selection of meats such as duck, chicken or smoked trout (platters from $26).

The wonderful karri forest begins immediately after the Karri Valley Resort, and it's worth detouring past 100m-high **Beedelup Falls**, even if it will add some short, sharp climbs to your day. The thrill of the final, free-wheeling descent into Pemberton will be tempered by the knowledge that you have to ride back out the same way the next day.

Day 6: Pemberton to Shannon
3–4 hours, 62.1km

The long and relatively strenuous stretch between Pemberton and Walpole is through gorgeous, isolated countryside. If

SOUTHWEST FORESTS & SEAS – DAYS 5-9

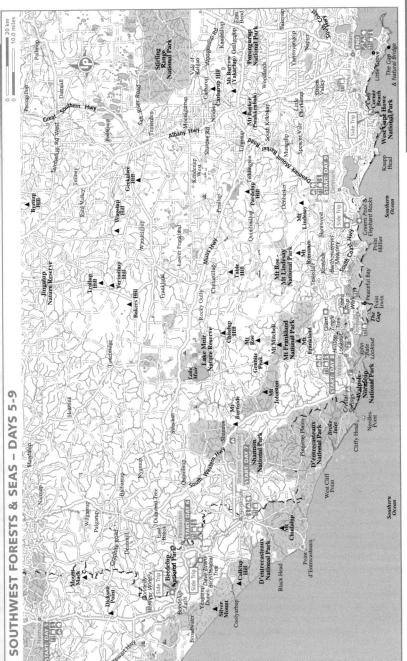

WHAT'S 'UP' IN WA?

In Western Australia's southwest it quickly becomes apparent that there's a theme to the place names. Why do so many end in 'up'? Nannup, Dwellingup, Manjimup, Gnowangerup…on and on and on; up and up and up. In the regional Aboriginal language, 'up' means 'place of'. Thus, Yallingup means 'place of love', Meelup is 'place of the moon', and Cowamarup, 'place of the parakeet'.

Nannup is said to mean 'stopping place' or 'meeting place by the water'.

you don't want to rough it at the Shannon campsite, there are two options: flog yourself to combine the two days into one (a 131km ride), or stop the night in Northcliffe (making for days of 32km and 99km). If you're riding a mountain bike, the shorter day to Northcliffe would give you the opportunity to play about on the mountain biking track at the **Round Tu-It Caravan Park** (☎ 08-9776 7276; Muirillup Rd; campsites $25, s/d $50/70). Formerly the state championship course (which has now moved to a site about 18km outside of Northcliffe), the 7km track now hosts the Round Tu-It Six-Hour Classic on the

SOUTHWEST FORESTS & SEAS – DAY 6

CUE			GPS COORDINATES
start		Pemberton visitors centre	116°02'05"N 34°26'40"S
0km		go SW on Brockman St	
1.3	▲	1.4km moderate climb	
{7.8	●●↰↱	Dave Evans Bicentennial Tree 6km ( ) }	
9.1	▲	2.5km moderate ▲	
30.3	↰	'to Walpole', Northcliffe"116°07'27"N	34°37'59"S
32.7	↱	Middleton Rd	
58.1	↱	South Western Hwy	
61.3	↱	'to Shannon National Park	116°24'30"N 34°35'37"S
		Campsite'	
62.1		Shannon Campsite	

third weekend of November. The park owner will also let you use his bike tools if you need them.

The side trip to the **Dave Evans Bicentennial Tree** adds in a climb of a different sort. Modelled on a series of fire-lookout trees around the southwest, the Bicentennial Tree is pierced with 130 metal spikes that serve as a ladder, allowing visitors to climb to a platform in the canopy of the karri tree. The tree is one of several such climbing trees in the region, but is the tallest at 75m (the Gloucester Tree, 3km outside of Pemberton, offers another climb near to the route).

From Northcliffe, Middleton Road undulates to Shannon National Park, where the karri forest is always thick but never dull. Look out along the way for the crossing of the Bibbulmun Track, WA's premier long-distance walking track, covering 964km between Kalamunda, on Perth's eastern fringe, and Albany. You'll intersect with it a number of times again before you reach Albany.

The turn-off to the Shannon Campsite is soon after Shannon River.

Day 7: Shannon to Walpole
3½–5 hours, 66.2km

The day begins through pickets of karri trees until, at around 20km, the forest cover gradually thins. You might think you'll miss these grand trees but the change also signals the flattening of the land…for a while, at least. If you fancy another night of bush camping (or need water) there's a turning to the pretty **Crystal Springs camp ground** at 53.2km (the campsite is less than 1km off the highway).

Fifteen kilometres from Walpole, the karri trees return, and the world looks a whole lot greener and straighter once more. Soon after, the day's longest climb begins as you cross ink-black Deep River, which also marks the western boundary of the

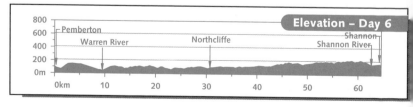

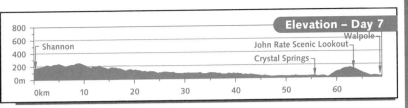

SOUTHWEST FORESTS & SEAS – DAY 7

CUE			GPS COORDINATES
start		Shannon Campsite	116°24′30″N 34°35′37″S
{0km	↺	to SW Hwy, go W}	
55.8	▲	4.3km moderate	
{60.8	★	John Rate Lookout}	
66.2		Walpole visitors centre	116°43′48″N 34°58′34″S

tingle tree (see boxed text p276). The hill rises to **John Rate Lookout**, where there's a keyhole view down to Nornalup Inlet and the coast.

From the lookout it's cruise control down into Walpole.

Day 8: Walpole to Denmark
3–5 hours, 73km

This day brings the chance to see a different giant of the forest, the remarkable tingle tree. The two loops out past the Giant Tingle Tree and the Valley of the Giants, in Walpole–Nornalup National Park, can be skipped by staying on the highway but

they are highly recommended, even if they require a little more grunt.

The road to the Giant Tingle Tree is a climbing dirt track (not suitable for road bikes), though the surface is generally good. En route, **Hilltop Lookout** offers a glimpse of the rugged coast around the mouth of Nornalup Inlet, even if the forest is continually trying to reclaim the view. In more laissez-faire times, visitors could park their motor vehicles inside the **Giant Tingle Tree** for a quirky photo. If you push your bike on the boardwalk, you can do the same with your bike.

In the suitably named Valley of the Giants there is the opportunity to walk not only past some of these giants, but also atop them. The **Tree Top Walk** (adult $6; 9am-4.15pm, 8am-5.15pm Christmas school holidays) is one of WA's major tourist stops. Its centrepiece is an aerial walkway, 600m long and rising to 40m from the ground, offering a possum-like perspective on both tingles and karris. Also here is the Ancient

SOUTHWEST FORESTS & SEAS – DAY 8

CUE			GPS COORDINATES	CUE CONTINUED			GPS COORDINATES
start		Walpole visitors centre	116°43′48″N 34°58′34″S	14.4	↰	'to Valley of the Giants'	116°53′24″N 34°58′40″S
0km		go E on South Coast Hwy		{19.4	★	Tree Top Walk}	
2.4	↰	'to Giant Tingle Tree'		19.4	↰	'to Denmark'	
	▲	3km steep		31.6	↰	South Coast Hwy, Bow Bridge	
{4.3	★	Hilltop Lookout}		40.6	▲	200m steep climb	
6.8	★	Giant Tingle Tree	116°45′13″N 34°58′59″S	{57.5	★	Bartholomews Meadery}	
6.8	↱	Gully Rd		57.9	▲	1.6km moderate	
8.7	↰	South Coast Hwy		{59.0	●● ↺	Greens Pool 8km ↺}	
10.5		Nornalup	116°52′47″N 34°59′48″S	73.0		Denmark visitors centre	117°21′10″N 34°57′39″S

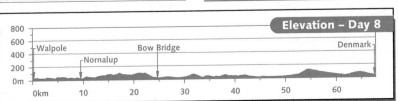

FOREST GIANTS

In WA's southwest, karri, tingle and jarrah trees are like a holy arboreal trinity. Found nowhere else in the world, they rule these forests with their height (karri) and their bulk (tingles). Karri can grow to 90m, making it one of the tallest trees in the world. It has a slender white trunk, turning pinkish in autumn, soaring 30m straight to the lowest branches.

There are three types of tingle tree – red, yellow and Rate's – and they occur only across a 6000-hectare area in Walpole–Nornalup National Park, between Deep River and Bow River. They are the only eucalyptus with buttressed trunks, and red tingles, the largest of the trees, can be as large as 16m around. Bushfires can burn through the heart of the trees (as at the Giant Tingle Tree), commonly leaving a huge hollow. The tree survives because its growth is concentrated in the outer layers of the trunk. Yellow and Rate's tingles can be difficult to distinguish from young red tingles.

Less spectacular, but more prevalent, is the jarrah, which has grooved, reddish-brown to grey bark.

Empire Walk, a 400m-long path through some of the most impressive tingles in the land. There are a few tingle trees along the road before you get here, but nothing nearly as impressive as the furrowed and grumpy-looking 'grandmother', a tree 12m around, 400 years old and bumpier than a desert track.

The land opens out (read: cleared for pasture) as the road weaves back to the highway at Bow Bridge – Cold Chisel fans may feel a nostalgic pang as they cross Bow River – passing through farmland, wetlands, low scrub and some attractive granite outcrops as it continues west.

Your sweet tooth might enjoy a stop at **Bartholomews Meadery** (☎ 08-9840 9349; 9am-4.30pm), where you can try honey wine and honey ice cream. Soon after the meadery, a side trip to **Greens Pool** marks your true arrival on Western Australia's south coast, which is a wonderful marriage of white sand and granite – people who spruik Queensland beaches have probably never been to this coast. There's good swimming in the protected lagoon at Greens Pool, or you can wander over the headland to another great beach at **Elephant Rocks**.

Back on the main route, the highway makes a short climb before rolling down into Denmark.

Day 9: Denmark to Albany
2½–4 hours, 56.8km
The final day is probably the easiest, offering a flatter finish to a hilly tour.

Leave town over the black Denmark River and past the black 'greens' of the golf

SOUTHWEST FORESTS & SEAS – DAY 9

CUE		GPS COORDINATES
start	Denmark visitors centre	117°21'10"N 34°57'39"S
0km	go E on South Coast Hwy	
17.4	`Alternative Scenic Route'	
19.1	Youngs Siding General Store	
{31.7 ● ● ● ⌐ Cosy Corner Beach 8.8km ⟲}		
40.9	Elleker	117°43'35"N 35°00'28"S
53.9	Frenchman Bay Rd	
54	Princess Royal Dr, `to centre'	
56.5	`to centre'	
56.6	Proudlove Pde	
56.8	Albany visitors centre	117°53'07"N 35°01'39"S

course, with the grand forest shrinking to a low, wind-ruffled scrub. At 17.4km the route turns on to the quieter Lower Denmark Rd, which meanders through pleasant dairy country. Ringed by hills and dunes, the road is mostly flat.

At around 28km, the road crests to a small rise with glorious views along the coast to the Albany wind farms and the cliffs of Torndirrup National Park. Shortly after, there's the option to detour back to the coast at **Cosy Corner Beach**, which is indeed one of the cosiest corners of beach imaginable. There are picnic tables, toilets and, back up the hill a few hundred metres, a turning down to the Cosy Corner East campsite.

Elleker General Store (40.9km) has the likes of fish and chips, burgers and salad rolls, plus a reasonable selection of groceries (and a more plentiful selection of alcohol). The route follows the railway line and the shore of Princess Royal Harbour into Albany.

MUNDA BIDDI TRAIL

Western Australia is home to one of Australia's premier bushwalking trails, with the Bibbulmun Track stretching almost 1000km from near Perth to Albany. Now, a mountain biking track is being created that parallels its path.

The **Munda Biddi Trail** (www.mundabiddi.org.au) begins in Mundaring, in the Perth Hills, and will eventually finish in Albany, following bush tracks, fire trails and abandoned sections of railway for around 950km. The idea for the trail was developed in the mid-1990s, with construction starting in 2001. The first stage from Mundaring to Collie (322km) opened in 2004, with the second stage to Nannup completed in 2009, bringing the trail's length to around 490km. The remainder of the trail is hoped to be finished by around 2012, though the date has been regularly pushed back.

Heading out through the valleys of the Darling Scarp and into the tall timber of the southwest's karri forests before trailing along the coast into Albany, it has the potential to become the finest long-distance cycling route in the country.

Like the Bibbulmun Track, the Munda Biddi will feature purpose-built campsites spaced along the trail; about every 35km to 40km between towns. Each campsite will have sheltered bike racks, picnic tables, sleeping quarters (bring a sleeping mat and sleeping bag), composting toilet and drinking water.

MOUNTAIN BIKE RIDES

For information about the Munda Biddi Trail, see above. The cycling page on the **Department for Planning & Infrastructure** (www.dpi.wa.gov.au/cycling/19620.asp#2) has a good list of mountain bike tracks.

Dwellingup

Beside the Munda Biddi Trail, the Turner Hill cycle trail is a 9km cross-country, singletrack loop with plenty of short climbs – and one extended climb about 4km into the route. The track has some good technical elements – drops, log jumps etc – and some flowing descents. The website for the **Perth Mountain Bike Club** (http://perthmtb .com) has a page dedicated to Turner Hill. There's an easier 8km mountain bike loop, the Marrinup Trail, nearby. Maps of the tracks can be picked up at the Dwellingup visitors centre.

Northcliffe

Northcliffe may well be the mountain bike capital of WA, with a selection of fine trails, included a private 7km track at the Round Tu-It Caravan Park that used to host the state mountain bike championships. These have since moved out of town to the 5.7km circuit at Boorara State Championship Trail, which also hosts part of the annual Karri Cup race. Closer to town, and simpler, are the Federation Track, a 600m route inside the Jubilee Park Arboretum; and the Northcliffe Forest Park mountain bike trail, which uses firebreaks, roads and a short section of the Bibbulmun Track in its 7.7km loop. Brochures about each of the trails can be picked up at the Northcliffe visitors centre.

Kep Track

For an extended MTB outing, the Kep Track is a 75km track from Mundaring Weir (near the start of the Munda Biddi Trail) to Northam, following the course of a pipeline constructed in the 1890s to carry water from the weir to goldfields. The track surface is good and the gradient gradual, making for a cruisy ride on trails that cyclists share only with walkers and horseback riders. Detailed information about the track can be found at www.goldenpipeline.com.au.

TOWNS & FACILITIES

ALBANY
☎ 08 / pop 28,600

Hugging the calm waters of King George Sound, Albany is the WA's oldest town. Established in 1826, three years before Perth, its raison d'être is its sheltered harbour, while its coastline also features some of Australia's most rugged and spectacular scenery.

Information
Pick up a copy of the *Go Cycle Amazing Albany* brochure, which maps cycling routes within a half-hour radius of town, at the **visitors centre** (☎ 1800 644 088, 9841 9290; www.amazingalbany.com; Proudlove Pde) inside the old train station. For national-park information, visit **DOC** (☎ 08-9842 4500; 120 Albany Hwy).

Supplies & Equipment
Rainbow Cycles (☎ 08-9841 6844; 154 Albany Hwy; 9am-5.30pm Tue-Fri, 10am-4pm Sat) has a good range of gear, including racks and panniers, plus repairs. **Albany Bicycle Hire** (☎ 08-9842 2468; www.albanybicyclehire.com; 1-/4-/7-day hire $18/45/50) will deliver rental bikes anywhere in the city.

Sleeping & Eating
Albany Bayview YHA (☎ 08-9842 3388; albanyyha@westnet.com.au; 49 Duke St; dm/s/d $23/40/52) In a quiet street 400m from the centre, this rambling backpackers has a lazy feel and is less frenzied than the hostel in town. Take an upstairs room if you want bay views.

Middleton Beach Holiday Park (☎ 1800 644 674; www.holidayalbany.com.au; Middleton Beach; unpowered sites $30-47, cabins $99-161, chalets $120-240) This park has prime real estate, just a dune from the ocean, and prices to match. A bikepath goes to Middleton Beach from the end of Princess Royal Dr.

Norfolk Sands (☎ 08-9841 3585; www.norfolksands.com.au; 18 Adelaide Cres, Middleton Beach; s/d $55/80) Just a few minutes' walk from Middleton Beach, this is simple accommodation with a touch of class. The share-facility rooms are tastefully decorated with Asian-style furnishings, and breakfast is served at the fantastic Bay Merchants cafe next door.

Beach House at Bayside (☎ 08-9844 8844; www.thebeachhouseatbayside.com.au; Barry Crt; r from $207) This B&B is midway between Middleton Beach and Emu Point, and offers touches such as port and chocs each evening.

Squid Shack (☎ 0417 170 857; Emu Beach; fish & chips $12; lunch & dinner) This local institution serves fish straight from the ocean, from what is literally a shack on the beach. Stick a bottle of wine in your bottle cage and plan a sunset picnic.

Nonna's (☎ 08-9841 4626; 135 Lower York St; lunch special $15; lunch & dinner) Classic Italian food served at reasonable prices and in a cosy setting.

Vancouver 51 (☎ 08-9841 2475; 65 Vancouver St; 2-course dinner $28; lunch Tue-Sun, dinner Fri & Sat) This great little cafe is perched above the coast, with balcony views and creative fusion food such as Szechuan duck and spicy plums.

Earl of Spencer Historic Inn (☎ 08-9841 1322; cnr Earl & Spencer Sts; mains $20; lunch & dinner) On a cold night you can't beat the warming qualities of the Earl's famous pie and pint or hearty lamb shanks. It's popular for a quiet drink or, on weekends, for live music.

Take your supermarket pick from **Coles** (cnr Albany Rd & Lockyer Ave) or **Woolworths** (Lockyer Ave); they are metres apart. Or there's an **IGA** (Proudlove Pde) by the visitors centre.

AUGUSTA
☎ 08 / pop 1700

Perth motor vehicles seem to run out of petrol before they reach Augusta, with Australia's most southwesterly town happily lacking the razzamatazz of Margaret River, Dunsborough and Busselton. If you haven't seen whales down the coast yet, whale-watching tours operate from Augusta.

Information
The **visitors centre** (☎ 08-9758 0166; cnr Blackwood Ave & Ellis St) has a range of brochures, including a free walking-trail guide of the town.

Sleeping & Eating
Turner Caravan Park (☎ 08-9758 1593; turnerpark@westnet.com.au; 1 Blackwood Ave; unpowered/powered sites $22/27) Grassy and shaded by melaleucas, with good views across to the mouth of the Blackwood River.

Baywatch Manor Resort (☎ 08-9758 1290; www.baywatchmanor.com.au; 88 Blackwood Ave; dm/s $23/45, d with/

without bathroom $70/55) Classier than it sounds, Baywatch has been regularly named the YHA Australian hostel of the year. The clean, modern rooms have great facilities and it also rents out several self-contained holiday cottages around town.

Riverside Cottages (☎ 08-9758 1545; www.riversidecottagesaugusta.com.au; Molloy St; cottages $60-95) A tad tatty but clean and great value, various-sized self-contained cottages sit on the river bank. Cottage number eight is perfect for two, with a small balcony overlooking the water.

Georgiana Molloy Motel (☎ 08-9758 1255; www.augustaaccommodation.com .au; 84 Blackwood Ave; r $99-$115) Good-sized, clean, well-equipped self-contained units are stand-out value here, each with a small garden area.

Augusta Bakery & Cafe (☎ 08-9758 1664; 121 Blackwood Ave; lunch $9-22; breakfast & lunch) Its claim to be 'Australia's best' is only an exaggeration by degrees. The coffee, cakes and light lunches are excellent.

Colourpatch Café (☎ 08-9758 1295; 38 Albany Tce; takeaway/dine-in $10/25; lunch & dinner) Watch the Blackwood River meet the waters of Flinders Bay at the self-styled 'last eating house before the Antarctic'. Takeaway fish and chips (the grassy bank of the Blackwood River is just a dozen steps away) are available until 8pm.

Augusta Hotel (☎ 08-9758 1944; Blackwood Ave; mains $21-39) Counter meals with a grandstand view of the wide Blackwood River. It's all things to all diners, from chicken parma to kangaroo fillets to the menu's star item, the 'land and dam': scotch fillet and marron.

Purchase your groceries at **SupaValu** (Blackwood Ave), opposite the hotel.

BUNBURY
☎ 08 / pop 56,180

Bunbury, 184km south of Perth, has started to remake its image as industrial port into that of seaside holiday destination, led by its dolphin swim encounters at Koombana Beach.

Information

The **visitors centre** (☎ 08-9721 7922; Carmody Pl; 9am-5pm Mon-Sat, 9.30am-4.30pm Sun) is located in the historic train station.

Supplies & Equipment

City Cycles (☎ 08-9721 6438; 15A Princep St) offers sales, service and a small range of panniers and racks.

Sleeping & Eating

Dolphin Retreat YHA (☎ 08-9792 4690; dolphinretreatbunburyyha@iinet.net.au; 14 Wellington St; dm/s/d $19/29/48) Just around the corner from the beach, this small hostel is well located with hammocks and a barbecue on the back vertanda.

Koombana Bay Holiday Resort (☎ 08-9791 3900; www.bestonparks.com.au; cnr Koombana Dr & Lyons St; unpowered/powered sites $28/32, cabins from $85) The great location of this caravan park – just over a towel's throw from Koombana Beach, and close to the dolphin centre – is reflected in its higher-than-usual price.

Rose Hotel (☎ 08-9721 4533; www .rosehotel.com.au; cnr Victoria & Wellington Sts; hotel s/d with shared bathroom $58/78, motel s/d $92/99) From the chandeliers hanging in the halls to the bloke wearing the armour in the lobby, this 1865 hotel oozes character. Go for the charming, old-style hotel rooms, even though you'll share a bathroom.

Lighthouse Beach Resort (☎ 08-9721 1311; www.lighthousehotel.com.au; Carey St; r $90-140, apt $130) With a fabulous setting above (funnily enough) Lighthouse Beach, the two-room self-contained apartment in this hotel is terrific value.

Clifton (☎ 08-9721 4300; www.the clifton.com.au; 2 Molloy St; ste $240) For luxurious accommodation with lots of heritage trimmings, go for the top-of-the-range rooms in the Clifton's historic Grittleton Lodge (1885), with sleigh beds, a spa and a grand piano for ivory-tinkling.

Mojo's (☎ 08-9792 5900; Victoria St; mains $20-30) This modern cafe's sunny outdoor tables are the place to watch the world and agonise over what you'll order from the local produce–focused menu.

Walkabout Café (☎ 08-9791 6922; Victoria St; mains $22; lunch & dinner) Themed around bush Australiana; you can eat kangaroo sausages and mash here and there's a good-value $12.50 lunch menu.

Check out the recent foodie options at Boat Harbour, where **VAT Two** (☎ 08-9791 8833; 2 Jetty Rd; mains $26-32; lunch

& dinner), the Bunbury sibling of Margaret River's see-and-be-seen VAT 107, overlooks the marina. In the next block, there's fish and chips on the deck at **Aristos Waterfront** (☎08-9791 6477; fish & chips $10; lunch & dinner), while upstairs **Barbados** (☎08-9791 6555; 11am-midnight) is the place to go for a sunset drink.

For good coffee, breakfast or a light lunch try **Benesse** (Victoria St), **Caf-fez** (20 Prinsep St) or **Cafe 140** (140 Victoria St).

Gather goodies at **Woolworths** (Bunbury Plaza, 12 Forrest Ave) or **Coles** (Bunbury Centrepoint, cnr Blair & Haley Sts).

DENMARK
☎ 08 / pop 4000

If this town could be likened to the other Denmark, it would be Christiania, the Copenhagen suburb that believes Woodstock never ended. An unabashed hippy haven, it's easy to see why the town attracts folk looking to opt out from city life – gorgeous coastline, rolling hills, magnificent forests and a vibrant artistic community.

Information
A flash new **visitors centre** (☎08-9848 2055; www.denmark.com.au; South Coast Hwy) opened on the highway in 2008, and is just about as big as the town it represents.

Sleeping & Eating
Riverbend Caravan Park (☎08-9848 1107; rivabend@omninet.net.au; East River Rd; unpowered sites $14-20, powered sites $17-23, cabins from $80) About 2km from town, on a quiet stretch of river, this lovely shaded site has excellent, well-equipped cabins with private vertandas and a vegie garden.

Blue Wren Travellers' Rest YHA (☎08-9848 3300; www.denmarkbluewren.com.au; 17 Price St; dm/tw/d $19/48/55) Chooks live under this little timber house and the goofy house dog is spoilt by everyone. Great info panels cover the walls, and it's small enough to have a homey feel.

Denmark Waterfront (☎08-9848 1147; www.denmarkwaterfront.com.au; 63 Inlet Dr; lodge $75, motel $85-110, cottages from $130) With great views of the water through the gum trees, there's a range of accommodation here. The four quiet lodge

rooms are good value, tucked off the road, with a communal kitchen and great views from the balconies.

Willowleigh B&B (☎08-9848 1089; kenannrn@wn.com.au; Kearsley Rd; r $100) Enjoy the two acres of gorgeous gardens from your conservatory or vertanda at this B&B on the edge of town.

Chimes Spa Retreat (☎08-9848 2255; www.chimes.com.au; Mt Shadforth Rd; r $230-355) Architect-designed and decorated with Indonesian furniture, this place will revive you if the tour is getting too long. A day spa (book ahead for pampering) completes the five-star offering. Prices depend on the view, the size of your bed and the number of bubbles in your bath.

Figtree Café (☎08-9848 2051; 27 Strickland St; breakfast $5-18; breakfast & dinner) Unhurried best describes the style at this coffee shop, popular with locals for long weekend breakfasts in the courtyard.

Organic Indigo (☎08-9848 2999; Strickland St; mains $16; dinner Thu-Sun) Spicy Indian food, organic and served with love; there are lots of vegie choices.

Denmark River Bistro (☎08-9848 2217; 6 Hollings St; mains $15-25) Grab one of the two small outdoor tables for a view over the river at this 'cafe by day, restaurant by night'. Not the most imaginative food – chicken parma, lasagne, green curry – but there's a lovely laid-back, Denmark kind of atmosphere and a 15% menu discount on Monday and Tuesday night.

If your cycling palate isn't too demanding, **Noakes Store** (Strickland St) is a good old-fashioned country grocer; you can top up on fancier items next door at **The Source** (Strickland St), which has the likes of organic vegetables, ground coffee and chutneys. Otherwise, there's the **Supa IGA** (cnr South Coast Hwy & Strickland St).

DUNSBOROUGH
☎ 08 / pop 3300

With its beaches protected by Cape Naturaliste, Dunsborough is one of southern WA's top holiday spots, despite the fact that it feels a bit like a beach-side suburb.

Information
The **visitors centre** (☎08-9755 3299; www.geographebat.com; Naturaliste Tce) has a free accommodation-booking service.

Sleeping & Eating

Dunsborough Lakes Holiday Resort (☎ 08-9756 8300; Commonage Rd; unpowered/powered sites $24/29, cabins $85-190) A large, cabin-dominated park on the town's eastern edge, the only things small here are the golf (mini) and tennis (half-court).

Dunsborough Inn (☎ 08-9756 7277; www.dunsboroughinn.com; 50 Dunn Bay Rd; dm/d $25/50, apt $90-139) The dorms are a bit cell-like but it is a case of location, location, location, with the hostel smack-dab in the centre of town.

Dunsborough Beachouse (☎ 08-9755 3107; www.dunsboroughbeachouse.com.au; 205 Geographe Bay Rd; dm/s/d $25/36/56) On the Quindalup beachfront, this friendly hostel has the best beach location in town; it's an easy 2km cycle from the centre.

Dunsborough Rail Carriages & Farm Cottages (☎ 08-9755 3865; www.dunsborough.com; Commonage Rd; carriages $100-120, cottages $140-190) Set among red gums on a 104-acre property 4km east of town, with resident, free-roaming roos, and lemon trees and herb gardens to help spruce up meals in the self-contained cottages.

Cape Wine Bar (☎ 08-9756 7650; 239 Naturaliste Tce; mains from $20; dinner Mon-Thu, tasting plates at the bar Fri & Sat, tapas Sun) Buzzing most nights, the wine bar has a well-deserved reputation for fresh seasonal food.

Artèzen (☎ 08-9755 3325; 234 Naturaliste Tce; mains from $20; 7am-5pm Sun-Thu, 7am-9pm Fri & Sat) Groovy cafe serving everything from great breakfasts to interesting Asian-influenced dishes like squid salad with soba.

Stock up for the walk at **Coles** (Dunsborough Centrepoint, Dunn Bay Rd) or **IGA** (cnr Dunn Bay Rd & Naturaliste Tce).

MARGARET RIVER

☎ 08 / pop 5600

Though it's famed for its surf, Margaret River is actually 10km from the coast, which probably explains why wine tasters and tourists outnumber board-riders in the streets. One of WA's most popular destinations, Margaret River gets very, very busy at Easter and Christmas (when you should book weeks, if not months, ahead for accommodation), during the annual food and wine bash in November, during surf competitions in March and November, and at the time of the renowned Leeuwin Estate open-air concerts in February.

Information

The sleek **visitors centre** (☎ 08-9757 2911; www.margaretriver.com; cnr Bussell Hwy & Tunbridge St) has wads of information, plus an on-site wine centre, and can make accommodation bookings.

Supplies & Equipment

Margaret River Cycles & Repairs (☎ 08-9758 7671; 31 Station Rd; 9.30am-5pm Mon-Fri, 9am-1.30pm Sat) does just as the label suggests. Also hires out bikes.

Sleeping & Eating

Riverview Tourist Park (☎ 1300 666 105; www.riverviewtouristpark.com; 8-10 Wilmott Ave; campsites $25-35, cabins $80-180) Less than 1km from town (albeit a roller-coaster ride), this park spruiks its riverside setting, though you have to pay for a top-dollar cabin to get anywhere near the bank. It's a quiet antidote, nonetheless, to the bustle of the town.

Margaret River Lodge (☎ 08-9757 9532; www.mrlodge.com.au; 220 Railway Tce; dm/s/d/f $25/55/63/73) About 1.5km southwest of the town centre, this YHA hostel is clean and modern with a pool and volleyball court in sizable gardens.

Bridgefield (☎ 08-9757 3007; www.bridgefield.com.au; 73 Bussell Hwy; s/d $100/120) A 19th-century coach house, this lovely higgledy-piggledy B&B is all wood panels, high ceilings, tiled floors and ancient clawfoot baths.

Riverglen Chalets (☎ 08-9757 2101; www.riverglenchalets.com.au; Carters Rd; chalets $130-250) Just north of town, these good-value timber chalets are spacious and fully self-contained, with vertandas looking out onto bushland; there's full disabled access to a couple of them.

Margaret River Resort Knight's Inn (☎ 08-9757 0000; www.margaret-river-resort.com.au; 40 Wallcliffe Rd; motel/hotel/villas $160/180/330) Ignore the dinky exterior: the jarrah-dense hotel rooms here are big and gorgeous, and the motel rooms luxurious. There's a Thai restaurant attached.

Urban Bean (☎ 08-9757 3480; 157 Bussell Hwy; lunch $7-10; 7.30am-4pm) A funky little place serving bleary-eyed locals their first daily brew, and making good quiche-y things for lunch.

GoodFellas Cafe (☎ 08-9757 3184; 97 Bussell Hwy; pizza $16-21, pasta $19-22; dinner daily summer, dinner Tue-Sat winter) At GoodFellas they believe in a theme: waiters in gangster hats, Godfather posters on the walls, pizzas with names such as Capone, Reservoir Dogs and Taxi Driver. Most importantly, the cooks are guns at wood-fired pizza.

Arc of Iris (☎ 08-9757 3112; 151 Bussell Hwy; mains $25; dinner) An old favourite, it's eclectic, lively and a throwback to the hippy generation.

VAT 107 (☎ 08-9758 8877; 107 Bussell Hwy; mains $35) Retaining its trendy reputation, the food here is inventive and excellent – like Jerusalem artichoke and black-cabbage risotto with seared scallops – and a simple coffee on the veranda makes for great people-watching.

Gather up groceries at **River Fresh IGA** (Bussell Hwy) or **Coles** (Bussell Hwy). On Station Rd there's a clutch of market-style produce stores: Foodroom Bakehouse, Station Road Greengrocers and Blue Ginger Fine Foods Delicatessen and Cafe.

NANNUP
☎ 08 / pop 1200

In the heart of the southwest forests and farmland, Nannup is a quiet, historical town in a picturesque setting. It's home to the legendary Nannup tiger, a striped wolflike animal similar to the Tasmanian tiger. In anticipation of the arrival of the Munda Biddi Trail (p277), the 26km section to Jarrahwood (currently known as the Sidings Trail) opened in late 2008, the town is going bike-friendly. There's a bike-repair stand at the start of the trail in Brockman St, and businesses are being encouraged to install bike racks.

Information

The helpful **visitors centre** (☎ 08-9756 1211; www.nannupwa.com; Brockman St) is in the 1922 police station.

Sleeping & Eating

Nannup Caravan Park (☎ 08-9756 1211; Brockman St; unpowered sites $17.50-20, cabins s/d $55/66) On the river bank beside the visitors centre. Check in at the visitors centre, or phone ahead for keys if arriving after 5pm. You're unlikely to take advantage of the pay-for-six-nights-get-the-seventh-free offer.

Black Cockatoo (☎ 08-9756 1035; 27 Grange Rd; d $20) This quirky guest house is full of eclectic objects (think wood sculptures and fabrics) and surrounded by a vibrant garden that encroaches on the vertandas.

Alice Cottage (d incl breakfast $110), **Nashie's Cottage** (d $100) and **Blyth Cottage** (d $100) all offer self-contained accommodation in the town. The visitors centre handles bookings and hold keys.

Koala Thai (☎ 08-9756 0075; 10 Warren Rd; Thai mains $13; breakfast & lunch daily, dinner Fri-Sun) Unlikely as it may seem, this pretty cafe transforms itself into a Thai restaurant for eat-in or takeaway dinner at the weekend.

Hamish's Café (☎ 08-9756 1287; 1 Warren Rd; mains $22-33; breakfast & lunch daily, dinner Mon & Thu-Sat) When you can start the day with a brunch of poached eggs and kippers, and end it with carpetbag steak, you know you're not eating in your average country restaurant. Highly recommended.

If the town supermarket, **eziway** (Warren Rd), is closed, the Caltex service station has rudimentary groceries.

PEMBERTON
☎ 08 / pop 950

A curious mix of tree-huggers and tree-fellers, Pemberton is home to both a milling operation and some of the country's most beautiful forest. It also happens to be a tourist favourite. If you've arrived in a sweat, the natural and pretty Pemberton Swimming Pool, surrounded by karri trees, is ideal.

Information

The **visitors centre** (☎ 08-9776 1133; www.pembertontourist.com.au; Brockman St) includes a pioneer museum and karri-forest discovery centre.

Sleeping & Eating

Pemberton Caravan Park (☎ 08-9776 1300; Pump Hill Rd; campsites $22, cabins

$60-80) Set in a shady clearing beside a creek, this pretty campsite has good-value cabins and is a walk away from the swimming pool.

Pemberton Backpackers YHA (☎ 08-9776 1105; pembertonbackpackers@wn.com.au; 7 Brockman St; dm/s/d/cottage $19/35/51/70) This friendly backpackers, right in the centre of town, has a self-contained cottage that can sleep up to eight people over the road; the cottage is popular, so book ahead if you can.

Gloucester Motel (☎ 08-9776 1266; Ellis St; s/d $75/85) The best of the town's motels, it's off the main road and the verandas aren't quite on the car park.

Old Picture Theatre Holiday Apartments (☎ 08-9776 1513; www.oldpicturetheatre.com.au; cnr Ellis & Guppy Sts; d $110) The town's old cinema has been revamped into lovely self-contained, spacious apartments with lots of jarrah detail and black-and-white movie photos; fantastic value.

Coffee Connection (☎ 08-9776 1159; Dickinson St; mains $8-10; breakfast & lunch) Attached to the Fine Woodcraft Gallery, this garden cafe makes good coffee and maybe the cheapest breakfasts in town.

Sadies Restaurant (☎ 08-9776 1266; Gloucester Motel, Ellis St, mains $22-42; dinner Tue-Sat) Who'd have thought a motel restaurant could be so good? With a chef named the best in the southwest in 2007, it's ample reward for the final pinch up the hill to get to the place.

Shamrock Restaurant (☎ 08-9776 1186; 18 Brockman St; mains $20-30; dinner) It's hardly surprising that there's a Shamrock amid all this greenery. Expect home-style cooking with Pemberton 'home' produce: trout, marron and its 'famous' kobe beef.

Grab your groceries at **IGA** (Dean St); supplies at the **Pemberton General Store** (Brockman St) are as basic as the town layout.

PERTH
☎ 08 / pop 1.4 million

With its nearest large neighbour, Adelaide, being around 2700km away, Perth is often called the world's most isolated city, and it is indeed a place of beaches and bush as much as buildings. A city that, until recently, was all but drunk on a mining boom, it is (with Canberra) one of Australia's most cycle-friendly cities, with a web of bike paths along the Swan River, the coast and the freeways. For maps of Perth bike paths, visit www.dpi.wa.gov.au/cycling/1518.asp.

Information
Buy park passes and gather literature on parks at **CALM Outdoors** (☎ 08-9399 9746; 40 Jull St, Armadale; 9am-2pm Mon, Tue, Thu & Fri).

Western Australian Visitors centre (☎ 1300 361 351; www.westernaustralia.net; Albert Facey House, cnr Forrest Pl & Wellington St) books tours, and you can flick through brochures over a coffee in the cafe attached.

Supplies & Equipment
Bike Force (www.bikeforce.com.au) has the greatest concentration of bike shops in Perth – Fremantle, Subiaco, Balcatta, Canning Vale – though **Mercer Cycles** (☎ 08-9335 9536; 97 South Tce, Fremantle; 9am-5.30pm Mon-Fri, 9am-5pm Sat) is the most comprehensive store. Stock includes panniers and racks.

About Bike Hire (☎ 08-9221 2665; www.aboutbikehire.com.au; Point Fraser Reserve, 1-7 Riverside Dr; bike hire per day/week $33/70) rents out road bikes, mountain bikes and hybrids, as well as panniers (per week $25) and BOB trailers (per week $70).

Perth Map Centre (☎ 08-9322 5733; www.mapworld.com.au; 900 Hay St; 9am-5.30pm Mon-Thu, 9am-6pm Fri, 10am-4pm Sat) has a full range of state and regional maps and travel guides.

Sleeping & Eating
Central Caravan Park (☎ 08-9277 1704; www.perthcentral.com.au; 34 Central Ave, Ascot; unpowered/powered sites $30/32, cabins d $95) Pinched between the Swan River and the airport, this somewhat cramped park is the closest camping option to the city.

Perth City YHA (☎ 08-9287 3333; www.yha.com.au; 300 Wellington St; dm $21-24, s $50, d with/without bathroom $75/62, non-YHA members add $5) This is the YHA experience at its best. Sure, it's a little predictable, and has that boarding-school feel in the halls, but the floorboards gleam (and charmingly creak) and the brightly painted rooms still smell new. In a well-preserved 1940s art-deco building in a quieter part of town, perhaps the best bit is the bathrooms: half the rooms have brand-spanking-new en suites. Family and twin rooms also available.

Governor Robinsons (☎ 08-9328 3200; www.govrobinsons.com.au; 7 Robinson Ave; dm $22, d from $60) More like a communal B&B than a backpackers, with leather sofas, a large dining table and a cottage-style kitchen, quietly removed from Northbridge's scruffier edges.

Hotel Northbridge (☎ 08-9328 5254; www.hotelnorthbridge.com.au; 210 Lake St; d with spa $120-140) Has an exterior like a country pub but is like a boutique hotel inside. The guest vertanda has perfect city views, and a recent refurbishment has dropped a spa in every single room.

Pension of Perth (☎ 08-9228 9049; www.pensionperth.com.au; 3 Throssell St; s/d from $115/145) Settle into a second home at this luxury B&B overlooking leafy Hyde Park. Exquisitely furnished and sociable, it has discounts over winter and for extended stays.

Riverview on Mount Street (☎ 08-9321 8963; www.riverview.au.com; 42 Mount St; d from $95) These converted, self-contained apartments have the best address in town, eye-balling the city high-rises but with Kings Park as their backyard. Front rooms overlook the Swan River.

No 44 King St (☎ 08-9321 4476; 44 King St; mains $18.50-33; 7am-late) Sift through a global list of coffees, cakes and wines, or settle in for a large breakfast or classy dinner from a menu that changes weekly.

Annalakshmi (☎ 08-9221 3003; www.annalakshmi.com.au; Jetty 4, Barrack St; pay by donation; lunch Tue-Fri, dinner Tue-Sun) Though it takes in 360-degree views of the Swan River and the city, this is no tourist cash cow: Annalakshmi is a curry house run by volunteers (formidable baby boomers, in the main) and you pay by donation. Assorted hippies and other locals line up for spicy potato-and-pumpkin curries and fragrant dhal. Chilled coconut milk and cardamom desserts cleanse the palate. It's all good fun.

Belgian Beer Café Westende (☎ 08-9321 4094; cnr Murray & King Sts; mains $21-41; lunch & dinner), Expect more than lager louts at this cafe-cum-pub, where the menu includes goat tagine and seared salmon; you will love the food even if you hate Brussels.

Perth is closer to parts of Asia than it is to Sydney, and this is reflected in the number and variety of Asian restaurants around the city.

Sparrow (☎ 08-9228 2238; 434A William St; lunch from $5.50, dinner from $6; lunch Fri & Sat, dinner Mon-Sat) is a popular Indonesian joint with the cheapest prices this side of Denpasar.

Lido Restaurant (☎ 08-9227 5545; 416 William St, Northbridge; mains $8-15; lunch Mon-Fri, dinner daily) straddles the Vietnam–China food border, making it possible to follow rice-paper rolls with any number of sweet-and-sour dishes.

Stock the larder at **Woolworths** (Murray St Mall), just 100m from the bus station. **City Provisions** (868 Hay St or 1266 Hay St, West Perth) has a small but excellent range of groceries, especially if your bush palette comes down on the gourmet side.

Getting There & Away
AIR
The domestic and international terminals of **Perth Airport** (☎ 08-9478 8888; www.perthairport.net.au) are 10km and 13km east of the city respectively.

Qantas (☎ 13 13 13; www.qantas.com.au; 55 William St), **Virgin Blue** (☎ 13 67 89; www.virginblue.com.au) and **Tiger Airways** (☎ 03-9335 3033; www.tigerairways.com) fly between Perth and other Australian state capitals. **Jetstar** (☎ 13 15 38; www.jetstar.com) runs cheapies from Avalon, Melbourne.

Skywest (☎ 1300 660 088; www.skywest.com.au) flies between Perth and regional destinations such as Albany and Broome, as well as flying to/from Melbourne (Tullamarine) three times a week.

Taxi fares from the airport to the city are around $25/35 from the domestic/international terminal. The **Perth Airport City Shuttle** (☎ 08-9277 7958; www.perthshuttle.com.au; domestic/international terminals $12/15, bike $5) provides transport to the city centre, hotels and hostels. It meets incoming domestic and international flights. Bookings are essential (24 hours ahead if possible) and bikes must be boxed. It is a simple task to ride into the city from the airports, joining the Swan River bike track by Ascot Racecourse.

BUS
The long-distance coach bookings office is located at the Perth train station.

For masochists, **Greyhound Australia** (☎ 13 14 99; www.greyhound.com.au) buses leave from the Wellington St bus station for Darwin ($810, 60 hours, one daily).

TRAIN
Perth has only one interstate rail link: the famous Indian Pacific transcontinental train journey, run by **Great Southern Railway** (☎ 13 21 47; www.trainways.com.au), which leaves from East Perth station. To Perth from Sydney, one-way fares are about $590 (seat only), $422 (seat only, backpacker rate) or $1320 (sleeper cabin). Between Adelaide and Perth, fares are $355 (seat only), $253 (seat only, backpacker), or $1005 (sleeper cabin). There are connections to the Ghan (to Alice Springs and Darwin) and the Overland (to Melbourne) trains.

You can buy train tickets at the Interstate and Country booking office at the Perth train station. The office is off Wellington St.

BICYCLE
Only the hardiest folk will approach Perth by bicycle because it means either riding across the Nullarbor or along the even more difficult west coast. If you are entering the city by bike you can download route maps at www.dpi.wa.gov.au/cycling.

CAR
All of the major car rental companies – **Avis** (☎ 13 63 33; 46 Hill St), **Budget** (☎ 13 27 27; 960 Hay St), **Hertz** (☎ 13 30 39; 39 Milligan St) and **Thrifty** (☎ 1300 367 227, within WA 13 61 39; 198 Adelaide Tce) – also have airport offices. Some local operators, such as **Bayswater Hire Car** (☎ 08-9325 1000; 160 Adelaide Tce), can be cheaper, but make sure you read the fine print. Note that some insurance policies, even with the bigger companies, don't cover you outside the metropolitan area after dark – in case you hit a roo.

ROTTNEST ISLAND
☎ 08

Tourist facilities and accommodation on Rottnest cling to the shores of Thomson and Geordie Bays, near to where the ferries dock.

Information
The **visitors centre** (☎ 08-9372 9752; 7.30am-5pm Sat-Thu, 7.30am-7pm Fri) is at the end of the main jetty.

Sleeping & Eating
There's no accommodation on Rottnest that you'd stick in the pages of *Luxury Traveller*, but that's the charm that Rotto's long-time visitors love. The island is wildly popular in summer and school holidays, when ferries and accommodation are booked out months in advance. There's even a ballot system for accommodation through the summer school holidays.

Allison campsite (☎ 08-9432 9111; Thomson Bay; campsites $8.50) Camping is restricted to this campsite beside the oval. It's known as Tentland by the surfers and students who colonise this patch of Rotto. Be vigilant about your belongings.

Kingston Barracks Youth Hostel (☎ 08-9432 9111; dm $24) These old army barracks are popular with school groups. Check in at the accommodation office at the main jetty before you make the 1.8km ride to Kingston.

Rottnest Island Authority Cottages (☎ 08-9432 9111; 4-bedroom oceanfront villas Sun-Thu/Fri-Sat $170/200, 4-bedroom oceanfront cottages Sun-Thu/Fri-Sat from $210/260) There are more than 250 villas and cottages, some with magnificent beachfront positions, for rent around the island. Linen provided. Note that there are off-season discounts.

Rottnest Lodge (☎ 08-9292 5161; www.rottnestlodge.com.au; Kitson St; d/f from $170/240) It's claimed there are ghosts in this comfortable complex, which is based around the former Quod and boys reform school. If that worries you, ask for one of the cheery rooms with a view in the new section fronting onto a salt lake.

Quokka Arms (☎ 08-9292 5011; quokkaarms@rottnestisland.com; 1 Bedford Ave; s/d $180/200) This beachfront building (1864) is Rotto's most popular watering

WESTERN AUSTRALIA

hole. The rooms are clean but nothing fancy; some have water views.

Rottnest Tearooms (☎ 08-9292 5171; Thomson Bay; mains $17.50-30) Grab an oceanfront table on the veranda for a burger or cuppa.

Vlamingh's (☎ 08-9292 5011; Quokka Arms, 1 Bedford Ave; mains $18-30) After a sunset drink at the pub, wander a few metres over to this beach-side restaurant, serving dishes such as mushroom, pumpkin and fennel risotto.

Marlins Restaurant (☎ 08-9292 5161; Rottnest Lodge, Kitson St; mains $24-32) Marlins is the other higher-end option on the island, focused on seafood-inflected risotto and pastas. The surrounds may be a bit dated, but it's intimate and relaxing nonetheless.

There's no exceptional dining to be had on the island; in general, self-catering is your best option. The general store, in the main mall, is like a small supermarket and even has a juice bar. **Rottnest Bakery** (☎ 08-9292 5023) is next door. If you like your food franchised, Rottnest now has a Subway and Red Rooster.

SHANNON

This attractive **campsite** (per person $7.50) has 23 sites sprinkled among the trees, or you can throw your stuff down in one of the basic stove-heated huts. The bunks consist of nothing more than wood slats so you'll need to be carrying a mattress and sleeping bag. There are hot showers (once you get the wood heater going), three walking trails and a BBQ shelter beside site No 6. Fill up with water at the picnic area across the highway – it's the literal long way between drinks from here.

There's also the basic **Shannon Lodge** (up to 10 people $66), which you can rent for the night. You must book ahead through the Donnelly district office of the **Department of Environment and Conservation** (☎ 08-9776 1207; donnelly.district@dec .wa.gov.au; Kennedy St, Pemberton) and a $150 bond is required. The lodge has single beds and hot water, including a shower.

WALPOLE
☎ 08 / pop 450
Surrounded entirely by the large forests of Walpole–Nornalup National Park, Walpole

might just as well have roots rather than foundation.

Information
Staff at the **visitors centre** (☎ 08-9840 1111; Pioneer Cottage, South Coast Hwy) are very helpful, while **CALM** (☎ 08-9840 1027; South Coast Hwy) is at the western end of town if you want national-park information.

Sleeping & Eating
Coalmine Beach (☎ 08-9840 1026; www .coalminebeach.com.au; Knoll Dr, Walpole; unpowered/powered sites per person from $13/16, cabins from $65) You couldn't get a better location than this, under shady trees above the beach. In quiet periods you might be lucky to hit a free fish night, when the owners cook up the day's catch.

Tingle All Over YHA (☎ 08-9840 1041; tingleallover2000@yahoo.com.au; Nockolds St; dm/s/d $22/38/50) A basic hostel presented with a touch of care; exercise your brain with the giant chess set in the garden.

Nornalup Riverside Chalets (☎/fax 08-9840 1107; Riverside Dr, Nornalup; chalets $80-125) If you press on the few kilometres to sleepy Nornalup, you'll find these comfortable, colourful self-contained chalets, just a rod's throw from the Frankland River.

Tree Top Walk Motel (☎ 1800 420 777; www.treetopwalkmotel.com.au; Nockolds St; d $125) Has an opportunistic name – the famous Tree Top Walk is about 20km away – but also large, neat rooms and Walpole's only genuine restaurant (mains $29 to $40; open for dinner).

Top Deck Cafe (☎ 08-9840 1344; 25 Nockolds St; breakfast & lunch) The best of Walpole's breakfast options, with pancakes, smoked-salmon scrambled eggs and standard artery blockers.

Walpole Hotel Motel (☎ 08-9840 1023; South Coast Hwy; mains $18-32; dinner) Old-fashioned pub grub; the sort that still believes peas and corn make decent companions. **Pioneer Store IGA** (Nockolds St) The best of Walpole's two supermarkets, with a decent range of supplies.

Queensland

HIGHLIGHTS

- Rolling beneath a toothy skyline of rock in the castaway **Numinbah Valley** (p291)
- Threading between the abstract peaks of the **Glass House Mountains** (p304)
- Hitting your stride amidst the throngs on **Cairns' foreshore promenade** (p316)
- Meeting the past preserved in the mining and mill towns of the **Atherton Tableland** (p322)
- Crossing paths with a cassowary on the rainforest road to **Cape Tribulation** (p317)

TERRAIN

Coast-hugging ranges make for a good mix of plains and hills, with most rides in this chapter at least banking onto the slopes.

Telephone code – 07	www.queenslandholidays .com.au	www.bq.org.au

You have to love a place where cycling in your boardshorts or bikini is considered *de rigueur*. Queensland is that place. Australia's reef and beef state is an enormous chunk of land, five times larger than Japan and twice the size of Texas, with a strip of coast that has become one of Australia's major tourist features, luring beach bums, sailors, divers, bushwalkers and a steady trickle of touring cyclists.

West of the Great Dividing Range, Queensland is a place for the frontier cyclist but east of the range, against the coast that launched 1000 postcards, there's some fantastic cycling. The rides in this chapter showcase some of the state's finest natural features – the Gold Coast hinterland, the Glass House Mountains, Magnetic Island, the World Heritage–listed Daintree – mostly from the comfort of back roads, away from the Bruce Hwy, which might be one of Australia's most unsuitable cycling roads (think large trucks and tiny road verges).

More than half of Australia's east coast is in Queensland, with the Great Barrier Reef running offshore for much of its length, so it's little surprise that popping in and out of beaches is one of the great pleasures of cycling here – Cape Tribulation and Horseshoe Bay will be proof enough of that. But it's the hinterland that is Queensland's surprise packet, with torrential waterfalls draining from the Atherton Tableland and sharp-tipped lava plugs piercing through rainforest and pineapple plantations behind the Gold and Sunshine Coasts.

Come for the beaches, but expect so much more.

QUEENSLAND

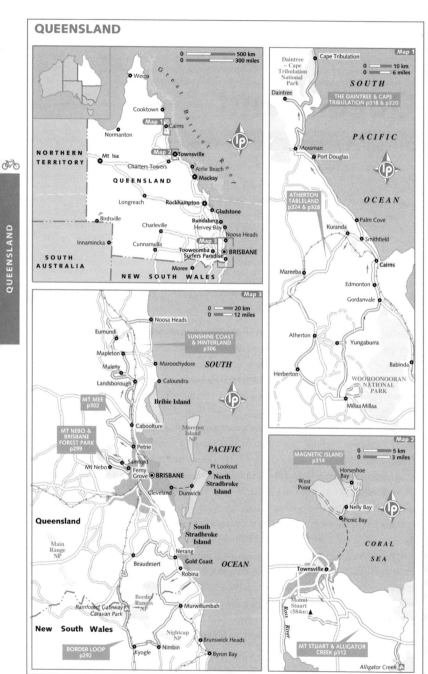

ENVIRONMENT

Queensland is Australia's second largest state, covering almost one quarter of the continent's area, ranging from the Great Barrier Reef, to Mitchell grass plains to the Simpson Desert in the west. It has almost 7000km of coastline on the mainland and almost as much again around its 1900-plus islands.

The spine of the Great Dividing Range separates a narrow, wet, coastal plain from the great, dry expanse of the outback. All of the rides described are east of the divide, where towns are closer together and the landscape is more lush and varied.

Protected lands, including around 220 national parks, make up just over 4% of Queensland's area, and the state is home to five of Australia's 17 Unesco World Heritage sites: the fossil sites at Riversleigh in the state's northwest, Fraser Island, the Great Barrier Reef, the Wet Tropics and the Gondwana Rainforests that sprawl across the Queensland–New South Wales border. Two of these areas feature in rides in this chapter, with the Border Loop ride showcasing parts of the Gondwana Rainforests, and the Daintree & Cape Tribulation ride burrowing into the Wet Tropics.

CLIMATE

Despite the images of sun, sun and sun, Queensland has one of the most varied climates of any of the Australian states – this may be the Sunshine State but Tully and Babinda in far north Queensland jostle for the title of Australia's wettest town, averaging more than 4m a year.

North Queensland has a pronounced Wet season (January to March) that delivers well above half the annual rainfall, which averages 2220mm in Cairns. Southeast Queensland has a less-pronounced Wet season (Brisbane's average annual rainfall is 1150mm), but winter (June to August) is markedly drier than the summer. January (with an average temperature of 29.4°C in Brisbane, 31.8°C in Cairns) is the hottest month, and enough rain falls statewide to drive the humidity up to sauna levels.

The combined sea breeze and trade wind give the state a predominantly southeasterly airflow. This makes for a good run if you are heading up the coast, but works like a handbrake if you are heading south.

PLANNING
When to Cycle

Queensland offers that rare Australian treat – good winter riding. While southern states shiver between June and August, Queensland is at its comfortable, dry best – Brisbane averages about 20°C in midwinter, and Cairns around 25°C.

Queensland is a holiday state and coastal areas are inundated with tourists over the summer holidays, particularly the two weeks after Christmas, and for the Easter break. Summer (December to February) is also best avoided for climatic reasons – the north of the state can be awash with rain, while even in the state's southern reaches humidity hovers around 70% (closer to 80% in the north).

Bike Hire

Brisbane has no suitable bike-hire outlets for touring outside of the city. In the north, **Cairns Scooter & Bicycle Hire** (☎ 07-4031 3444; www.cairnsbicyclehire.com.au; 47 Shields St) hires out mountain bikes for $60 a week.

Maps

The **Royal Automobile Club of Queensland** (RACQ; ☎ 13 1905; www.racq.com.au) produces a series of road maps covering the whole state, but at 1:1,250,000 they can lack detail. Southeast Queensland is better covered at 1:420,000. The maps are available from RACQ offices.

Hema's 1:2,500,000 *Queensland State Map* and its associated regional maps are great for travel planning. Sunmap has a 1:2,500,000 state map, regional maps and a series of 1:25,000 and 1:50,000 topographic maps.

Books

Lonely Planet's *Queensland & The Great Barrier Reef* guide makes a useful companion. For a good selection of rides in and around the capital, the Gold Coast and the Sunshine Coast, pick up a copy of *Where to Ride South East Queensland* by Ian Melvin. Off-roaders can find guidance in *Where to Mountain Bike in South East Queensland*.

Cycling Events

Fleche Opperman All Day Trial (www.audax.org.au; Mar) Teams of three to five

QUEENSLAND

cyclists ride over a course at least 360km in length, finishing in Brisbane.

Coot-tha Challenge (www.bq.org.au; Mar) Part of Queensland's Bike Week, this is a 2.3km, 9%-grade climb to Mt Coot-tha.

Brissie to the Bay (www.brissietothebay .com.au; Jul) A 50km fundraising ride from Brisbane to Wynnum (and return), or ease back on the 25km or 10km courses.

Cycle Queensland (www.bq.org.au; Sep) A week-long supported tour in changing locations around the state.

Brisbane to the Gold Coast Cycle Challenge (www.bq.org.au; Oct) A mass of riders pedalling 100km from South Brisbane to Southport (or a shorter 60km route).

Crocodile Trophy (www.crocodile -trophy.com; Oct) Billed as the hardest, longest and hottest mountain bike race in the world, with competitors racing around far north Queensland.

Information Sources

Begin your quest for information at the following places:

Bicycle Queensland (☎ 07-3844 1144; www.bq.org.au; 28 Vulture St, West End) Queensland's cycling-advocacy body, organising rides and selling books and other cycling gear.

Queensland Parks and Wildlife Service (www.epa.qld.gov.au) Official site with extensive information about Queensland's national parks and conservation areas.

Queensland Transport (www.transport .qld.gov.au/cycling) State government webpage on all things cycling around the state.

Tourism Queensland (www.queens landholidays.com.au) Official tourism site, providing comprehensive information on destinations, accommodation, attractions, tours and more.

Cycle Tours

Bicycle Tours of Queensland (www.bicycle toursqld.com.au) One- and two-day tours around the Sunshine Coast and hinterland.

Bushranger Bikes (☎ 07-3139 1402; www.bushrangerbikes.com.au) Range of off-road tours, both day and overnight, in southeast Queensland.

Revolution Cycling (☎ 07-3103 2617; www.revolutioncycling.com.au) Tours around the Sunshine Coast and hinterland.

GETTING AROUND

Greyhound Australia (☎ 13 14 99; www .greyhound.com.au) The most extensive bus network in the state, servicing the coast from Coolangatta to Cairns; to carry a boxed or disassembled bike costs $25, while assembled bikes cost $49.

Premier Motor Service (☎ 13 34 10; www.premierms.com.au) is the main competitor on the Brisbane–Cairns route. It charges $25 for a boxed bike and $55 for unboxed.

Queensland has a good rail network that services the coast between Brisbane and Cairns, operated by Travel Train (www .traveltrain.com.au), a wing of **Queensland Rail** (☎ 1300 131 722; www.qr.com.au). The two trains of use to cyclists are the *Sunlander*, which travels between Brisbane and Cairns three times a week, and the *Tilt* train, which also runs between Brisbane and Cairns three times a week. Pedals must be removed from the bike and the handlebars turned parallel to the frame. Bikes are charged at 20% of the adult economy fare for the journey. Note that the *Tilt* train to Rockhampton and Bundaberg do not carry bikes.

GATEWAYS

See Brisbane (p333) and Cairns (p336).

THE SOUTHEAST

As if by force of gravity, the majority of Queensland's population is scrunched into a corner around Brisbane, the Gold Coast and Sunshine Coast. Cycling networks have sprung up around them, making the area perhaps Queensland's finest for cycling.

Most visitors come to beach themselves on the sands of the Gold or Sunshine Coasts, but for cyclists most of the interest is inland, amid the ranges that hold the coast at arm's length from the vast outback beyond. Behind the Gold Coast, the hinterlands' ranges are cloaked in vestiges of the Gondwana Rainforests; out of Brisbane the hills offer quiet climbs and wide views back over the city; and the Blackall Range and Mary Valley will keep you fuelled on Devonshire teas, cheeses and coastal views.

BORDER LOOP

Duration 5 days
Distance 325.3km
Difficulty demanding
Start Robina
Finish Nerang

Summary Loop out and back across the Border Ranges, switching between two states and two states of mind: the glam Gold Coast and the hippie haven of the northern New South Wales hinterland.

Behind the beaches of the Gold Coast lurks southeast Queensland's true gold, the hinterland of hills and ancient forest that wrap around Mt Warning, constituting the rim of the largest volcanic caldera in the southern hemisphere. Mt Warning, one of the centrepieces of this ride, is a remnant of the volcanic plug from inside the chamber of the ancient volcano.

There are no lava flows here today, but the climbs to cross and recross the Queensland–New South Wales border through the rugged McPherson Range will certainly burn your thighs. Compensation comes in a string of beautiful valleys, some fascinating rock formations, a landscape that changes from rainforested ranges to dry grazing lands near Beaudesert, and a virtual loop of Mt Warning – the upturned nose of which is one of the most striking sights in the region.

If you plan to take any of the side trips, allow an extra day or two.

PLANNING
When to Cycle
The cool heights of the McPherson Range make this one of the few Queensland rides that's feasible in summer, though you'll pay for it on the climbs. Spring and autumn are the best seasons, but it is possible to ride this route year-round.

Maps
The RACQ 1:420,000 *Gold Coast–Northern Rivers* map is one of the few that cover the whole border area. The NRMA 1:200,000 *Far North Coast* map offers far greater detail for the sections of riding south of Burleigh Heads and Numinbah.

GETTING TO/FROM THE RIDE
Beginning in Robina, this ride can be easily accessed from both Brisbane (p333) and Surfers Paradise (p345). From Roma St station in Brisbane, **Translink** (☎ 13 1230; www.translink.com.au) trains run to Robina ($11.50, 1¼ hours) and return to Roma St from Nerang ($10, 70 minutes).

From Surfers Paradise, bike routes link to Nerang and Robina – maps of the routes can be downloaded at www.goldcoast.qld .gov.au. Type 'cycling' into the search box and click on the 'Cycling & Bikeways' link.

THE RIDE
Day 1: Robina to Murwillumbah
4–7½ hours, 72.3km
Leave the high-rises for the high hills, passing through the rainforest beauty of Springbrook National Park before dipping into two of the country's most beautiful valleys.

From Robina, a short bike lane guides you out of the scrum of the Gold Coast, warming up your legs on the rises over the first 10km until the climb begins in earnest. The road to Springbrook National Park is a favourite training ground for race cyclists – it's a lovely coiling ascent, relentless but without any particularly steep stretches as its rises through dry evergreen forest into pockets of subtropical rainforest.

Prepare to ride your brakes as the road drops steeply (350m over 4.5km) off the back of the Wunburra Range into the **Numinbah Valley**, arguably the most beautiful valley in southeast Queensland. Leaving the township of Numinbah (31.7km), the valley closes in beneath Turtle Rock and the honeycombed escarpment at the eastern edge of Lamington National Park. For a time the route also follows the route of the Gold Coast Hinterland Great Walk, a 54km bushwalking route linking the Springbrook and Lamington plateaus – the walk turns away from the road beneath Turtle Rock.

Natural Bridge, a short side trip at 43km, is an impressive formation, where Cave Creek plunges into a cave. A 1km circuit walk passes through some gorgeous rainforest, and there are a couple of accommodation options nearby if you want to stick around and see the glowworms in the forest.

QUEENSLAND

QUEENSLAND

BORDER LOOP

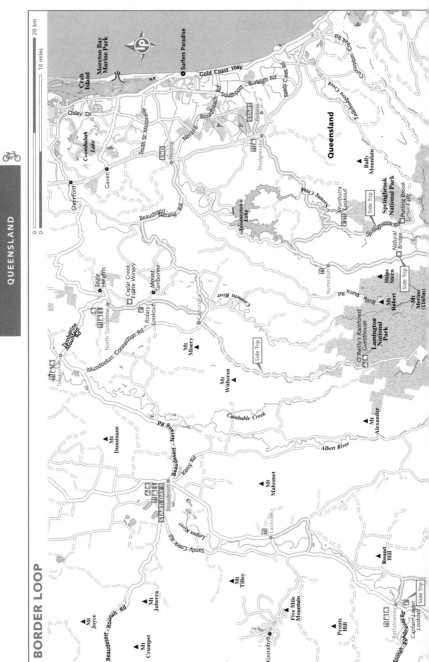

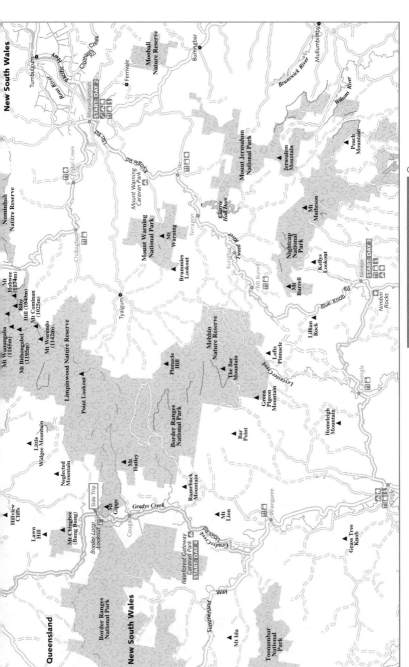

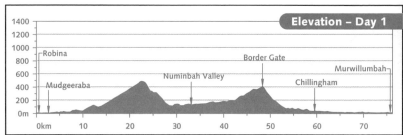

Elevation – Day 1

BORDER LOOP – DAY 1

CUE		GPS COORDINATES
start	Robina train station (west exit)	153°23'21"E 28°04'41"S
0km	go S on station access road	
0.1	Robina Centre Dr	
1.6	Railway St	
2.3	Mudgeeraba	153°21'54"E 28°04'42"S
2.5	to Springbrook'	
2.9	Gold Coast-Springbrook Rd	
9.5	2.2 moderate	
13.2	7.8km moderate	
21.0	to Natural Bridge'	
	straight on Purling Brook Falls 11km	

CUE CONTINUED		GPS COORDINATES
22.1	4.5km steep descent	
28.1	to Natural Bridge'	
30.0	1.1km moderate	
31.7	Numinbah	153°13'34"E 28°08'38"S
40.5	5.7km moderate	
43.0	Natural Bridge 0.8km	
46.2	NSW/Qld border	
56.9	Chillingham	153°16'40"E 28°18'51"S
60.6	Crystal Creek	153°19'41"E 28°18'42"S
65.2	to Alt. Murwillumbah'	
71.4	Wollumbin St	
72.3	Murwillumbah visitors centre	153°23'36"E 28°19'38"S

From the border (46.2km) there are views of Mt Warning all the way into **Chillingham**, an interesting little town, as you'll probably note from the caterpillar shadehouse, the flute workshop and the bush tucker garden with its finger-lime marmalades, rosella jams and seasonal fruits. The road wriggles east from Chillingham, along the Rous Valley, into Murwillumbah.

SIDE TRIP: PURLING BROOK FALLS
¾–1 hour, 11km

A whole day could easily be spent exploring the lush Springbrook Plateau, fringed with delightful waterfalls and lookouts to the coast and beyond. There's a range of accommodation strung along the plateau if you do decide to stay.

Continue along Springbrook Rd, climbing steeply up an intriguing one-way section. After 800m, the road passes **Wunburra lookout**, from where the view is like a road map of your ride thus far, peering through the valley to the spiky skyline of the Gold Coast – the large white building at the forefront of the strip is the stadium beside Robina train station. Opposite the lookout is **Paddymelons**

Restaurant & Cafe (☎ 07-5533 5126; lunch & dinner Fri-Sun).

After about 5km turn left on Forestry Rd and follow it to the park's entrance, from where it's a 300m walk to a lookout over the high **Purling Brook Falls** (or you can walk a 6km loop to a swimming hole). If you're staying the night, make a booking with the **Springbrook Research Observatory** (☎ 07-5533 5055; $15) for a telescopic viewing of the evening sky.

Enjoy the steep descent (16%) to complete the loop.

Day 2: Murwillumbah to Nimbin
3–5½ hours, 48.9km

Today's ride creeps gradually up the rural Tweed Valley before clambering out of the caldera and into the catchment of the Richmond River, where Nimbin stands frozen in a cannabis cloud of time. Learn to love pick-a-plank bridges, you have to thread your way across seven of them this day.

Mt Warning dominates the first half of the route and, at 10.2km, the ride passes the turning into the mountain. It's a spectacular peak, and the first place in

THE ENDLESS AGE OF AQUARIUS

In Nimbin it has been the Age of Aquarius for more than 35 years. Founded as a timber town in the 19th century, Nimbin came to prominence in 1973 when the Australian Union of Students organised the Aquarius Festival in the Nimbin Valley.

The festival ran for 10 days and was like a lingering piece of the 1960s; Woodstock with a Strine accent. And though the stage was dismantled, the spirit of the festival was not. Many who attended the festival chose to stay on in Nimbin, sometimes pooling their money to buy land to establish communes. Nimbin, a conservative dairying town, was transformed into a peace- and pipe-loving kind of place.

Today, the area around Nimbin is known as the 'Rainbow District'; the town is awash in a swirl of murals, and the young blokes in the main street asking if you 'wanna smoke' aren't tobacconists.

If you want to indulge in the Nimbin vibe, pay a visit to the wacky and wonderful **Nimbin Museum** (☎ 02-6689 1123; 62 Cullen St; admission free; 9am-5pm), which pays homage to crashed Kombis in psychedelic garb and the pursuit of 'loving the child within yourself'; or visit the **Hemp Embassy** (Cullen St; 9am-5pm), which features none-too-subtle displays about hemp and marijuana.

On the third and fifth Sunday of the month, Nimbin holds the **Aquarius Fair Markets**, a spectacular affair of produce, art and live music where locals revel in their culture.

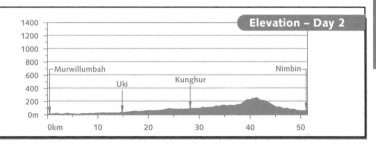

BORDER LOOP – DAY 2

CUE			GPS COORDINATES
start		Murwillumbah visitors centre	153°23'36"E 28°19'38"S
0km		go W on Alma St	
1.0		Riverview St	
8.3	★	fruit stall	
14.1		Uki	153°20'12"E 28°24'51"S
25.3	⚠	pick-a-plank bridge	
31.1		Mt Burrell	153°12'59"E 28°29'14"S
31.4	⚠	pick-a-plank bridge	
33.7	⚠	pick-a-plank bridge	

CUE CONTINUED			GPS COORDINATES
34.9	⚠	pick-a-plank bridge	
35.2	⚠	pick-a-plank bridge	
36.3		to Nimbin'	
	⚠	1.3km moderate climb	
38.2	⚠	400m moderate climb	
47.8	⚠	pick-a-plank bridge	
48.6	⚠	pick-a-plank bridge	
48.9		Nimbin visitors centre	153°13'24"E 28°35'38"S

Australia to see the rising sun, but it's only worth making the side trip if you intend to climb the mountain, which is sacred to the Indigenous Bundjalung people. Under their law, only specific people are allowed to climb the peak, so they request that visitors choose also not to climb it. If you decide to do so, it's a 750m climb from the car park and you will probably need to stay the night: **Mt Warning Caravan Park & Tourist Retreat** (☎ 02-6679 5120; Mt Warning Rd; campsites from $18, cabins from $55), on the approach road, has good kitchen facilities and a well-stocked kiosk.

At 8.3km, stock up on fruit at the stall, or there's time to compile a shopping list from the trail of handmade signs in the kilometres before another fruit stall at Mt Burrell.

The road into Nimbin, the capital of the so-called 'Rainbow District' (see boxed text p295), is bumpy and potholed, a reflection, perhaps, on the local culture. Are the road workers distracted by the beauty of the area, cash-strapped, or just stoned?

Day 3: Nimbin to Gradys Creek
3½–6 hours, 58.5km

A roller-coasting day of small climbs and wide views, though the second half of the day, along the Richmond Valley, is as flat as the first half is hilly.

As the ride leaves town, it passes beneath **Nimbin Rocks**, spearing Warrumbungles-like out of the hillsides. The rocks are an important part of the Bundjalung Aboriginal folklore. One story tells of Nimbun, who was imprisoned in a cave in the rock known as the Cathedral. He escaped by charging through the wall, creating a hole visible today. In 1990 the site was handed back to the traditional owners. Glance back for a final view of the rocks as you crest the first climb, where Mt Warning also reappears to

the north, framed by other peaks but still the most striking feature of the landscape.

Cawongla (18.1km) is an easy place to pause, especially with the day's toughest climb just beginning. The Cawongla Store has a licensed cafe (there's wood-fired pizza on Friday, Saturday and Sunday) and picnic tables but the real highlight is the rustic building.

At around 27km, the route pops out above the Richmond Valley, winding down into its green expanses and the town of Kyogle. Stock up on food here because there are no stores at Gradys Creek. If you're desperate for bike parts, **Doug Campbell Saw Works** (☎ 02-6632 1619; 12 Geneva St) has tyres and wheels but little else.

The Lions Clubs of Kyogle and Beaudesert combined forces in the early 1970s to join existing roads along Gradys and Running Creeks; thus the **Lions Rd tourist route** was born (you can pick up a guide to the road at the general store in Wiangaree). It begins by crossing Richmond River and heads up-valley, crossing and recrossing Gradys Creek, its tributaries and the Sydney–Brisbane railway line.

Day 4: Gradys Creek to Beaudesert
4–7½ hours, 73.2km

After some solid climbing early on and a whooping descent into Queensland, this day's route becomes mostly flat, touching down at the edge of the plains that stretch out for eternity west of the Great Dividing Range.

At the foot of the climb out of Gradys Valley, **Cougal** feels a little like the OK Corral with its line of abandoned, rusted farm buildings. It's a tough grind out of the valley, cutting through the rainforested edge of Border Ranges National Park to the

BORDER LOOP – DAY 3

CUE			GPS COORDINATES
start		Nimbin visitors centre	153°13'24"E 28°35'38"S
0km		go S on Cullen St	
1.6	⌐►	Stony Chute Rd	
6.1	▲	2.5km moderate climb	
11.7	▲	1.8km moderate climb	
13.7	⌐↰	Kyogle Rd	
14.6	▲	600m moderate climb	
17.7	▲	4.1km steep climb	
18.1		Cawongla	153°06'11"E 28°35'30"S
29.8	⌐↰	Kyogle Rd	
31.5	⌐►	to Brisbane', Kyogle"	153°00'17"E 28°37'15"S
44.8		Wiangaree	152°58'03"E 28°30'21"S
49.8	⌐►	Lions Rd	
58.5		Rainforest Gateway Caravan Park, Gradys Creek	152°58'24"E 28°22'40"S

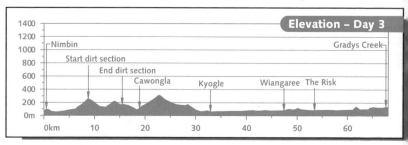

Elevation – Day 3

| 1400 |
| 1200 |
1000	Nimbin					Gradys Creek
800	Start dirt section
600	End dirt section
400	Cawongla	Kyogle	Wiangaree	The Risk
200
0m
0km	10	20	30	40	50	60

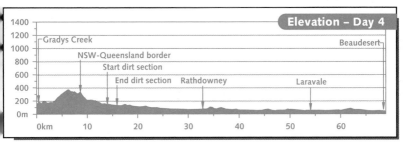

BORDER LOOP – DAY 4

CUE		GPS COORDINATES	
start	Rainforest Gateway Caravan Park, Gradys Creek	152°58'24"E	28°22'40"S
0km	go N on Lions Rd		
6.9	1.5km moderate climb		
10.0	3km steep climb		
12.9	Border Loop Lookout 1km		
14.7	400m steep climb		
15.1	NSW/Qld border		
	1km steep descent		
38.3	Captain Logan Lookout 700m		
38.4	Mt Lindesay Hwy, Rathdowney	152°51'51"E	28°12'39"S
50.3	Tamrookum Church Rd		
50.8	All Saints Church		
54.1	Christmas Creek Rd		
58.7	Mt Lindesay Hwy, Laravale"	152°56'09"E	28°5'16"S
72.8	Brisbane St		
73.2	Beaudesert Historical Museum & Information Centre	152°59'48"E	27°59'13"S

Border Loop Lookout road, a side trip at 12.9km. It's known as Border Loop because, below, the Sydney–Brisbane railway does a loop, and from the lookout you can see the line at three different points. If you're desperate to see a train, the XPT from Brisbane passes through at around 9am – trainspotters, go nuts.

The **border crossing** is a stark experience as the landscape changes from deep forest to rural, open hills (though it's still a good view). A roller-coaster road and a series of cattle grids welcome you back to Queensland, with the road squeezed tight against Running Creek until the valley widens out.

The short but steep detour to **Captain Logan Lookout** (a side trip at 38.3km) has views of Mts Lindesay, Ernest, Barney, Ballow, May and Maroon – collectively southern Queensland's premier bushwalking region, in Mt Barney National Park.

Try not to squirm as you pass the sign for the 'knackery' outside of Rathdowney and head out onto the plains. At 50.8km, the beautiful, timber **All Saints Church** looks a little like a midwestern barn out of the USA. It was built in 1915 in memory of Robert Collins, a philanthropic grazier who helped to establish national parks, particularly Lamington National Park. Inspections of the church can be arranged for a donation (if the caretaker's there).

Mt Lindesay Hwy has a decent verge for the approach into Beaudesert.

Day 5: Beaudesert to Nerang
4–7½ hours, 72.4km

Another day, another 500m climb. Cycling over the top of Mt Tamborine is certainly not the easiest way to the coast, but this oasis of galleries, cafes and resplendent rainforest remnants is its own reward, as is the screaming descent.

Out of Beaudesert, the route bumps along the plain to Tamborine, take note of the land's dryness so that the contrast will be complete when you're thick in forest atop the mountain.

Tamborine Mountain looms as soon as you turn out of Tamborine and, winding up the range, the forest suddenly canopies the road. The magnificent grove of piccabeen palms and towering rose gums means you've entered Tamborine National Park.

On the way out of North Tamborine, it's worth checking out **Cedar Creek Estate Winery** (☎ 07-5545 1666; www .cedarcreekestate.com.au; 104 Hartley Rd), not necessarily for its wines but for its artificial glowworm caves. Tours depart every half-hour. A few hundred metres on, **Rotary Lookout** stares down into the Canungra Valley – yes, you've climbed a long way.

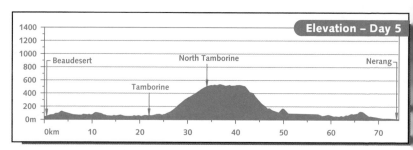

Elevation – Day 5

BORDER LOOP – DAY 5

CUE			GPS COORDINATES
start		Beaudesert Historical Museum & Information Centre	152°59'48"E 27°59'13"S
0km		go N on Brisbane St	
0.4	⌐▶🏢	Beaudesert Nerang Rd	
21.0	⌐▶	to Tamborine Mountain'	
23.9	▲	8.7km moderate climb	
32.6	↰	unsigned road, North Tamborine	153°11'05"E 27°55'39"S
35.0	★	Rotary Lookout	
37.2	⌐▶◎	unsigned road	
38.0	⌐▶	White Rd	
41.3	⚠	800m steep, narrow descent"	

CUE CONTINUED			GPS COORDINATES
43.0	⚠	2km very steep descent	
45.9	↰	Beaudesert Nerang Rd	
	●●⌐▶	Green Mountains 74.5km (↻)	
46.7	↘	to Gold Coast'	
48.1	▲	700m steep climb	
64.2	▲	200m steep climb	
66.7	↰	Beaudesert Nerang Rd	
70.7	⌐▶🏢	Ferry St, 'to Broadbeach'	
71.2	↗	to Broadbeach'	
72.1	↰🏢	Warrener St, 'to Nerang Station'	
72.2	⌐▶◎	Warrener St	
72.4		Nerang train station	153°20'11"E 27°59'22"S

The township of Mt Tamborine has become a fashionable weekend getaway for Brisbane and Gold Coast residents, so for a time the ride is encased by boutique B&Bs, wineries, day spas and a gaggle of galleries, before it's suddenly all downhill. The so-called 'goat track' that plunges off the mountain is an exhilarating bit of road, haring beneath loose cliffs and past a live military firing range, just the thing to give you the adrenaline needed for the final kilometres. If you have a day or two in hand, it's well worth the long climb of a side trip to Lamington National Park.

The ride leads to Nerang train station, so cyclists can head back to Brisbane. There's also a bikepath from Nerang to Surfers Paradise.

SIDE TRIP: LAMINGTON NATIONAL PARK

4-6 hours, 74.5km

Lamington National Park is one of the treasures of Queensland's national park system: dripping with waterfalls; peeping open to views across the Mt Warning caldera; and containing pockets of Antarctic beech forest, isolated since the last ice age.

Travelling through the rustic township of Canungra, you will eventually come to the park's Green Mountains section, where a treetop walk and a vast network of walking tracks show off the rainforest and rugged landscape. The birdlife in the park is prolific and colourful – the regent bowerbird is one of Lamington's iconic sights.

The climb to Green Mountains is beautifully graded, averaging 3.5% most of the way. There are great views, tall forest and some emerald dairy fields before entering the rainforest proper. The return descent is simply magic.

The famous **O'Reilly's Rainforest Guesthouse** (☎ 1800 688 722, 07-5544 0644; www.oreillys.com.au; Lamington National Park Rd; guesthouse s/d from $155/265, villas 1-/2-bedroom from $310/360) at Green Mountains is still run by the O'Reilly family. A number of luxury villas have recently been built but the original guesthouse (looking dated and faded) still manages to retain its old-world rustic charm – and sensational views. There's a plush restaurant (mains $25 to $40; breakfast, lunch & dinner) or a more affordable cafe.

There's a national park **campsite** (☎13 13 04; www.epa.qld.gov.au; per person $5) close to O'Reilly's. Camping permits can be obtained on-site, by phone, or online. During weekends and school holidays all permits must be booked in advance.

MT NEBO & BRISBANE FOREST PARK

Duration 3–5 hours
Distance 50.1km
Difficulty moderate–demanding
Start/Finish Ferny Grove train station
Summary Climb out of the suburbs and into the D'Aguilar Range's thick forest, which seems to part purely to present views east over the city and coast.

A ride through suburbs that aren't suburbs – with just a few turns of the pedals it feels as though you've left the city behind. The ride climbs into the thick bush around Mt Nebo along one of Brisbane's most fun (and best named) cycling roads, the quiet Goat Track.

If you want to turn the ride into an overnighter, there are B&Bs at Mt Glorious and Mt Nebo.

PLANNING
When to Cycle
Starting after 9am, makes train travel easier, but try to avoid the peak hour (5pm) traffic on Settlement Rd at the end of the day.

Bike Hire
Valet Cycle Hire & Tours (☎0408-003 198; www.cyclebrisbane.com) hires out bikes for $35 a day. Bikes can be delivered to your hotel or picked up at the City Botanic Gardens in Alice St.

Maps
The ride is covered by the RACQ 1:420,000 *Brisbane–Sunshine Coast* map.

Information Sources
For a retrospective look at the forest areas you will have cycled through, stop at the **Brisbane Forest Park Information Centre**

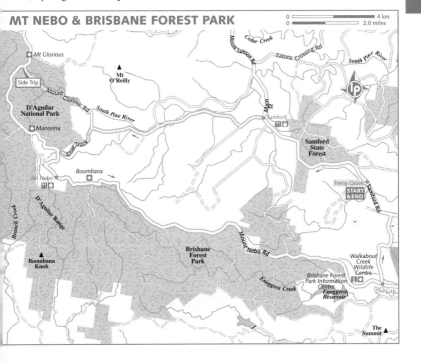
MT NEBO & BRISBANE FOREST PARK

(☎ 1300 723 684; 60 Mt Nebo Rd, The Gap) at the 42km mark of the ride.

GETTING TO/FROM THE RIDE
Ferny Grove (start/finish)
TRAIN

Translink (☎ 13 1230; www.translink .com.au) trains run to Ferny Grove from Brisbane's Roma St Station ($3.40, 30 minutes). It's possible to finish in the city by continuing from The Gap along Waterworks Rd for a further 10km, though traffic will become progressively heavier on this route.

THE RIDE

As you leave Ferny Grove station you may be excited by the sight of a bike lane on Samford Rd, but sadly it lasts for only 50m – a shared bikepath also runs beside the road for 1.7km but the road is wide enough for vehicles and bikes.

The ride leaves the suburbs immediately, climbing gradually through dry eucalypt forest before descending into the Samford Valley and the outlier suburb of Samford.

The road rises gently from Samford through a chain of acreage lifestyle blocks,

with the D'Aguilar Range becoming prominent at around 11km – the next few kilometres are a warm-up for the big climb.

Road signs encourage motorists to stay off the narrow, winding **Goat Track**, making it a cyclists' haven. Intimately surrounded by bush and nicely graded, it's in sharp contrast to the main Mt Glorious Rd with its deadly 15% pinches. It's also a one-way road so you don't need to worry about any vehicles approaching head-on. In fact, don't be surprised if you share the road only with a few goannas. A glance behind as you climb will reveal views east over the Samford Valley to the distant dunes of Moreton Island.

Manorina (20.1km), the ride's turnaround point, is inside the D'Aguilar National Park and makes for the ideal lunch spot. Two walking tracks depart from this point: the 750m Atrax track through the range's only stand of cabbage palms; and the 6km Morelia track to **Mt Nebo Lookout**.

The road undulates to Mt Nebo (24.2km), where the only spot for lunch at the time of research was **Cafe Boombana** (☎ 07-3289 8110; 1863 Mt Nebo Rd; Devonshire tea

MT NEBO & BRISBANE FOREST PARK

CUE			GPS COORDINATES
start		Ferny Grove train station	152°56′15″E 27°24′00″S
0km		go W on Samford Rd	
2.8	▲	1.2km moderate climb	
6.8		Samford	152°53′12″E 27°22′22″S
15.7	◄┐	Goat Track	
	▲	4.6km moderate climb	
16.2	⚠	2.6km dirt road	
18.8	┌►	Mt Nebo Rd	
20.1	★	Manorina	
	●●↑	Mt Glorious 15.2km ↻	
		retrace outward route	

CUE CONTINUED			GPS COORDINATES
21.4	▲	1.5km moderate climb	
24.2	▲	Mt Nebo	152°47′04″E 27°23′51″S
24.9	★	Boombana	
25.6	▲	500m moderate climb	
39.4	▲	1.6km moderate climb	
42.0	★	Brisbane Forest Parks Information Centre	
44.1	◄┐🏠	Settlement Rd	
44.6	▲	1.8km moderate	
47.9	◄┐🏠	Samford Rd	
48.5	↗	to Samford'	
50.1		Ferny Grove train station	152°56′15″E 27°24′00″S

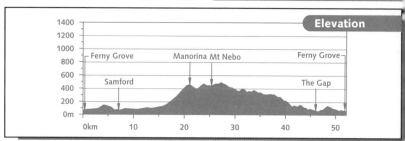

Elevation profile showing Ferny Grove, Samford, Manorina, Mt Nebo, The Gap, Ferny Grove. Elevation axis 0m–1400m; distance axis 0km–50km.

8.50, breakfast & lunch; Wed-Sun), which n typical Queensland fashion boasts of laving the world's best scones. They might e just the fuel for another walking stop at **Boombana** (24.9km), where a 1.1km circuit neanders through subtropical rainforest, grove of piccabeen palms and a giant trangler fig.

The descent offers a variety of lookouts, out the road itself has views just as good, o enjoy the ride. Stop at the **Brisbane Forest Park Information Centre** (42km) o learn more about all you have seen. The djacent **Walkabout Creek Wildlife Centre** 9am-4pm) has 80 species of native fauna, ncluding platypus and rainforest birds.

Once back on Samford Rd, a bike lane eads back to the train station.

SIDE TRIP: MT GLORIOUS
−1½ hours, 15.2km

From Manorina you can continue along Mt Nebo Rd (which becomes Mt Glorious Rd), following a roller-coaster ridge to **Mt Glorious** village, though it does add considerably to the day's effort. A popular lay-trip destination from Brisbane (and, as you will have noticed, a particular favourite with motorcyclists), it has some nice cafes, ea rooms and galleries. Continue 500m past the village and you'll come to the **Maiala** section of D'Aguilar National Park, where a trio of walking tracks include a 2km rainforest circuit and a 4.3km stroll to a lookout over Greene's Falls. If you're conserving energy you can always just flop by the picnic tables at the park entrance.

MT MEE

Duration 4–7½ hours

Distance 74.8km

Difficulty moderate–demanding

Start Petrie

Finish Caboolture

Summary An energetic ride to a hilltop village that has the clear mountain air and views that should attract tourists and developers, but somehow doesn't.

At the northern end of the D'Aguilar Range, Mt Mee offers a bucolic escape that's good either as a solid day out or as a ride to build up fitness for longer tours. Detours into the forest offer a chance to walk among large piccabeen palms, or you can simply admire the views from Mt Mee, including a panorama across the abstract skyline of the Glass House Mountains.

This ride is possible in either direction, but the climb is easier from Petrie. This also creates scope to link to the Sunshine Coast & Hinterland ride (p304) to make a four- or five-day tour.

PLANNING
Bike Hire
Valet Cycle Hire & Tours (☎ 0408-003 198; www.cyclebrisbane.com) hires out bikes for $35 a day. Bikes can be delivered to your hotel or picked up at the City Botanic Gardens in Alice St.

Maps
The ride is covered by the RACQ 1:420,000 *Brisbane–Sunshine Coast* map.

GETTING TO/FROM THE RIDE
Both Petrie and Caboolture are easily reached by train from Brisbane. Suburban **Translink** (☎ 13 1230; www.translink.com .au) trains run to Petrie station ($4.80, 35 minutes) from Roma St station. The same service returns from Caboolture to Roma St ($5.70, 65 minutes). You can continue riding north, linking with the Sunshine Coast & Hinterland ride by following the alternative route.

THE RIDE
It's an undulating run – alternately farm and forest – from Petrie to Dayboro, with the chance to go back in time at **Old Petrie Town** (☎ 07-285 5934; www.oldpetrietown .com; 9am-3pm Tue-Fri & Sun), which contains many of Petrie's buildings from the days when it was the first horse change for Cobb and Co Coaches heading to the Gympie goldfields. The buildings are now home to more than a dozen speciality stores, from homewares and sweets to a rock 'n' roll emporium and rum and cheese tastings. There's a market each Sunday.

It's a short detour, with a couple of steep pinches (especially on the return), to **MacGavin View**, where there are picnic areas with a view over North Pine Dam.

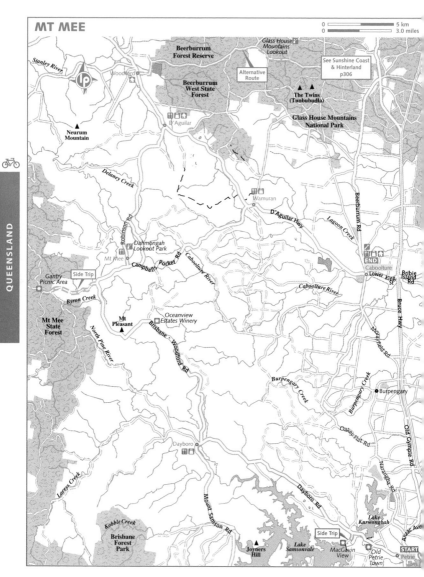

MT MEE

See Sunshine Coast & Hinterland p306

The climb to Mt Mee is long but never difficult, with good views that act as a balm. If the hill works up a thirst, **Oceanview Estates Winery** (☎ 07-3425 3900; 10am-9pm Thu-Sat) has tastings that can be soaked up with a cheese or antipasto platter. And if the hill destroys your legs, the winery also has two cottages.

A side trip (at 37.8km) to **Mt Mee State Forest** undulates along a ridge, with a steep 100m climb over the final 1km to Gantry picnic area. From here a walking track wanders for 1km through piccabeen palms and blue gum. In summer and autumn the fruit of the giant piccabeens makes a favourite snack for gorgeous

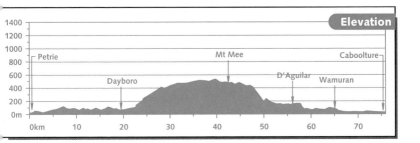

MT MEE

CUE			GPS COORDINATES	
start		Petrie train station	152°58'32"E	27°16'08"S
0km		go S on Station St		
0.1		Station St		
0.1		Anzac Ave		
0.4		to Dayboro'		
3.0	<★>	Old Petrie Town		
4.4	●●	MacGavin View 2.8km		
18.6		Mt Mee Rd, Dayboro"	152°49'21"E	27°11'47"S
21.7	▲	5.6km moderate climb		
28.7	★	Oceanview Estates Winery		
37.8	●●	Mt Mee State Forest 10km		
40.7		Mt Mee	152°46'11"E	27°04'28"S

CUE CONTINUED			GPS COORDINATES	
43.2	★	Dahmongah Lookout Park		
45.5	⚠	2.3km steep, winding descent		
53.8		D'Aguilar Hwy, D'Aguilar	152°47'52"E	26°59'14"S
		alt route: Landsborough 43.3km		
63.0		Wamuran	152°51'56"E	27°02'21"S
68.7		Williams Rd		
68.9		to Caboolture'		
69.3		King St		
74.2		George St		
74.3		Hasking St		
74.8		Caboolture train station	152°57'04"E	27°05'05"S

QUEENSLAND

king parrots. From the turn-off, look east for views across Moreton Bay to North Stradbroke Island.

As the route approaches Mt Mee, there are glimpses ahead to the Glass House Mountains, looking like a set of broken fingers, and back over Brisbane's suburbs. The only business capitalising on Mt Mee's spectacular location is **Birches Restaurant** (☎ 07-5498 2244; 1350 Mt Mee Rd; lunch mains $17-40; breakfast, lunch & dinner Wed-Sun). The view widens even further just beyond Mt Mee, at **Dahmongah Lookout Park**, with the Glass House Mountains spread out to the north.

On the final stretch, along the D'Aguilar Hwy (which has a decent shoulder), there are signs for a bike/horse/walk trail – this is the Bicentennial Trail, a 5330km route from Healesville (Victoria) to Cooktown (Queensland) along the bumpy spine of the Great Dividing Range.

ALTERNATIVE ROUTE: LANDSBOROUGH
1¼–2 hours, 43.3km

This scenic and mostly unsealed back route connects to the Sunshine Coast & Hinterland ride (p304) about halfway through Day 1.

The full Petrie to Landsborough journey is almost 80km in length, and difficult, so it would be better to break it into two days, staying at the **D'Aguilar Motel** (☎ 07-5496 4060; 2036 D'Aguilar Hwy; s/d/tw $80/90/95) or 4km further at the **Woodford Village Motel** (☎ 07-5496 1044; www.woodfordhotel.com.au; 76-81 Archer St; s $80, tw $100). Both motels are beside the respective town pubs, where dinner is available .

In Woodford, turn right at George St (by the hotel) and then left at Golf Course Rd before beginning 11km of dirt road. Turning left at 14.3km, the route winds around to the **Glass House Mountains Lookout** (17.6km), where the view is dominated by the bulk of Beerwah and the sharp tip of Coonowrin. There's also a cafe just before the lookout where you can take a break and relax, whilst sipping a coffee made with locally grown Arabica beans. With great views of Mount Coonowrin, you may even have the pleasure of meeting the cafe's 3 wild geese who like to greet guests on arrival.

Turn left at Old Gympie Rd and then follow the Day 1 cues for the Sunshine Coast & Hinterland ride.

QUEENSLAND

SUNSHINE COAST & HINTERLAND

Duration 4 days
Distance 184.3km
Difficulty moderate
Start Caboolture
Finish Noosa Heads
Summary Ride among the ancient volcanic plugs of the Glass House Mountains and up to the lush Blackall Range before looping through bucolic lands towards Queensland's most chic beach town.

For those who inexplicably don't like their beaches shadowed by high-rises and theme parks, the Sunshine Coast has long been some sort of antidote to the Gold Coast. Though development has crept along its shores, it's broken up by a series of reserves and fades away quickly into a hinterland of sugar cane, pineapple plantations, misshapen peaks and some of the state's most appealing and quirky small towns.

This ride concentrates on the hinterland, rising up and over the bump of the Blackall Range with its thriving arts scene and expansive views, before dropping into the food bowl that is the Mary Valley and meandering to the coast at Noosa Heads, where you can celebrate the end of a rewarding ride on the beach or on one of Australia's best eating strips.

PLANNING
When to Ride
Avoid, if possible, the December to January summer holiday peak: accommodation prices can double and traffic volumes go through the roof.

What to Bring
If you intend to climb Ngungun (p305) or any other of the Glass House Mountains, cleated cycling shoes will not be sufficient. If possible, squeeze in a pair of hiking boots for ankle support on the tricky terrain.

Bike Hire
Noosa Bike Hire & Tours (☎ 07-5474 3322; www.bikeon.com.au; four-day hire $79) rents out front-suspension mountain bikes suited to touring and will deliver them to hotels or apartments in Noosa.

Maps
The Sunmap 1:130,000 *Sunshine Coast & Hinterland* map covers the ride with good detail. The RACQ 1:420,000 *Brisbane-Sunshine Coast* map is less detailed but adequate for this route.

Information Sources
The hinterland section of the ride passes by three national parks – Glass House Mountains, Kondalilla and Mapleton Falls. The **national parks office** (☎ 07-5494 3983; 61 Bunya St; 7.30am-4pm Mon-Fri) for these parks is in Maleny.

GETTING TO/FROM THE RIDE
It's possible to append this ride to the Mt Mee ride (p305) to make a longer four- or five-day trip.

Caboolture (start)
TRAIN
Citytrain (☎ 13 1230) services connect Brisbane's Roma St station with Caboolture ($5.70; 65 minutes; half-hourly).

Noosa Heads (finish)
BUS
Intercity buses stop near the corner of Noosa Dr and Noosa Pde. **Greyhound Australia** (☎ 1300 473 946; www.greyhound.com.au) has several daily connections from Brisbane ($27, three hours) while **Premier Motor Service** (☎ 13 34 10; www.premierms.com .au) has one ($20, 2 hours). **Sunbus** (☎ 13 12 30) has frequent services to Maroochydore ($5, one hour) and the Nambour train station ($5, one hour).

THE RIDE
Day 1: Caboolture to Landsborough
2½–4 hours, 36.7km
This is a short, mostly flat day allowing you time to catch the train up from Brisbane and to explore the striking peaks of the Glass House Mountains. Named by James Cook for a supposed likeness to the glass foundries of Yorkshire, the mountains are the cores of 13 volcanoes.

The route heads out of Caboolture between the railway line and the showgrounds. At 2.5km the **Caboolture Historical Village** (☎ 07-5495 4581; admission $10; 9.30am-3.30pm) has over 70 buildings, including a barber shop, a licensed hotel, the original railway station, a maritime museum and a few vintage bikes.

At Beerburrum the ride turns briefly inland, winding through pine plantations and the volcanic plugs of the Glass House Mountains. The side trip to the **Glass House Mountains Lookout** (19.9km) is a worthwhile detour, even if it is reasonably steep (climbing 120m over 2.7km). If short on puff, the side trip passes the **Lookout Cafe** 1km before the lookout and just before the worst of the climb – the cafe has views almost equal to those of the lookout. From either spot, the view is dominated by the Beerwah and Coonowrin peaks, and it's easy to appreciate the Aboriginal legend of the mountains as a family frozen in stone. The pleasant picnic area at the lookout has toilets and water.

Another side trip at 22km runs between the organ-pipe escarpment of **Ngungun** and the hulking Tibrogargan, a mountain known locally as the Gorilla, to the start of the walking track to the summit of 253m Ngungun. The easiest climb of the main peaks, it has superb views of its neighbours. The 2.2km return walk is steep, and in places loose, but not difficult. Climbing Beerwah or Tibrogargan requires more time, confidence and scrambling experience, while Coonowrin is recommended only for those with rock-climbing experience.

Beyond Ngungun the road passes directly beneath the nose of **Coonowrin**, the most striking of the Glass House Mountains: it's summit as sharp as the pineapples growing at its foot. Old Landsborough Rd is fairly narrow, but there's a bikepath beside the road for most of the journey into Landsborough.

If you still have time at day's end you might want to take the short side trip out from Landsborough to **Australia Zoo** (☎ 07-5494 1134; www.australiazoo.com .au; Steve Irwin Way; admission $49; 9am-4.30pm), one of Queensland's most popular tourist attractions – and even more popular since the death of its famous founder, Steve Irwin. The amazing wildlife menagerie has a Cambodian-style Tiger Temple, the Asian-themed Elephantasia and the famous 'crocoseum'. There are macaws, birds of prey, giant tortoises, snakes, otters, camels, and more crocs and critters than you can poke a stick at.

Day 2: Landsborough to Mapleton
2½–4½ hours, 41.6km

The Blackall Range, like its waterfalls, is cool, fresh, inviting and utterly deserved after the hard grind up from Landsborough. It's a gorgeous, if at times steep, run along the top of the Blackall Range with the Sunshine Coast laid out below. The range is an artsy-crafty kind of place, so you could finish the day with panniers stuffed full of patchwork quilts and cuckoo clocks.

The biggest climb, that onto the range, begins just 1.2km out of Landsborough, with lingering views over the Sunshine Coast and along the line of the Blackall Range to abate any pain. After the climb, it's worth prolonging your entry into Maleny by touring around the rim of the range to **Mary Cairncross Park** (10.6km), which comprises 52 hectares of rainforest preserved by the philanthropic Thynne family. It also has a cafe, picnic area and rainforest walk. Across the road, there's an expansive view over the Glass House Mountains – on a clear day Brisbane's skyline is visible between Coonowrin and Beerwah. This very Australian view can be savoured in the next few kilometres at a German or Irish restaurant, or at **McCarthy's Lookout** for a subtly different angle on the mountains.

Maleny (18.6km) is a laid-back place with a superb local art scene, where bookstores

SUNSHINE COAST & HINTERLAND – DAY 1

CUE			GPS COORDINATES
start		Caboolture train staion	152°57′04″E 27°05′05″S
0km		go N on Matthew Tce	
0.2	⌐°🚲	Beerburrum Rd	
1.4	⌐°🚲	Beerburrum Rd	
2.5	★	Caboolture Historical Village	
8.5		Elimbah	152°56′40″E 27°0′54″S
13.7	↰	to Glass House Mountains Lookout'	
17.7	↙	Old Gympie Rd	
19.9	●●↰	Glass House Mtns Lookout 5.4km ↺	
22.0	●●⌐°	Ngungun 7.4km ↺	
29.1	⌐°	Kilcoy-Beerwah Rd	
31.1	↰�	Old Landsborough Rd, " Beerwah	152°57′41″E 26°51′32″S
36.5	↑	Cribb St	
	●●⌐°	Australia Zoo 6.6km ↺	
36.7		Landsborough train station	152°57′57″E 26°48′35″S

QUEENSLAND

SUNSHINE COAST & HINTERLAND

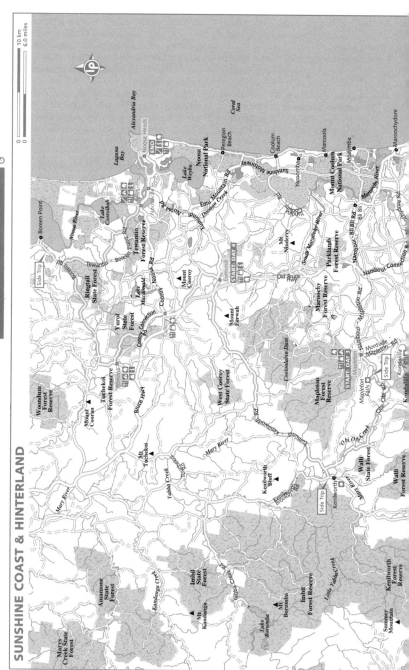

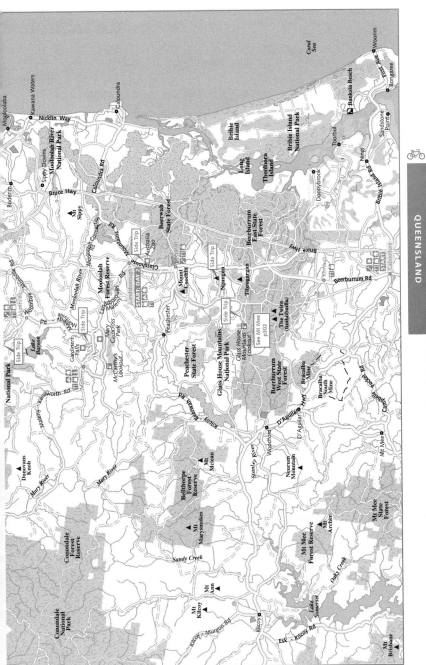

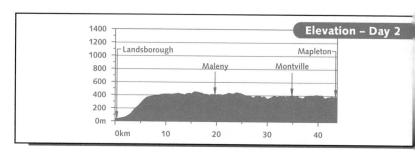

SUNSHINE COAST & HINTERLAND – DAY 2

CUE		GPS COORDINATES
start	Landsborough train station	152°57′57″E 26°48′35″S
0km	go S on Cribb St	
0.2	Blackall Range Tourist Dr (unsigned)	
1.2	4.5km steep climb	
9.2	Mountain View Rd	
10.6	Mary Cairncross Park	
14.7	McCarthy's Lookout	
15.4	Maleny-Stanley River Rd	
18.3	to `Landsborough'	

CUE CONTINUED		GPS COORDINATES
18.6	Maleny	152°50′57″E 26°45′36″S
21.6	Gardiners Falls 2.5km	
22.7	to Montville'	
25.9	400m steep climb	
29.5	400m steep climb	
32.7	Montville	152°53′43″E 26°41′30″S
35.2	200m steep climb	
35.6	Kondalilla Falls 1.8km	
41.6	Mapleton Tavern	152°52′04″E 26°37′28″S

and galleries proliferate. **Gardiners Falls** (a side trip at 21.6km) aren't particularly grand, but on a hot day the plunge pool below is well worth missing school for, as the local truants will attest. The falls are a five-minute walk downstream from the car park so you should have no trouble pushing your bike along the path. The only downside to this detour is the steep climb back out , when whatever sweat you've just washed off will soon be back.

There are a number of lookouts along the top of the Blackall Range even though the road is one long viewpoint. Chintzy **Montville** (32.7km) is the Blackall Range's fashionable heart, where every building that isn't already a boutique B&B seems to be aspiring to become one. It's not to everyone's liking, but the produce from the fudge emporiums may help propel you through the afternoon.

At 35.6km there's a diversion to 80m-high **Kondalilla Falls**. Quite prosaically, Kondalilla is a local Aboriginal word meaning 'rushing water' and the falls were reputedly a popular meeting spot for the locals clans. You can swim at the top of the falls, or walk a trio of longer circuits, including to the rainforest at the base of the falls, before rolling on into Mapleton.

Day 3: Mapleton to Eumundi
3–5 hours, 49.4km

Roll off the back of the Blackall Range into the Mary Valley before swinging back towards the coast. If possible, ride this section on a Tuesday or Friday so that you can be in Eumundi for its famed morning market on Wednesday or Saturday. If you intend to camp, you will need to stop at Kenilworth or else push on 20km to Pomona.

It's another day, another waterfall with the side trip (at 2.8km) to **Mapleton Falls**. From

SUNSHINE COAST & HINTERLAND – DAY 3

CUE		GPS COORDINATES
start	Mapleton Tavern	152°52′04″E 26°37′28″S
0km	go W on Obi Obi Rd	
2.8	Mapleton Falls 1.8km	
4.2	1.8km dirt road	
	1.8km steep, winding descent	
14.5	600m moderate climb	
19.4	Eumundi-Kenilworth Rd	
	Kenilworth 3.2km	
20.3	500m moderate climb	
46.8	Memorial Dr	
47.1	Memorial Dr	
49.1	turn onto Memorial Dr (unsigned)	
49.4	Discover Eumundi Heritage & Visitors centre	152°57′05″E 26°28′28″S

the car park you can just about ride straight out onto the lookout platform, which has great views out over the head of the falls, past the piccabeen palm-topped rainforest and into the Obi Obi Valley. It's a preview of the next section of this day's ride, for soon you will be down in the Obi Obi Valley.

The descent from the range is on a dirt road but it's often as smooth as a sealed road. It's tight, twisting and fun, but be sure to check your brakes at the top as it drops 170m in around 1.7km. The road has two factors in its favour: it's a one-way road and caravans and trucks are banned (always a good thing). When it flattens out into the Obi Obi Valley, look back up to the right, one of those creases in the range is Mapleton Falls.

What goes down must come back up, though the climb out from the Mary Valley near Kenilworth back over the hills has little sting as it dives in and out of farmland and bush. East of the range, on the approach to Eumundi, the green landscape is dotted with hills that resemble the Glass House Mountains before they were taken to with a pencil sharpener.

SIDE TRIP: KENILWORTH
10-15 minutes, 3.2km

If you've dropped into the Mary Valley it's also worth dropping into the small town of Kenilworth for a gourmet treat. North of town, two wineries, **Kenilworth Bluff Wines** (☎ 07-5472 3723; Bluff Rd; 10am-4pm Fri-Sun) and **Blind Man's Bluff Vineyards** (☎ 07-5472 3168; cnr Bluff & Wilcox Rds; 10am-5pm Wed-Sun), offer tastings, but it's wine's great mate, cheese, that is the real king of Kenilworth. The **Kenilworth Cheese Factory** (☎ 07-5446 0144; 45 Charles St; 9am-4pm Mon-Fri, 10.30am-3pm Sat & Sun) has free cheese tastings, ice cream produced on the premises and some wonderful yoghurt concoctions such as banana and honey and mango and macadamia.

Day 4: Eumundi to Noosa Heads
3–5½ hours, 56.6km

A meandering journey through the Sunshine Coast's northern hinterland, passing through quirky Pomona before skirting Lake Cootharaba to finish at the coast's glitziest town.

The day begins with a climb through the Eumundi Range, rounding Mt Cooroy, which stands starkly to the east – it's not steep but it might feel it first thing in the morning. At the top of the climb the route joins the Noosa Shire's marked cycle ways: route 9 goes to Cooroy, where you join route 10 to Tewantin and route 8 into Noosa.

The gum trees in the **Yurol State Forest** are as straight as barcodes, and when the trees open out, Mt Cooroora looms large above Pomona. On the fourth Sunday each July, this mountain is the stage for the **King of the Mountain** (www.kingofthemountain .com.au) race, in which runners barrel up and down the steep peak. The race record is a smidge under 23 minutes; if you're walking up, allow another couple of hours.

Entering Pomona, the route passes the wonderful **Majestic Theatre** (☎ 07-485

QUEENSLAND

EVERYTHING'S BIG IN...

Poke about in Tewantin for a while and you will become acquainted with Queensland's obsession for big pieces of representative roadside kitsch. Here, the Big Shell and the Big Bottle stand proud and mutant, towering over passersby.

It's a phenomenon that is said to have started with the Big Banana in Coffs Harbour in the 1960s, but which Queensland has well and truly adopted as its own. It's even claimed that the Big Pineapple near Nambour was once the second-most visited tourist attraction in the country…and if that fact inspires you, you can always just drive up the highway to a second Big Pineapple in Gympie.

In this state you can climb inside the Big Pineapple, salivate at the Big Mango, shoot it out with the Big Ned Kelly, mourn the closure of the Big Cow or visit the Big Fish near Caboolture, where there's not actually a fish.

Queensland is not alone in its fondness for colossal fruit, bushrangers and animals, with around 150 big things sprinkled around Australia (Queensland has about 50 of them). If you're on a pilgrimage, visit the Big Bicycle in Chullora, in Sydney's western suburbs.

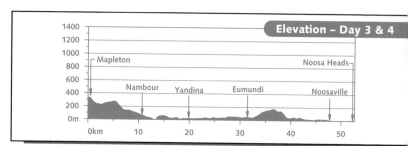

QUEENSLAND

SUNSHINE COAST & HINTERLAND – DAY 4

CUE		GPS COORDINATES
start	Discover Eumundi Heritage & Visitors centre	152°57'05"E 26°28'28"S
0km	go N on Memorial Dr	
0.3	Eumundi Range Rd	
0.6	Eumundi Range Rd	
1.1	2.1km moderate climb	
8.4	to Cooroy'	
10.0	Elm St, Cooroy	152°54'46"E 26°25'01"S
14.3	Yurol Forest Dr	
20.0	Pomona	152°51'21"E 26°22'01"S
21.8	Louis Bazzo Dr	
35.3	McKinnon Dr, `to Tewantin'	
●● ↑	Boreen Point 9km ↺	
40.6	Illoura Place	

CUE CONTINUED		GPS COORDINATES
44.3	unsigned road	
44.7	unsigned road	
45.9	McKinnon Dr	
49.6	Poinciana Ave (unsigned)	
50.2	Tewantin	
50.5	Doonella St	
50.5	Lake St	
50.6	Memorial Ave	
51.9	Gympie Tce	
53.8	Howard St	
53.9	Noosa Pde	
56.4	Noosa Dr	
56.6	Noosa visitors centre	153°05'24"E 26°23'40"S

2330; www.majestic.spiderweb.com.au; 3 Factory St, Pomona; Thu-Sun nights), one of the only places in the world where you can see a silent movie accompanied by the original Wurlitzer organ soundtrack. For 21 years (until 2007) the theatre played only one film, Rudolph Valentino's *The Son of the Sheikh*, every Thursday night. A recent spruce-up has seen the addition of a restaurant and the reintroduction of talkies but the focus remains firmly on the silent screen. For a step back in history, catch a **screening** (tickets $10, meal deal $25; 8pm) of the iconic *The Son of the Sheikh* on the first Thursday of each month.

At around 29km there's a glimpse of Lake Cootharaba and the dunes of Great Sandy National Park, but for a decent look, take the side trip at 35.3km to **Boreen Point**. This heads through paperbarks to the lake, which is part of the outlet for the Noosa River. There's good swimming (well, wading) in the shallow lake or, if you have a spare day or two, the paddling through the Noosa Everglades is fantastic. Canoes and

kayaks can be hired from the **Elanda Point Canoe Company** (☎ 07-5485 3165; www .elanda.com.au; canoes per day $40, sea kayaks per day $80). There's also camping and accommodation by the lake if you prefer this to busy Noosa.

Noosa gets suburban a long way out, as new homes mix with paperbark swamp along Illoura Pl, though good bike lanes make it a cruisey finish into Noosa Heads.

WARNING

The waters of the tropical north harbour particular hazards. Saltwater crocodiles inhabit the mangroves, estuaries and open water north from around Lucinda. Just as lethal are marine stingers such as the Chironex box jellyfish and Irukandji, which generally only appear from October through May, but even protective nets can't keep out the tiny Irukandji. Heed warning signs and check with locals before swimming. See p403 for more details.

AROUND TOWNSVILLE

Tired of living in the shadow of Cairns and Airlie Beach, Townsville, 1400km northwest of Brisbane, has transformed itself. Originally a shipping port and service centre to the region's agricultural industries, the city has had a reputation as a fairly dour northern outpost. Re-greened with 100,000 new trees and coloured by a spruced-up waterfront promenade and revitalised restaurant row, Townsville has proudly shed its reputation as the dreary 'Brownsville' backwater of North Queensland. Convincingly tropical, its sun is hot, beer cold, characters large and the cane toads sometimes prolific. The authorhrty charged with protecting the offshore 2000km endangered expanse of Great Barrier Reef (GBRMPA, see this page) has its headquarters here.

ENVIRONMENT

The flora surrounding Townsville is more hardy and sparse than the rainforests further north. Up to 280 bird species, including vast flocks of migratory magpie geese, brolgas and finches visit the area's immense seasonal wetlands, the closest of which is the Town Common Conservation Park.

The Great Barrier Reef quells any surf, but there are still some nice, sandy beaches, especially Townsville's vibrant manmade Strand, national winner of the 2008 Keep Australia Beautiful Clean Beaches Awards. World-class diving and snorkelling trips are available.

CLIMATE

Townsville has a monsoonal climate with a turbulent and wet summer season followed by nine months of much drier weather. Although cyclones and storm surges are uncommon, when precipitation is forecast, it can really heave down and flooding sometimes ensues. February 2009 was the wettest on record, nearly surpassing in just one month the normal annual average rainfall (1143mm). The average maximum temperature ranges from 24°C in July to 31°C in January. Winds tend to be southeasterly sea breezes, which strengthen as the day warms.

PLANNING
When to Cycle

To avoid temperature extremes and monsoon wet, April to November is best. June, July and August are the coolest and driest months.

Information Sources

The central **Great Barrier Reef Marine Park Authority** (GBRMPA; ☎ 07-4750 0700; www.gbrmpa.gov.au; Reef HQ, 2-68 Flinders St, Townsville; 9.30am-5pm Mon-Fri) purveys detailed and technical information about the Reef. For details about the area's protected lands, the **Queensland Parks & Wildlife Service** (☎ 07-4722 5211; www.epa.qld.gov.au; Old Quarantine Station at Cape Pallarenda; 10am-4pm Mon-Fri) is inconveniently located 10km northwest of town. General information about Townsville and vicinity is available at visitors centres in town (see Information p347), where you can ask for the *Bikeways in Thuringowa* brochure that traces routes in the surrounding communities.

GETTING THERE & AWAY

See Townsville (p347).

MT STUART & ALLIGATOR CREEK

Duration	2 days
Distance	62.2km
Difficulty	easy
Start/Finish	Townsville

Summary Beautiful, reptile-free Alligator Creek is the mid-point of this easy pedal: either a two-day introduction to cycle camping or a solid day-ride with a tough optional climb.

Keen to try a short and simple trip that involves one overnight in a tent? This is an easy primer to self-contained touring. Alternatively, it has all the qualities of a moderately long day-ride, made tougher if you include the Mt Stuart side trip and/ or the hike to Alligator Falls. Whatever you decide, plan for a dip in the cool, clear waters of Alligator Creek, which, despite its ominous name, has no toothy predators.

QUEENSLAND

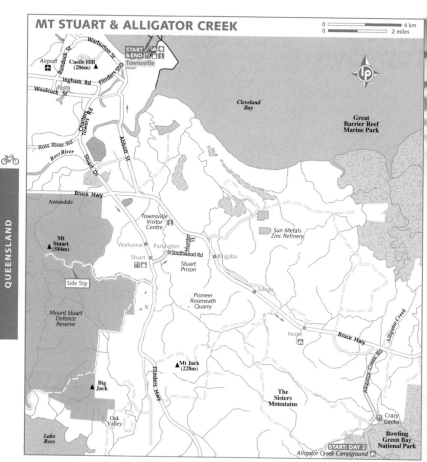

ENVIRONMENT

The 1234m granite peak of Mt Elliot and its neighbouring Saddle Mountain dominate the 579-sq-km Bowling Green Bay National Park and flank Alligator Creek. Mount Elliot's steep upper eastern slopes drop precipitously into Australia's most southerly tropical rainforest. The lower slopes and surrounding coastal plains contain diverse habitats, from sand spits to mangrove communities and bird-rich wetlands of international importance. The most common trees in the wooded areas are species resistant to, and dependent on, fire – eucalypts, acacias, cycads, grass trees and native kapok.

PLANNING

When to Cycle

Even in winter, Townsville temperatures are rarely cool, so hit the road early, especially if you're climbing Mt Stuart. The Alligator Creek campsite can be popular on weekends and holidays, so pre-book one of the four sites (see p332).

What to Bring

Camping, cooking gear and mosquito repellent are essential at Alligator Creek. Bring enough food for all meals.

Bike Hire

Park and Pedal (☎ 0421-007 863; park andpedal@bigpond.com; Strand Park,

Townsville; 8am-5pm Mon-Fri, 9am-4pm Sat & Sun) has mountain bikes available for $35/60/100 per day/two days/week. Helmets and locks are included.

Maps

Geoscience Australia's 1:100,000 *Townsville* map covers the route, which is simple and short enough not require much cartographic support.

THE RIDE
Day 1: Townsville to Alligator Creek
2–3½ hours, 34.2km

Fortunately the roads and shoulders around Townsville are broad. They make escaping the already low-key urban buzz easy as you roll along the Flinders Hwy and watch the scenery change from suburban to industrial to rural in the span of a few kilometres. It then stays delightfully country for the rest of the day. The optional, challenging side-trip up Mt Stuart is the only topographical trial.

At 11.4 km the **Stuart Snack Bar** (☎ 07-4778 4977; 485 Stuart Dr; 5am-7.30pm Mon-Fri, 5am-4pm Sat, 7am-4pm Sun) has a full stock of drinks, groceries, sandwiches and grilled meals. It's your last chance to take on water before the Mt Stuart side trip (at 12.1km) and, a short backtrack from the end of the side trip, your only chance to purchase forgotten supplies for the overnight at **Alligator Creek**.

Pedalling southeast on the Bruce Hwy you may encounter a headwind and some traffic. With luck it'll all behind you on the spin back to town tomorrow.

The sign to Bowling Green Bay National Park points up Alligator Creek Rd, which weaves languidly through mango and pawpaw farms. Bowling Green Bay National Park is the largest coastal park in the region, protecting a diverse range of habitats and is set against a backdrop of stark granite mountains. You end up on good-quality gravel for the final 600m before the campsite.

SIDE TRIP: MT STUART
1¼–2 hours, 21km

The 9.3km climb up Mt Stuart begins 1.9km south of the Stuart Snack Bar. The overall average gradient of 5.5% tells you little since there are several dips and compensating steep bits along the way. At the summit, a short distance beyond the Rotary Lookout parking area, is a weatherworn waterless picnic site. At least the view northeast to Townsville, Cape Pallarenda and Magnetic Island is excellent.

On the return, after 200m, turn left down a small road towards a telecommunications tower. There, a rough track leads to a scenic reserve at the top of the cliffs. This popular rock-climbing area is much more attractive than the summit lookout.

Day 2: Alligator Creek to Townsville
1½–3 hours, 28km

Retrace more than half of the outward route, continuing on the Bruce Hwy to Abbott St, the most direct route back to the city centre. Keep your eye out for here-again-gone-again bikepaths and brief respites from traffic. Townsville's main tourist office (19km) is on the highway but can only really provide information already available at the more central facilities.

MT STUART & ALLIGATOR CREEK – DAY 1

CUE			GPS COORDINATES
start		Townsville visitor kiosk	146°48'53"E 19°15'44"S
0km		go SW on Flinders St	
1.3	↘	Morris St	
1.7	↑	Charters Towers Rd/Flinders Hwy	
4.0	↘	Bowen Rd 'to Charters Towers'	
11.4		Stuart	146°50'02"E 19°20'38"S
12.1	↰	Southwood Rd	
{	●●↑	Mt Stuart 21km ↺}	
14.1	↰	Hunter St	
15.4	↱	Bruce Hwy	
25.3		Nome	146°55'42"E 19°22'55"S
28.1	↱	'to Bowling Green Bay NP'	
34.2		Alligator Creek Campsite	146°56'41"E 19°25'56"S

MT STUART & ALLIGATOR CREEK – DAY 2

CUE			GPS COORDINATES
start		Alligator Creek Campsite	146°56'41"E 19°25'56"S
0km		go NW on Alligator Ck Rd	
6.1	↰	Bruce Hwy	
19.0		Townsville visitors centre	
20.8	↱	Abbott St	
24.9	⚠	200m narrow bridge	
27.2	↰	Rooney St	
27.7	↱	Flinders St Mall	
28.0		Townsville visitor kiosk	146°48'53"E 19°15'44"S

QUEENSLAND

QUEENSLAND

MAGNETIC ISLAND

Duration 1¼–2¼ hours
Distance 22km
Difficulty easy–moderate
Start/Finish Nelly Bay
Summary Abundant wildlife, stunning beaches, great eating, scenic riding and thrilling water sports make Magnetic Island appealing to everyone. This short day-ride is a fun spin for all levels of ability.

There's no better way around 'Maggie' than by bike. Named by Captain Cook in 1770 when he mistakenly thought it influenced his ship's compass, the 11km-long island teems with wildlife, has sandy beaches, good snorkelling and four tiny villages each with its own distinct personality. It is completely unpretentious, but also staggeringly gorgeous. Although this is a short return ride, its hills under the tropical sun will still make you sweat. The West Point and Radical Bay Rds are off limits to hired vehicles – a bonus for cyclists.

ENVIRONMENT

All of Magnetic Island is part of the Great Barrier Reef World Heritage area. A bit more than half of it is national park and its surrounding reefs are zoned within the Great Barrier Reef Marine Park and Townsville–Whitsunday State Marine

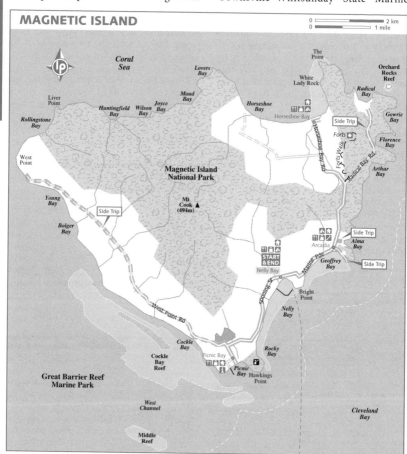

Park. Its rugged surface of smooth grey boulders and open eucalypt woodland are a vast natural sanctuary (one of Australia's biggest) for koalas, rock wallabies, brush-tailed possums and a host of bird species, while the fringing coral reef attracts a spectacular diversity of marine life. Information signs across the island help explain its unique natural characteristics; the *Magnetic Island World Heritage* brochure is also particularly edifying. There are marine stinger enclosures at Picnic and Horseshoe Bays from November to May.

PLANNING

Although the ride is easily manageable in a day, you can stay overnight and laze on a long, sandy beach or hike some of the bush trails in the adjacent national park. There's a **Queensland Parks & Wildlife Service office** (QPWS; ☎ 07-4778 5378; 22 Hurst St, Picnic Bay; 8am-4pm), but for general information and free maps, pop into a mainland visitors information centre (p347) before boarding a ferry.

ATMs are scattered throughout the island, but there are no banks.

What to Bring

There are ample outlets for food and drink, but water should be carried on the side trips.

Bike Hire

Many accommodations have bikes available for guests, but for bike hire and repair try **Townville and Magnetic Island Bike Hire** (☎ 07-4758 1333; Shop 5, Bright Av, Arcadia; $20/30 for 24 hours/three days). Call ahead to arrange bike pick up at the ferry terminal in Nelly Bay.

GETTING TO/FROM THE RIDE

A frequent service by **SunFerries** (☎ 07-4726 0800; www.sunferries.com.au; $29 return, bikes free; 20 minutes, 14 to 19 daily) departs from Townsville's Breakwater terminal (Sir Leslie Thiess Dr) from 7.05am; the last boat leaves the island at 10.35pm. **FantaSea** (☎ 07-4772 5422; www .magneticislandferry.com.au) also operates a car and passenger ferry ($25 return, bikes free; 20 minutes; seven or eight daily) from the south side of Ross Creek.

THE RIDE

The route follows the only road that goes anywhere, between Picnic Bay and Horseshoe Bay. For a cool-down dip, you can swim year-round in the stinger enclosures at Picnic and Horseshoe Bays, or in winter at any of the island's secluded coves.

All ferries now dock at Nelly Bay, from which you first head south to Picnic Bay. A side trip (at 3.8km) along the quiet West Point Rd serves up an intimate look at the island's forests and bird life. The surface is paved for 3.5km, then turns to dirt, which progressively deteriorates. West Point is a great place to watch the sunset over the mainland, but since there is no camping, you'll need lights for the return.

From Picnic Bay head back north through Nelly Bay towards Arcadia. Don't skip the detour (at 10.6.5km) to the jetty at Geoffrey Bay to spy rock wallabies and, in the clear water, schools of diamond scale mullet, all waiting for a feed from the next tour group. Alma Bay (10.8km) is an absolute gem, cool off there before the 100m gain in elevation to Horseshoe Bay.

The 3km-return Forts walk (at 12.8km) around abandoned WW2 emplacements offers good views of the coast and an

MAGNETIC ISLAND

CUE		GPS COORDINATES
start	Nelly Bay Ferry Terminal	146°51'20"E 19°09'29"S
0km	go SW on Sooning St {follow signs to Picnic Bay}	
3.8	↰ Granite St	
{	●●↑ West Point 16.6km (↻) }	
4.4	Moran Restaurant, Picnic Bay 146°50'23"E 19°10'44"S	
{retrace outward route}		
5.5	▲ 300m steep climb	
7.7	Nelly Bay	
8.8	↖ Arcadia Rd	
10.1	↑ Marine Pde	

CUE CONTINUED		GPS COORDINATES
10.6	Arcadia	
{	●●↳ Geoffrey Bay Jetty 1km (↻) }	
{10.8	★ Alma Bay}	
11.0	▲ 1.1km moderate climb	
{12.8	★ Forts Walk}	
{	●●↳ Radical Bay 6.1km (↻) }	
15.2	↳ Pacific Dr	
15.4	↱ Maggie's, Horseshoe Bay 146°51'41"E 19°07'02"S
{retrace outward route}		
22.0	Nelly Bay Ferry Terminal 146°51'20"E 19°09'29"S

excellent chance of seeing koalas. Afterwards, the Radical Bay side trip on unpaved roads traverses national park for visits to the delightful, secluded Arthur Bay and Florence Bay. Radical Bay itself has a sandy beach spoiled by the ruins of a resort.

Throughout the island, don't ride on any of the walking paths, punishable by a steep fine and confiscation of your bike.

Return to Nelly Bay via the outward route.

FAR NORTH QUEENSLAND

With your wheels, you have the kind of mobility some people never need, content as they are to remain within Cairns' city limits. You won't believe what they're missing: lush tropical rainforests, temperate and green uplifted hinterlands and workaday agricultural villages home to good honest folk. Of course, that's without even mentioning the underwater spectacle, idyllic beach communities and coral-fringed islands. Although Cairns and Port Douglas are the Far North's tourism hubs, really, it's beyond these centres that the true attractions abound.

HISTORY
The colonial history of Far North Queensland mimics that of other areas in the state. In the 1870s red cedar, gold and tin attracted the aspirant to the Palmer and Hodgkinson Rivers. Overland routes were opened, allowing access for grazing and agriculture. Much of the lowland rainforest was slashed and burned for sugarcane growing. Throughout, little account was taken of the original inhabitants. More recently, the economic value of preserving the region's natural wonders and Aboriginal culture is being realised and developed in a much more sustainable way.

ENVIRONMENT
The 900,000-hectare Wet Tropics World Heritage Area was declared in 1988 to protect and manage remnant forest areas between Townsville and Cooktown. Spectacular and diverse, it incorporates coastal mangroves, eucalypt forest and some of the world's oldest rainforest. The biodiversity is so rich that an average two hectares of Daintree rainforest contains more tree species than either the continents of North America or Europe. Also diverse is the wildlife, which includes remarkable tree kangaroos and cassowaries. Offshore, the 2000km Great Barrier Reef is one of the world's natural wonders.

PLANNING
When to Cycle
Any time is fine as long as it's not the Wet season (December to April), during which storms, flooding and stingers make travel difficult. Many tourism ventures, particularly north of Port Douglas, close or cut back services in this period.

Bike Hire
See Cairns (p336).

Maps
In Cairns, if you decide that the free maps described in each ride section aren't up to snuff, check out the impressive range of options at **Absell's Chart & Map Centre** (☎ 07-4041 2699; Main Street Arcade, 85 Lake St).

Information Sources
For general regional coverage, check in with **Tropical North Queensland** (www .tropicalaustralia.com.au), housed in the Gateway Discovery Centre (see p336). The **Queensland Parks & Wildlife Service** (QPWS; ☎ 07-4046 6600; www.epa.qld .gov.au; 5B Sheridan St, Cairns) disseminates details about national parks, state forests, biking trails and camping permits. The **Wet Tropics Management Authority** (www .wettropics.gov.au) is specifically enjoined

---

WARNING

From late October to May swimming in coastal waters is highly inadvisable due to the presence of lethal Chironex box jellyfish, Irukandji and other marine stingers. Saltwater crocodiles inhabit the mangroves, estuaries and open water of the far north, so avoid swimming or wading in these places. Do not ignore the posted warning signs. See p403 for more details.

to sustainably exploit the Wet Tropics World Heritage Area.

GETTING THERE & AWAY
See Cairns (p336).

THE DAINTREE & CAPE TRIBULATION

Duration 3 days
Distance 173.3km
Difficulty moderate
Start Cairns
Finish Cape Tribulation
Summary Edge from Cairns, the gateway to the Tropical North, up to Cape Tribulation, the frontier of Far North Queensland. Along the way, revel in the Wet Tropics and Great Barrier Reef World Heritage Areas.

You'll love being suspended between blue and green. During your journey to the frontier of Australia's Far North Queensland, off to the west are the deep and robust shades of the Daintree tropical rainforests; to the east, the sparkling waters of the Coral Sea. Two World Heritage Areas run parallel here, the Wet Tropics and the Great Barrier Reef – the only place in the world where this is the case. At a two-wheeled pace, you can really take this all in, as well as the contrasting communities – Aborigines, cane growers and back-to-nature ferals.

PLANNING
A popular cyclists' route is the 106km Bloomfield Track between Cape Tribulation and Cooktown. Seek advice on the road condition and accommodation before proceeding, since most of the route is dirt and sometimes very steep. There are also some unbridged water crossings. Buses and local aircraft depart from Cooktown to Cairns. If you don't want to go that far, consider the 14km return trip from Cape Tribulation to Emmagen Creek, a wild stream that flows from the rainforest wilderness. Resist the temptation to swim here, as it's crocodile country.

Maps
Several free maps available at visitors centres do justice to the ground you will cover. Great

Tropical Drive's 1:400,000 *Northern Region* map includes all but the day from Cairns to Port Douglas, for which no map is needed. A closer look at the Mossman to Daintree area is on the back of the Daintree Village Tourism Association's *Daintree…Naturally* brochure. The *Free Cape Tribulation Map* zeroes in on the roads and services north of the Daintree River.

GETTING TO/FROM THE RIDE
The Atherton Tableland ride (p322) could precede or follow this ride.

Cairns (start)
See p336.

Cape Tribulation (finish)
BUS
Sun Palm (☎ 07-4087 2900; www .sunpalmtransport.com) runs three buses daily from Cape Tribulation to Cairns ($75, 3-3½ hours) via Port Douglas ($45, two hours). Bikes officially cost $10 extra and you must box or bag it and warn the company in advance.

Country Road Coachlines (☎ 07-4045 2794; www.countryroadcoachlines.com.au) also runs from Cape Tribulation to Cairns ($42, 3½ hours) via Port Douglas ($32, 2¼ hours) on its thrice-weekly (Tuesday, Thursday and Saturday) coastal route. Bikes cost $20 extra but require no special packing, although you should still call the company to advise about the extra luggage.

THE RIDE
Day 1: Cairns to Port Douglas
3¾–6¾ hours, 68.3km
Today is like a staging ride for the real action to come. Hampered by a busy stretch of urban sprawl north of Cairns and then more development as you approach Port Douglas, the pleasant pedalling is limited to a coastal World Heritage Area that serves as a glimpse of the verdant majesty to come. You rarely leave the Captain Cook Hwy, but you've got a generous shoulder as far as Ellis Beach.

Just north of Cairns proper, the road to the airport skirts a large mangrove flat, part of a muddy, unglamorous breeding ground for many commercial fish species, and home to Queensland's culinary icon, the mud crab. A side trip at 4.1km leads to a

QUEENSLAND

THE DAINTREE & CAPE TRIBULATION – DAY 1

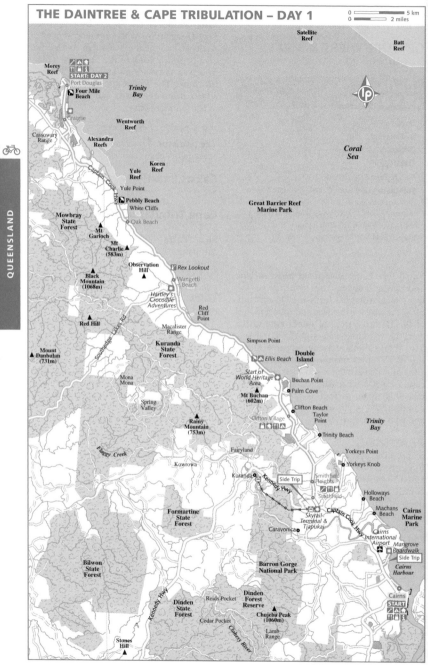

QUEENSLAND

THE DAINTREE & CAPE TRIBULATION – DAY 1

CUE			GPS COORDINATES
start		Gateway Discovery Centre, Cairns	145°46'42"E 16°55'16"S
0km		go NW on Esplanade bikepath	
2.6	⤴	Smith St (at end of bikepath)	
2.7	⤵◎	Lake St bikepath	
3.4	⤴	Rutherford St	
3.7	⤵	Captain Cook Hwy	
{4.1 ●● ⤵		mangrove boardwalk 3.8km (🍴)}	
{13.1 ●● ⤴		Skyrail & Tjapukai 200m (🍴)}	
14.8		Smithfield	145°41'34"E 16°50'22"S

CUE CONTINUED			GPS COORDINATES
23.8		Clifton Village	145°40'12"E 16°46'08"S
26.7		World Heritage section starts	
{29.8	★	Ellis Beach}	
{41.7	★	Hartley's Crocodile Adventures}	
42.2	▲	1.4km moderate climb	
{43.6	★	Rex Lookout}	
62.4	⤵	'to Port Douglas'	
67.9	⤴	Macrossan St	
68.3		Port Douglas visitors centre	145°27'49"E 16°28'57"S

mangrove boardwalk, which has excellent interpretive signs explaining the ecology.

Just northwest of a large roundabout (13.7km) are two of Cairns' finest commercial tourist attractions. The **Tjapukai Aboriginal Cultural Park** (☎ 07-4042 9900; www.tjapukai.com.au ; Captain Cook Hwy) features live performances of the Tjapukai tribe's corroboree dances. The cultural displays are excellent. Next door, the **Skyrail Rainforest Cableway** (☎ 07-4038 1555; www.skyrail.com.au; cnr Captain Cook Hwy & Cairns Western Arterial Rd; adult/child $40/20, return $58/29) gondola gives a bird's-eye view of tropical rainforest and Barron Gorge National Park. A rainforest boardwalk at Red Peak Station breaks up the 90-minute, 7.5km journey to Kuranda. Bikes are not allowed on the cableway.

The **World Heritage Area** on Captain Cook Hwy north of Buchan Point (26.7km) is a noted accident zone. Drivers not gawking at the rolling scenery are probably rushing to ferry another load of tourists to Port Douglas or beyond, so beware, especially once the road shoulder disappears and blind turns begin. The scenery is indeed superb and there are plenty of quiet beaches to stop at. The last stinger enclosure for summer swimming is at **Ellis Beach** (29.8km).

At 44.3km **Hartley's Crocodile Adventures** (☎ 07-4055 3576; www.crocodileadventures.com; Captain Cook Hwy; adult/child $31/15.50) is one of the better parks of its type. The highlight is the daily Crocodile Attack show at 3pm.

Palm-lined Port Douglas Rd adds a bit of pomp to your arrival. It's a fitting introduction to a town focused on making people feel good about themselves and spend lots of money.

Day 2: Port Douglas to Daintree
3–5½ hours, 55.7km
Seen from the sky the land flanking today's ride is a grand patchwork of cane fields that feed the Mossman sugar mill. From road level, depending on the season, you can be walled in by mature, 4m-high cane or find yourself alone in a vast expanse of ploughed pasture. After the beach-side hamlet of Wonga the road skirts parts of Daintree National Park, more teasers of the rainforest to come.

For a first and early taste at 5.6km, though, **Rainforest Habitat** (☎ 07-4099 3235; www.rainforesthabitat.com.au; Port

THE DAINTREE & CAPE TRIBULATION – DAY 2

CUE			GPS COORDINATES
start		Port Douglas visitors centre	145°27'49"E 16°28'57"S
0km		go SE on Macrossan St	
0.4	⤵	Davidson St/Port Douglas Rd	
{5.6	★	Rainforest Habitat}	
5.8	⤵	'to Mossman'	
{19.5 ●● ⤴		Mossman Gorge 10.4km (🍴)}	
19.8		Mossman	145°22'25"E 16°27'39"S
22.0	⤴	Captain Cook Hwy	

CUE CONTINUED			GPS COORDINATES
{24.5	★	Scommazon's Fruit & Veg}	
27.7	⤴	'to Daintree'	
37.3		Wonga	145°24'36"E 16°20'45"S
45.7	↑	pass turn to ferry	
52.9	⚠	50m narrow bridge	
55.0	⤡	Osborne St	
55.6	⤵	Stewart St	
55.7		Daintree visitors centre	145°19'06"E 16°15'00"S

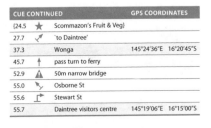

QUEENSLAND

THE DAINTREE & CAPE TRIBULATION – DAYS 2-3

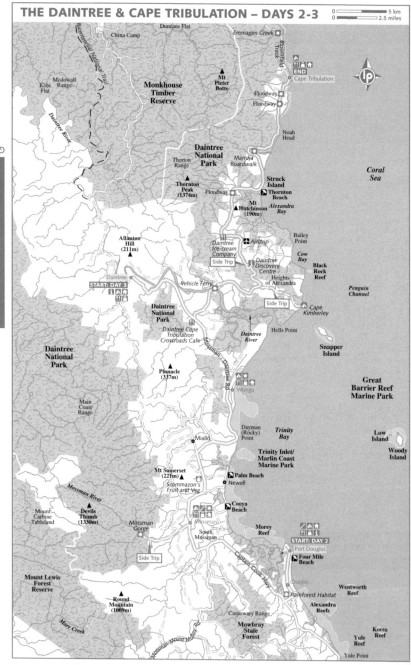

0 ————— 5 km
0 ————— 2.5 miles

Duncans Flat
China Camp
Emmagen Creek
Bloomfield Track
Bicentennial National Trail
Mcdowall Range
Kobi Flat
END
Cape Tribulation
Mt Pieter Botte
Monkhouse Timber Reserve
Floodway
Floodway
Daintree River
Noah Head
Daintree National Park
Thorton Range
Marrdja Boardwalk
Coral Sea
Thornton Peak (1374m)
Floodway
Struck Island
Thornton Beach
Mt Hutchinson (190m)
Alexandra Bay
Allanton Hill (211m)
Daintree Ice-cream Company
Airstrip
Bailey Point
Side Trip
Daintree Discovery Centre
Cow Bay
Black Rock Reef
Daintree
START: DAY 3
Vehicle Ferry
Heights of Alexandra
Penguin Channel
Daintree National Park
Side Trip
Cape Kimberley
Daintree Cape Tribulation Crossroads Cafe
Mossman–Daintree Rd
Daintree River
Hells Point
Snapper Island
Daintree National Park
Pinnacle (337m)
Great Barrier Reef Marine Park
Main Coast Range
Wonga
Dayman (Rocky) Point
Trinity Bay
Low Island
Woody Island
Miallo
Trinity Inlet/Marlin Coast Marine Park
Mossman River
Mt Somerset (221m)
Palm Beach
Newell
Scommazon's Fruit and Veg
Cooya Beach
Mossman
Morey Reef
Mount Carbine Tableland
Devils Thumb (1330m)
Mossman Gorge
South Mossman
START: DAY 2
Port Douglas
Side Trip
Four Mile Beach
Mount Lewis Forest Reserve
Craiglie
Rainforest Habitat
Wentworth Reef
Round Mountain (1009m)
Captain Cook Hwy
Alexandra Reefs
Mary Creek
Mossman–Mount Molloy Rd
Cassowary Range
Mowbray State Forest
Korea Reef
Yule Reef
Yule Point

Douglas Rd; adult/child $29/14.50; 8am-5pm) is one of the best wildlife tourist parks in north Queensland.

Down-to-earth Mossman (19.8km) is an unpretentious working town, focused on its **sugar mill** (tours possible; www.mossag.com.au) and seemingly impervious to the tourist turbulence around it. From its centre, detour to Mossman Gorge, a side trip in the Daintree National Park.

Scommazon's fruit shed (24.5km) is a cornucopia of locally grown produce – coffee, honey and tropical fruit. Choose what's in season from among soursop, mangosteen, durian and creamy-lemon-flavoured rollinia.

As you turn inland from Wonga (37.3km), whose peaceful 7km ribbon of **beach** unfortunately has no stinger enclosure, the rainforest at last closes in around you. Winding through the Daintree Valley, you get a real sense of the wild north. The first thing you'll probably notice is the prolific and vocal winged life.

SIDE TRIP: MOSSMAN GORGE
½–1 hour, 11km

The term 'gorge' is a bit exaggerated, but the water has certainly incised a valley through the granite. Turtles and hovering perch lurk beneath the river's surface, while dazzling blue Ulysses butterflies flutter above. A short **walk** links riverbank lookouts, and a 2.7km **rainforest loop** just scratches the surface of this 560-sq-km park.

From Mossman, turn left on Johnston Rd (signed to Mossman Gorge), which climbs gently up the valley – watch the slippery cobbles at the entrance to Daintree National Park. **Mossman Gorge Gateway** (☎ 07-4098 2595; www.yalanji.com

.au; 8.30am-5pm Mon-Sat), right at the entrance, is an Aboriginal community-run visitors centre, gallery and shop, from which excellent 1½-hour **Kuku Yalanji Dreamtime guided walks** (adult/child $32/18.50; 9am, 11am, 1pm and 3pm) are run.

Day 3: Daintree to Cape Tribulation
2¾–5 hours, 49.3km

Retracing the Day 2 route for 10km, the ride continues north, crossing the Daintree River by ferry and passing into largely intact tropical lowland rainforest, much of it protected as Daintree National Park. The 200m Heights of Alexandra range is the physical challenge of the day. From here the scenery alternates between cleared freehold blocks and dense woodlands. Three floodway crossings can prove barriers during heavy rains. If in doubt wait a few hours as the waters usually subside quickly.

The 10-minute ferry trip (bikes $1) is the cheapest cruise on the Daintree. The river really is a frontier. Beyond it there's no sugarcane, less traffic and lots of trees. However, with 1000 freehold properties, it's no wilderness. At least the development is low-key and many blocks are being bought back for conservation.

The first worthy side trip (at 18.9km) to **Cape Kimberley** is typically Daintree, a gravel road to a quiet resort and an almost deserted beach. It's on roads like this that you might happen upon a magnificent cassowary.

The second detour (at 23.6km) takes in the **Daintree Discovery Centre** (☎ 07-4098 9171; www.daintree-rec.com.au; Tulip Oak Rd; adult/child $28/15; 8.30am-5pm), an award-winning rainforest interpretive centre. Entry includes displays

THE DAINTREE & CAPE TRIBULATION – DAY 3

CUE		GPS COORDINATES
start	Daintree visitors centre	145°19'06"E 16°15'00"S
0km	go S on Stewart St	
0.1	Osborne St	
0.6	Douglas St	
2.8	50m narrow bridge	
10.0	'to Ferry Crossing'	
13.7	ferry jetty	
{ferry across Daintree River}		
{18.9	Cape Kimberley 10.9km}	
	2.6km moderate	

CUE CONTINUED		GPS COORDINATES
{23.6	Discovery Centre 600m}	
{28.3	Daintree Ice-Cream Co}	
33.4	floodway on Cooper Creek	
40.4	50m pick-a-plank bridge	
{41.7	Marrdja Boardwalk}	
43.6	1.3km moderate climb	
47.5	floodway on Thomson's Creek	
47.9	floodway on Myall Creek	
49.3	PK's Jungle Village, Cape Tribulation	145°27'35"E 16°05'56"S

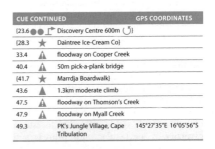

WET TROPICS WORLD HERITAGE AREA

Most of Australia was covered in rainforest 50 million years ago, but continental shift and climate change saw it dwindle to about 1% of the continent by the time Europeans arrived. After 200 years of logging, clearing and settlement, less than a third of that remains, half of which is in Queensland.

Despite strenuous resistance from the timber industry and state government the Wet Tropics World Heritage Area was declared in 1988, protecting the earth's oldest continually surviving tropical forest from commercial logging. Stretching from Townsville to Cooktown, it covers 9000 sq km of the coast and hinterland and includes Queensland's highest peak, Mt Bartle Frere (1622m), the Daintree–Cape Tribulation National Park and 2800 plant species, of which more than 700 are endemic.

Local residents now overwhelmingly support the World Heritage listing, with ecotourism easily eclipsing sugar as Far North Queensland's biggest industry. For more information on the Wet Tropics, visit www.wettropics.gov.au.

---

on rainforest animals and Gondwanan history, a 23m canopy-viewing tower and guided walks.

The **Daintree Ice-Cream Company** (☎ 07-4098 9114; Cape Tribulation Rd; ice cream $5; 11am-5pm) at 28.3km is the third must-stop kind of place, fabled for its exotic-fruit flavours. Whether wattleseed, black sapote (chocolate-pudding fruit) or jackfruit, they're all delicious.

The **Maardja boardwalk** (41.7km) takes advantage of its 'where-rainforest-meets-the-sea' geography to show off three distinct plant communities. The amazing fan palms are an icon of Cape Tribulation, the 'centre' of which is upon you before you know it.

ATHERTON TABLELAND

Duration 5 days
Distance 242.3km
Difficulty moderate
Start Kuranda
Finish Cairns
Summary Spin your wheels through cool climes, waterfalls, crater lakes, rainforest giants and historic towns. A quick visit to the highest point in the Queensland road system promises some great downhills.

Although Cairns' marine orientation is for very good reason, climbing back from its coast are highlands known as the Atherton Tableland. Far from being flat, though, the region is an unpredictable patchwork of richly fertile fields, extended forests, a diversity of spectacular natural areas and endearing country towns and people. This ride takes in a little of it all.

HISTORY

The coastal ranges were a formidable challenge to non-Indigenous settlers, who arrived in the 1870s in search of shiny saleable metal. In addition to what was found in the ground, they located a rich volcanic soil that would later make the Tableland the fertile food bowl of the region. Many who stayed in the area turned to agriculture. Curiously, a sizeable Chinese population in the late 19th-century grew 80% of Tableland crops, the clearing for which displaced the original inhabitants (from the Djirbal language group).

The history of Gillies Hwy is of some interest. Originally a mule-train route, a single-lane road was cut, largely by hand, over a three-year period. There were 611 bends in the range section and the one-way traffic was controlled by a gate system that remained in place until 1959.

PLANNING
When to Cycle

Although milder and drier than the coast, the Tableland is still subject to Far North weather patterns (see p316).

What to Bring

With elevations reaching up to 1100m, the Tableland often obliges people to don good raincoats and warm clothes even in summer. If you choose to camp in Granite Gorge (see Day 2 side trip) instead of a hotel in Mareeba, pack a tent and food supplies.

Maps

The free maps distributed at visitors centres are more than sufficient for this ride. Great Tropical Drive's 1:300,000 *Central Region* map covers it all, as does the Panorama Publications' 1:250,000 *Tropical Atherton Tableland* map. Also useful is the QPWS's *Tablelands Parks and Forest Area Guide for the Cairns Highlands*, with a map and heaps of details about different park facilities.

GETTING TO/FROM THE RIDE

Link this ride with The Daintree & Cape Tribulation ride (p317), which starts from Cairns.

Kuranda (start)

BUS

John's Kuranda Bus (☎ 0418-772 953; tickets $4) runs a service between Cairns and Kuranda five times a day, but won't take bikes. Buses depart from Cairns' Lake St Transit Centre.

TRAIN

The **Kuranda Scenic Railway** (☎ 07-4036 9333; www.ksr.com.au) is justly famous. Trains depart Cairns daily at 8.30am and 9.30am ($40, bikes $10; 1¾ hours). Arrive early since it's only two bikes per train.

BICYCLE

Kuranda is 27km northwest of Cairns. Follow Day 1 of The Daintree & Cape Tribulation ride (p317) to Smithfield, and turn left onto the Kennedy Hwy. It's busy but scenic, steadily climbing 400m before descending 100m to Kuranda.

Cairns (finish)

See p336.

THE RIDE
Day 1: Kuranda to Mareeba
2–2¾ hours, 36.9km

This easy, undulating ride has a gradual overall climb. The rainforest is quickly supplanted first by open eucalypt forest and then, around Mareeba, by irrigated farmland growing a rich variety of crops. There are no services between Kuranda and Mareeba, so stock everything you'll need. For self-sufficient cyclists an overnight alternative to Mareeba is the Granite Gorge campsite 15km further (see Day 2 side trip).

ATHERTON TABLELAND – DAY 1

CUE			GPS COORDINATES
start		Kuranda visitors centre	145°38'01"E 16°49'10"S
0km		go SE on Therwine St	
0.0	↱	(70m) Coondoo St	
0.2	↘	Rob Vievers Dr	
1.4	↰	Kennedy Hwy `to Mareeba'	
18.5	↑	cross Davies Creek	
{22.8 ●●	↰	Davies Creek 12.5km (↻)}	
{29.3 ●●	↱	Jacques Coffee 9km (↻)}	
35.5	↘	`to Town Centre'	
35.4	↱	Byrnes St	
36.9		Mareeba visitors centre	145°25'15"E 16°59'17"S

Detour (at 23.9km) down a gravel road to **Davies Creek**, where the granite bed runs with cool, clear water year-round. Lace monitors (goannas) and birds are common throughout the picnic area and some nice swimming holes; self-registration camping costs $4.80 per person. The 75m-high Davies Creek Falls are 2km (one hour return) further along the road.

Approaching Mareeba, you can't miss the signs for **Jacques Coffee Plantation** (29.3km; ☎ 07-4093 3284; www .jacquescoffee.com; 137 Leotta Rd). They point 4.5km northwest to one of the area's several working coffee farms open for tours and tastings (adult/child $12/5).

Day 2: Mareeba to Herberton
3½–6 hours, 61km

Today's route climbs almost imperceptibly for most of the distance, generally through rich agricultural land that finally gives way to the forested hills of the Herberton Range.

Along Chewko Rd the farms tackle tobacco (look for the covered drying sheds) or, more commonly, avocado, macadamia, mango, coffee, sugarcane and Indigenous tea tree. In one pleasantly shaded area stop at the **Mt Uncle Distillery** (20.4km; ☎ 07-4086 8008; www.mtuncle.com; 1819 Chewko Rd; 10am-5pm), which produces seasonal liqueurs using local banana, coffee, mulberry and lemon.

The Kennedy Hwy, despite its weighty name, is usually light on traffic. During WW2 that was probably not the case, as the **Rocky Creek War Memorial Park** (31.2km) attests. From 1943 to 1945 the Tableland was the largest military base in

QUEENSLAND

QUEENSLAND

ATHERTON TABLELAND – MAP 1

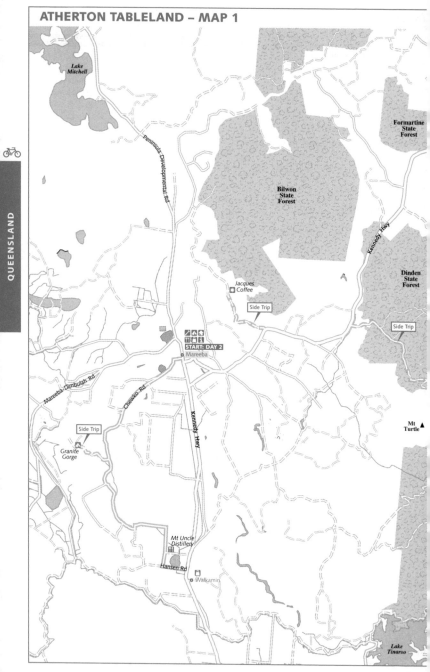

Lake Mitchell

Peninsula Developmental Rd

Formartine State Forest

Kennedy Hwy

Bilwon State Forest

Dinden State Forest

Jacques Coffee

Side Trip

Side Trip

START: DAY 2
Mareeba

Mareeba-Dimbulah Rd

Chewko Rd

Kennedy Hwy

Side Trip

Granite Gorge

Mt Turtle

Mt Uncle Distillery

Hansen Rd

Walkamin

Lake Tinaroo

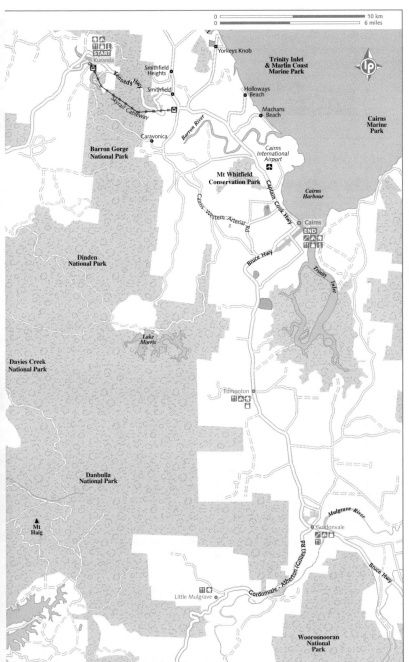

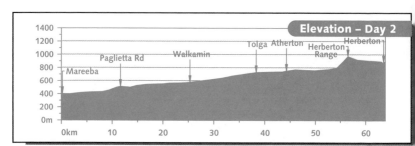

Elevation – Day 2

ATHERTON TABLELAND – DAY 2

CUE		GPS COORDINATES
start	Mareeba visitors centre	145°25'15"E 16°59'17"S
0km	go NE on Byrnes St	
1.6	Rankin St 'to Granite Gorge'	
2.2	Chewko Rd	
{11.2	Granite Gorge 8.2km}	
13.0	Chewko Rd 'Tourist Drive 2'	
19.1	unsigned road	
{20.4	Mt Uncle Distillery}	
21.7	Hansen Rd 'to Atherton'	
23.4	Kennedy Hwy	

CUE CONTINUED		GPS COORDINATES
24.4	Walkamin	145°25'34"E 17°07'44"S
{31.2	Rocky Creek War Memorial}	
37.1	Tolga	145°28'46"E 17°13'06"S
41.6	'to Herberton'	
42.3	Atherton	145°28'29"E 17°16'07"S
{43.5	Hou Wang Temple (LHS)}	
51.7	2.3km steep climb	
60.4	200m steep descent to Wild River	
61.0	Herberton post office	145°23'07"E 17°23'03"S

Australia and the park is located on the site of the largest field hospital in the wartime southern hemisphere.

Tolga (37.1km) is the first community of any size since leaving Mareeba. Its **Tolga Woodworks Gallery & Cafe** (☎ 07-4095 4488; www.tolgawoodworks.com.au; Kennedy Hwy) features an exceptional range of crafted products. The adjoining cafe serves light meals.

Atherton (42.3km) is a large centre with all facilities. It's a good place for lunch and, as home of the **Tablelands Cycle Sports Club** (☎ 07-4091 3838), for gathering information about social rides in the area (one regularly scheduled group leaves from the Atherton pool at 7am on Sundays).

Don't miss the **Atherton Chinatown** (☎ 07-4091 6945; www.houwang.org.au; 86 Herberton Rd; adult/concession/child $10/7.50/5; 10am-4pm), which provides insight into the lives of more than 500 Chinese migrants who came to the region in the late 1800s. There's a museum and a guided tour of the only remaining building, the historic **Hou Wang Temple**.

The Herberton Range is a solid climb, but the reverse is good fun. It's not all downhill though – a crazy swoop to the

Wild River precedes a hard grind up to the centre of town at the end of the day. Just before the final drop, take a look at the **Herberton Historic Village** (www.herbertonhistoricvillage.com.au), a remarkable collection of 30 or so 19th-century historic Australian structures.

SIDE TRIP: GRANITE GORGE
30–45 minutes, 8.2km
Popular **Granite Gorge** (www.granitegorge.com.au) is signed all the way along Paglietta Rd. The campsite backs onto Granite Creek – a jumble of granite boulders populated by rock wallabies. The marked walk around the gorge takes an hour, and the swimming hole, though permanent, can get pretty soupy. The facilities are fairly basic, but at $12 per person (including the $7.50 nature park entry fee), everyone's happy. Bring everything you need.

Day 3: Herberton to Millaa Millaa
2–3¾ hours, 38km
Today you hit the state's highest road, which means you're either wowed by views or trapped inside a cloud. The distance is short to allow for the hilly but advisable side trip (at 15.1km) to

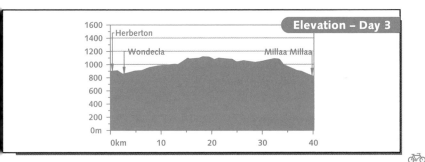

ATHERTON TABLELAND – DAY 3

CUE		GPS COORDINATES
start	Herberton post office	145°23'07"E 17°23'03"S
0km	go S on Perkins St	
3.0	Wondecla	145°23'32"E 17°24'40"S
13.0	1.7km steep climb	
15.1	`to Ravenshoe'	
{	The Crater 10.2km	
{17.4	Qld's highest road 1.2km	
23.7	East Evelyn Rd `to Millaa Millaa'	
28.7	follow paved road	
31.4	2km steep descent	
{	McHugh Lookout 1.5km	
36.0	`to Millaa Millaa'	
37.8	`to Main Street'	
38.0	Tobin's Market, Millaa Millaa	145°36'47"E 17°30'48"S

the **Crater**. The highlight, although not highest point, of the route, is the **Millaa Millaa Lookout**.

Like the last two days, you're faced with a long but easy climb, this time up to the dairy pastures of the Evelyn Tableland, which is, of course, anything but flat. The vegetation becomes gradually greener, tending to rainforest near the Kennedy Hwy. More WW2-era reminders mark the sites of camps used by Allied forces when the Tableland was used as a **wartime training area** and staging post.

The short (0.6km) additional rise on the side trip (at 17.4km) to the highest point of the Queensland road system is a must. The summit has a reasonable view and a sign for the obligatory photograph.

Detour (at 33.4km) to the Millaa Millaa or **McHugh Lookout,** known colloquially as the Gentle Annie, a sarcastic reference to the 10% climb there from town. Fortunately, it's all downhill for a cruisey conclusion to the day.

SIDE TRIP: THE CRATER
¾–1 hour, 10.2km

The key feature of Mt Hypipamee National Park is the Crater, a vertical-sided vent blasted through solid granite. It's a giddying 58m to the water's surface, and the sheer walls continue 85m underwater.

Although small, the park sits astride the transition zone from wet, open forest to rainforest. The upshot is a remarkable diversity of plants and animals. The mammals are nocturnal, but not the raucous birdlife.

Pedalling through superb rainforest, you almost forget the steep ups and downs, but the long final descent to the park does mean a 150m return climb. The park has picnic tables, toilets and drinking water, and the crater is a 400m stroll from the car park.

Day 4: Millaa Millaa to Yungaburra
2–3¾ hours, 37.4 km

This short ride allows plenty of time for the 18.5km Falls Circuit side trip. Ride it without panniers before heading to Yungaburra. The rolling hills of the central Tableland area have been heavily cleared, but the scenic highlights preserved.

Tarzali (14.3km) was a major timber centre and retains one of the Tableland's few operating mills. Malanda (23.4km) is the milk capital of North Queensland, although it delivers internationally as well. The town features the **Malanda Hotel**, reputedly the southern hemisphere's largest timber building, and the **Majestic Theatre** (www.majestictheatre.com.au ; 10 Station St), perhaps Australia's longest continually running theatre (since 1928).

Malanda Falls, a 1.8km return side trip from town, drops 2m into an artificial pool –

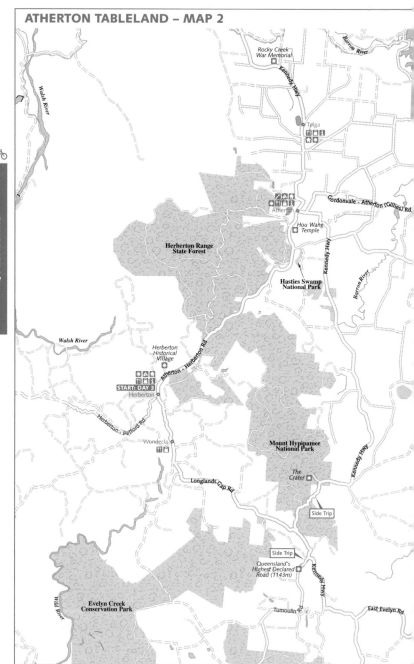

ATHERTON TABLELAND – MAP 2

Walsh River

Rocky Creek War Memorial

Barron River

Kennedy Hwy

Tolga

Atherton

Cordonvale – Atherton (Gillies) Rd

Hou Wang Temple

Herberton Range State Forest

Hasties Swamp National Park

Barron River

Kennedy Hwy

Walsh River

Herberton Historical Village

Atherton – Herberton Rd

START: DAY 3
Herberton

Herberton – Petford Rd

Wondecla

Mount Hypipamee National Park

The Crater

Longlands Gap Rd

Side Trip

Side Trip

Queensland's Highest Declared Road (1143m)

Kennedy Hwy

Evelyn Creek Conservation Park

Wild River

Tumoulin Rd

East Evelyn Rd

QUEENSLAND

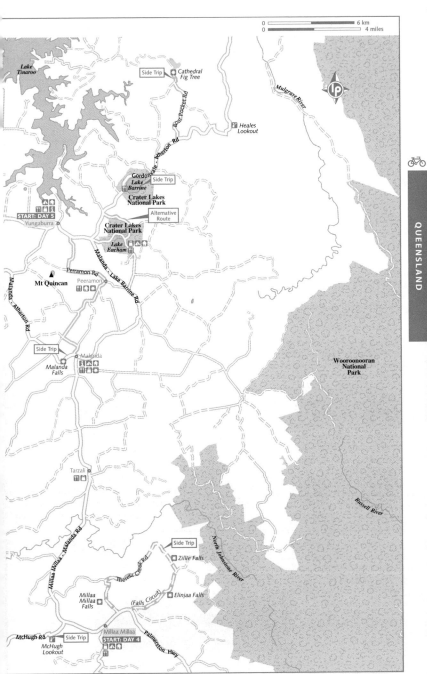

QUEENSLAND

no visual marvel, but a good place to cool off. The adjacent **Malanda Environmental Centre** has a good display on the region's geology.

The 1908 **Peeramon Hotel** (30.3km) is the archetypal Australian country pub – broad verandas, cold beer and old number plates nailed over the bar.

From Peeramon the route passes close to the cinder cone of **Mt Quincan**, a sign of the Tableland's ancient volcanic history.

SIDE TRIP: FALLS CIRCUIT
1–1¾ hours, 18.5km

There's plenty of up and down on this well-established and well-marked tour of three waterfalls. Take snacks and water, but leave your gear in Millaa.

A 300m walk from the Elinjaa Falls picnic area leads through regenerating rainforest to the base of the falls. The undercut

ATHERTON TABLELAND – DAY 4

CUE		GPS COORDINATES
start	Tobin's Market, Millaa Millaa	145°36'47"E 17°30'48"S
0km	go SW on Main St	
0.2	⬆ `to Malanda'	
▲	3.3km gradual climb	
{ ● ●⬆	Falls Circuit 18.7km (↺) }	
14.3	Tarzali	
145°36'12"E	17°25'26"S	
22.9	⬆ `to Atherton'	
23.4	★ Malanda	145°35'34"E 17°21'06"S
	⬆ Mary St	
{ ● ●↘	Malanda Falls 1.8km (↺) }	
24.2	↘ Pound Rd	
30.3	Peeramon	145°36'56"E 17°18'25"S
36.9	⬆ Rte 52 `to Yungaburra'	
37.4	⤳ Cedar St `to info centre'	
37.4	(50m) Yungaburra info centre	145°34'55"E 17°16'13"S

Zillie Falls have a big jumble of basalt blocks at the base, reachable via a slippery 200m trail from the head of the falls, just 50m from the road. Millaa Millaa Falls are the Tableland's most scenic. They're 400m down a steep side road in well-preserved rainforest. The circular plunge pool is great for a swim, but don't expect tropical warmth.

From town follow the Palmerston Hwy towards Innisfail. Pass the turn-off to Millaa Millaa Falls – saving the best for last – and turn left, after 2.3km, onto Theresa Creek Rd (signed to Elinjaa and Zillie Falls).

Day 5: Yungaburra to Cairns
3¾–7 hours, 69km

All that hard-earned elevation is lost in one dreamlike descent. It's preceded by two of the Tableland's finest natural attractions (see alternative route and side trip).

Yungaburra is famous for its two nearby crater lakes, Eacham and Barrine, now part of Crater Lakes National Park. Formed by volcanic explosions when hot magma met ground water, they are now tranquil pools surrounded by lush rainforest. **Lake Barrine** (the side trip at 9.3km) is larger and less disturbed than **Lake Eacham** (see alternative route). An elegant old **teahouse** (www.lakebarrine.com.au) overlooks Lake Barrine and regular cruises give commentary on the forest and animals. Enjoy a swim and the 5km walking track past 50m-tall bull kauri pines, some of which are estimated to be more than 1000 years old.

The long and winding descent of the Lamb Range through World Heritage-listed park will not be quickly forgotten. You cover almost 20km and 260 bends

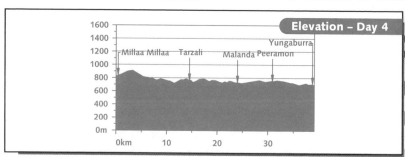

Elevation – Day 4

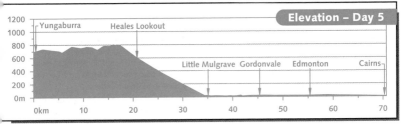

ATHERTON TABLELAND – DAY 5

CUE		GPS COORDINATES
start	Yungaburra info centre	145°34'55"E 17°16'13"S
0km	go SE on Cedar St	
0	↑ (50m) Gillies Way	
{3.6	⌐ alt route: Lake Eacham 7.4km}	
{5.1	alt route rejoins ⌐▸}	
{9.3	●● ⌐▸ Lake Barrine 800m (⟳)}	
{13.0	●● ⌐⌐ Cathedral Fig Tree 11.5km (⟳)}	
34.2	Little Mulgrave	145°43'24"E 17°08'28"S
35.5	⚠ tram tracks	
36.5	⚠ tram tracks	
43.8	⌐⌐ 'to Cairns', Gordonvale	145°46'48"E 17°06'00"S
54.3	⌐⌐ Edmonton	145°44'41"E 17°01'09"S
67.1	⤢🛗 'to City via Spence St'	
67.9	⌐⌐ Spence St	
68.9	⌐⌐ Esplanade	
69.0	Gateway Discovery Centre, Cairns	145°46'42"E 16°55'16"S

before you need to touch the pedals. A quick stop at **Heales Lookout** (23.8km) takes in the views south over the Mulgrave Valley.

Traffic on the valley floor gets heavy due to local quarrying industries, but is nothing like the congestion, heat and humidity when headed back to Cairns. At least the road is flat, has a good shoulder and there's usually a tailwind.

ALTERNATIVE ROUTE: LAKE EACHAM
30–45 minutes, 7.4km

Lake Eacham is a great place for a swim, picnic and 4.5km walk around its perimeter. Saw-shelled turtles and water dragons are common.

At 3.6km turn right to Malanda and Lake Eacham. After 50m turn left still following signs to Lake Eacham. To return, backtrack 300m from the lake's edge and veer right on Wrights Creek Rd, signed to Cairns. Go right when you hit the highway.

SIDE TRIP: CATHEDRAL FIG TREE
¾–1 hour, 11.5km

It's totally worth pedalling 11.5km over hilly terrain just to see this tree. This banyan, or green fig, is immense and makes an impression that outlasts the pain of getting there. The supporting root network has a girth of 43m. The canopy, 50m overhead, covers the area of two Olympic swimming pools, and the limbs support epiphyte colonies the size of small cars.

Turn left on Boar Pocket Rd (at 13km) and follow signs.

MOUNTAIN BIKE RIDES

BRISBANE
Gap Creek Reserve

On the slopes of Mt Coot-tha, a series of mountain bike (MTB) trails radiating out from the Gap Creek picnic area offer some of the best off-road riding near to the city. The contouring Echidna Trail and Rocket Frog Trail are good starting rides for newcomers to MTB, while Whipbird Way and Bandicoot Byway can be linked for a good singletrack circuit. The tighter, more technical Pipeline Track is the challenge for experienced riders, with rock gardens, log jumps and some narrow boards.

SUNSHINE COAST
Noosa Trail Network

At the northern end of the Sunshine Coast, the Noosa Shire has created five marked off-road trails, cutting through state forest and along back roads. The majority of the trails converge at the town of Kin Kin, making this a good base for the routes to Lake Macdonald, Cooran or the countryside loop around town. The

ATHERTON TABLELAND MOUNTAIN BIKING

Although at the time of writing it doesn't yet have an official bike park or any waymarked bike trails, the Atherton Tableland around Atherton, Herberton and Mareeba has already secured an international reputation as a first-rate mountain biking area. Hundreds of kilometres of existing track have lured in several world-class endurance mountain bike events that, in part because of the location, are drawing ever-larger and increasingly diverse rosters of riders.

Pending council cooperation and completion of feasibility studies, special recognised bike facilities in the Atherton Tableland could be the new permanent home of mountain bike races like the Herberton 8-Hour Mountain Bike Challenge and the **Crocodile Trophy** (www.crocodile-trophy.com), the latter claiming to be the world's most brutal mountain bike race. Any new infrastructure will of course be open to the public.

For the latest updates ask at the visitors centres in Herberton (p339) or Atherton, or contact the **Cairns Mountain Bike Club** (www.cairnsmtb.com) or **Tableland Cycle Sports Club** (☎ 0418-878 391, 07-4091 3838).

routes to Lake Macdonald (through the Ringtail State Forest) and Cooran (through Woondum Forest Reserve) require permits; these can be obtained free from Queensland Parks & Wildlife Service. The five routes are marked on the *Noosa Shire Cycling & Walking Map*, which can be picked up at visitors centres in the region. There's also some good singletrack in the Tewantin State Forest that's not shown on the map.

CAIRNS
Smithfield Mountain Bike Park
In 1996 Cairns hosted the mountain biking world championship, an event that became the origin of this MTB park set in the hills of the city's northern suburbs. Operated by the Cairns Mountain Bike Club, it has downhill, cross country and mountain X tracks. The cross country tracks are made up of singletrack and doubletrack; expect plenty of climbing. Access the park from McGregor Rd.

TOWNS & FACILITIES

ALLIGATOR CREEK
As the only easily accessible campsite with facilities in Bowling Green Bay National Park, Alligator Creek is very popular with both day-trippers and overnighters. The stream, fed by the clouded upper slopes of Mt Elliot, rarely stops flowing and is the prominent feature of the 16km (five hours return) easy–moderate track to the

spectacular Alligator Falls. Otherwise, cool off in the creek's rock pools and watch the agile rock wallabies and scrub turkeys roam around the campsite.

Camping is the only option at Alligator Creek. Four sites can be booked in advance (☎ 13 13 04; www.qld.gov.au/camping; per person $4.85), while you must self-register for the remaining spaces on a first-come-first-served basis. Showers, picnic shelters and gas barbeques are available.

Bring food and cooking gear for all meals, although the **Crazy Gecko** family restaurant 3.1km from the campsite may also be open.

BEAUDESERT
☎ 07 / pop 4900
Beaudesert is country Australia when it's not aspiring to be something else: big hats, utes, wide streets, a pub on each corner, thongs as dress attire. There are no real sights, just a bit of authentic, dusty charm.

Information
The **visitors centre** (☎ 07-5541 4495; 2 Enterprise Dr) is 3km north of the town centre. A more convenient option is the information desk at the **historical museum** (Beaudesert Historical Museum and Visitor Information Centre; ☎ 07-5541 3740; Brisbane St).

Sleeping & Eating
Beaudesert Caravan & Tourist Park (☎ 07-5541 1368; Albert St; unpowered/powered sites for two $17/20, cabins $65) More residential than a holiday park,

campsites are limited to a small grassed area at the back of the park, but it's unlikely that you'll ever have more friendly or down-to-earth neighbours.

Kerry Court Motel (☎ 07-5541 1593; kerrycourtmotel@optusnet.com.au; cnr Albert & Brisbane Sts; s/d/tw $66/88/98) Beaudesert's best motel has beautifully presented rooms and well-considered touches: microwave, DVD players (and libraries), blow dryers, stubby holders, even hand cream to soften those handlebar-roughened palms. Bikes can be locked up in a rear enclosure.

Baggs B&B (☎ 07-5541 0555; www .baggs.com.au; 41 Tina St; s $100-115, d $115-130) About 1km from the town centre, by the hospital, with neat, themed rooms and a self-contained unit. There's buffet breakfast or you can splurge ($12.50) on a tropical gourmet spread to start the day.

Everydays Cafe (☎ 07-5541 1226; 105 Brisbane St; breakfast $7-13; breakfast & lunch) Real style and real coffee in a real surprising location. The juices and cakes are as fresh as the shaded courtyard.

bh! (☎ 07-5541 1044; 80 Brisbane St; mains $15-25; lunch & dinner Mon-Sat) Chic name, standard pub grub in the central Beaudesert Hotel.

Railway Hotel (☎ 07-5541 3848; 121 Brisbane St; mains $11-24, steak $21-41; dinner) You've entered beef country, so head to the Railway's steakhouse, which is that rare kind of pub that prefers not to cook well-done. The big beef here is the elite-cut Wagyu rib-eye on the bone.

The Border Loop ride passes **Foodworks** (Mt Lindesay Hwy) as it enters town. Otherwise try **Coles** (cnr Anna & William Sts) or **Woolworths** (Beaudesert Plaza, Brisbane St).

BRISBANE
☎ 07 / pop 1.8 million
It may be Australia's third-largest city, but for the longest time Brisbane was seen as something of a poor cousin to Sydney and Melbourne: a sleepy country town hiding behind a big city façade. In recent years, however, Brisbane has stirred from its slumber as people become aware of its perfect lifestyle, world-class art galleries, a

booming live music scene and fabulous cafe culture. For all that, the city still retains the laid-back, easy attitude of a small community.

For ride information around the city, pick up a copy of the city council's *Brisbane Bicycle Experience Guide* booklet from visitors centres. Maps of Brisbane bikepaths and bike lanes can be downloaded at www .brisbane.qld.gov.au; type 'bikeways' into the search box and then click on the 'Bikeway maps' link.

Information
Brisbane Visitors Information Centre (☎ 07-3006 6290; Queen St Mall; 9am-5.30pm Mon-Thu, 9am-7pm Fri, 9am-4.30pm Sat, 9.30am-4pm Sun) Located between Edward and Albert Sts. Great one-stop information counter for all things Brisbane.

Brisbane Visitors Accommodation Service (☎ 07-3236 2020; 3rd fl, Roma St Transit Centre, Roma St; 7.30am-6pm Mon-Sat, 8am-6pm Sun) Privately run outfit specialising in backpacker travel, tours and accommodation in Brisbane and elsewhere in Queensland.

Naturally QLD (☎ 1300 130 372; 160 Ann St; 8.30am-5pm Mon-Fri) The Queensland Parks & Wildlife Service (QPWS) runs this excellent information centre. You can get maps, brochures and books on national parks and state forests, as well as camping information. You can also visit **South Bank Visitors Centre** (☎ 07-3867 2051; www.visitsouthbank .com.au; Stanley St Plaza, South Bank Parklands; 9am-5pm)

Supplies & Equipment
City-centre bike stores include **Lifecycle** (☎ 07-3831 2611; 276 Petrie St; 10am-6pm Mon & Tue, 10am-7pm Wed-Fri, 9am-4pm Sat) and **Victor Cycles** (☎ 07-3211 0111; 125 Margaret St; 8.30-6pm Mon-Fri, 10am-3pm Sat). The small shopfront at **Ridgway Cycles** (☎ 07-3355 9653; 609 Stafford Rd, Stafford Heights), 8km north of the city centre, belies the fact that it's like a cycling bric-a-brac store inside. It stocks a huge range of spares and will track down the unusual. There's also a **Goldcross** (☎ 07-3205 1096; 751 Gympie Rd, Lawton; 8.30am-5.30pm Mon-Wed & Fri, 8.30am-

9pm Thu, 9am-5pm Sat, 10am-5pm Sun) bike store about 2km from the start of the Mt Mee ride.

World Wide Maps & Guides (☎ 07-3221 4330; www.worldwidemaps.com.au; Shop 30, Anzac Square Arcade, 267 Edward St, Brisbane) has a comprehensive range of travel guides and Queensland maps. RACQ road maps can be obtained from the **RACQ head office** (☎ 13 19 05; www.racq.com.au; 261 Queen St).

Sleeping & Eating

Newmarket Gardens Caravan Park (☎ 07-3356 1458; www.newmarketgardens.com.au; 199 Ashgrove Ave, Ashgrove; unpowered/powered sites for two $27/30, caravans $47, cabins $80-100; pi) This clean site is just 4km north of the city centre and is connected to town by several bus routes and the Citytrain (Newmarket station). There aren't too many trees, but the bathrooms are spotless and there are good laundries and BBQs on-site. There are shady spots in the bottom corner of the park (around sites 193 and 194). Book in advance for cabins.

Homestead (☎ 1800 658 344, 07-3358 3538; 57 Annie St, New Farm; dm $22-26, d $69) A great old house in a top location, Homestead has four-, six- and eight-bed dorms (mixed and female-only). There's a large, clean kitchen and a cool lounge room with leather couches. Dorm 12 has the newest bunks, while room 6 is the best double with heaps of space for your bikes. There's a courtesy bus into the city and Fortitude Valley on weekends.

Brisbane Backpackers Resort (☎ 07-3844 9956; www.brisbanebackpackers.com.au; 110 Vulture St, West End; dm $24-28, d $73) 'Resort' is not in the title of this backpackers by accident – it's a class act. Perks include TVs, en suites and private balconies in the dorms, and a tiled outdoor area around the bar, which is spacious with a nice tropical feel. The hostel provides a courtesy bus, tours and meals, and is a very professionally run outfit. It's also very close to cafes and bars in the funky West End, as well as to South Bank.

Allender Apartments (☎ 07-3358 5832; www.allenderapartments.com.au; 3 Moreton St, New Farm; r $100-155) The yellow-brick façade may not grab you, but Allender's studios and one- and two-bedroom apartments are tasteful and immaculate. The cool, shaded interiors of the heritage and deluxe apartments are a fusion of funky décor and homely amenities and there's plenty of room to spread out. Allender also owns more contemporary apartments on nearby Villiers St.

One Thornbury House (☎ 07-3839 5334; www.onethornbury.com; 1 Thornbury St, Spring Hill; d $140-170) Behind a trellised frontage lies this classy guesthouse in a two-storey Queenslander, built in 1886. There are four rooms (three are en suite), all beautifully furnished in warm contemporary decor that contrasts vividly against rendered brick and weatherboard walls. The pick of the rooms is No 1, with a king-size bed and opulent bathroom: a speck of dirt would feel lonely in here. Other bonuses include the lovely rear courtyard designed for hours of quiet contemplation.

Brisbane's CBD has a number of fine eating options, but there is also an extensive array of culinary offerings outside the city centre. In Fortitude Valley you'll find inexpensive cafes and a smorgasbord of Asian flavours. Nearby, stylish New Farm is becoming the place to eat out in Brisbane with a large selection of multicultural eateries, including some very fine restaurants. West End is a distinctly cosmopolitan corner, with trendy cafes and eclectic cuisine. In every pocket of town, eateries take advantage of Brisbane's perfect winter climate with open-air courtyards or tables out on the street.

Java Coast Cafe (☎ 07-3211 3040; 340 George St; mains $6-10; 7.30am-4pm Mon-Fri) Fancy recapturing your zen while lunching under a canopy of trees in the middle of the CBD? Tables in the rear courtyard at this special city nook feel a mile away from the busy streets outside, and the tranquillity is accompanied by some quality tucker. Goodies include giant muffins, bagels, paninis and quiche. There are also 20 different varieties of tea and decent coffee.

Cha Cha Char (☎ 07-3211 9944; shop 5, Eagle St Pier; mains $30-40; lunch Mon-Fri, dinner daily) Wallowing in awards, many consider this Brisbane's best restaurant. Although you can tuck into fish, veal or duck dishes, it is primarily a steak restaurant – and a supremely good one at that. It's very classy without being pretentious as demonstrated by the diverse clientele.

There's a Coles Express on Queen St, just west of the mall, and a Woolworths on Edward St in the city. In Fortitude Valley there's a great produce market inside **McWhirters Marketplace** (cnr Brunswick & Wickham Sts). The Asian supermarkets in Chinatown mall also have an excellent range of fresh vegies, Asian groceries and exotic fruit. Not a potato, asparagus, pear or Lisbon lemon sits out of place at the upmarket **James St Market** (James St, Fortitude Valley). It's pricey, but the quality is excellent.

Getting There & Away

AIR

Brisbane's main airport is about 16km northeast of the city centre at Eagle Farm, and has separate international and domestic terminals almost 3km apart, linked by the **Airtrain** (☎ 07-3215 5000; www.airtrain .com.au; tickets $4), which runs every 15 to 30 minutes.

Qantas (☎ 13 13 13; www.qantas.com .au; 247 Adelaide St) connects Brisbane with Sydney (1½ hours), Melbourne (2½ hours), Adelaide (2½ hours), Canberra (two hours), Hobart (four hours), Perth (five hours) and Darwin (four hours). **Virgin Blue** (☎ 13 67 89; www.virginblue .com.au) flies between Brisbane and other Australian capitals, while **Jetstar** (☎ 13 15 38; www.jetstar.com.au) flies to all capitals (except Perth), as well as Cairns.

BUS

Bus companies have booking desks on the 3rd level of the Roma St Transit Centre. **Greyhound Australia** (☎ 13 14 99; www .greyhound.com.au) is the main company on the Sydney–Brisbane run; you can go via the New England Hwy (17 hours) or the Pacific Hwy (16 hours) for $125. **Premier Motor Service** (☎ 13 34 10; www.premierms.com.au) operates the same routes often, with slightly cheaper deals.

You can also travel between Brisbane and Melbourne ($230, 24 to 28 hours) or Adelaide ($300, 40 hours), although competitive airfares should enable you to fly for less.

Premier Motor Service runs one direct service daily to Cairns ($255, 29 hours), while Greyhound runs four. Places in this chapter along the route include Noosa ($20, 2½ hours), Townsville ($215, 23 hours).

TRAIN

Brisbane's main station for long-distance trains is the Roma St Transit Centre. For reservations and information contact the **Queensland Rail Travel Centre** (☎ 131 617; www.qr.com.au) Central Station (☎ 07-3235 1323; Ground fl, Central Station, 305 Edward St; 8am-5pm Mon-Fri); Roma St (☎ 07-3235 1331; Roma St Transit Centre, Roma St; 6am-5pm Mon-Fri).

CountryLink (☎ 13 22 32; www .countrylink.info) has a daily XPT (express passenger train) service between Brisbane and Sydney. The northbound service runs overnight, and the southbound service runs during the day (economy seat/1st-class seat $92/130; 15 hours).

The *Sunlander* travels between Brisbane and Cairns three times a week, leaving Brisbane on Tuesday, Thursday and Sunday morning and departing Cairns on Tuesday, Thursday and Saturday morning (economy seat/economy sleeper/1st-class sleeper/ Queenslander-class $215/270/415/760; 30 hours). The *Tilt Train*, a high-speed economy and business train, makes the trip from Brisbane to Cairns (business seat $310; 25 hours) leaving Brisbane at 6.25pm on Monday, Wednesday and Friday, and Cairns at 9.15am on Sunday, Wednesday and Friday. Economy seats are only available from Brisbane to Rockhampton ($105, eight hours).

CAR

Hertz (☎ 13 30 39), **Avis** (☎ 13 63 33), **Budget** (☎ 13 27 27), **Europcar** (☎ 13 13 90) and **Thrifty** (☎ 1300 367 227) have offices at the Brisbane airport terminals and throughout the city.

There are also several smaller companies in Brisbane that advertise slightly cheaper deals:

Abel Rent A Car (☎ 1800 131 429, 07-3236 1225; www.abel.com.au; cnr Wickham & Warren Sts, Fortitude Valley)

Ace Rental Cars (☎ 1800 620 408, 07-3862 2158; www.acerentals.com.au; 35 Sandgate Rd, Albion)

QUEENSLAND

East Coast Car Rentals (☎ 1800 028 881, 07-3839 9111; www.eastcoastcarrentals .com.au; 76 Wickham St, Fortitude Valley)

Hawk Rent A Car (☎ 07-3236 0788; www.hawkrentacar.com; 3rd fl, Roma St Transit Centre, Roma St)

Getting Around

Bicycles are allowed on Citytrains, except during weekday peak hours (7am to 9.30am going into the CBD and 3pm to 6.30pm heading out of the CBD). You can take bikes on CityCats and ferries for free.

CABOOLTURE
☎ 07 / pop 17,500

Fifty kilometres north of Brisbane, Caboolture is a modern centre with all amenities, though it offers little as a tourist stop; it's better to travel from Brisbane rather than stay overnight here.

Supplies & Equipment

Caboolture Cycle Sports (☎ 07-5495 7499; 31 Morayfield Rd), south of the centre, is a large store with a huge range of gear and spares.

Sleeping & Eating

Riverlakes Motel (☎ 07-5499 1766; www .riverlakesmotel.com.au; 14 Morayfield Rd; s & d $105-160), overlooking the Caboolture River, is the town's best motel.

Woolworths (Market Plaza, Morayfield Rd) is nearby and opens seven days a week.

CAIRNS
☎ 07 / pop 122,700

Popular Cairns, gateway to the Tropical North and the Great Barrier Reef, is unashamedly a tourist town. Take time before and after your pedalling to absorb its infectious holiday vibe. Start at the Esplanade foreshore and just follow your Havaianas.

Information

Ignore the glut of baffling tourist information centres and head straight for the government-run Gateway Discovery Centre (☎ 07-4051 3588; www.tropicalaustralia. com.au; 51 The Esplanade; 8.30am-6.30pm), which offers impartial advice, books tours and houses an interpretive centre. As always, the QPWS (see p316) disburses national park information and permits.

For information about cycling in and around Cairns, including social rides, check out the website of the Cairns Bicycle User Group (www.cairnsbug.org).

Supplies & Equipment

Bike hire, sales and repair are all possible at The Bike Man (☎ 07-4041 5566; www .bikeman.com.au; 99 Sheridan St; $15/50 per day/week).

Sleeping & Eating

Cairns Holiday Park (☎ 1800 259 977; 07-4051 1467; www.cairnscamping.com .au; 12-30 Little St; unpowered/powered sites $29/36, cabins from $60) is the closest campsite to the city centre with good facilities including backpacker cabins.

Serpent Hostel (☎ 1800 737 736, 07-4040 7777; www.serpenthostel.com; 341 Lake St; dm $14-28, d $50-85) is a bit away from the centre but a backpacker bubble with a huge pool, sports bar, free evening meals and free shuttle bus.

Northern Greenhouse (☎ 1800 000 541, 07-4047 7200; www.friendlygroup.com.au; 117 Grafton St; dm $25, tw $95, apt $120) has a laid-back vibe and is a cut above the backpackers. There's a central deck, pool, friendly staff and lots of free facilities such as internet and luggage storage.

Behind the train station, on and around Bunda St, is a group of colourful low-key hostels with similar facilities and prices. Cairns also has plenty of comfortable self-contained accommodation good for groups or families; virtually identical motels line Sheridan St with stand-by rates from as little as $75 a standard room.

The Esplanade between Shields and Aplin Sts and the Pier waterfront have every sort of eatery, operating at all hours. Some of Cairns' pubs also dish up surprisingly good budget meals. If you want something cheap and quick, the Night Markets, between the Esplanade and Abbott St, has a busy Asian-style food court.

Rattle & Hum (☎ 07-4031 3011; 65-67 The Esplanade; mains $13-23; 10am-midnight) has a prime people-watching position from which you can also watch the wood-fired pizzas being prepared or slip into the rustic 'outback saloon'-style restaurant.

Pier Bar & Grill (☎ 07-4031 4677; www .pierbar.com.au; Pier Point Rd; mains $13-

32; lunch & dinner) is hard to beat for informal waterfront dining. Its big deck overlooking the foreshore lagoon makes it very popular.

Donnini's Ciao Italia (☎ 07-4051 1133; Marina Boardwalk; mains $18-35; lunch & dinner) is rated by many locals as the best Italian in town. With its boardwalk location it's hard not to be lured in by the Mediterranean aromas.

Self-caterers can visit **Woolworth's** (btwn Lake & Abbott Sts) or the two **supermarkets** in Cairns Central Shopping Centre (McLeod St).

Getting There & Away
AIR
Cairns is the major **airport** servicing North Queensland, with both international flights and frequent domestic flights to/from all Australian capital cities. The terminal is a flat and easy 7km ride north of the city, just turn left from Airport Av onto the highway. Alternatively, **Australia Coach** (☎ 07-4040 1000; adult/child $10/5) shuttle buses meet all incoming flights and run to the CBD. **Black & White Taxis** (☎ 131 008) charges around $20.

BUS
Cairns is the hub for far north Queensland buses. **Greyhound Australia** (☎ 1300 473 946; www.greyhound.com.au; Reef Fleet Terminal) has four daily services down the coast to Brisbane ($298, 29 hours), via Townsville ($80, six hours), Airlie Beach ($135, 11 hours) and Rockhampton ($207, 18 hours). You can stop over at any point as long as you hop back on within six days. Buses leave from outside Reef Fleet Terminal at the southern end of the Esplanade.

TRAIN
The *Sunlander* departs Cairns on Tuesday, Thursday and Saturday for Brisbane (economy seat/sleeper $213/271, 31 hours), returning on Tuesday, Thursday and Sunday. The swifter *Tilt Train* operates over the same route (business-class seat $311, 24 hours) southbound on Sunday, Wednesday and Friday, northbound on Monday, Wednesday and Friday. The **train station**, on the southwest side of the Cairns Central shopping centre, is also the point of departure of the Scenic Railway to Kuranda

($40, $10 for bikes; 1¾ hours). Contact **Queensland Rail** (☎ 1800 872 467; www.traveltrain.com.au).

BICYCLE
Plenty of cyclists ride the main highway from Brisbane to Cairns but it's generally uninspiring and unpleasant. Riding in the other direction, into the wind, would be even worse.

CAPE TRIBULATION
☎ 07 / pop 600

The two principal attractions here are the beaches, Myall and Cape Tribulation, and the rainforest that tumbles down to meet them. In fact, backpackers and outdoor enthusiasts are so rapt by nature that there's no need for a town. It would just detract from this slice of paradise so inaptly named by Captain Cook.

Information
Most lodgings and Mason's Store (see Sleeping & Eating) offer information and can book from an extensive menu of guided outdoor activities. Otherwise, most just relax, swim, snorkel, fish and hike. The **ranger station** (☎ 07-4098 0052; 9-11am) is 1.4km to the north.

PK's Jungle Village has the only ATMs, although some accommodations have Eftpos facilities.

Sleeping & Eating
Cape Tribulation Camping (☎ 07-4098 0077; www.capetribcamping.com.au; unpowered/powered sites $30/36, d $65) has beach frontage and a good range of facilities, such as grassy campsites and safari-tent cabins with fans.

PK's Jungle Village (☎ 1800 232 333, 4098 0040; www.pksjunglevillage.com; unpowered sites per person $10, dm $23-28, d $92-115) is a long-time budget favourite, staffed by overworked backpackers. Its boozy bar/restaurant is the local entertainment hub.

Cape Trib Beach House (☎ 07-4098 0030; www.capetribbeach.com.au; dm $25-36, d $79-249) is a low-key alternative to PK's party house. Neat rainforest huts range from air-con dorms to overpriced private timber cabins. The breezy restaurant-bar keeps a pool table and games.

Rainforest Hideaway (☎ 07-4098 0108; www.rainforesthideaway.com; 19 Camelot Close; d $95-135) is a colourful, rambling B&B single-handedly built by the owner. It's extremely private, if you don't count the intruding cassowary.

Dragonfly Gallery Cafe (☎ 07-4098 0121; Lot 9, Camelot Close; mains $13-28; lunch & dinner) is a timber pole-house set in delightfully serene surrounds. The bar is open till late.

Myall Creek Takeaway (meals $5-10; 8am-7pm), next to Mason's, is the place for burgers, sandwiches and coffee.

Stock up at the **IGA Supermarket** (at PK's Jungle Village; 7am-8pm) or the adjacent **Mason's Store** (☎ 07-4098 0070; Cape Tribulation Rd; 8am-6pm).

EUMUNDI
☎ 07 / pop 490

Eumundi is an artsy small town without attitude. Beer is still its most famous export (even if it's no longer brewed) and a dental spa can sit side-by-side with a pub that has weekly gigs from Uncle Bob's Jug Band. The historic streetscape blends well with modern cafes, unique boutiques, silversmiths, craftsmen and body-artists doing their thing.

The **Eumundi markets** (6.30am-2pm Sat, 8am-1pm Wed) are the big gig in town, attracting thousands of visitors to 300-plus stalls and have everything from hand-crafted furniture and jewellery to homemade clothes and alternative healing booths.

Information

Pick up a copy of the *Noosa Shire Cycling & Walking Map*, which shows all bike routes around the region, at the **Discover Eumundi Heritage Visitors centre** (☎ 07-5442 8762; cnr Gridley St & Memorial Dr; 10am-4pm Mon-Fri, 9am-3pm Sat, 10am-2pm Sun).

Sleeping & Eating

If you want to camp, you'll need to stop in Kenilworth or push on to Pomona.

Hidden Valley B&B (☎ 07-5442 8685; www.eumundibed.com; 39 Caplick Way; r $175-195, railway carriage from $105) This not-so-hidden retreat is on 1.5 hectares of land only 1km from Eumundi on the Noosa road. Inside the attractive Queenslander you

can choose a themed room to match your mood – Aladdin's Cave, the Emperors Suite or the Hinterland Retreat. All have private balconies but there are simpler rooms in the converted railcar in the garden.

Harmony Hill Station (☎ 07-5442 7469; 81 Seib Rd; carriage $120) Perched on a hilltop, this restored and self-contained 1912 purple railway carriage is the perfect place to relax at day's end. Share the grounds with grazing kangaroos, watch the sunset from Lover's Leap…or even get married (the owners are celebrants!). Breakfast and dinner hampers are available on request.

Berkelouw Café (☎ 07-5442 8422; 87 Memorial Dr; dishes $5-15; 7.30am-5pm) One of the few cafes to open every day, this is the place for coffee, cakes and muffins. Take your coffee for a browse through the massive Berkelouw Books next door.

Treefellers Café (☎ 07-5442 7766; 69 Memorial Dr; mains $16-21; breakfast Wed, Sat & Sun, lunch Wed-Sun, dinner Thu-Sat) Eumundi's most cosmopolitan eatery was named after Eumundi legend, Dick Caplick, a tree-feller turned ecofriend. The cafe is famous for its humungous Treefellers 'all day breakfast' (with enough calories to fuel a lumberjack).

Modernprimitive (☎ 07-5442 7946; 101 Memorial Dr; mains $20-35; dinner Tue-Sat) The Mod Oz menu changes weekly but is always full of variety, be it five-spiced cuttlefish, lamb rogan josh or a gorgonzola, almond and courgette pizza. Awarded the Sunshine Coast's best new restaurant in 2008.

Eumundi General Store (Memorial Dr), opposite the Imperial Hotel, has a basic line of groceries, while **Hinterland Organics** (Caplick Way; 2-6pm) can satisfy your stomach and your conscience together.

DAINTREE
☎ 07 / pop 80

The sedate main street of Daintree Village is only a few pedal turns long, but what it packs into that short stretch carries travellers on river and forest tours beyond. The surrounding coastal lowland is a mix of cleared fields once used for dairy herds, a fragile rainforest national park and the home of the traditional owners, the Kuku Yalanji people. Today the economy relies heavily on ecotourism.

Information

Although nearly every storefront in town brandishes the information 'i', the **Daintree Tourist Information Centre** (☎ 07-4098 6120; 5 Stewart St) is reliable. Before arrival, perusing the websites of the **Daintree Village Tourism Association** (www .daintreevillage.asn.au) and **Wet Tropics Management Authority** (www.wettropics .gov.au) will also help. The Daintree Store has Eftpos facilities.

Sleeping & Eating

Daintree Riverview (☎ 07-4098 6119; www.daintreeriverview.com; 2 Stewart St; unpowered/powered sites $18/21, cabins $99) has lovely riverside camping and good-value en suite cabins.

Kenadon Homestead Cabins (☎ 07-4098 6142; www.daintreecabins.com; Dagmar St; s/d incl breakfast $100/120) cluster together near a pool but face out to the pastures of a 400-acre family cattle farm.

Red Mill House (☎ 07-4098 6233; www .redmillhouse.com.au; 11 Stewart St; s $140, d $180) is favoured by bird-watchers, who find kindred souls in the owners. The large veranda overlooks a rainforest garden, a great setting for breakfast while watching resident wildlife.

Daintree Eco Lodge & Spa (☎ 07-4098 6100; www.daintree-ecolodge.com. au; 20 Daintree Rd; s/d from $510/550) is 15 luxurious villas propped on stilts in the rainforest canopy a few kilometres south of town. Expect special things from **Julaymba Restaurant** (mains $32 to 34; breakfast, lunch & dinner), like the Flaming Green Ant cocktail – made with crushed green ants!

Daintree is very quiet in the evenings. Two restaurants open for dinner are **Ellenor's Place** (mains $16-25), adjoining the **Daintree Store** (☎ 07-4098 6146; 1 Stewart St), and **Papaya Cafe** (☎ 07-4098 6173; 3-5 Stewart St; mains $7-25; lunch & dinner Wed-Sun).

GRADYS CREEK
☎ 02

A geographic location rather than a town, the beautiful Gradys Creek is surrounded by the Border Ranges National Park. The park can be accessed from The Lions Rd, but it's a major undertaking. It's best to stock up on food and cash in Kyogle.

Sleeping & Eating

Rainforest Gateway Caravan Park (☎ 02-6636 6114; Lions Rd; unpowered site per person $8, powered site $18, motel r $60, cottage $70) Beautiful, bird-rich setting at the confluence of Gradys and Cedargetters Creeks. Basically the yard of a property, the best sites are back by the creek, which is home to platypus, offering the chance to see one of the country's most elusive creatures. The set-up is a little ad hoc (when the owners are out, it's closed) so call ahead to make certain it will be open.

If you want something plusher, **Ripples on the Creek** (☎ 02-6636 6132; www .ripplesonthecreek.com.au; Lions Rd; d $195), 2.5km before the caravan park, has luxurious yurt-style cabins, while **Cougal Park B&B** (☎ 02-6636 6213; www .cougalpark.com; 145 Lions Rd; s $100, d $140) is 8.5km up the road. The latter offers home-cooked dinners (two courses $30 to $35).

HERBERTON
☎ 07 / pop 1000

Peaceful Herberton is nestled in the crease of one of the area's rolling hills. It took root on the Wild River almost overnight when tin-mining leases were pegged in 1880. Its rapid growth decimated the Indigenous Bar Barrum community. Mining and smelting ceased in 1978 and Native Title has since been reinstated; the cultural significance of certain areas to the Bar Barrum has also been acknowledged. Today's Herberton hosts many fine, timber buildings and is crisscrossed by historical and nature walking trails through old mining areas and pioneer routes. In time, many of these trails may also be open to cyclists (see boxed text p332).

Information

The **Herberton Mining & Information Centre** (☎ 07-4096 3474; www .herbertonvisitorcentre.com.au; 1 Jacks Rd; 9am-4pm) on the site of an old tin mine, has an informative display ($5) on the region's mining history and geology. It's the starting point for a number of walks and stocks trail guides and brochures.

There are no banks in town, but the convenience store and caravan park have Eftpos facilities.

QUEENSLAND

Sleeping & Eating

Wild River Cafe Caravan Park (☎ 07-4096 2121; 23 Holdcroft Dr; unpowered/powered sites $12/18, s/d cabins $40/60) is on the edge of town, with its own BYO restaurant (meals $15 to $20; weekends only).

Royal Hotel (☎ 07-4096 2231; wattosroyalhotel@bigpond.com; 46-48 Grace St; r $30), the town's hospitable social hub, has well-maintained old-fashioned pub rooms and a surprisingly good counter menu (mains $15 to $25; dinner Wed-Sun & lunch).

Australian Hotel-Motel (☎ 07-4096 2263; 44 Grace St; s $40, d $65; mains $12-16; lunch & dinner) offers uninspiring meals and motel-style rooms.

Herberton Heritage Cottage B&B (☎ 07-4096 2032; www.herbertoncottage .com; 2 Perkins St; s $170, d $180), located in the original post office, has charming heritage-style rooms and modern features.

Jacaranda Coffee Lounge (52 Grace St) serves up eat-in and takeaway hamburgers, fish and chips, pizzas and some groceries.

The **Herberton Convenience Store** (Grace St) carries all the essentials and even stocks a basic bike bits.

KURANDA

☎ 07 / pop 750

Kuranda, famed for its craft markets (on Therwine St and Rob Veivers Dr), is the most popular daytripping destination on the tableland. While the shopping can seem a bit tacky, the Kuranda area's other significant attractions – such as truly beautiful and refreshing rainforest walks – could fill an entire day if you've got time to linger. Kuranda reverts to a mellow mountain village at night.

Information

The **visitors centre** (☎ 07-4093 9311; www.kuranda.org; 10am-4pm) is centrally located in Centenary Park. Get a copy of the *Kuranda and Mowbray National Parks Visitor Guide*, which shows the trails on which mountain biking is permitted.

Sleeping & Eating

Kuranda Rainforest Accommodation Park (☎ 07-4093 7316; www.kuranda rainforestpark.com.au; 88 Kuranda Heights Rd; unpowered/powered sites $24/28, s/d

$30/55, bungalows $90-105) lives up to its name. The budget rooms suit backpackers, while self-contained units enjoy poolside or garden views.

Kuranda Backpackers Hostel (☎ 07-4093 7355; www.kurandabackpackers hostel.com; cnr Arara & Barang Sts; dm $19, s $46, d $49) is a rambling timeworn home surrounded by a large garden. Spacious common areas and a laid-back attitude compensate for its slightly bleak feel.

Kuranda Hotel Motel (☎ 07-4093 7206; www.kurandahotel.com.au; cnr Coondoo & Arara Sts; s/d from $85/100) hides out behind a local hotel. Its basic motel-style rooms here are tidy enough, with private facilities, fridge and TV.

Kuranda Resort & Spa (☎ 07-4093 7556; www.kurandaresort.com.au; 3 Green Hills Rd; dm $40, d $129-199) feels like a magazine spread for stylish eco-friendly apartments. There're even four-bed backpacker rooms for the budget-conscious.

Annabel's Pantry (☎ 07-4093 7605; Therwine St; pies $3.50-4.50; breakfast & lunch) carries around 25 pie varieties, from kangaroo to curry.

Banjo's Bar & Grill (☎ 07-4093 9399; 17 Therwine St; mains $10-22; breakfast & lunch daily, dinner Thu-Sat), Kuranda's liveliest restaurant, serves up organic fruit crepes for breakfast, gourmet burgers, focaccias and pizzas with occasional live music.

Fanny O'Reilly's Bar & Grill (☎ 07-4093 7206; cnr Coondoo & Arara Sts; mains $10-25; lunch daily, dinner Mon-Sat) occupies the corner deck of the Kuranda Hotel Motel. Good pub food – the Guinness potpie is the specialty.

Self-caterers should turn to **Foodworks** (Coondoo St; 7am-7pm weekdays, until 6pm on weekends).

LANDSBOROUGH

☎ 07 / pop 1400

Pinched between the Sunshine Coast beaches, the cutesy Blackall Range and the Glass House Mountains, Landsborough hasn't yet capitalised on its position, serving mostly as a distant commuter belt for Brisbane. There's little to do in town but get on the road early to make the most of the Blackall Range.

Sleeping & Eating

The town's only accommodation is **Landsborough Pines Caravan Park** (☎ 07-5494 1207; Steve Irwin Way; campsites for 2 $26, cabins $65), with a beautiful rainforest location at the edge of town. Otherwise you will need to push another 20km uphill to Maleny, where the rambling **Maleny Lodge Guest House** (☎ 07-5494 2370; www.malenylodge.com; 58 Maple St; s incl breakfast $130-160, d incl breakfast $150-170) boasts gorgeous rooms with cushy, four-poster beds and lashings of stained wood and antiques. There's an open fire for cold winter days and an open pool house for warm summer ones.

Just 4 Gossip (☎ 07-5494 1548; 40 Cribb St; breakfast $6-16; 7am-5pm) Landsborough's newest cafe is also its best. Part giftware store, part cafe, it has a mix of healthy and heart-clogging breakfasts - try the Swiss panini for a twist on the bacon-and-eggs theme.

Landsborough Hotel (☎ 07-5494 1001; Cribb St; lunch & dinner) The standard run of lounge-bar meals, with steak specials Tuesday and Thursday nights.

Woodfire Pizza Parlour (☎ 07-5494 8333; pizza $12-19; dinner Tue-Sun) Hidden away behind the main shopping strip, churning out a variety of wood-fired pizzas and homemade pastas. It's mostly geared towards takeaways but there are a couple of tables.

Both the **IGA** (Mill St) and **Landsborough Supermarket Country Store** (34 Cribb St) are near the train station.

MAPLETON

☎ 07 / pop 550

The tiny village of Mapleton is perched at the northern end of the Blackall Range. It has a couple of craft and pottery galleries and flanks the Mapleton Falls National Park, where Pencil Creek cascades 120m over an escarpment to form Mapleton Falls.

Sleeping & Eating

Lilyponds Holiday Park (☎ 1800 003 764, 07-5445 7238; www.lilyponds.com.au; 26 Warruga St; unpowered/powered sites for two from $22/25, cabins $70-95) Overlooking the Mapleton Lily Ponds, just north of town, you can camp in the orchard and pick fresh avocados off the trees.

Obilo Lodge (☎ 07-5445 7705; www.obilolodge.com.au; Lot 9, Suses Pocket Rd; r incl breakfast $160-190) This friendly B&B has unpretentious rooms but great views of the Obi Obi Valley. The most expensive room also has a spa.

Taman Sari (☎ 07-5478 6868; www.tamansari.com.au; Obi Obi Rd; d per night $320, minimum 2-night stay) Two private pavilions in a luxurious, Asian-inspired rainforest sanctuary overlooking the Obi Obi Valley. Behind the impressive wooden doors the attention to detail is extraordinary, from the heated towel racks to the huge spa room with its pebbled floor.

Mapleton Tavern (☎ 07-5445 7499; cnr Maleny–Montville & Obi Obi Rds; mains $16-25; lunch daily, dinner Mon-Sat) Lunch on the wide veranda at this iconic pink Queenslander comes with sweeping views of the hinterland and the distant ocean.

Bellavista Pizza & Pasta (☎ 07-5445 7722; shop 8, 1 Post Office Rd; mains $19-30; dinner Tue-Sun) Stylish presentation elevates Bellavista above the usual pizza parlour, as does the long wine list and specials such as seafood chowder and Margaret River Wagyu rump.

The **IGA** (28-32 Flaxton Dr) supermarket is in the BP service station at the southern edge of town (on the ride in from Montville). It has an attached bakery-cafe for that caffeine-and-cake start to the day. Montville organic coffee is the star of the show.

MAREEBA

☎ 07 / pop 10,500

Mareeba is the busy agricultural/pastoral hub of cattle, coffee and sugar enterprises. As such it's essentially an administrative and supply town for the northern tablelands. Once the centre of a major tobacco industry, Mareeba has shifted its focus to fruit, vegetables, coffee and sugar cane. A growing number of food producers – particularly boutique coffeemakers – have opened their doors for tours. The region's natural beauty is typified by the expansive wetlands (www.mareebawetlands.com) to the north. Every July Mareeba hosts one of Australia's largest rodeos.

Information

The **tourist centre** (☎ 07-4092 5674; www.mareebaheritagecentre.com.au; Centenary

QUEENSLAND

Park, 345 Byrnes St; museum donation encouraged; 9am-5pm Mon-Fri, 8am-4pm Sat & Sun) is also the Mareeba Heritage Museum with displays ranging from local Aboriginal artefacts to white settlement and the rural industries.

Supplies & Equipment
For bike parts and repairs (Tuesday to Friday), call at **Sports North** (☎ 07-4091 1469; sportsnorthmareeba@bigpond.com; 153 Byrnes St), which also has a branch in Atherton.

Sleeping & Eating
Riverside Caravan Park (☎ 07-4092 2309; 13 Egan St; camping per person $8, unpowered/powered sites $18/22), the closest campsite to town, nudges up against the steep-sided Barron River.

Peninsula Hotel (☎ 07-4092 1032; Byrnes St; dm $13, s $30, d $40) has good-value backpacker-style beds.

Mareeba Motor Inn (☎ 07-4092 2451; Kennedy Hwy; s, $80, d $100) boasts immaculate and functional rooms with a licensed restaurant.

Jackaroo Motel (☎ 07-4092 2677; www .jackaroomotel.com; 340 Byrnes St; r $100) has a great range of facilities, including a saltwater swimming pool, BBQ and laundry.

Curcio's Bakery (cnr Walsh & Rankin Sts) is an amazing drive-through bakery that churns out loaves of incredible size.

Nastasi's (☎ 07-4092 2321; 10 Byrnes St; meals $4-10; breakfast, lunch & dinner) can prepare fried everything: burgers, pizzas and sandwiches. It doubles as the local internet cafe.

Ant Hill Hotel & Steakhouse (☎ 07-4092 1011; 79 Byrnes St; mains $12-22; lunch & dinner) has daily specials with all the pub favourites – steak, barra and burgers. Classic simple pub rooms are also available (s $35, d $50).

Mareeba's **supermarkets** and range of **cafes** and **takeaways** along Byrnes St are proof that farm work, like cycling, generates big appetites.

MILLAA MILLAA
☎ 07 / pop 400
'Millaa', established in 1909, had a short heyday of timber milling and dairying. The forests are now all cleared and although the surrounding farmland is dotted with black-and-white Friesian cows, the dairy industry's centralised on Malanda, 24km to the north. Millaa is now a sleepy settlement whose only real claim to fame is the nearby Waterfalls Circuit (see p330). The town's name is an Aboriginal word meaning 'many waters'.

Information
Tobin's Supermarket (☎ 07-4097 2250; Main St; 7am-6pm Mon-Fri, 7am-2pm Sat) has a small stand of tourist information next to the cash register. There are no banks in town, but several businesses with Eftpos facilities.

Sleeping & Eating
Millaa Millaa Tourist Park (☎ 07-4097 2290; www.millaapark.com; cnr Malanda Rd & Lodge Av; unpowered/powered sites $10/20, s $30, d $40, cabins from $30) has a range of cabins and rooms set in large grounds.

Millaa Millaa Hotel Motel (☎ 07-4097 2212; 15 Main St; s $70, d $80) runs attractive and very central en suite motel units and a busy pub-style restaurant (mains $15-20; breakfast, lunch & dinner).

Falls Teahouse (☎ 07-4097 2237; www .fallsteahouse.com.au; Palmerston Hwy; s $105, d $120; mains $15-20; 10am-5pm) overlooks the rolling tableland where the Millaa Millaa Falls turn-off meets the highway. The country-style kitchen is always busy and the three guest rooms have period fixtures.

De Millaa's Coffee Shop (☎ 07-4097 2327; www.demillaas.com.au; Main St; meals $10; breakfast & lunch) brings new culinary chic to town. Dinners may soon also be an option.

Tobin's Supermarket will meet all your supply needs, although the **Millaa Millaa Takeaway** (61 Main St) also sells a few groceries in addition to the standard fried and grilled fodder.

MURWILLUMBAH
☎ 02 / pop 7700
Sitting on the banks of the Tweed River, Murwillumbah is a charming town and an agricultural focal point for the region. Peppered with heritage façades, its streets tumble on top of one another, with

stunning views of Mt Warning from almost every corner.

Information

The **Murwillumbah visitors centre** (☎ 02-6672 1340; www.tweedcoolangatta.com.au; cnr Alma St & Tweed Valley Way), across the Tweed River from the town centre, sells national park passes, and has information on accommodation and a great rainforest display.

Supplies & Equipment

Jim's Cycle Centre (☎ 02-6672 3620; 58 Wollumbin St) has spares and repairs.

Sleeping & Eating

Greenhills Caravan Park (☎ 02-6672 2035; ghillscp@onthenet.com.au; 488 Tweed Valley Way; unpowered/powered $20/25, cabins without/with bathroom $65/85) On the Ballina road, 1.7km east of the visitors centre, the park is rudimentary but grass is plentiful.

Mount Warning Murwillumbah Riverside YHA (☎ 02-6672 3763; www.yha.com .au; 1 Tumbulgum Rd; dm/d from $25/54) Gorgeous position, all but swimming in the Tweed River, in a house as colourful as Murwillumbah's residents. It has eight-bed dorms and free ice cream at night but signs warn that it takes no 'flea bitten tramps' or 'smelly people who don't shower', which sounds awfully like cyclists.

Imperial Hotel (☎ 02-6672 2777; fax 6672 8188; 115 Main St; s/d with shared bath $30/45, d $55) These grand old pub rooms look like they haven't been altered since the pub opened – shabby chic without even trying. Snug interiors stock antique robes and floral bedspreads. The sprawling bistro (mains $15; lunch & dinner) has a short but snazzy menu, including tempura barramundi and gourmet bangers and mash.

Murwillumbah Motor Inn (☎ 1800 687 224, 1800 023 105; www .murwillumbahmotorinn.com.au; 17 Byangum Rd; s $84, d $96) They're a mite frumpy, but all rooms here have cable TV and microwave. There's also a pleasant courtyard out the back.

New Leaf Café (☎ 02-6672 2667; shop 10, Murwillumbah Plaza; meals $5-10; breakfast & lunch) The food here is creative and vegetarian, with plenty of Middle Eastern flavours and salads. Dine inside, alfresco, or takeaway.

Sugar Beat (☎ 02-6672 2330; shop 2, 6-8 Commercial Rd; mains $10; breakfast & lunch) Park yourself by the sunny window or settle into a corner on the long bench seating. Then tuck into tofu and vegetable gado-gado, sesame chicken with Japanese dressing or an equally elaborate salad or burger.

Spar (Brisbane St), **Singh's IGA** (Warina Walk, Main St) and **Coles** (Sunnyside Mall, cnr Brisbane & Wollumbin Sts) are huddled around the main intersection.

NIMBIN

☎ 02 / pop 400

Cycling into Nimbin can be like entering a social experiment, particularly in the middle of the day, when Byron Bay day trippers arrive en masse and find themselves hectored by dreadlocked, tie-dyed pot dealers on the main street. This is the stereotype, of course (not all the pot dealers wear tie-dye), and Nimbin's residents and culture are actually far more eclectic, with the town boasting a growing artist community, a New Age culture and welcoming locals.

Information

Nimbin Connexion (☎ 02-6689 1764; www.nimbinconnexion.com; Cullen St; 9am-4pm), at the northern end of town, has a wealth of town information, bike hire (per day $20) and internet access (per hour $6).

Sleeping & Eating

Nimbin Tourist Caravan Park (☎ 02-6689 1402; 29 Sibley St; unpowered/powered sites for two $17/19) Wrapped around the public pool. Good, grassy sites in the town all but founded on 'grass'.

Nimbin Backpackers at Granny's Farm (☎ 02-6689 1333; Cullen St; dm $20, d $54) The closest hostel to town offers warm and colourful doubles and dorms, with enough room to swing a tofu cow. Friendly drinking fests are a common night-time occurrence.

YHA Nimbin Rox Hostel (☎ 02-6689 0022; www.yha.com.au; 74 Thorburn St; dm $24, d $56) Tumbling down a landscaped native garden, this excellent hostel has clean and contemporary accommodation and spectacular national-park views. There are also safari tents.

Grey Gum Lodge (☎ 02-6689 1713; 2 High St; s/d from $40/55) The rooms at this beautifully worn and creaky house fit better than your favourite jacket, and the high, comfy beds are the snugly silver lining. The back veranda provides outstanding sunsets.

Rainbow Café (☎ 02-6689 1997; 70 Cullen St; mains $6-13; breakfast & lunch) Pack a healthy appetite for this Nimbin institution – the burgers, wraps, nachos and salads are generous and creative. The sunny courtyard is a time vacuum.

Nimbin Hotel (☎ 02-6689 1246; Cullen St; mains $15; lunch & dinner) Nimbin's local boozer dishes up hearty pub nosh on the back porch, where the views are stunning. At weekends it gets rolling with live music.

Nimbin Trattoria & Pizzeria (☎ 02-6689 1427; 70 Cullen St; mains $10-20; lunch Thu-Sun, dinner daily) Outstanding pizzas and delicious pastas are churned out in ample supply at this toasty trattoria.

Nimbin Organics (Cullen St) has a good range of foods, while the **general store** (Cullen St) can fill out the rest of your shopping list.

NOOSA HEADS
☎ 07 / pop 9110

The stylish resort town of Noosa Heads, at the northern tip of the Sunshine Coast, is one of Queensland's star attractions. The town's stunning natural landscape of crystalline beaches and tropical rainforests blends seamlessly with its fashionable boulevard, Hastings Street, and the sophisticated beach elite that flock here. On long weekends and school holidays, though, the flock becomes a migration and narrow Hastings St a slow-moving file of traffic.

Noosa's trendy cafe landscape has been cultivated without losing sight of simple seaside pleasures, and strict council laws prohibit any building to be higher than the trees. Despite the designer boutiques, pricey restaurants and air of exclusivity, the beach and bush are still free, so glammed-up fashionistas simply share the beat with thongs, boardshorts and bronzed bikini bods baring their bits.

Information

The **Noosa visitors centre** (☎ 07-5430 5020; www.visitnoosa.com.au; Hastings St; 9am-5pm) is very helpful.

Supplies & Equipment

Le Cyclo Sportif (☎ 07-5447 4466; www.lecyclosportif.com; 36 Sunshine Beach Rd, Noosa Junction), up the hill towards Sunshine Beach, has good brands and a large range of cycling gear – it's the sort of store you just want to poke about in for a while.

If you want to stick around and explore some more areas by bike, **Noosa Bike Hire & Tours** (☎ 07-5474 3322; www.noosabikehire.com; tours $69) offers half-day mountain bike tours down nearby Mt Tinbeerwah. **Pedal & Paddle** (☎ 07-5474 5328; tours $89) operates great four-hour hike, bike and kayak combo tours. Prices include morning and afternoon tea and local transfers.

Sleeping & Eating

Bougainvillia Holiday Park (☎ 1800 041 444, 07-5447 1712; jsjs@optusnet.com.au; 141 Cooroy-Noosa Rd, Tewantin; unpowered/powered sites for two from $30/34, cabins $65-135; sw) Neat as a pin and meticulously landscaped, this is the best camping option in the area. The facilities are spotless and there's an on-site cafe.

YHA Halse Lodge (☎ 1800 242 567, 07-5447 3377; www.halselodge.com.au; 2 Halse Lane, Noosa Heads; members/nonmembers dm $29/32, d $74/82; meals $9-12) Don't expect serenity; this splendid colonial-era timber Queenslander is a legend on the backpacker route. The dorms and kitchen are a tad cramped, but the bar is a mix-and-meet bonanza and serves great meals. The steep driveway may be the greatest challenge.

Noosa River Retreat (☎ 07-5474 2811; www.noosariverretreat.net; cnr Weyba Rd & Reef St, Noosaville; 1-bedroom unit $130) Your buck goes a long way at this orderly complex, which houses spick, span and spacious units. There's a central BBQ and laundry and the corner units are almost entirely protected by small native gardens.

Sheraton Noosa Resort (☎ 07-5449 4888; www.starwoodhotels.com/sheraton; 14-16 Hastings St, Noosa Heads; r $290-540) This five-star hotel has tastefully decorated rooms with suede fabrics, fabulous beds, balconies, kitchenettes and spas. The hotel has a day spa.

Sierra (☎ 07-5447 4800; 10 Hastings St; mains $15-25; breakfast, lunch & dinner)

This hot little pavement cafe has great coffee, killer cocktails and an assortment of interesting dishes, including gourmet salads, steaks, burgers and seafood dishes such as grilled prawns with Cajun bananas and black sticky rice. Daiquiri Hour is between 5pm and 7pm and there's live music on Wednesday and Sunday.

Bistro C (☎ 07-5447 2855; On the Beach, Hastings St; mains $15-32; breakfast, lunch & dinner) The menu at this yuppie beachfront brasserie is an eclectic blend of everything that seems like a good idea at the time. The egg-fried calamari with chilli lime coriander dip is legendary.

Berardo's on the Beach (☎ 07-5448 0888; Hastings St; mains $15-30; lunch & dinner) Reminiscent of the French Riviera, this stylish bistro is only metres from the waves. Classy without being pretentious, this is Noosa in a seashell. The Mod Oz menu has Asian and Italian influences.

Self-caterers can stock up at the **Noosa Fair Shopping Centre** (Lanyana Way, Noosa Junction).

PORT DOUGLAS
☎ 07 / pop 1000

Port Douglas, known locally as 'Port Dougie', is the flashy and sophisticated up-market playground of tropical North Queensland. Entrepreneurs only recognised the town's potential – ready access to the reef and rainforest, and a sandy beach that Cairns could only ever wish for – in the 1980s and turned it into a five-star retreat. The fine-sand Four Mile Beach just east of town has a stinger enclosure. Snorkelling and diving trips to the reef are popular.

Information
There's no independent visitors centre, but the **Port Douglas Tourist Information Centre** (☎ 07-4099 5599; 23 Macrossan St) is a helpful accommodation- and tour-booking office.

Supplies & Equipment
Port Douglas Bike Hire (☎ 07-4099 5799; www.portdouglasbikehire.com; cnr Wharf & Warner Sts; per day/week $19/89; 9am-5pm) promises speedy repairs, free delivery for multiday hires and advice about local-area rides.

Sleeping & Eating
Tropic Breeze Van Village (☎ 07-4099 5299; 24 Davidson St; unpowered/powered sites $24/31, cabins $80) is a little cramped, but the closest campsite to Port central and with a path straight through to the beach.

Port o' Call Lodge (☎ 1800 892 800, 07-4099 5422; www.portocall.com.au; cnr Port St & Craven Close; dm $29.50-33, d $99-119) is the YHA-associated hostel with a bar, bistro, communal kitchen and laundry.

Port Central (☎ 07-4099 4488; www.portcentral.com.au; 36 Macrossan St; d $69-89) is indeed very central. It's also tidy, tiny and cheap enough. No reception, just a phone and keypad.

Port Douglas Motel (☎ 07-4099 5248; www.portdouglasmotel.com; 9 Davidson St; d $70-110) can't be beat for value and location. Its bright and well-furnished rooms (no views) are often full.

Stacks of quality restaurants ornament Port, with correspondingly high prices. Most are along or near Macrossan St.

Mocka's Pies (☎ 07-4099 5295; 9 Grant St; pies $4-7; breakfast & lunch) has a great selection of gourmet pies, quiches and sweet pastries that pack a quick calorie punch.

Mango Jam Cafe (☎ 07-4099 4611; 24 Macrossan St; mains $10-25; lunch & dinner) is a casual licensed family restaurant with a menu that'll keep kids and adults happy. Gourmet, wood-fired pizza is a speciality.

On the Inlet (☎ 07-4099 5255; www.portdouglasseafood.com; 3 Inlet St; mains $18-37; lunch & dinner) occupies a sublime location on Dickson Inlet. Tables here are spread along a sprawling water-view deck. The menu is big on seafood.

For self-caterers the well-stocked **Coles** supermarket (☎ 07-4099 5366; 11 Macrossan St) is in the Port Village shopping centre.

SURFERS PARADISE
☎ 07 / pop 18,510

The signature high-rise settlement of Surfers Paradise is a giddy, frenetic, brash pleasure dome of nightclubs, shopping and relentless entertainment. Imagine Daytona Beach or Miami shifted down under, and you'll have some idea of what to expect.

If sun-worship is your thing, head to the beach early as the density of high-rise apartments shades the sand from midafternoon, though the beach is hardly Surfers' main attraction these days – most people are here for the nearby theme parks or to party. The backpacker places particularly go all out to ensure that the town goes off every night of the week.

Information

The **Gold Coast Tourism Bureau** (☎ 07-5538 4419; Cavill Ave Mall; h8.30am-5.30pm Mon-Fri, 8.30am-5pm Sat, 9am-4pm Sun) information booth also sells theme-park tickets if you fancy a ride of a different kind.

Sleeping & Eating

Main Beach Tourist Park (☎ 07-5581 7722; www.gctp.com.au/main; Main Beach Pde, Main Beach; unpowered/powered sites for two from $29/32, cabins $129-205) Just across the road from Main Beach, around 4km north of Surfers, this caravan park offers a tight fit between sites but the facilities are good. Rates are for two people.

Cheers Backpackers (☎ 1800 639 539, 07-5531 6539; www.cheersbackpackers .com.au; 8 Pine Ave; dm $24, d $56) Amid the friendly blur of theme nights, karaoke, pool comps, pub crawls, happy hours and BBQs, you'll also find adequate rooms and good facilities. Cheers is undeniably a party hostel, and the fun frequently trickles out to the action of Surfers.

Surf 'n' Sun Backpackers (☎ 1800 678 194, 07-5592 2363; www.surfnsun-gold coast.com; 3323 Surfers Paradise Blvd; dm $24, d $60) A very friendly, family-run business that rivals Cheers as party central, this hostel is the best option for Surfers' beach and bars. There's a constant hum of music, surfboards for hire and a TV in every room.

International Beach Resort (☎ 1800 657 471, 07-5539 0099; www.internationalresort .com.au; 84 The Esplanade; apt $120-165) This high-rise place is just across from the beach, and has good studios and one- and two-bedroom units. The cafe downstairs is open for breakfast, lunch and cocktails.

Breakfree Cosmopolitan Resort (☎ 07-5570 2311; www.breakfree.com.au; cnr Surfers Paradise Blvd & Beach Rd; r from $143) Set back from the beach but still very central, this complex contains 55 privately owned, self-contained apartments, each uniquely furnished by the owners. There's

also a BBQ area, spa and sauna, but it can be noisy at night.

Q1 Resort (☎ 1300 792 008, 07-5630 4500; www.q1.com.au; Hamilton Ave; 1-/2-/3-bedroom apt from $284/444/654) Spend a night in the world's tallest residential tower. This stylish 80-storey resort is a modern mix of metal, glass and fabulous wraparound views. Each unit has glass-enclosed balconies. There's a lagoon-style pool, a fitness centre and a day spa.

Bumbles Café (☎ 07-5538 6668; 21 River Dr; dishes $11-18; 7am-4pm) One of the few tranquil spots in Surfers, this cute cafe is located in a quiet nook opposite the Nerang River. The menu isn't extensive and the service is a bit slow but the food is well worth the wait. For a light lunch try the roasted vegetables with feta and cashew-nut pesto.

Beer Thai Garden (☎ 07-5538 0110; cnr Chelsea Ave & Gold Coast Hwy; mains $13-21; dinner) Reputed to dish up the best Pad Thai on the Gold Coast, this lovely restaurant brims with atmosphere. Two glitzy elephants flank the entrance, and soft lighting makes the most of the outdoor Thai garden bar. Good value and easy on the pocket.

Tandoori Place (☎ 07-5538 0808; Aegean Resort, Laycock St; mains $15-20; lunch & dinner) An Indian restaurant that boasts a swag of awards and is highly recommended by locals. On the extensive menu you'll find seafood, poultry, lamb, beef and hot, hot, hot vindaloo roo. Vegetarians are also spoiled for choice.

Costa D'oro (☎ 07-5538 5203; 27 Orchid Ave; mains $17-29; lunch & dinner) The Italian village setting painted into the backdrop of this popular restaurant goes nicely with the authentic, if not predictable, pasta, pizzas, salads and mains. It's in a good people-watching possie and if you have an early dinner between 3pm and 7pm you get a 40% discount.

Self-caterers will find supermarkets in **Centro Surfers Paradise** (Cavill Ave Mall), **Chevron Renaissance Shopping Centre** (cnr Elkhorn Ave & Gold Coast Hwy) and **Circle on Cavill** (cnr Cavill & Ferny Aves).

Getting There & Away

AIR

The Gold Coast international airport at Coolangatta is 25km south of Surfers

Paradise. **Qantas** (☎ 13 13 13; www
.qantas.com), **Jetstar** (☎ 13 15 38; www
.jetstar.com.au) and **Virgin Blue** (☎ 13 67
89; www.virginblue.com) fly from Sydney
and Melbourne. **Tiger Airways** (☎ 03 9335
3033; www.tigerairways.com) has flights to/
from Melbourne and Adelaide.

BUS
The transit centre is on the corner of Beach
and Cambridge Rds. All the major bus
companies have desks here.

Greyhound Australia (☎ 1300 473 946;
www.greyhound.com.au) has frequent
services to/from Brisbane ($20, 1½
hours), Byron Bay ($30, 2½ hours) and
Sydney ($154, 15 hours). **Premier Motor
Service** (☎ 13 34 10; www.premierms
.com.au) serves the same routes and is
less expensive. **Kirklands** (☎ 02-6686
5254; www.kirklands.com.au) travels to
Surfers Paradise from Byron Bay ($28) and
Brisbane ($16).

Coachtrans (☎ 07-3358 9700; www
.coachtrans.com.au) operates the Airporter
direct services from Brisbane airport to
anywhere on the Gold Coast ($39) and
also has services from Brisbane City to
Surfers ($28, 1½ hours). **Aerobus** (☎ 1300
664 700; www.aerobus.net) has transfers
from Brisbane airport to Gold Coast
accommodation ($35).

TRAIN
Translink (☎ 13 1230; www.translink
.com.au) trains travel from Brisbane's Roma
Street station to Nerang railway station
($10, 70 minutes), where bike routes link
to Surfers Paradise. Maps of the bike routes
can be downloaded at www.goldcoast.qld
.gov.au. Type 'cycling' into the search box
and click on the 'Cycling & Bikeways' link.
You will need map Nos eight and nine.

TOWNSVILLE
☎ 07 / pop 170,000
Underrated Townsville is the unofficial
capital of North Queensland. It mixes
real-city services for cattle grazing and
sugar industries with a renewed attention
to tourism. It's also a university town
and home to a large military contingent.
Until recently, Townsville hadn't rated
highly on most travellers' 'to do' lists, but
the times they are a-changing, and fast:

Sojourners have awakened to Townsville's
laidback charm. Despite the heat, cycling
in and around town is easy and common,
facilitated by a good network of lanes and
paths and a young, fit population.

Information
Townsville's most accessible of three **visitors centres** is in the Flinders St Mall
(☎ 1800 801 902; www.townsvilleholidays
.info; Flinders St Mall, between Stokes &
Denham Sts; 9am-5pm Mon-Fri, 9am-1pm
Sat & Sun), the other two are located on
the Bruce Hwy 8km south of town and
inside the Museum of Tropical Queensland
(Flinders St East), both open 9am-5pm
daily. In the Flinders St Mall information
kiosk **Barrier Reef Dive Cruise & Travel**
(☎ 07-4772 5800, 1800 636 778; www
.divecruisetravel.com) has a comprehensive
list of dive operators and deals.

Supplies & Equipment
Top Brand Cycles (☎ 07-4725 4269;
www.topbrandcycles.com.au; 200 Charters
Towers Rd; 8.15am-5.30pm Mon-Wed &
Fri, 8.15am-7pm Thu, 8.15am-2.30pm Sat)
handles bike sales and repairs and is in
touch with the local cycling clubs. For bike
rental, see p289.

Sleeping & Eating
Rowes Bay Caravan Park (☎ 07-4771
3576; www.rowesbaycp.com.au; Heatley
Pde, Rowes Bay; unpowered/powered sites
$17/29, cabins without/with bathroom
$62/77, villas $89) is nestled snugly on the
beachfront 3km north of town. The leafy
campsite has a pool, kiosk and well-stocked
campers' kitchen.

Adventurers Resort (☎ 07-4721 1522;
www.adventurersresort.com; 79 Palmer
St; dm $22, s $40, d $48) promises roomy
dorms at the northeastern end of Palmer St.
This good hostel has a massive kitchen and
fantastic rooftop pool and barbecue area
with awesome views.

Orchid Guest House (☎ 07-4771
6683; 34 Hale St; dm $26, s without/with
bathroom $50/70, d with/without bathroom
$62/80) is a guesthouse in every sense of the
word. The dorms are a surprise with TV,
fridge and air-con. The doubles are even
better value. Think peace, quiet and money
well spent.

QUEENSLAND

Strand Motel (☎ 07-4772 1977; www .strandmotel.com.au; 51 The Strand; s $75, d $85) has pokey but affordable rooms with house-proud cleanliness. Right opposite the watery esplanade, they're particularly good value.

Coral Lodge B&B (☎ 07-4771 5512; www.corallodge.com.au; 32 Hale St; downstairs s/d/tw $60/65/75, upstairs s/ d/t $75/85/95) divides its upstairs homey self-contained units from the downstairs guestrooms that share male and female bathrooms. It's a safe, friendly, good old-fashioned Aussie home away from home.

Betty Blue & the Lemon Tart (☎ 07-4724 2554; 254 Sturt St; meals $7-$9; breakfast & lunch) boasts just-baked muffins and tarts. It's as funky as Townsville gets.

Harold's Seafood (☎ 07-4724 1322; cnr The Strand & Gregory St; meals $4-10; lunch & dinner) is more than your average fish 'n' chip joint. Order at the counter and then pull up a seat outside.

Zolli's Trattoria Cafe (☎ 07-4721 2222; 113 Flinders St E; mains $8-25; dinner) may sometimes seem like disorganised chaos, but if you can turn a blind eye to the mayhem around you, you'll find that the food is worth it.

Naked Fish (☎ 07-4724 4623; 60 The Strand; mains $17-25; dinner Mon-Sat) having snookered prime position, serves an ocean-inspired menu that keeps punters coming. Seafood melds with Cajun, Moroccan and other influences on the extensive menu. Limited vegetarian options.

All other supplies are on shelves at **Woolworth's** (cnr Stanley & Walker Sts) and **Coles** (Urban Quarter Plaza, cnr Ogden & Stanley Sts).

Getting There & Away
AIR
Townsville **airport** is 5km northwest of the city centre at Garbutt. Virgin Blue, Qantas and Jetstar fly to/from Brisbane, Sydney and Melbourne. To cycle to the city follow John Melton Black Dr and then Bundock and Warburton Sts around the northern side of Castle Hill. A regular **Airport Shuttle** (☎ 07-4775 5544, 1300 554 378; one-way/ return $10/18) with luggage trailer services all arrivals and departures and will drop off/pick up anywhere within the CBD. A taxi (☎ 13 10 08) costs around $20.

BUS
The long-distance bus station is at the **Townsville Transit Centre** (☎ 07-4721 3082; cnr Palmer & Plume Sts). You'll find agents for the major companies, including Greyhound Australia with services at least daily to Brisbane ($249, 23 hours) and Cairns ($76, six hours).

TRAIN
The Brisbane-to-Cairns *Sunlander* travels through Townsville three times a week in each direction. From Brisbane to Townsville takes approximately 24 hours (one-way economy seat/sleeper $184/242), while Townsville to Cairns is 7¼ hours (economy seat $64). The *Tilt Train* also runs thrice weekly each way, only 17¾ hours between Brisbane and Townsville (one-way business-class seat $270) and 6¼ hours between Townsville and Cairns ($95). The **train station** is about 1km south of the centre.

YUNGABURRA
☎ 07 / pop 1000
The belle of the Tablelands, this attractive, unassuming and heritage-listed former mill town was established in the 1880s as an overnight stop for travellers headed to/ from Herberton. The quaint chocolate-box prettiness of its historic timber buildings and superb boutique accommodation has made it a popular weekend retreat and convenient centre for the nearby rainforest and lake attractions (see Day 5). A platypus hiding where the Gillies Hwy crosses Peterson Creek rewards the patient.

The **Yungaburra Folk Festival** (www .yungaburrafolkfestival.org) is a fabulous community event held annually over a late October weekend; it features music, workshops, poetry readings and kids' activities.

Information
Follow the golden platypus signs to the **visitors centre** (☎ 07-4095 2416; www .yungaburra.com; Cedar St; 10am-6pm), staffed by local volunteers. There's a map signboard adjacent to the Lake Eacham Hotel.

Atherton, 13km away, has the nearest banks and bike shop, but there are Eftpos facilities in town.

Sleeping & Eating

On the Wallaby (☎ 07-4095 2031; www
.onthewallaby.com; 34 Eacham Rd;
camping $10, dm $22, d $55), with its
mountain chalet feel, instantly puts you at
ease. Camping is allowed in the backyard
and mountain bikes are available for hire
($15/70 per day/week).

Lake Eacham Hotel (☎ 07-4095 3515;
6-8 Kehoe Pl; d $75-85; meals $20) is
better known as the 'Yungaburra Pub'. The
downstairs dining room of this grand old
hotel is as inspirational as its circular pool
table is unconventional.

Gables B&B (☎ 07-4095 2373;
thegables1@bigpond.com; 5 Eacham Rd; s
$65, d $85) fills a historic Queenslander.
Rates include self-serve breakfast.

Kookaburra Lodge (☎ 07-4095 3222;
www.kookaburra-lodge.com; cnr Oak St &
Eacham Rd; s $75, d $90) stands out for
its affordability, especially with so much

pricey boutique accommodation around.
Stylish little rooms open out to an inviting
pool and garden.

Whistlestop Cafe (☎ 07-4095 3913; cnr
Cedar St & Gillies Hwy; mains $8.50-12.50;
7.30am-5pm Wed-Mon) serves home-
cooked meals in a shady tea garden.

Nick's Restaurant & Yodeller's Bar
(☎ 07-4095 3330; www.nicksrestaurant.
com.au; 33 Gillies Hwy; mains $25-36;
lunch Wed-Sun, dinner Tue-Sun) makes
for a fun night out with costumed staff and
piano-accordion serenade. The food is a
mix of Swiss, Italian and Mod Oz.

Flynn's (☎ 07-4095 2235; 17 Eacham
Rd; mains $28-31; lunch Sun, dinner
Fri-Wed) guides you to its door with the
continental aromas of authentic French and
Italian cooking.

The **Yungaburra Food Market** (Eacham
Rd; 7am-7pm) is open daily for food and
camping supply needs.

Cyclists Directory

CONTENTS

In Australia, it's easy to get a good night's sleep at the end of a hard day's ride, with the country offering everything from the tent-pegged confines of campsites and the communal space of hostels to gourmet breakfasts in guesthouses, chaperoned farmstays and everything-at-your-fingertips resorts, plus the gamut of hotel and motel lodgings.

In most areas of the country you will find seasonal price variations. During the high season over summer (Dec to Feb) and at other peak times, particularly school and public holidays, prices are usually at their highest, whereas outside these times you will find useful discounts and lower walk-in (or ride-up) rates. One exception is the Top End, where the Wet season (roughly Oct to Mar) is the low season, and prices can drop substantially, even though you will have to content with the weather.

The weekend escape is a notion that figures prominently in the Australian psyche, meaning accommodation from Friday night through to Sunday can be in greater demand and significantly pricier in almost of all the major holiday areas, especially along the coasts.

ACCOMMODATION
Camping & Caravan Parks

Caravan parks are thick on the ground in Australia – you will find one in just about every town (or roadhouse) that imagines itself to have a tourist attraction or three. The nightly cost of camping for two people is usually between $15 and $25, slightly more for a powered site. Note that most city campsites lie at least several kilometres from the town centre, so be prepared to jostle with some city traffic to get to them.

Almost all caravan or holiday parks are equipped with hot showers, flushing toilets and laundry facilities, and frequently a pool. Some still have old on-site caravans for rent, and most have on-site cabins. Cabin sizes and facilities vary, but expect to pay $70 to $80 for a small cabin with a kitchenette and up to $130 for a two-bedroom cabin with a fully-equipped kitchen, lounge room, TV and stereo, veranda, and beds for up to six people. Regardless of the vintage or style of cabin, they're generally excellent value if you're on the road for a while, or are cycling in a group. They allow you to be completely self-sufficient and often provide more space than a motel or hotel room.

Caravan parks, which encompass tent sites, caravan sites and cabins, are popular along coastal areas. In summer months and school holidays they're often booked out well in advance.

If you intend on doing a lot of camping, consider joining one of the major chains, such as **Big 4** (www.big4.com.au), which offer discounts at member parks.

On many rides, cyclists have the option of staying at designated campsites in national parks. These normally cost between $5 and $9 per person. It is rare for them to have showers. Running water is a rarity but there is almost always a water tank (be sure to treat the water). National park campsites invariably also have better locations than caravan parks.

Bear in mind that camping is best done during winter (ie the Dry season) across the north of Australia, and during summer in the south of the country.

PRACTICALITIES

- *Australian Cyclist* magazine has a strong touring focus. *Bicycling Australia* is geared towards roadies, while *Mountain Biking Australia* gets down and dirty on the singletrack.

- Look for the program *Cycling Central* on television station SBS, focussing on pro racing and a variety of cycling topics.

- Videos you might buy or watch will be based on the PAL system, also used in New Zealand and most of Europe.

- Use a three-pin adaptor (different from British three-pin adaptors) to plug into the electricity supply (240V AC, 50Hz).

- Australia uses the metric system: you will buy your milk and petrol in litres, and you will walk kilometres.

- On the box watch the ad-free ABC, the government-sponsored and multi-cultural SBS, or one of three commercial TV stations; Seven, Nine and Ten.

WILD CAMPING

In areas away from towns and cities there will often be the temptation to camp in undesignated areas, with a flat piece of earth, grass or sand seemingly custom-made to fit your back. Such wild camping should be done with sensitivity to the surrounding environment: don't leave rubbish; bury toilet waste at least 100m from watercourses; avoid using detergents and lighting fires; clean up food waste to prevent possums and the like from scavenging through the night. Ask permission if camping on private property, and never camp beneath red gums – notorious for dropping branches, they are not known as 'widow makers' for nothing.

Guesthouses & B&Bs

B&Bs in Australia might be restored miners' cottages, converted barns, rambling old houses, upmarket country manors, beachside bungalows or a simple bedroom in a family home (though invariably they will be more floral than the Chelsea Flower Show). Prices are typically around $100 to $200 (per double), though in cutesy weekender destinations such as the Blue Mountains and the Great Ocean Road this might just be your deposit. Local tourist offices can usually provide a list of places.

Online resources:

australianbandb.com.au (www.australian bandb.com.au)
babs.com.au (www.babs.com.au)
OZBedandBreakfast.com (www.ozbedand breakfast.com)

Hostels

Backpacker hostels are exceedingly popular in Australian cities and along coastal tourist trails. In the outback and rural areas you'll be hard pressed to find one. Highly social affairs, they're generally overflowing with 18 to 30 year olds, but some have reinvented themselves to attract other travellers who simply want to sleep for cheap.

Hostels provide varying levels of accommodation, from the austere simplicity of wilderness hostels to city-centre buildings with a cafe-bar and some en suite rooms. Most of the accommodation is in dormitories (bunk rooms), which can range in size from four bunk beds to 60. If you want to spread out your panniers, you might do better searching out hostels that also provide twin rooms and doubles. Typically a dorm bed costs $19 to $26 per night and a double (usually without bathroom), $70 to $90. Hostels generally have cooking facilities, a communal area with a TV and laundry facilities. Bed linen is often provided; sleeping bags are not welcome due to hygiene concerns and the risk of introducing bed bugs.

Some places will only admit overseas backpackers; this mainly applies to city hostels that have had problems with locals sleeping over and bothering the backpackers. Hostels that discourage or ban Aussies say it's only a rowdy minority that makes trouble, and will often just ask for identification in order to deter potential troublemakers, but it can be annoying and discriminatory for people genuinely trying to travel in their own country. Also watch out for hostels catering expressly to working backpackers, where facilities can be minimal but rent can be high.

HOSTEL ORGANISATIONS & CHAINS

Australia has over 140 hostels that are part of the **Youth Hostels Association** (YHA; ☎ 02-9261 1111; www.yha.com.au). The YHA is part of Hostelling International (HIH; www.hihostels.com), also known as the International Youth Hostel Federation (IYHF), so if you're already a member of that organisation in your own country, your membership entitles you to YHA rates in the relevant Australian hostels. Nightly charges are between $10 and $30 for members; most hostels also take non-YHA members for an extra $3.50. Preferably, visitors to Australia should purchase an HI card in their country of residence, but you can also buy one at major local YHA hostels at a cost of $37 for 12 months; see the HI or YHA websites for further details. Australian residents can become full YHA members for $52/85 for one/two years; join online, at a state office or at any youth hostel.

A new trend in hostels is represented by **base BACKPACKERS** (www.baseback packers.com), an upmarket hostel chain that emphasises comfort and offers extensive facilities – one of its innovations is a women-only floor.

Bicycle storage facilities in hostels are variable, so check ahead.

Other international hostel organisations:

Nomads Backpackers (☎ 02-9299 7710; www.nomadsworld.com; 89 York St, Sydney) Membership ($34 for 12 months) entitles you to numerous discounts.
VIP Backpacker Resorts (☎ 07-3395 6111; www.vipbackpackers.com) Membership is $43/57 for one/two years and entitles you to many discounts.

Hotels & Motels

Except for pubs, the hotels that exist in cities or well-touristed places are generally of the business or luxury variety (insert the name of your favourite chain here), where you get a comfortable, anonymous and mod con-filled room in a multistorey block. These places tend to have a pool, restaurant/cafe, room service and various other facilities. For these

hotels we quote 'rack rates' (official advertised rates), though significant discounts can be offered when business is quiet.

Motels (or motor inns) offer comfortable budget to midrange accommodation and are found all over Australia. Prices vary and there's rarely a cheaper rate for singles, so motels are better for couples or groups of three. Most motels are modern, low rise and have similar facilities (tea- and coffee-making, fridge, TV, air-con, bathroom) but the price will indicate the standard. You will mostly pay between $60 and $120 for a room.

Useful discount booking agencies:

Lastminute.com (www.lastminute.com.au)
Quickbeds.com (www.quickbeds.com.au)
Wotif.com (www.wotif.com.au)

Pubs

Hotels in Australia are generally the ones that serve beer, and are commonly known as pubs (from the term 'public house'). In country towns, pubs are invariably found in the town centre. Many were built during boom times, so they're often vying with the church to be the largest, most extravagant building in town. In tourist areas some of these pubs have been restored as heritage buildings, but generally the rooms remain small, old fashioned and weathered, with a long amble down the hall to the bathroom. They're usually cheap and central, but if you're a light sleeper, avoid booking a room right above the bar and check whether a band is playing downstairs that night.

Standard pubs have singles/doubles with shared facilities starting at around $35/60, more if you want a private bathroom.

Other Accommodation

There are lots of less-conventional and, in some cases, uniquely Australian accommodation possibilities scattered across the country.

A decent number of country farms offer a bed for a night, while a few outback stations also allow you to stay in homestead rooms or shearers' quarters. Check out **Australian Farmstays** (www.australiafarmstay.com .au) for your options. State tourist offices can also let you know what's available.

Within city limits, it's sometimes possible to stay in the hostels and halls of residence normally occupied by university students, though you'll need to time your stay to coincide with university holiday periods.

BUSINESS HOURS

Hours vary a little from state to state but most shops and businesses open about 9am and close at 5pm Monday to Friday, with Saturday hours usually from 9am to either noon or 5pm. Sunday trading is becoming increasingly common but is currently limited to major cities, urban areas and tourist towns. In most towns there are usually one or two late shopping nights a week, normally Thursday and/or Friday, when doors stay open until about 9pm. Most supermarkets are open until at least 8pm and are sometimes open 24 hours. Milk bars (general stores) and convenience stores are often open until late.

Banks are normally open from 9.30am to 4pm Monday to Thursday and until 5pm on Friday. Some large city branches are open from 8am to 6pm weekdays, and a few are also open until 9pm on Friday. Post offices are open from 9am to 5pm Monday to Friday, but you can also buy stamps on Saturday morning at post office agencies (operated from newsagencies) and from Australia Post shops in all the major cities.

Restaurants typically open at noon for lunch and between 6pm and 7pm for dinner; most dinner bookings are made for 6.30pm to 8pm.

CLIMATE

Australia's climate typically errs on the hot side, but as should be expected from the sixth-largest country on the planet, there is tremendous variation. The southern third of the country has cold (though generally not freezing) winters (June to August). Tasmania and the High Country in Victoria and New South Wales get particularly chilly (at Crackenback, above Thredbo, the average July maximum temperature is 0.1˚C). Summers (December to February) in the south are pleasant and warm, though sequences of days above 36˚C are quite common. Spring (September to November) and autumn (March to May) are transition months, offering comfortable conditions throughout the south.

As you head north the climate changes dramatically – 40% of the continent lies north of the Tropic of Capricorn. Seasonal variations become fewer until, in the far north around Darwin and Cairns, you are in the monsoon belt where there are basically just two seasons: hot and wet, and hot and dry. The Dry roughly lasts from April to September, and the Wet from October to March; the build-up to the Wet (from early October) is often when the humidity is at its highest. The centre of the continent is arid – hot and dry during the day, but often bitterly cold at night.

Outside of Antarctica, Australia is the driest continent; more than half the country receives less than 300mm of rain annually. The wettest place in the country is Mt Bellenden Ker (not far from the Atherton Tableland ride), with an average of around 8m a year. Rainfall decreases steadily away from the coast; a large part of the interior receives less than 100mm annually.

See When to Cycle (p21) for an overview on how the seasons might influence your cycling plans.

Weather Information

The best source of weather information is the website of the **Bureau of Meteorology** (BoM; www.bom.gov.au), which includes detailed regional forecasts and all kinds of warnings. Some national park offices also post daily local forecasts to help you keep a watch on the heat or approaching rain.

For a good overview of climate averages for destinations throughout Australia, take a look at www.weatherbase.com.

CYCLING WITH CHILDREN

Whether you're towing them in a trailer or trailer-bike, or they're pedalling along beside you, cycle touring is a great way to share time and activity with your children – even if it might preclude the silences you once favoured when riding.

Take into account your child's capabilities (both in fitness and concentration) as you plan your ride. It's likely you'll need to break down the days into smaller portions than those described in this book. If your child is riding along with you, take note before you begin as to their comfortable time and distance in the saddle. If you're towing younger children, anything beyond about three hours of riding a day can begin to test their equilibrium.

Key to the enjoyment of a ride with children is your choice of route. You're unlikely to want to set off on the Tassie's West Coast ride, or jostle with holiday traffic on the Great Ocean Road, but there are a number of rides in this book well suited to children. Rottnest Island (p236) has the best of everything for kids: short distances, no traffic, inviting water, and beaches sometimes just a few minutes apart.

Tassie's East Coast (p165) offers similar scenes (if colder water), as does the run along the Fleurieu Peninsula coast (p229) around Port Elliot and Victor Harbor.

For a kid-happy experience away from roads, try the Murray to the Mountains Rail Trail that forms a part of the Riches of the Northeast (p129) ride. Not only is the riding great, but wineries and cafes in the region cater well to child-toting visitors, with the likes of toy boxes and colouring pencils.

At day's end, most motels and the better-equipped caravan parks around the country have playgrounds and swimming pools, and can supply cots and baby baths – motels may also have in-house children's videos and child-minding services. Top-end hotels and many (but not all) midrange hotels are well versed in the needs of guests with children. B&Bs, on the other hand, often market themselves as sanctuaries from all things child related. Many cafes and restaurants lack a specialised children's menu, but others do have kids' meals, or will provide small serves from the main menu. Some also supply highchairs.

Lonely Planet's *Travel with Children* contains plenty of useful information about getting around with little ones.

CUSTOMS

For information on customs regulations, contact the **Australian Customs Service** (☎ 1300 363 263, 02-6275 6666; www .customs.gov.au).

When entering Australia you can bring most articles in free of duty provided that customs is satisfied they are for personal use and that you'll be taking them with you when you leave. There's a duty-free quota per person of 2.25L of alcohol, 250 cigarettes and dutiable goods up to the value of $900 ($450 for people under 18).

When arriving or departing the country, you'll need to declare all animal and plant material (wooden spoons, straw hats, the lot) and show them to a quarantine officer. Some items may require treatment to make them safe before they are allowed in. Bikes are certain to come under scrutiny for any dirt stuck in the tread of tyres or splashes on the frame. Give your bike a thorough clean before departure if you want to hurry through customs.

Australia takes quarantine very seriously. All luggage is screened or X-rayed - if you fail to declare quarantine items on arrival and are caught, you risk a hefty on-the-spot fine of up to $220, or prosecution, which may result in much more significant fines and up to 10 years imprisonment. For more information on quarantine regulations contact the **Australian Quarantine and Inspection Service** (AQIS; ☎ 1800 020 504, 02-6272 3933; www.aqis .gov.au).

DANGERS & ANNOYANCES

Australia is a relatively safe place to visit but you should still take reasonable precautions. Don't leave hotel rooms or your bike unlocked, and don't leave your valuables unattended in panniers or handlebar bags.

Cyclists should be alert to the presence of bushfires, which are a regular occurrence in Australia. In hot, dry and windy weather, be extremely careful with any naked flame, and on days of Total Fire Ban it's forbidden to use a camping stove, campfires or solid fuel barbecue. The penalties for doing so are severe. Given that people have lost their homes and worse to bushfires in rural Australia, locals will not be amused if they catch you breaking this law, and they'll happily turn you in.

Australia's profusion of dangerous creatures is legendary but often overstated. Travellers don't need to be constantly alarmed and the chances of being attacked are minimal. Hospitals have antivenin on hand for all common snake and spider bites, but it helps to know what it was that bit you.

For more information about safe travel among these critters, and on the roads in general, see the Health & Safety chapter (p393).

EMBASSIES & CONSULATES

Australian Embassies & Consulates

The website of the **Department of Foreign Affairs & Trade** (www.dfat.gov.au) provides a full listing of all Australian diplomatic missions overseas.

Canada (☎ 613-236 0841; www.ahc-ottawa .org; Suite 710, 50 O'Connor St, Ottawa, Ontario K1P 6L2) Also in Vancouver and Toronto.

France (☎ 01-40 59 33 00; www.france .embassy.gov.au; 4 rue Jean Rey 75724 Cedex 15, Paris)

Germany (☎ 030-880 08 80; www.germany .embassy.gov.au; Wallstrasse 76-79, Berlin 10179) Also in Frankfurt.

Indonesia (☎ 0212 550 5555; www.indo nesia.embassy.gov.au; Jalan HR Rasuna Said Kav C15-16, Jakarta Selatan 12940) Also in Medan (Sumatra) and Denpasar (Bali).

Ireland (☎ 01-664 5300; www.ireland .embassy.gov.au; 7th fl, Fitzwilton House, Wilton Tce, Dublin 2)

Japan (☎ 0352 324 111; www.australia .or.jp/english; 2-1-14 Mita, Minato-Ku, Tokyo 108-8361) Also in Osaka, Nagoya, Sendai, Sapporo and Fukuoka City.

Malaysia (☎ 03-2146 5555; www.malaysia .embassy.gov.au; 6 Jalan Yap Kwan Seng, Kuala Lumpur 50450) Also in Penang, Kuching (Sarawak) and Kota Kinabalu (Sabah).

Netherlands (☎ 070 310 8200; www.nether lands.embassy.gov.au; Carnegielaan 4, The Hague 2517 KH)

New Zealand Wellington (☎ 04-473 6411; www.newzealand.embassy.gov.au; 72-76 Hobson St, Thorndon, Wellington); Auckland (☎ 09-921 8800; Level 7, Price Waterhouse Coopers Bldg, 186-194 Quay St, Auckland)

Singapore (☎ 6836 4100; www.singapore .embassy.gov.au; 25 Napier Rd, Singapore 258507)

South Africa (☎ 12-423 6000; www .southafrica.embassy.gov.au; 292 Orient Street, Arcadia, Pretoria 0083) Also in Johannesburg.

Thailand (☎ 02 344 6300; www.thailand .embassy.gov.au; 37 South Sathorn Rd, Bangkok 10120)

UK (☎ 020-7379 4334; www.uk.embassy .gov.au; Australia House, The Strand, London WC2B 4LA) Also in Edinburgh.

USA (☎ 202-797 3000; www.usaembassy .gov.au; 1601 Massachusetts Ave NW, Washington DC 20036-2273) Also in Los Angeles, New York and other major cities.

Embassies & Consulates in Australia

The main diplomatic representations are in Canberra. There are also representatives in other major cities, particularly from countries with a strong link to Australia, such as the USA, the UK or New Zealand.

Canada Canberra (☎ 02-6270 4000; www .dfait-maeci.gc.ca/australia; Commonwealth Ave, Canberra, ACT 2600); Sydney (☎ 02-9364 3000; Level 5, 111 Harrington St, Sydney, NSW 2000)

France Canberra (☎ 02-6216 0100; www .ambafrance-au.org; 6 Perth Ave, Yarralumla, ACT 2600); Sydney (☎ 02-9261 5779; www.consulfrance-sydney.org; Level 26, St Martins Tower, 31 Market St, Sydney, NSW 2000)

Germany Canberra (☎ 02-6270 1911; www.germanembassy.org.au; 119 Empire Circuit, Yarralumla, ACT 2600); Sydney (☎ 02-9328 7733; 13 Trelawney St, Woollahra, NSW 2025); Melbourne (☎ 03-9864 6888; 480 Punt Rd, South Yarra, Vic 3141)

Ireland Canberra (☎ 02-6273 3022; irishemb@cyberone.com.au; 20 Arkana St, Yarralumla, ACT 2600); Sydney (☎ 02-9231 6999; Level 30, 400 George St, Sydney, NSW 2000)

Japan Canberra (☎ 02-6273 3244; www .japan.org.au; 112 Empire Circuit, Yarralumla, ACT 2600); Sydney (☎ 02-9231 3455; Level 34, Colonial Centre, 52 Martin Pl, Sydney, NSW 2000)

Malaysia Sydney (☎ 02-9327 7596; 67 Victoria Rd, Bellevue Hill, NSW 2023)

Netherlands Canberra (☎ 02-6220 9400; www.netherlands.org.au; 120 Empire Circuit, Yarralumla, ACT 2600); Sydney (☎ 02-9387 6644; Level 23, Tower 2, 101 Grafton St, Bondi Junction, NSW 2022)

New Zealand Canberra (☎ 02-6270 4211; www.nzembassy.com/australia; Commonwealth Ave, Canberra, ACT 2600); Sydney (☎ 02-8256 2000; Level 10, 55 Hunter St, Sydney, NSW 2001)

Singapore Canberra (☎ 02-6271 2000; www.mfa.gov.sg/canberra; 17 Forster Cres, Yarralumla, ACT 2600)

South Africa Canberra (☎ 02-6272 7300; www.sahc.org.au; cnr Rhodes Pl & State Circle, Yarralumla, Canberra, ACT 2600)
Thailand Canberra (☎ 02-6273 1149; www.thaiembassy.org.au; 111 Empire Circuit, Yarralumla, ACT 2600); Sydney (☎ 02-9241 2542; http://thaisydney.idx .com.au; Level 8, 131 Macquarie St, Sydney, NSW 2000)
UK Canberra (☎ 02-6270 6666; www .britaus.net; Commonwealth Ave, Yarra-lumla, ACT 2600); Sydney (☎ 02-9247 7521; 16th fl, 1 Macquarie Pl, Sydney, NSW 2000); Melbourne (☎ 03-9652 1600; 11th fl, 90 Collins St, Melbourne, Vic 3000)
USA Canberra (☎ 02-6214 5600; http: //usembassy-australia.state.gov; 21 Moonah Pl, Yarralumla, ACT 2600); Sydney (☎ 02-9373 9200; Level 59, 19-29 Martin Pl, Sydney, NSW 2000); Melbourne (☎ 03-9526 5900; Level 6, 553 St Kilda Rd, Melbourne, Vic 3004)

FESTIVALS & EVENTS

Some of the most enjoyable Australian festivals are also the most typically Australian – like the surf life-saving compe-titions on beaches all around the country during summer, or outback race meetings, which draw together isolated communities. There are also big city-based street festivals, sporting events and arts festivals that show-case comedy, music and dance, and some important commemorative get-togethers.

The Australian Government's Culture and Recreation Portal (www.culturean drecreation.gov.au/articles/festivals) has a comprehensive list of festivals, with links to many of them.

Cycling Events

Australia has hundreds of cycling events, from the opening pro race of the year to organised, thousands-strong cycle tours.

JANUARY

Bay Classic Criteriums (Victoria; www .jaycobayclassic.com) Based in Geelong, the so-called world's fastest criteriums also attract the country's biggest cycling names.

Tour Down Under (South Australia; www.tourdownunder.com.au) It's the only pro tour race held outside Europe (see the boxed text, p228).

Australian Open Road Championships (Victoria; www.aorcc.com) Australia's top roadies on a tough course around Buninyong, near Ballarat.

Alpine Classic (Victoria; www.audax .org.au) The premier Audax event of the year is held on Australia Day long weekend. Cyclists pedalling 200km and over two mountain tops (Mts Hotham, Buffalo and Falls Creek) plus two ascents through steep Tawonga Gap. Also has routes of between 70km and 140km.

Amy's Ride (Victoria; www.amygillett .org.au) Ride on the Bellarine Penin-sula (120km, 65km or 22km) to promote cycling safety and raise money for the Amy Gillett Foundation – Olympian Gillett was killed during a training ride in Germany in 2005. Amy's Ride is also held in Adelaide (November) and Albury (March).

FEBRUARY

Penny Farthing Championships (Tasmania; www.evandalevillagefair.com) Penny farthings trundle through the streets of Evandale in northern Tasmania.

Otway Odyssey (Victoria; www.rapid ascent.com.au/OtwayOdyssey) A 100km mountain-bike challenge from Apollo Bay, on the Great Ocean Rd, to Forrest. Also has 50km and 15km courses.

MARCH

Fleche Opperman All Day Trial (www .audax.org.au) Modelled on France's Fleche Velocio, involving teams of three to five cyclists riding over a course at least 360km in length. The set finish points are Dapto (New South Wales), Rochester (the birth-place of Sir Hubert Opperman in Victoria), Brisbane (Queensland), Adelaide (South Australia), Fremantle (Western Australia) and Hobart (Tasmania).

Great Escapade (www.bv.com.au) A nine- to 14-day supported tour organised by Bicycle Victoria. Past destinations have included Western Australia, New Zealand, the Blue Mountains and (regularly) Tasmania.

Loop the Lake (New South Wales; www .loopthelake.com.au) An 85km circuit of Lake Macquarie near Newcastle, or go easy on the 16km or 50km course.

Great Ocean & Otway Classic Ride (Victoria; www.supersprint.com.au) A

145km (or 60km) ride along the Great Ocean Rd and through the Otways.

JULY

Brissie to the Bay (Queensland; www.brissie tothebay.com.au) A 50km fundraising ride from Brisbane to Wynnum (and return), or ease back on the 25km or 10km courses.

SEPTEMBER

Simpson Desert Bike Challenge (South Australia; www.sdbc.org.au) Five-day, 590km mountain-bike event across the myriad dunes of the Simpson Desert from Purnie Bore to a welcome beer at Birdsville.

OCTOBER

Around the Bay (Victoria; www.bv.com .au) Melbourne's biggest cycling event, with thousands of riders circuiting Port Phillip Bay – choose from 250km, 210km, 100km, 80km or 50km routes.

Fitz's Challenge (Australian Capital Territory; www.pedalpower.org.au) Choose from four distances (207km, 165km, 105km, 50km) in the ACT's premier one-day event. Expect plenty of hills.

Brisbane to the Gold Coast Cycle Challenge (Queensland; www.bq.org.au) Bicycle Queensland event, with around 5000 riders pedalling 100km from South Brisbane to Southport (or a shorter 60km route).

Crocodile Trophy (Queensland; www .crocodile-trophy.com) Billed as the hardest, longest and hottest mountain bike race in the world, with competitors racing around far north Queensland.

On Your Bike (Western Australia; www .ctawa.asn.au) Supported nine-day tour organised by the Cycle Touring Association of Western Australia; riders must be members of the CTAWA.

Melbourne to Warrnambool Cycling Classic (Victoria; www.melbourneto warrnambool.com) First held in 1895, this is the world's second-longest-running one-day cycling event; open to licensed riders.

NOVEMBER

Sydney to the Gong (New South Wales; www.msaustralia.org.au/gongride) This is Sydney's top one-day event, a 90km (or 56km) charity ride from the city to Wollongong.

Kelly Country Classic (Victoria; www .nhw.hume.org.au) Three courses (150km, 100km, 50km) out from Glenrowan, the heart of Ned Kelly Country, raising funds for the local hospital.

DECEMBER

Great Victorian Bike Ride (www.bv.com .au) The country's most colossal cycle tour, with around 4000 cyclists pedalling for nine days to a different destination each year.

FOOD

Australia is not renowned for having a unique cuisine, but many people are surprised by the range and wealth of food available in restaurants, markets, delicatessens (delis) and cafes, especially in the major cities but often in far less populated places as well. Australians have coined their own phrase, Modern Australian (Mod Oz), to describe their cuisine. If it's a melange of East and West, it's Mod Oz. If it's not authentically French or Italian, it's Mod Oz – the term is an attempt to classify the unclassifiable. The cuisine doesn't really alter from one region to another, but some influences are obvious, such as the Italian migration to Melbourne and the Southeast Asian migration to Darwin.

Vegetarian eateries and vegetarian selections in nonvegie places (including menu choices for vegans and coeliac sufferers) are becoming more common in large cities and are forging a stronger presence in the smaller towns visited by tourists, though rural Australia – as exemplified by pub grub – mostly continues its stolid dedication to meat. Those who enjoy a pre- or postdigestive cigarette will need to go outside, as smoking has been made illegal in most enclosed public places in all Australian states and territories, including indoor cafes, restaurants, clubs and (sometimes only at meal times) pub dining areas.

Not many actual dishes can lay claim to being uniquely Australian – the meat pie was long the country's culinary standard bearer. Even the humble 'pav' (pavlova), the meringue dessert with cream and passionfruit, may be from New Zealand. Ditto for lamingtons, large cubes of cake dipped in chocolate and rolled in desiccated coconut. The nearest thing you will find to a truly local experience is to eat some of the wild-

CYCLISTS DIRECTORY

RECIPE TO RIDE BY

My cycling meal of choice is usually whatever's ahead at the next bakery, but when the bakeries close before dinner (curse them) out comes the camp stove. One of my favourite – and simplest – meals on the road is the sort of thing your mum might have called 'surprise soup': a bit of this, a bit of that. But it doesn't weigh down the panniers, stores away some carbs for the next day and actually tastes pretty good (for camp food anyway). The following recipe is for two people:

- 250g couscous
- a handful of pistachio nuts or cashews
- two sachets of tomato paste
- a half packet of dried peas and carrots
- mixed herbs
- stock cube

Stir the tomato paste and stock cube into water, add the dried vegetables and bring to the boil. After a few minutes, add mixed herbs and couscous. Boil for about one minute, then remove from heat and let the couscous sit in the hot water. Add the nuts, stir and eat.

Chocolate-chip-cookie chaser optional but recommended.

Andrew Bain

---

life – kangaroo, emu or crocodile – that you may have been admiring as you ride.

On the Ride

Unless you're in the outback, you'll rarely need to carry more than snacks, with even the smallest towns having some sort of eatery, often disguised under the name 'general store', with a pie-warmer sat behind the counter.

In between towns there's always the great roadhouse, usually with an attached dining room. You wouldn't come here for a night out with a loved one, but they will fill that hole created by a morning of cycling. Indeed, there's an argument that roadhouses produce some of the best burgers to be found anywhere in the country.

BUYING FOOD

You will find at least some sort of grocery store in most Australian towns, though the smaller ones are often short on variety. In this book, supermarkets and other self-catering options are listed in the town descriptions and noted on maps. Where possible, we have stressed where you will need to shop elsewhere in order to find a decent range of goods.

HOLIDAYS

The Australian calendar is strewn with holidays. Cyclists need to keep alert to school-holiday dates and major public holidays such as Easter, Australia Day and

Anzac Day, when the roads are busy with holiday traffic and campsites and hotels may be full.

Public Holidays

The following is a list of the main national public holidays. Each state and territory also has its own public holidays, such as bank holidays and Labour Day. For precise dates check locally.

New Year's Day 1 January
Australia Day 26 January
Easter (Good Friday to Easter Monday inclusive) March/April
Anzac Day 25 April
Queen's Birthday (except WA) Second Monday in June
Queen's Birthday (WA) Last Monday in September
Christmas Day 25 December
Boxing Day 26 December

School Holidays

The Christmas holiday season, from about mid-December to late January, is the main school break – it is the time you are most likely to find yourself weaving through traffic jams on holiday coasts. There are three shorter school holiday periods during the year (except in Tasmania, where there are two). Dates vary by a week or two from state to state, but they fall roughly from early to mid-April, late June to mid-July and late September to early October.

For school-holiday dates, visit the Australian government website www .australia.gov.au/School_Term_Dates.

INSURANCE

Don't underestimate the importance of a good travel insurance policy that covers theft, loss and medical problems – nothing is guaranteed to ruin your tour quicker than an accident or having that brand-new digital camera stolen. Most policies offer lower and higher medical-expense options; the higher ones are chiefly for countries that have extremely high medical costs, such as the USA. There is a wide variety of policies available, so compare the small print.

Some policies specifically exclude designated 'dangerous activities' such as scuba diving, bungee jumping, motorcycling, skiing and even bushwalking, so check carefully what it says about cycling.

You may prefer a policy that pays doctors or hospitals directly rather than requiring you to pay on the spot and claim later. If you have to claim later make sure you keep all documentation. Check that the policy covers ambulances and emergency medical evacuations by air.

See also p394 for details on health insurance.

INTERNET ACCESS

Internet cafes have become so ubiquitous throughout Australia it is easy to imagine that bytes and not bites are now a menu item. Connection speeds and prices vary significantly, but they all offer straightforward internet access. Most public libraries also have internet access, though this is provided primarily for research needs, not for travellers to check their email, so it's usually best to head for an internet cafe. You will find them in cities, large towns and pretty much anywhere that travellers congregate. The cost ranges from $3 per hour in cut-price places such as Sydney's King's Cross to $10 per hour in more remote locations. The average is about $6 per hour, usually with a minimum of 10 minutes' access. Most youth hostels and backpacker places can hook you up, as can many hotels and caravan parks. Telecentres (community centres providing web access and other hi-tech facilities to locals and visitors) provide internet access in remote areas of Western Australia, South Australia and NSW, while Tasmania has access centres in some local libraries and schools.

See p27 for some useful sites when planning your cycle tour.

MAPS

A good map is about as essential as a bike seat – a wrong turn can add hours of hard pedalling to a day. Anybody used to bushwalking or trekking will be familiar with maps scaled at around 1:50,000 or 1:100,000 but you will rarely need such detail, or want the bulk of so many maps in your panniers.

The best maps for cycle touring are often those produced by the state automobile clubs (with scales of around 1:200,000 to 1:350,000), which include road names and tourist features but not topographical information

If you desperately need to know about the climbs and need contours to count, the NATMAP series, produced by **Geoscience Australia** (www.ga.gov.au), the Australian government's national mapping agency, covers the entire country in 1:250,000 topographic maps.

Bike maps of cities and large towns are often available from visitors centres or bike shops (or downloadable) – see the regional chapters for details.

Buying Maps

It's a good idea to stock up on all the maps you'll need in capital cities. Each capital has at least one decent map shop and offices of the state automobile association, but

---

WATER

Australia has some of the finest drinking water in the world (you might disagree if you have only tasted it from Adelaide's taps), though drinking from streams without treating the water is not advised. Rarely can you be certain that another person or animal hasn't contaminated it upstream. Some treatments, especially iodine, can leave an unpalatable flavour in the water – if this is a concern, think about carrying powdered flavour sachets. For information on treating water, see, p396.

MAPS IN THIS BOOK

The maps in this book are based on the best available references, combined with GPS data collected in the field. They are intended to show the general routes of the tours we describe. They are primarily to help locate the route within the surrounding area. They are not detailed enough in themselves for route finding or navigation. You will still need a properly surveyed map at an adequate scale – specific maps are recommended in the Planning section for each hike. Most chapters also have a regional map showing the gateway towns or cities and other major features. Map symbols are interpreted in the legend on the inside front cover of this book.

On the maps in this book, natural features such as river confluences and mountain peaks are in their true position, but sometimes the location of towns and routes is not always so. This may be because a town is spread over a hillside, or the size of the map does not allow for detail of the road's twists and turns. However, by using the cue sheets provided, you should have few problems following our descriptions. For more information see p359.

there are few outside these cities. Small-scale maps showing the entire country or state or a region are plentiful and can also be purchased at map shops, visitors centres, some newsagents and even petrol stations. If you want to get a head start, the **Melbourne Map Centre** (☎ 03-9569 5472; www.melbmap.com.au) has online purchasing, and stocks topographic maps and road maps from around the country.

MONEY

Australia's currency is the Australian dollar, comprising 100 cents. Although the smallest coin in circulation is 5c, prices are marked in single cents, and the total price rounded to the nearest 5c when you pay. The Australian dollar has been on a yo-yo ride the last few years, so be ready for it to climb or slip in value at any time – see the inside front cover for exchange rates at the time of writing. For an idea of local costs, see p26.

Unless otherwise stated, all prices in this book are given in Australian dollars.

ATMs

ATMs are plentiful throughout Australia, though don't expect to find them too far off the beaten track or in very small towns. Most ATMs accept cards issued by other banks and are linked to international networks.

Credit & Debit Cards

Arguably the best way to carry most of your money around is in the form of a plastic card. Australia is well and truly a card-carrying society, and credit cards such as Visa and MasterCard are widely accepted for everything from a hostel bed to a bike repair. They can also be used to get cash advances over the counter at banks and from many ATMs, depending on the card, though these transactions incur immediate interest. Charge cards such as Diners Club and American Express (Amex) are not as widely accepted.

The obvious danger with credit cards is maxing out your limit and racking up a steaming pile of debt and interest charges. A safer option is a debit card from which you can draw money directly from your bank account using ATMs, banks or Eftpos devices. Any card connected to the international banking network (Cirrus, Maestro, Plus and Eurocard) should work, provided you know your PIN. The most flexible option is to carry both a credit and a debit card.

Moneychangers

Changing foreign currency or travellers cheques is usually no problem at banks throughout Australia, or at licensed money-changers such as Travelex or Amex in cities and major towns. Black-market exchange is almost unheard of.

On the Ride

Rides in this book rarely take you too far from civilisation so you'll never be more than a day or two from an ATM. Cash should be kept on hand for snacks – make sure to allow for a cycling appetite – and camping fees, especially if you plan to pitch in national parks or other reserves where rangers (or honesty boxes) don't come equipped with credit-card swipe machines.

Taxes & Refunds

The Goods and Services Tax (GST) is a flat 10% tax on all goods and services – accommodation, eating out, transport, electrical goods, books, clothing etc. There are exceptions, however, such as basic foods (milk, bread, fruits and vegetables). By law the tax is included in the quoted or shelf prices, so all prices in this book are GST-inclusive. International air and sea travel to/from Australia is GST-free, as is domestic air travel when purchased outside Australia by nonresidents.

If you are an overseas resident and purchase new or second-hand goods with a total minimum value of $300 from any one supplier no more than 30 days before you leave Australia, you are entitled under the Tourist Refund Scheme (TRS) to a refund of any GST paid. The scheme doesn't apply to all goods but mainly to those taken with you as hand luggage or worn onto the plane or ship. Also note that the refund is valid for goods bought from more than one supplier, but only if at least $300 is spent in each. For more details, contact the **Australian Customs Service** (☎ 1300 363 263; www .customs.gov.au).

Tipping

Tipping is the exception rather than the norm in Australia, though by some law of the jungle it is expected in more expensive restaurants – 10% of the bill is the usual amount if you think the food and service has warranted it. Nobody is going to be offended if you tip, but some people will happily think they have taken you for a ride (in more than their taxi) if you are extravagant about it.

Travellers Cheques

The ubiquity and convenience of internationally linked credit- and debit-card facilities in Australia means that travellers cheques are not heavily relied upon. Nevertheless, Amex, Thomas Cook and other well-known international brands of travellers cheques are easily exchanged. Transactions at their bureaux are commission-free if you use their cheques, while local banks charge hefty fees for the same service. You need to present your passport for identification when cashing travellers cheques. There are no notable restrictions on importing or exporting travellers cheques.

PERMITS & FEES
National Park Fees

It is becoming more commonplace to be charged an entry fee on arrival at a national park – this can range from a bit of chump change to $16 a day at Kosciuszko National Park. Only Queensland allows free access to all of its national parks. Increasingly you can also buy park passes that allow you entry into all, or a selection of, national parks in each state. Each state has its own system and pricing.

TELEPHONE

Local calls from private phones cost 15c to 30c, while local calls from public phones cost 50c; both allow unlimited talk time. Calls to mobile phones attract higher rates and are timed. Long-distance calls are cheaper during off-peak hours – generally between 7pm and 7am.

International calls from Australia are cheap and subject to specials that reduce the rates even more, so it's worth shopping around. When calling overseas you will need to dial the international access code from Australia (☎ 0011 or 0018), the country code and then the area code (without the initial 0). In addition, certain operators will have you dial a special code to access their service.

If dialling Australia from overseas, the country code is ☎ 61 and you need to drop the 0 in state/territory area codes.

Numbers starting with ☎ 190 are usually recorded information services, charged at anything from 35c to $5 or more per minute (more from mobiles and payphones). To make a reverse-charge (collect) call from any public or private phone, dial ☎ 1800 REVERSE (738 3773) or ☎ 12 550. Toll-free numbers (prefix ☎ 1800) can be called free of charge from almost anywhere in Australia, although they may not be accessible from certain areas or from mobile phones. Calls to numbers beginning with ☎ 13 or ☎ 1300 are charged at the rate of a local call – the numbers can usually be dialled Australia-wide, but may be applicable only to a specific state or district. Telephone numbers beginning with ☎ 1800, ☎ 13 or ☎ 1300 cannot be dialled from outside Australia.

Mobile Phones

Local numbers with the prefixes ☎ 04xx or ☎ 04xxx belong to mobile phones. Australia's two mobile networks, digital GSM and digital CDMA, service more than 90% of the population but leave vast tracts of the country uncovered. The east coast, southeast and southwest have good reception, but elsewhere (apart from major towns) it is haphazard or nonexistent.

Australia's digital network is compatible with GSM 900 and 1800 (used in Europe), but generally not with the systems used in the USA or Japan. It is easy and cheap enough to get connected short term as the main service providers have prepaid mobile systems.

Phone Codes

For long-distance calls, Australia uses four STD (Subscriber Trunk Dialling) area codes. Area-code boundaries don't necessarily coincide with state borders – NSW, for example, uses each of the four neighbouring codes – but the main area codes are as follows:

State/Territory	Area code
ACT	☎ 02
NSW	☎ 02
NT	☎ 08
QLD	☎ 07
SA	☎ 08
TAS	☎ 03
VIC	☎ 03
WA	☎ 08

Phonecards

A variety of phonecards can be bought at newsagents, hostels and post offices for a fixed dollar value (usually $10, $20 etc)

CYCLING ORGANISATIONS

Cycling is a lonely pursuit but you need not be alone in organising your tour in Australia. Each state has a cycling-advocacy organisation, headed by the national **Bicycle Federation of Australia** (☎ 02-6249 6761; www.bfa.asn.au) and sprinkled around the country are various touring clubs if you're feeling social or just want to pick a knowing mind.

You can find a list of more than 70 cycling clubs at www.bicycles.net.au – follow the links through the Australian Cycling Directory.

STATE CYCLING ORGANISATIONS

Bicycle Institute of South Australia (www.bisa.asn.au)

Bicycle New South Wales (☎ 02-9218 5400; www.bicyclensw.org.au; level 5, 822 George St, Sydney)

Bicycle Queensland (☎ 07-3844 1144; www.bq.org.au; 28 Vulture St, West End)

Bicycle Tasmania (www.biketas.org.au)

Bicycle Transportation Alliance (☎ 08-9420 7210; www.btawa.org.au; suite 4, City West Lotteries House, 2 Delhi Street, West Perth) West Australian cycling-advocacy group.

Bicycle Victoria (☎ 03-8636 8888; www.bv.com.au; level 10, 446 Collins St, Melbourne)

Pedal Power (☎ 02-6248 7995; www.pedalpower.org.au; 20 Genge St, Canberra; noon-2pm Tue-Fri) The ACT's volunteer-run bicycle advocacy group.

OTHER ORGANISATIONS

Audax Australia (www.audax.org.au) Runs noncompetitive, long-distance rides, on- and off-road, including the Alpine Classic (p356). Visitors are welcomed. The website lists events in each state.

Cycling Australia (www.cycling.org.au) The national body for competitive cycling (road, track, mountain biking and BMX); it has separate associations in each state.

Mountain Bike Australia (www.mtba.asn.au) A coalition of mountain bike clubs around the country.

and can be used with any public or private phone by dialling a toll-free access number and then the PIN number on the card. Some public phones also accept credit cards.

TIME

Australia is divided into three time zones: the Western Standard Time zone (GMT/UTC plus eight hours) covers WA; Central Standard Time (plus 9½ hours) covers the NT and SA; and Eastern Standard Time (plus 10 hours) covers Tasmania, Victoria, NSW, the ACT and Queensland. There are minor exceptions – Broken Hill (NSW), for instance, is on Central Standard Time. For international times, see www.timeanddate .com/worldclock.

'Daylight saving', for which clocks are put forward an hour, operates in most states during the warmer months (Oct to Mar). However, NT and Queensland stay on standard time (WA began a three-year trial of daylight savings in 2006).

TOURIST INFORMATION

Tourism Australia (www.australia.com) is the peak national tourist organisation. The website (which comes in 10 languages) is a good planning resource, though not heavy on cycling information. Run a search for 'cycling' and you will uncover a good few tour operators.

Within Australia, tourist information is disseminated by various regional and local offices. In this book, the main state tourism authorities are listed in the introductory Planning section of each chapter. Almost every major town in Australia seems to maintain a tourist office of some type, providing local information not readily available from the state offices. Invariably, local offices have better knowledge of cycling routes than state offices or Tourism Australia. Details of local tourism offices are given in the relevant city and town sections throughout this book.

VISAS

All visitors to Australia need a visa – only New Zealand nationals are exempt, and even they receive a 'special category' visa on arrival. Application forms for the several types of visa are available from Australian diplomatic missions overseas (p355), travel agents or at www.immi.gov.au.

Electronic Travel Authority (ETA)

Many visitors can get an ETA through any International Air Transport Association (IATA)-registered travel agent or overseas airline. They make the application direct when you buy a ticket and issue the ETA, which replaces the usual visa stamped in your passport – it's common practice for travel agents to charge a fee, in the vicinity of US$25, for issuing an ETA. This system is available to passport holders of 32 countries, including the UK, USA and Canada, most European and Scandinavian countries, Malaysia, Singapore, Japan and Korea.

You can also apply for the ETA online (www.eta.immi.gov.au), which incurs a non-refundable service charge of $20.

Tourist Visas

Short-term tourist visas have largely been replaced by the ETA. However, if you are from a country not covered by the ETA, or you want to stay longer than three months, you'll need to apply for a visa. Standard Tourist Visas (which cost $70) allow one (in some cases multiple) entry, for a stay of up to 12 months, and are valid for use within 12 months of issue.

Transport

CONTENTS

GETTING THERE & AWAY

ENTERING THE COUNTRY

Arrival in Australia is a straightforward affair, with only the usual customs declarations (p354) to endure. As an island nation, Australia has strict quarantine requirements. If you are bringing in a bike with dirt or mud on the wheels or frame, you might find yourself getting a lecture – and your bike getting a decent spit and polish – from quarantine officers.

Passport

There are no restrictions when it comes to citizens of foreign countries entering Australia. If you have a visa (p363), you should be fine.

AIR

There are lots of competing airlines and a wide variety of air fares to choose from if you're flying in from Asia, Europe or North America, but you'll still pay plenty for a flight. Because of Australia's size and diverse climate, any time of year can prove busy for inbound tourists – if you plan to fly at a particularly popular time of year (Christmas is notoriously difficult for Sydney and Melbourne) or on a particularly popular route (such as Hong Kong, Bangkok or Singapore to Sydney or Melbourne), make your arrangements well in advance of your trip.

The high season for flights into Australia is roughly over the country's summer (Dec to Feb), with slightly less of a premium on fares over the shoulder months (Oct/Nov and Mar/Apr). The low season generally tallies with the winter months (Jun to Aug).

Airports & Airlines

Australia has several international gateways, with Sydney and Melbourne being the busiest. The full list of international airports follows.

Adelaide (code ADL; ☎ 08-8308 9211; www.aal.com.au)
Brisbane (code BNE; ☎ 07-3406 3190; www.brisbaneairport.com.au)
Cairns (code CNS; ☎ 07-4052 9703; www.cairnsport.com.au/airport)
Darwin (code DRW; ☎ 08-8920 1811; www.ntapl.com.au)
Melbourne (Tullamarine; code MEL; ☎ 03-9297 1600; www.melbourne-airport.com.au)
Perth (code PER; ☎ 08-9478 8888; www.perthairport.net.au)
Sydney (Kingsford Smith; code SYD; ☎ 02-9667 9111; www.sydneyairport.com.au)

Australia's overseas carrier is Qantas, which, despite a few recent mishaps, is regarded as one of the world's safest airlines. It flies chiefly to runways across Europe, North America, Asia and the Pacific.

Airlines that visit Australia include the following (all phone numbers listed here are for dialling from within Australia):

THINGS CHANGE...

The information in this chapter is particularly vulnerable to change. Check directly with the airline or a travel agent to make sure you understand how a fare (and ticket you may buy) works and be aware of the security requirements for international travel. Shop carefully. The details given in this chapter should be regarded as pointers and are not a substitute for your own careful, up-to-date research.

CYCLE-FRIENDLY AIRLINES

There aren't too many airlines that will carry a bike free of charge these days – at least according to the official policy. Most airlines regard the bike as part of your checked luggage. With European, Asian and Australian carriers, the usual luggage allowance is 20kg – which doesn't leave much room for your gear – and being over the limit can mean hefty excess baggage charges.

US and Canadian-based carriers work on a slightly different system: you are generally allowed two pieces of luggage, each of which must be 32kg or less. Excess baggage fees are charged for additional pieces, rather than for excess weight. On some airlines a bike may be one of your two pieces; others charge a set fee for carrying a bike, which may then be carried in addition to your two other pieces.

When we looked into the policies of different carriers, we found that not only does the story sometimes change depending on who you talk to – and how familiar they are with the policy – but the official line is not necessarily adhered to at the check-in counter. If your flight is not too crowded, the check-in staff are often lenient with the excess charges, particularly for sporting equipment.

The time when you are most likely to incur excess baggage charges is on full flights – and, of course, if you inconvenience the check-in staff. If you suspect you may be over the limit, increase your chances of avoiding charges by checking in early, being well organised and being friendly and polite – a smile and a thank you can go a long way!

Air Canada (airline code AC; ☎ 1300 655 767; www.aircanada.ca)

Air New Zealand (airline code NZ; ☎ 13 24 76; www.airnz.com.au)

British Airways (airline code BA; ☎ 1300 767 177; www.britishairways.com)

Cathay Pacific (airline code CX; ☎ 13 17 47; www.cathaypacific.com)

Emirates (airline code EK; ☎ 1300 303 777; www.emirates.com)

Freedom Air (airline code SJ; ☎ 1800 122 000; www.freedomair.com)

Garuda Indonesia (airline code GA; ☎ 1300 365 330; www.garuda-indonesia.com)

Gulf Air (airline code GF; ☎ 1300 366 337; www.gulfairco.com)

Hawaiian Airlines (airline code HA; ☎ 1300 669 106; www.hawaiianairlines.com.au)

Japan Airlines (airline code JL; ☎ 02-9272 1111; www.jal.com)

Jetstar (☎ 13 15 38; www.jetstar.com.au)

KLM (airline code KL; ☎ 1300 392 192; www.klm.com)

Lufthansa (airline code LH; ☎ 1300 655 727; www.lufthansa.com)

Malaysia Airlines (airline code MH; ☎ 13 26 27; www.malaysiaairlines.com.au)

Pacific Blue (airline code DJ; ☎ 13 16 45; www.flypacificblue.com)

Qantas (airline code QF; ☎ 13 13 13; www.qantas.com.au)

Royal Brunei Airlines (airline code BI; ☎ 1300 721 271; www.bruneiair.com)

Singapore Airlines (airline code SQ; ☎ 13 10 11; www.singaporeair.com.au)

South African Airways (airline code SA; ☎ 1800 221 699; www.flysaa.com)

Thai Airways International (airline code TG; ☎ 1300 651 960; www.thaiairways.com.au)

Tiger Airways (airline code TR; ☎ 03-9335 3033; www.tigerairways.com)

United Airlines (airline code UA; ☎ 13 17 77; www.unitedairlines.com.au)

Tickets

Automated online ticket sales work well if you're doing a simple one-way or return trip on specified dates, but are no substitute for a travel agent with the low-down on special deals, strategies for avoiding stopovers and other useful advice.

Paying by credit card offers some protection if you unwittingly end up dealing with a rogue fly-by-night agency, as most card issuers provide refunds if you can prove you didn't get what you paid for. Alternatively, buy a ticket from a bonded agent, such as one covered by the **Air Travel Organiser's Licence** (ATOL; www.atol.org.uk) scheme in the UK. If you have doubts about the service provider, at the very least call the airline and confirm that your booking has been made.

If you are flying to Australia from the other side of the globe, round-the-world (RTW) tickets can be a real bargain. They are generally put together by the three biggest airline alliances – **Star Alliance** (www.staralliance.com), **Oneworld** (www.oneworldalliance.com) and **Skyteam** (www.skyteam.com). An alternative type of RTW ticket can be put together by a travel agent. These are usually more expensive than airline RTW fares but allow you to create your own itinerary.

For online ticket bookings, start with the following websites:

Air Brokers (www.airbrokers.com) This US company specialises in cheap tickets. Fly Los Angeles or San Francisco-Hong Kong-Bangkok-Singapore-Bali-Perth or Darwin.

Cheap Flights (www.cheapflights.com) Informative site with specials, airline information and flight searches from the USA and other regions.

Cheapest Flights (www.cheapestflights.co.uk) Cheap worldwide flights from the UK; but you need to get in early for the bargains.

Expedia (www.expedia.msn.com) Microsoft's travel site; mainly USA-related.

Flight Centre International (www.flightcentre.com) Respected operator handling direct flights, with sites for Australia, New Zealand, the UK, the USA, Canada and South Africa.

Flights.com (www.flights.com) International site for flights; offers cheap fares and an easy-to-search database.

Roundtheworldflights.com (www.roundtheworldflights.com) This excellent site allows you to build your own trips from the UK with up to six stops.

STA Travel (www.statravel.com) Prominent in international student travel but you don't have to be a student; site linked to worldwide STA sites.

Travel Online (www.travelonline.co.nz) Good place to check worldwide flights from New Zealand.

Travel.com.au (www.travel.com.au) Good Australian site; look up fares and flights to/from the country.

Travelocity (www.travelocity.com) US site that allows you to search fares (in US dollars) to/from practically anywhere.

Asia

Most Asian countries offer competitive air-fare deals, but Bangkok, Singapore and Hong Kong are the best places to shop around for discount tickets.

Flights between Hong Kong and Australia are notoriously heavily booked. Flights to/from Bangkok and Singapore are often part of the longer Europe-to-Australia route so they are also in demand. Plan your preferred itinerary well in advance.

You can get cheap short-hop flights between Darwin and Indonesia, a route serviced by Garuda Indonesia and Qantas. Airnorth runs flights between Darwin and Dili, East Timor.

Royal Brunei Airlines flies between Darwin and Bandar Seri Begawan Airport, while Malaysia Airlines flies from Kuala Lumpur. Budget carrier Tiger Airways flies from Singapore to Darwin and Perth.

Excellent bargains are sometimes available in Hong Kong. Some Asian agents **No 1 Travel** (☎ 03-3205 6073; www.no1-travel.com) In Japan. **STA Travel** Bangkok (☎ 02-236 0262; www.statravel.co.th); Singapore (☎ 6737 7188; www.statravel.com.sg); Tokyo (☎ 03-5391-2922; www.statravel.co.jp)

Canada

The air routes from Canada are similar to those from mainland USA, with most Toronto and Vancouver flights stopping in one US city such as Los Angeles or Honolulu before heading on to Australia. Air Canada now also flies direct from

BAGGAGE RESTRICTIONS

Airlines impose tight restrictions on carry-on baggage. No sharp implements of any kind are allowed onto the plane, so pack items such as pocket knives, camping cutlery and first-aid kits into your checked luggage.

If you're carrying a camping stove you should remember that airlines also ban liquid fuels and gas cartridges from all baggage, both check-through and carry-on. Empty all fuel bottles, wash them thoroughly and buy what you need at your destination.

Vancouver to Sydney, unofficially dubbed the 'Miss America' flight because, well, it does just that.

The air fares sold by Canadian discount air-ticket sellers (consolidators) tend to be about 10% higher than those sold in the USA. **Travel Cuts** (☎ 866-246-9762; www.travelcuts.com) is Canada's national student travel agency and has offices in all major cities.

Continental Europe

From major European destinations, most flights travel to Australia via one of the Asian capitals. Some flights are also routed through London before arriving in Australia via Singapore, Bangkok, Hong Kong or Kuala Lumpur.

In Germany, good travel agencies include **Adventure Travel** (www.adventure-holidays.com), which specialises in Australian travel, and the Berlin branch of **STA Travel** (☎ 069 743 032 92; www.statravel.de). In France try **Usit Connect Voyages** (☎ 0825 082 525; www.usitconnections.fr) or **OTU Voyages** (☎ 01 55 82 32 32; www.otu.fr) – both of these companies are student/youth specialists and have offices in many French cities. Other recommendations include **Voyageurs du Monde** (☎ 08 92 23 56 56; www.vdm.com/vdm) and **Nouvelles Frontières** (☎ 08 25 00 07 47; www.nouvelles-frontieres.fr); the phone numbers given are for offices in Paris, but again both companies have branches elsewhere.

Travel agencies in Holland include Australian specialist **BarronTravel** (☎ 020-625 8600; www.barron.nl), **Holland International** (☎ 0900-8858; www.hollandinternational.nl) and **Wereldcontact** (☎ 0343 530 530; www.wereldcontact.nl).

New Zealand

Air New Zealand and Qantas operate a network of flights linking key New Zealand cities with most major Australian gateway cities, while quite a few other international airlines include New Zealand and Australia on their Asia-Pacific routes.

Another trans-Tasman option is the no-frills budget airline Freedom Air, an Air New Zealand subsidiary that offers direct flights between destinations on Australia's east coast and New Zealand cities.

Pacific Blue, a subsidiary of budget airline Virgin Blue, flies between both Christchurch and Wellington and several Australian cities, including Perth and Adelaide.

There's usually not a significant difference in price between seasons, as this is a popular route year-round.

For reasonably priced fares, try one of the numerous branches of **STA Travel** (☎ 0800 474 400; www.statravel.co.nz). Another good option is **House of Travel** (☎ 0800 367 468; www.houseoftravel.co.nz).

UK & Ireland

There are two routes from the UK: the western route via the USA and the Pacific; and the eastern route via the Middle East and Asia. Flights are usually cheaper and more frequent on the latter. Some of the best deals around are with Emirates, Gulf Air, Malaysia Airlines, Japan Airlines and Thai Airways International. British Airways, Singapore Airlines and Qantas generally have higher fares but may offer a more direct route.

Discount air travel is big business in London. Advertisements for travel agencies appear in the travel pages of the weekend broadsheet newspapers, in *Time Out*, the *Evening Standard* and in the free magazine *TNT*.

Popular agencies in the UK include the ubiquitous **STA Travel** (☎ 0871 230 0040; www.statravel.co.uk), **Trailfinders** (☎ 020-7938 3939; www.trailfinders.co.uk) and **Flight Centre** (☎ 0870 499 0040; www.flightcentre.co.uk).

At peak times such as mid-December, fares go up by as much as 30%.

USA

Most of the flights between the North American mainland and Australia travel to/from the USA's west coast, with the bulk routed through Los Angeles but some coming through San Francisco. Numerous airlines offer flights via Asia or various Pacific islands.

San Francisco is the ticket consolidator capital of America, although good deals can be found in Los Angeles, New York and other big cities.

STA Travel (☎ 800-781 4040; www.statravel.com) has offices in all major cities all over the USA.

TRANSPORT

GETTING AROUND

AIR
Airlines
Qantas is the country's chief domestic airline, represented at the so-called 'budget' end of the national air-travel market by its subsidiary Jetstar. Another highly competitive carrier that flies all over Australia is Virgin Blue, while as Singapore Airlines subsidiary, Tiger Airways, joined the domestic air battle in 2007. Keep in mind if flying with Jetstar the no-frills airline, check-in closes 30 minutes prior to a flight.

Australia also has many smaller operators flying regional routes. Many of these airlines operate as subsidiaries or commercial partners of Qantas. Some regional airlines that may be of use for rides in this book include the following:

Aeropelican (☎ 13 13 13; www.aeropelican .com.au) Flies between Newcastle (Williamtown Airport), Inverell and Sydney.
Air Link (☎ 13 17 13; www.airlinkairlines .com.au) Flies between Sydney and Bathurst as well as NSW destinations further west.
Brindabella Airlines (☎ 1300 668 824; www.brindabellaairlines.com.au) Flies to Canberra, Albury, Newcastle, Port Macquarie, Coffs Harbour and Brisbane.
Jetstar (☎ 13 15 38; www.jetstar.com.au) Flies to all the capital cities and around 15 east-coast destinations from Cairns to Hobart.
Macair (☎ 13 13 13; www.macair.com.au) Links Brisbane, Townsville and Cairns with western Queensland towns.
Qantas (☎ 13 13 13; www.qantas.com.au) Australia's chief domestic airline.
QantasLink (☎ 13 13 13; www.qantas .com.au) Flying across Australia under this Qantas subsidiary brand is a collective of regional airlines that includes Eastern Australia Airlines, Airlink and Sunstate Airlines.
Regional Express (Rex; ☎ 13 17 13; www .regionalexpress.com.au) Flies to Sydney, Melbourne, Adelaide, Burnie and around 30 other destinations in New South Wales (NSW), Victoria, South Australia (SA) and Tasmania.

Skywest (☎ 1300 660 088; www.skywest .com.au) Flies from Perth to many western towns, including Albany, plus twice-weekly flights from Melbourne to Perth.
Tiger Airways (☎ 03-9335 3033; www .tigerairways.com) Budget flights between destinations that include Adelaide, Perth, Hobart, Launceston, Canberra, Melbourne, Sunshine Coast and the Gold Coast.
Virgin Blue (☎ 13 67 89; www.virginblue .com.au) Highly competitive Virgin Blue flies all over Australia.

Air Passes
With discounting being the norm these days, air passes are not great value. Qantas' **Boomerang Pass** (☎ 13 13 13) can only be purchased overseas and involves buying coupons for either short-haul flights (up to 1200km, eg Hobart to Melbourne) or multizone sectors (including New Zealand and the Pacific). You must purchase a minimum of two coupons before you arrive in Australia, and once here you can buy more.

Regional Express has the **Rex Backpacker** (☎ 13 17 13) scheme, where international travellers with a VIP, YHA, ISIC or IYTC card (Australian residents are not eligible) buy one or two months' worth of unlimited travel on the airline; it applies to standby fares only.

BOAT
Australia might be an island nation but there are few opportunities to practically use the ocean as a means of transport. The one major ferry that might be of use is the Spirit of Tasmania (☎ 1800 634 906; www .spiritoftasmania.com.au), which operates between Melbourne and Devonport (Tasmania).

BUS
Australia's extensive bus network is a relatively cheap and reliable way to get around, though it can be a tedious means of travel and requires planning if you intend to do more than straightforward city-to-city trips. Most buses are equipped with air-con, toilets and videos, and all are smoke-free zones. The smallest towns eschew formal bus terminals for a single drop-off/pick-up point, usually outside a post office, newsagent or shop.

A national bus network is provided by **Greyhound Australia** (☎ 13 14 99; www .greyhound.com.au). Fares purchased online are roughly 5% cheaper than over-the-counter tickets. A boxed or disassembled bike costs $25 (disassembled bikes must have the front wheel off and taped to the frame, the pedals removed and the chain covered) and assembled bikes cost $49.

Due to convoluted licensing arrangements involving some regional bus operators, there are some states and smaller areas in Australia – namely SA, Victoria and parts of NSW and northern Queensland – where you cannot buy a Greyhound ticket to travel between two destinations within that state/area. Rather, your ticket needs to take you out of the region or across a state/territory border. For example, you cannot get on a Greyhound bus in Melbourne (Victoria) and get off in Ballarat (Victoria), but you can travel from Melbourne to Bordertown (SA). This situation does not apply to bus passes (see this page), which can be used freely.

Regional operators running routes that may be of use for rides in this book include the following:

Firefly Express (☎ 1300 730 740; www .fireflyexpress.com.au) Runs between Sydney, Melbourne and Adelaide. Bikes do not have to be disassembled (on busy runs, the front wheel may have to be removed) and cost $30 to transport.
Premier Motor Service (☎ 13 34 10; www .premierms.com.au) Runs along the east coast between Cairns and Melbourne. A boxed bike will cost $25; an unboxed bike costs $55.
Premier Stateliner (☎ 08-8415 5555; www.premierstateliner.com.au) Services towns around SA, including Victor Harbor. Carriage of disassembled bicycles costs between $7 and $15, and for assembled bikes, $12 to $25, depending on the destination.
Redline Coaches (☎ 1300 360 000; www .tasredline.com.au) Services Hobart and Tasmania's northern and eastern coasts. Bikes cost $15 and do not need to be disassembled.
TassieLink (☎ 1300 300 520; www .tassielink.com.au) Crisscrosses Tasmania, with extra summer links to bushwalking

locales. Bikes cost $10, the front wheel must be removed and you should book ahead as buses have space for only two bikes.
Transwa (☎ 1300 662 205; www.transwa .wa.gov.au) Hauls itself around the southern half of WA. Bicycles ($10) can be carried if space permits; book ahead to ensure there is room.
V/Line (☎ 13 61 96; www.vline.com.au) Runs to most major towns and cities in Victoria. Bikes (except folding bikes) cannot be carried on V/Line buses.

Bus Passes

The following Greyhound passes are subject to a 10% discount for members of YHA, VIP, Nomads and other approved organisations, as well as card-carrying seniors/pensioners.

AUSSIE EXPLORER PASS

This popular pass gives you from one to 12 months to cover a set route - there are 23 in all and the validity period depends on the distance of the route. You don't have the go-anywhere flexibility of the Aussie Kilometre Pass (you can't backtrack), but if you can find a route that suits you it generally works out cheaper.

The Aussie Highlights pass allows you to loop around the eastern half of Australia from Sydney to Melbourne, Adelaide, Coober Pedy, Alice Springs, Darwin, Cairns, Townsville, the Whitsundays, Brisbane and Surfers Paradise for $1600, including tours of Uluru-Kata Tjuta and Kakadu National Parks. Or there are one-way passes, such as the Aussie Reef & Rock, which goes from Sydney to Alice Springs (and Uluru) via Cairns and Darwin (and Kakadu) for $1220; and the Top End Explorer, which takes in Cairns to Darwin (and Kakadu) for $555.

AUSSIE KILOMETRE PASS

This is the simplest pass and gives you a specified amount of travel, starting at 2000km ($340), going up in increments of 1000km to a maximum of 20,000km ($2450). It's valid for 12 months and you can travel where and in what direction you please, and stop as many times as you like. For example, a 2000km pass will get you from Cairns to Brisbane, 4000km ($620) from Cairns to Melbourne, and 12,000km ($1520) will cover

TRANSPORT

a loop from Sydney through Melbourne, Adelaide, central Australia, Darwin, Cairns and back to Sydney.

Phone at least a day ahead to reserve a seat if you're using this pass, and bear in mind that side trips or tours off the main route may be calculated at double the actual kilometre distance.

Reservations

Over summer, school holidays and public holidays, book well ahead on the more popular routes, including intercity and east-coast services. Make a reservation at least a day in advance if you're using a Greyhound pass.

CAR

The easiest way to access most of the rides in this book is by public transport, but if you want to hop quickly between rides, or want to mix cycling with general sightseeing, travelling by car is also an option.

Automobile Associations

Each state (and the NT) has its own automobile association, providing emergency breakdown services, excellent touring maps and detailed guides to accommodation and campsites. They each have reciprocal arrangements with associations in other states (and overseas), so if you are a member of the NRMA in NSW, for example, you can use RACV facilities in Victoria. Similarly, if you are a member of the AAA in the USA, you can use any of the Australian organisations' facilities. Bring proof of your membership with you.

Association details for each state:

National Roads & Motorists Association (NRMA; ☎ 13 11 22; www.nrma.com.au) NSW and the ACT.
Royal Automobile Association of South Australia (RAA; ☎ 08-8202 4600; www.raa.net)
Royal Automobile Club of Queensland (RACQ; ☎ 13 19 05; www.racq.com.au)
Royal Automobile Club of Tasmania (RACT; ☎ 13 27 22; www.ract.com.au)
Royal Automobile Club of Victoria (RACV; ☎ 13 72 28; www.racv.com.au)
Royal Automobile Club of Western Australia (RACWA; ☎ 13 17 03; www.rac.com.au)

Driving Licence

You can generally use your home country's driving licence in Australia, as long as it is in English (otherwise you will need a certified translation) and carries your photograph for identification. You can also use an International Driving Permit (IDP), which must be supported by your home licence. It is easy enough to get an IDP – just go to your home country's automobile association and it should issue it on the spot. The permits are valid for 12 months.

Fuel & Spare Parts

Fuel (predominantly unleaded and diesel) is available from service stations sporting well-known international brand names. LPG (liquefied petroleum gas) is not always stocked at more remote roadhouses; if you're on gas it's safer to have dual-fuel capacity.

Prices vary from place to place but basically fuel is heavily taxed and continues to rise in price, much to the disgust of local motorists. Unleaded petrol is now hovering between \$1.40 and \$1.60. Once out into the country, prices soar – prices in the outback can be up to 50% higher than in the cities. Distances between fuel stops can be long in the outback. On main roads there'll be a small town or roadhouse roughly every 150km to 200km (up to 300km in the west). Note, though, that while many roadhouses on main highways are open 24 hours, this does not apply to every fuel stop and you can't always rely on a service station being open in the dead of night.

Hire

For cheaper alternatives to the big-name international car-hire firms, try one of the many local outfits. Remember, though, that if you want to travel a significant distance you will want unlimited kilometres, and that cheap car hire often comes with serious restrictions.

You must be at least 21 years old to hire from most firms – if you are under 25 you may have to pay a surcharge. It is cheaper if you rent for a week or more and there are often low-season and weekend discounts. Credit cards are the usual payment method.

Large firms sometimes offer one-way rentals (eg pick up a car in Adelaide and leave it in Sydney) but there are many limitations, including a substantial drop-off fee.

Major companies offer a choice: either unlimited kilometres, or 100km or so a day free plus so many cents per kilometre over this.

If you are carrying your bike, it may be best to avoid so-called compact cars because space can be very tight – you will undoubtedly have to remove your front wheel to fit the bicycle inside (once you've lowered the back seats) and even then it can be a pinch.

You can compare prices between companies at www.carhire.com.au.

Rental companies with offices in the capital cities include the following:

Airport Rent-A-Car (☎ 03-9335 3355; www.airportrentacar.com.au)
Apex (☎ 1800 804 392; www.apexrentacar.com.au)
Avis (☎ 13 63 33; www.avis.com.au)
Budget (☎ 1300 362 848; www.budget.com.au)
Europcar (☎ 1300 131 390; www.europcar.com.au)
Hertz (☎ 13 30 39; www.hertz.com.au)
Rent-a-Bomb (☎ 13 15 53; www.rentabomb.com.au) Offices in NSW, Victoria and Queensland.
Thrifty (☎ 1300 367 227; www.thrifty.com.au)

Insurance

In Australia, third-party personal injury insurance is included in the vehicle registration cost, ensuring that every registered vehicle carries at least minimum insurance. We recommend extending that minimum to at least third-party property insurance – minor collisions can be amazingly expensive.

When it comes to hire cars, understand your liability in the event of an accident. Rather than risk paying out thousands of dollars, you can take out your own comprehensive car insurance or (the usual option) pay an additional daily amount to the rental company for an 'insurance excess reduction' policy. This reduces the excess you must pay in the event of an accident from between $2000 and $5000 to a few hundred dollars.

Be aware that if travelling on dirt roads you will not be covered by insurance unless you have a 4WD. Also, most companies' insurance won't cover the cost of damage to glass (including the windscreen) or tyres.

TRAIN

Long-distance rail travel in Australia is something you do because you really want to – not because it's cheaper or more convenient, and certainly not because it's fast. That said, trains are more comfortable than buses, and on some of Australia's long-distance train journeys the romance of the rails is alive and kicking. The *Indian Pacific* across the Nullarbor Plain and the *Ghan* from Adelaide to Darwin are two of Australia's great rail journeys.

Rail services within each state are run by that state's rail body, either government or private – see the relevant state chapter for details.

The three major interstate services in Australia are operated by **Great Southern Railways** (☎ 13 21 47; www.gsr.com.au), namely the *Indian Pacific* between Sydney and Perth, the *Overland* between Melbourne and Adelaide, and the *Ghan* between Adelaide and Darwin via Alice Springs. Bikes (boxed/unboxed $30/40) can be taken on the trains.

CountryLink (☎ 13 22 32; www.countrylink.info) is a rail and coach operation servicing destinations in NSW, the ACT, Queensland and Victoria. Trains have only three spaces available for carrying bicycles, which must be boxed and booked ahead. It costs $12 for a bike.

Costs

Following are some standard one-way train fares. Note that 'rail saver' tickets are non-refundable, no changes are permitted, they are only available on travel seats and payment has to be made at the time of the booking.

Adelaide–Darwin Adult/child/rail saver in a travel seat $700/460/430, from $1390/1025 in a cabin.
Adelaide–Melbourne Adult/child/rail saver in a travel seat $90/55/60, from $140/100 in a cabin.
Adelaide–Perth Adult/child/rail saver in a travel seat $395/190/245, from $1005/610 in a cabin.
Brisbane–Cairns $205 per adult (economy seat).
Canberra–Melbourne $65 per adult (economy seat); involves a bus ride from Canberra to Cootamundra, then a train to Melbourne.

Canberra–Sydney $35 per adult (economy seat).

Sydney–Brisbane $125 (economy seat).

Sydney–Melbourne $75 per adult (economy seat).

Sydney–Perth Adult/child/rail saver in a travel seat $600/325/260, from $1320/860 in a cabin.

Reservations

As the railway-booking system is computerised, any station (other than those on metropolitan lines) can make a booking for any journey throughout the country. For reservations call ☎ 13 22 32; this will connect you to the nearest main-line station.

Discounted tickets work on a first-come, first-served quota basis, so it helps to book in advance.

Train Passes

The **Great Southern Railways Pass** (☎ 13 21 47; www.gsr.com.au), which is available only to non-Australian residents, allows unlimited travel on the rail network for a period of six months. The pass costs $690/590 per adult/concession (relatively inexpensive considering the amount of ground you could cover over the life of the pass), but note that you'll be travelling in a 'Daynighter' reclining seat and not a cabin. You need to prebook all seats at least 24 hours in advance.

CountryLink (☎ 13 22 32; www.countrylink.info) is a rail and coach operation that visits destinations in NSW, the ACT, Queensland and Victoria, and offers two passes to foreign nationals with valid passports. The East Coast Discovery Pass allows one-way economy travel between Melbourne and Cairns (in either direction) with unlimited stopovers, and is valid for six months – the full trip costs $470, while Sydney to Cairns is $380 and Brisbane to Cairns is $270. The Backtracker Rail Pass allows for travel on the entire CountryLink network and has four versions: a 14-day/one-/three-/six-month pass costing $235/275/300/420 respectively.

YOUR BICYCLE

Fundamental to any cycle tour you plan is the bicycle you choose to ride. In this chapter we look at choosing a bicycle and accessories, setting it up to best accommodate your needs and learning basic maintenance procedures. In short, everything you need to gear up and get going.

CHOOSING & SETTING UP A BICYCLE

The ideal bike for cycle touring is (strangely enough) a touring bike. These bikes look similar to road bikes but generally have relaxed frame geometry for comfort and predictable steering; fittings (eyelets and brazed-on bosses) to mount panniers and mudguards; wider rims and tyres; strong wheels (at least 36 spokes) to carry the extra load; and gearing capable of riding up a wall (triple chainrings and a wide-range freewheel to match). If you want to buy a touring bike, most tend to be custom-built these days, but Cannondale (www.cannondale .com) and Trek (www.trekbikes.com) both offer a range of models.

Of course you can tour on any bike you choose, but few will match the advantages of the workhorse touring bike.

Mountain bikes are a slight compromise by comparison, but are very popular for touring. A mountain bike already has the gearing needed for touring and offers a more upright, comfortable position on the bike. And with a change of tyres (to those with semi-slick tread) you'll be able to reduce the rolling resistance and travel at higher speeds with less effort.

Hybrid, or cross, bikes are similar to mountain bikes (and therefore offer similar advantages and disadvantages), although they typically already come equipped with semi-slick tyres.

Racing bikes are less appropriate: their tighter frame geometry is less comfortable on rough roads and long rides. It is also difficult to fit wider tyres, mudguards, racks and panniers to a road bike. Perhaps more significantly, most racing bikes have a distinct lack of low gears.

Tyres – Unless you know you'll be on good, sealed roads the whole time, it's probably safest to choose a tyre with some tread. If you have 700c or 27-inch wheels, opt for a tyre that's 28–35mm wide. If touring on a mountain bike, the first thing to do is get rid of the knobby tyres – too much rolling resistance. Instead, fit 1–1½ inch semi-slick tyres or, if riding unpaved roads or off-road occasionally, a combination pattern tyre (slick centre and knobs on the outside).

To protect your tubes, consider buying tyres reinforced with Kevlar, a tightly woven synthetic fibre very resistant to sharp objects. Although more expensive, Kevlar-belted tyres are worth it. An added benefit is that they are usually light and 'foldable' (they can literally be folded flat), which makes them very simple to pack for long-haulers wishing to carry a spare.

Pedals – Cycling efficiency is vastly improved by using toe clips, and even more so with clipless pedals and cleated shoes. Mountain-bike or touring shoes are best – the cleats are sufficiently recessed to allow comfortable walking. However, you should avoid shoes with excessive flexibility as they reduce pedalling efficiency and can create hotspots on the balls of the feet.

FOLD & GO BIKES

Another option is a folding bike. Manufacturers include: Brompton (www .bromptonbike.com), Bike Friday (www .bikefriday.com), Birdy (www.birdybike .com), Slingshot (www.slingshotbikes .com) and Moulton (www.alexmoulton .co.uk). All make high-quality touring bikes that fold up to allow hassle-free train, plane or bus transfers. The Moulton, Birdie, Brompton and Slingshot come with suspension and the Bike Friday's case doubles as a trailer for your luggage when touring.

YOUR BICYCLE

TOURING BIKE

YOUR BICYCLE

PHOTOS BY JEFF CROW

Handlebar Bag

Combined Brake-Gear Levers

Front Pannier Rack (obscured)

Front Pannier

Headset

Stem

Head Tube

Down Tube

Top Tube

Seat Tube

Seat Post

Seat-Post Bolt

Rear Pannier Rack (obscured)

Rack Pack

Rear Pannier

Freewheel (9-Speed Sprocket Set)

Cable Adjusting Barrel

Rear Derailleur

Seat Stay

Chainstay

Front Derailleur

Crank

Chainwheel (with triple chainring set)

Mudguards – Adding mudguards to your bike will reduce the amount of muddy water and grit that sprays you when it rains or the roads are wet. Plastic clip-on models are slightly less effective but not as expensive, and they can be less hassle.

Water Bottles & Cages – Fit at least two bottle cages to your bike – in isolated areas you may need to carry more water than this. Water 'backpacks', such as a Camelbak, make it easy to keep your fluids up.

Reflectors & Lights – If riding at night, add reflectors and lights so you can see, and others can see you. Modern LED technology has revolutionised light efficiency, and a small headlight can also double as a torch (flashlight). Flashing LED tail-lights are cheap, compact and highly effective.

Pannier Racks – It's worth buying good pannier racks. The best are aluminium racks made by Blackburn. They're also the most expensive, but come with a lifetime guarantee. Front racks come in low-mounting and mountain bike styles. Low-mounting racks carry the weight lower, which improves the handling of the bike, but if you're touring off-road it is a better idea to carry your gear a bit higher.

Panniers – Panniers range from cheap-and-nasty to expensive top-quality waterproof bags. Get panniers that fit securely to your rack and watch that the pockets don't swing into your spokes.

Cycle Computer – Directions for rides in this book rely upon accurate distance readings, so you'll need a reliable cycle computer, preferably GPS enabled.

Other Accessories – A good pump is essential. Make sure it fits your valve type (see boxed text 'Valve Types'). Some clip on to your bicycle frame, while others fit 'inside' the frame. The stroke volume and high-pressure capability of mini-pumps vary considerably, so shop around. Also carry a lock. Although heavy, U- or D-locks are the most secure; cable locks can be more versatile.

RIDING POSITION SET UP

Cycling is meant to be a pleasurable pursuit, but that isn't likely if the bike you're riding isn't the correct size for you and isn't set up for your needs.

In this section we assume your bike shop did a good job of providing you with the correct size bike (if you're borrowing a bike get a bike shop to check it is the correct size for you) and concentrate on setting you up in your ideal position and showing you how to tweak the comfort factor. If you are concerned that your bike frame is too big or small for your needs get a second opinion from another bike shop.

The following techniques for determining correct fit are based on averages and may not work for your body type. If you are an unusual size or shape get your bike shop to create your riding position.

Saddle Height & Position

Saddles are essential to riding position and comfort. If a saddle is poorly adjusted it can be a royal pain in the derriere – and legs, arms and back. In addition to saddle height, it is also possible to alter a saddle's tilt and its fore/aft position – each affects your riding position differently.

Saddle Tilt – Saddles are designed to be level to the ground, taking most of the weight off your arms and back. However, since triathletes started dropping the nose of their saddles in the mid-1980s many other cyclists have followed suit without knowing why. For some body types, a slight tilt of the nose might be necessary. Be aware, however, that forward tilt will place extra strain on your arms and back. If it is tilted too far forward, chances are your saddle is too high.

Fore/Aft Position – The default setting for fore/aft saddle position will allow you to run a plumb bob from the centre of your forward pedal axle to the protrusion of your knee (that bit of bone just under your knee cap).

Fore/Aft Position: To check it, sit on your bike with the pedals in the three and nine o'clock positions. Check the alignment with a plumb bob (a weight on the end of a piece of string).

Saddle Height – The simplest method of roughly determining the correct saddle height is the straight leg method. Sit on your bike wearing your cycling shoes. Line one crank up with the seat-tube and place your heel on the pedal. Adjust the saddle height until your leg is almost straight, but not straining. When you've fixed the height of your saddle pedal the cranks backwards (do it next to a wall so you can balance yourself). If you are rocking from side to side, lower the saddle slightly. Otherwise keep raising the saddle (slightly) until on the verge of rocking.

The most accurate way of determining saddle height is the Hodges Method. Developed by US cycling coach Mark Hodges after studying the position of dozens of racing cyclists, the method is also applicable to touring cyclists.

Hodges Method

Standing barefoot with your back against a wall and your feet 15cm apart, get a friend to measure from the greater trochanter (the bump of your hip) to the floor passing over your knee and ankle joints. Measure each leg (in mm) three times and average the figure. Multiply the average figure by 0.96.

Now add the thickness of your shoe sole and your cleats (if they aren't recessed). This total is the distance you need from the centre of your pedal axle to the top of your saddle. It is the optimum position for your body to pedal efficiently and should not be exceeded; however, people with small feet for their size should lower the saddle height slightly. The inverse applies for people with disproportionately large feet.

If you need to raise your saddle significantly do it over a few weeks so your muscles can adapt gradually. (Never raise your saddle above the maximum extension line marked on your seat post.)

Handlebars & Brake Levers

Racing cyclists lower their handlebars to cheat the wind and get a better aerodynamic position. While this might be tempting on windy days it doesn't make for comfortable touring. Ideally, the bars should be no higher than the saddle (even on mountain bikes) and certainly no lower than 75mm below it.

YOUR BICYCLE

Pedals

For comfort and the best transference of power, the ball of your foot should be aligned over the centre of the pedal axle (see right).

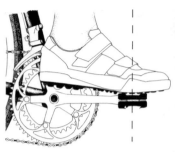

If using clipless pedals consider the amount of lateral movement available. Our feet have a natural angle that they prefer when we walk, run or cycle. If they are unable to achieve this position the knee joint's alignment will be affected and serious injury may result. Most clipless pedal systems now have some rotational freedom (called 'float') built in to allow for this, but it is still important to adjust the cleats to each foot's natural angle.

Pedal Alignment: The ball of your foot should be over the centre of the pedal axle for comfort and the best transfer of power.

COMFORT CONSIDERATIONS

Now that you have your optimum position on the bike, there are several components that you can adjust to increase the comfort factor.

Handlebars come in a variety of types and sizes. People with small hands may find shallow drop bars more comfortable. Handlebars also come in a variety of widths, so if they're too wide or narrow, change them.

With mountain bike handlebars you really only have one hand position, but 'riser' bars tend to have a more comfortable angle for touring than 'flat' bars; adding a pair of bar-ends increases hand position options. On drop bars the ends should be parallel to the ground. If they're pointed up it probably means you need a longer stem; pointed down probably means you need a shorter stem.

On mountain bikes the **brake levers** should be rotated downwards to around 45 degrees from horizontal, which ensures your wrist is straight – it's the position your hand naturally sits in. For drop bars the bottom of the lever should end on the same line as the end section.

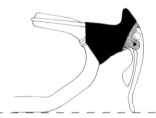

Getting the right **saddle** for you is one of the key considerations for enjoyable cycling. Everybody's sit bones are shaped and spaced differently, meaning a saddle that suits your best friend might be agony for you. A good bike shop will allow you to keep changing a new (undamaged) saddle until you get one that's perfect. Women's saddles tend to have a shorter nose and a wider seat, and men's are long and narrow.

Brake Levers: Adjust your drop bars so the end section is parallel to the ground and the brake lever ends on this same line.

If you feel too stretched out or cramped when riding, chances are you need a different length **stem** – the problem isn't solved by moving your saddle forward/aft. Get a bike shop to assess this for you. Height-adjustable stems (with a pivot) are also a versatile option, but the correct length is still required.

RECORD YOUR POSITION

When you've created your ideal position, mark each part's position (scratch a line with a sharp tool like a scribe or use tape) and record it, so you can recreate it if hiring a bike or when reassembling your bike after travel. The inside back cover of this book has a place to record all this vital data.

MAINTAINING YOUR BICYCLE

If you're new to cycling or haven't previously maintained your bike, this section is for you. It won't teach you how to be a top-notch mechanic, but it will help you maintain your bike in good working order and show you how to fix the most common touring problems.

If you go mountain biking it is crucial you carry spares and a tool kit and know how to maintain your bike, because if anything goes wrong it's likely you'll be miles from anywhere when trouble strikes.

If you want to know more about maintaining your bike there are dozens of books available (*Richard's 21st Century Bicycle Book*, by Richard Ballantine, is a classic; if you want to know absolutely everything get *Barnett's Manual: The Ultimate Technical Bicycle Repair Manual* or *Sutherland's Handbook for Bicycle Mechanics*) or inquire at your bike shop about courses in your area.

PREDEPARTURE & DAILY INSPECTIONS

Before going on tour get your bike serviced by a bike shop or do it yourself. On tour, check over your bike every day or so (see the boxed text 'Predeparture & Post-Ride Checks').

SPARES & TOOL KIT

Touring cyclists need to be self-sufficient and should carry some spares and, at least, a basic tool kit. How many spares/tools you will need depends on the country you are touring in – in countries where bike shops aren't common and the towns are further spread out you may want to add to the following.

Multi-tools (see right) are very handy and a great way to save space and weight, and there are dozens of different ones on the market. Before you buy a multi-tool though, check each of the tools is usable – a chain breaker, for example, needs to have a good handle for leverage otherwise it is useless.

Adjustable spanners are often handy, but the trade-off is that they can easily burr bolts if not used correctly – be careful when using them.

THE BARE MINIMUM:
o pump – ensure it has the correct valve fitting for your tyres (look for one that adapts to both types)
o water bottles (2)
o spare tubes (2)
o tyre levers (2)
o chain lube and a rag
o puncture repair kit (check the glue is OK)
o Allen keys to fit your bike
o small Phillips screwdriver
o small flat screwdriver
o spare brake pads
o spare screws and bolts (for pannier racks, seat post etc) and chain links (2)

FOR THOSE WHO KNOW WHAT THEY'RE DOING:
o spoke key
o spare spokes and nipples (8); can be taped to the lower rear forks
o tools to remove cassette/freewheel
o chain breaker
o pliers with side-cutters
o spare chain links; Shimano HyperGlide chains require new rivets once broken, but quick-release chain links such as the SRAM Powerlink and Wipperman Connex are an excellent alternative
o spare rear brake and rear gear cables

ALWAYS HANDY TO TAKE ALONG:
o roll of electrical/gaffer tape
o nylon cable ties (10) – various lengths/sizes
o hand cleaner (store it in a film canister)

YOUR BICYCLE

FIXING A FLAT

Flats happen. And if you're a believer in Murphy's Law then the likely scenario is that you'll suffer a flat just as you're rushing to the next town to catch a train or beat the setting sun.

Don't worry – this isn't a big drama. If you're prepared and know what you're doing you can be up and on your way in five minutes flat.

Being prepared means carrying a spare tube, a pump and at least two tyre levers. If you're not carrying a spare tube, of course, you can stop and fix the puncture then and there, but it's unlikely you'll catch that train and you could end up doing all this in the dark. There will be days when you have the time to fix a puncture on the side of the road, but not always. If it's a wet day, be aware that patches may not glue satisfactorily. Carry at least two spare tubes; ones with holes can be patched at day's end.

1 Note which cog the chain sits on, for reference when refitting. Take the wheel off the bike. Remove the valve cap and locknut (see 'Valve Types') on Presta valves. Deflate the tyre completely, if it isn't already.

2 Make sure the tyre and tube are loose on the rim – moisture and tube-pressure often fuse the tyre and rim.

3 Work the tyre bead as far into the central well of the rim as possible to create maximum play where the tyre is being lifted over the rim (removal and fitment). If the tyre is really loose you should be able to remove it by hand. Otherwise you'll need to lift one side of the tyre over the rim with tyre levers. Pushing the tyre away from the lever as you insert it should ensure you don't pinch the tube and puncture it again.

4 When you have one side of the tyre off, you'll be able to remove the tube. It's imperative before inserting the replacement tube that you carefully inspect the tyre (inside and out) for what caused the puncture; it's often easier to remove the tyre completely. Remove anything embedded in the tyre. Also check that the rim tape covers all spoke nipples and that none protrude through it.

VALVE TYPES

The two most common valve types are Presta (sometimes called French) and Schraeder (American or 'car'). To inflate a Presta valve, first unscrew the round nut at the top (and do it up again after you're done); depress it to deflate. The valve may need to be depressed before pumping as they can stick closed with time. To deflate Schraeder valves depress the pin (inside the top). Ensure your pump is set up for the valve type on your bike.

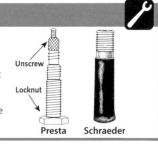

Unscrew

Locknut

Presta   Schraeder

5 Time to put the new tube in. Start by partially pumping up the tube (this helps prevent it twisting or being pinched) and insert the valve in the rim-hole. Tuck the rest of the tube in under the tyre, making sure you don't twist it. Make sure the valve is straight – most Presta valves come with a locknut to help achieve this.

6 Work the tyre back onto the rim with your fingers (refer to Step 3). If this isn't possible, and again, according to Murphy's Law, it frequently isn't, you might need to release a little air and even use your tyre levers for the last 20cm to 30cm. If you need to use the levers, make sure you don't pinch the new tube, otherwise it's back to Step 1. All you need to do now is pump up the tyre and put the wheel back on the bike. Don't forget to fix the puncture that night.

FIXING THE PUNCTURE

To fix the puncture you'll need a repair kit, which usually comes with glue, patches, sandpaper and, sometimes, chalk. (Always check the glue in your puncture repair kit hasn't dried up before heading off on tour.) The only other thing you'll need is clean hands.

1. The first step is to find the puncture. Inflate the tube and hold it up to your ear. If you can hear the puncture, mark it with the chalk; otherwise immerse it in water and watch for air bubbles. Once you find the puncture, mark it, cover it with your finger and continue looking – just in case there are more.

2. Dry the tube and lightly roughen the area around the hole with the sandpaper. Sand an area larger than the patch.

3. Follow the instructions for the glue you have. Generally you spread an even layer of glue over the area of the tube to be patched and allow it to dry until it is tacky.

4. Patches also come with their own instructions – some will be just a piece of rubber and others will come lined with foil (remove the foil on the underside but don't touch the exposed area). Press the patch firmly onto the area over the hole and hold it for 2–3 minutes. If you want, remove the excess glue from around the patch or dust it with chalk or simply let it dry.

5. Leave the glue to set for 10–20 minutes. Inflate the tube and check the patch has worked.

CHAINS

Chains are dirty, greasy and all too often the most neglected piece of equipment on a bike. There are about 120 or so links in a chain and each has a simple but precise arrangement of bushes, bearings and plates. Over time all chains stretch, but if dirt gets between the bushes and bearings this 'ageing' will happen prematurely and will likely damage the teeth of your chainrings, sprockets and derailleur guide pulleys.

To prevent this, chains should be cleaned and lubed frequently (see your bike shop for the best products to use).

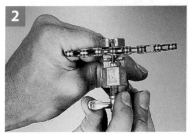

No matter how well you look after a chain it should be replaced regularly – wear depends on the quality of the chain and riding conditions, but about every 5000–8000km on average. Seek the advice of a bike shop to ensure you are buying the correct type for your drivetrain (the moving parts that combine to drive the bicycle: chain, freewheel, derailleurs, chainwheel and bottom bracket).

If you do enough cycling you'll need to replace a chain (or fix a broken chain), so here's how to use that funky-looking tool, the chain breaker. Of course, if you use a quick-release chain link you can avoid all of the following steps (see 'Chain Options' boxed text).

1 Remove the chain from the chainrings – it'll make the whole process easier. Place the chain in the chain breaker (on the outer slots; it braces the link plates as the rivet is driven out) and line the pin of the chain breaker up with the rivet.

2 Wind the handle until the rivet is clear of the inner link but still held by the outer link plate.

3 Flex the chain to 'break' it. If it won't, you'll need to push the rivet out some more, but not completely – if you push it all the way out, you'll have to remove two links and replace them with two spare links. If you're removing links, you'll need to remove a male and female link (ie, two links).

4 Rejoining the chain is the reverse. If you turn the chain around when putting it on you will still have the rivet facing you. Otherwise it will be facing away

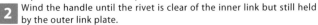

CHAIN OPTIONS

Check your chain; if you have a Shimano HyperGlide chain you'll need a special HyperGlide chain rivet to rejoin the chain. This will be supplied with your new chain, but carry a spare.

A really cool alternative is to fit a two-piece joining link, such as Sachs Powerlink or Wipperman Connex Speed Connector – available for all 8-, 9- and 10-speed chains. You'll still need a chain breaker to fix a broken chain or take out excess links.

5

from you and you'll need to change to the other side of the bike and work through the spokes.

Join the chain up by hand and place it in the breaker. Now drive the rivet in firmly, making sure it is properly lined up with the hole of the outer link plate. Stop when the rivet is almost in place.

5 Move the chain to the spreaders (inner slots) of the chain breaker. Finish by winding the rivet into position carefully (check that the head of the rivet is raised the same distance above the link plate as the rivets beside it). If you've managed to get it in perfectly and the link isn't 'stiff', well done!

Otherwise, move the chain to the spreaders on the chain breaker and gently work the chain laterally until the link is no longer stiff.

If this doesn't work (and with some chain breakers it won't), take the chain out of the tool and place a screwdriver or Allen key between the outer plates of the stiff link and carefully lever the plates both ways. If you're too forceful you'll really break the chain, but if you're subtle it will free the link up and you'll be on your way.

PREDEPARTURE & POST-RIDE CHECKS

Each day before you get on your bike and each evening after you've stopped riding, give your bike a quick once-over. Following these checks will ensure you're properly maintaining your bike and will help identify any problems before they become disasters. Go to the nearest bike shop if you don't know how to fix any problem.

PREDEPARTURE CHECKLIST
o **brakes** – are they stopping you? If not, adjust them.
o **chain** – if it was squeaking yesterday, it needs lube.
o **panniers** – are they all secured and fastened?
o **cycle computer** – reset your trip distance at the start.
o **gears** – are they changing properly? If not, adjust them.
o **tyres** – check your tyre pressure is correct (see the tyre's side wall for the maximum psi); inflate, if necessary.

POST-RIDE CHECKLIST
o **pannier racks** – check all bolts/screws are tightened; do a visual check of each rack (the welds, in particular) looking for small cracks.
o **headset** – when stationary, apply the front brake and rock the bike gently; if there is any movement or noise, chances are the headset is loose.
o **wheels** – visually check the tyres for sidewall cuts/wear and any embedded objects; check the wheels are still true and no spokes are broken.
o **wrench test** – pull on the saddle (if it moves, tighten the seat-post bolt or the seat-clamp bolt, underneath); pull laterally on a crank (if it moves, check the bottom bracket).

YOUR BICYCLE

BRAKES

Adjusting the brakes of your bike is not compli-cated and even though your bike shop will use several tools to do the job, all you really need is a pair of pliers, a spanner or Allen key, and (some-times) a friend.

Check three things before you start: the wheels are true (not buckled), the braking surface of the rims is smooth (no dirt, dents or rough patches) and the cables are not frayed. With disc brakes the wheel should spin freely without any noticeable drag.

Begin by checking that the pads strike the rim correctly: flush on the braking surface of the rim (see right and opposite) and parallel to the ground.

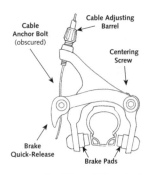

Dual-Pivot Calliper Brakes

Calliper Brakes

It's likely that you'll be able to make any minor adjustments to calliper brakes by winding the cable adjusting barrel out. If it doesn't allow enough movement you'll need to adjust the cable anchor bolt:

1 Undo the cable anchor bolt – not complete-ly, just so the cable is free to move – and turn the cable adjusting barrel all the way in.

2 Get your friend to hold the callipers in the desired position, about 2–3mm away from the rim. Using a pair of pliers, pull the cable through until it is taut.

3 Before you tighten the cable anchor bolt again, check to see if the brake lever is in its normal position (not slack as if somebody was ap-plying it) – sometimes they jam open. Also, ensure the brake quick-release (use it when you're remov-ing your wheel or in an emergency to open the callipers if your wheel is badly buckled) is closed.

4 Tighten the cable anchor bolt again. Make any fine-tuning to the brakes by winding the cable adjusting barrel out.

BRAKE CABLES

If your brakes are particularly hard to apply, you may need to replace the cables. Mois-ture can cause the cable and housing (outer casing) to bond or stick. If this happens it's often possible to prolong the life of a cable by removing it from the housing and apply-ing a coating of grease (or chain lube) to it.

If you do need to replace the cable, take your bike to a bike shop and get the staff to fit and/or supply the new cable. Cables come in two sizes – rear (long) and front (short) – various thicknesses and with different types of nipples.

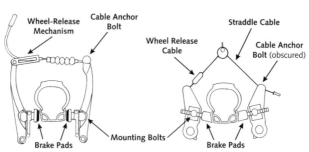

Cantilever Brakes (new style)   **Cantilever Brakes** (old style)

Cantilever Brakes

These days most touring bikes have cantilever rather than calliper brakes. The newest generation of cantilever brakes (V-brakes) are more powerful and better suited to stopping bikes with heavy loads.

On cantilever brakes ensure the leading edge of the brake pad hits the rim first (see left). This is called toe-in; it makes the brakes more efficient and prevents squealing. To adjust the toe-in on cantilever brakes, loosen the brake pad's mounting bolt (using a 10mm spanner and 5mm Allen key). Wiggle the brake pad into position and tighten the bolt again.

If you only need to make a minor adjustment to the distance of the pads from the rim, chances are you will be able to do it by winding the cable adjusting barrel out (located near the brake lever on mountain bikes and hybrids). If this won't do you'll need to adjust the cable anchor bolt:

Cantilever Brake Toe-In: This is how the brake pads should strike the rim (from above) with correct toe-in.

1 Undo the cable anchor bolt (not completely, just so the cable is free to move) and turn the cable adjusting barrel all the way in. Depending on the style of your brakes, you may need a 10mm spanner (older bikes) or a 5mm Allen key.

2 Hold the cantilevers in the desired position (get assistance from a friend if you need to), positioning the brake pads 2–3mm away from the rim. Using a pair of pliers, pull the cable through until it is taut.

3 Before you tighten the cable anchor bolt again, check to see if the brake lever is in its normal position (not slack as if somebody was applying it) – sometimes they jam open.

4 Tighten the cable anchor bolt again. Make any fine-tuning to the brakes by winding the cable adjusting barrel out.

Disc Brakes

Disc brakes have traditionally only been used on mountain bikes, but they are starting to make an appearance in the touring bike market these days. The higher-end models offer the advantage of strong, fade-free stopping power in wet and dry conditions, plus none of the rim wear associated with all calliper and cantilever brakes. Once correctly adjusted to eliminate dragging, they are relatively trouble-free, and they are well worth considering when looking at a new bike purchase or upgrade.

Due to the many different brands and adjustment systems available for disc brakes, unless you are very familiar with your particular model, we recommend taking your bike to a reliable repairer for any maintenance or adjustment.

YOUR BICYCLE

GEARS

If the gears on your bike start playing up – the chain falls off the chainrings, it shifts slowly or not at all – it's bound to cause frustration and could damage your bike. All it takes to prevent this is a couple of simple adjustments: the first, setting the limits of travel for both derailleurs, will keep the chain on your drivetrain, and the second will ensure smooth, quick shifts from your rear derailleur. Each will take just a couple of minutes and the only tool you need is a small Phillips or flat screwdriver.

Front Derailleur

If you can't get the chain to shift onto one chainring or the chain comes off when you're shifting, you need to make some minor adjustments to the limit screws on the front derailleur. Two screws control the limits of the front derailleur's left and right movement, which governs how far the chain can shift.

When you shift gears the chain is physically pushed sideways by the plates (outer and inner) of the derailleur cage. The screws are usually side by side (see photo No 1) on the top of the front derailleur. The left-hand screw (as you sit on the bike) adjusts the inside limit and the one on the right adjusts the outside limit.

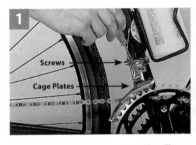

After you make each of the following adjustments, pedal the drivetrain with your hand and change gears to ensure you've set the limit correctly. If you're satisfied, test it under strain by going for a short ride.

Front Derailleur: Before making any adjustments, remove any build up of grit from the screws (especially underneath) by wiping them with a rag and applying a quick spray (or drop) of chain lube.

Outer Limits – Change the gears to position the chain on the largest chainring and the smallest rear sprocket. Set the outer cage plate as close to the chain as you can without it touching. Adjust the right-hand limit screw to achieve this.
Inner Limits – Position the chain on the smallest chainring and the largest rear sprocket. For chainwheels with three chainrings, position the inner cage plate between 1–2mm from the chain. If you have a chainwheel with two chainrings, position the inner cage plate as close to the chain as you can without it touching.

Rear Derailleur

If the limit screws aren't set correctly on the rear derailleur the consequences can be dire. If the chain slips off the largest sprocket it can jam between the sprocket and the spokes and could then snap the chain, break or damage spokes or even break the frame.

The limit screws are located at the back of the derailleur (see photo No 2). The top screw (marked 'H' on the derailleur) sets the derailleur's limit of travel on the smallest sprocket's (the highest gear) side of the freewheel. The bottom screw ('L') adjusts the derailleur's travel towards the largest sprocket (lowest gear).

Outer Limits – Position the chain on the smallest sprocket and largest chainring (see photo No 3). The derailleur's top guide pulley (the one closest to the sprockets) should be in line with the smallest sprocket; adjust the top screw ('H') to ensure it is.
Inner Limits – Position the chain on the largest rear sprocket and the smallest chainring (see photo No 4). This time the guide pulley needs to be lined up with the largest sprocket; do this by adjusting the bottom screw ('L'). Make sure the chain can't move any further towards the wheel than the largest sprocket.

Cable Adjusting Barrel

If your gears are bouncing up and down your freewheel in a constant click and chatter, you need to adjust the tension of the cable to the rear derailleur. This can be achieved in a variety of ways, depending on your gear system.

The main cable adjusting barrel is on your rear derailleur (see photo No 5). Secondary cable adjusting barrels can also be found near the gear levers (newer Shimano combined brake-gear STI levers) or on the downtube of your frame (older Shimano STI levers and Campagnolo Ergopower gear systems) of some bikes. Intended for racing cyclists, they allow for fine tuning of the gears' operation while on the move.

Raise the rear wheel off the ground – have a friend hold it up by the saddle, hang it from a tree or turn the bike upside down – so you can pedal the drivetrain with your hand.

To reset your derailleur, shift gears to position the chain on the second smallest sprocket and middle chainring (see photo No 6). As you turn the crank with your hand, tighten the cable by winding the rear derailleur's cable adjusting barrel anti-clockwise. Just before the chain starts to make a noise as if to shift onto the third sprocket, stop winding.

Now pedal the drivetrain and change the gears up and down the freewheel. If things still aren't right you may find that you need to tweak the cable tension slightly: turn the cable adjusting barrel anti-clockwise if shifts to larger sprockets are slow, and clockwise if shifts to smaller sprockets hesitate.

If you've made all these adjustments and gear changes are still not smooth over the entire range, it is highly likely that there is fine grit contaminating the cable housing or a minute crimp in the inner cable. Even very slight friction in the cabling can cause shifting problems, and the easiest solution is to completely replace the inner cable and outer housing. There are devices available that seal out dirt (especially useful for bikes with cables running down the rear frame stay, which allow water to run directly into the cable outer) and aid in reducing friction at the sharp bend into the rear derailleur; a good combo is the Avid Rollamajig and the SRAM Nightcrawler.

REPLACING A SPOKE

Even the best purpose-made touring wheels occasionally break spokes. When this happens the wheel, which relies on the even pull of each spoke, is likely to become buckled. When it is not buckled, it is considered true.

If you've forgotten to pack spokes or you grabbed the wrong size, you can still get yourself out of a pickle if you have a spoke key. Wheels are very flexible and you can get it roughly true – enough to take you to the next bike shop – even if two or three spokes are broken.

If you break a spoke on the front wheel it is a relatively simple thing to replace the spoke and retrue the wheel. The same applies if a broken spoke is on the nondrive side (opposite side to the rear derailleur) of the rear wheel. The complication comes when you break a spoke on the drive side of the rear wheel (the most common case). In order to replace it you need to remove the cassette, a relatively simple job in itself but one that requires a few more tools and the know-how.

If you don't have that know-how fear not, because it is possible to retrue the wheel without replacing that spoke and without damaging the wheel – see 'Truing a Wheel' (below).

1 Remove the wheel from the bike. It's probably a good idea to remove the tyre and tube as well (though not essential), just to make sure the nipple is seated properly in the rim and not likely to cause a puncture.

2 Remove the broken spoke but leave the nipple in the rim (if it's not damaged; otherwise replace it). Now you need to thread the new spoke. Start by threading it through the vacant hole on the hub flange. Next lace the new spoke through the other spokes. Spokes are offset on the rim; every second one is on the same side and, generally, every fourth is laced through the other spokes the same way.

3 With the spoke key, tighten the nipple until the spoke is about as taut as the other spokes on this side of the rim. Spoke nipples have four flat sides – to adjust them you'll need the correct size spoke key. Spoke keys come in two types: those made to fit one spoke gauge or several. If you have the latter, trial each size on a nipple until you find the perfect fit.

Truing a Wheel

Truing a wheel is an art form and, like all art forms, it is not something mastered overnight. If you can, practise with an old wheel before leaving home. If that's not possible – and you're on the side of the road as you read this – following these guidelines will get you back in the saddle until you can get to the next bike shop.

1 Start by turning the bike upside-down, so the wheels can turn freely. Check the tension of all the spokes on the wheel: do this by squeezing each pair of spokes on each side. Tighten those spokes that seem loose and loosen those that seem too tight. Note, though, the spokes on the drive side of the rear wheel (on the same side as the freewheel) are deliberately tighter than the non-drive side.

2 Rotate the wheel a couple of times to get an idea of the job at hand. If the wheel won't rotate, let the brakes off (see 'Brakes').

3 Using the chalk from your puncture repair kit, mark all the 'bumps'. Keep the chalk in the same position (brace the chalk against the pannier rack or bike's frame) and let the bumps in the wheel 'hit' the chalk.

4 In order to get the bumps out you'll need a constant point of reference – to gauge if the bumps are being removed. Often, if it is not a severe buckle, you can use a brake pad. Position the brake pad about 2–3mm from the rim (on the side with the biggest buckle).

5 With your spoke key, loosen those spokes on the same side as the bump within the longest chalked area, and tighten those on the opposite side of the rim. The spokes at the start and the finish of the chalked area should only be tightened/loosened by a quarter-turn; apply a half-turn to those in between.

6 Rotate the wheel again; if you're doing it correctly the buckle should not be as great. Continue this process of tightening and loosening spokes until the bump is as near to gone as you can get it – as the bump is removed turn the nipples less (one-eighth of a turn on the ends and a quarter-turn in between). Experienced exponents can remove buckles entirely, but if you can get it almost out (1mm here or there) you've done well.

7 If the wheel has more than one bump, move onto the second-longest chalk mark next. As each bump is removed you might find it affects the previous bump slightly. In this case, remove the previous chalk mark and repeat Steps 4–6. Continue to do this until all the buckles are removed.

Don't forget to readjust the brakes.

If you've trued the wheel without replacing the broken spokes, have them replaced at the next bike shop.

YOUR BICYCLE

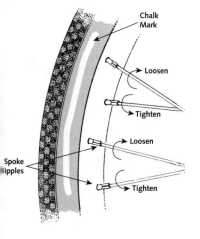

Chalk Mark

Loosen

Tighten

Loosen

Spoke nipples

Tighten

LOADING YOUR BICYCLE

If you've ever been to Asia and seen a bike loaded with boxes piled 2m high or carrying four, five or six people, plus a chicken or two, you'll realise that there are more ways to carry your gear than would otherwise seem. More realistic options for you come from a combination of front and rear panniers, a handlebar bag or trailer.

'Credit-card tourists', who are intent on travelling lighter, further and faster and who are happy to stay in hotels or hostels, can get by with a handlebar bag and/or rear panniers (see top right). The downside to this configuration is poor bike-handling; the steering feels particularly 'airy'. It's possible to adopt the 'lighter, further, faster' principle and still camp, but it means frugal packing.

If you want to be more self-sufficient or you're carrying 20kg or more, you'll probably find it easier (and your bike will handle better) with front and rear panniers. The tried-and-tested configuration that works best for a touring bike is to use four panniers: two low-mounting front panniers with two high-mounting rear panniers (see bottom right). The only other thing you might want to add is a small handlebar bag for this book, snacks, sunblock, money, camera etc.

Pannier configurations: the four-pannier system is the best way of carrying your gear and having a bike that handles well; packing light saves weight but the compromise can be poor bike handling.

This combination, with a few light but bulky items on the rear rack (eg, tent, sleeping mat etc), allows you to carry a large load and still have predictable and manageable bike-handling.

If you're riding a mountain bike and riding off-road you'll probably want high-mounting front panniers to give you more clearance.

PACKING YOUR GEAR

It's frequently said that, in packing for a cycle tour, you should lay out everything you need to take and then leave half of it behind. The skill is in knowing which half to leave behind. Almost as much skill is needed in organising the gear in your panniers. Here are some tried and tested tips.

Compartmentalise Pack similar items into nylon drawstring bags (stuff sacks), to make them easier to find again (eg, underwear in one, cycling clothes in another, and even dinner food separated from breakfast food). Using different coloured stuff sacks makes choosing the right one easier.

Waterproof Even if your panniers are completely waterproof, and especially if they're not, it pays to put everything inside heavy-duty plastic bags. Check bags for holes during the trip; replace them or patch the holes with tape.

Reduce Flood Damage If your panniers are not waterproof and they pool water, you can reduce problems by putting things that are unaffected by water, say a pair of thongs, at the bottom of the bag. This keeps the other stuff above 'flood level'. Try using seam sealant on the bags' seams beforehand, too.

Load Consistently Put things in the same place each time you pack to avoid having to unpack every bag just to find one item.

Balance the Load Distribute weight evenly – generally around 60% in the rear and 40% in the front panniers – and keep it as low as possible by using low-mounting front panniers and packing heavy items first. Side-to-side balancing is just as critical.

Group Gear Pack things used at the same time in the same pannier. Night/camp things like your mat, sleeping bag and pyjamas, which you don't need during the day, could all be in the bag most difficult to access – likely to be on the same side as the side of the road you are riding on, since you will probably lean that side of the bike against a tree, pole or roadside barrier.

Put all clothing in one pannier, if possible, sorted into separate bags of cycling clothes, 'civilian' clothes, underwear, wet weather gear and dirty clothes. Keep a windproof jacket handy on top for descents.

In the Front Food and eating utensils are convenient to have in a front pannier along with a camping stove. Toiletry items, towel, first-aid kit, reading material, torch and sundry items can go in the other front bag.

In the Pockets or Bar Bag Easily accessible pockets on panniers or on your cycling shirt are useful for items likely to be needed frequently or urgently during the day, such as snacks, tool kit, sun hat or sunscreen. A handlebar bag is good for these items if your panniers don't have pockets, but remember that weight on the handlebars upsets a bike's handling.

Keep Space Spare Remember to leave some spare space for food and, if using a camping stove, for the fuel canister. Be mindful when packing foods that are squashable or sensitive to heat and protect or insulate them – unless you're working on a gourmet pasta sauce recipe that includes socks.

ANOTHER OPTION – TRAILERS

Luggage trailers are gaining in popularity and some innovative designs are now on the market. By spreading the load onto more wheels they relieve the bike and can improve rolling resistance. Their extra capacity is a boon for travelling on a tandem or with a young family. They can be combined with racks and panniers, but the hitch (point it connects with the bike) of some trailers may interfere with your panniers, so check first.

PHOTO BY PETER HINES

Two-wheeled trailers are free standing and can take very heavy loads, including babies and toddlers. Often brightly coloured, they give a strong signal to car drivers who tend to give you a wide berth. However, their relatively wide track can catch a lot of wind and makes them ungainly on rough, narrow roads or trails. Single-wheeled trailers such as the BOB Yak share the load with the bike's rear wheel.
They track well and can be used on very rough trails and may be the easiest option for full-suspension bikes. The load capacity of these units is somewhere between that of a bike with a rear rack only and a fully loaded (four panniers plus rack-top luggage) touring bike.

YOUR BICYCLE

Prevent 'Internal Bleeding' Act on the premise that anything that can spill will, and transfer it to a reliable container, preferably within a watertight bag. Take care, too, in packing hard or sharp objects (tools, utensils or anything with hooks) that could rub or puncture other items, including the panniers. Knives or tools with folding working parts are desirable.

Fragile Goods Valuables and delicate equipment such as cameras are best carried in a handlebar bag, which can be easily removed when you stop. Alternatively, carry these items in a 'bum bag', which will accompany you automatically.

Rack Top Strap your tent lengthways on top of the rear rack with elastic cord looped diagonally across from front to rear and back again, and maybe across to anchor the rear end. Be sure the cord is well tensioned and secure – deny its kamikaze impulses to plunge into the back wheel, jamming the freewheel mechanism, or worse.

WHAT TO LOOK FOR IN PANNIERS

Panniers remain the popular choice for touring luggage. They offer flexibility, in that one, two or four can be used depending on the load to be carried and they allow luggage to be arranged for easy access.

Many people initially buy just a rear rack and panniers, and it is wise to buy the best quality you can afford at this stage. These bags will accompany you on all of your tours as well as for day-to-day shopping and commuting trips for years to come. The attachment system should be secure, but simple to operate. That big bump you hit at 50km/h can launch a poorly designed pannier and your precious luggage.

The stiffness of the pannier backing is another concern – if it can flex far enough to reach the spokes of the wheel the result can be catastrophic. Good rack design can also help avoid this. The fabric of the panniers should be strong and abrasion- and water-resistant. You can now buy roll-top panniers, made from laminated fabrics, that are completely waterproof. Bear in mind that these bags are only waterproof until they develop even the smallest hole, so be prepared to check them and apply patches occasionally. Canvas bags shed water well, but should be used in conjunction with a liner bag to keep things dry. Cordura is a heavy nylon fabric with excellent abrasion resistance. The fabric itself is initially waterproof, but water tends to find the seams, so using a liner bag is a good idea once again.

Pockets and compartments can help to organise your load, but the multitude of seams increase the challenge of keeping the contents dry in the wet. A couple of exterior pockets are great for sunscreen, snacks and loose change that you need throughout the day. Carrying front panniers as well as rear ones allows more opportunities to divide and organise gear. When fitting rear panniers check for heel strike. Long feet, long cranks and short chainstays will all make it harder to get the bags and your body to fit.

YOUR BICYCLE

Health & Safety

Road yobbos and road trains aside, Australia's greatest hazards are more topographical than infectious – you are more likely to grimace through knee soreness than you are to be felled by disease. Some tropical maladies such as malaria and yellow fever are unheard of, as are diseases of insanitation such as cholera and typhoid. By taking care to treat any water you may gather from watercourses, covering yourself against the sun and exercising basic caution on the roads, you are likely only to carry this chapter as ballast.

Keeping healthy on your travels depends on your predeparture preparations, your daily health care and diet while on the road, and how you handle any medical problem that develops. Few touring cyclists experience anything more than a bit of soreness, fatigue and chafing, although there is potential for more serious problems.

BEFORE YOU GO

Since most vaccines don't produce immunity until at least two weeks after they're given, visit a physician four to eight weeks before departure. Ask your doctor for an International Certificate of Vaccination

FIRST-AID KIT

- Acetaminophen (paracetamol) or aspirin
- Adhesive or paper tape
- Antibacterial ointment (for cuts, abrasions and saddle rash or sores)
- Antibiotics
- Antidiarrhoeal drugs (eg loperamide)
- Antihistamines (for hay fever and allergic reactions)
- Anti-inflammatory drugs (eg ibuprofen)
- Antiseptic wipes
- Bandages, gauze swabs, gauze rolls
- Calamine lotion, sting-relief spray or aloe vera (for sunburn and insect bites or stings)
- Elasticised support bandage (for knees, ankles etc)
- Iodine tablets or water filter (for water purification)
- Insect repellent, sun block and lip balm
- Latex gloves
- Nonadhesive dressing
- Oral rehydration salts
- Paper stitches
- Scissors, safety pins, tweezers
- Steroid cream or cortisone (for allergic rashes)
- Sticking plasters (Band-Aids, blister plasters)
- Sutures
- Syringes and needles (for removing gravel and dirt from road-rash wounds) – ask your doctor for a note explaining why you have them
- Thermometer
- Tweezers

(otherwise known as 'the yellow booklet'), which will list all the vaccinations you've received. This is mandatory for countries that require proof of yellow fever vaccination upon entry (sometimes required in Australia, see Required & Recommended Vaccinations, p395), but it's a good idea to carry a record of all your vaccinations wherever you travel.

Bring medications in their original, clearly labelled containers. A signed and dated letter from your physician describing your medical conditions and medications, including generic names, is also a good idea. If carrying syringes or needles, be sure to have a physician's letter documenting their medical necessity.

Australia has an excellent health-care system. It is a mixture of privately run medical clinics and hospitals alongside a system of public hospitals funded by the Australian government. The Medicare system covers Australian residents for some health-care costs. Visitors from countries with which Australia has a reciprocal health-care agreement are eligible for benefits specified under the Medicare program. Agreements are currently in place with New Zealand, the UK, the Netherlands, Sweden, Finland, Italy, Malta and Ireland – check the details before departing these countries. In general the agreements provide for any episode of ill-health that requires prompt medical attention.

INSURANCE

If your health insurance doesn't cover you for medical expenses abroad, consider getting extra insurance. Make sure this covers you for remote-area rescue if you plan to ride outside of the major city centres.

For Australian residents, Medicare doesn't cover ambulance costs, though ambulance service is free for Queensland and Tasmanian residents. Residents of other states should check their health insurance covers them for remote-area ambulance rescue services. Some health insurers offer ambulance-only cover, and in Victoria, South

---

GETTING FIT FOR TOURING

Ideally, a training program should be tailored to your objectives, specific needs, fitness level and health. However, if you have no idea how to prepare for your cycling holiday, the following guidelines will help you get the fitness you need to enjoy it most. Things to think about include the following:

Foundation You will need general kilometres in your legs before you start to expose them to any intensive cycling. Always start out with easy rides – even a few kilometres to the shops – and give yourself plenty of time to build towards your objective.

Tailoring Once you have the general condition to start preparing for your trip, work out how to tailor your training rides to the type of tour you are planning. Someone preparing for a three-week ride will require a different approach to someone building fitness for a one-day or weekend ride. Some aspects to think about are the ride length (distance and days), terrain, climate and weight to be carried on the bike. If your trip involves carrying 20kg in panniers, incorporate this weight into some training rides, especially the longer ones. If you are going to be touring in mountainous areas, choose a hilly training route.

Recovery You usually adapt to a training program during recovery time, so it's important to do the right things between rides. Recovery can take many forms, but the simple ones are best. These include getting quality sleep, maintaining an adequate diet to refuel the system, doing recovery rides between hard days (using low gears to avoid pushing yourself), stretching and enjoying a relaxing bath. Other forms of recovery include massage, spas and yoga.

If you have no cycling background the program below will help you get fit for your cycling holiday. If you are doing an easy ride (each ride in this book is rated; see p19), aim to at least complete Week 4; for moderate rides, complete Week 6; and complete the entire program if you are doing a demanding ride. Experienced cycle tourers could start at Week 3, while those who regularly ride up to four days a week could start at Week 5.

Australia and country Western Australia you can take out ambulance cover direct with the ambulance service.

REQUIRED & RECOMMENDED VACCINATIONS

If you're entering Australia within six days of having stayed overnight or longer in a yellow fever-infected country, you'll need proof of yellow fever vaccination. For a full list of these countries visit the **World Health Organisation** (WHO; www.who.int/wer) or **Centres for Disease Control & Prevention** (www.cdc.gov/travel) websites.

If you're really worried about health when travelling, there are a few vaccinations you could consider for Australia. The WHO recommends that all travellers should be covered for diphtheria, tetanus, measles, mumps, rubella, chickenpox and polio, as well as hepatitis B, regardless of their destination.

Planning to travel is a great time to ensure that all routine vaccination cover is complete. The consequences of these diseases can be severe, and while Australia has high levels of childhood vaccination coverage, outbreaks of these diseases do occur.

FIRST AID

It's a good idea at any time to know the appropriate responses in the event of a major accident or illness, and it's especially important if you are intending to ride off-road in a remote area. Consider learning basic first aid through a recognised course before you go, and carrying a first-aid manual and small medical kit.

Although detailed first-aid instruction is outside the scope of this guidebook, some basic points are listed in the section on Traumatic Injuries (p404). Undoubtedly the best advice is to avoid an accident in the first place. The Safety on the Ride section (p405) contains tips for safe on-road and off-road riding, as well as information on how to summon help should a major accident or illness occur.

Don't treat this as a punishing training schedule: try cycling to work or to the shops, join a local touring club or get a group of friends together to turn weekend rides into social events.

	Monday	Tuesday	Wednesday	Thursday	Friday	Saturday	Sunday
Week 1	10km*	–	10km*	–	10km*	–	10km*
Week 2	–	15km*	–	15km*	–	20km*	–
Week 3	20km*	–	20km†	25km*	–	25km*	20km†
Week 4	–	30km*	–	35km*	30km†	30km*	–
Week 5	30km*	–	40km†	–	35km*	–	40km†
Week 6	30km*	–	40km†	–	–	60km*	40km†
Week 7	30km*	–	40km†	–	30km†	70km*	30km*
Week 8	–	60km*	30km†	–	40km†	–	90km*

* steady pace (allows you to carry out a conversation without losing your breath) on flat or undulating terrain
† solid pace (allows you to talk in short sentences only) on undulating roads with some longer hills

The training program shown here is only a guide. Ultimately it is important to listen to your body and slow down if the ride is getting too hard. Take recovery days and cut back distances when you feel this way. Don't panic if you don't complete every ride, every week; the most important thing is to ride regularly and gradually increase the length of your rides as you get fitter.

For those with no exercise background, be sure to see your doctor and get a clearance to begin exercising at these rates. This is especially important for those over 35 years of age with no exercise history and those with a cardiac or respiratory condition of any nature.

Kevin Tabotta

PHYSICAL FITNESS

Most of the rides in this book are designed for someone with a moderate degree of cycling fitness. As a general rule, however, the fitter you are, the more you'll enjoy riding. It pays to spend time preparing yourself physically before you set out, rather than let a sore backside and aching muscles draw your attention away from some of the world's finest cycle-touring countryside.

Depending on your existing level of fitness, you should start training a couple of months before your trip. Try to ride at least three times a week, starting with easy rides (even 5km to work, if you're not already cycling regularly) and gradually building up to longer distances. Once you have a good base of regular riding behind you, include hills in your training and familiarise yourself with the gearing on your bike. Before you go you should have done at least one 60km to 70km ride with loaded panniers.

As you train, you'll discover how to adjust your bike to increase your comfort.

STAYING HEALTHY

The best way to have a lousy holiday (especially if you're relying on self-propulsion) is to become ill. Heed the following simple advice and the only thing you're likely to suffer from is that rewarding tiredness at the end of a full day.

Reduce the chances of contracting an illness by washing your hands frequently, particularly after working on your bike and before handling or eating food.

HYDRATION

You may not notice how much water you're losing as you ride, because it evaporates in the breeze. However, don't underestimate the amount of fluid you need to replace, particularly in warmer weather. The magic figure is supposedly 1L per hour, though many cyclists have trouble consuming this much – remembering to drink enough can be harder than it sounds. Sipping little and often is the key; try to drink a mouthful every 10 minutes or so and don't wait until you get thirsty. Water 'backpacks' can be great for fluid regulation since virtually no physical or mental effort is required to drink. Keep drinking before and after the day's ride to replenish fluid.

Use the colour of your urine as a rough guide to whether you are drinking enough. Small amounts of dark urine suggest you need to increase your fluid intake. Passing reasonable quantities of light-yellow urine indicates that you've got the balance about right. Some other obvious signs of dehydration include headache and fatigue. For more information on the effects of dehydration, see p400.

Water

Tap water is universally safe in Australia, but all other water should be treated. The simplest way of purifying water is to boil it thoroughly. Vigorous boiling for five minutes should do the job.

Simple filtering will not remove all dangerous organisms, so if you can't boil water, treat it chemically. Chlorine tablets will kill many pathogens, but not giardia. Iodine is very effective in purifying water and is available in tablet and liquid form, but follow the directions carefully and remember that too much iodine can be harmful. Flavoured powder such as Tang will disguise the taste of treated water and is a good thing to carry if you are spending time away from town water supplies.

Sports Drinks

Commercial sports drinks such as Gatorade and PowerAde are an excellent way to satisfy your hydration needs, electrolyte replacement and energy demands in one. On endurance rides especially, it can be difficult to keep eating solid fuels day in, day out, but sports drinks can supplement these energy demands and allow you to vary your solid fuel intake a little. The bonus is that those all-important body salts lost through perspiration get re-stocked. Make sure you drink plenty of water as well; if you have two water bottles on your bike (and you should), it's a good idea to fill one with sports drink and the other with plain water.

If using a powdered sports drink, don't mix it too strong (follow the instructions) because, in addition to being too sweet, too many carbohydrates can actually impair your body's ability to absorb the water and carbohydrates properly.

NUTRITION

One of the great things about bike touring is that it requires lots of energy, which means you can eat more of Australia's fabulous food. Depending on your activity levels, it's not hard to put away huge servings of food and be hungry a few hours after.

Because you're putting such demands on your body, it's important to eat well – not just lots. As usual, you should eat a balanced diet from a wide variety of foods.

The main part of your diet should be carbohydrates rather than proteins or fats. While some protein (for tissue maintenance and repair) and fat (for vitamins, long-term energy and warmth) is essential, carbohydrates provide the most efficient fuel. They are easily digested into simple sugars, which are then used in energy production. Less-refined foods such as pasta, rice, bread, fruits and vegetables are all high in carbohydrates.

Eating simple carbohydrates (sugars, such as lollies or sweets) gives you almost immediate energy – great for when you need a top-up (see the boxed text, p397); however, because they are quickly metabolised, you may get a sugar 'high' then a 'low'. For cycling it is far better to base your diet around complex carbohydrates, which take longer to process and provide slow-release energy over a longer period. (But don't miss the opportunity to indulge guiltlessly in pastries and that delicious cheese every now and then…)

If you can get hold of a copy, the out-of-print *Cycle Food: A Guide to Satisfying Your Inner Tube*, by Lauren Hefferon, is a handy reference for nutrition and health advice with practical recipes.

Day-to-Day Needs

Eat a substantial breakfast – wholegrain cereal or bread is best, if you can find them – and fruit or juice for vitamins. You may get cooked breakfasts in hotels, but if you're camping and preparing your own breakfast, include carbohydrates (such as porridge, toast or potatoes). Try to avoid foods high in fat, which take longer to digest.

Bread is the easiest food for lunch, topped with ingredients such as cheese,

---

AVOIDING THE BONK

The bonk, in a cycling context, is not a pleasant experience; it's that light-headed, can't-put-power-to-the-pedals feeling that engulfs you (usually quite quickly) when your body runs out of fuel.

If you experience it, the best move is to stop and refuel immediately. It can be quite serious and risky to your health if it's not addressed as soon as symptoms occur. It won't take long before you are ready to get going again (although most likely at a slower pace), but you'll also be more tired the next day so try to avoid it.

The best way to do this is to maintain your fuel intake while riding. Cycling for hours burns considerable body energy, and replacing it is something that needs to be tailored to each individual's tastes. The touring cyclist needs to target foods that have a high carbohydrate source. Foods that contain some fat are not a problem, as cycling at low intensity (when you're able to ride and talk without losing your breath) will usually trigger the body to draw on fat stores before stored carbohydrates.

Good on-bike cycling foods include:

- bananas (in particular) and other fruits
- bread with jam or honey
- breakfast and muesli bars
- rice-based snacks
- prepackaged high-carbohydrate sports bars (eg, PowerBar)
- sports drinks

During lunch stops (or for breakfast) you can try filling potato-based dishes, spaghetti, cereal, pancakes and baked beans.

It's important not to get uptight about the food you eat. As a rule of thumb, base all your meals around carbohydrates of some sort, but don't be afraid to also indulge in local culinary delights.

peanut butter, salami and fresh salad vegetables. If you're in a town, filled bread rolls make for a satisfying meal (chips or pizza, with their high fat content, will feel like a lump in your stomach if you ride on straight away).

Keep topping up your energy during the ride – see the boxed text, p397.

Try to eat a high-carbohydrate meal in the evening. If you're eating out, Italian or Asian restaurants tend to offer more carbohydrate-based meals.

Rice, pasta and potatoes are good staples if you're self-catering. Team them with fresh vegetables and ingredients such as instant soup, canned beans, fish or bacon. Remember that even though you're limited in terms of what you can carry on a bike, it's possible – with some imagination and preparation – to eat delicious as well as nutritious camp meals.

AVOIDING CYCLING AILMENTS
Saddle Sores & Blisters

While you're more likely to get a sore bum if you're out of condition, riding long distances does take its toll on your behind. To minimise the impact, always wear clean, padded bike shorts (also known as 'knicks'). Brief, unfitted shorts can chafe, as can underwear. Shower as soon as you stop a day's ride and put on clean, preferably nonsynthetic, clothes. Moisturising or emollient creams (or nappy-rash cream) also help guard against chafing – apply liberally around the crotch area before riding. For information on correctly adjusting your bike seat, see the Your Bicycle chapter (p373).

If you do suffer from chafing, wash and dry the area and carefully apply a barrier (moisturising) cream.

You probably won't get blisters unless you do a very long ride with no physical preparation. Wearing gloves and correctly fitted shoes will reduce the likelihood of blisters on your hands and feet. If you know you're susceptible to blisters in a particular spot, cover the area with medical adhesive tape before riding.

Knee Pain

Knee pain is common among cyclists who pedal in too high a gear. While it may seem faster to turn the pedals slowly in a high gear, it's actually more efficient (and better for your knees) to 'spin' the pedals – that is, use a low enough gear so you can pedal quickly with little resistance. For touring, the ideal cadence (the number of pedal strokes per minute) ranges from 70 to 90. Try to maintain this cadence even when you're climbing.

It's a good idea to stretch before and after riding, and to go easy when you start each day. This reduces your chances of injury and helps your muscles to work more efficiently.

You can also get sore knees if your saddle is too low, or if your shoe cleats (for use with clipless pedals) are incorrectly positioned. Both are discussed in greater detail in the Your Bicycle chapter (p373).

Numbness & Backache

Pain in the hands, neck and shoulders is a common complaint, particularly on longer riding days. It's generally caused by leaning too much on your hands. Apart from discomfort, you can temporarily damage the nerves and experience numbness or mild paralysis of the hands. Prevent it by wearing padded gloves, applying less weight on your hands and changing your hand position frequently (if you have flat handlebars, fit bar ends to provide more hand positions).

When seated your weight should be fairly evenly distributed through your hands and seat. If you're carrying too much weight on your hands there are two ways of adjusting your bike to rectify this: either by raising the height of your handlebars or, if you are stretched out too much, fitting a shorter stem (talk to your local bike shop). For more guidance on adjusting your bicycle for greater comfort, see the Your Bicycle chapter (p373).

Fungal Infections

Warm, sweaty bodies are ideal environments for fungal growth, and physical activity, combined with inadequate washing of your body and/or clothes, can lead to fungal infections. The most common are athlete's foot (tinea) between the toes or fingers, and infections on the scalp, in the groin or on the body (ringworm). You can get ringworm (which is a fungal infection, not a worm) from infected animals or other people.

STRETCHING

Stretching is important when stepping up your exercise levels: it improves muscle flexibility, which allows freer movement in the joints; and prevents the rigidity developing in muscles that occurs through prolonged cycling activity.

Ideally, you should stretch for 10 minutes before and after riding and for longer periods (15 to 30 minutes) every second day. Stretching prepares muscles for the task ahead, and limits the stress on muscles and joints during exercise. It can reduce post-exercise stiffness (decreasing the recovery time between rides) and reduce the chance of injury during cycling.

You should follow a few basic guidelines:

- before stretching, warm up for five to 10 minutes by going for a gentle bike ride, jog or brisk walk
- ensure you follow correct technique for each stretch
- hold a stretch for 15 to 30 seconds
- stretch to the point of discomfort, not pain
- breathe freely (ie, don't hold your breath) and try to relax your body whenever you are stretching
- don't 'bounce' the stretch; gradually ease into a full stretch
- repeat each stretch three times (on both sides, when required)

Do not stretch when you have an injury to a muscle, ligament or tendon (allow it to heal fully), as it can lead to further injury and/or hinder recovery. Warming up the muscles increases blood flow to the area, making it easier to stretch and reducing the likelihood of injury.

The main muscle groups for the cyclist to stretch are: quadriceps, calves, hamstrings, lower back and neck. Use the following stretches as a starting point, adding extra stretches that are already part of your routine or if you feel 'tight' in other areas (eg, add shoulder rolls if your shoulders feel sore after a day's cycling).

QUADRICEPS

Facing a wall with your feet slightly apart, grip one foot with your hand and pull it towards the but-tocks. Ensure the back and hips are square. To get a better stretch, push the hip forward. You should never feel pain at the knee joint. Hold the stretch, before lowering the leg and repeating the stretch with the other leg.

CALF

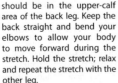

Stand facing a wall, placing one foot about 30cm in front of the other. Keep the heels flat on the ground and bend the front leg slowly toward the wall – the stretch should be in the upper-calf area of the back leg. Keep the back straight and bend your elbows to allow your body to move forward during the stretch. Hold the stretch; relax and repeat the stretch with the other leg.

HAMSTRINGS

Sit with one leg extended and the other leg bent with the bottom of the foot against the inside of the extended leg. Slide your arms down the extended leg – bending from the waist – until you feel a pull in the hamstring area. Hold it for 15 seconds, before returning to the start position. Keep the toes pointed up; avoid hunching the back.

LOWER-BACK ROLL

Lie on your back (on a towel or sleeping mat) and bring both knees up towards the shoulders until you feel a stretch in the lower back. Hold the stretch for 30 seconds; relax.

'CAT STRETCH' HUNCH

Another stretch for the lower back. Move to the ground on all fours (hands shoulder-width apart; legs slightly apart), lift the hips and lower back towards the sky until you feel a stretch. Hold it for 15 seconds; return to start position.

NECK

Gently and smoothly stretch your neck each of the four ways: forward, back and side to side. Do each stretch separately. (Do not rotate the head in a full circle.) For the side stretches, use your hand to pull the head very gently in the direction of the stretch.

To prevent fungal infections, wash frequently and dry yourself carefully. Change out of sweaty bike clothes as soon as possible.

If you do get an infection, wash the infected area at least daily with a disinfectant or medicated soap and water, and rinse and dry well. Apply an antifungal cream or powder such as tolnaftate. Expose the infected area to air or sunlight as much as possible, avoid artificial fibres and wash all towels and underwear in hot water, changing them often and letting them dry in the sun.

Staying Warm

Except on extremely hot days, put on another layer of clothing when you stop cycling – even if it's just for a quick break. Staying warm when cycling is as important as keeping up your water and food intake. Particularly in wet or sweaty clothing, your body cools down quickly after you stop working. Muscle strains occur more easily when your body is chilled and hypothermia (p401) can result from prolonged exposure. Staying rugged up will help prevent picking up chest infections, colds and the flu.

It's not advisable to cycle at high altitude during winter; however, you can get caught suddenly in bad weather at any time of year, especially in the mountains. No matter when you ride, always be prepared with warm clothing and a waterproof layer. Protect yourself from the wind on long downhill stretches – even stuffing a few sheets of newspaper under your shirt cuts the chill considerably.

MEDICAL PROBLEMS & TREATMENT

ENVIRONMENTAL HAZARDS
Sun

You can get sunburnt quite quickly, even on cool or cloudy days, especially during spring and summer and at higher altitudes. Take sun protection seriously – unless you want to be fried and increase your chances of heatstroke and skin cancer:

○ Cover yourself up: wear a long-sleeved top with a collar, and a helmet with a sun peak – you may want to go the extra step and add a 'legionnaire's flap' to your helmet to protect the back of your neck and ears. Make sure your shirt is sunproof: very thin or loosely woven fabrics still let sun through. Some fabrics are designed to offer high sun protection.

○ Use a high-protection sunscreen (SPF 30+ or higher). Choose a water-resistant sunscreen and reapply every few hours as you sweat it off. Protect your neck, ears, hands (if not wearing gloves), and feet. Zinc cream is good for sensitive noses, lips and ears.

○ Wear good sunglasses; they will also protect you from wind, dust and insects and are essential protection against sticks and flying objects if you're mountain biking, and from stones thrown up by vehicles.

○ Sit in the shade during rest breaks.

○ Wear a wide-brimmed hat when off the bike.

Mild sunburn can be treated with calamine lotion, aloe vera or sting-relief spray.

Heat

Very hot weather is experienced year-round in northern Australia and during summer for most of the country. When arriving from a temperate or cold climate, remember that it takes two weeks for acclimatisation to occur, so don't set yourself a demanding touring schedule as soon as your arrive. Before the body is acclimatised, an excessive amount of salt is lost in perspiration, so increasing the salt in your diet is essential.

DEHYDRATION & HEAT EXHAUSTION

Dehydration is a potentially dangerous and easily preventable condition caused by excessive fluid loss. Sweating and inadequate fluid intake are common causes of dehydration in cyclists, but others include diarrhoea, vomiting and high fever – see p401 for details on appropriate treatment for diarrhoea.

The first symptoms of dehydration are weakness, thirst and passing small amounts of very concentrated urine. This may progress to drowsiness, dizziness or fainting when standing up and, finally, coma.

It's easy to forget how much fluid you are losing through perspiration while you are cycling, particularly if a strong breeze is drying your skin quickly. Make sure you drink sufficient liquids (see p396). You should refrain from drinking too many caffeinated drinks such as coffee, tea and some soft drinks (which act as a diuretic, causing your body to lose water through urination) throughout the day; don't use them as a water replacement.

Dehydration and salt deficiency can cause heat exhaustion. Salt deficiency is characterised by fatigue, lethargy, headaches, giddiness and muscle cramps; salt tablets may help, but adding extra salt to your food is probably sufficient.

If one of your party suffers from heat exhaustion, lie the person down in a shady spot and encourage them to drink slowly but frequently. If possible, seek medical advice.

HEATSTROKE

This serious and occasionally fatal condition can occur if the body's heat-regulating mechanism breaks down and the body temperature rises to dangerous levels. Continuous periods of exposure to high temperatures and insufficient fluids can leave you vulnerable to heatstroke.

The symptoms are feeling unwell, not sweating very much (or at all) and a high body temperature (39°C to 41°C or 102°F to 106°F). Where sweating has ceased, the skin becomes flushed and red. Severe, throbbing headaches and lack of coordination will also occur, and the sufferer may be confused or aggressive. Eventually the victim will become delirious or convulse.

Hospitalisation is essential, but in the interim get the person out of the sun, remove their clothing, cover them with a wet sheet or towel and then fan continuously. Give them plenty of fluids (cool water), if conscious.

Cold
HYPOTHERMIA

Hypothermia occurs when the body loses heat faster than it can produce it and the core temperature of the body falls. It is surprisingly easy to progress from very cold to dangerously cold due to a combination of wind, wet clothing, fatigue and hunger, even if the air temperature stays above freezing.

Symptoms of hypothermia are exhaustion, numb skin (particularly toes and fingers), shivering, slurred speech, irrational or violent behaviour, lethargy, stumbling, dizzy spells, muscle cramps and powerful bursts of energy. Irrationality may take the form of sufferers claiming they are warm and trying to take off their clothes.

To prevent hypothermia, dress in layers. A strong, waterproof outer layer is essential. Protect yourself against wind, particularly for long descents. Eat plenty of high-energy food when it's cold; it's important to keep drinking too, even though you may not feel like it.

To treat mild hypothermia, get the person out of the wind and/or rain, remove wet clothing and replace it with dry, warm clothing. Give them hot liquids – not alcohol – and some high-kilojoule, easily digestible food. Do not rub victims: instead, allow them to slowly warm themselves. This should be enough to treat the early stages of hypothermia; however, medical treatment should still be sought, urgently if the hypothermia is severe. Early recognition and treatment of mild hypothermia is the only way to prevent severe hypothermia, a critical condition.

Hay Fever

If you suffer from hay fever, bring your usual treatment.

INFECTIOUS DISEASES
Diarrhoea

Simple things like a change of water, food or climate can cause a mild bout of diarrhoea, but a few rushed toilet trips with no other symptoms are not indicative of a major problem. More serious diarrhoea is caused by infectious agents transmitted by faecal contamination of food or water, by using contaminated utensils or directly from one person's hand to another. Paying particular attention to personal hygiene, drinking purified water and taking care of what you eat are important measures to take to avoid getting diarrhoea while touring.

Dehydration is the main danger with any diarrhoea, as it can occur quickly. Under all circumstances, the most important thing is to replace fluids (at least equal to the volume being lost). Urine is the best guide to this – if you have small amounts of dark-coloured urine, you need to drink more. Weak black tea with a little sugar, soda water, or soft

HEALTH & SAFETY

drinks allowed to go flat and diluted 50% with clean water are all good. With severe diarrhoea it's better to use a rehydrating solution to replace lost minerals and salts. Commercially available oral rehydration salts should be added to boiled or bottled water. In an emergency, make a solution of six teaspoons of sugar and a half teaspoon of salt in a litre of boiled or bottled water. Keep drinking small amounts often. Stick to a bland diet as you recover.

Gut-paralysing drugs such as diphenoxy-late or loperamide can be used to bring relief from the symptoms, although they do not actually cure the problem. Only use these drugs if you do not have access to toilets, that is, if you must travel. These drugs are not recommended for children under 12 years of age, or if you have a high fever or are severely dehydrated.

Seek medical advice if you pass blood or mucus, are feverish or suffer persistent or severe diarrhoea.

Another cause of persistent diarrhoea in travellers is giardiasis (see below).

Dengue Fever

Dengue fever occurs in northern Queensland, particularly from October to March, during the Wet. Also known as 'breakbone fever', because of the severe muscular pains that accompany it, this viral disease is spread by a species of mosquito that feeds primarily during the day. Most people recover in a few days but more severe forms of the disease can occur, particularly in residents who are exposed to another strain of the virus (there are four types) in a subsequent season.

Giardiasis

Giardiasis is widespread in waterways around Australia. This intestinal disorder is contracted by drinking water contaminated with the giardia parasite. The symptoms are stomach cramps, nausea, a bloated stomach, watery and foul-smelling diarrhoea, and frequent gas. Giardiasis can appear several weeks after you have been exposed to the parasite. The symptoms may disappear for a few days and then return; this can go on for several weeks. Seek medical advice if you think you have giardiasis but, where this is not possible, tinidazole or metronidazole are the recommended drugs. Treatment is

a 2g single dose of tinidazole or 250mg of metronidazole three times daily for five to 10 days.

Meningococcal Disease

This disease occurs worldwide and is a risk if you have prolonged stays in dormitory-style accommodation. A vaccine exists for some types of this disease, namely meningococcal A, C, Y and W. No vaccine is presently available for the viral type of meningitis.

Ross River Fever

The Ross River virus is widespread throughout Australia and is spread by mosquitoes living in marshy areas. In addition to fever, it causes headache, joint and muscular pains and a rash, and resolves after five to seven days.

Tetanus

This disease is caused by a germ that lives in soil and in the faeces of horses and other animals. It enters the body via breaks in the skin. The first symptom may be discomfort in swallowing, or stiffening of the jaw and neck; this is followed by painful convulsions of the jaw and whole body. The disease can be fatal. It can be prevented by vaccination.

Tick Typhus

Cases of tick typhus have been reported throughout Australia, but are predominantly found in Queensland and New South Wales. A week or so after being bitten, a dark area forms around the bite, followed by a rash and possible fever, headache and inflamed lymph nodes. The disease is treatable with antibiotics (doxycycline), so see a doctor if you suspect you have been bitten.

Viral Encephalitis

Also known as Murray Valley encephalitis virus, this is spread by mosquitoes and is most common in northern Australia, especially during the Wet season (Oct to Mar). This potentially serious disease is normally accompanied by headache, muscle pains and sensitivity to light. Residual neurological damage can occur and no specific treatment is available. However, the risk to most travellers is low.

BITES & STINGS
Dogs
You're bound to encounter barking dogs while riding in Australia, and some are likely to be untethered, especially away from towns and cities. The best thing to do is ride through their territory quickly and try shouting at them. A squirt from the water bottle or tap with the bike pump may provide added deterrent if the animal won't take the hint – though use the pump as a last resort, especially if the owner is in sight.

Leeches
Often present in damp rainforest conditions, leeches attach themselves to your skin to suck your blood. Salt or a lighted cigarette end will make them fall off. Do not pull them off, as the bite is then more likely to become infected. Clean and apply pressure if the point of attachment is bleeding. An insect repellent may keep them away.

Marine Animals
Marine spikes, such as those found on sea urchins, stonefish, scorpion fish, catfish and stingrays, can cause severe local pain. If this occurs, immediately immerse the affected area in hot water (as high a temperature as can be tolerated). Keep topping up with hot water until the pain subsides and medical care can be reached. The stonefish is found only in tropical Australia, from northwestern Australia around the coast to northern Queensland. An antivenin is available.

Marine stings from jellyfish such as box jellyfish and Irukandji also occur in Australia's tropical waters, particularly during the Wet season (Oct to Mar). The box jellyfish and the Irukandji have an incredibly potent sting and have been known to cause fatalities. Warning signs exist at affected beaches, and stinger nets are in place at the more popular beaches. Never dive into water unless you have checked – with local beach life-savers – that it's safe. If you are stung, first aid consists of washing the skin with vinegar (there's often a vinegar bottle near the beach) to prevent further discharge of remaining stinging cells, followed by rapid transfer to a hospital; antivenin is widely available.

Mosquitoes & Sandflies
Mosquitoes appear after dusk. Avoid bites by covering bare skin and using an insect repellent. Mosquitoes may be attracted by perfume, aftershave or certain colours. They can bite you through thin fabrics or on any small part of your skin not covered by repellent.

The most effective insect repellent is called DEET, an ingredient in many commercially available repellents. Look for a repellent with at least a 28% concentration of DEET. Note that DEET breaks down plastic, rubber, contact lenses and synthetic fabrics, so be careful what you touch after using it. It poses no danger to natural fibres.

Sharks & Crocodiles
Despite extensive media coverage, the risk of shark attack in Australian waters is no greater than in other countries with extensive coastlines. Check with surf life-saving groups about local risks.

Only one ride in this book – The Daintree & Cape Tribulation (p317) – is in crocodile country, and the risk of crocodile attack is real but predictable and largely preventable. Discuss the local risk with police or tourist agencies in the area before swimming in rivers, water holes and in the sea.

Snakes
Australian snakes have a fearful reputation that is justified in terms of the potency of their venom, but unjustified in terms of the actual risk to travellers and locals. Snakes are usually quite timid in nature and, in most instances, will move away if disturbed. They have only small fangs, making it easy to prevent bites to the lower limbs (where 80% of bites occur) by wearing protective clothing (such as gaiters) around the ankles when bushwalking. The bite marks are very small and may even go unnoticed.

In the warmer months, snakes are often seen warming their bellies on roads. Keep a watch for them ahead of your bike, though they are often difficult to spot until the last moment. Take comfort that it'll be hard for a snake to strike an object as elusive as a foot turning on a pedal.

If bitten, wrap the bitten limb tightly, as you would for a sprained ankle, and immobilise it with a splint. Keep the victim still and seek medical assistance; it will help if you can describe the offending reptile. Torniquets and sucking out the poison are now totally discredited.

Spiders

Australia has a number of poisonous spiders. The Sydney funnel-web spider causes severe local pain, as well as generalised symptoms (vomiting, abdominal pain, sweating). An antivenin exists, so apply pressure to the wound and immobilise the area before transferring to a hospital.

Redback spiders are found throughout the country. Bites cause increasing pain at the site, followed by profuse sweating and generalised symptoms (including muscular weakness, sweating at the site of the bite, nausea). First aid includes application of ice or cold packs to the bite, then transfer to hospital.

White-tailed spider bites may cause an ulcer that is very slow and difficult to heal. Clean the wound thoroughly and seek medical assistance.

Ticks

Always check all over your body if you have taken a rest in a potentially tick-infested area as ticks can cause skin infections and other more serious diseases. Ticks are most active from spring to autumn, especially where there are plenty of sheep or deer. They usually lurk in overhanging vegetation, so avoid brushing against trees and shrubs if possible.

If a tick is found attached to the skin, press down around the tick's head with tweezers, grab the head and gently pull upwards. Avoid pulling the rear of the body as this may squeeze the tick's gut contents through its mouth into your skin, increasing the risk of infection and disease. Smearing chemicals on the tick will not make it let go and is not recommended.

TRAUMATIC INJURIES

Although we give guidance on basic first-aid procedures here remember that, unless you're an experienced first aider and confident in what you're doing, it's possible to do more harm than good. Always seek medical help if it is available, but if you are far from any help, follow these guidelines.

Cuts & Other Wounds

Here's what to do if you suffer a fall while riding and end up with road-rash (grazing) and a few minor cuts. If you're riding in a hot, humid climate or intend continuing on your way, there's a risk of infection, so the wound needs to be cleaned and dressed. Carry a few antiseptic wipes in your first-aid kit to use as an immediate measure, especially if no clean water is available. Small wounds can be cleaned with an antiseptic wipe (only wipe across the wound once with each). Deep or dirty wounds need to be cleaned thoroughly:

○ Clean your hands before you start.
○ Wear gloves if you are cleaning somebody else's wound.
○ Use bottled or boiled water (allowed to cool) or an antiseptic solution such as povidone-iodine.
○ Use plenty of water – pour it on the wound from a container.
○ Embedded dirt and other particles can be removed with tweezers or flushed out using water squirted from a syringe (you can get more pressure if you use a needle as well) – this is especially effective for removing gravel.
○ Dry wounds heal best, so avoid using antiseptic creams that keep the wound moist; instead apply antiseptic powder or spray.
○ Dry the wound with clean gauze before applying a dressing – alternatively, any clean material will do as long as it's not fluffy (avoid cotton wool), as it will stick.

Any break in the skin makes you vulnerable to tetanus infection (p402) – if you didn't have a tetanus injection before you left, get one now.

A dressing will protect the wound from dirt, dust and flies. Alternatively, if the wound is small and you are confident you can keep it clean, leave it uncovered. Change the dressing regularly (once a day to start with), especially if the wound is oozing, and watch for signs of infection.

If you have any swelling around the wound, raising the affected limb can help the swelling settle and the wound to heal.

It's best to seek medical advice for any wound that fails to heal after a week or so.

BLEEDING WOUNDS

Most cuts will stop bleeding on their own, but if a blood vessel of any size has been cut it may continue bleeding for some time. Wounds to the head, hands and at joint creases tend to be particularly bloody.

To stop bleeding from a wound:

○ Wear gloves if you are dealing with a wound on another person.

○ Lie the casualty down if possible.

○ Raise the injured limb above the level of the casualty's heart.

○ Use your fingers or the palm of your hand to apply direct pressure to the wound, preferably over a sterile dressing or clean pad.

○ Apply steady pressure for at least five minutes before looking to see if the bleeding has stopped.

○ Put a sterile dressing over the original pad (don't move this) and bandage it in place.

○ Check the bandage regularly in case bleeding restarts.

Never use a tourniquet to stop bleeding as this may cause gangrene – the only situation in which this may be appropriate is if the limb has been amputated.

Major Accident

Crashing or being hit by an inattentive driver in a motor vehicle is always possible when cycling. When a major accident does occur, what you do is determined to some extent by the circumstances you are in and how readily available medical care is. However, remember that emergency services may be different from what you're used to at home. And, as anywhere, if you are outside a major town they may be much slower at responding to a call, so you need to be prepared to do at least an initial assessment and to ensure that the casualty comes to no further harm. First of all, check for danger to yourself. If the casualty is on the road ensure oncoming traffic is stopped or diverted around you. A basic plan of action is:

○ Keep calm and think through what you need to do and when.

○ Get medical help urgently; send someone to phone ☎ 000.

○ Carefully look over the casualty in the position in which you found them (unless this is hazardous for some reason, eg, on a cliff edge).

○ Call out to the casualty to see if there is any response.

○ Check for pulse (at the wrist or on the side of the neck), breathing and major blood loss.

○ If necessary (ie, no breathing or no pulse), and you know how, start resuscitation.

○ Check the casualty for injuries, moving them as little as possible; ask them where they have pain if they are conscious.

○ Don't move the casualty if a spinal injury is possible.

○ Take immediate steps to control any obvious bleeding by applying direct pressure to the wound.

○ Make the casualty as comfortable as possible and reassure them.

○ Keep the casualty warm by insulating them from cold (use whatever you have to hand, such as a sleeping bag).

SAFETY ON THE BIKE

ROAD RULES

Generally cyclists must follow the same rules as motorists in Australia. You must ride on the left-hand side of the road, and at intersections you must give way to vehicles entering from the right.

Helmets are compulsory in Australia – you risk being fined if you ride without one. Your bike must be fitted with an effective brake (so now is not the time to indulge your fancy in brakeless, fixed-gear bikes), plus a bell or warning device. For night riding, a red rear light, white front light and reflectors are also necessary.

HEALTH & SAFETY

TIPS FOR BETTER CYCLING

The following tips on riding technique are designed to help you ride more safely, comfortably and efficiently.

- Ride in bike lanes if they exist.
- Ride about 1m out from the edge of the kerb or from parked cars; riding too close to the road edge makes you less visible and more vulnerable to rough surfaces or car doors opening without warning.
- Stay alert; especially on busy, narrow, winding and hilly roads, it's essential to constantly scan ahead and anticipate the movements of other vehicles, cyclists, pedestrians or animals – and keep an eye out for potholes and other hazards.
- Keep your upper body relaxed, even when you are climbing.
- Ride a straight line and don't weave across the road when you reach for your water bottle or when climbing.
- To negotiate rough surfaces and bumps, take your weight off the saddle and let your legs absorb the shock.

At Night

- Only ride at night if your bike is equipped with a front and rear light; consider also using a reflective vest and/or reflective ankle bands.

Braking

- Apply front and rear brakes evenly.
- When your bike is fully loaded you'll find that you can apply the front brake quite hard and the extra weight will prevent you doing an 'endo' (flipping over the handlebars).

Climbing

- When climbing out of the saddle, keep the bike steady; rock the handlebars from side to side as little as possible.
- Use your gears to keep your legs 'spinning'.

Cornering

- Loaded bikes are prone to sliding out in corners: approach corners slowly and don't lean into the corner as hard as you normally would.
- If traffic permits, straighten corners; hit the corner wide, cut across the apex and ride out of it wide – but never cross the dividing line on the road.
- Apply the brakes before the corner, not in it (especially if it's wet).

Descending

- Stay relaxed, don't cramp up; let your body go with the bike.

Other road rules that cyclists should be aware of include the following:

- Riding two abreast is permitted, though cyclists should ride no more than 1.5m apart.
- In Queensland, Tasmania, the Australian Capital Territory (ACT) and the Northern Territory (NT), cyclists can ride on footpaths unless otherwise signed. In other states, it's not allowed unless the cyclist is under 12 years of age or is accompanying a child rider.
- Cyclists must ride in bicycle lanes when they are marked on roads.
- On paths shared with pedestrians, cyclists must ride in single file, keep to the left and give way to pedestrians.
- In all states hand signals are required if a cyclist is turning or diverging to the

- Be aware that a loaded bike is more likely to wobble and be harder to control at speed.
- Pump the brakes to shed speed rather than applying constant pressure, to avoid overheating the rims.

Gravel Roads

- Avoid patches of deep gravel (often on the road's edge); if you can't, ride hard – like you're driving a car through mud.
- Look ahead to plan your course; avoid sudden turning and take it slowly on descents.
- Brake in a straight line using your rear brake and place your weight over the front wheel if you need to use that brake.
- On loose gravel, loosen your toe-clip straps or clipless pedals so you can put your foot down quickly.

Group Riding

- If you're riding in a group, keep your actions predictable and let others know, with a hand signal or shout, before you brake, turn, dodge potholes etc.
- Don't overlap the wheels of fellow cyclists.
- Ride in single file on busy, narrow or winding roads.

In Traffic

- Obey the rules of the road and signal if you are turning.
- To tell if a car is moving or not (if it's at a T-junction or about to join the road) look at its wheels.
- Scan for trouble: look inside the back windows of parked cars for movement – that person may open the door on you.
- Look drivers in the eye; make sure they've seen you.
- Learn to bunny hop your bike (yes, it can be done with a fully-loaded touring bike; just not as well) – it'll save you hitting potholes and other hazards.

In the Wet

- Be aware that you'll take longer to slow down with wet rims, and exercise appropriate caution.
- On descents apply the brakes lightly to keep the rims free of grit/water etc and encourage quicker stopping.
- Don't climb out of the saddle (unless you want a change); shift down a gear or two and climb seated.

On Cycle Paths

- Use a bell or call out to warn others of your approach on cycle paths.

right. The ACT and NT require you to also signal when stopping; WA requires signals for all turns; and NSW, for all turns and when stopping.
- Overtaking on the left is allowed unless the vehicle is turning or indicating left.
- Cyclists are allowed to tow trailers only if the cyclist is aged over 16, the trailer passenger aged under 10, and the trailer is no wider than 66cm.

RIDING OFF-ROAD

If riding off-road or mountain biking, never go alone. It's best, if possible, to go in a small group – four is usually considered the minimum number. This way, if someone has an accident, one person can stay with the casualty and the others can go for help.

Always tell someone where you are going and when you intend to be back – and

EMERGENCY NUMBERS

In event of an emergency, call ☎ 000. If you don't have mobile-phone reception, and you have a GSM phone, you can dial ☎ 112; this will connect you to an emergency call service if another carrier has network coverage in the area.

make sure you contact them when you do get back. Take warm clothing, matches, a first-aid kit and enough food and water in case of emergency. Carry enough tools so you can undertake any emergency repairs (see p379).

Carry a map and take note of your surroundings (terrain, landmarks, intersections etc) so that if you do get lost, you are more likely to find your way out again. If you really get lost, stay calm and stop. Try to work out where you are or retrace your route. If you can't, or it's getting dark, find a nearby open area, put on warm clothes and find or make a shelter. Light a fire for warmth and help searchers by making as many obvious signs as you can (creating smoke, displaying brightly coloured items, making symbols out of rocks or wood etc).

EMERGENCY PROCEDURES

If you or one of your group has an accident (even a minor one), or falls ill during your ride, you'll need to decide on your best course of action, which is not always easy. Obviously, you will need to take into consideration your individual circumstances, including where you are and whether you have some means of direct communication with emergency services, such as a mobile phone. Some basic guidelines:

○ Use any first-aid knowledge and experience, as well as the information in this guide if necessary, to make a medical assessment of the situation.
○ For groups of several people, the accepted procedure is to leave one person with the casualty, together with as much equipment, food and water as you can sensibly spare, and for the rest of the group to go for help.
○ If there are only two of you, the situation is more tricky, and you will have to make an individual judgement as to the best course of action.
○ If you leave someone, mark their position carefully on the map (take it with you); you should also make sure they can be easily found by marking the position with something conspicuous, such as bright clothing or a large stone cross on the ground.
○ You can try attracting attention by using a whistle or torch, lighting a smoky fire (use damp wood or green leaves) or waving bright clothing; shouting is tiring and not very effective.

The uncertainties associated with emergency rescue in remote wilderness areas should make it clear to you how important careful planning and safety precautions are, especially if you are going in a small group.

Glossary

See the labelled bicycle diagram in the Your Bicycle chapter for technical bike terms.

A

ACT – Australian Capital Territory
arid – having little or no rain; arid regions are usually defined as those receiving less than 250mm of rain a year
autumn – fall (season)

B

B&B – bed and breakfast accommodation
barbie – barbecue (BBQ)
bathers – swimming costume (also togs, cozzie)
beanie – warm hat
bitumen – tar or asphalt; surfaced road
bloke – man
bore water – water from an artesian (underground) well
booze – alcohol
brekky – breakfast
brumby – wild horse
bull dust – fine, sometimes deep, dust on outback roads
bush, the – country, anywhere away from the city
bushfire – fire in bushland
bush tucker – native foods found naturally in the bush
bushie – someone who lives in 'the bush'
bushranger – colonial term for a robber, usually armed, with operations based in the bush
bushwalking – hiking, tramping, walking; walking for pleasure in the bush
BYO – 'bring your own' (usually alcohol)

C

camping ground – designated campsite with facilities
campsite – area suitable for camping, often without facilities
canyon – gorge or ravine, usually formed by a river
carbo – carbohydrates
cascade – small waterfall
CBD – Central Business District
come a cropper – fall (literally or metaphorically)

cooee – a long, loud, high-pitched call
corrugated road – rutted dirt road
counter meal – pub meal
creek – stream or small river
criterium – circuit race
croc – crocodile
cyclone – violent tropical storm, bringing high winds and rain to northern Australia

D

damper – Australian bush bread, made of flour and water and cooked in the ashes of a fire
deli – corner store or general store; also *milk bar*
dieback – microscopic fungus called *Phytophthora cinnamomi*, which attacks, and usually kills, some species of native plants by rotting their roots
dolerite – coarse-grained volcanic rock
donga – small, transportable building widely used in the outback
drag – (as in 'the main drag') main street
Dreaming (Dreamtime) – the rough European translation for the complex concept that forms the basis of Aboriginal spirituality. It incorporates the creation of the world and the spiritual energies operating around us.
Dry, the – Dry season in northern Australia (Apr to Oct)
dunny – (outdoor) toilet

E

escarpment – line of cliffs along the edge of a ridge

F

fire trail – 4WD track, usually in national parks, built for fire-fighting vehicles
ford – to cross a river by wading
fork – point where a road or track splits into two
freshie – freshwater crocodile
fuel stove – cooker, usually portable, using liquid fuel or gas canisters

G

g'day – good day, traditional Australian greeting

gorge – large, steep-sided valley, usually surrounded by cliffs

GPS – Global Positioning System; an electronic means of accurately fixing location using microwave satellite signals

granite – light-coloured, coarse-grained volcanic rock

GST – Goods & Services Tax

gully – small valley

gum tree – eucalypt tree

H

happy hour – period during which pubs offer cheap drinks

High Country – the Victorian and New South Wales Alps

hut – simple building used for accommodation, mainly in national parks, generally unsupervised and without facilities

I

inlet – indentation in the coast, usually with a narrow opening to the sea

isthmus – narrow stretch of land connecting two larger landmasses

J

jumper – sweater or pullover

K

knackered – broken, tired

knicks – padded bike shorts

L

limestone – sedimentary rock composed mainly of calcium carbonate

long weekend – three-day weekend created by a public holiday on the Friday or Monday

loo – toilet

M

mangrove – coastal tree that grows in salt water

march fly – biting fly; horsefly; gadfly

mate – general term of familiarity

midden – mound of discarded shells and bone fragments

milk bar – corner store or general store; also deli

Mod Oz - Australian cuisine, typified by its multi-cultural influences and ambivalence to claim any dish or meal as uniquely Australian

mozzie – mosquito

MTB – mountain bike

N

never never – remote country in the outback

NPWS – National Parks and Wildlife Service (New South Wales)

NSW – New South Wales

NT – Northern Territory

O

ocker – uncultivated Australian man

ocky strap – elastic strap to tie things down; also octopus strap, bungee cord

outback – remote, sparsely inhabited interior areas of Australia

Oz – slang for Australia

P

paddock – fenced area of land, usually for livestock; field

petrol – motor vehicle fuel (gas)

pick-a-plank bridge – timber bridge with planks that run parallel to the road

pissed – drunk

plateau – elevated area of land that's almost flat

pub – bar or hotel

Q

Queenslander – high-set traditional Queensland weatherboard house

R

rip – a strong ocean current or undertow

road train – long truck towing several trailers

roo – kangaroo

roundabout – traffic circle

S

SA – South Australia

saddle – pass or gap; low point on a ridge or between summits

saltie – saltwater crocodile

sandblow – large, unstable dune of sand that's slowly driven forward by a prevailing wind

sandstone – sedimentary rock comprising sand grains

sclerophyllous forest – woody, evergreen forest, typically with small, leathery leaved plants

scree – weathered rock fragments at the foot of a cliff or on a hillside

scrub – low dense vegetation

sealed road – surfaced road

service station – petrol (gas) station
Shellite – liquid fuel derived from petroleum and used in camp stoves
shout – to buy a round of drinks, as in 'it's your shout'
smoko – tea break
snag – sausage
snow line – level below which snow seldom falls or lies on the ground
sparrow's fart – dawn
spur – small ridge that leads up from a valley to a main ridge
station – large sheep or cattle farm
stinger – extremely poisonous box jellyfish found in northern Australia
stubby – 375mL bottle of beer
surf 'n' turf – a slab of steak topped with seafood, usually served in a pub
swag – bed roll
swimming hole – large pool on a creek or river, safe for swimming
switchback – route that follows a zig-zag course up or down a steep incline

T

takeaway – takeout food; place selling takeaway food
tap – faucet
tarn – small alpine lake

taxi – cab
thongs – flip-flops, rubber slippers
tor – high, bare, rocky hill
torch – flashlight
Total Fire Ban – prohibition of all open flames on days of extreme fire danger
tree line – highest natural level of tree growth
tucker – food

U

uni – university
ute – utility; pick-up truck

V

vego – vegetarian

W

WA – Western Australia
waterhole – small pool or lake
Wet, the – rainy season in the north (Nov to Mar)
whoop-whoop – remote town or area
World Heritage area – area included on a list of places deemed by Unesco to be of world significance

Y

yobbo – uncouth, aggressive person

Behind the Scenes

THIS BOOK
This guidebook was commissioned in Lonely Planet's Melbourne office, and produced by the following:
Publisher Chris Rennie
Associate Publisher Ben Handicott
Commissioning Editor Bridget Blair, Janine Eberle
Coordinating Cartographer James Regan
Assisting Cartographers Tadhgh Knaggs, Tom Webster, Valeska Canas, Barb Benson
Managing Cartographer David Connolly
Cover Designer Mary Nelson Parker
Cover Layout Designer Indra Kilfoyle
Project Manager Jane Atkin
Thanks to Shahara Ahmed, Rebecca Dandens, Wayne Murphy, Darren O'Connell, Julie Sheridan, Simon Tillema
Production [recapture]

OUR READERS
Many thanks to the travellers who used the last edition and wrote to us with helpful hints, useful advice and interesting anecdotes:
Liz Abbott, Steven & Cath Abbott, Thelma Anderson, Raymond Ang, Erin Arsenault, Paul Dixon, Paul Evenblij, Neil Glick, Aine Gliddon, Jonathan Ide, James Lamb, Tony Lang, Chai Lee, Gabrielle Methou, Keith Moon, Russell O'Brien, Thomas Palfy, Noelene Proud, Melinda Richards, Tobias Roller, David Rutter, Andrew Sharpe, Helen Spurling, Matt Wielgosz, John Willems

ACKNOWLEDGMENTS
All photographs by Lonely Planet Images, and by: Richard I'Anson p5 (#4); Andrew Bain p2 (#1), p3 (#2), p3 (#3), p6 (#1), p7 (#3), p7 (#4), p8 (#2), p9 (#1, #3), p10 (#2), p12; Ross Barnett p11 (#3); Glenn Beanland p5 (#2); Grant Dixon p6 (#2); David Hannah p4 (#5); Rodney Hyett p4 (#3); Paul Sinclair p2 (#5); David Wall p8 (#1), p11 (#4)

THANKS FROM THE AUTHORS
ANDREW BAIN
For beds, beers and bike sheds, a wheelie in the direction of Greg and Angie Kemp, Matt Brown, Carina Tan-Van Baren, Geoff Bain and Sue Lobo – and their various herds of kids. To Janette, Kiri and Cooper – thanks is not enough. To the book's *domestiques*, Bridget Blair and Janine Eberle, thanks for continual guidance, and a hurrah also to Ethan Gelber for taking the floods and fires.

ETHAN GELBER
The scramble to get everything done requires patience and resources beyond those I sometimes can muster. What would I do without the network of support that somehow always develops?

My sincere thanks to all ranks of Lonely Planet, particularly those of the Trade and Reference team for keeping the train on the tracks.

THE LONELY PLANET STORY
Fresh from an epic journey across Europe, Asia and Australia in 1972, Tony and Maureen Wheeler sat at their kitchen table stapling together notes. The first Lonely Planet guidebook, *Across Asia on the Cheap*, was born.

Travellers snapped up the guides. Inspired by their success, the Wheelers began publishing books to Southeast Asia, India and beyond. Demand was prodigious, and the Wheelers expanded the business rapidly to keep up. Over the years, Lonely Planet extended its coverage to every country and into the virtual world via lonelyplanet.com and the Thorn Tree message board.

As Lonely Planet became a globally loved brand, Tony and Maureen received several offers for the company. But it wasn't until 2007 that they found a partner whom they trusted to remain true to the company's principles of travelling widely, treading lightly and giving sustainably. In October of that year, BBC Worldwide acquired a 75% share in the company, pledging to uphold Lonely Planet's commitment to independent travel, trustworthy advice and editorial independence.

Today, Lonely Planet has offices in Melbourne, London and Oakland, with over 500 staff members and 300 authors. Tony and Maureen are still actively involved with Lonely Planet. They're travelling more often than ever, and they're devoting their spare time to charitable projects. And the company is still driven by the philosophy of *Across Asia on the Cheap*: 'All you've got to do is decide to go and the hardest part is over. So go!'

To Jane and Rohan: You are pillars of hope and joy, whose confidence I have too long abused. My hand may have been holding the pen, but you gave the hand reason to write.

To Leonie Higgins: Shelter and warmth matter most when you have neither. Who knows what we would have done without your open door and cupboards? Eternal gratitude.

Along the way there were other couches unfolded, stores of wisdom shared and words of encouragement proffered. May Miller-Dawkins (and friends), Sofiah Mackay, Barbara and Drew Parker, Quentin Frayne, Elizabeth Hole and Bicycle NSW, Garry Brennan and Tom Lester of Bicycle Victoria, and, of course, all the Gelbers and Higgins – for services known and unknown – I am beholden.

Lastly, to my co-author and fellow two-wheel devotee, Andrew Bain: congrats mate on a job well done.

SEND US YOUR FEEDBACK

We love to hear from travellers – your comments keep us on our toes and help make our books better. Our well-travelled team reads every word on what you loved or loathed about this book. Although we cannot reply individually to postal submissions, we always guarantee that your feedback goes straight to the appropriate authors, in time for the next edition. Each person who sends us information is thanked in the next edition – and the most useful submissions are rewarded with a free book.

To send us your updates – and find out about Lonely Planet events, newsletters and travel news – visit our award-winning website: **lonelyplanet.com/contact.**

Note: we may edit, reproduce and incorporate your comments in Lonely Planet products such as guidebooks, websites and digital products, so let us know if you don't want your comments reproduced or your name acknowledged. For a copy of our privacy policy visit www.lonelyplanet.com/privacy.

Index

LONELY PLANET OFFICES

Australia
Head Office
Locked Bag 1, Footscray, Victoria 3011
☎ 03 8379 8000, fax 03 8379 8111
talk2us@lonelyplanet.com.au

USA
150 Linden St, Oakland, CA 94607
☎ 510 893 8556, toll free 800 275 8555
fax 510 893 8572
info@lonelyplanet.com

UK
2nd fl, 186 City Rd,
London EC1V 2NT
☎ 020 7106 2100, fax 020 7106 2101
go@lonelyplanet.co.uk

Although the authors and Lonely Planet have taken all reasonable care in preparing this book, we make no warranty about the accuracy or completeness of its content and, to the maximum extent permitted, disclaim all liability arising from its use.

PUBLISHED BY LONELY PLANET PUBLICATIONS PTY LTD

ABN 36 005 607 983

© Lonely Planet Publications Pty Ltd 2009

© photographers as indicated 2009

Cover photograph: Blue sky and countryside near Perth, Mark Karrass/Corbis Many of the images in this guide are available for licensing from Lonely Planet Images: www.lonelyplanetimages.com.

Printed by Hang Tai Printing Company.
Printed in China.

Mixed Sources
Product group from well-managed forests and other controlled sources
www.fsc.org Cert no. SGS-COC-005002
© 1996 Forest Stewardship Council